Global Economic Prospects

Realizing the Development Promise
of the Doha Agenda

2004

© 2003 The International Bank for Reconstruction and Development / The World Bank
1818 H Street, NW
Washington, DC 20433
Telephone 202-473-1000
Internet www.worldbank.org
E-mail feedback@worldbank.org

All rights reserved.

1 2 3 4 04 03

This volume is a product of the staff of the World Bank. The findings, interpretations, and conclusions expressed herein do not necessarily reflect the views of the Board of Executive Directors of the World Bank or the governments they represent.

The World Bank does not guarantee the accuracy of the data included in this work. The boundaries, colors, denominations, and other information shown on any map in this work do not imply any judgment on the part of the World Bank concerning the legal status of any territory or the endorsement or acceptance of such boundaries.

Rights and Permissions

The material in this work is copyrighted. Copying and/or transmitting portions or all of this work without permission may be a violation of applicable law. The World Bank encourages dissemination of its work and will normally grant permission promptly.

For permission to photocopy or reprint any part of this work, please send a request with complete information to the Copyright Clearance Center, Inc., 222 Rosewood Drive, Danvers, MA 01923, USA, telephone 978-750-8400, fax 978-750-4470, www.copyright.com.

All other queries on rights and licenses, including subsidiary rights, should be addressed to the Office of the Publisher, World Bank, 1818 H Street NW, Washington, DC 20433, USA, fax 202-522-2422, e-mail pubrights@worldbank.org.

ISBN 0-8213-5582-1
ISSN 1014-8906

Cover photo credit: AFP/CORBIS.

Workers at the Los Ausoles coffee plantation in Ahuachapan, El Salvador, clean coffee beans, August 14, 2002.

Contents

Foreword ix

Acknowledgments xi

Overview xiii

Abbreviations and Data Notes xxxi

Chapter 1 Global Outlook and the Developing Countries 1
　　The industrial countries: Deficits, confidence, capital spending, and the dollar 4
　　The external environment for developing countries: Gradual improvement, but a bumpy road ahead 19
　　The developing countries: Back on track toward growth? 28
　　Trade, growth, and poverty in developing countries 38
　　Looking ahead to the Doha Round 47
　　Annex 1 Historical trade dynamics for developing countries 55
　　Notes 59
　　References 60

Chapter 2 Trade Patterns and Policies: Doha Options to Promote Development 63
　　Changing patterns in developing-country exports 65
　　Behind the patterns: Economic and policy determinants 73
　　Market access for development: The agenda 78
　　From Doha to Cancún and beyond: How should protection be reduced? 88
　　Notes 98
　　References 98

Chapter 3 Agricultural Policies and Trade 103
　　Poverty, rural households, and trade in agriculture 105
　　Trade and export growth in agriculture 109
　　Global agricultural protection: The bias against development 114
　　Proposals for reforms in the Doha Round 131
　　Notes 138
　　References 139

Chapter 4 Labor Mobility and the WTO: Liberalizing Temporary Movement   143
    The bigger picture: Global migration and remittance trends   145
    Temporary movement of workers   150
    Bilateral and regional approaches to labor mobility   152
    Understanding the impact of temporary foreign workers   155
    Mode 4 and the WTO   166
    Notes   172
    References   174

Chapter 5 Reducing Trading Costs in a New Era of Security   179
    Why transport, trade facilitation, and logistics matter   181
    The new international security dimension in trade   182
    The anticompetitive effects of international transport regulations   188
    Trade facilitation   191
    Trade facilitation and the WTO agenda   195
    Lowering transport costs, increasing security, and facilitating trade   198
    Notes   200
    References   202

Chapter 6 Development and the Doha Agenda   205
    Special and differential treatment and the WTO   207
    Market access for development   208
    Toward a new regime for WTO rules   220
    Putting development into the Doha agenda   227
    Notes   228
    References   229

Appendix 1 Regional Economic Prospects   233

Appendix 2 Global Commodity Price Prospects   257

Appendix 3 Global Economic Indicators   279

Figures
1.1   Growth in the OECD countries falters   4
1.2   OECD manufacturing shows a distinct "double dip"   5
1.3   Consumer confidence recovers from pre-war lows   6
1.4   The drop in U.S. household net worth has been offset by real estate appreciation   8
1.5   Capital spending has been hesitant in all industrial countries   9
1.6   Corporate profits have risen moderately in the United States and Japan   9
1.7   Business confidence remains poor, but better in the United States than in Europe   10
1.8   The U.S. fiscal deficit is widening quickly   11
1.9a   The U.S. current account deficit is at record levels   11
1.9b   The U.S. current account deficit is at record levels   13
1.10   Market interest rates have dropped   14
1.11   Is deflation a danger for Europe and the United States?   15

1.12	Output gaps are widening, bringing deflationary pressures to bear	16
1.13	The dollar has fallen sharply since early 2002	16
1.14	OECD recovery begins in the United States	18
1.15	OECD-area imports have declined sharply since April 2000	21
1.16	China's share of East Asian exports keeps rising	21
1.17	The price of oil fell sharply before the war in Iraq	23
1.18	Agricultural prices have begun to decline as crop prospects improve	25
1.19	Emerging-market spreads rallied sharply after late 2002	26
1.20	Bond issuance dominates capital market flows in 2003	27
1.21a	Regional trends in industrial production are mixed	29
121b	Inflation is moderating in the developing world	29
1.21c	Major currencies in Latin America and East Asia are firming up	30
1.22	Developing countries are on track toward long-term growth	31
1.23	Growth rates in developing countries will rise through 2005	31
1.24	Before the SARS outbreak, East Asian GDP was growing robustly	32
1.25	Argentina, Brazil, and Chile see strong upturn in production	33
1.26	Growth will cool in CIS while picking up in Central and Eastern Europe	34
1.27	Middle East oil production has increased to prevent shortages	35
1.28	Indian production of food and automobiles recovered sharply in early 2003	37
1.29	Growth in Africa is expected to improve modestly	38
1.30	Income elasticity has risen globally, but particularly in the developing world	40
1.31	Export-to-GDP ratios have risen sharply in developing countries	41
1.32	Productivity will contribute more to GDP growth through 2015 than will capital or labor	44
1.33	The pro-poor reform scenario promises substantial income gains	50
1.34	Exports should rise sharply	52
1.35	Millions of people would be moved out of poverty	52
1.36	Gains for most, but adjustment costs for some	53
1.37	Significant shifts in global output patterns	54
2.1	Developing countries have become important exporters of manufactured products	65
2.2	Manufactures account for a growing share of exports in all regions	67
2.3	Technology-laden manufactures have increased as a share of exports from each group of countries, while the share of resource-based exports has diminished	70
2.4	Global production sharing is increasingly important for China and India	71
2.5	Soaring exports from China and India had only a moderate effect on China's and India's terms of trade	72
2.6	Many developing countries face an adjustment when quotas are lifted	80
2.7	Antidumping barriers by sector and by country group	88
3.1	Countries that produce more cash crops also produce more food	109
3.2	Import growth rates of nontraditional export commodities decreased in industrial countries but increased in developing countries	112
3.3	Developing countries' exports of nontraditional products have surged, but industrial countries' exports have changed little	114
3.4	Developing countries lowered tariffs on manufactured products more than on agricultural products	119

3.5 Rich countries use non–ad valorem tariffs more often than do developing countries   122
3.6 Throughout the world, tariff rates escalate with degree of processing   123
3.7 The proportion of tariff lines containing non–ad valorem duties increases with degree of processing   125
3.8 Tariff rate quotas protect a substantial portion of output in many industrial countries   126
3.9 High protection of sugar and wheat has increased domestic production and reduced net imports   128
4.1 Workers' remittances are an important source of income for many developing countries   149
5.1 Customs clearance takes longer in the developing world than in the OECD, lowering the competitiveness of developing-country trade   185
5.2 Higher trade costs reduce global welfare   186
5.3 Facilitating trade in less-efficient countries would bring significant gains   194
5.4 The impact of individual trade-facilitation measures differs significantly from region to region   195
5.5 Domestic reforms alone would produce many of the same gains as global reform   196
6.1 The benefits of U.S. trade preferences are distributed unequally   211
6.2 Countries "graduating" from U.S. generalized system of preferences have better export performance than those still in program   212
6.3 Preferences have not increased the share of the least developed countries in imports into the European Union and the United States   215
6.4 Market shares of countries eligible for three U.S. "deep preference" programs have not increased   215
6.5 Preferred countries' apparel exports to the United States have risen   216
6.6 Agricultural exports from Mexico and Spain rose dramatically after the two countries joined regional trade blocs   217
6.7 The trade policies of countries in the U.S. generalized system of preferences are more protectionist than those of countries not in the program   218
6.8 Countries enjoying preferences have increased their exports of apparel to the United States   219

Tables

1.1 Global growth should accelerate, but risks persist   3
1.2 Weak fundamentals underlie sluggish growth in the rich countries   5
1.3 The difficult environment for developing-country growth should improve   20
1.4 Developing countries' exports will grow faster than those of the high-income countries   22
1.5 GDP per capita will grow faster in the developing world than in the OECD area   43
1.6 Global poverty will decrease significantly, but not uniformly across regions   46
1.7 Tariffs could be cut clearly and simply   48
1.8 The pro-poor tariff scenario would significantly lower protection   49
1.9 A large share of real income gains comes from lowering of barriers in agriculture and food   51
1.A1 Sectoral export decomposition for developing countries   55

1.A2	Regional export decomposition for developing countries	57
2.1	Developing countries are becoming exporters of high-value products	68
2.2	Developing countries' exports became more competitive in the 1990s	74
2.3	Investment in people and in capital grew rapidly	75
2.4	Tariffs hurt exports—but less so in the 1990s than in the 1980s	77
2.5	Quota abolition in China will move resources from other activities to textiles and clothing	81
2.6	Industrial countries levy higher tariffs on imports from developing countries than from other industrial countries—and some regions have high tariff walls	82
2.7	Developing countries pay large amounts in tariffs to their neighbors	83
2.8	Most antidumping actions are filed by developing countries against other developing countries	86
2.9	Antidumping rates are much higher than tariff rates	86
2.10	Antidumping duties are high	87
2.11	Competing formulas make a big difference for tariffs	95
2A.1	The various liberalization proposals have very different features	97
3.1	Most of the world's poor live in rural areas outside the least developed countries	106
3.2	Rural poverty is higher in poorer countries	107
3.3	Even in subsistence economies, cash is important	107
3.4	U.S. farmers earn less from farming than from other sources	107
3.5	Manufacturing exports grew much faster than agricultural exports	110
3.6	South-South exports in agriculture are rising as South-North export shares fall	110
3.7	Developing countries have shared unequally in export market gains	117
3.8	Agricultural tariffs are higher than manufacturing tariffs in both rich and poor countries	118
3.9	Agricultural tariffs: High peaks and deep valleys	119
3.10	Most subsidies go to producers—and come from border protection	120
3.11	Subsidies account for a large share of farmers' revenues	121
3.12	Specific tariffs are higher than ad valorem rates	123
3.13	Tariffs rise with level of processing	124
3.14	The Harbinson proposals could greatly reduce applied tariffs in the European Union and the United States	133
3.15	The Harbinson proposals would not significantly reduce protection in the developing world—if reductions were taken from bound rates	133
3.16	U.S. trade preferences—a plethora of programs	136
4.1	Migration is rising in many OECD countries	147
4.2	Workers' remittances are the second-largest source of external funding for developing countries	148
4.3	Remittances are a significant source of income in all regions of the developing world	149
4.4	Temporary movement is rising in rich countries	150
4.5	Foreign-born workers meet skill shortages in rich countries	152
4.6	The distribution of costs and benefits associated with Mode 4 trade	157
4.7	TMNP is the smallest of the four modes of international service supply	168
4.8	Most Mode 4 commitments by WTO members are in management categories	169

5.1   Elimination of anticompetitive private practices can cut costs drastically   190
6.1   Developing countries rarely receive significant preferences in sectors in which they would have a comparative advantage   209
6.2   Utilization rates for preference-eligible products with high MFN tariffs are low   210
6.3   Actual use of preference programs is declining   211

Boxes
1.1   Consumer confidence and U.S. private consumption   7
1.2   Financing the U.S. current account deficit: From equity to debt   12
1.3   OPEC struggles to achieve higher prices amid growing supply competition   24
1.4   Economic effects of Severe Acute Respiratory Syndrome (SARS)   33
1.5   AIDS is taking a rising toll in Sub-Saharan Africa   39
2.1   Poor export performance in 43 countries   69
2.2   Swimming upstream: The case of Vietnamese catfish   85
2.3   The scourge of the specific   89
2.4   "Average cuts," the cut you have when you're not having a cut   92
2.5   The implications of five tariff-cutting proposals   93
3.1   The impact of national trade integration and reform on poverty   106
3.2   Did agricultural exports slow down solely because of falling prices?   111
3.3   Decomposing export growth in manufacturing   113
3.4   Food safety standards: From barriers to opportunities   115
3.5   Decoupling agricultural support from production decisions   127
3.6   Fewer subsidies, stronger agricultural sector   132
3.7   The potential impact of real preferences   134
3.8   Rules of origin in preferential schemes are complicated—and often contradictory   136
3.9   Food aid principles   137
4.1   Population aging and migration   146
4.2   Temporary labor movement and the East Asian crisis of 1997–98   151
4.3   Recent initiatives to facilitate temporary movement of highly skilled workers   153
4.4   A trade facilitation approach to labor mobility: NAFTA and APEC   154
4.5   Initiatives to encourage return migration   160
4.6   Wages and conditions   163
4.7   E-commerce and temporary movement   164
4.8   Boosting intra-EU labor mobility   165
4.9   Measuring Mode 4 is still imprecise   167
4.10 Key impediments to Mode 4 trade   169
4.11 Elements of a possible GATS visa/permit regime   171
5.1   The evolving definition of trade facilitation   181
5.2   The logistics needs of a German car part manufacturer in Tunisia   192
5.3   Tackling corruption in customs: Peru   197
5.4   Customs reform in Lebanon   198
6.1   EU and U.S. preference programs   213
6.2   Major WTO provisions allowing developing countries greater freedom to use restrictive trade policies   221
6.3   A "development box" for the Agreement on Agriculture?   223

Foreword

THE INTERNATIONAL COMMUNITY finds itself at a crossroads as it goes into the last quarter of 2003. Will the Doha Agenda regenerate the multilateral consensus that has been the hallmark of successive rounds of trade liberalization since 1947 and in doing so provide new impetus for global integration? Or will the Doha Agenda collapse in stalemate and perhaps be viewed as the moment when the international community retreated from multilateralism and opened the floodgates for less desirable bilateral and regional arrangements?

The answers to these questions matter a great deal to the world's poor. The round of trade talks launched in November 2001 in Doha, Qatar, is the first negotiation focused primarily on issues of concern to developing countries, and the first trade round since the birth of the World Trade Organization (WTO). Moreover, the Doha round is the first trade round for many new WTO members, including the world largest developing economy, China. Consequently, the round has the opportunity to remove many of the inequities in the global trading system that put developing countries—and poor people in particular—at a disadvantage in their trade.

Three trade barriers are of particular concern. Poor people work in agriculture, and agricultural products are subject to the highest barriers to trade. In addition, poor people produce labor-intensive manufactures, which are subject to peak tariffs in a world that has already reduced average tariffs in manufactures to historic lows. Poor people could benefit from greater temporary migration.

Governments everywhere have worked hard to create the opportunity to reduce these and other barriers. And they will have to work hard to capitalize on that opportunity. To fulfill the development promise of the Doha Agenda, rich countries will have to reduce protection of their (relatively wealthy) farmers. Their tariff walls and huge subsidies depress global prices of the products that poor farmers produce throughout the developing world. These subsidies cost the average working family in the European Union, Japan, and the United States more than $1,000 a year. Middle-income countries, though their protection is generally lower and less distorting in agriculture, have high average tariffs in all sectors, and are more restrictive in services. As south-south trade increases in importance, protection of sectors in middle-income countries undermines their poorer trading partners and often undercuts the countries' own productivity growth. Finally, low-income countries should look to the international system to meet their very reasonable demands—not for special preferences *to some markets* and exemptions from rules, but for nondiscriminatory market access *to every market* in products in which they have a comparative advantage, for appropriately phased introduction of international regulations, and for development assistance in implementing administratively costly WTO rules. Like other countries, low-income countries will find it in their interest to reduce their own external levels of protection as part of an integrated development strategy aimed at reducing poverty.

Reducing barriers to trade is not enough to fulfill the development promise of Doha. Trade must be part of a larger development strategy for each country, a strategy that includes attention to macroeconomic policy, infrastructure, education, and health as well as to accountable and responsible governance. These elements of investment climate take time to develop but are essential for growth and poverty reduction and are crucial to make a sound trade strategy pay its growth and poverty reduction dividends.

The World Bank, working in partnership with the other international institutions and bilateral donors, is committed to supporting a pro-poor Doha outcome. Our objectives in trade are twofold: promoting a world trading system in which global, regional, and bilateral rules are conducive to development and poverty reduction, and helping individual developing countries leverage trade to promote their own growth. The latter objective hinges on integrating appropriately sequenced trade reforms into national development and poverty reduction strategies.

The Bank is increasing its investment in research, technical assistance, and lending for trade. A casual perusal of the bibliography in each chapter of this report will give the interested reader an idea of the scope of the Bank's research program. Moreover, in the last two years, the Bank has undertaken at the request of governments more than 20 diagnostic studies of obstacles to trade integration. In conjunction with six partner institutions, the Bank has led the Integrated Framework program—studies of trade obstacles in a dozen least-developed countries to date. It has completed several regional studies of trade.

In addition to studies and policy advice, the Bank has provided technical assistance in the form of lending to improve trade-related institutions and transport logistics. The Bank has programs that finance activities in 49 countries (approximately one-third of its active client countries). These projects span all regions and range from export competitiveness projects in Ghana and Bangladesh, to transport and trade facilitation projects in Eastern Europe, to support for improving customs–border control agencies and training the trading community in Pakistan. The Bank is also implementing projects to improve quality standards and is leading the "Standards and Trade Development Facility," an interagency partnership with the WTO, the FAO, and the World Health Organization, to deliver technical assistance for food safety and related standards. Should trade ministers reach an agreement on the Doha Agenda, the Bank will expand its lending and technical assistance to help countries take advantage of new market access, to use trade to promote their domestic competitiveness, and to manage any transitional costs—such as those arising from erosion of trade preferences, changes in prices of imports, or reallocation of domestic resources from inefficient sectors to more efficient ones.

A pro-poor outcome in the Doha Agenda is only one step toward a world more supportive of development. But this step is an important one. And it can be achieved only if everyone understands what is at stake in this historical moment—and moves purposefully and together to seize the opportunity.

Nicholas Stern
Chief Economist and Senior Vice President
World Bank

Acknowledgments

THIS REPORT WAS prepared by the World Bank Development Prospects Group, drawing on resources throughout the Development Economics Vice Presidency and the World Bank's operational units. Richard Newfarmer was the lead author and manager of the report, under the direction of Uri Dadush. The principal chapter authors were Richard Newfarmer (Overview); Elliot Riordan and Dominique Van der Mensbrugghe (Chapter 1); William Martin and Vlad Manole (Chapter 2); Ataman Aksoy (Chapter 3); Pierre Sauvé, drawing on work by the OECD (Chapter 4); John Wilson, Shweta Bagai, and Carsten Fink (Chapter 5); and Bernard Hoekman and Caglar Ozden (Chapter 6). We are grateful for the ideas and insights of several peer reviewers who provided comments at various stages: Bijit Bora (World Trade Organization); J. Michael Finger (American Enterprise Institute); Gary Hufbauer (Institute for International Economics); Mari Pangestu (Center for Strategic and International Studies), Gary Horlick (Wilmer, Cutler, and Pickering), and Julia Nielson (OECD); Julio Nogues (United Nations Development Programme); and Olivier Cattaneo (Agence Française de Développement). The report was prepared under the general guidance of World Bank Chief Economist and Senior Vice President Nicholas Stern.

Many staff from inside and outside the World Bank contributed to the report. In the Overview, Aart Kraay contributed a note on trade and poverty, and Carsten Fink, Bernard Hoekman, William Martin, and Aaditya Mattoo provided helpful suggestions. In Chapter 1, Hans Timmer, Caroline Farah, Himmat Kalsi, Robert Keyfitz, Annette I. De Kleine, Robert Lynn, Fernando Martel Garcia, Mick Riordan, and Bert Wolfe contributed to the global trends analysis; Dominique Van der Mensbrugghe provided the long-term analysis; Shaohua Chen and Martin Ravallion contributed to the poverty analysis; and Katherine Rollins was the staff assistant. Chapter 2 benefited from background papers and other inputs from J. Michael Finger and Andri Zlate. For Chapter 3, John Beghin, Donald Mitchell, John Baffes, Harry De Gorter, Ndiame Diop, Paul Brenton, Steve Jaffee, and Mirvat Sewadeh provided background papers, and Baris Sivri, Tarek Soueid, Konstantin Senyut, and Gaston Gohou undertook data collection and analysis. Chapter 4 drew on research papers prepared by the OECD Trade Directorate and on the annual OECD report *Trends in International Migration*; the chapter reflects insights from Jeffrey Lewis, Julia Nielson (OECD), and Olivier Cattaneo (AFD). Tsunehiro Otsuki and Katherine Mann (IIE) worked closely with the team on Chapter 5, and Ranga Rajan Krishnamani provided research assistance. Chapter 6 draws on research by Bernard Hoekman, Constantine Michalopoulos, and L. Alan Winters. The regional annexes benefited from the written input of regional chief economists around the Bank and their staff, particularly Milan Brahmbhatt. John Baffes, Betty Dow, Donald Mitchell, and Shane Streifel prepared the commodity annex. The staff assistant for the report was Awatif Abuzeid. Steven Kennedy provided editorial assistance. Denis

Medvedev provided research assistance. Dorota Nowak coordinated the report's publication and dissemination activities, working closely with the World Bank's Office of the Publisher.

Several experts provided written comments that have immeasurably improved the quality of the report at various stages: Paul Brenton, Robin Carruthers, Jean-Jacques Dethier, Shahrokh Fardoust, Coralie Gevers, Ian Goldin, Gary Horlick, Elena Ianchovichina, Mark Juhel, Hans Peter Lankes, Jeffrey Lewis, Patrick Low (WTO), Kunio Mikuriya (World Customs Organization), John Nash, David Rosenblatt, John Panzer, Luiz Perreira da Silva, Byungdoo Sohn, Mark Sundberg, Helena Tang, Yvonne Tsikata, and L. Alan Winters.

Overview

ON THE EVE of the World Trade Organization's (WTO) Fifth Ministerial Meeting in Cancún in September 2003, the world's trade ministers—and the governments they represent—face enormous challenges. The global trade talks are stalled in several policy domains vital to developing countries—agriculture, nonfarm trade, access to patented drugs for countries without domestic drug industries, special and differential treatment, and dispute settlement. Nor is there much progress in other contentious areas, such as the "Singapore issues" of investment, competition, trade facilitation, and government procurement.

At the same time, the global recovery continues to sputter. Although some signs of a turnaround have been evident in the United States, Europe seems to be losing momentum, and Japan appears positioned for another disappointing year. The Chinese economy, reinforced by a positive performance in East Asia in 2002, continues to bustle along, but concerns over Severe Acute Respiratory Syndrome (SARS) and lost export momentum in the face of the world slowdown haunted the regional outlook. South Asia continues to grow more rapidly than the world average. Latin America is showing signs of an upturn, driven in part by renewed confidence in Brazil, a tentative rebound in Argentina, and an increase in Mexico's growth; however, the recession in the República Bolivariana de Venezuela, when coupled with political difficulties in the Andean countries, continues to weigh down regional performance. Africa, suffering from low commodity prices, is growing slowly; although faster than in the 1980s and 1990s, today's growth is far short of the pace necessary to make significant dents in the poverty headcount or to achieve the Millennium Development Goals in health and education. War has adversely affected regional performance in the Middle East and North Africa; sluggish performance in Europe, especially Germany, has adversely affected many countries in Central and Eastern Europe. Even though progress on trade would undoubtedly boost investor confidence, politicians coping with slow growth and high unemployment at home have been finding it more difficult to risk alienating influential constituencies by accepting bold proposals in the world trade talks.

The outlook for the remainder of this year and for 2004, though somewhat improved, is unlikely to produce growth strong enough to cut sharply into unemployment rates (figure 1). Uncertainty in the global environment remains unusually high. Structural problems persist—overcapacity in high-tech industries globally, rising twin deficits in the U.S. fiscal and current accounts, and lingering bad loans in Japanese and (to a lesser extent) European banks. Other problems may prove more transitory. The cessation of conflict in Iraq has not yet produced complete calm, and the inability to reach consensus at the UN Security Council

GLOBAL ECONOMIC PROSPECTS

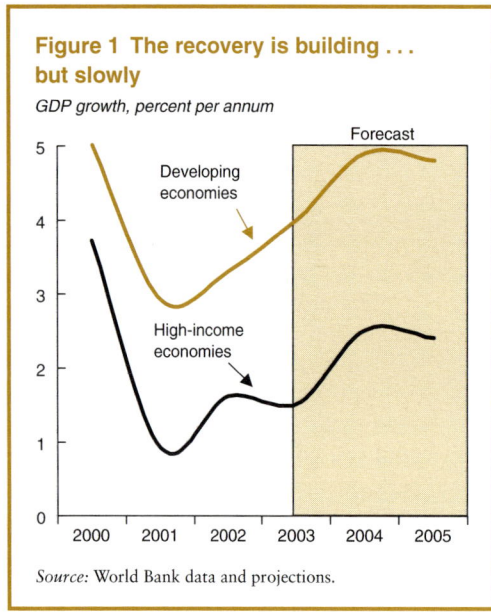

Figure 1 The recovery is building... but slowly
GDP growth, percent per annum
Source: World Bank data and projections.

has created a lingering distrust among multilateral partners that clouds the global business environment. Nonetheless, policy responses are promising. Governments in the United States and Europe reacted to weak economic conditions with fiscal and monetary policy to stimulate their economies. And at the global political level, the June meeting of the G-8, together with several subsequent bilateral meetings, began to mend frayed multilateral relations. It remains to be seen whether this new positive momentum will extend into multilateral collaboration in trade.

The precarious international environment is only one reason why the global trade talks have progressed slowly. Deeper explanations can also be found in the history of multilateral trade talks themselves. With the incorporation of ever more countries—mainly from the developing world—the sheer number of actors has expanded, making coalitions more difficult to build and consensus more elusive. Moreover, previous multilateral rounds produced agreements in areas of primary interest to the rich countries that dominated these discussions, particularly in manufactured goods. It was only with the Uruguay Round, concluded in 1994, that tentative steps toward freeing up trade in products of particular interest to developing countries—notably agriculture and textiles—were included. Consequently, many of the hardest issues for rich countries have been left to this negotiation.

Realizing the development promise of the Doha agenda

The challenge is daunting. But so is the reward to success. With room for additional fiscal and monetary stimulus rapidly vanishing, progress on structural reforms such as trade is important. In addition to bolstering investor confidence in the short term, a Doha Round agreement that slashed trade barriers, particularly in agriculture, would stimulate trade and raise incomes around the world, leading to a substantial reduction in global poverty.

The open question is whether a new multilateral agreement will live up to the development promise of the Doha Agenda. Several issues under discussion are pivotal to development outcomes. They are the focus of this report:

- Because most poor people live in rural areas, trade barriers in *agriculture* are among the most important to poverty reduction.
- *Labor-intensive manufactures* have been the most dynamic market segment for every major region, including Africa, yet many developing countries find that their exports meet obstacles in foreign markets—high tariffs, quotas, specific duties, and "anti-development" tariff structures that discourage adding value in poor countries.
- In *services,* the potential for development-promoting reciprocal gains is especially high. Regulations in some developing countries still protect some inefficient state monopolies from competition—a drag on growth. (To be sure, proper regulation in some sectors must precede liberalization to avoid potential disruptions in socially important markets, such as finance or basic services.) Also,

access for developing countries' services exports to industrial countries has yet to be fully bound in the General Agreement on Trade in Services (GATS) (World Bank 2001). Finally, national laws prevent greater labor mobility that would otherwise contribute to higher standards of living in both receiving and sending countries.
- Reducing the costs of trading by improving international transportation services, customs and ports, and logistics management—*trade facilitation*—requires substantial new investment, additional technical assistance, and coordinated multilateral efforts. Trade facilitation is fundamental to realizing the expanded trade promise of Doha, but the WTO agenda constitutes a small part of the challenge.
- Finally, the issue of *special treatment for developing countries* cuts across all of these policy domains and affects trade preferences and exemptions from WTO regulations. The pursuit of trade preferences and exemptions from multilateral rules have not always served developing countries particularly well, both because preferences have not proven reliable and because selective coverage has often left productivity-detracting trade barriers in place. The residual barriers sap growth in the protected economies and in developing-country trading partners that are denied access. Perhaps most important, the majority of the world's poor do not live in the least developed countries (LDCs). Trade preferences targeted at these countries do not benefit the three-quarters of the world's poor that live on US$1 per day in other countries. In implementing new WTO rules, new accords will be most effective if they recognize differences among individual countries' capacity to undertake new, resource-intensive rules. These differences require a new approach to special and differential treatment.

These areas pose difficult political challenges for all segments of the international community—rich countries, middle-income developing countries, and low-income countries alike. Rich countries account for two-thirds of world trade and comprise nearly three-quarters of world GDP, so their domestic policies—most evident in agriculture—have the greatest effect on the global marketplace. Despite the fact that agricultural protection, tariff peaks, and antidumping measures shield powerful lobbies, rich-country leadership in reducing this protection is a prerequisite for a pro-poor development outcome.

Today's middle-income developing countries have increased their global market share in the last two decades. Because they include many of the most dynamic global economies, their domestic policies no longer have only minor consequences for trade. With protection rates in manufactures three times the level of those in rich countries and with ubiquitous restrictions on services, the middle-income countries have ample scope for undertaking reductions in protection that will accelerate their growth and provide access and a growth impulse to neighboring countries. High protection in these countries taxes their growth and their poor in much the same way as protection in the North.

Low-income countries have a special interest in greater market access, but they cannot succumb to the siren calls of preferential market access nor opt out of reducing border protections at home, which tax exports and cut into productivity growth. Preferences for LDCs can help, but would be more effective if they were made less restrictive and more reliable than at present—and if benefiting countries take the necessary policy steps, including reductions in border protection, to promote a supply response. Moreover, because other developing countries are unlikely to be granted new trade preferences, global reciprocal reduction in trade barriers holds the most promise for the world's poor.

Market access is not the whole development story. Even if developing countries succeed in obtaining access to new markets, they will have to adopt complementary policies—removing obstacles to private investment, improving public investment in infrastructure, and providing education—to ensure that domestic firms respond to new opportunities associated with greater integration, and that the benefits of integration are transmitted to the poor. Put differently, trade policies must be embedded in a coherent national development strategy—they are not a substitute for it. For all of these reasons, realizing the development promise of the Doha Agenda requires the participation of all groups of the international community.

This report: toward a pro-poor Doha outcome

This report analyzes central elements of the Doha Agenda that are important to developing countries. Chapter 1 describes the prospects for the global economy that form the backdrop to the Doha trade negotiations. Chapters 2–6 focus on agriculture, nonagricultural trade, services, transport and trade facilitation, and special development provisions. In each area, we expand on themes that have received less analysis in previous World Bank reports—among them specific duties in agriculture, antidumping in manufactures trade, temporary movement of labor in services, security issues in trade facilitation, and trade preferences and exemptions from rules as part of special and differential treatment (SDT). The remainder of this overview weaves these findings together with those of previous Bank studies[1] to lay out the principal elements of a pro-poor outcome for the Doha Agenda.

A Doha deal for development

Agriculture is at the heart of a development round

Agriculture is central to the development promise of this trade round for two reasons: most of the world's poor work in agriculture and most of the world's protection is directed at agriculture. Some 70 percent of the world's poor live in rural areas and earn their income from agriculture. Largely exempt from pre-Uruguay Round trade agreements to reduce protection, agriculture is among the most distorted sectors in international trade. Even though levels of average tariff protection are comparable in rich and poor countries, the extensive use of producer subsidies in the OECD countries and the fact that the OECD constitutes two-thirds of world agricultural trade underscore the centrality of their policies to development outcomes. Reducing protection in agriculture alone would produce roughly two-thirds of the gains from full global liberalization of all merchandise trade.

A few facts are enough to establish the context: protection facing developing country exporters in agriculture is four to seven times higher than in manufactures in the North and two to three times higher in developing countries (IMF-World Bank 2002). Tariff peaks are particularly high in rich countries against products from poor countries. Tariff escalation that discourages development of further processing is more pronounced in agriculture in both rich and poor countries (figure 2). Hefty specific duties are particularly common in rich countries; they automatically increase protec-

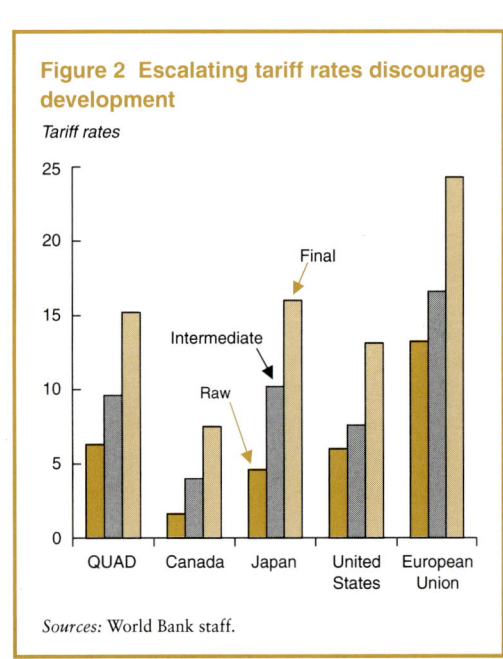

Figure 2 Escalating tariff rates discourage development

Sources: World Bank staff.

tion when commodity prices fall, throwing the burden of adjustment onto global prices and poor countries. Subsidies in OECD countries amount to US$330 billion—of which some US$250 billion goes directly to producers. The effect is to stimulate overproduction in high-cost rich countries and shut out potentially more competitive products from poor countries. It is no wonder that agricultural exports from developing countries to rich countries grew in the 1990s at just half the rate they did to other developing countries.

Consider how agricultural protection plays through individual commodity markets. Sugar in the European Union (EU), Japan, and the United States is commonly protected through a combination of quotas, tariffs, and subsidies allowing domestic sugar producers in those countries to receive more than double the world market price. OECD governments support sugar producers at the rate of US$6.4 billion annually—an amount nearly equal to all developing country exports. Prices are so high that it has become economic to grow sugar beets in cold climates and to convert corn to high-fructose corn syrup. Sugar imports in the OECD have shrunk to next to nothing. U.S. subsidies to cotton growers totaled US$3.7 billion last year, three times U.S. foreign aid to Africa. These subsidies depress world cotton prices by an estimated 10–20 percent, reducing the income of thousands of poor farmers in West Africa, Central and South Asia, and poor countries around the world. In West Africa alone, where cotton is a critical cash crop for many small-scale and near-subsistence farmers, annual income losses for cotton growers are about US$250 million a year. Rice support in Japan amounts to 700 percent of production at world prices, stimulating inefficient domestic production, reducing demand, and denying export opportunities to India, Thailand, Vietnam, and other countries.

More than 70 percent of subsidies in rich countries are directed to large (often corporate) farmers. These farmers have incomes that are higher—often substantially so—than average incomes in Europe, Japan, and, to a lesser extent, the United States. The net effect of subsidizing the relatively rich in wealthy countries at the expense of adverse price penalties for the products of the relatively poor in developing countries is to aggravate global income inequalities. Said differently, subsidies make the relatively rich even richer and the poor even poorer.

Realizing the development potential of Doha requires phased reductions of border protection and subsidies. Of these, border protection is the most important. These reductions ought to be done in a way that cuts off antidevelopment tariff peaks, reduces tariff escalation, and phases out specific duties. A propoor reform also means reforming policies that distort particular commodities of importance to developing countries—sugar, cotton, rice, wheat, and dairy products.

Because global prices may rise in some commodities, the international community may want to design—and help finance—a program of adjustment in vulnerable countries that suffer deterioration in their terms of trade. These effects are likely to be confined to a few countries for several reasons: many food importers also export other agricultural products that will experience positive terms-of-trade changes from liberalization; others now have tariffs on those same food imports, tariffs that can be reduced to offset any increase in global prices; some food importers will gain access to new markets in nonagricultural products and be able to export; and, because prices will change relatively slowly, some food importers will increase domestic production in response to higher prices and become self-sufficient or even net exporters. Nonetheless, even though the changes are likely to be manageable at the global level, the issue requires study and in some countries may require action.

Because rich and poor countries alike will benefit from liberalization, all must make the policy changes necessary to realize its development promise. The rich countries, whose policies arguably distort international trade the most, cannot escape leadership on agriculture. Moreover, leadership among donors to finance a program to cushion adjustment is

Box 1 Trade and poverty: what are the links?

Countries that trade more grow faster, according to evidence emerging from case studies of trade liberalization and from large cross-country and time-series econometric studies. Although the links from specific trade policy instruments to trade outcomes and growth is less clear, the basic association between increased trade and growth is clear (box figure 1).[a]

Even when trade raises average incomes, its effects on poverty will depend on whether poverty in a given country is sensitive to growth in average incomes, and on how the increase in trade affects the distribution of income in the country. The first of these issues is empirically well understood. The sensitivity of poverty to growth in average incomes depends in an important way on initial inequalities in a country (Ravallion 1997). When incomes and opportunities are distributed relatively equally, the effect of growth on poverty is larger than when initial inequality is high. Thus, growth associated with increased trade (or from any other source) is likely to have larger proportional effects on poverty in countries where initial inequality is low.

More interesting and potentially more important are the effects of increased trade on the distribution of income. Almost by definition, if increased trade disproportionately benefits the poor, poverty will fall faster than if trade disproportionately benefits the nonpoor. Understanding the likely distributional consequences of trade liberalization is therefore crucial to understanding the overall effects of trade on poverty. In many cases, there are very direct channels through which trade liberalization is likely to disproportionately benefit the poor. For example, agricultural trade liberalization that allows previously suppressed prices of agricultural goods to rise to world levels will benefit farmers, who are net producers, but will hurt consumers. If farmers are more likely to be poor, the liberalization will be, on average, pro-poor. Similarly, reductions in tariffs on manufacturers will hurt previously protected urban workers, who

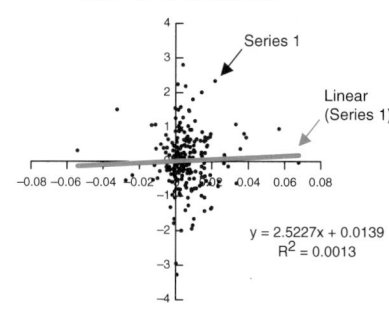

Box Figure 2 Changes in trade have little relation to inequality
Average annual change in Gini coefficient

Note: This figure shows changes in trade as a fraction of GDP and changes in the Gini measure of income inequality, for a large sample of growth episodes of at least five years in duration.
Source: Dollar and Kraay (2001).

in many developing countries are likely to be relatively well off, but will benefit poorer consumers of their products by lowering prices.

At the same time, however, the distributional consequences of trade liberalization can also work against poor people. For example, reductions in tariffs imply reductions in trade tax revenues that can be important in developing countries that rely disproportionately on this source of revenue. To the extent that public spending disproportionately benefits poor people (and this is by no means universal), reductions in tax revenues that accompany trade liberalization can have adverse distributional consequences.

The likely distributional consequences of trade liberalization, therefore, are complex and country-specific. Determining whether a given action would be pro- or anti-poor requires careful analysis. Looking back across countries, there is little evidence that increased trade is *systematically* associated with either increases or decreases in inequality (box figure 2).

On average, trade can be a powerful force for poverty reduction, especially over longer horizons where the cumulative effects of growth on incomes of the poor are large. But this will not be true for all countries at all times—underscoring the importance of complementary pro-poor policies at the country level to ensure maximum positive effects in every situation.

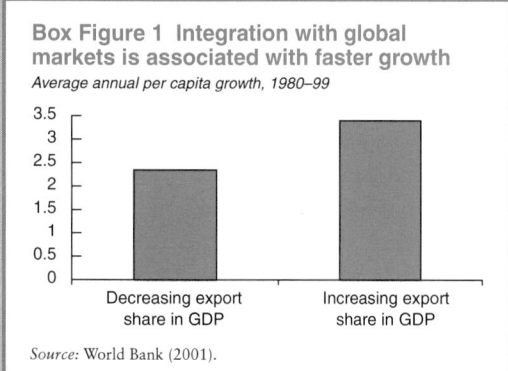

Box Figure 1 Integration with global markets is associated with faster growth
Average annual per capita growth, 1980–99
Source: World Bank (2001).

[a] For contrasting views on the state of the evidence on trade, trade policies, and growth, see Srinivasan and Bhagwati (2000), Rodriguez and Rodrik (1997), Bernanke and Rogoff (2001).
Source: World Bank staff.

essential; their technical assistance to help implement standards and facilitate trade is needed to help developing countries take advantage of new trade opportunities. Middle-income countries, whose own policy reforms would produce a large share of the benefit to developing countries from global liberalization in agriculture, have to move more assertively than in the past. Their high tariffs have an adverse impact on growing South-South trade, especially with neighboring countries. In a pattern common to all regions, agricultural exporters in East Asia, for example, paid one-third of all their tariff duties to other East Asian governments (second only to tariffs paid to get into rich countries). Agricultural exporters in the Middle East paid 44 percent of their tariff duties to regional neighbors.

Nonfarm trade is increasingly essential to growth in poor countries

Over the past two decades, developing countries have increased their share of global trade from just under one-quarter to about one-third. As a group, they have moved beyond their traditional specialization in agricultural and resource exports into manufactures trade. Exports of manufactures have grown at nearly twice the rate of agriculture, and now constitute nearly 80 percent of exports from all developing countries. Countries that were low income in 1980 managed to raise their exports of manufactures from roughly 20 percent of their total exports to more than 80 percent (figure 3). As a result, many grew quickly and entered the ranks of today's middle-income countries. The middle-income group of 1980 also increased its manufactures share, but somewhat less rapidly, to reach nearly 70 percent. This dramatic change in trade magnitudes and composition has given developing countries a new interest—and a powerful voice—in the ongoing Doha Round.

One reason for this change was the dramatic reduction in border barriers in developing countries since the mid-1980s, in combination with increased access to rich-country markets. Because import tariffs indirectly tax exports, reducing trade barriers in developing countries stimulated trade. The burden of import protection on all export activities in developing countries declined, but more so for manufactures than for agriculture and natural resources. At the same time, the fact that successive multilateral trade rounds liberalized global manufactures, while rich countries continued to protect their agriculture (and developing countries eventually began to follow suit) meant that developing countries' exports of manufactures were free to grow more rapidly than those in agriculture.

Today, trade in manufactures is still impeded. Although tariffs on manufacturing in rich countries are on average lower than in developing countries, the tariffs rich countries charge developing countries are substantially higher than those they charge other industrial countries. For example, exporters of manufactures from industrial countries face, on average, a tariff of 1 percent on their sales to other industrial countries; exporters in developing countries pay anywhere from 2 percent if they are from Latin America (where NAFTA weighs heavily) to 8 percent if they are from South Asia. Overall, rich countries collect from developing countries about twice the tariff revenues per dollar of imports that they collect from other rich countries. However, the problem is not solely a North-South issue. Latin American exporters of manufactures, for example, face tariffs in neighboring Latin American markets that are seven times higher than in industrial countries. In Sub-Saharan Africa, the same multiple is six; in South Asia, two.

Protection takes forms other than tariffs—among them quotas, specific duties, and contingent protection measures such as antidumping duties. As with tariffs, these measures tend to be used more frequently against labor-intensive products from developing countries. The quota arrangements in the WTO Agreement on Textiles and Clothing (ATC) still shackle the exports of many poor countries. Although these arrangements are scheduled to be removed in only 15 months, rich countries

GLOBAL ECONOMIC PROSPECTS

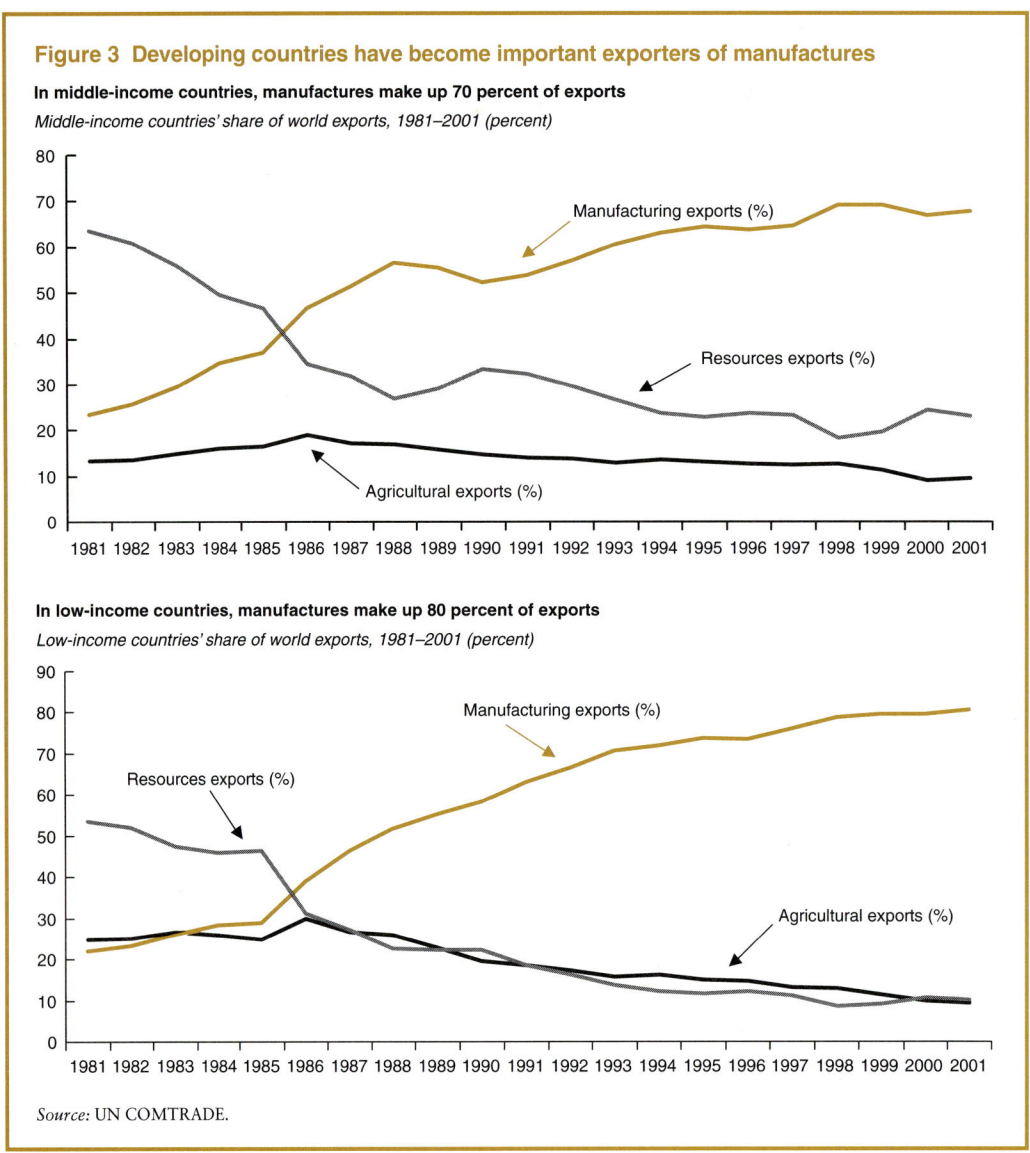

Figure 3 Developing countries have become important exporters of manufactures

to date have freed up only 15 percent of the quotas, obliging them to implement major changes at the end of the phase-in period. Average antidumping duties are seven to ten times higher than tariffs in industrial countries, and about five times higher in developing countries. Today's protection remains heavily concentrated in the most politically sensitive areas—textiles, clothing, and other labor-intensive manufactures, as well as agriculture—in both rich and poor countries.

Realizing the development promise of Doha depends particularly on three efforts.

- First, rich countries desirous of promoting development can do so by ensuring that the now lagging phase-out of the ATC is completed according to the agreement—and not reversed through antidumping actions. The ATC phase-out will also require reforms by some exporters facing increased competition, many of which are LDCs, to ensure a

smooth adjustment; trade-related development assistance could play a role in easing the transition.
- Second, in both rich and poor countries, efforts to cut back on antidumping measures that create a patchwork of ad hoc protection are essential if market access granted by the right hand of quota elimination and tariff reductions is not to be withdrawn by the left hand of antidumping suits. Developing countries themselves have become accomplished practitioners of contingent protection.
- Third, moving forward in nonfarm trade requires a Swiss-type formula approach that will require disproportionately greater reductions in high tariffs so as to mitigate the antidevelopment bias embedded in most tariff structures around the world. The choice of the formula, and of its coefficients of reduction, is important. Applying these cuts to bound rates will effectively credit developing countries that have unilaterally reduced their applied tariffs since the end of the Uruguay Round.

Services liberalization could raise productivity

Services are the fastest-growing component of the global economy. Even in developing countries, services exports grew more rapidly than manufactures in the 1990s (World Bank 2001, chapter 3). More efficient backbone services—in finance, telecommunications, domestic transportation, retail and wholesale distribution, and professional business services—improve the performance of the whole economy because they have broad linkage effects. Yet most developing regions trail the industrialized world in exposing service sectors to competition. Figure 4 shows that only Latin American countries are beginning to approximate the high-income countries in their degree of competition. Estimates suggest that, after controlling for other determinants of growth, countries that fully liberalized trade and investment in finance and telecommunications grew on average 1.5 percentage points faster than other countries over the past decade (Mattoo, et al. 2001).

No less important, developing countries have an interest in locking in market access for their services exports to rich-country markets—exports that are growing more rapidly than merchandise exports. Examples include China's incipient software industry as well as software and back-office services from India.

The Doha Round has the potential of locking in access to foreign markets for services exports. Just as many rich countries have not yet bound access for developing countries' services exports, many developing countries have yet to schedule with the WTO liberalizing reforms that have already been undertaken. Offering to bind unilateral reforms can be used to lock in existing access to overseas services markets. Active participation in the services negotiations could help accelerate these twin processes (Mattoo 2003).

The GATS process allows governments to liberalize services at their own pace. It does not require that a government forgo its regulatory responsibilities. Nor does the GATS framework require a cessation of subsidies or preempt pro-poor regulation on universal service access. The main requirement is that, once a sector is scheduled, governments are required to have transparent regulations, treat domestic and foreign companies alike, and permit all foreign companies access to the domestic market on the same terms as domestic companies. In fact, many governments have chosen to liberalize—but not to make commitments with the GATS that would bind this opening. Some two-thirds of the WTO members have scheduled fewer than 60 sectors of the approximately 160 sectors covered by the GATS. For example, only 12 developing countries have made commitments in education. None have made commitments in the provision of water.

Why the reluctance? Liberalization in services is more complicated than in goods markets. Privatization without competition and proper regulation may achieve nothing more than transforming a public monopoly into a private monopoly—with no improvement in services. And too many developing countries have been content to change ownership

GLOBAL ECONOMIC PROSPECTS

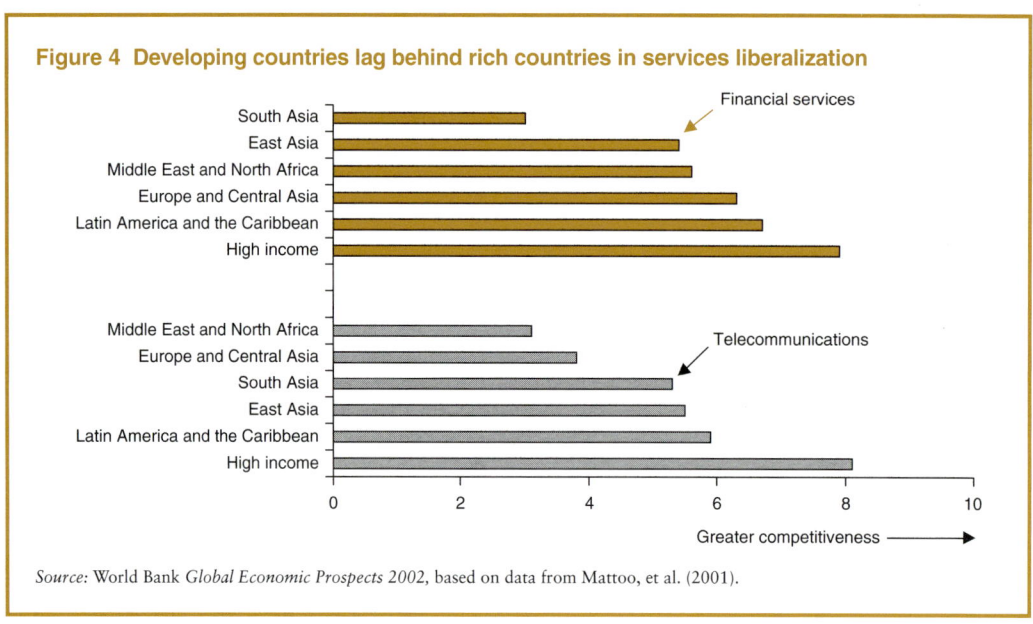

Figure 4 Developing countries lag behind rich countries in services liberalization

Source: World Bank *Global Economic Prospects 2002,* based on data from Mattoo, et al. (2001).

through privatization while retaining limits on entry that buttress monopolies.

Effective regulation is critical to ensure that the poor have access to basic services (World Bank 2002a, 2002b). Some sectors, such as retail and wholesale services, can be opened expeditiously because competition can be relied on to discipline firms' pricing and investment decisions. Others, however, require well-formulated regulations before liberalization to ensure proper market functioning and adequate access for low-income groups to services. In China's financial sector, for example, the World Bank recommended that financial markets be opened gradually to allow regulations and institutional developments to precede liberalization. The goal was to avoid destabilizing financial losses by state banks saddled with poor portfolios as efficient banks, domestic and foreign, entered the market (World Bank 1996). China's WTO accession agreement generally reflected this phased approach. In network sectors, such as telecommunications and water, ensuring adequate pricing and universal access are similarly important if the poor are to benefit from the expansion of the system (World Bank 2001, chapter 3). Trade ministers wishing to harness the reciprocal negotiating framework of the GATS to spur domestic reforms while leveraging market access abroad must ensure that sectoral ministries have properly sequenced regulations to support liberalization.

Liberalized trade in labor services could contribute much more

To date, virtually all GATS commitments have focused on the first three "modes" of international service delivery. Most trade in services has occurred through those same modes. Twenty-eight percent of the value of services trade, for example, has been in Mode 1, "cross-border supply of services." Another 14 percent has been in Mode 2, "consumption abroad," such as tourism. Fifty-six percent has been in Mode 3, "commercial presence," such as through foreign direct investment in services.

Mode 4, which involves the temporary movement of labor to provide services, accounts for only 1.4 percent of services trade (figure 5). Temporary movement has some advantages over permanent migration for both developed and developing countries. Rich countries can obtain workers whose skills are

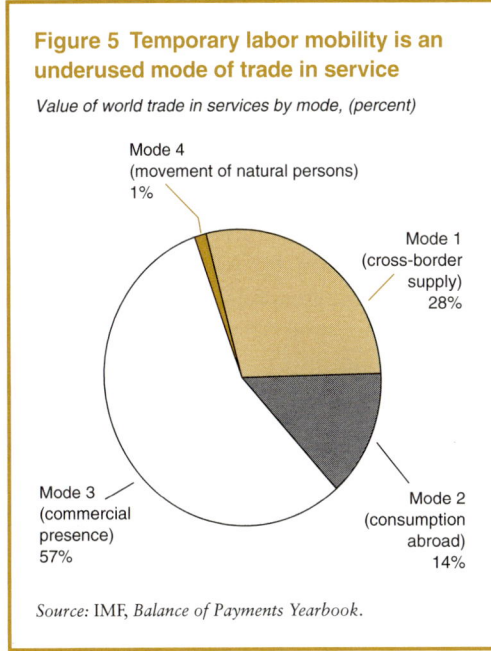

Figure 5 Temporary labor mobility is an underused mode of trade in service

Value of world trade in services by mode, (percent)

Source: IMF, Balance of Payments Yearbook.

in short supply, with minimal disruption of labor markets and without taxing social services. Temporary migration allows developing countries to obtain access to new, higher-paying jobs without necessarily suffering the "brain drain" that would occur with permanent migration. Poor countries also gain from remittances sent home by temporary migrants, and returning workers bring new skills back to the sending country. In 2001, remittances from permanent as well as temporary migrants provided some US$71 billion to developing countries, nearly 40 percent more than all official development assistance and significantly more than net debt flows to developing countries. If temporary movement of labor up to 3 percent of the total labor force in rich countries were permitted, developing countries would stand to gain as much as US$160 billion in additional income (Walmsley and Winters 2003).

To date, however, even after the significant liberalization of trade in services during the Uruguay Round, little has been done to loosen conditions governing the temporary movement of natural persons (TMNP) supplying services. Present commitments refer almost exclusively to higher-level personnel. More than 40 percent of workers covered by existing Mode 4 commitments are intracorporate transferees whose mobility is intimately related to foreign direct investment (often in services); another 50 percent are executives, specialists, and sales personnel who are business visitors. To date, therefore, Mode 4 has been of limited significance for developing countries, whose comparative advantage lies in the export of medium and low-skilled, labor-intensive services.

In addition to other concerns associated with broader migration issues, two fundamental tensions hamper progress on Mode 4 temporary labor mobility. The first is that governments are reluctant to undertake permanent commitments when employment demand varies with cyclical conditions. Wanting to maintain policy flexibility, immigration and labor market officials have made GATS commitments far below the degree of TMNP access already afforded under domestic laws and regulations. TMNP liberalization has been greatest in sectors (and for categories of workers) where labor demand routinely exceeds supply—tourism, information technology, health services. The second tension stems from the fact that regional patterns of migration create domestic political support for programs that favor neighboring countries, whereas Mode 4 programs necessarily are open to all countries on a most-favored-nation (MFN) basis. Preferential migration schemes are commonly negotiated at the bilateral and regional levels—and MFN-based liberalization would undermine these. Because many bilateral labor agreements are usually not tied to trade policy or other agreements, they afford governments a greater degree of flexibility to adjust programs to evolving migration trends and labor-market needs.

Tensions notwithstanding, present levels of Mode 4 use fall far short even of Mode 4's relatively modest potential. To rectify this, developing countries should expand their requests and offers in the Doha Round. Only six requests had been tabled by June 2003, and only two from developing countries (India and Colómbia). Also, WTO members should adopt rules that would provide greater clarity and predictability. To help regularize entry and exit while improving security, countries could adopt a GATS visa system that would facilitate national visas for up to one year, subject to appropriate security checks and oversight (see Hatcher 2003 and Self and Zutshi 2003).

Reducing transport costs and facilitating trade can have a powerful effect

The cost of moving goods across international borders is often as important as formal trade barriers in determining the cost of landed goods—and ultimately of market share. One study estimated that every day spent in customs adds nearly 1 percent to the cost of goods (Hummels 2001). In developing countries, transit costs are routinely two to four times higher than in rich countries. Transparent customs regimes, modern port facilities, dense transportation networks, and access to information and telecommunications systems—all can help lower transit costs.

Since September 11, 2001, security has become a dominant issue in international trade. Border inspections, cargo review, and other measures have increased transport times and driven up costs. Each 1 percent increase in costs to trade from programs to tighten border security reduces world income by US$75 billion per year. Developing countries, too, are vulnerable to security threats and terrorism, but limited budgets, dependence on foreign trade and investment, and outdated infrastructure and technology present serious challenges for these countries. New security protocols being deployed at ports, customs offices, and border posts around the world have the potential to add costs and diminish market access for developing countries—at least in the short term. But managed correctly, the same measures can streamline trade transactions while promoting safety and security. To achieve this trade-expanding result, a global framework must be established to ensure that the needs of developing countries are addressed as enhanced security regimes take shape.

To counter any trade-reducing effects of security measures, every effort to cut trade-related costs in other areas is imperative. Regulatory restrictions on international air and maritime transport services inflate transport costs—on some routes by amounts that dwarf the value of tariffs. International air transport, which carries about 30 percent of developing countries' exports by value, is heavily protected from international competition. Bilateral air service agreements commonly bar entry to efficient outside carriers, thereby raising export costs for developing countries. City-pair routes on which more than two passenger airlines or dedicated freight airlines operate can cut costs by an average of 10.7 percent. Maritime transport, too, is often subject to practices, such as cargo-reservation schemes and limitations on port services, which protect inefficient service providers. Such competition-restricting practices among shipping lines and port-terminal operators can increase freight rates up to 25 percent on some routes. Rising concentration in the market for port-terminal services has increased the risk that private firms may capture the benefits of government reforms. Abusive practices by private operators are of special concern in developing countries, where traffic volumes are lower and competitive forces inherently more limited. Regulations governing such practices are now outside the WTO mandate, but logically they should be reviewed for reformulation.

Facilitating trade by eliminating delays in developing countries would lower trading costs significantly, particularly if accompanied by liberalization of transport and telecommunications, and streamlined regulations to promote domestic competition. Trade facilitation requires modernizing customs, improving port facilities, and making investments in trade-related information technology—a huge institutional and infrastructural agenda. Countries display wide variation in customs efficiency and clearance times, for example (figure 6). If those whose trade-facilitation capacity was below average could be brought halfway up to

OVERVIEW

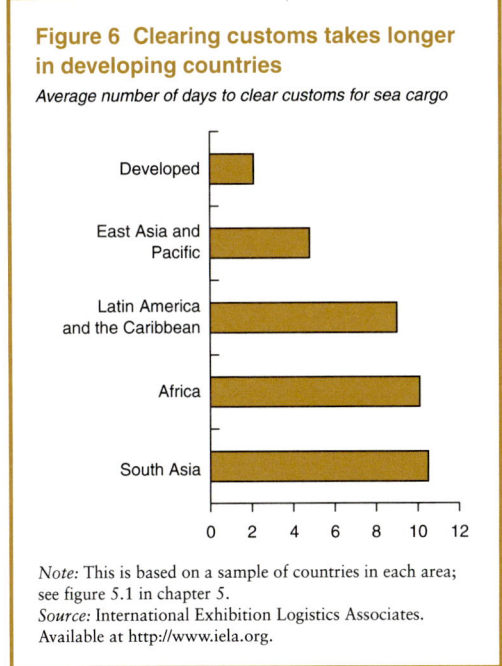

Figure 6 Clearing customs takes longer in developing countries
Average number of days to clear customs for sea cargo

Note: This is based on a sample of countries in each area; see figure 5.1 in chapter 5.
Source: International Exhibition Logistics Associates. Available at http://www.iela.org.

the global average, international trade would increase by US$380 billion annually.

Multilateral efforts are under way outside the WTO to promote—and in some cases finance—institutional changes in trade facilitation. Key players include the World Customs Organization, the regional development banks, and the World Bank. Their efforts focus on policy reform, technical assistance, and infrastructure modernization.

Should trade facilitation, investment, and competition be the subject of new multilateral disciplines in the WTO?
As one of the four Singapore issues, trade facilitation is under discussion in Geneva for possible inclusion in the Doha Agenda. Already the WTO, through the GATS, has a potentially important role to play in international transport and trade logistics—many of the transport service sectors could be immediately scheduled with the GATS if countries saw fit to do so. However, few countries have taken advantage of its provisions.

Aspects of trade facilitation are part of the WTO's trade-related disciplines, particularly the provisions that encourage uniform treatment of transit trade and transparency of fees. Strengthening provisions related to transit, fees, and transparency, issues originally in the General Agreement on Tariffs and Trade (GATT), would be helpful. However, best practice cannot be established in a vacuum; it has to be gradually created in sound domestic laws, regulations, and practices. A sustained program of institutional reform must be tailored to each country, and it often requires technical assistance. The bilateral donors and multilateral development banks and agencies are best positioned to provide the thorough diagnostics and technical assistance required to promote needed institutional change.

If the dynamics of the Doha negotiations propel the WTO into a role in the broader trade-facilitation agenda, any agreement, if it is to be effective, should recognize limitations in domestic capacity for implementation. An agreement would be most effective if it included a serious commitment by developed nations to finance new trade-facilitation systems. Development assistance delivered under the commitment could be provided by the World Customs Organization, the multilateral development banks, and bilateral donors. The obligations of developing countries should be tailored to their implementation capacity. And because the WTO's dispute settlement provisions are largely inappropriate to promoting institutional changes, conventional enforcement of dispute settlement through trade sanctions ought to be set aside.

Other Singapore issues would stretch the WTO mandate into yet new areas, probably with only marginal development benefits if taken up in isolation. As discussed in *Global Economic Prospects 2003*, there is no evidence that an investment agreement would, by itself, promote new foreign investment. Similarly, adopting an agreement in competition policy—as currently framed in the negotiations—would

XXV

have minimal effects on the terms of trade of developing countries, unless the agreement were to establish new disciplines on national export cartels and illegal international cartels (World Bank 2002a, chapter 4). Finally, a new agreement on government procurement that focuses on transparency is unlikely to improve market access substantially (Evenett 2002). Virtually all of the disciplines proposed in these arrangements would require new policy actions only in developing countries. Although some of these may promote development, the main benefits of WTO agreements in these areas would be in the market access that new agreements leverage (Newfarmer 2003).

Securing the benefits of trade for the poorest countries

More favorable and differential treatment of developing countries is a prominent feature of multilateral trade rules. Selected subsets of countries have been granted trade preferences. Some countries were granted exemptions or allowed to defer implementing some multilateral agreements; many have benefited from technical assistance to help implement mandates.

The present patchwork system has not worked especially well. Countries benefiting from trade preferences have generally underperformed in exports. One reason is that rich countries grant preferences voluntarily rather than as part of a binding multilateral negotiation. Those preferences often come laden with restrictions, product exclusions, and administrative rules that prevent beneficiaries from taking full advantage of them. For example, only 39 percent of potentially preferred imports under the Generalized System of Preferences (GSP) into the Quad countries—Canada, the EU, Japan, and the United States—actually took advantage of preferential access—and usage rates are declining (figure 7). At times, protectionist lobbies have weighed in to pressure for reductions in the preference, either before a country was deemed eligible or even later, when the first signs of export success for developing countries become evident. Beyond GSP, the Quad countries sponsor their own

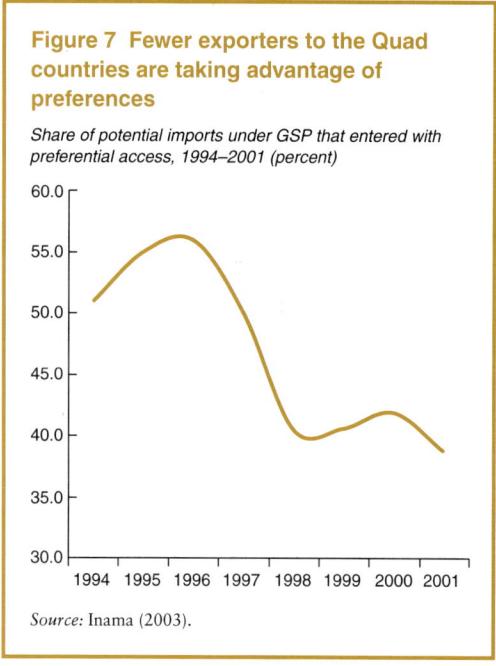

Figure 7 Fewer exporters to the Quad countries are taking advantage of preferences

Share of potential imports under GSP that entered with preferential access, 1994–2001 (percent)

Source: Inama (2003).

"deep preference" programs, such as the EU's Everything But Arms program and the U.S. African Growth and Opportunity Act, but each has different rules and exceptions. For these reasons, preferences cover only a portion of exports from even poor developing countries—and among eligible countries and products, only a fraction of preferences are actually used. Even when effective, preferences tend to divert trade away from other poor countries, effectively "robbing Peru to pay Panama."

Existing preferences do relatively little for most of the world's poor people (those living on less than US$1 per day), most of whom live in China, India, Nigeria, Pakistan, Northeast Brazil, and the ASEAN countries, which may enjoy only partial preferences at best. Although some of these countries enjoy limited preferential access to some markets, all would be better off with across-the-board, nondiscriminatory binding access.

Finally, the extensive use of voluntary preference schemes has created perverse incentives in both rich and poor countries to avoid liberalization that would otherwise benefit the poor. Too often, rich countries have offered differential treatment to a subset of poor countries instead of arriving at MFN reductions in trade barriers that would benefit all developing countries. And, too often, developing countries have sought preferential access and exemptions from agreed MFN reductions in trade barriers that would benefit themselves and other developing countries. In other words, the present system of preferences reduces the incentives to negotiate effectively for reductions in trade barriers abroad and with domestic protectionist constituencies at home.

Making trade regime more supportive of development therefore involves four important policy directions.

- Central to any new regime is improvement in market access for all developing countries on an MFN basis, especially in products that have hitherto escaped WTO disciplines, such as agriculture and labor-intensive products. Broad market access would allow trade reform to reach the 70 percent of the world's poor not living in the 49 least developed countries.
- Trade preferences would be more effective if they were consistent and uniform, shorn of restrictions that raise the cost of taking advantage of preferences. WTO rules that require institutional improvements—especially "behind the border" policies, as distinct from trade policy changes that can be implemented at the "stroke of the pen"—would be more effective if they were calibrated to developing countries' capacity to implement them. As countries move up the ladder of development, they should be expected to assume the full obligations of WTO members.
- Integrating technical assistance into the national priorities for development while increasing "aid for trade"—a part of the Monterrey consensus—could help poor developing countries identify and address trade-capacity priorities. Increased development assistance—for ports, customs, and logistics management—would augment the capacity of developing-country firms to benefit from market-access opportunities.
- Finally, the WTO membership must learn which of its policies promote, and which defeat, the interests of developing countries. Getting the rules right is arguably the major challenge confronting WTO members from a development perspective. Among other things, getting the rules right means limiting new rule-making to cases in which the payoff for developing countries is clearly positive.

TRIPS and Public Health

Negotiations at the WTO on patents and public health have stalemated over the question of improving access to generic drugs for poor countries. The WTO's Agreement on Trade Related Aspects of Intellectual Property Rights (TRIPS), which took effect in 1995, obliges countries to extend patent protection to pharmaceutical products and processes after a phase-in period linked to level of development (World Bank 2001, chapter 5). Under these rules, countries that are able to manufacture the drugs themselves would continue to have legal access to generics if they chose to issue compulsory licenses. These tend to be the larger and better-off developing countries such as Brazil, China, India, and Thailand. Countries that lack sufficient manufacturing capability—typically the world's poorest and often most disease-ravaged states—may be barred from importing generic versions of patent-protected drugs, once rules take effect. Hence, the Doha mandate on TRIPS and Public Health included finding a mechanism by which such countries can import generic drugs protected by patents abroad.

These rules are important for poor people. For example, one day's supply of patented antiretrovirals to treat a single HIV/AIDS patient can cost as much as US$30 in rich countries. Such prices are prohibitive for the nearly 3 billion people who live on less than US$2 per day. Generics are not always cheaper, but the threat of competition has helped to reduce prices of patented antiretrovirals supplied to developing-country governments (Fink 2003).

Patents create incentives for research by offering temporary monopolies on new drugs, and developing countries need that research as much as the rest of the world. Indeed, increased R&D for medicines to treat diseases that are more prevalent in developing countries is desperately needed. Yet poor countries that lack pharmaceutical manufacturing capability form only a tiny portion—perhaps less than 1 to 2 percent—of the global pharmaceuticals market. In the 12 months to October 2002, developed countries accounted for more than 95 percent of the US$270 billion of sales in the world's leading 20 country markets worldwide. The group of developing countries that may benefit from a WTO agreement on importing generic drugs under compulsory licensing probably accounts for less than 1 or 2 percent of global pharmaceutical sales. Permitting the export to these markets of generic versions of patented medicines developed for rich-country markets is unlikely to erode incentives for research and development (Fink 2003). Despite this unlikelihood, the negotiations going into the summer of 2003 were stalemated on possible restrictions of the list of diseases that would be covered by any new agreement.

Governments everywhere have potentially competing interests. They have an interest in maintaining R&D and in preventing illegal generics entering rich-country markets from undercutting patent rights that finance it. Strengthening mechanisms that prevent such illegal trade is important, such as by prohibiting generic manufacturers from mimicking the packaging of patented drugs. At the same time, governments everywhere have an interest in ensuring that limited budgets for drugs to improve health in poor countries go as far as possible, and this means that all developing countries have access to drugs at the cheapest most competitive prices. In balancing these objectives, any eventual agreement should put the developing countries with insufficient manufacturing capacity on the same footing as those countries that have manufacturing capacity.

Resolving the Doha issue is only one small piece of the larger problem of delivering drugs and health care to sick people in developing countries. Of equal importance to the health of the poor is undertaking the large investments in complementary health infrastructure, including hospitals, roads, warehouses, and doctors and nurses. For example, even in some countries that manufacture anti-AIDS generics or that get AIDS drugs free, governments have not succeeded in providing medicines to significant shares of the needy population. Second, funding for fighting the developing world's health crisis needs to be scaled up—and massively. For example, the latest projections by UNAIDS put the cost of the global struggle against AIDS at US$10.5 billion a year by 2005 and US$15 billion a year by 2007; even if governments in affected countries cover part of this amount, estimated aid flows of about US$3 billion in 2002 are still insufficient. The *Global Fund to Fight Aids, Tuberculosis, and Malaria* remains cash-strapped. The recent U.S. commitment of US$15 billion to fight HIV/AIDS will, when disbursed, partially relieve resource constraints, but a substantial funding gap remains. The TRIPS issue is small when compared with the real obstacles preventing access to better health in developing countries, and it concerns a small corner of the global pharmaceutical market—two reasons why the international community should move swiftly to resolve it.

Delivering the Doha deal for development

The potential for reciprocal reductions in trade protection holds the promise of better lives for everyone. To illustrate, we consider the effects of a pro-poor agreement in which rich countries cut tariff peaks to 10 percent in agriculture and to 5 percent in manufacturing, and in which these reductions are reciprocated with cuts to 15 and 10 percent in developing countries (table 1). This program, combined with reductions in prevailing tariff averages, a decoupling of agricultural subsidies, and an end to agricultural subsidies could realize nearly three-quarters of the gains that might be anticipated from full merchandise liberalization.

Table 1 A pro-poor tariff reduction program
(percent)

	Rich	Developing
Agriculture		
Average	5	10
Maximum	10	15
Manufacturing		
Average	1	5
Maximum	5	10

This illustrative pro-poor program, discussed in detail in chapter 1, if implemented progressively over the five years to 2010 and accompanied by a realistic productivity response, would produce gains for developing countries of nearly US$350 billion in additional income by 2015. Rich countries would benefit, too, with gains on the order of US$170 billion. All of this would mean that 8 percent fewer people would be living in poverty in 2015—140 million fewer people living below US$2 per day. If greater opening of services, including Mode 4, were to occur, the benefits would be substantially greater.[2]

Delivering a Doha deal that spurs development will not be easy. Negotiators may well have to transcend the mercantilist mind-set that tends to dominate trade negotiations. All segments of the international community must keep their focus on potential gains, not only from "winning concessions" from foreign partners, but also on the gains from domestic reforms that "pay for" foreign concessions. Rich-country negotiators will do better, for themselves and for the developing world, if they keep in mind that their own countries can benefit by directing agricultural subsidies away from production subsidies for large farmers toward income subsidies to relatively small family farms, delivered in a form that is decoupled from output. Middle-income country negotiators likewise have to keep in mind that their telecommunications and financial services could be much more efficient and less expensive if more competitors were allowed to enter well-regulated markets. Low-income countries that have high protection will find they benefit from domestic reforms that lower costs of imported inputs, increase domestic competition that spurs productivity growth, and expand exports. Study after study has shown that trade reforms redound first and fastest to the reformer.

Negotiations will determine the pace and details of a final package, but the broad outlines of a potentially good deal for development are already evident from this analysis. Realizing that agricultural reform in a time of rapidly rising budget deficits will contribute positively to their own economic growth, rich countries would benefit from reforms in agriculture. Lopping off tariff peaks and phasing out the ATC at the end of 2004 will benefit developed-country poor who are forced to pay more for food and clothing because of external protection (Gresser 2002). Further progress on the part of all countries in reducing tariffs in manufactures would benefit developing countries and stimulate healthy South-South trade. For the rich countries, the prospect of greater access to markets in developing countries—home to 80 percent of the world's population with markets growing two to three times faster than their own—is also a worthy prize.

Developing countries, too, have much to gain. Middle-income countries—continuing a process begun over the last two decades—may do well to open selected services markets, often plagued by inefficiency that dampens productivity of the whole economy, in exchange for greater access in agriculture and labor-intensive goods. Because many countries have already lowered tariffs, the issue is now to bind those new lower levels. Finally, low-income countries would benefit if, in relinquishing demands for exemption from disciplines on their own tariffs, they succeed in obtaining commitments to greater market access in products and services of importance to them, a new commitment to consistency in the administration of preferences, and development assistance to facilitate trade and implement new WTO rules in accord with domestic capacities and development priorities. Delivering this type of deal would go far toward fulfilling the development promise of the Doha Agenda.

Notes

1. *Global Economic Prospects 2002: Making Trade Work for the World's Poor* (World Bank 2001), in addition to analyzing agriculture, labor-intensive manufactures, and services, dealt with regulatory impediments in transportation (chapter 4) and intellectual property rights and TRIPS (chapter 5). *Global Economic Prospects 2003: Investing to Unlock Global Opportunities* (World Bank 2002a) analyzed two of the Singapore issues—investment and competition policy—from a development perspective (chapter 4).

2. *Global Economic Prospects 2002* presents illustrations of the gains from services liberalization. While we do not have firm estimates of relative parameters, several studies have shown that gains are likely to be a multiple of merchandise liberalization. See World Bank (2001), chapter 6.

References

Bernanke, Ben, and Kenneth Rogoff, eds. 2001. *Macroeconomics Annual 2001*. Cambridge, Mass.: MIT Press.

Dollar, David, and Aart Kraay. 2001. "Trade, Growth, and Poverty." World Bank Policy Research Department Working Paper 1615.

Evenett, S. 2002. "The WTO Government Procurement Agreement: An Assessment of Current Research and Options for Reform." Paper presented at the roundtable "Informing the Doha Process: New Trade Research for Developing Countries." Egypt. May 20–21.

Fink, C. 2003. "Implementing the Doha Mandate on TRIPS and Public Health." *Trade Note 5*. Washington, D.C.: World Bank. May (www.worldbank.org/trade).

Gresser, E. 2002. "America's Hidden Tax on the Poor: The Case for Reforming U.S. Tariff Policy." Progressive Policy Institute Policy Report. Washington, D.C.: Progressive Policy Institute. March.

Hatcher, Mark. 2003. Draft Model Schedule for Mode 4: A Proposal. In Aaditya Mattoo and Antonia Carzaniga, eds., *Moving People to Deliver Services*. Washington, D.C.: Oxford University Press and World Bank, 2003.

Hummels, D. 2001. "Time as a Trade Barrier." Mimeo. Department of Economics, Purdue University, Lafayette, Ind.

Inama, Stefano. 2003. "Trade Preferences and the WTO Negotiations on Market Access." Mimeo. UNCTAD.

International Monetary Fund (IMF). *Balance of Payments Statistics Yearbook*. Washington, D.C.: IMF.

IMF-World Bank. 2002. "Market Access for Developing Country Exports—Selected Issues." Washington, D.C.: World Bank, September 26.

Mattoo, Aaditya. 2003. "Services in a Development Round." Paper presented to the OECD Global Forum on Trade, OECD, Paris, June 5–6, 2003.

Mattoo, A., R. Rathindran, and A. Subramanian. 2001. "Measuring Services Trade Liberalization and Its Impact on Economic Growth: An Illustration." World Bank Policy Research Working Paper 2655. World Bank, Washington, D.C.

Newfarmer, R. 2003. "From Singapore to Cancún: Investment." *Trade Note* 2. Washington, D.C.: World Bank. May (www.worldbank.org/trade).

Ravallion, Martin. 1997. "Can High-Inequality Countries Escape Absolute Poverty?" *Economics Letters* 56(1): 51–57.

Rodriguez, Francisco, and Dani Rodrik. 1999. "Trade Policy and Economic Growth: A Skeptic's Guide to the Cross-National Evidence." NBER Working Paper W7081. NBER, Cambridge, Mass.

Self, R. J., and B. K. Zutshi. 2003. "Mode 4: Negotiating Challenges and Opportunities." In Aaditya Mattoo and Antonia Carzaniga, eds., *Moving People to Deliver Services*. Washington, D.C.: Oxford University Press and World Bank, 2003.

Srinivasan, T.N., and Jadgish Bhagwati. 2000. "Outward-Orientation and Development: Are Revisionists Right?" *Macroeconomics Annual 2000*. Cambridge: MIT Press.

Walmsley, T. L., and A. Winters. 2003. "Relaxing the Restrictions on the Temporary Movements of Natural Persons: A Simulation Analysis." CEPR Discussion Paper 3719. London: Center for Economic Policy Research.

World Bank. 1996. *The Chinese Economy: Fighting Inflation, Deepening Reforms*. Washington, D.C.: World Bank. April.

———.2001. *Global Economic Prospects 2002: Making Trade Work for the World's Poor*. Washington, D.C.: World Bank.

———.2002a. *Global Economic Prospects 2003: Investing to Unlock Global Opportunities*. Washington, D.C.: World Bank.

———.2002b. *World Development Report 2003: Sustainable Development in a Dynamic World*. Washington, D.C.: World Bank.

Abbreviations and Data Notes

ACE	Automated commercial environment
ACP	African Caribbean and Pacific states
ACPC	Association of Coffee Producing Countries
AGOA	African Growth and Opportunity Act
APEC	Asia Pacific Economic Cooperation
ASAs	Air service agreements
ASCM	Agreement on Subsidies and Countervailing Measures
ASEAN	Association of Southeast Asian Nations
ASECNA	Agency for Air Transport Security in Africa
ATC	Agreement on Textiles and Clothing
ATPA	Andean Trade Preferences Act
ATPDEA	Andean Trade Promotion and Drug Eradication Act
CACM	Central American Common Market
CAP	Common Agricultural Program
CARICOM	Caribbean Community
CBERA	Caribbean Basin Economic Recovery Acts
CBI	Caribbean Basin Initiative
CBTPA	Caribbean Basin Trade Partnership Act
CEE	Central and Eastern Europe
CEPR	Center for Economic and Policy Research
CIS	Commonwealth of Independent States
COMTRADE	U.S. Commodity Trade Statistics
CSI	Container Security Initiative
C-TPAT	Customs-Trade Partnership Against Terrorism
DFID	Department for International Development
DRIFE	Danish Research Institute of Food Economics
DTIS	Diagnostic Trade Integration Study
ECB	European Central Bank

EEA	European Economic Area
EMBI	Emerging Markets Bond Index
EU	European Union
FAO	Food and Agricultural Organization
FDA	Food and Drug Administration
FDI	Foreign direct investment
FTA	Free Trade Area
GATS	General Agreement on Trade in Services
GATT	General Agreement on Tariffs and Trade
GCC	Gulf Cooperation Council
GDP	Gross domestic product
GSP	Generalized System of Preference
GTAP	Global Trade Analysis Project
HITS	Harmonized Tariff Schedule
HIV/AIDS	Human immunodeficiency virus/acquired immune deficiency syndrome
HKSC	Hong Kong Shippers Council
IADB	Inter-American Development Bank
ICAO	International Civil Aviation Organization
ICO	International Coffee Organization
ICTSD	International Center for Trade and Sustainable Development
IISD	International Institute for Sustainable Development
ILO	International Labour Organization
IMF	International Monetary Fund
IMO	International Maritime Organization
INS	Immigration and Naturalization Service
ISM	Institute for Supply Management
LDCs	Least developed countries
LME	London Metals Exchange
LNG	Liquid natural gas
MFN	Most favored nation
NAFTA	North America Free Trade Agreement
NASDAQ	National Association of Security Dealers
NAV	Non-ad-valorem
NIEs	Newly industrialized economies
OECD	Organisation for Economic Co-operation and Development
OPEC	Organization for Petroleum Exporting Countries
PECC	Pacific Economic Cooperation Council
PPI	Purchasing Parity Index

ABBREVIATIONS AND DATA NOTES

PROCAMPO	Programa de Apoyos Directos al Campo (National Program for Agricultural Direct Support)
PSRE	Program de soutien à la relance economique
QUAD	Canada, European Union, Japan, and United States
RDS	Research, development, and statistics
SAARC	South Asian Association for Regional Cooperation
SARS	Severe Acute Respiratory Syndrome
SDT	Special and differential treatment
SMEs	Small and medium-sized enterprises
SOLAS	Safety of Life at Sea Convention
SOPEMI	Continuous Reporting System on Migration
STAR	Secure Trade in the APEC Region
TMNP	Temporary movement of natural persons
TN	Trade NAFTA
TRIPS	Trade-related aspects of intellectual property rights
TRQs	Tariff rate quotas
UN/ECE	United Nations Economic Commission for Europe
UNCTAD	United Nations Conference for Trade and Development
UNDCP	United Nations International Drug Control Program
UNECE	United Nations Economic Commission for Europe
USAID	United States Agency for International Development
USCS	U.S. Customs Service
USDA	U.S. Department of Agriculture
USTR	U.S. Trade Representative
WCO	World Customs Organization
WFP	World Food Program
WITS	World Integrated Trade Solutions
WTO	World Trade Organization

Data notes

The "classification of economies" tables at the end of this volume classify economies by income, region, export category, and indebtedness. Unless otherwise indicated, the term "developing countries" as used in this volume covers all lower- and middle-income countries, including countries with economies in transition.

All dollar figures are U.S. dollars.

1

Global Outlook and the Developing Countries

The global economy continues to be weak
For the third year in a row the global economy in 2003 is growing well below potential, at an expected rate of 2 percent. The global slowdown that began in 2001 with the bursting of the equity-market bubble evolved into a subdued recovery during 2002. Initially, the sharp downturn in business investment was a critical factor behind sluggish growth, as corporations worldwide redressed the substantial financial imbalances that had emerged during the boom of the late 1990s. The pace of activity faltered again at end-2002 and early 2003 in response to events that undermined confidence: the buildup to war in Iraq, transatlantic tensions, persistent concerns about terrorism, and the outbreak of Severe Acute Respiratory Syndrome (SARS). Consumer and business confidence waned again—and so did spending.

Manufacturing production as well as GDP growth in the rich countries slowed considerably at the turn of the year. The momentum of goods production retrenched to negative territory, and G-7 GDP growth braked from an annualized pace of 2.8 percent during the third quarter of 2002 to 0.8 percent by the first quarter of 2003.

Developing countries faced a difficult environment in 2002 to mid 2003. Latin America's GDP contracted in 2002 because of political problems in Venezuela, investor concerns about Brazil in the run-up to elections, and fallout from Argentina's default. Per capita incomes will barely rise this year, despite an encouraging rebound in most countries of the region. Activity in South Asia is holding up well. Countries in East Asia lost some growth momentum due to SARS, but its apparent containment has opened the way to a resumption of rapid growth. Africa continues to underperform: although the region's commodity prices have firmed, they are still well below long-term trends. War has affected regional performance in the Middle East and North Africa; while many countries in Central and Eastern Europe are undergoing sluggish growth tied to lackluster conditions in Western Europe, especially in Germany.

Macro policy response has been strongly supportive, but it is approaching limits
Policymakers, particularly in the United States, reacted to the slowdown in 2001 with significant monetary easing and fiscal stimulus. The stimulus and the effects of automatic stabilizers prevented a sharper downturn in the global economy and helped improve the external environment for developing-country growth.

But the scope for substantial further macroeconomic stimulus is rapidly dissipating. Fiscal deficits threaten to become part of the problem instead of part of the solution, especially since a quick reversal of the deficit is not anticipated. The U.S. general government budget position (including Social Security), for example, shifted dramatically from a surplus of 2.3 percent of GDP in 2000 to a deficit of 3.2 percent as of the first quarter of 2003. The

Congressional Budget Office projects that the budget position is unlikely to return to surplus until 2012. In Europe, several large countries have breached the 3-percent-of-GDP fiscal deficit limits embedded in the Maastricht criteria for the common currency. And Japan has limited fiscal scope, given persistent deficits in the 6–7 percent range. Interest rates have been brought down sharply in the United States as well as in Japan, where they stand at an effective rate of zero. Following the recent 50-basis point cut in rates, Europe still has modest headroom for monetary easing should the European Central Bank choose to relax its inflation target. In fact, downward price trends in the United States and Europe have triggered concerns of possible deflation.

Activity should build gradually through 2004–05, but risks remain

Barring additional shocks, global growth should pick up to 3 percent in 2004, as firms in the rich countries make progress in adjusting balance sheets and begin to upgrade capital stock and replenish inventories (table 1.1). The financial headwinds that have constrained investment are apparently diminishing across the OECD centers. Early signs of renewed economic activity are appearing in the United States—including an upturn in orders, production, and exports, as well as firming equity markets. Yet conditions in Europe and Japan remain extremely slack. Improvement in confidence will prove the key to a revival in capital spending and growth. Following an advance of 4 percent in 2003, developing countries are likely to grow at 4.9 percent in 2004, grounded in a revival of world trade, the fading of global tensions, and the rekindling of domestic demand.

But risks to the outlook remain. First, the pace of stabilization in the Middle East remains uncertain. Second, SARS, though now apparently under control, could reemerge next flu season and would present challenges to policymakers worldwide, especially in China. Third, and more broadly, a reversal of the incipient investment rebound in the industrial countries cannot be ruled out, as investment growth dropped sharply during the first quarter of 2003. Finally, the U.S. current account deficit is surpassing historic levels. During 2002, U.S. external financing needs claimed 10.3 percent of the savings of the rest of the world—more than double the levels of 1998. Moreover, the composition of finance also shifted toward short-term flows: net FDI flows were negative by almost $100 billion; U.S. banks' overseas lending had ceased; and foreign official inflows (most from East Asia) increased to nearly $100 billion, from $5 billion in 2001. A sudden reversal in these short-term flows could undercut U.S. and world growth. The 25 percent fall of the U.S. dollar against the euro in the last 18 months represents at least a partial adjustment.

Structural reforms could boost confidence

With scope for additional macroeconomic stimulus fading, the focus of policy in the rich countries should arguably shift toward structural reforms that help restore business and consumer confidence. These could include efforts to resolve the nonperforming loan problem in the Japanese banking system and to achieve positive inflation rates there; addressing corporate governance and related issues in the United States, and needed labor market reforms in Europe. A rekindling of multilateral consensus on economic policy would also contribute to renewed confidence, which had been shaken by geopolitical tensions and security concerns.

Intensified trade underpins strong developing country growth in the long run

One important and ongoing program is the Doha Development Agenda, where progress could do much for near-term sentiment and eventually for global growth. Intensified trade relations during the 1990s and the increasingly global nature of production and distribution have sharply increased productivity in tradable sectors and drastically changed trade patterns, laying the foundation for future growth. Productivity growth in manufacturing sectors that compete in international markets

Table 1.1 Global growth should accelerate, but risks persist
Global conditions affecting growth in developing countries and world GDP

	2001	Current estimate 2002	Current forecasts 2003	2004	2005	GDF2003 forecasts 2003	2004
Global conditions							
World trade (volume)	−0.7	3.0	4.6	7.9	7.9	6.2	8.1
Inflation (consumer prices)							
G-7 OECD countries[a, b]	1.5	1.0	1.4	0.9	1.4	1.4	1.3
United States	2.8	1.6	1.9	1.2	2.3	2.5	2.3
Commodity prices (nominal $)							
Commodity prices, except oil ($)	−9.1	5.1	6.9	1.1	1.5	8.2	2.3
Oil price ($, weighted average), $/bbl	24.4	24.9	26.5	22.0	20.0	26.0	21.0
Oil price (percent change)	−13.7	2.4	6.3	−17.0	−9.1	4.3	−19.2
Manufactures export unit value ($)[c]	−4.5	−0.1	4.0	−0.4	1.5	5.6	−0.1
Interest rates							
LIBOR, 6 months ($, percent)	3.5	1.8	1.0	2.0	3.8	1.7	3.2
EURIBOR, 6 months (Euro, percent)	4.2	3.4	2.1	2.1	3.1	2.4	2.3
GDP (growth)[d]							
World	1.3	1.9	2.0	3.0	2.9	2.3	3.2
Memo item: World GDP (PPP)[e]	2.3	3.0	3.1	3.9	3.8	3.2	4.1
High-income countries	0.9	1.6	1.5	2.5	2.4	1.9	2.9
OECD countries	1.0	1.6	1.5	2.5	2.3	1.8	2.8
United States	0.3	2.4	2.2	3.4	2.8	2.5	3.5
Japan	0.4	0.1	0.8	1.3	1.3	0.6	1.6
Euro Area	1.5	0.8	0.7	1.7	2.1	1.4	2.6
Non-OECD countries	−1.1	2.4	2.1	4.1	4.4	3.0	4.3
Developing countries	2.9	3.3	4.0	4.9	4.8	4.0	4.7
East Asia and Pacific	5.5	6.7	6.1	6.7	6.6	6.4	6.6
Europe and Central Asia	2.2	4.6	4.3	4.5	4.1	3.7	3.7
Latin America and the Caribbean	0.3	−0.8	1.8	3.7	3.8	1.7	3.8
Middle East and North Africa	3.2	3.1	3.3	3.9	3.5	3.7	3.9
Oil exporters	2.9	3.2	3.9	3.9	3.3	4.0	3.7
Diversified economies	3.8	2.8	2.4	3.7	3.8	3.1	4.2
South Asia	4.9	4.2	5.4	5.4	5.4	5.3	5.2
Sub-Saharan Africa	3.2	2.8	2.8	3.5	3.8	3.0	3.6
Memorandum item							
Developing countries: excluding China and India	1.7	2.0	3.1	4.1	4.1	2.9	3.9

a. Canada, France, Germany, Italy, Japan, the United Kingdom, and the United States.
b. In local currency, aggregated using 1995 GDP weights.
c. Unit value index of manufactures exports from G-5 to developing countries, expressed in U.S. dollars.
d. GDP in 1995 constant dollars: 1995 prices and market exchange rates.
e. GDP measured at 1995 PPP (international dollar) weights.
Sources: Development Prospects Group, baseline, July 2003 and GDF 2003 forecasts of March 2003.

is traditionally 1.5 percentage points higher than economy-wide productivity growth. This differential has increased to 2.5 percentage points during the last decade. Sharp technological progress in manufacturing was partly an autonomous process—driven by advances in computer technology—but was also triggered by increased competition on a global scale. Developing countries as a group have benefited from the intensification of trade in manufactures and associated productivity gains, as the share of manufactured goods in their exports increased from 20 percent in 1980 to more than 70 percent in 2001.

Under a set of favorable but plausible assumptions, developing countries are expected to experience an acceleration of per capita income growth through 2015. The East Asia region is an exception because its already high growth of 6 percent annually over the last decades will be difficult to maintain, as economies mature and the gap with high-income countries narrows, even though it is likely to remain the fastest-growing region in the developing world.

Poverty remains a challenge, especially for Africa

Broad acceleration of per capita growth would translate into a sharp reduction in the incidence of poverty, from 28.3 percent in 1990 to a projected 12.5 percent by 2015, meeting, on average, the millennium development goal (MDG) of 14.8 percent. However, the gap between strong and weak performers will remain large. Even if Sub-Saharan Africa could turn falling per capita incomes into annual increases of 1.6 percent—as assumed in the baseline scenario—its rate of growth would be less than one-third the rate of growth that is expected in East Asia. The relatively poor performance of Sub-Saharan Africa makes the MDGs for that region especially challenging. For example, under the baseline scenario the percentage of people living on $1 per day or less will be only 42.3 percent in 2015 instead of 24 percent as targeted by the MDGs.

The industrial countries: Deficits, confidence, capital spending, and the dollar

Confidence is the key to the long-awaited breakthrough to growth

The high-income OECD countries have faced substantial difficulties in overcoming the legacies of the second half of the 1990s, including the equity market downturn. The recovery that began in early 2002 faltered after the summer of that year as the rebound in investment showed signs of weakness. Government expenditure could not continue to grow at the high rates achieved in the early phase of recovery, though deficits continued to widen. Late in 2002 and through early 2003, U.S. consumption, a major driver of global demand, slowed from an earlier pace of 4 percent to near 2 percent—partly as a reflection of the dramatic drop in consumer confidence on the eve of the Iraqi conflict and partly in reaction to high oil prices and weakening of the dollar. By the first quarter of 2003, GDP growth had slowed from generally stronger first-half 2002 rates to 1.4 percent (saar) in the United States, to 0.6 percent in Japan, to 0.2 in the Euro Area (figure 1.1).

Manufacturing output advances slowed discernibly at the turn of the year, and intensified during the spring. Growth momentum in goods production suffered a "double dip," to stand at –1.2 percent for the Euro Area, –2.0 percent for Japan, and –2.3 percent for the United States as of April–June 2003 (figure 1.2). The end to combat in the Iraqi campaign helped to boost U.S. consumer confidence from nine-year troughs reached in March; but response of consumers in Japan and especially in Europe was muted, despite an incipient up-

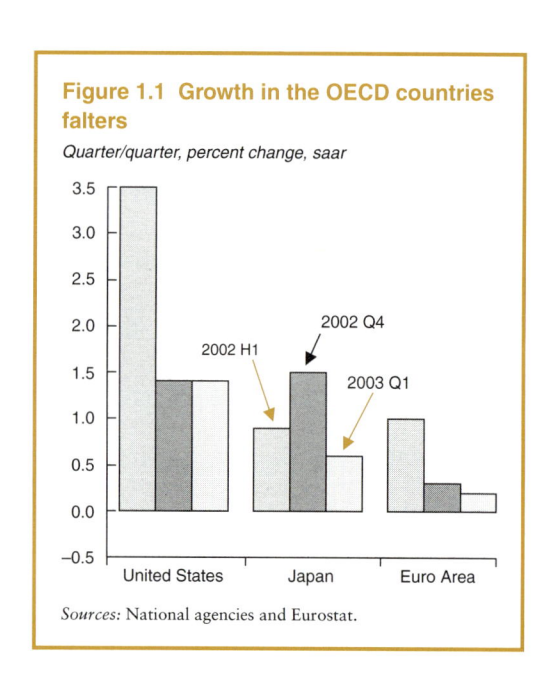

Figure 1.1 Growth in the OECD countries falters

Quarter/quarter, percent change, saar

Sources: National agencies and Eurostat.

Figure 1.2 OECD manufacturing shows a distinct "double dip"

Manufacturing IP, 3-month/3-month, percent change, saar

Sources: National agencies and Eurostat.

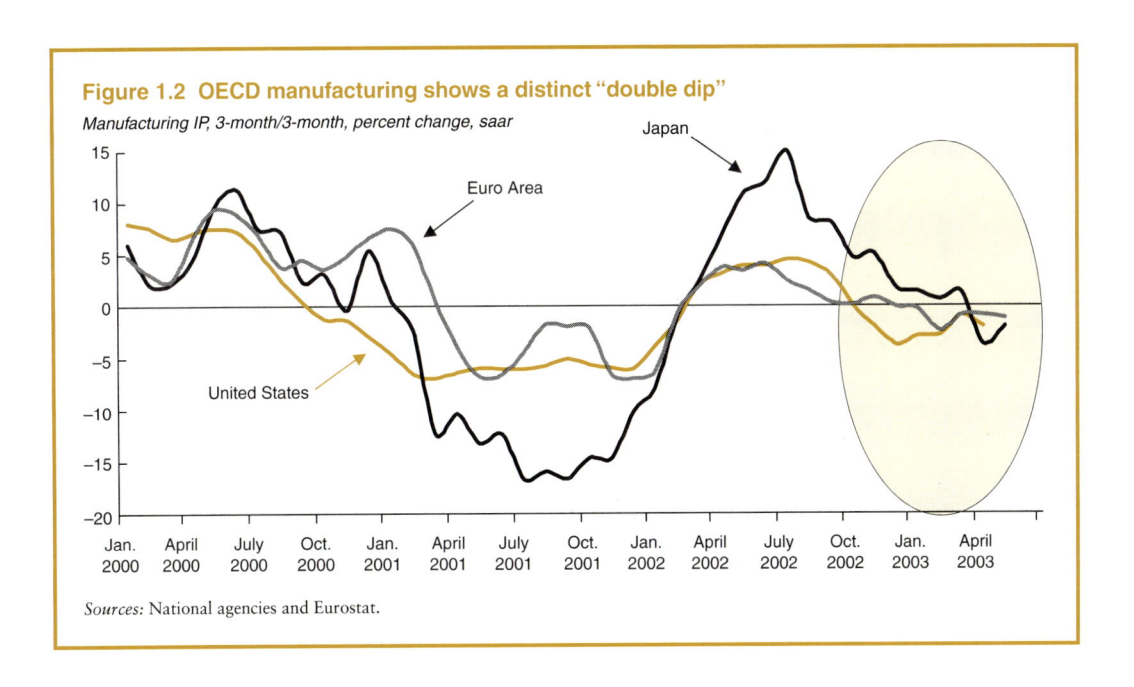

turn in equity markets. Rather, focus returned to the set of weak fundamentals underlying sluggish growth in the rich countries—notably substantial debt overhangs in the U.S. corporate, household, and, increasingly, government sectors.

The sharp depreciation of the dollar began to yield shifts in the contribution of net exports to GDP growth (table 1.2). In the United States, a contribution of −1.0 percentage points during the first half of 2002 changed into one of +0.9 percentage points in the first quarter of 2003. The opposite occurred in Europe and Japan. There, during the first half of 2002, net exports added respectively 0.9 and 1.4 percentage points to GDP growth, but these rates turned around in the first quarter of 2003, to −1.8 and −0.2 percentage points.

Table 1.2 Weak fundamentals underlie sluggish growth in the rich countries

Recent developments in GDP and components, United States, Euro Area, and Japan (percent)

	United States				Euro Area				Japan			
Growth	H1-02	H2-02	Q4-02	Q1-03	H1-02	H2-02	Q4-02	Q1-03	H1-02	H2-02	Q4-02	Q1-03
GDP	3.5	2.7	1.4	1.4	1.0	1.1	0.3	0.2	0.9	3.0	1.5	0.6
Private consumption	3.5	3.0	1.7	2.0	0.0	1.6	1.4	1.7	2.0	1.5	−0.2	0.8
Fixed investment	−2.8	0.7	4.4	−0.2	−3.2	−0.9	0.9	−4.8	−5.3	1.0	3.2	−1.9
Government	5.7	3.0	4.6	0.4	3.3	2.0	1.2	1.4	2.4	1.7	0.4	2.5
Growth contributions												
Private consumption	2.4	2.1	1.2	1.4	0.0	0.9	0.8	1.0	1.1	0.9	−0.1	0.4
Investment	1.0	0.9	1.0	−0.9	−0.5	−0.2	0.7	0.8	−2.0	1.5	0.1	0.0
Fixed capital	−0.5	0.1	0.7	0.0	−0.7	−0.2	0.2	−1.0	−1.4	0.3	0.8	−0.5
Change in stocks	1.5	0.7	0.3	−0.9	0.2	0.0	0.5	1.8	−0.6	1.2	−0.7	0.5
Government	1.0	0.5	0.8	0.1	0.7	0.4	0.2	0.3	0.4	0.3	0.1	0.4
Net exports	−1.0	−0.9	−1.9	0.9	0.9	0.0	−1.4	−1.8	1.4	0.4	1.6	−0.2

Note: H=half year; Q=quarter year.
Sources: National agencies, OECD, and World Bank data.

Although the depreciation of the dollar and turnaround in U.S. exports was a movement toward more balanced conditions, weak demand in external markets now poses special challenges for Europe and Japan. For the latter, the near-term effects of SARS in East Asia will likely exact an additional toll on exports.

Recently, the issue of deflation has emerged in the United States, and more so in Europe in the wake of 25 percent currency appreciation and flat output growth there. Labor market conditions continued to deteriorate across the OECD centers, with expectations widely held for a more prolonged period of sub-par growth in the global economy.

From this set of initial conditions, a breakthrough to stronger growth will hinge on a restoration of confidence among consumers and businesses. Under these circumstances, and in an environment of low interest rates (coupled with moderate gains in financial markets), the standard factors that boost investment after a recession—increasing obsolescence of the capital stock, improved expectations for demand—are likely to yield a gradual upturn in the pace of investment growth, and with it a resumption of economic recovery. Indeed, some signs of revival in the U.S. economy are now emerging, but the worst may not be over for Europe and Japan.

Consumer spending has slowed

From late 2002 to early 2003, anticipation of war in Iraq provided a "non-economic" overlay to the fundamental factors dampening consumer sentiment. Consumer confidence plunged to near-record lows on both sides of the Atlantic in the months leading up to war (figure 1.3). Though the estimated sensitivity of personal spending to changes in sentiment is surprisingly small, the relationship suggests that for the United States, the decline in confidence since late 2000, tied to economic conditions and war jitters, yielded a fall-off in consumption of a cumulative 1.2 percent, or $75 billion (box 1.1). Recovery of U.S. sentiment since that time, boosted by incipient gains in equity markets, has been moderately encouraging. However, the Conference Board index flattened-out in May and fell in June (to 83.5) to bring the measure to its level of late Fall 2002. European confidence has recovered little, as economic growth slows and developments in Germany in particular have deteriorated markedly.

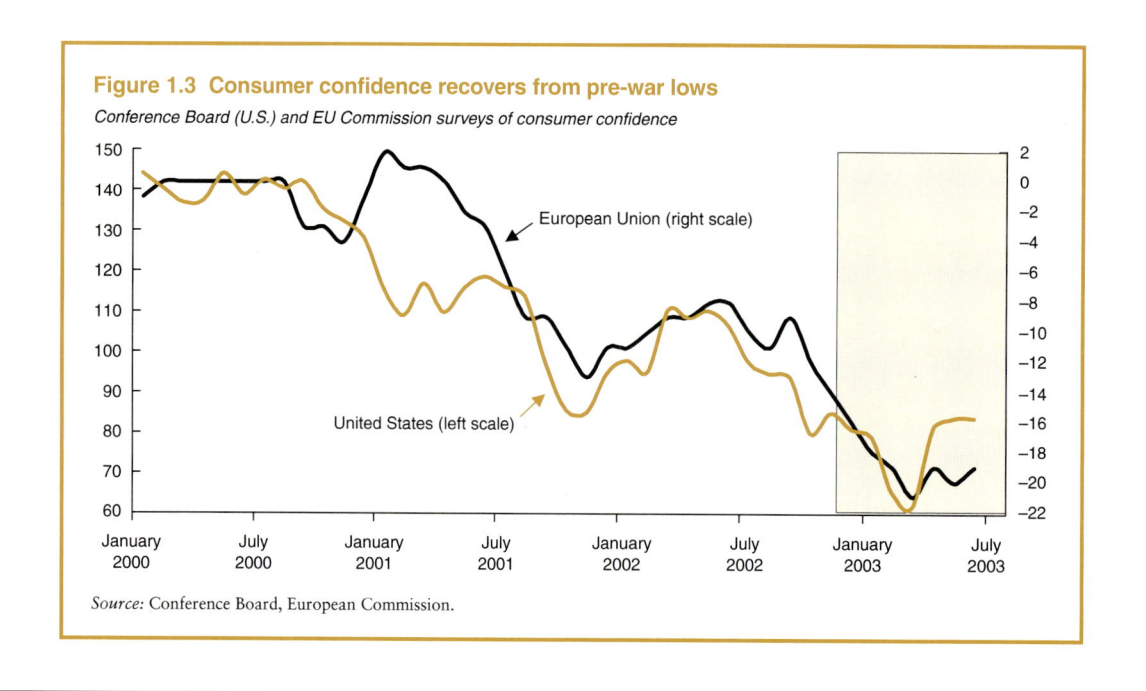

Figure 1.3 Consumer confidence recovers from pre-war lows

Conference Board (U.S.) and EU Commission surveys of consumer confidence

Source: Conference Board, European Commission.

Box 1.1 Consumer confidence and U.S. private consumption

The U.S. consumer accounts for more than two-thirds of U.S. and 20 percent of world expenditure, and has contributed nearly one-third to total world GDP growth since the onset of slower growth in 2001. Consumers seemed able to shake off the depressing effects of lower confidence during this period. The bursting of the stock market bubble, with its contractionary effects on household wealth, slowed consumption and growth and revealed substantial overinvestment in telecommunications and other high-technology industries. These developments left confidence levels vulnerable to short-term events, which came in the form of the Iraq war.

The Conference Board's index of consumer confidence was down 20 percent on average in the first eight months of 2001 and dropped another 25 percent after September 11. Yet in the fourth quarter of 2001 consumers flocked back to the malls in response to generous incentives and spending surged by 6 percent (saar). By mid-2002, confidence had recouped most of the losses suffered after September, but as war in Iraq seemed more likely, confidence tumbled again, dropping a further 45 percent by March 2003, when military action began.

Economic and noneconomic determinants of confidence. The impact of noneconomic factors such as 'terrorist threats' and 'war jitters' on consumer confidence and spending can be significant. Moreover, their dynamics are different from traditional economic factors insofar as they can appear and reverse suddenly. For instance, the Conference Board's index soared 32 percent in April 2003 after a quick resolution in Iraq.

The decomposition of consumer confidence into economic and non-economic components is not straightforward. By definition, the economic component should track coincident and leading indicators such as unemployment, household debt, and stock prices. However, objective proxies for war jitters or perceptions of terrorist threats are problematic. Thus, instead of measuring the role of non-economic factors directly, we take the indirect route of regressing confidence on a set of economic variables and interpreting the residual as representing the non-economic component.[1] The results are illustrated in the figure. Note the large negative residual that appeared after September 11, 2001, although this

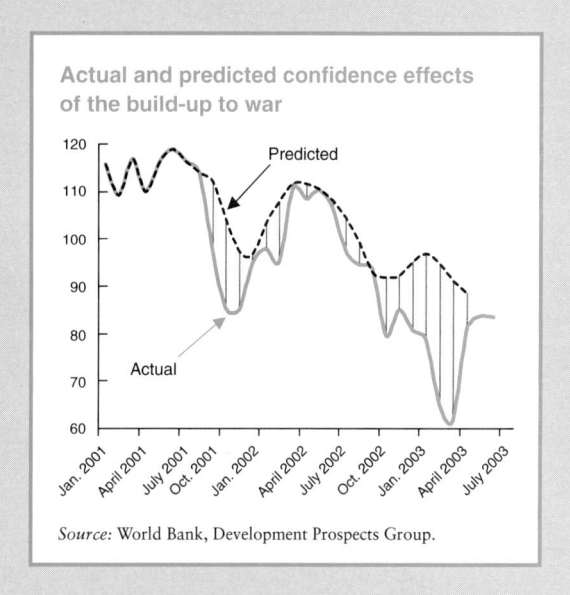

Actual and predicted confidence effects of the build-up to war

Source: World Bank, Development Prospects Group.

turned out to be short lived. But, starting in the fourth quarter of 2002 and first quarter of 2003, economic factors began yielding a sustained and substantial over-prediction. The mean squared prediction error is more than five times larger after September 2002 than before—compelling evidence of the war jitters story. By March 2003, when the war began, confidence was only two-thirds of what economic conditions alone would have indicated—the biggest discrepancy since the first Gulf War in 1991. In April, however, confidence rebounded sharply, narrowing the discrepancy to only 9 percent.

The impact on consumer spending. Many studies have found that variations in consumer confidence help to explain aggregate consumer spending, above and beyond what household disposable income and wealth can predict alone, though the effects are relatively small. A simple regression carried out for the purposes of this study yields a typical result, which implies that a 1 percent increase in confidence would raise real consumption growth by .023 percent over the subsequent year. Using this estimate, a cumulative 1.2 percent reduction in consumption, or around $75 billion since late 2000, is attributable to the fall in confidence.

(Box continues on next page)

> **Box 1.1 (continued)**
>
> **What happens next?** The equation predicts that the 30 percent improvement in confidence after the war, if sustained, could add as much as an additional 30*.023 = 0.7 percent, or around $45 billion to consumption levels over the next year. It is likely that durables such as housing and automobiles would be the main beneficiaries. But the experience after the 1991 Gulf War sounds a note of caution. Then, too, confidence dipped sharply as the war approached, and surged by 36 percent in March 1991 following the ceasefire. Less than a year later, however, it had more than given up this gain. The reason? Soaring unemployment. It was not until 1993 that U.S. consumption again recovered to near its long-run average growth rate. Moreover, our model attributes a cumulative 1.2 percent reduction in consumption since 2000 to confidence, but 9.2 percent to changes in income and wealth. In short, the future course of employment, income, and asset prices will be by far the most important determinants of consumption spending.
>
> *Source:* World Bank staff.

Since 2000, spending in the rich countries has been buffeted by divergent trends in net worth; most households suffered sharp declines in the value of financial assets. In the United States and the United Kingdom, however, rapid appreciation of housing values has partially offset the deterioration in financial worth (figure 1.4). For example, U.S. households suffered loss of $7.7 trillion in net financial worth since peak levels of the first quarter of 2000—mitigated to $4.4 trillion by real estate appreciation. Moreover, low interest rates have encouraged widespread refinancing and equity cash-outs to supplement flows of personal income and spending. On the other hand, rapid buildup of mortgage and other consumer debt has placed U.S. households in an exposed position should interest rates begin to rise with eventual recovery. At record levels of $8.9 trillion, representing 80 percent of GDP or 111 percent of disposable income as of the first quarter of 2003, burgeoning household debt could hamper vigorous spending responses in later stages of the anticipated recovery.

And the investment rebound relapsed

The sluggish pace of economic recovery is also linked to hesitant patterns of business capital spending, common across the industrial countries. After picking up to a 2.5 percent pace in the final quarter of 2002, G-7 fixed investment relapsed to growth of just 0.3 percent during the first quarter of 2003. U.S. business outlays dropped by a disappointing 3.4 percent, capital spending in Japan fell by 2 percent, and Euro Area investment plummeted by 4.8 percent, as that in Germany fell 6.8 percent (figure 1.5).

At midpoints of the business cycle, the prime mover for growth would normally transition from consumer spending and inventory building to more robust advances in fixed capital formation. Unlike in previous business cy-

Figure 1.4 The drop in U.S. household net worth has been offset by real estate appreciation

Trillions of dollars

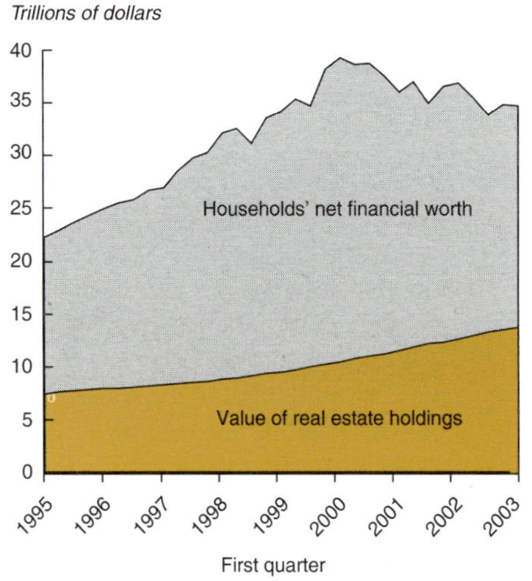

Source: Federal Reserve Board.

GLOBAL OUTLOOK AND THE DEVELOPING COUNTRIES

Figure 1.5 Capital spending has been hesitant in all industrial countries

Real fixed investment, quarter/quarter, percent change, Q/Q, saar

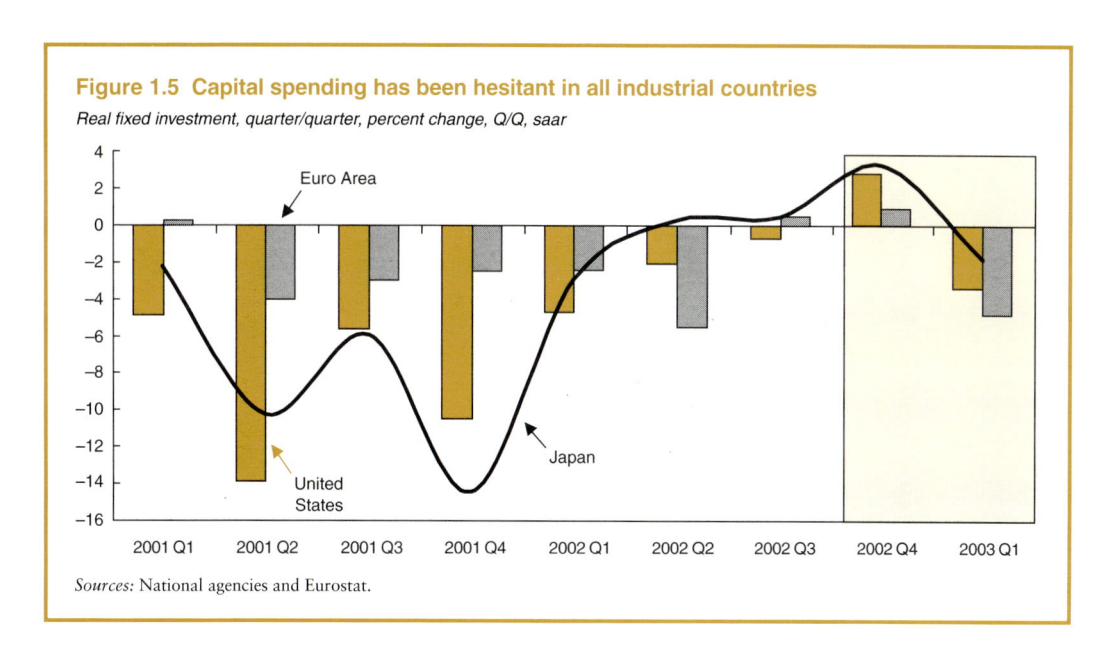

Sources: National agencies and Eurostat.

cles, however, several factors have combined to inhibit a vigorous rebound in investment.

Corporate debt legacies of the 1990s' boom continue to curtail investment plans across the OECD. For example, U.S. non-financial corporate debt as a proportion of GDP rose from 38 percent in 1995 to 47 percent in 2002. Recent data, however, show U.S. debt rates stabilizing over the last quarters of 2002 and the first of 2003—a positive sign that adjustment efforts are beginning to yield fruit. *Corporate profits* fell 10 percent in the United States in 2001, while those of Japanese manufacturers plummeted 48 percent, reflecting onset of recession. The tortuous road toward restoration of profit growth has involved substantial cuts to capital spending and to employment over the last years. However, there is evidence that profits are staging recoveries in the United States and Japan, as well as in several sectors of industry in Europe. U.S. profits enjoyed a 15 percent rebound in 2002, but growth eased to a 5 percent pace in the first quarter of 2003. In Japan, profits of major manufacturers experienced a substantial comeback, rising 38 percent in recent quarters (y/y)—despite numerous challenges (figure 1.6). These developments offer additional evidence that the corner to growth in capital spending, at least for the United States—and possibly for Japan—may be approaching.

Business sentiment is now displaying distinct divergence between the United States and

Figure 1.6 Corporate profits have risen moderately in the United States and Japan

Adjusted profits in billions of dollars (2Q-ma) and trillions of yen (3Q-MA)

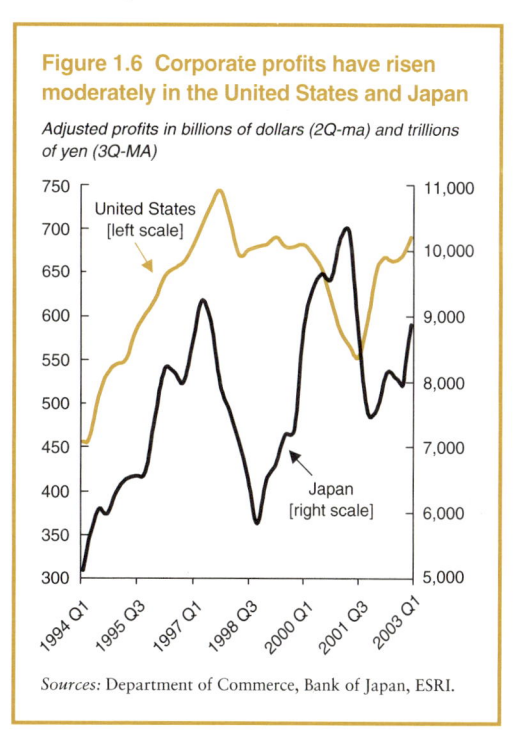

Sources: Department of Commerce, Bank of Japan, ESRI.

9

GLOBAL ECONOMIC PROSPECTS 2004

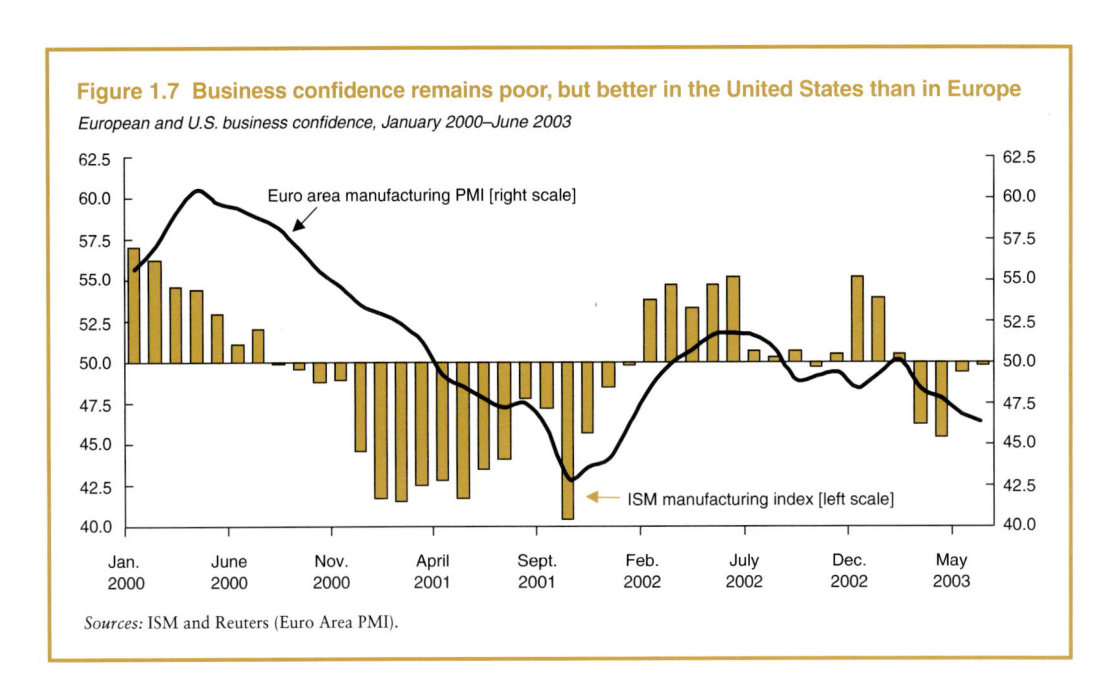

Figure 1.7 Business confidence remains poor, but better in the United States than in Europe
European and U.S. business confidence, January 2000–June 2003

Sources: ISM and Reuters (Euro Area PMI).

Europe and Japan, where assessments of conditions have worsened. The ISM survey covering U.S. manufacturing and non-manufacturing sectors fell below the 50 percent line that divides expansion from contraction during March and April—before manufacturing rebounded to 49.8 in June—and services sharply to 54.5 in May. In contrast, the composite PMI for the Euro Area entered the "contraction zone" in March, and fell further to 48.1 in June, reflecting declines in both services and manufacturing indicators (figure 1.7). It appears that financial conditions weighing against capital spending are easing across the OECD, and business sentiment is now reviving in the United States. Yet a key uncertainty persists: the robustness of future demand, which is strongly tied to the effects of policy.

After providing substantial stimulus, economic policy is reaching limits

On both fiscal and monetary fronts, policymakers in the rich countries injected significant stimulus, first to limit the global economic downturn of 2001, and over the last 18 months to foster conditions conducive for stronger recovery. On the *fiscal* front, the U.S. government's general budget position shifted dramatically from a surplus of 2.3 percent of GDP in 2000 to a deficit of 3.2 percent during the first quarter of 2003. In part this reflects reduced revenues associated with sluggish activity and the operation of automatic stabilizers. But the shift to deficit has been more pronounced due to tax reduction and funding of the Iraqi campaign at the federal level, and by increasing shortfalls at the state and local levels (figure 1.8). Before the recent additional $350 billion tax reduction was enacted, the Congressional Budget Office projected that the federal on-budget fiscal position was unlikely to return to surplus until 2012. Persistent deficits of such magnitude carry the potential to constrain growth in the medium term and beyond, largely as long-term interest rates rise in response to much-increased supply of Treasury securities.

Fiscal deterioration and the current account

The deterioration of the fiscal position has played a role in the doubling of the U.S. current account deficit from 2.3 percent of GDP in 1998 to 4.6 percent in 2002. The public-sector financial balance (saving less investment)

GLOBAL OUTLOOK AND THE DEVELOPING COUNTRIES

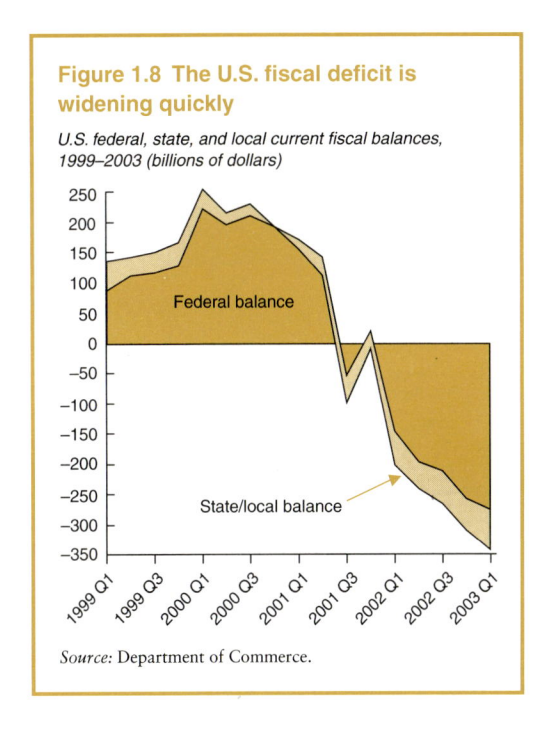

Figure 1.8 The U.S. fiscal deficit is widening quickly

U.S. federal, state, and local current fiscal balances, 1999–2003 (billions of dollars)

Source: Department of Commerce.

shifted from balance in 1999 to deficit of 3.6 percent of GDP in 2002, and further to a shortfall of 4.3 percent in the first quarter of 2003. At the same time, improvement in the private-sector balance (largely through compression of investment), although substantial, was far from sufficient to make up the gap (figure 1.9a).

Aside from the underlying savings-investment imbalance that drives the need for foreign capital, the widening of the U.S. external deficit is attributable to several factors. Booming domestic conditions during the second half of the 1990s attracted imports at a growth rate of 10 percent annually, while the strong dollar and only moderate growth in U.S. trade partners served to constrain export growth to 6 percent. In turn the trade balance deteriorated from a deficit of $175 billion in 1995 to $485 billion in 2002. Foreign capital flows funding the current account deficit have become increasingly volatile over the last years, shifting rapidly in composition and in region of origin. The effects of sustaining such capital inflows over an extended period remain a question of some concern (box 1.2).

The present level of the current account deficit, at 5.1 percent of GDP in the first quarter of 2003, is an historic record. Of particular concern is the unprecedented level of deficit occurring at an *early phase* of economic recovery, when external positions are normally closer to balance given only moderate changes in

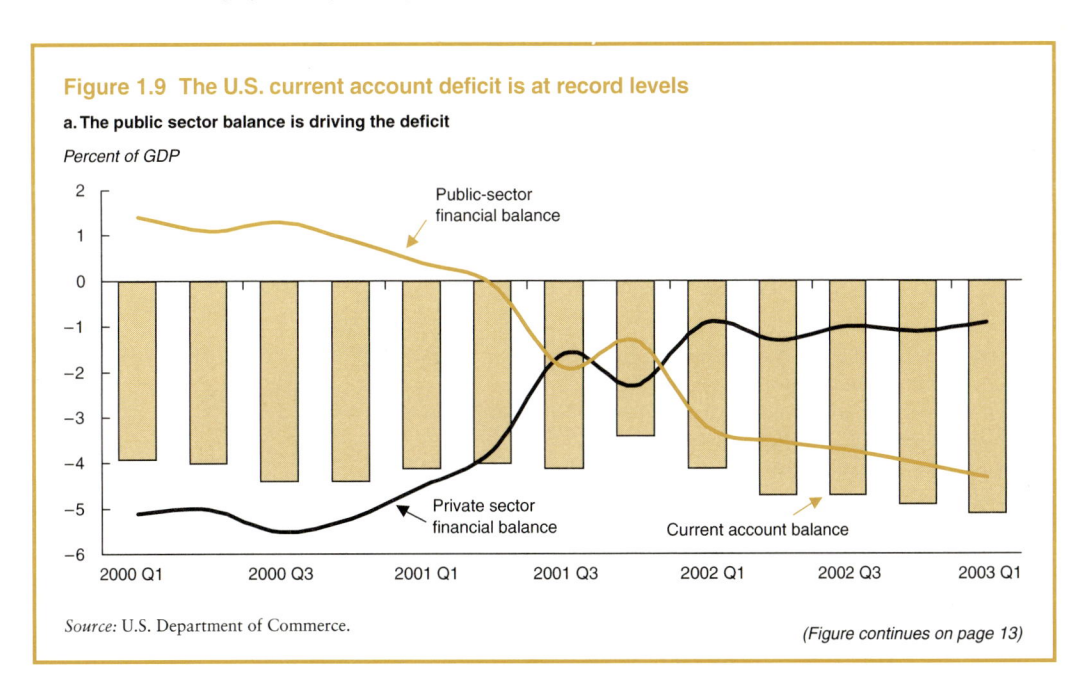

Figure 1.9 The U.S. current account deficit is at record levels

a. The public sector balance is driving the deficit

Percent of GDP

Source: U.S. Department of Commerce.

(Figure continues on page 13)

11

Box 1.2 Financing the U.S. current account deficit: From equity to debt

As the U.S. current account deficit more than doubled in dollar terms between 1998 and 2002 to reach $480 billion, U.S. calls on international financial markets increased in tandem. The country's external financing requirement climbed to 4.6 percent of GDP in 2002, representing some 10.3 percent of the savings of the rest of the world. U.S. financing requirements largely have been smoothly met by net inflows from abroad. But the form of financing (that is, the composition of the net foreign-asset flow) has changed dramatically over just the last three years, while the region of origin of the inflow has shifted as well. The underlying nature of the capital inflow can, as demonstrated aptly in recent years, lead to questions of medium-term sustainability of the external deficit; while shifts in origin of flows can influence market expectations for adjustment in the value of the dollar against its major partner currencies.

During 2000, the final year of the boom, the United States required net inflows of some $457 billion to cover its current account deficit. Financing was readily available, through increased mergers-and-acquisitions activity that yielded net purchases of corporate bonds of $281 billion; complemented by strong $160 billion in FDI flows and some $85 billion attracted to 45 percent gains in NASDAQ (see first figure). Together the equity component of flows (FDI and stocks) accounted for more than 50 percent of requirements—a strong fundamental position. The onset of recession in the United States during 2001 was clearly a transition year for investor perceptions. The fall of equity markets (NASDAQ down 50 percent) forced a compression of the highly diversified flows of 2000, as equity and FDI dropped to negligible amounts and investors flocked into debt instruments. Long-term debt-related securities almost covered the U.S. requirement of some $420 billion in the year. The transition in composition of inflows evolved more fully in the difficult environment of 2002. FDI recorded net *outflow* of almost $100 billion; purchases of Treasuries by risk-averse investors increased by $100 billion; a virtual cessation in overseas lending by U.S. banks yielded a net buildup in bank liabilities of $70 billion; and foreign official assets (largely East Asian) increased by $90 billion from an inflow of $5 billion during the previous year.

U.S. external financing requirements and net financial flows
Billions of dollars

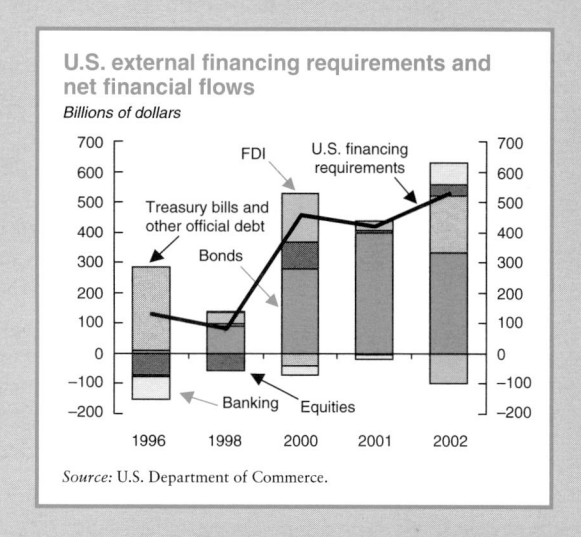

Source: U.S. Department of Commerce.

The source of inflows to U.S. equity and "corporate" bond markets shifted over recent years (second figure). Although the United Kingdom's status as a major financial hub for the European region dominates flows, a discernible shift is clear: from "other Western Europe" (Euro Area) and Japan as centers of demand for U.S. securities to "other countries" (East Asia and Latin America). During 2000, the Euro Area accounted for 25 percent of total net

Net flows into U.S. private securities by region of origin
Billions of dollars

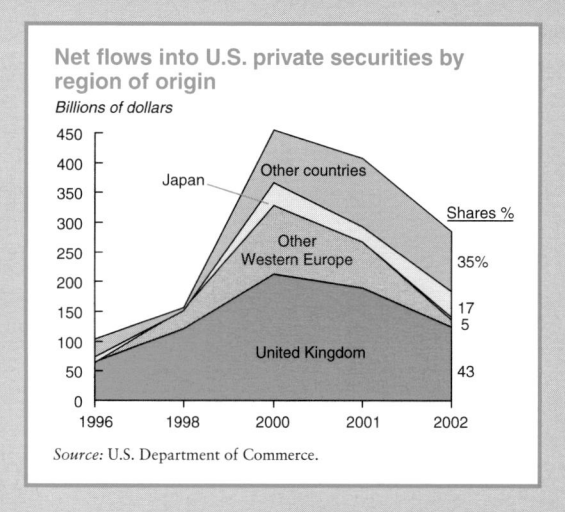

Source: U.S. Department of Commerce.

(Box continues on next page)

GLOBAL OUTLOOK AND THE DEVELOPING COUNTRIES

Box 1.2 (continued)

foreign purchases, falling to 5 percent in 2002—a large decline in relative demand for dollar-based assets, tending to boost the value of the euro; in contrast Japan's share increased from 9 to 17 percent, while East Asia and Latin America almost doubled their shares in purchases from 19 to 35 percent by 2002. Such a shift in the origin of funds may set the stage for future currency movements.

In looking ahead, the downshift in equity, persistence of large debt flows and dependence on volatile official reserve assets for some 20 percent of coverage, and the fall of the U.S. dollar against the euro, augur poorly for the inherent stability of financing in the short to medium terms. A "less than virtuous" circle may result, as sources of finance become less stable. Greater volatility may be imparted to the dollar, leading in turn to higher and more volatile interest rates. When combined with perceptions of a persistently growing current account deficit, the confidence of foreign investors in dollar-denominated assets may be adversely affected.

Implications for the availability of finance for developing countries also arise from the increasing U.S. share of international capital flows. Although "crowding out" has yet to be in clear evidence, the potential for it exists should deficits continue to rise. The U.S. current account appears to have increased as a source of financial risk for the global outlook.

---

demand (figure 1.9b). In looking forward, with continued requirements for massive net inflows of foreign capital, the U.S. income-account deficit is likely to widen, while terrorism-related issues may continue for an extended period, pressuring U.S. services and net transfer positions. Yet assuming a gradual buildup of global economic activity, an expected improvement in the goods balance should build, bringing about medium-term stabilization of the deficit in dollar terms, declining as a proportion to GDP.

Member states of the Euro Area have struggled to cope with the requirements of the Stability and Growth Pact of the Maastricht

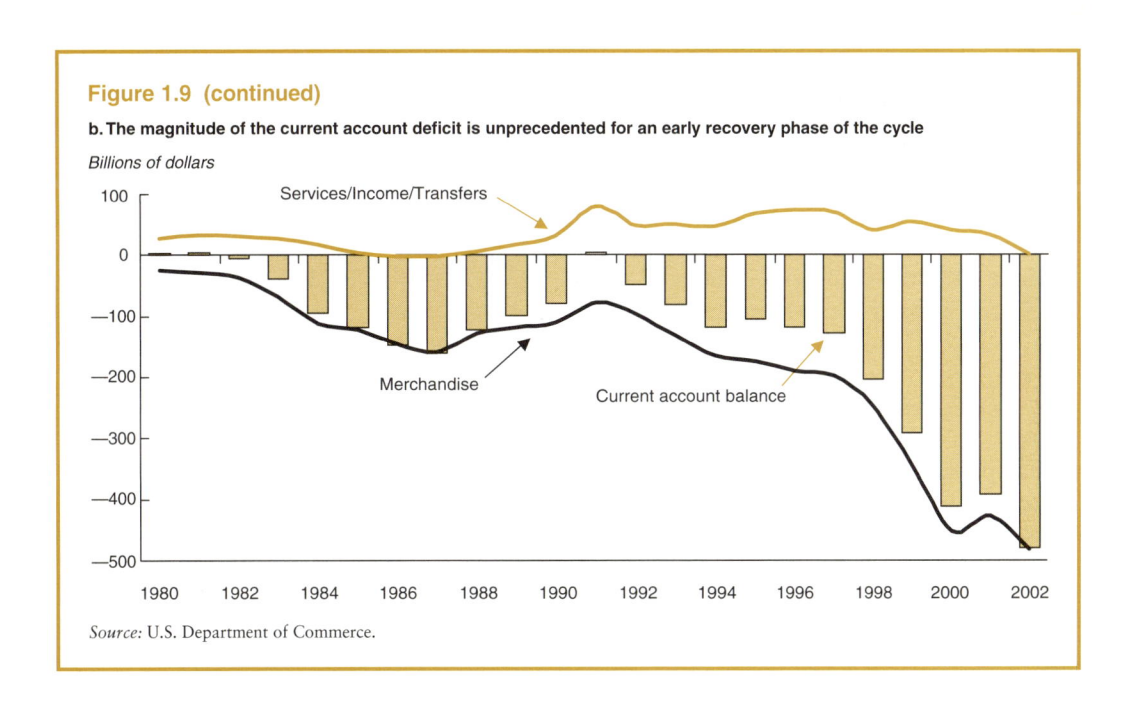

Figure 1.9 (continued)

b. The magnitude of the current account deficit is unprecedented for an early recovery phase of the cycle

Billions of dollars

Source: U.S. Department of Commerce.

Figure 1.10 Market interest rates have dropped

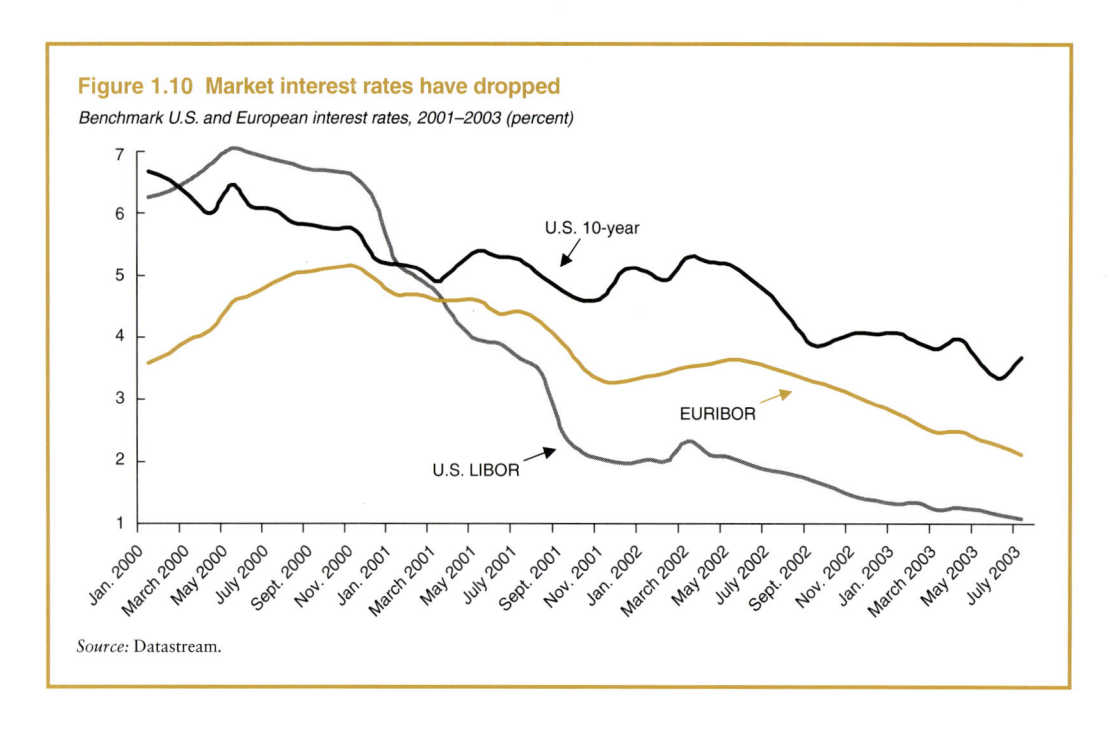

Benchmark U.S. and European interest rates, 2001–2003 (percent)

Source: Datastream.

Treaty, which, to set a foundation for the single currency, limits fiscal deficits to 3 percent of GDP and outstanding government debt levels to about two-thirds of GDP. During 2004 Italy is anticipated to join France, Germany, and Portugal in the group of countries that have breached the 3 percent limit. The consolidated balance for the Euro Area has deteriorated by 1.5 points of GDP over the period since early 2000, while that for Germany has shifted markedly from a 1.1 percent surplus to a 3.8 percent deficit. For the latter, especially, the tightening of policy to return to within the limits by 2005–06 is inopportune because economic conditions have deteriorated sharply; fiscal "austerity" only adds to these tendencies.

Japan's fiscal stance continues to deteriorate, moving from a deficit of 6 percent of GDP in 2000 to 7 percent during 2002. Although public-sector investment outlays associated with public works and other traditional supplementary budget measures have been curtailed in recent years (falling by a cumulative 4.5 percent since 2000), more public monies have been allocated to shoring up the banking system and underpinning social safety nets for those falling into unemployment. Japan's public-debt burden, however, at some 150 percent of GDP, against the background of a rapidly aging demographic profile, suggests that a required movement toward balance in current budget terms will present considerable challenges to policymakers.

In *monetary* policy, authorities in the industrial countries have been aggressive—more so in the United States, less in Europe (figure 1.10). While operating with effective policy interest rates at zero, the Bank of Japan (BOJ) has proposed a wide range of policy measures aimed at easing the deflationary state of the economy. But evidence to date suggests that little has been achieved in this area. Aggressive easing of policy rates by the Federal Reserve, from 6.5 percent at end-2000 to 1 percent at present, clearly supported consumer and housing-related activity, though with little apparent effect on business capital formation. Consumption of durable goods, especially autos, has found support from record low interest rates. And mortgage refinancings have been spurred to new highs, placing extra disposable income into consumers' pockets.

The European Central Bank (ECB) has adopted a more conservative approach to policy ease, given its central mandate of controlling inflation for the group of EMU countries. The ECB repurchase rate has been lowered in steps from 4.75 percent in late 2000 to 2 percent at present. The rapid appreciation of the euro has placed downward pressure on import prices, which eventually will compress prices at the consumer level, thereby creating an opportunity for the ECB to lower interest rates somewhat further. Policy in Japan has been geared, first, to lifting the economy from its deflationary state—which began in 1998 in the aftermath of the East Asian financial crisis and has intensified since—and to redressing the tenuous conditions in the commercial banking sector. Core consumer price inflation in Japan has ranged between −0.5 and −1.5 percent over 2000–03, defying the BOJ's attempts to support higher price levels through various measures. Broader money remains stagnant, as the decline in commercial bank lending effectively cancels intermediation through the economy. By intervening in the non-performing loan market (NPL), the BOJ now intends to expand the number of channels available to inject liquidity into the system, while supporting workouts of bad loans. The challenges are daunting.

Deflation risk? After two decades of disinflation in high-income countries, set off in the early 1980s by monetary tightening to curb self-enforcing inflationary pressures, a spread of deflation has become a real risk. While Japan is experiencing its fourth consecutive year of falling prices, core-CPI inflation fell to 1.7 percent in the Euro Area and eased to 1.5 percent in the United States in June (figure 1.11). As these measures of inflation probably overstate "true" inflation by 0.5–1 percentage points, the world's major economies could be balanced on the edge of deflation.

Deflation need not be damaging if it reflects gains from deregulation, technological advances and rapid productivity growth. Today, the computer and telecoms revolution, along with globalization, is pushing down prices. Yet

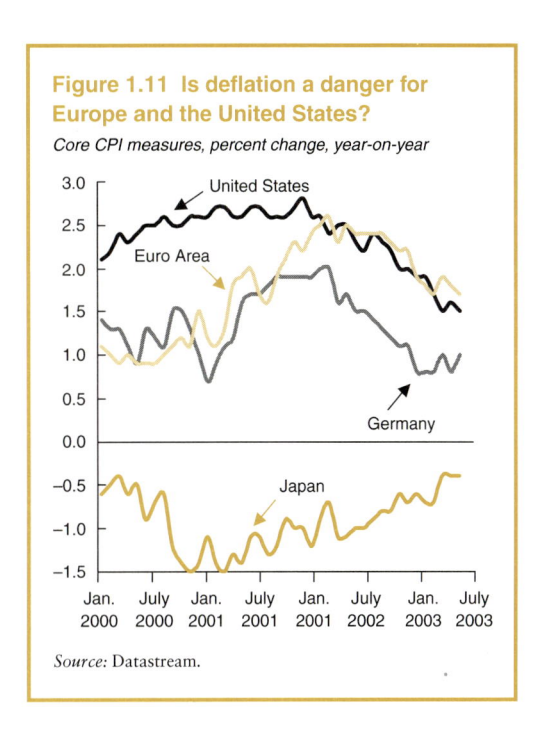

Figure 1.11 Is deflation a danger for Europe and the United States?
Core CPI measures, percent change, year-on-year

Source: Datastream.

deflation can be dangerous when it reflects demand shocks, such as the bursting of an asset price bubble. These have the potential to set in motion a downward spiral of falling prices, delayed consumption, and declining profits and production.

Monetary authorities should shift their focus more decisively, if they have not done so already, from avoiding inflation to maintaining low inflation, fighting deflation as aggressively as they would high inflation. Asymmetric price targets and careful monitoring of output gaps are important ingredients in such a policy. Output gaps for the rich countries turned negative as of 2001 and have widened precipitously over the last two years (figure 1.12). OECD estimates place the U.S. output gap at 1.5 percent in 2002, rising to 2.1 percent during 2003. And the gap in Germany is particularly severe, shifting by a full point from 1.3 to 2.3.

However, as fiscal stimulus becomes quickly ineffective in the fight against stubborn underperformance, so, after time, can monetary policy. Both fiscal and monetary stimulus may at some point become part of

GLOBAL ECONOMIC PROSPECTS 2004

Figure 1.12 Output gaps are widening, bringing deflationary pressures to bear

Deviation of actual from potential GDP as proportion of potential

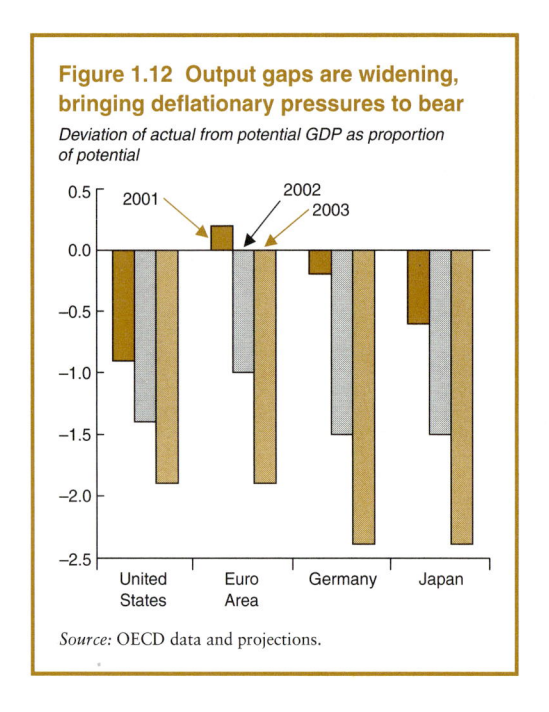

Source: OECD data and projections.

The dollar's fall means near-term pressure on growth, medium-term benefits

Recent developments in foreign exchange markets, reflecting an intensification of the dollar's decline from early 2002 peaks, have come to influence trends in OECD trade growth and the pace of economic activity. Over the period, the dollar has fallen by 12.5 percent on a real trade-weighted basis. But the 25 percent fall of the dollar vis-à-vis the euro—linked in part to diminishing European demand for dollar-denominated financial assets—is especially of concern to the future pace of growth in Europe (figure 1.13).

Euro-Area export prices expressed in dollar terms rose by 2.5 percent during 2002, but with the dollar's rapid fall they are anticipated to rise by nearly 12 percent in 2003. Growth of German and French exports fell sharply to negative territory (10 percent decline) as of early 2003. While diminished impetus from exports will detract from GDP advances, the stronger euro should imply a rise in real incomes, potentially supporting domestic demand. The 11 percent depreciation of the yen-

the problem instead of the solution. High fiscal debt could curb a recovery, and low interest rates for too long could encourage the accumulation of excessive debt that could increase debt service burdens once the economy starts recovering again. To the extent that market participants position their balance sheets around the expectation of low rates for an extended period, then the risk of sudden, violent movements in bond (and possibly currency) markets increases, not unlike what happened in 1993–94.

To avoid that underperformance, policies that address the structural foundations of economies become increasingly more important than macro stimulus. Such policies can not only address specific inefficiencies, but also provide a boost to confidence. A breakthrough in the Doha trade negotiations (see the end of this chapter) is an example of such structural improvements. Other examples are the strengthening of corporative governance, especially in the United States; labor and product market reforms in Europe; and decisive elimination of bad loans in Japan.

Figure 1.13 The dollar has fallen sharply since early 2002

Euro and yen per USD and REER, January 2002 = 100

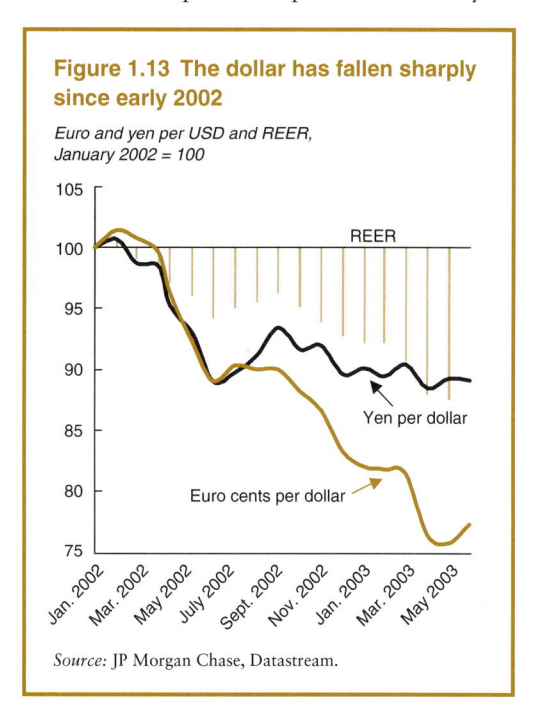

Source: JP Morgan Chase, Datastream.

dollar rate poses complications, in a manner similar to Europe, for sustaining economic activity in Japan. Momentum underlying Japanese exports plummeted from 35 percent growth during spring 2002 to decline in early 2003, tied to a sharp 35 percent fall-off in shipments to the United States and slowing exports to Asia, from 45 to 3.5 percent rates. Authorities have been active in market intervention to slow the pace of dollar depreciation.

Ongoing realignment of currency values, however, will carry medium-term benefits. Recent moves are in a balancing direction, as the strength of the dollar over most of the 1990s raised the question of overvaluation against a longer-term equilibrium rate for the currency based on fundamental factors. The strong dollar contributed to the massive U.S. external imbalance, but at the same time maintained downward pressures on inflation, allowing room for substantial interest rate reductions. A medium term boost to U.S. competitiveness may be expected, provided that the dollar stabilizes or moves only gradually. Still, prospects for stabilization of the current account deficit remain at some risk.

Expansion is likely by 2004

As *additional* impetus to growth from policy action is anticipated to be small, recovery among the rich countries will hinge on the effects of policy actions taken to date, and importantly, a restoration of confidence. The momentum of economic activity will likely build over 2003, reaching more robust proportions by 2004. Recovery should be paced by advances in the United States and by a return to stronger domestic demand in the emerging and high-income economies of East Asia. Revival of growth in the Euro Area will be tortuous, lagging that of the United States, and may find its focus in domestic rather than external demand. A lower dollar will help European consumers—as real incomes rise with lower inflation, and a virtuous cycle of stronger business output and eventually more substantial increases in capital expenditure could emerge.

The risk of weaker growth is substantial, however, given deterioration of conditions in Germany. Short-to-medium-term growth in Japan will be conditioned to a large degree by developments in export markets, especially in broader East Asia; the competitiveness of the yen; and the success or failure of policy in mitigating the deep-seated problems in the banking system.

Some positive developments have become apparent in the U.S. landscape. If sustained, these developments may augur well for gradual recovery. Since September 2002, consumer confidence has recovered moderately, while the Dow Jones index has recouped some 20 percent of its value (figure 1.14a). Manufacturing sentiment has improved and production risen, while sentiment for services has returned to its early fall levels. A possible upturn in the high-tech/semiconductor cycle has been underpinned by near 30 percent gains in orders for computers and communications equipment. And the effects of dollar depreciation may be coming into evidence as export momentum breached positive territory with a 3 percent advance from April to May. Yet the pace of consumer demand remains cloudy, and evidence for incipient recovery in capital spending is sketchy.

Against this background, the projections posit a subdued 1.5 percent growth outturn in 2003 for the high-income OECD countries, marking a 0.1 point deterioration of growth from 2002, largely because of sluggish conditions in the United States and particularly in Europe during the first half of the year. The advance in aggregate GDP is anticipated to rise to 2.5 percent by 2004—closer to long-term averages—as momentum builds in U.S. investment and output growth achieves 3.4 percent rates there. A revival in world trade toward 8 percent growth should help buoy performance in Europe and Japan. Interest rates will begin to respond to improved economic prospects, leading U.S. growth to taper off moderately into 2005, while Europe and Japan continue to register improvement, given the later start of their recoveries (figure 1.14b).

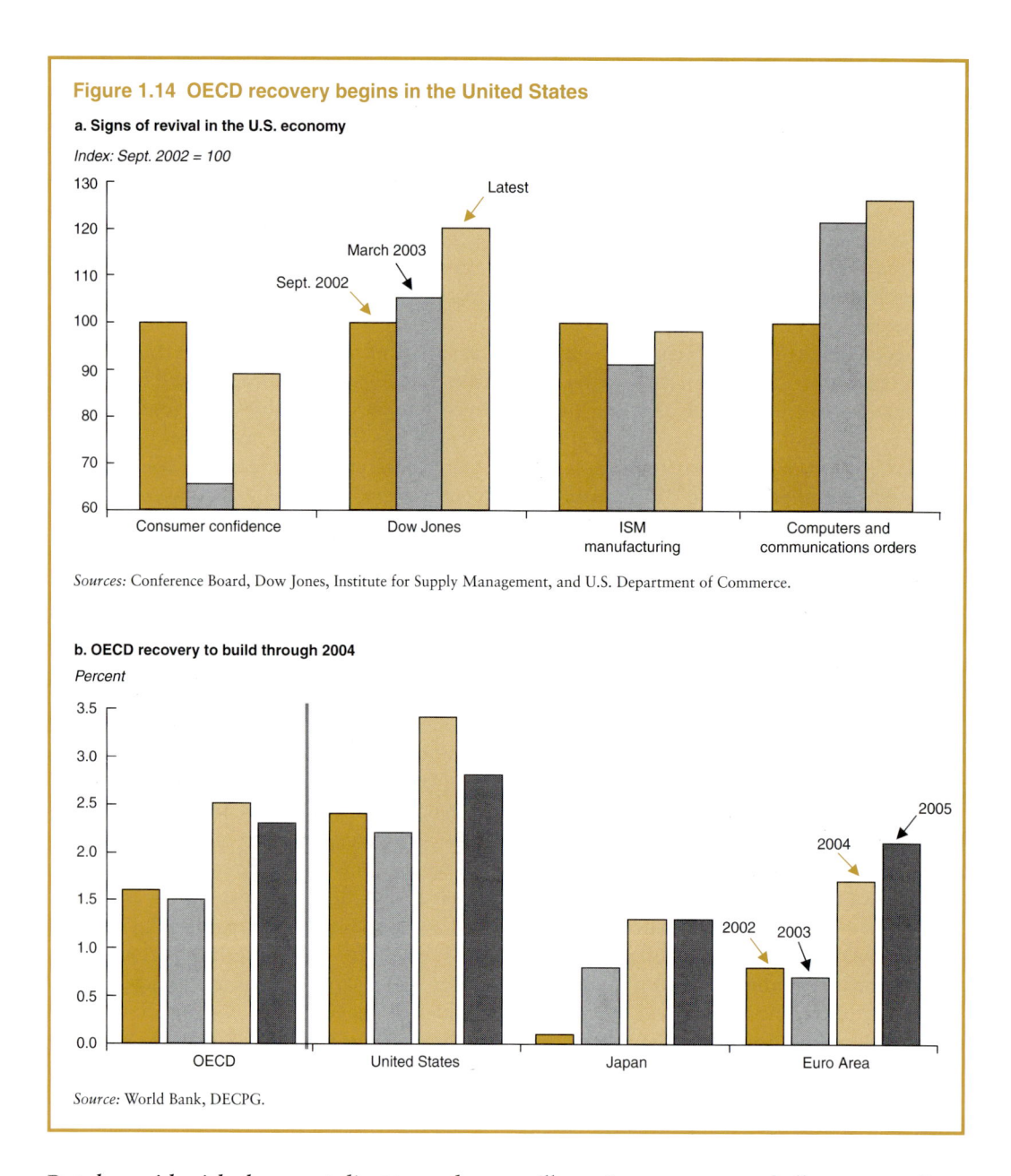

GLOBAL ECONOMIC PROSPECTS 2004

Figure 1.14 OECD recovery begins in the United States

a. Signs of revival in the U.S. economy

Index: Sept. 2002 = 100

Sources: Conference Board, Dow Jones, Institute for Supply Management, and U.S. Department of Commerce.

b. OECD recovery to build through 2004

Percent

Source: World Bank, DECPG.

But downside risks have not disappeared

Some of the global uncertainties related to noneconomic events—the war in Iraq and SARS—have eased, but have not completely disappeared. Prospects for eventual stabilization and resolution of developments in the Middle East remain uncertain, and the potential for adverse events remains, while SARS will continue to present challenges to policymakers worldwide (box 1.4). However, these uncertainties do not constitute the most serious risk to the global recovery. More important risks are to be found in the high-income countries.

A noteworthy feature of current global prospects is that many of the downside risks originate in high-income countries, and that a strong recovery is not predicted for any of these countries in the near term. The rebound in the investment cycle, which is crucial to the overall recovery, remains uncertain. Although economic and financial conditions—low interest rates, rising equity prices, improved corporate balance sheets, and increased profits—are favorable for a recovery in investment, a lack of confidence could delay or even abort the rebound. Other risks are of a financial nature. The weakening of the dollar has, until now, been a movement toward equilibrium. But the dollar's fall is likely not enough to sustain demand for dollar-denominated assets, as the burgeoning U.S. fiscal and current account deficits are likely to call for an additional $1.5 trillion in net foreign inflows over the period through 2005. A further sharp fall in the dollar could destabilize the recovery in the high-income countries. Additional risk may arise if vulnerabilities in the banking sector of the main industrialized economies intensify in response to deflationary pressures. Risks in the high-income countries call for decisive policy initiatives to improve the structure of economies. Moreover, uncertainties surrounding the recovery in high-income countries transmit to the international environment and to the medium-term outlook for developing countries, implying that expected improvement in developing-country growth should not be taken for granted.

The external environment for developing countries: Gradual improvement, but a bumpy road ahead

The external environment facing developing countries has been shaped by the set of recent developments in the rich countries as well as expectations for OECD growth and import demand. The evolution of trade prices, interest rates, and financial flows will play a major role in determining external balances, while influencing reserves and liability management decisions in emerging markets. Overall, the environment of the last few years has been a difficult one, but conditions should improve gradually through 2005 (table 1.3).

Although export market growth for developing countries chalked-up a meager 2.5 percent advance during 2002, export volumes for the group accelerated from nil in 2001 to 7.7 percent in the year, implying substantial gains in market share. As market growth rises toward a 7–8 percent range by 2003–05, emerging-market exports should continue to gain share and expand at rates around 10 percent. Trade prices bode well for improvement in export revenues during 2003, with terms of trade anticipated to rise by 0.4 percent, but moderation in non-oil commodity prices and in oil markets by 2004–05 should serve to dampen initial gains.

Advanced market interest rates are expected to trough during 2003, to rise moderately in 2004, and return to long-term average rates by 2005, a net increase of some 280 basis points from current 1 percent levels of US$-LIBOR, and 100 points for EURIBOR, as European growth fundamentals remain subdued for a longer period. Meanwhile, there has been sharp compression in average emerging-market spreads, and a continuation of that trend would help keep the cost of capital for developing countries at moderate levels.

The near-term outlook for capital flows to developing countries is mixed, however, as continued restraint on the part of commercial banks in extending new loans is offset by much stronger trends in bond issuance. Gross capital market flows are anticipated to rise by some 9 percent in 2003. But FDI flows in the current economic and geopolitical environment, potentially exacerbated by the SARS epidemic in China (the major recipient country), are anticipated to experience no growth during 2003—an assessment that may prove somewhat optimistic. On balance, the outlook envisions an environment increasingly conducive for growth, but a potentially bumpy road for policymakers to navigate.

GLOBAL ECONOMIC PROSPECTS 2004

Table 1.3 The difficult environment for developing-country growth should improve
External factors affecting developing-country growth, 2001–05 (percent change, except as noted)

	2001	2002	2003	2004	2005
OECD import demand	−0.7	1.7	4.1	6.3	6.7
Export market growth[a]	−0.2	2.5	6.8	8.0	7.7
Developing export volume	1.1	7.7	10.0	10.9	9.7
Non-oil commodity prices	−9.1	5.1	6.9	1.1	1.5
Oil price $/bbl	24.4	24.9	26.5	22.0	20.0
MUV[b]	−4.5	−0.1	4.0	−0.4	1.5
Terms of trade	−0.7	−1.1	0.4	−1.5	−2.7
US LIBOR	3.5	1.8	1.0	2.0	3.8
EURIBOR	4.2	3.4	2.1	2.1	3.1
Emerging market spread (bp)	797	728	610	—	—
Financial flows ($ billion)	326	293	309	—	—
FDI inflow	171	143	145	—	—
Gross capital market flows	155	150	164	—	—
Equity placement	7	11	12	—	—
Bond financing	62	55	70	—	—
Bank lending	86	84	82	—	—

— Not available.
a. Import demand in partner markets.
b. Manufactures Unit Value index, expressed in U.S. dollars.
Source: World Bank data and projections.

World trade is growing more slowly than expected in 2003, but fundamentals suggest a buildup of momentum into 2004

A decidedly soft patch in trade momentum developed over the second half of 2002 and through early 2003. Demand was bogged down by widespread weakness in the automotive, air travel, and technology sectors. And slackening of domestic demand conditions in the OECD countries compounded these trends. European import demand went through sharp compression: trade among EU member states especially affected by recession-like conditions on the Continent, and demand from outside the Union falling rapidly as well. After a pick-up to 12 percent rates at year-end, U.S. import volumes retrenched to a decline of 5 percent by April 2003—a pattern echoed by Japanese foreign demand—before rising again in May (figure 1.15). Against this background, following an advance of 3 percent in 2002, estimates for world trade growth in the current year have been marked down from 6.2 percent anticipated in spring 2003 projections to 4.6 percent.

A gradual advance in OECD industrial production and investment, combined with somewhat diminished strength in East Asian intraregional trade, underpin the anticipated recovery of trade volumes over the second half of 2003 and into 2004. And the medium-term outlook appears generally positive, as domestic demand in the rich countries, as well as low-and-middle income countries, should eventually rise in response to substantial policy stimulus. In contrast, the view for a revival of trade related to the global semiconductor cycle is uncertain at present. Sales may have reached a local peak, as unit shipments are now close to 2000 levels, while prices are likely to remain soft, reflecting the recent shift of production toward developing East Asia.

East Asia has been generating strong trade momentum on its own account, led by China. Chinese nominal imports (excluding oil) have grown at a compound rate of 12.2 percent since 1995, with much of the demand being met by regional producers. China's share in the merchandise exports of East Asia (Indonesia,

GLOBAL OUTLOOK AND THE DEVELOPING COUNTRIES

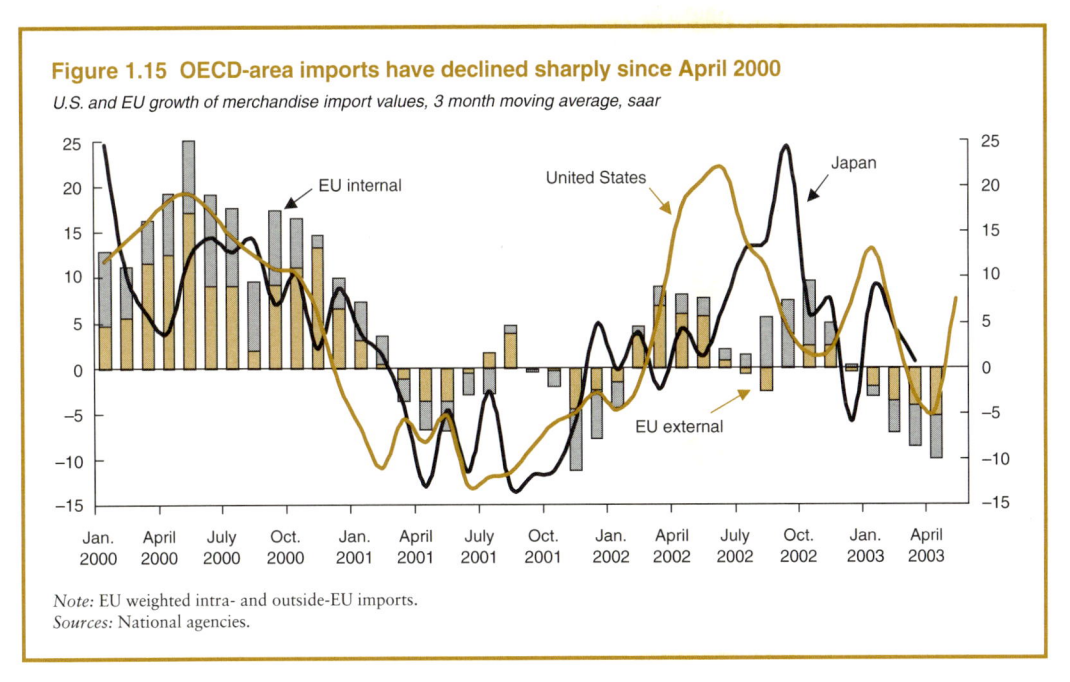

Figure 1.15 OECD-area imports have declined sharply since April 2000

U.S. and EU growth of merchandise import values, 3 month moving average, saar

Note: EU weighted intra- and outside-EU imports.
Sources: National agencies.

Republic of Korea, Taiwan (China), Malaysia, Thailand) has doubled over the last two years and quadrupled over the last ten (figure 1.16).

The dollar's weakness may improve merchandise trade balances for developing countries

For exporters who sell at a markup to local currency costs, dollar weakness implies higher dollar revenues per unit sold. Over the last two years developing countries' export prices have tended to grow at higher rates than those of high-income countries, yielding a cumulative improvement in the terms of trade. Yet, this development must be interpreted as a double-edged sword, with much of the improvement explained by higher oil prices.

As a group, developing countries are net energy exporters; but within the group there are significant net importers, many of which have been experiencing deterioration in their terms of trade. Indeed, *two-thirds* of developing countries, with GDP of $2.9 trillion (56 percent of total developing-country GDP) and population of 3.5 billion (75 percent of the developing world) are net energy importers. To a

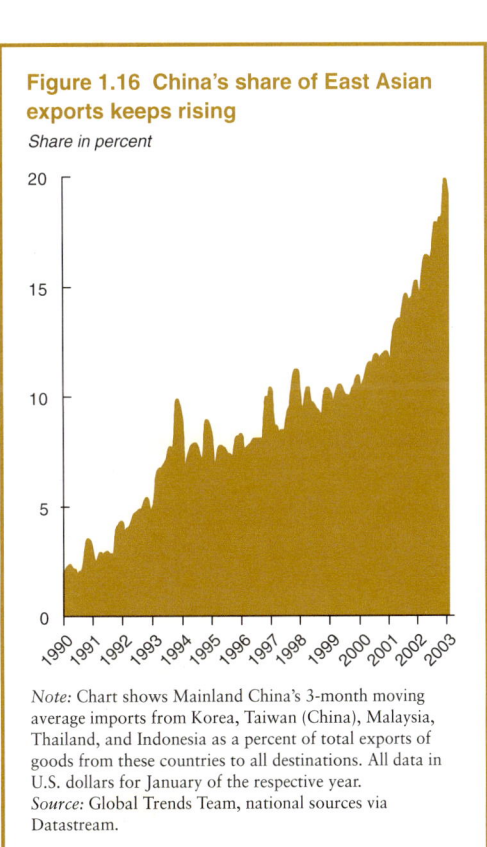

Figure 1.16 China's share of East Asian exports keeps rising

Share in percent

Note: Chart shows Mainland China's 3-month moving average imports from Korea, Taiwan (China), Malaysia, Thailand, and Indonesia as a percent of total exports of goods from these countries to all destinations. All data in U.S. dollars for January of the respective year.
Source: Global Trends Team, national sources via Datastream.

GLOBAL ECONOMIC PROSPECTS 2004

Table 1.4 Developing countries' exports will grow faster than those of the high-income countries
Merchandise export volumes, 2001–05 (percent change)

	2001	2002	2003	2004	2005
World	−0.7	3.2	4.6	7.9	7.9
High-income countries	−1.2	2.1	3.2	7.1	7.4
OECD	−0.5	1.5	2.6	7.0	7.4
United States	−5.9	−4.2	0.0	7.6	9.7
Japan	−8.3	7.3	6.7	7.0	6.5
Euro Area	3.2	1.1	2.1	5.7	7.1
Other high income	−6.8	7.1	7.7	8.1	7.3
Developing countries	1.1	7.7	10.0	10.9	9.7
East Asia and Pacific	−0.6	15.5	14.5	13.7	11.4
Latin America and Caribbean	−1.2	2.6	7.9	11.4	10.4
Europe and Central Asia	4.9	6.3	8.5	8.7	8.5
South Asia	2.1	−1.8	5.4	7.7	8.2
Middle East and North Africa	5.0	−0.2	4.2	5.5	5.2
Sub-Saharan Africa	2.5	1.2	2.7	5.4	5.7

Source: World Bank data and projections.

degree, the decline in terms of trade for net energy importers may have been moderated by price increases for non-oil commodities, but much of the improvement in price has been limited to a few products—among them cocoa, rubber, and coarse grains. True terms-of-trade gains for this group are likely to wait further softening in oil price and a firming in non-oil prices associated with global economic recovery.

The medium-term outlook for developing country exports is encouraging, given expected growth in export markets, combined with continuing pickup in market shares. East Asia is likely to dominate developing country trade flows over the forecast period, but better performance is anticipated for Latin America, Europe and Central Asia, and South Asia (table 1.4).

The eventual return of Iraqi oil exports will pressure OPEC and the oil price . . .
Oil prices averaged $31.3/bbl during the first quarter of 2003. Fears of loss of oil supplies from war in Iraq, low stocks, strong weather-related demand, and sharply reduced exports from Venezuela all contributed to the price hike. In response to the rise, supplies from other OPEC countries increased significantly. Saudi Arabia raised output to more than 9mb/d to help offset the prevailing and potential shortfall, and other OPEC members outside Venezuela added more than 1mb/d. The global oil price began falling shortly *before* the Iraq war began, as traders did not want to be caught short as the conflict commenced, particularly if a release of strategic stocks were to cause prices to crash as they did at the start of the Gulf War in 1991. Iraq's oil infrastructure was only minimally damaged during the war, and prices declined below $25/bbl during April. But Iraqi exports did not resume shortly after the war's end, as widespread looting of oil field equipment and of service industries that supply the oil sector, such as electricity and water, significantly delayed restart of production. Global crude oil inventories have remained persistently low, particularly in the United States, as OPEC has well-managed sales of its surplus production into the market. While U.S. imports have risen, continued tightness in physical markets has caused prices to rebound to around $27/bbl as of mid-June 2003 (figure 1.17).

Conditions surrounding Iraqi oil exports will likely be the most important drivers of oil

GLOBAL OUTLOOK AND THE DEVELOPING COUNTRIES

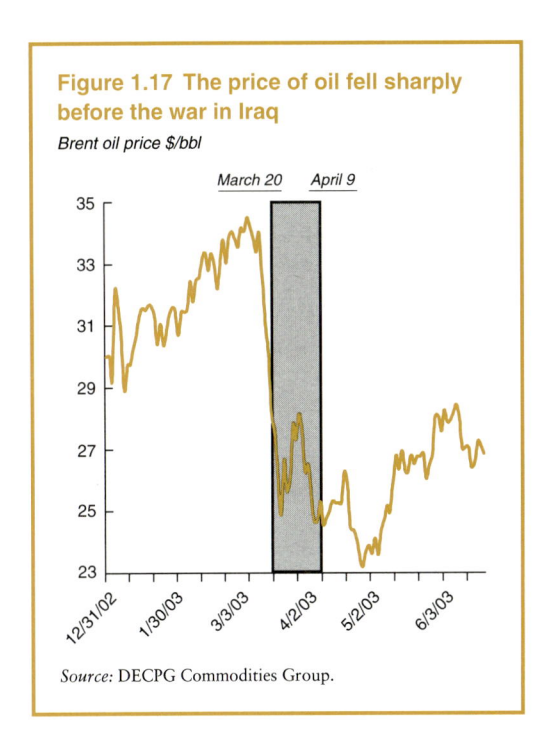

Figure 1.17 The price of oil fell sharply before the war in Iraq
Brent oil price $/bbl

Source: DECPG Commodities Group.

prices in the near term. Iraq's production for domestic needs resumed quickly after the war, but export volumes were limited to pre-war storage that was shipped in late June. Oil exports are scheduled to resume in the third quarter of the year, but technical difficulties as well as recent pipeline explosions will initially constrain shipments to about 1mb/d. However, the risk of further disruption is high, and it is unlikely that Iraq will achieve pre-war production levels of some 2.5mb/d during 2003. A gradual return of exports should enable OPEC to curtail production in a timely manner and keep the oil price within its target band of $22–28/bbl during 2003, particularly given the extremely low level of global inventories. Difficulties for OPEC could deepen in 2004 when Iraq's exports are anticipated to reach pre-war levels.

Initial investment in Iraq's oil sector will focus on refurbishing and improving efficiency of the present infrastructure. Limited growth in capacity could occur in 2004, but production is not expected to rise significantly above pre-war levels until 2005 and beyond. There are sugges-

tions to double or triple capacity, but such an endeavor would take several years to achieve and require substantial investment. Nevertheless higher capacity in Iraq, along with growing capacity within other OPEC members and significant expansion outside OPEC, is expected yield lower prices over the forecast period (box 1.3). Large increases in non-OPEC supplies that will capture much of the expected moderate growth in world oil demand are expected in the next several years. A "high-side" risk to the medium-term outlook for the oil price is that OPEC might exert stronger discipline to sustain higher prices. Such a policy, however, would raise incentives for non-OPEC producers to bring additional supplies to market.

But the dollar's decline and supply-side conditions outweigh the effects of the Iraq war on non-oil prices

Non-oil commodity prices have patently been affected by the war in Iraq—through increased freight costs, a buildup of inventories prior to the war, and the continuing reduction of stocks in the wake of military engagement. In addition, the war generally dampened consumer and industrial demand. Other factors, however, have been more important in influencing recent commodity price trends—among them the weakening of the dollar, supply conditions in individual commodities, and extremely depressed levels of some commodity prices before the recent recovery. The index of non-oil commodity prices rose 5.1 percent in 2002 after having declined by a cumulative 33 percent from 1997 to 2001. Prices are anticipated to increase an additional 7 percent during 2003 and advance at a modest 1 percent per year for the following three years. But even after recovery in 2003, nominal prices will remain well below their peaks of the mid-1990s.

The recovery in agriculture prices is expected to be modest

The index of nominal agricultural prices rose 8.5 percent in 2002. It is projected to increase by 7 percent in 2003 and by a more modest 1 percent per year for the next three years. The

23

Box 1.3 OPEC struggles to achieve higher prices amid growing supply competition

Oil markets suffered minimal disruption as a result of the Iraqi conflict, as other OPEC producers, particularly Saudi Arabia, raised production in anticipation of reduced Iraqi output and to replace Venezuelan exports. Oil prices peaked at $34.2/bbl just before the conflict commenced but quickly fell below $25/bbl. Oil stocks have stayed persistently low and prices have since recovered.

Oil prices have been extremely volatile during the last few years, largely because of fluctuations in OPEC production. Beginning in 2000, OPEC has targeted a price band of $22–$28/bbl for its basket of crude. By and large the organization has been successful. With the exception of the post-September 11th slump, oil prices have averaged about $27/bbl since late 1999. This compares with an average price of about $17.6/bbl over the 1986–99 period when OPEC was mainly concerned with regaining market share.

OPEC's new strategy is to keep inventories low and prices high, but doing so requires it to both raise and lower production during the year because of the seasonal pattern of oil consumption. Typically the industry builds stocks in the summer for use during the peak-demand winter season. However, it is difficult to precisely anticipate demand and supply three to six months forward, and this can result in large imbalances and volatile prices.

Achieving higher prices has been counterbalanced by loss of OPEC's market share. In recent years virtually all of the modest growth in world oil demand (less than 1 percent annually from 1997 to 2002) has been captured by non-OPEC producers—and much by the former Soviet Union. For OPEC 10 (excluding Iraq), its crude oil production as a share of total world supply fell from 35 percent in 1996–97 to 30 percent in 2002. Continued high oil prices will dampen future demand growth and, more importantly, stimulate development of non-OPEC supplies. Rising capacity within OPEC, desires for higher quotas (Algeria and Nigeria), and a recovery of Iraq's exports could strain OPEC's efforts to support higher prices.

Oil prices are expected to decline from $26.5/bbl in 2003 to $22/bbl in 2004 because of rising supply competition and below-trend demand growth, and to fall below $20/bbl by mid-decade. By 2006–07, significant new supplies from West Africa, the Caspian, Russia, deepwater-areas of the Atlantic basin, and elsewhere are expected to come on stream and, coupled with rising capacity within OPEC, exert severe downward pressure on prices. A risk to the forecast is that OPEC could maintain strong production discipline over the next few years to keep prices at or above $25/bbl. To achieve this goal, however, the cartel would have to yield market share for higher prices. High prices would add to the growing pressures on world demand and competing supplies. In the end, it is probable that prices would still fall below $20/bbl within a few years.

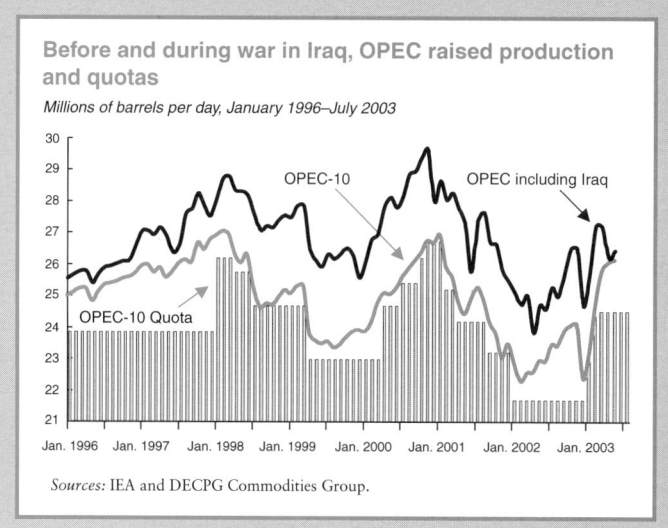

In the longer term, demand growth will be moderate, as it has been for the past 20 years, but new technologies, environmental pressures, and government policies could further reduce growth. Prices below $20/bbl are sufficiently high to generate adequate development of conventional and unconventional oil supplies, and there are no apparent resource constraints far into the future. In addition, new areas continue to be developed (for example, deep-water offshore sites and the Caspian Sea), and development costs continue to fall because of new technologies, shifting supply curves outward.

Before and during war in Iraq, OPEC raised production and quotas

Millions of barrels per day, January 1996–July 2003

Sources: IEA and DECPG Commodities Group.

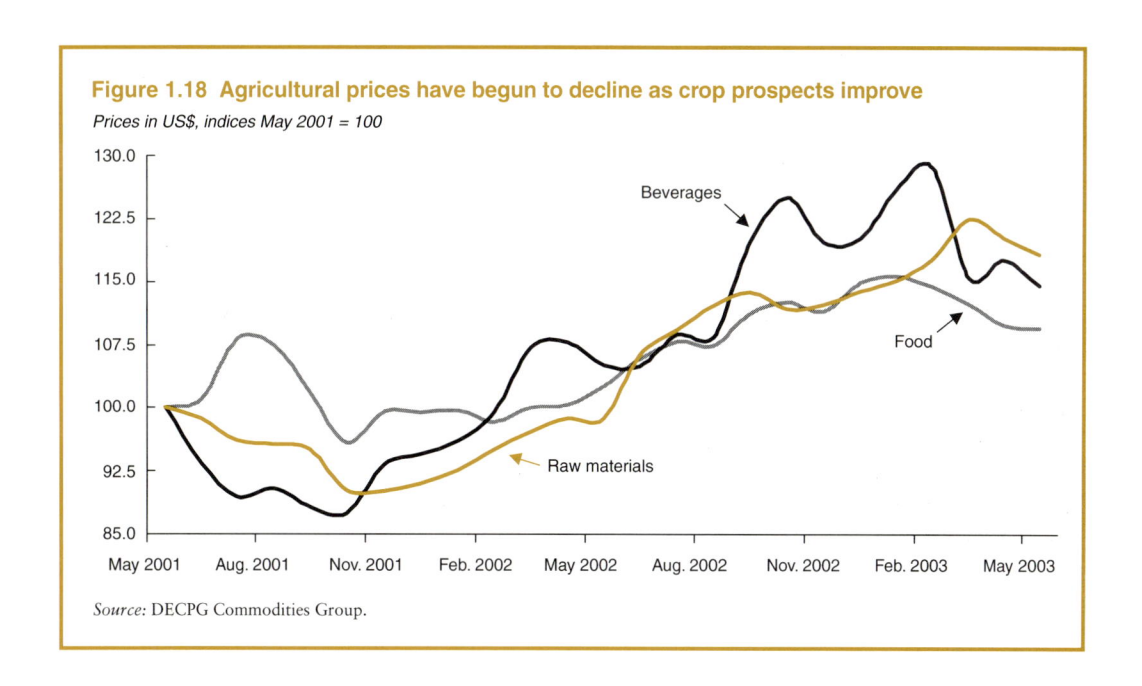

Figure 1.18 Agricultural prices have begun to decline as crop prospects improve

Prices in US$, indices May 2001 = 100

Source: DECPG Commodities Group.

advance in 2003 is driven primarily by the recovery of coffee, rubber, and vegetable oil prices after severe declines from 1997 to 2001. Most other agricultural commodity prices are expected to show only modest gains, however, because of high stock levels, excess production capacity, and slow demand growth associated with the modest recovery of global economic activity. Sharp increases in wheat prices at mid-2002 were quickly reversed as supply conditions in the United States improved and nontraditional exporters—Ukraine and Russia—increased international shipments. Other commodities, such as coffee and sugar, are burdened by large stock overhang; price increases are not anticipated despite historically low levels (figure 1.18).

Metals prices have undergone rallies over the past years but have faltered—mainly because of renewed expectations of weak demand. Recently, worries about the impact of the SARS virus on East Asian demand has also taken the luster out of metals prices. Inventories remain high for most metals and most markets are expected to remain in surplus this year. Nickel is the exception; stocks are low, there has been strong demand for stainless steel—especially in China—and prices have risen quite sharply. Gold also posted higher prices tied to reduced producer hedging and concerns about U.S. equity markets and the dollar. Although production cutbacks have been made for most metals, idle capacity will haunt the market even after the anticipated recovery in demand is finally underway. Metals prices are expected to increase by about 6 percent per year for the next two years, after decreasing by about 3 percent in 2002. Copper, the most balanced market among base metals, could tilt into deficit next year along with nickel. Other metals are expected to remain in surplus for a longer period, unless further production cuts occur, and prices are likely to lag behind that of copper during the recovery.

Financial markets have shown some surprises

The divergence between the sharp rally in developing countries' fixed-income asset prices and the fairly tepid capital flows in response to those prices has been the hallmark of market-based financing during early 2003. This development was not expected at the start of the year (see World Bank 2003). While asset prices

GLOBAL ECONOMIC PROSPECTS 2004

have evolved along expected trends—though more sharply and swiftly than anticipated—advances in gross capital flows have been lower than expected—and lower than warranted by the spectacular pickup in market prices.

The rally in developing-country debt prices that commenced in fall 2002, once concerns over elections in Brazil and Turkey had faded, gained momentum through mid-2003. As investors pursued yields higher than those in industrialized countries, the availability of capital for investment in developing-country debt increased swiftly, outpacing demand for debt financing from developing-country borrowers. The outcome was not new volumes of financing but a sharp adjustment in benchmark prices. These dynamics played out differently than they have since the late 1990s, when low industrial-country yields failed to promote a surge in availability of capital for developing countries (because investors were focusing more on credit risk than returns).

Benchmark spreads on emerging markets dropped from a peak of 869 basis points in September 2002 to 500 basis points by mid-year, the lowest level since 1998 (figure 1.19). The decline in spreads for several countries that had attracted investor concern was more spectacular. Benchmark spreads for Brazil, Argentina, and Uruguay declined by 1,700, 1,300, and 700 basis points, respectively over the period. Spreads on Turkish debt, which had escalated to 1,100 basis points by end-March 2003, dropped close to 700 basis points by mid-May. Gains in fixed-income prices stand out more clearly when benchmarked against the volatility and performance of global equity markets, which returned, on average, barely any gains between October and mid-May, even when taking into account the fall of the U.S. dollar.

Despite the narrowing of benchmark spreads, gross market-based capital flows to developing countries lost some ground during the early months of 2003 after mustering strength late in 2002 (figure 1.20). During the first quarter, capital flows slumped to $34 billion, down about 14 percent over fourth-quarter levels. After a strong start to the year, flows eased in February and dropped further in March. But a revival in both bond issuance and banking lending during April–May brought

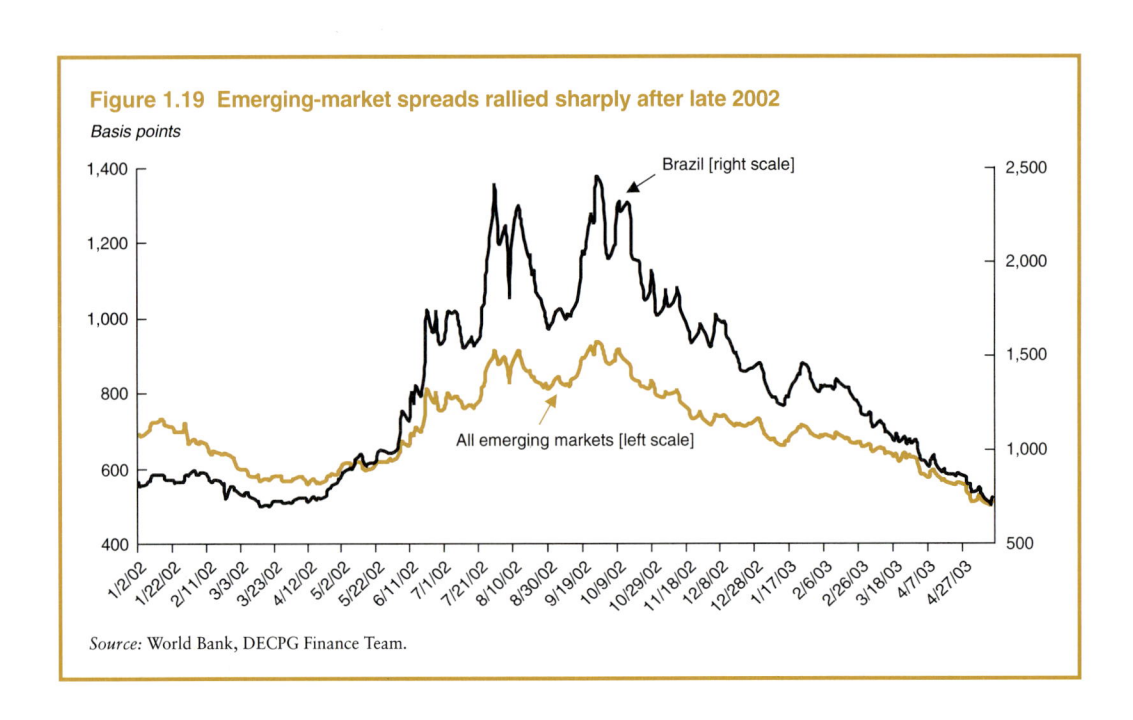

Figure 1.19 Emerging-market spreads rallied sharply after late 2002

Source: World Bank, DECPG Finance Team.

26

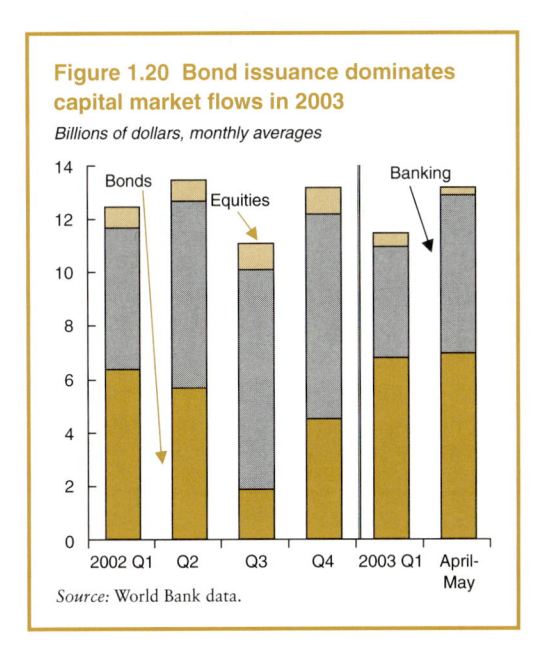

Figure 1.20 Bond issuance dominates capital market flows in 2003
Billions of dollars, monthly averages

Source: World Bank data.

flows to a rate of $40 billion, comparable to the patterns established during the second quarter of 2002. The ups and downs in overall capital flows were led by bond financing, which is sensitive to short-run developments. A noteworthy feature in bond financing was the easing of access for Latin American borrowers compared with 2002. Brazil was able to come to the market with a $1 billion issue after being absent for a year. However, the major portion of bond issuance from Latin America has been accounted for by investment-grade-rated countries. Contrasted with 2002 outturns, bank lending to developing countries has remained subdued, with monthly lending standing some 20 percent below comparable 2002 levels, as banks of almost all domiciles have been slow in extending credit to developing countries.

Market-based capital flows to developing countries have so far performed below the estimates set out for 2003 earlier this year, by about $2 billion a month on average. The subdued response of capital flows to the strong performance of asset prices can be traced to several factors: (a) uncertainty in the runup to the Iraq war, (b) renewed concerns over the strength of the economic recovery, and (c) increased volatility in financial markets during the early months of 2003. Many borrowers avoided or postponed borrowing.

The demand for external debt financing by developing countries remained limited, as many (especially in East Asia) have learned to live with less debt, while others are being kept in check even though financing conditions have eased relative to 2002. Capital flows could strengthen during the remainder of 2003. Borrowers may (a) take advantage of favorable financing conditions and move up their financing targets; (b) establish benchmarks for the purpose of setting favorable pricing in the future, or (c) undertake liability management, given the improvement in terms of borrowing over terms on previously contracted debt. Novel aspects of financing are already being encouraged. Mexico arranged a $2 billion bank loan to retire some of its Brady debt. And bond issues with collective action clauses have swiftly become more acceptable with relatively little or no premium. Mexico, Brazil, and South Africa issued bonds with such clauses between March and April.

The stimulus to developing-country capital flows from low industrial-country yields could persist over the short-to-medium terms, as yields in the G-3 countries are unlikely to rise sharply and swiftly even if they do turn the corner. Barring major fallout, investors may continue to grow less risk averse. Most of the vulnerabilities in emerging-market economies and in high-yield industrial-country markets have been exposed and have evolved through changes in market prices. Substantial fallout from the troubled Latin American borrowers was largely avoided. Foreign exchange reserve positions of developing countries in general are holding steady, and their dependency on external debt is falling. Vulnerability to adverse external shocks appears to have been reduced from the high levels of the last two years, and flexible exchange rates have helped in this area. And for several countries, the macroeconomic implications of accession to the European Union have vastly improved credit risk perceptions.

The developing countries: Back on track toward growth?

Developing countries appear poised for growth to resume at more rapid rates. Despite continuing geopolitical uncertainties and subdued conditions in the rich countries at present, developments in several areas are converging to support the expectation of a step-up in output growth. Should conditions in the external environment improve as expected over the next years, countries should have the opportunity to advance export-market shares and grow export volumes at more robust rates. International financial markets have become more accessible to developing countries, and compression of spreads has reduced the cost of raising capital. International reserves have risen to record proportions, especially in developing East Asia, providing a degree of cushioning against potential vagaries in global financial markets.

Developing-country fundamentals are improving

On the domestic front, fiscal positions have generally improved across developing regions, allowing a degree of stimulus to be undertaken to bolster domestic demand, and prospectively, more can be achieved here. While industrial production supporting both external and internal demand growth is currently mixed across regions, the seeds of firmer recovery appear to be fairly widespread. Inflation is moderating, and this trend should be enhanced as the oil price moves downward over the next years—and for several countries, currency appreciation will abet improved inflation performance. Finally, recent political and financial difficulties in Latin America appear to have moderated, though uncertainties persist. In contrast, developments in the Middle East and North Africa region (MENA) remain unsettled in the aftermath of conflict, and heightened uncertainty and risk aversion among exporters, investors, and tourists is likely to affect growth for the countries of the region for some time.

Recent trends in industrial production highlight the current mixed picture across key regions, to a large degree, integrated with ongoing global developments. For developing countries as a group, output has recovered to 7 percent year-over-year rates from troughs experienced in early 2002 (figure 1.21a). The MENA region, which accounts for some 9 percent of developing-country value added, has enjoyed a 15 percent surge in crude petroleum and other energy production, as OPEC members have exceeded quota levels in expectation of the loss of Iraqi output. In contrast, some underlying influences of SARS may be discerned in drooping production figures for the East Asia and Pacific region (EAP), though other factors, including the slowdown of world trade and poor conditions in high-tech markets, are likely the more important elements at work. Latin America, meanwhile, is building on revitalization of output in Argentina, and earlier in Brazil and Mexico, but activity in the latter countries appears to have eased recently. Europe and Central Asia (ECA) has benefited from Turkey's dramatic recovery from its financial crisis of 2001, while hydrocarbon exporters in the Commonwealth of Independent States (CIS), including Russia, have ramped up oil and gas production to fill part of the gap left by loss of Iraqi crude oil. As some of the near-term distortions to production dissipate—the recovery now underway for low- and middle-income countries should firm and broaden over the coming quarters and into 2004.

Inflation has moderated for developing countries as a group, from recent peaks of 5.5 percent as of mid-2001 toward a 3 percent year-over-year pace at present (figure 1.21b). Improvement has been spearheaded by developments in the EAP region, where tendencies toward deflation in China (largely productivity driven), and easing of price pressures in most ASEAN countries have yielded a reduction of 3 percentage points in annual inflation, from 5 toward 2 percent rates. And developments in the ECA region have been quite promising as well, with a 4 point fall in CPI over the like period, from 6 to 2 percent, reflecting improvement in Turkey, Russia, and many of the countries of Central Europe. In-

GLOBAL OUTLOOK AND THE DEVELOPING COUNTRIES

Figure 1.21a Regional trends in industrial production are mixed
IP, 3-month/3-month, percent change, year/year

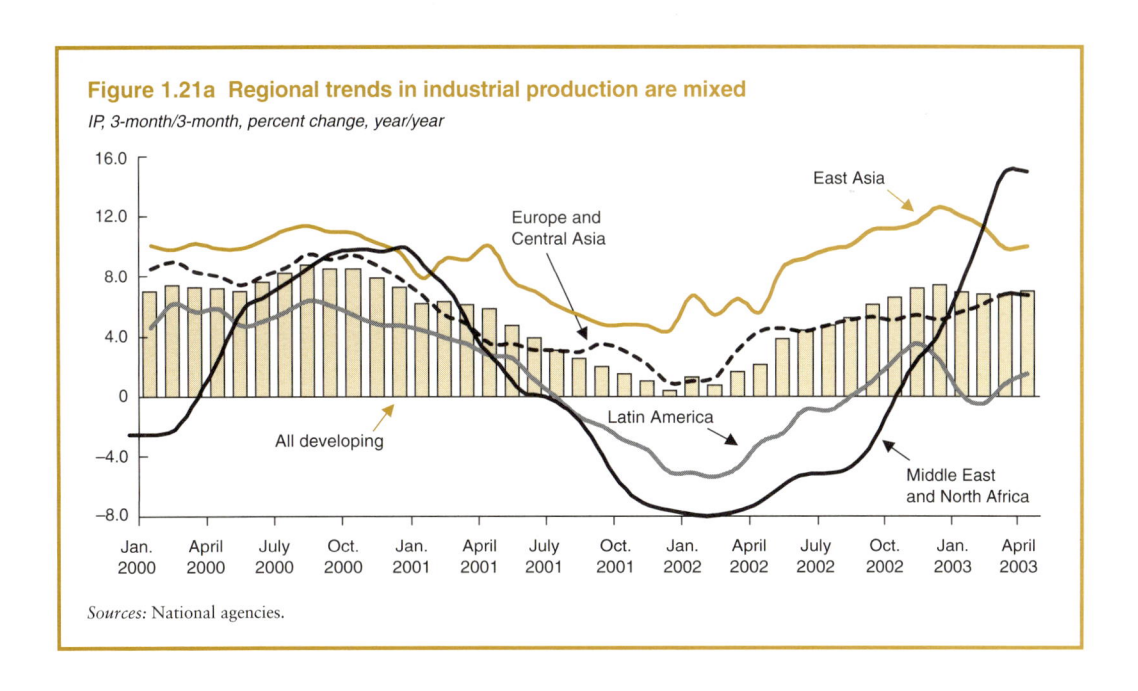

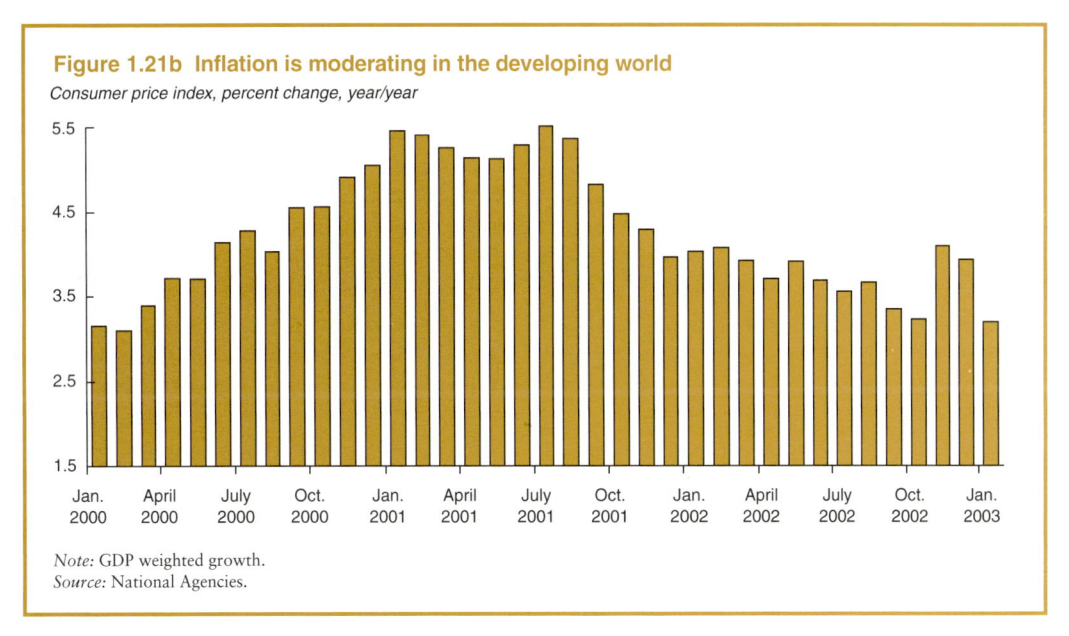

Sources: National agencies.

Figure 1.21b Inflation is moderating in the developing world
Consumer price index, percent change, year/year

Note: GDP weighted growth.
Source: National Agencies.

flation remains at moderate 3 percent rates in South Asia (SA), but has re-accelerated in Latin America and Sub-Saharan Africa, reflecting earlier currency devaluations in the former region, and adverse fiscal conditions and large-scale currency decline in several large African states.

The fall of the dollar vis-à-vis partner currencies has affected more than the cross-rates for the euro, yen, or sterling. Since October 2002, the brunt of dollar depreciation has fallen upon several Latin American currencies, importantly the Brazilian real and Argentine peso (20–25 percent appreciation), reflecting

GLOBAL ECONOMIC PROSPECTS 2004

Figure 1.21c Major currencies in Latin America and East Asia are firming up

Dollar depreciation against major currencies since October 2002, percent change

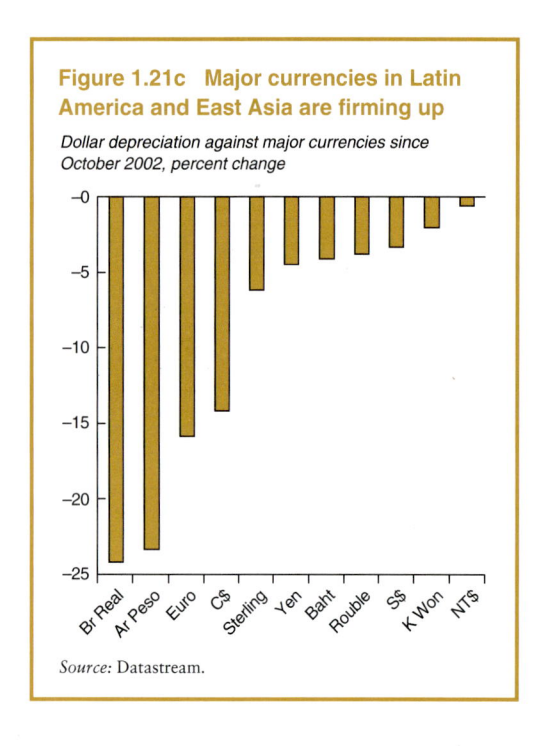

Source: Datastream.

in part strong rallies in financial markets in those countries, along with sharply narrowing spreads on benchmark bonds and fixed-income funds (figure 1.21c). Several East Asian currencies have also appreciated more moderately against the U.S. unit—notably the Thai baht and Korean won, while the Russian rouble has risen in like proportion. Currency appreciation in Latin America is likely to deliver mixed results: while serving to dampen export prospects—an important vehicle for economic recovery—appreciation will help to reduce inflationary tendencies in both Argentina and Brazil, providing room for needed interest rate reductions and a stronger foundation for domestic growth.

Growth should pick up across regions during 2004–05

Over the last years, GDP growth for the developing and transition countries has undergone dramatic shifts and suffered volatility associated with global business-cycle developments, as during the recessions of the early 1980s and 1990s. Several region-specific crises and transformations also have induced sharp variations in aggregate growth—among them the Latin debt crisis of the early 1980s, the period of recession associated with transition in the former COMECON countries during the early 1990s, the East Asian financial crisis of 1997–98, and the Russian devaluation of 1999 (figure 1.22). The global downturn of 2001 exacted a toll on developing country growth, but the deceleration of output has been much less dramatic than in earlier episodes.

In the base-case projections, developing-country growth is expected to reaccelerate in all regions from the relatively sluggish performance of 2001–02 to an average GDP advance of 4 percent during 2003, reaching about 5 percent growth by 2004–05, consistent with previous peaks in 2000 and 1996–97 (figure 1.22). Latin America is expected to see the most substantial gain, as the region consolidates following the Argentine crisis. A return to stronger growth in India powers the South Asia region, while more moderate gains are achieved in Europe and Central Asia—tracking the slower pace of revival in EU activity. The pickup in growth will be lower in the Middle East and North Africa, where uncertainty regarding the regional political and economic situation is likely to persist, and in Sub-Saharan Africa, where only moderate gains in commodity prices and sluggish European growth play a role (figure 1.23).

SARS carries some adverse economic affects for the East Asian economy

The East Asia and Pacific region was able to overcome a retrenchment in world trade, a sluggish high-tech sector, geopolitical uncertainty, and soaring oil prices in 2002 to register solid 6.7 percent growth (figure 1.24). China and Vietnam, at 8 percent and 6 percent respectively, were the engines of the regional economy, as exports spilled over into domestic demand and generated strong demands for intermediate imports from other countries in the region, including Korea, Thailand, Malaysia, and the Philippines. The main exceptions to the

Figure 1.22 Developing countries are on track toward long-term growth

GDP growth, percent per annum, 1981–2005

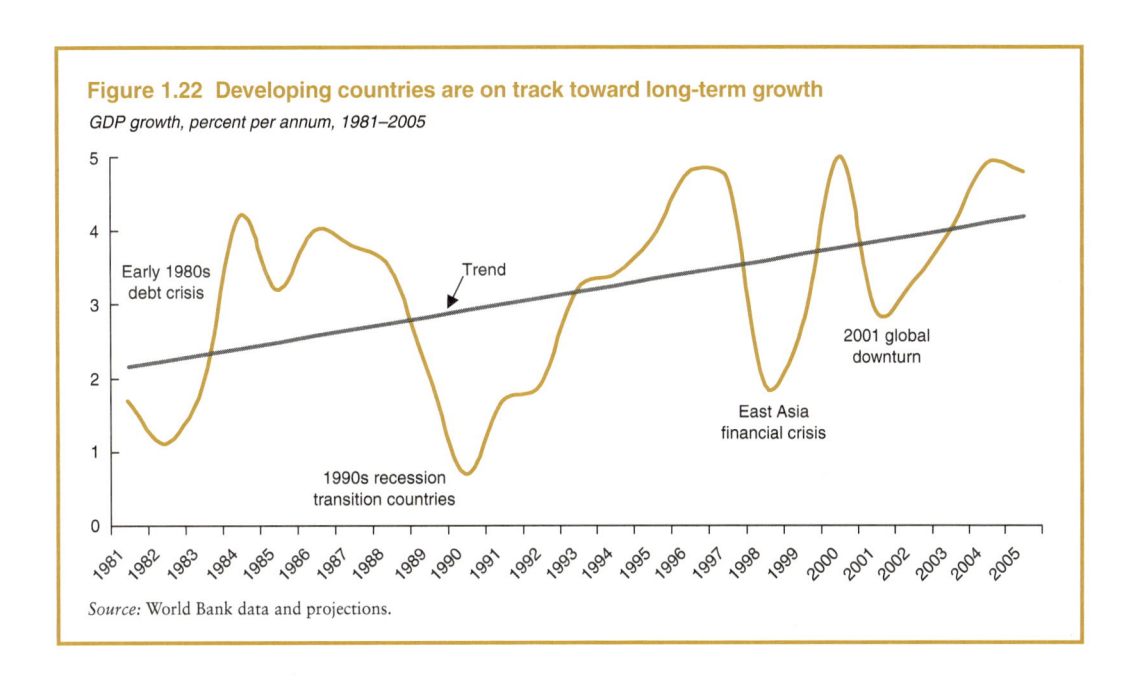

Source: World Bank data and projections.

Figure 1.23 Growth rates in developing countries will rise through 2005

GDP growth, 2001–02 and 2003–05 (percent)

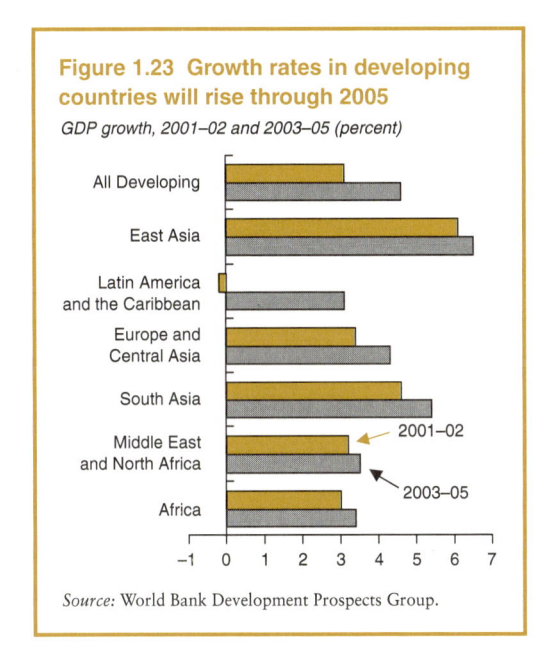

Source: World Bank Development Prospects Group.

buoyant performance were Hong Kong (China) and Singapore, which failed to capitalize on burgeoning intraregional trade, and Indonesia.

Growth in East Asia is expected to slow by more than half a percent to 6.1 percent in 2003, in part because of the outbreak of SARS centered in China and Hong Kong. According to favorable World Bank estimates, SARS may subtract about 0.5 percent from regional growth during 2003 through its effects on travel, tourism, and domestic consumption and investment (box 1.4). Some countries are likely to be more affected than others—because of high tourism shares in GDP or their importance as hubs of international trade. In Hong Kong (China) and Singapore, growth may drop by several percentage points from 2002 results. Meanwhile, growth in the Philippines is expected to ease because of consolidation of government finance, and Indonesia is vulnerable to a fall in confidence, especially in conjunction with high levels of household debt.

Though near-term prospects are muted, longer-term performance is expected to remain strong. In 2004, growth is expected to reach 6.7 percent based on a quick containment of the SARS epidemic, together with recovery in industrial countries and an upturn in the high-tech cycle. By 2005, the EAP region is expected to return to a long-term trend rate of output growth of around 6.5 percent.

GLOBAL ECONOMIC PROSPECTS 2004

Figure 1.24 Before the SARS outbreak, East Asian* GDP was growing robustly

GDP growth, percent change, Q/Q saar

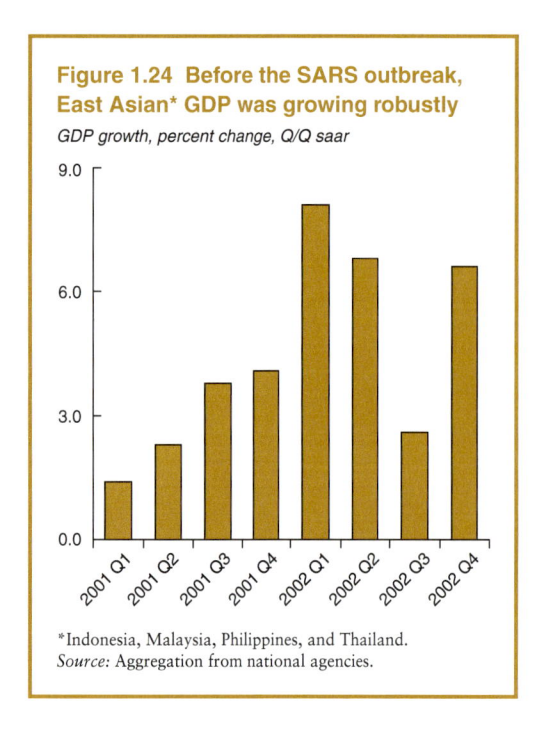

*Indonesia, Malaysia, Philippines, and Thailand.
Source: Aggregation from national agencies.

Latin America shows signs of renewed recovery

Latin America showed increasing evidence of a recovery during 2003, after growth fell to –0.8 percent in 2002. In fact, the negative growth performance for 2002 results exclusively from severe contractions in Argentina, Uruguay, and Venezuela; and a regional average excluding these countries registers positive growth of 1.6 percent, underscoring that contagion had been limited. Industrial production returned to positive growth during the fourth quarter of 2002, up 5.6 percent, underpinned by gains in Argentina, Chile, and Brazil (figure 1.25). Falling yield spreads confirmed the impression of an improvement in financial health. In Brazil, for example, spreads declined from a peak of 2,067 basis points in October 2002 to 754 basis points by April 2003, as risk aversion eased among global investors. Though capital flows, especially bank lending, to Latin America and the Caribbean remain weak, the strengthening of several local currencies against the dollar (Argentine peso, Brazilian real, Chilean and Mexican pesos) has occurred in parallel with improving investor sentiment regarding local equity and fixed-income markets. Though still dependent on an accommodating external environment, threats of financial crises and attendant spillovers appear to have receded.

In Brazil, President Lula da Silva's commitment to balanced macroeconomic policies has helped to restore confidence, and has already facilitated access to international finance, while additional support from the International Monetary Fund should be forthcoming. Meanwhile, rising consumer confidence and receding unemployment in Argentina indicate a growing consensus that the worst may be over. Yet inflation risks persist, and the credibility of economic policy will need to be established by the new president. Both countries continue to face the challenges of supporting growth in the context of tight constraints to fiscal and monetary policy. In contrast, the Republica Bolivariana de Venezuela restarted its oil exports following a strike-induced shut-in lasting some 60 days. But, there the political crisis appears to be unresolved and macroeconomic performance continues to suffer, with GDP declining by 9 percent in 2002 and forecasted to fall 14 percent for 2003. Peru's performance has been remarkable for 2002 and prospects for 2003 are still favorable, but recent political turmoil will potentially be a drag on growth and raise public deficits. Recent political unrest in Bolivia also had damaging repercussions, and in the Dominican Republic a massive bank fraud triggered the collapse of the second-largest financial institution, with potentially heavy financial and economic costs.

Given the extent of recent difficulties and remaining uncertainties, near-term growth prospects remain subdued. However, the longer-term outlook is more optimistic. Multilateral trade agreements and regional market-opening initiatives in the European Union (EU) and U.S. markets bode well for external performance. Exports are diversifying into areas such as tourism and other services. Macroeconomic stability and commitment to sound

Box 1.4 Economic effects of Severe Acute Respiratory Syndrome (SARS)

While the threat of Severe Acute Respiratory Syndrome (SARS)—a virus that spreads easily and has no known antidote—has shaken China, Canada, and the world at large, the spread of the outbreak has stopped and public panic has largely subsided. The outbreak seems to have been brought under control as a result of stringent public health measures in the affected countries, though there may also be a seasonal component to the disease. The economic impact should thus be concentrated in the second quarter of 2003, and is expected to be largely limited to the East Asia region, with a relatively small impact on global growth. As of end-June 2003, it is estimated that SARS had infected 8,450 people in 32 countries and to have killed over 800 people.

Short-term economic activity—particularly in 'face-to-face' exchanges such as in the retail sector—slowed in the most affected countries. Overall, the economic impact was largely transmitted through aggregate demand, but also to a lesser extent through supply mechanisms. Tourism and trade-related services declined as people became less willing to travel to areas where there were SARS outbreaks. The airline industry was hit especially hard, as the SARS virus came at an already difficult time, following the September 11 attack and the war in Iraq, which already diminished vacation travel, in particular, but also corporate travel, given sluggish world growth. Manufacturing trade was also affected. International firms with production lines in affected countries suffered some interruptions to production because of restrictions on travel. Some (temporary) substitutions may have been made; however, sustained losses in market share are unlikely. Finally, the SARS outbreak temporarily depressed consumer and business confidence in the countries most affected, but containment of the outbreak should result in a quick return to pre-SARS confidence levels. The macroeconomic policy response to the outbreak is expected to be most evident in increased fiscal outlays through transfers and tax breaks, in addition to increased health care expenditures to respond to the outbreak.

Source: World Bank staff.

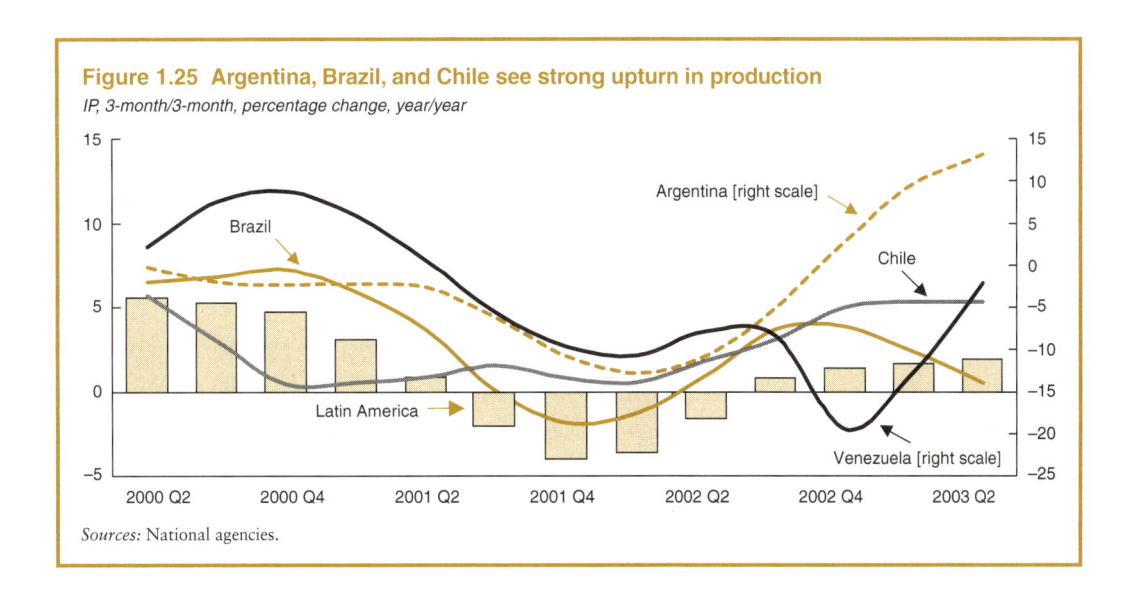

Figure 1.25 Argentina, Brazil, and Chile see strong upturn in production

IP, 3-month/3-month, percentage change, year/year

Sources: National agencies.

GLOBAL ECONOMIC PROSPECTS 2004

fiscal and monetary policies are becoming the norm and already yielding benefits in the form of less costly international borrowing and more robust domestic financial markets.

The outlook for Europe and Central Asia is mixed: greater EU demand, but flagging oil prices

Output expanded by 4.6 percent in the ECA region during 2002, primarily resulting from the strength of domestic demand, which more than offset lackluster growth in the region's main export markets. A number of economies enjoyed a pickup in growth during the year (Croatia, Estonia, Lithuania, Poland, Slovak Republic, Turkey, Armenia, Azerbaijan, Belarus, Georgia), though excluding Turkey activity was marked down about half a point to 3.9 percent. Output in the Commonwealth of Independent States (CIS) eased to 4.7 percent growth in 2002, from robust 5.8 percent outturns of 2001, and from the spike in growth of 8.4 percent posted in 2000. The critical factor in this development was erosion of stimulus to the Russian economy stemming from the *rouble* devaluation of 1998 and the rents from strong energy prices. In turn, diminished import demand from Russia—representing an important export market for the remaining CIS countries—contributed to the slowdown for the rest of the group. Activity in the Central and Eastern European Countries (CEECs), excluding Turkey, was unchanged in 2002 relative to 2001, at 2.9 percent. Including Turkey, growth averaged 4.5 percent for the group, a sharp upswing from contraction of 0.8 percent in 2001, reflecting a 7.8 percent recovery enjoyed by Turkey in 2002. For the CEECs, domestic demand was spurred by fiscal policy (Hungary, Czech Republic, Poland, Slovenia, Slovakia) and/or easing of monetary policy (Czech Republic, Latvia, Lithuania, Romania).

Aggregate growth for the region is anticipated to slow moderately to 4.3 percent in 2003, as a return to more modest advances in Turkey, under the burden of required fiscal consolidation and related issues, will carry some weight (figure 1.26). Among the CEECs,

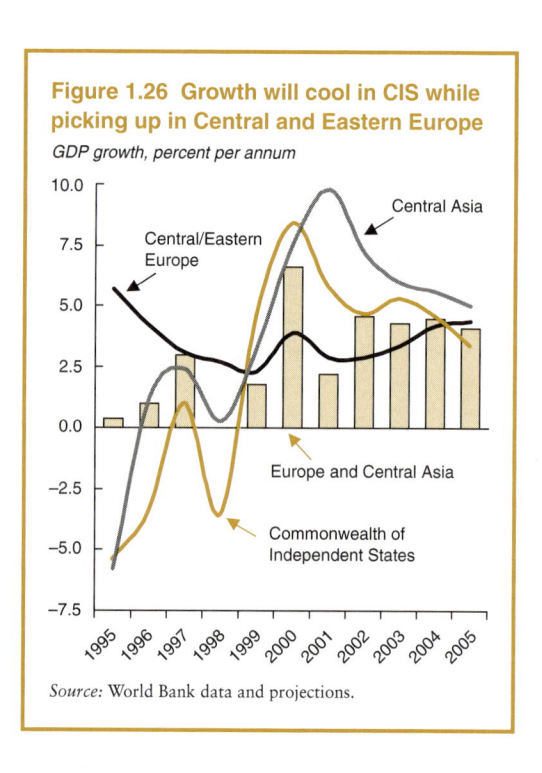

Figure 1.26 Growth will cool in CIS while picking up in Central and Eastern Europe
GDP growth, percent per annum

Source: World Bank data and projections.

excluding Turkey, growth in 2003 is projected to ramp-up moderately (by 0.5 points) as a result of three factors: a gradual recovery toward year-end in the EU, the group's main export market; notable acceleration of growth in Poland (representing about 13 percent of the region's GDP); and expected improvement in growth performance in the Czech Republic, Slovenia, and Albania. An expected boost to consumer confidence is likely because of progress in the EU accession process.[2] Growth is projected to strengthen slightly among the CIS countries in 2003, as domestic demand has begun to firm in Russia, which in turn should support growth in other CIS countries dependent on Russia's import demand. ECA regional growth is expected to accelerate to 4.5 percent in 2004 and then to slow to 4.1 percent in 2005, reflecting divergent trends at the sub-regional level. Growth in the CEEC sub-region (including Turkey) is likely to accelerate from 3.5 in 2003 to 4.3 and 4.7 percent in 2004 and 2005, respectively, in part because of firming of external demand and significant inflows of FDI to new EU members, in addition to EU transfers. Growth is likely to slow in the CIS from 5.3 percent in 2003 to 4.6 and 3.4 percent in 2004 and 2005, respectively, assuming a substantial fall in the oil price in both 2004 and 2005 and a decline in growth impetus through fiscal linkages, especially in Russia.

The war in Iraq and its aftermath are the key factors for the Middle East and North Africa region

The buildup to the war in Iraq and its aftermath have dominated events in the Middle East and North Africa region over the past year. The developments were, on balance, positive for oil exporters. The oil price surged, peaking at $38/bbl, and production quotas were raised in early 2003 (figure 1.27). Buoyant oil revenues boosted economic performance by supporting higher fiscal expenditures. Elsewhere in the region, however, tourism and trade, not fully recovered from the effects of September 11, 2001, were further battered by the prospect of conflict in Iraq. The most affected countries were those closest to the conflict. Tourism in Jordan and Egypt was seriously affected; for Jordan, where tourism accounts for some 10 percent of GDP, the consequences were particularly adverse. For Egypt, lower non-oil trade also affected revenues from the Suez Canal.

Short-term prospects for the region will be conditioned by political resolution in post-conflict Iraq. Uncertainties over the future of the country, with respect to governance, aid flows, and reconstruction, will continue to affect the region for some time. Nevertheless, growth should accelerate somewhat during 2003. The oil-exporting countries are expected to grow more quickly in 2003 as a result of fiscal pump priming and increased oil production quotas. For the diversified exporters, particularly Jordan and Egypt, a gradual recovery in tourism and other sectors affected by the conflict could unfold in the second half of 2003, but such recovery would be fragile. Other factors, not directly associated with recent developments in Iraq, will shape the near-term outlook. Egypt is suffering from a period of extended weakness in the domestic sector, and despite reforms to the exchange rate regime earlier in 2003, growth expectations for the year have dimmed as private investment remains subdued. Moroccan agriculture will provide a substantial boost to output in 2003 following the severe drought in that country. A

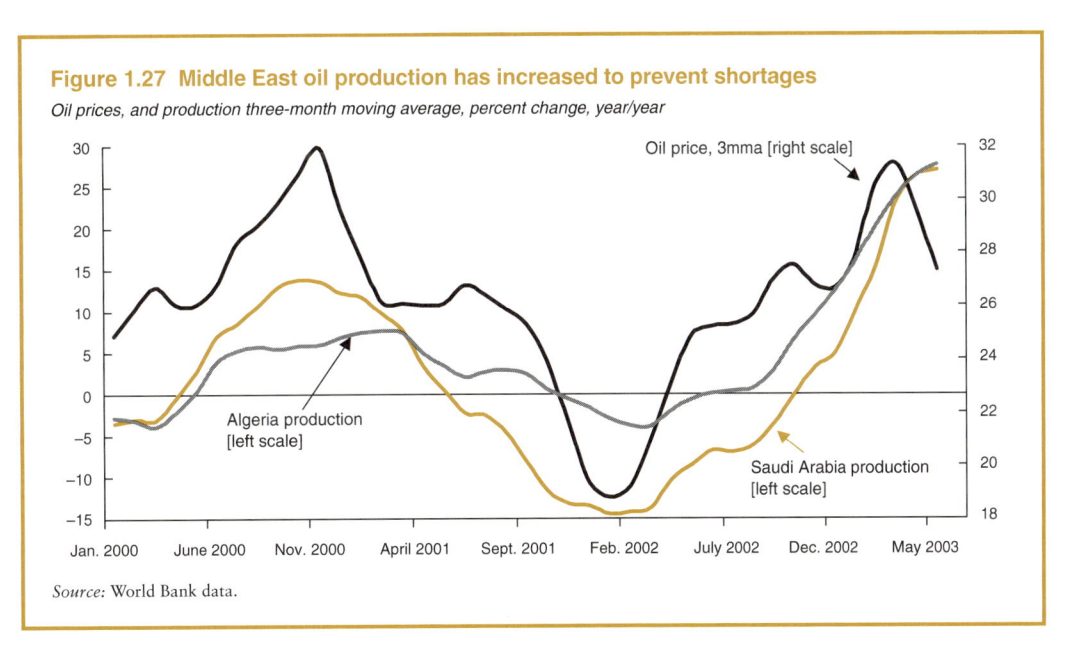

Figure 1.27 Middle East oil production has increased to prevent shortages

Oil prices, and production three-month moving average, percent change, year/year

Source: World Bank data.

similar situation exists in Tunisia, where agricultural output fell by an estimated 11 percent during 2002.

The economic consequences of the conflict in Iraq will play out through its impacts on confidence and investment spending. A protracted process of reconstruction could exacerbate these problems. A downward trend in the oil price presents a further risk. With sluggish growth in world demand, oil prices could trend lower than anticipated, cutting exporters' incomes and putting fiscal expenditure programs at risk. Moreover, further political instability in the tense environs of the region cannot be ruled out, a development that would hamper investment and growth for an extended period of time.

A stronger external environment, upswing in agricultural cycle, should boost South Asian growth

Growth in the South Asia region slowed to 4.2 percent during 2002 from 4.9 percent in 2001, marking a downward revision from previous estimates, largely because of adverse weather conditions and declines in agricultural output in India, Bangladesh, and Nepal. Nepal experienced a plunge in tourism receipts and a sharp fall in manufacturing output, as domestic insurgency intensified. Pakistan and Sri Lanka both enjoyed a pickup in growth during the year linked to strong government spending in Pakistan; and for Sri Lanka, a recovery in the services sector and improved political stability tied to progress in peace talks and implementation of a year-long cease-fire. Current account balances for the two largest economies, India and Pakistan, posted surpluses and the region's aggregate external balance strengthened. A number of economies experienced a significant increase in remittances during 2002. These were driven largely by: incentives introduced by the Bangladeshi government to channel remittances through official sources; high interest rate differentials in India—reflecting significant government borrowing requirements there; and improvements in the security situation and progress in macroeconomic stabilization in both Pakistan and Sri Lanka.

Growth is anticipated to accelerate throughout the region in 2003, to an average of 5.4 percent, assuming a return to trend agricultural production, a recovery in external demand, continued improvement in political stability and regional security, and a firming of domestic demand, especially in India (figure 1.28). In the medium term South Asian growth is likely to be sustained near 5.4 percent, assuming a continued recovery in external demand and establishment of normal trends in agricultural output. Bangladesh and India should benefit from an ongoing recovery in domestic demand. Both Pakistan and Sri Lanka are projected to enjoy continued macroeconomic stability and an associated acceleration of growth. Similarly, Nepal is anticipated to experience a pick-up in growth, assuming continued improvement in the security situation there, with a recovery in domestic demand and in tourism receipts.

Furthermore, recently improved relations between India and Pakistan are hoped to lead to greater stability in the region, paving the way for increased business confidence and stability. The fiscal positions of the South Asian economies are forecast to improve moderately, assuming some progress in raising budget revenues (as a share of GDP) and improvement in the management of government expenditure. Inflation is projected to increase somewhat, albeit still at moderate levels, because of stronger growth and assumptions of a more accommodative monetary stance in many countries. Falling oil prices are expected to provide some offset to these domestic factors.

Sub-Saharan Africa maintains positive per capita growth in spite of a difficult external environment

A subdued world economy together with familiar problems of drought and civil strife held growth in Sub-Saharan Africa (SSA) to 2.8 percent in 2002. Import demand from Europe, the region's main trading partner, was particularly weak. Though most (dollar denominated) com-

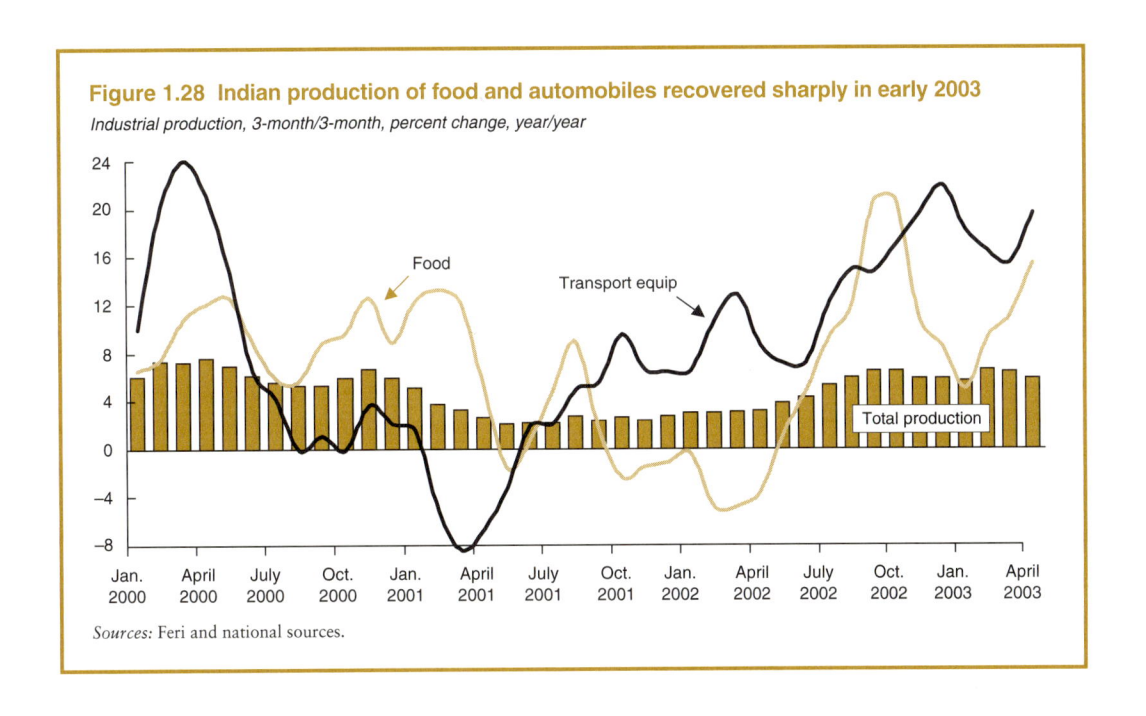

Figure 1.28 Indian production of food and automobiles recovered sharply in early 2003

Industrial production, 3-month/3-month, percent change, year/year

Sources: Feri and national sources.

modity prices have rebounded from recent lows, terms of trade for non-oil exporters have recovered little of their losses of the past few years. At the same time, travel and tourism suffered not only from slower world income growth, but also from terrorist fears and the buildup to war in Iraq. As a result, foreign trade made a negative contribution to the region's growth. Domestic economies also slowed as poor weather or civil disorder disrupted agricultural production in countries containing over half the region's population, depressing incomes and demand. Notably, though, investment spending was relatively resilient. There were pluses to note as well. South Africa overcame the depressed tourism market to become the world's fastest growing tourist destination in 2002, with arrivals up over 20 percent. Nontraditional exports covered by AGOA preferences—transportation equipment, textiles and apparel, and agricultural products—registered strong growth despite the slowdown in the U.S. economy, indicating that with the right incentives and opportunities, SSA countries can be competitive. Most encouraging of all, according to preliminary estimates 12 countries in the region achieved growth of 4 percent or better and average per capita income rose for a fourth successive year—the longest sustained rise in over two decades.

The region's largest economy, South Africa, registered relatively sound performances during 2002. Growth slowed toward the end of the year, but remained in positive territory as it has since 1999. Because of the increasing strength of the rand, foreign trade contributed negatively to growth, but domestic absorption was strong enough to offset that impact and growth overall reached 3.0 percent. Investment was particularly strong, up 6.5 percent in spite of high real interest rates. In Nigeria, the picture was mixed. The successful presidential election helped cement the fledgling democratic process; however, progress on fiscal and economic reforms continues to be frustratingly slow. Despite high oil prices, budget gridlock and a reduced OPEC quota held growth to only 1.9 percent. Progressively weaker oil prices over the next few years will put pressure on fiscal and external accounts, though expansion of the energy sector, especially of liquid natural gas (LNG), should sustain moderate real growth in the medium term.

In the medium term, the economic performance of Sub-Saharan Africa should benefit as the global recovery consolidates. Yet, with expectations for Europe at best moderate, the external impetus to growth will remain weak. For the region as a whole, growth is expected to remain unchanged at 2.8 percent in 2003, then rise to 3.5 percent in 2004. Both oil and non-oil producers will share in the acceleration. For oil producers—including additions to the list such as Côte d'Ivoire—rising capacity presages substantial growth in medium-term production and exports, even though prices and terms of trade are expected to fall sharply. Major energy-related infrastructure projects will further support demand. For the rest of the region, the recent rebound in commodity prices has largely run its course, but at least the expectation is for a measure of stability in key export markets at levels where exporters in Sub-Saharan Africa can continue to compete. With luck, better weather conditions will stimulate domestic incomes and expenditure as well (figure 1.29).

In the longer term, per capita growth is expected to average 1.6 percent—a substantial improvement on long-run historical trends, though barely half what would be needed to achieve the MDGs. The region continues to face immense development challenges from HIV/AIDS, to low savings and investment, poor infrastructure, shortages of human capital, and negative perceptions of international investors (box 1.5). Nor does the forecast anticipate any significant help from a reversal of recent terms of trade losses. But the region's most critical need is to re-establish civil order, where lacking, and to raise standards of governance and policymaking, for these are the most powerful predictors of economic performance. Here there is encouraging progress to report, with signs of institutional strengthening at both the country and regional levels. On balance, assuming a continuation of this trend, the forecast of positive, albeit moderate growth for the region should be achievable.

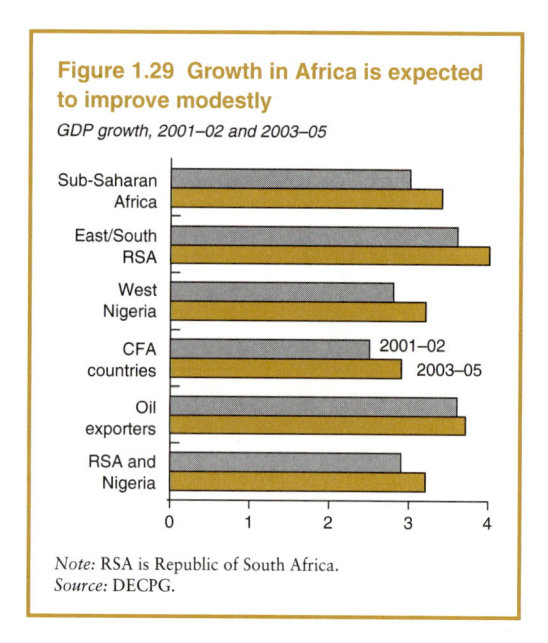

Figure 1.29 Growth in Africa is expected to improve modestly
GDP growth, 2001–02 and 2003–05

Note: RSA is Republic of South Africa.
Source: DECPG.

Trade, growth, and poverty in developing countries

World trade growth reached unprecedented levels in the 1990s, accompanied by accelerating flows of foreign direct investment (FDI). The sectoral and regional composition of trade changed dramatically with the spectacular growth of export volumes. While natural resource–based commodities—agriculture, oil and gas, minerals—were driving factors in developing countries' export growth in the past, more recent trade growth has been driven largely by manufactured goods—high-tech products as well as low-skill-intensive goods. These trends have led to stronger economic growth in many countries and significant reductions in global poverty.

Can these trends be sustained over the next 10–15 years? And can they be broadened to include countries that have not benefited from trade growth, but have very large proportions of poor people? The answer to both questions is "probably." The long-term forecast anticipates that the MDG of halving the number of the world's people living in extreme poverty will be reached by 2015. Nonetheless, significant pockets of poverty will persist, and the goal will not be achieved in all developing regions.

Box 1.5 AIDS is taking a rising toll in Sub-Saharan Africa

Sub-Saharan Africa continues to be the epicenter of the AIDS epidemic. According to UNAIDS, 28.5 million Africans were infected in 2001 and 2.2 million died, lowering population growth by one-third of a percentage point. Given social and financial hurdles, treatment and care programs are likely to have at best a modest impact on the course of the epidemic. UNAIDS predicts 55 million deaths attributable to AIDS in Africa between 2000 and 2015 (UNAIDS 2002).

Although effective antiretroviral therapies have been developed, they are not in widespread use. Part of the explanation is cost. Providing these drugs to the entire infected population of Sub-Saharan Africa would cost nearly $9 billion, about 70 percent of current official development assistance to the region. Nevertheless, it can be argued that such an expenditure, equivalent to just 0.04 percent of OECD GDP, would be cost effective from a development standpoint, by alleviating the burden on health-care systems and raising productivity (Moatti and others 2002). While more money is becoming available, it remains only a fraction of what is needed.

In addition to the financial obstacles to treatment, there is a deadly culture of denial to be overcome. In Botswana, the most afflicted country in the region, the incidence rate in the adult population is near 40 percent and life expectancy has dropped from more than 65 to less than 40. Yet a $100 million partnership between the Bill and Melinda Gates Foundation and Merck to provide free antiretrovirals to all who need them has, so far, achieved only limited success. Less than 5 percent of Botswanans have been tested for HIV, and fewer than 0.1 percent of those thought to be infected are enrolled for free treatment.

Many researchers have explored the economics of HIV/AIDS using macroeconometric and CGE models. The magnitudes of impact appear surprisingly small, seemingly out of proportion to the human tragedy. From a macroeconomic standpoint, impacts of HIV/AIDS arise from:

- Slower labor-force growth and a higher proportion of younger, less-skilled, and less productive workers

- Lower productivity because of illness or worry on the job, or more time off work

- Higher costs to governments and employers of health care, training, and sick pay

- Reduced household savings after payments for treatment or funerals, and, simultaneously, less public and private investment because of financing constraints, uncertainty, and lower expected profits.

Quantifying these channels is not straightforward, but the preponderance of results suggests an overall reduction of per capita growth somewhere between 0.5 and 1 percentage point. This reduction is a significant cost to a region where long-term growth lies in the 0.8 to 1.6 percent per capita range, and it underscores Greener's point (2002) that economic policy is important so that better economic performance can offset the enormous devastation.

HIV/AIDS has major implications for public finance and the provision of health services. Even without the epidemic, African public health budgets, which average $50 per capita, would be woefully inadequate. In addition, the disease may have major, though not well studied, implications for income distribution. An individual household is either affected or not; and for those vulnerable to being tipped into poverty by the loss of one or more breadwinners, the effect can be tragic. The threat posed by large numbers of homeless, uneducated, angry youths with no parents and no prospects may, in the long run, turn out to be the greatest cost of the epidemic.

Sources: Greener (2002), Moatti et al. (2002).

Trade performance over the 1990s was unprecedented

From several points of view, trade performance during the 1990s was unprecedented. The overall volume of trade accelerated relative to output, growing nearly 2.5 times faster than GDP, compared to an historical average of 1.5. Such increase in income elasticity was a global phenomenon, although it was clearly more pronounced in developing countries, which had experienced a sharp fall in trade during the debt crises of the 1980s, and a sharp boom just before the financial crises of 1997 and 1998 (figure 1.30).

The robustness of the recent trade expansion was highlighted following the East Asian financial collapse. Trade flows recovered from that crisis much more quickly than they did after the Latin American debt crises of the early 1980s. During the 1990s, developing countries' merchandise exports increased at an annual rate of 8.5 percent, up from growth trends of less than 2 percent during the 1980s. Despite the financial crisis of 1997, exports from East Asia increased on average by 13.4 percent per year during the decade, almost doubling the strong performance of the 1980s.

Within a decade export revenues in developing countries rose from less than 15 percent of GDP to almost 25 percent (figure 1.31).

The change in the composition of exports was a major factor underpinning growth

More remarkable than the overall growth of trade was the transformation in the product mix of exports. Developing countries now rely less on shipments of primary commodities than on manufactured goods. Whereas two decades ago developing countries derived 70 percent of merchandise export revenue from sales of primary commodities—agriculture and energy—the situation is now completely reversed, with 80 percent of revenue coming from exports of manufactures. Even exports from Sub-Saharan Africa are no longer primarily resource-based, as the share of manufactures in African exports has risen from 25 percent during the late 1970s to 56 percent today. Almost all of the increase was realized during the last decade.

With the rising share of manufactures in total exports, underlying high growth rates in most manufacturing sectors have an increasingly large impact on overall export growth. The shift toward manufacturing clarifies some

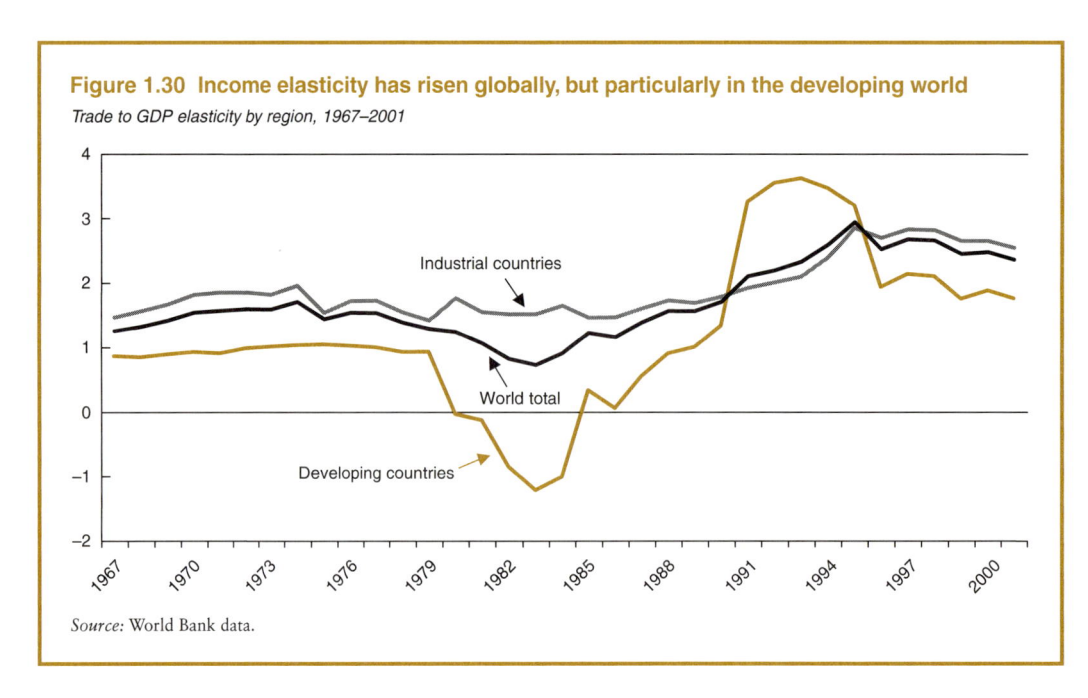

Figure 1.30 Income elasticity has risen globally, but particularly in the developing world

Trade to GDP elasticity by region, 1967–2001

Source: World Bank data.

Figure 1.31 Export-to-GDP ratios have risen sharply in developing countries
Merchandise exports, percent of GDP, 1980–2002

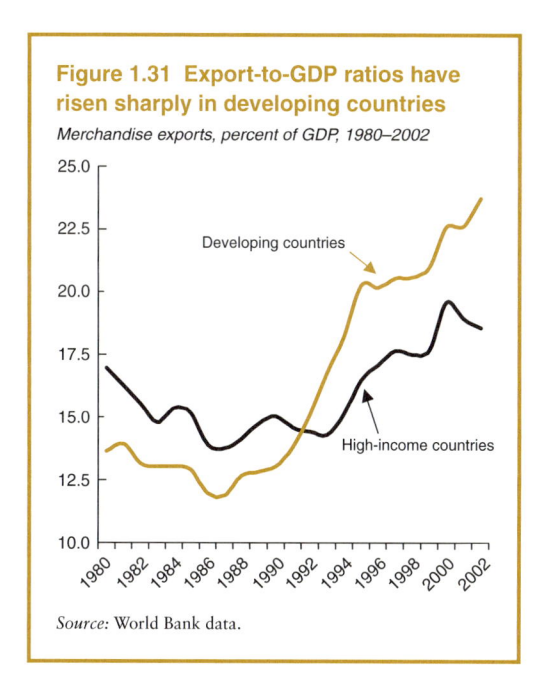

Source: World Bank data.

of the regional differences in overall trade performance—growth has been fastest where the share of manufactured products in total exports was already large—and suggests that the acceleration of overall trade growth was not a temporary phenomenon, as the share of manufactured products is likely to increase further.

To illustrate the importance of the export mix, annual growth of export revenue during the 1990s for East Asia and Sub-Saharan Africa are calculated with different sectoral weights, while using *actual* growth rates at a sectoral level. Merchandise export revenue in Sub-Saharan Africa advanced at an annual rate of 5.4 percent during the 1990s. However, if the region had already reached the maturity of East Asia, with a significantly larger share of manufactures in total exports, the same sectoral growth rates—double digit for manufacturing and small for natural resources—would have led to 10.6 percent overall revenue growth. Alternatively, applying East Asian growth rates to Sub-Saharan shares would have led to 10 percent growth, instead of the 17 percent annual growth actually realized. This suggests that roughly half of the difference in overall growth between the two regions was due to differences in sectoral growth rates, the other half to the larger share of manufactures in East Asia.

Such compositional effect will continue to influence overall growth numbers during the coming decade as the share of manufactured products rises further. Should all developing countries achieve the same growth of export revenue at a sector level as during the 1990s, overall revenue growth would rise to 20 percent per year, instead of the 11 percent realized annually during the 1990s. The composition effect of 9 percent a year applies to most regions, with regional effects ranging from 5.1 percent in Latin America to 10.6 percent in Europe and Central Asia.

Changes in the composition of trade can be traced to several factors

What accounts for the growth in manufactured exports? Will trade continue to grow at such robust rates? The driving forces are a combination of policy reforms, structural change in global production processes, and general economic trends related to continuous increases in real per capita incomes. The contribution of these various forces cannot be decomposed in a linear fashion, because some are tightly linked with others. However, because the strong links work in a virtuous circle, it is likely that the combined effects evident in current trends will continue into the coming years.

Policy reforms began in the 1970s in East Asia. They were later initiated in other regions, culminating in a rapid acceleration of reforms during the 1990s. A key element of the policy change was lowering of trade barriers in manufacturing—unilaterally, regionally, and multilaterally. But in all successful cases, change was embedded in broader domestic institutional reforms. Technological progress lowered transportation costs, improved communications and business practices, and made it possible to build global production networks. The last change radically altered geographic specialization patterns and intensified trade in intermediate products. Income growth triggered consumers' desire for more and newer varieties of goods, creating markets for foreign products. These factors reinforced one another: Lower trade barriers triggered a new, global organization of production to take advantage of diversity in comparative advantage across the world. Desire for new products and a search for new markets provided a strong incentive for lower trade barriers. And importantly, technological progress and income growth were spurred by increased global competition and efficiency gains through global networks.

The decline in manufactures trade prices relative to domestic price deflators is a clear indicator of strong productivity growth in sectors operating on global markets. Prices of merchandise exports from high-income countries fell by almost 2 percent per year relative to domestic prices. This marked a significant acceleration of the price differential compared to the 1980s, when relative export prices fell 1 percent per year. A similar indication of accelerating productivity growth in sectors producing for global markets was observable in East Asia, where exports were already heavily concentrated in manufactures. In that region the price differential changed almost 2 percentage points during the 1990s. Though for other developing regions price trends are mixed—partly because of different specialization patterns, partly because of imperfections in domestic-factor markets—an acceleration of productivity growth in manufacturing sectors that compete in global markets appears to be a worldwide phenomenon.

While there are several key factors driving the changes in trade, there is no doubt that the sustained dismantling of trade barriers has been a primary driver. For example, the growth of production networks and their association with trade growth would not have been possible if trade barriers had remained high. Expanding the benefits of trade to a broader range of countries will require significant further decline in trade barriers, particularly for those commodities in which poor countries have a comparative advantage—agriculture and low-skill-intensive manufacturing. While expanding market access is not a sufficient condition to catalyze the economies of poor countries, it is a necessary condition to be able to justify indispensable investments—in public and private infrastructure and education—to enable these economies to take off. The Doha Round will be a key complement to other more limited efforts to reduce trade barriers, for example, regional free trade agreements and unilateral reform efforts.

Greater trade will build on ongoing reforms to spur per capita growth in all regions

Intensified trade relations have laid the foundations for continuation of a virtuous circle in which access to new markets, increased competition, and productivity growth reinforce each other. Such an upward spiral would accelerate per capita income growth in many developing countries, especially those in which the effect of reforms is visible in certain sectors—even if not yet on an aggregate level. As competitive manufacturing sectors grow and reforms spread further, the results will become evident in economic figures over the next 10 years (table 1.5). The growing reliance on manufacturing will also reduce vulnerability to sharp and disruptive commodity cycles.

The impact of industrialization on productivity is reflected, for example, in the sharp acceleration of per capita income growth in Sub-Saharan Africa, from annual decline of 0.2 percent during the 1990s to an increase of 1.6 percent per year during the coming years. On the other hand, countries that, over the last decades, have experienced a rapid catching-up in productivity as a result of integration in global markets are bound to experience some slowdown, as the gap with the technological frontier narrows in some sectors. However, East Asia is still anticipated to outperform other regions, with average per capita income growth of 5.4 percent—lower than the 6.4 percent growth achieved during the 1990s.

As these fundamental structural shifts promote development, other conditions across countries are improving. Reduced imbalances in the external and internal accounts of developing countries have lowered their vulnerabil-

Table 1.5 GDP per capita will grow faster in the developing world than in the OECD area
Real GDP per capita, annual average percentage change, 1980s, 1990s, and forecasts

	1980s	1990s	Forecast Medium term 2001–05	Forecast Long term 2006–15
World total	1.3	1.2	1.0	2.2
High-income countries	2.5	1.8	1.4	2.5
OECD	2.5	1.8	1.4	2.4
United States	2.2	2.2	1.5	2.5
Japan	3.5	1.2	0.7	1.9
European Union	2.1	1.7	1.5	2.3
Non-OECD countries	3.1	3.8	1.1	4.2
Developing countries	0.7	1.7	2.7	3.4
East Asia and the Pacific	5.6	6.4	5.4	5.4
Europe and Central Asia	0.6	–1.8	3.8	3.3
Latin America and the Caribbean	–0.9	1.7	0.3	2.5
Middle East and North Africa	–0.6	1.2	1.4	2.5
South Asia	3.6	3.3	3.4	4.1
Sub-Saharan Africa	–1.1	–0.2	1.0	1.6

Note: Aggregations are moving averages, reweighted annually after calculations of growth in constant prices.
Source: World Bank.

ity to swings in international interest rates and exchange rates and provided governments with some room to manage economic downturns. And macroeconomic conditions have improved—for example, lower inflation and interest rates are providing an improved environment for long-term investment by both domestic and foreign entities.

Apart from acceleration in growth, the relative importance of growth-supporting factors is likely to change. Productivity will likely increase in importance relative to population growth and capital accumulation (figure 1.32). This is especially true for countries in Latin America, where population growth during the coming 10 years is expected to be 0.5 percentage points lower than during the 1990s, capital accumulation will slow, and countries will be less able to rely on continued large current-account deficits. Reforms will have created the right environment to absorb technological innovations.

For the high-income countries, the scenario suggests per capita growth of around 2.5 percent over 2006–15, an acceleration of 0.7 percentage points from the average growth rate of the 1990s. Acceleration in the developing countries will be more dramatic, with a projection of per capita growth of 3.4 percent for 2006–15, driven partly by a turnaround in Europe and Central Asia—an improvement already under way in the late 1990s. With adhesion to the European Union only months away, the accession countries can anticipate the type of growth experienced by Portugal and Spain upon their accession—built on solid investment flows, improved market access, and financial assistance from Brussels. The other countries in the region will benefit through trade linkages; they, too, will continue to consolidate the benefits from reforms initiated during their transition from planned economies.

Somewhat more tentatively, the scenario also presumes improved economic performance in Sub-Saharan Africa, which has witnessed two decades of negative per capita income growth. Despite the nearly 2 percentage point turnaround in per capita growth, a rate of 1.6 percent per capita if achieved, would still leave Sub-Saharan Africa at the low end of the developing-country growth spectrum, inadequate to make much of a dent

GLOBAL ECONOMIC PROSPECTS 2004

Figure 1.32 Productivity will contribute more to GDP growth through 2015 than will capital or labor

a. Decomposition of GDP growth, 1990–2000

Average percent per annum

b. Decomposition of GDP growth, 2005–2015

Average percent per annum

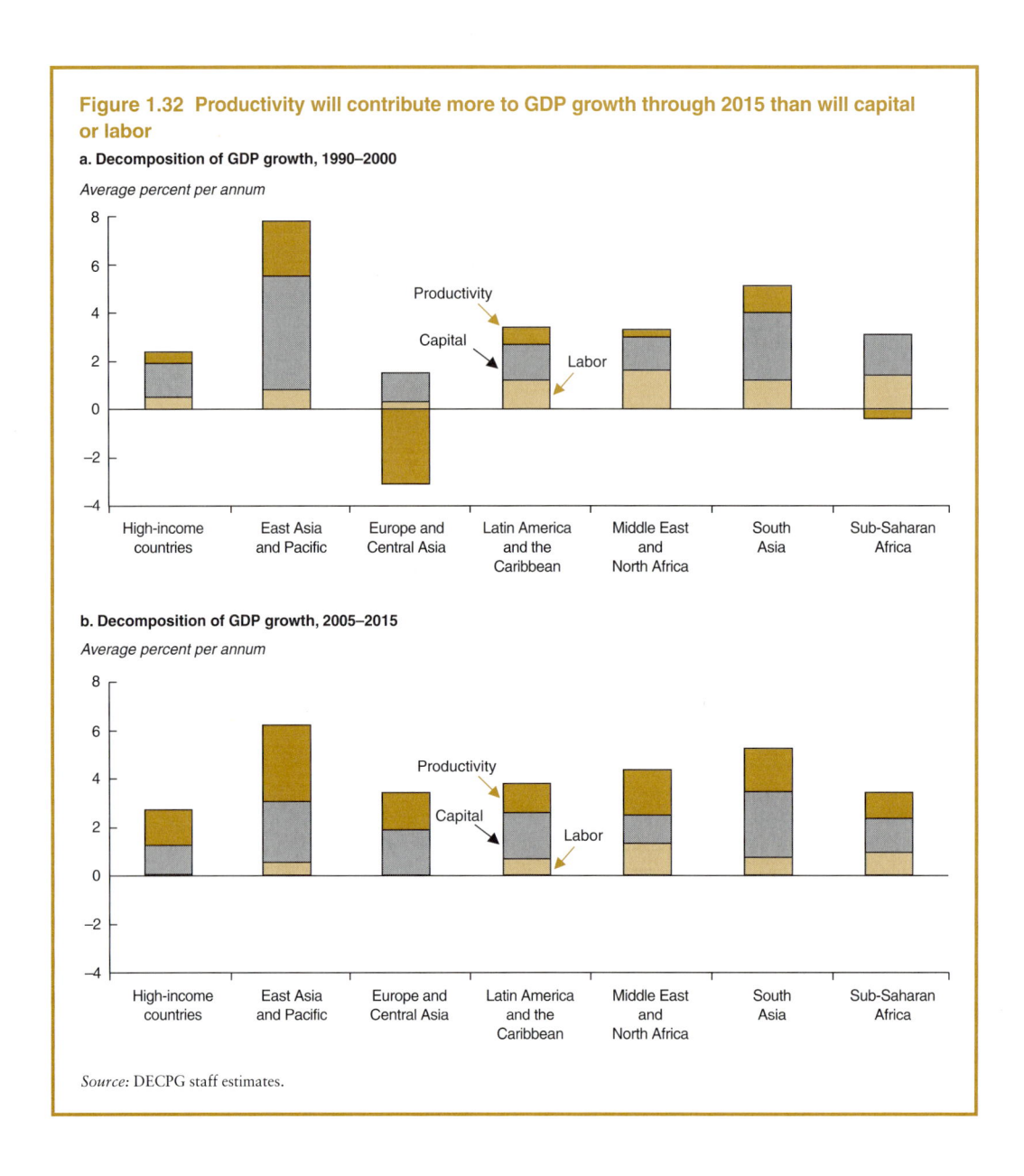

Source: DECPG staff estimates.

in poverty and other MDGs. Nonetheless there are positive signs emerging from parts of Sub-Saharan Africa, with per capita income growth positive for the fourth consecutive year, and a dozen countries achieving growth rates in excess of 4 percent per annum.

The main difference with the long-term scenarios contained in *Global Economic Prospects 2003* resides in the Middle East and North Africa. Recent and prospective policy changes suggest that the region could attain a per capita growth rate of 2.5 percent over the next 10 years. Such an achievement would facilitate effort—particularly in private-sector development—to absorb the rapid increase in the labor force.

Growth rates in East Asia and Pacific are expected to remain strong through the long term. At official exchange rates, incomes in rich countries remain more than 20 times higher than the average in East Asia and Pacific, and even at purchasing-power exchange rates, incomes are six times higher.

After the Middle East and North Africa, South Asia is the region least integrated into the global economy. Growth over the last decade can be attributed partly to trade policy reforms. Those reforms are expected to be pursued by local governments over the next decade, giving rise to sustained growth at rates approaching those of East Asia.

Latin America, like many of the other regions, has significantly diversified its exports over the last years and gained a strong foothold in global production networks. It is still, on average, relatively closed compared to some other developing regions and therefore will benefit from pursuing trade reforms within the hemisphere and beyond. Improved macroeconomic conditions—lower inflationary expectations and more flexible exchange rates—will provide better starting conditions to achieve higher potential growth of around 2.5 percent in per capita terms.

The risks to the long-term forecast are nevertheless not to be minimized. Many countries are still grappling with relatively low revenue-collection rates, which could become critical as countries attempt to make up for lost tariff revenues. The limits on government revenues are straining the capacity for required investment in public infrastructure—roads, ports, education, and other social services. The private sector can (and will) fill in some of the gaps, provided the right structures are in place. Conflict could affect growth prospects, particularly at the regional level, as we have seen in some parts of Sub-Saharan Africa in recent years or in the Middle East and Central Asia. Finally, a lack of progress in trade reforms or, worse yet, a return to protectionist tendencies could curb the expansion of trade and the ensuing benefits. The final section of this chapter assesses some of the economic benefits to be derived from further trade reform, above and beyond the baseline forecast presented here.

And growth will greatly reduce poverty

Strong economic growth—particularly in China and India, with yet-high concentrations of poor—will lead to substantial reductions in the incidence of poverty through 2015, with the MDG of halving extreme poverty being achieved on a global level—if not in each country or region. Sub-Saharan Africa—unless dramatic changes occur—almost surely will not reach the goal. Even under a somewhat optimistic economic forecast, the percentage of the African population living on $1/day or less will remain above 42 percent through 2015, far from the goal of 23.7 percent. Sub-Saharan Africa will have nearly three times the incidence of poverty as the next poorest region (table 1.6).

South Asia, having approximately the same initial level of poverty as Sub-Saharan Africa in 1990, had already achieved impressive gains by 2000 (from 42 percent to 32 percent according to the latest figures) and will likely almost halve that level by 2015.[3]

According to current projections, Latin America will reach 2015 some 38 percent above the target, and Europe and Central Asia, 90 percent above—the latter after recovering sharply from the large rise in poverty during the transitional 1990s.

This year's poverty forecast contains some noteworthy changes from last year. The changes can be attributed to four factors—changes in the initial estimation of the number of poor,[4] changes in the macroeconomic relation between per capita consumption growth and poverty reduction, changes in the economic forecast, and changes in the population forecast. The first two factors are derived from updated surveys and National Account data. The third factor—changes to the economic forecast—are mainly attributable to changes in the short- and medium-term forecast with little or no change to the long-term forecast (with one exception, noted below). The poverty forecast also incorporates the World Bank's most recent population projections. Growth in population has been revised downward in many regions. If per capita consumption

GLOBAL ECONOMIC PROSPECTS 2004

Table 1.6 Global poverty will decrease significantly, but not uniformly across regions
Regional breakdown of poverty estimates in developing countries, various measures

	GEP 2003			GEP 2004		
Region	1990	1999	2015	1990	2000	2015
Number of people living on less than $1 per day (millions)						
East Asia and Pacific	486	279	80	470	261	44
China	377	223	73	361	204	41
Rest of East Asia and Pacific	110	57	7	110	57	3
Europe and Central Asia	6	24	7	6	20	6
Latin America and the Caribbean	48	57	47	48	56	46
Middle East and North Africa	5	6	8	5	8	4
South Asia	506	487	264	466	432	268
Sub-Saharan Africa	241	315	404	241	323	366
Total	1,293	1,168	809	1,237	1,100	734
Excluding China	917	945	735	877	896	692
$1 per day headcount index (percent)						
East Asia and Pacific	30.5	15.6	3.9	29.4	14.5	2.3
China	32.9	17.8	5.3	31.5	16.1	3.0
Rest of East Asia and Pacific	24.2	10.6	1.1	24.1	10.6	0.5
Europe and Central Asia	1.4	5.1	1.4	1.4	4.2	1.3
Latin America and the Caribbean	11.0	11.1	7.5	11.0	10.8	7.6
Middle East and North Africa	2.1	2.2	2.1	2.1	2.8	1.2
South Asia	45.0	36.6	15.7	41.5	31.9	16.4
Sub-Saharan Africa	47.4	49.0	46.0	47.4	49.0	42.3
Total	29.6	23.2	13.3	28.3	21.6	12.5
Excluding China	28.5	25.0	15.7	27.2	23.3	15.4
Number of people living on less than $2 per day (millions)						
East Asia and Pacific	1,114	897	339	1,094	873	354
China	819	627	219	800	599	256
Rest of East Asia and Pacific	295	269	120	295	273	98
Europe and Central Asia	31	96	45	31	101	48
Latin America and the Caribbean	121	132	117	121	136	124
Middle East and North Africa	50	68	62	50	72	38
South Asia	1,010	1,128	1,139	971	1,052	968
Sub-Saharan Africa	386	480	618	386	504	612
Total	2,711	2,801	2,320	2,653	2,737	2,144
Excluding China	1,892	2,173	2,101	1,854	2,138	1,888
$2 per day head count index (percent)						
East Asia and Pacific	69.7	50.1	16.6	68.5	48.3	18.2
China	71.6	50.1	15.7	69.9	47.3	18.4
Rest of East Asia and Pacific	64.9	50.2	18.4	64.9	50.8	17.6
Europe and Central Asia	6.8	20.3	9.3	6.8	21.3	10.3
Latin America and the Caribbean	27.6	26.0	18.9	27.6	26.3	20.5
Middle East and North Africa	21.0	23.3	16.0	21.0	24.4	10.2
South Asia	89.8	84.8	68.0	86.3	77.7	59.2
Sub-Saharan Africa	76.0	74.7	70.4	76.0	76.5	70.7
Total	62.1	55.6	38.1	60.8	53.6	36.4
Excluding China	58.7	57.5	44.7	57.5	55.7	42.0

Source: World Bank staff estimates.

growth rates remain unchanged, the revised rates of population growth will have no effect on the poverty headcount index (all else equal), but it would lower the absolute number of poor.

One of the changes in table 1.6 is the use of the year 2000, rather than 1999, as the base year for the forecast. Because developing countries were booming in 2000, the headcount index—assuming distribution neutrality—would have declined substantially.[5] Most regions indeed witnessed a decline in the headcount index in 2000, compared with the 1999 headcount index reported last year, except for the Middle East and North Africa, and Sub-Saharan Africa.[6] At the global level, the estimate of the headcount index in 2000 is 21.6 percent, compared with the 23.2 percent estimate for 1999 in last year's report—representing a decline of 6.9 percent.

However, not all of the changes can be attributed to the change in the base year. This year's estimates are also based on new surveys and methodology affecting, among others, the two largest developing countries—China and India. The estimate of the number of poor in China has been revised downward for two reasons. The first is that, for the first time, consumption-based data—deemed more appropriate for poverty analysis—are available on a time-series basis. The second is that rural/urban population shares have been revised, with the urban share higher than previously estimated. The lower incidence of poverty in urban areas accounts for the downward revision in the overall poverty level for China. The new survey used in India has also led to a downward revision in the estimate of the poverty level. A new household survey provided the basis for our revision of Pakistan's poverty profile. The Middle East and North Africa regime benefits from new surveys in Morocco and Tunisia. The estimated level of initial poverty in Yemen has raised the regional level of poverty, but from a very low base.[7] There are eleven new surveys for Latin American countries, including Brazil and Mexico.

Looking forward to 2015, there are some rather sharp changes in the poverty forecast, focusing on the $1/day indicator. At a global level, the new forecast for 2015 for the headcount index drops to 12.5 percent, compared with 13.3 percent in last year's report—a 5.9 percent decline. The projected number of poor in 2015 declines to 734 million, from 809 million last year. Part of the decline in the number of poor can be attributed to a decline in the population growth rate through 2015.

Compared with last year's forecast, the headcount index for East Asia declines by 44 percent, from 3.9 percent to 2.3 percent. By and large, the decline is the result of a new estimate of the headcount elasticity, since the long-term GDP growth rates remain largely unchanged. The other key difference is for the Middle East and North Africa region. The incidence of poverty starts from a low level (between 2 and 3 percent). With growth prospects revised upward, the headcount index is expected to drop to 1.2 percent, compared with last year's 2.1 percent, despite the upward revision in the base number of poor. In South Asia, the headcount index in 2015 has been revised upward from 15.7 percent to 16.4 percent, despite the decrease in the initial level. The new survey information suggests that the estimate of the headcount elasticity has declined, as the shape of the income distribution curve has shifted the poor toward the left end of the distribution tail, away from the poverty line. For Sub-Saharan Africa, the 2015 headcount index is forecast at 42.3 percent, a drop from last year's 46 percent. This improvement incorporates some new survey information, but positive trends in the short- and medium-term forecast, particularly for the oil exporters, account for most of the change.

Looking ahead to the Doha Round

A successful outcome of the multilateral trade negotiations known as the Doha Development Agenda, or the Doha Round, would greatly improve the growth and poverty outcomes discussed above. This section analyzes an illustrative pro-poor scenario of multilateral trade reform, using the World Bank's global trade model.

An illustrative pro-poor scenario

Several proposals to improve market access for merchandise trade have been tabled in advance of the upcoming WTO ministerial meetings in Cancun in September 2003 (see chapter 2). Most observers concur that any agreement reached in Cancun should meet at least three criteria—it should be simple, it should address tariff peaks, and it should be development-friendly. An illustrative pro-poor scenario and its potential impact on incomes, trade, and poverty are discussed below.

Rich countries would be subject to a maximum tariff in agriculture of 10 percent—that is, all peaks would be cut back to a maximum of 10 percent (table 1.7). The average tariff target would be 5 percent. On the manufacturing side, tariff peaks would be scaled back to 5 percent, with a 1 percent target on the average manufacturing tariff rate, which is already low. Developing countries would be subject to a maximum agricultural tariff of 15 percent, with a targeted average of 10 percent (double the rich-country average). In manufacturing, the peak would be capped at 10 percent; the targeted average would be 5 percent.

The pro-poor scenario includes elimination of export subsidies, decoupling of all domestic subsidies, and the elimination of the use of specific tariffs, tariff rate quotas (TRQs), and antidumping duties and sanctions. Specific tariffs and TRQs have unpredictable and perhaps unintended consequences for exporters[8] and consumers, and—in the case of TRQs—have proven difficult to administer. Antidumping measures, in increasing use since 1995, have a chilling effect on many exporters by presenting them with the possibility of losing market access on short notice.

Analyzing the impact of the pro-poor scenario is not a trivial exercise, partly because of data issues—the difficulty in quantifying specific tariffs and TRQs—and partly because of methodological issues—modeling TRQs and the impact of antidumping measures raises a number of thorny problems. Nonetheless, drawing on the work published in *Global Economic Prospects 2002*, the next section describes the impact of the foregoing scenario, using the World Bank's trade model (with modifications).

Assessing the impact of the pro-poor scenario is complex

The starting point is the GTAP database—used by trade analysts worldwide for trade assessments. The base year is 1997, with more recent agricultural protection data, but excluding other developments—such as recently signed regional trade agreements, China's WTO accession offer, and future changes to farm programs (such as the recently agreed reform of the EU's Common Agricultural Program). Taking these points into consideration, together with other features of the GTAP dataset, the impact assessment likely will overstate some of the benefits of the pro-poor scenario. It is also possible, however, that other factors, such as the pro-competitive and dynamic effects of trade reform, could prove our impact assessment to be an underestimate.

Summary indications of the scenario's impact on *tariffs* using the GTAP level of protection are presented in table 1.8. The table is divided into two broad sectors—agriculture (in-

Table 1.7 Tariffs could be cut clearly and simply
Pro-poor tariff targets by type of country and sector (percent)

	Industrial	Developing
Agriculture		
Average	5	10
Maximum	10	15
Manufacturing		
Average	1	5
Maximum	5	10

Source: World Bank.

Table 1.8 The pro-poor tariff scenario would significantly lower protection

Analysis of initial and final average tariffs in agriculture and manufacturing under the World Bank's tariff scenario, using World Bank trade model (percent)

	Agriculture			Manufacturing		
	\multicolumn{2}{c	}{Average tariff}	Percent reduction in non-peak tariffs	\multicolumn{2}{c	}{Average tariff}	Percent reduction in non-peak tariffs
	Initial	Final		Initial	Final	
OECD Cairns countries	15.9	6.0	100.0	2.2	1.0	56.3
European Union with EFTA	22.4	7.4	100.0	4.2	1.2	100.0
United States	10.8	5.0	60.6	2.4	1.0	57.7
Japan	50.3	10.0	100.0	1.6	0.9	0.0
Korea, Rep. of, and Taiwan (China)	49.4	8.2	100.0	5.7	3.1	100.0
Hong Kong (China) and Singapore	1.6	1.6	0.0	0.0	0.0	0.0
Brazil	12.0	10.0	21.3	14.6	6.9	100.0
China	38.8	11.0	100.0	13.8	8.6	100.0
India	25.9	13.2	100.0	21.7	8.8	100.0
Indonesia	9.0	7.4	0.0	8.6	5.0	29.0
Russian Federation	11.8	10.0	12.3	12.3	5.6	100.0
Mexico	23.6	10.0	61.5	2.7	2.3	0.0
Southern African Customs Union	45.7	12.2	100.0	9.4	5.0	32.4
Vietnam	32.5	11.4	100.0	16.9	5.2	100.0
Rest of South Asia	23.6	10.3	100.0	31.3	9.9	100.0
Rest of East Asia	22.9	11.9	100.0	7.9	5.0	29.6
Rest of Latin America and Caribbean	14.5	10.0	77.9	12.0	6.3	100.0
EU accession countries	24.9	12.8	100.0	7.5	5.0	35.5
Rest of Europe and Central Asia	22.4	10.0	92.5	5.0	4.7	0.0
Middle East	76.4	12.8	100.0	8.4	5.0	49.4
North Africa	35.5	10.2	100.0	18.6	9.1	100.0
Rest of Sub-Saharan Africa	20.6	10.5	100.0	16.0	8.8	100.0
Rest of WORLD	8.1	6.0	0.0	7.5	5.0	15.6

Note: Agricultural tariff peaks are cut to 10 and 15 percent respectively in high-income and developing countries. Manufacturing tariff peaks are cut to 5 and 10 percent respectively in high-income and developing countries. The targets for average agricultural tariffs are respectively 5 and 10 percent, respectively, for high-income and developing countries. Targets for the average manufacturing tariff are 1 and 5 percent, respectively, for high-income and developing countries.
Sources: GTAP release 5.3 and World Bank staff calculations.

cluding processed foods) and manufacturing. The first column in each sector provides the (import weighted) average tariff.[9] Thus for Japan, the average tariff is 50 percent in agriculture but less than 2 percent in manufacturing.

The second column shows the targeted average tariff rate. The rich-country agricultural target of 5 percent is achieved in the United States, for example. In Japan and some regions, it is not achieved. In Japan, for example, the scenario would lead to an average rate of 10 percent, twice the target rate, because Japan's peaks are high and cover a wide percentage of agricultural trade. Initial tariffs below the peaks would have to become negative for the target to be achieved.[10] In some cases cutting the peaks is sufficient to achieve or surpass the targeted tariff level. This is the case, for example, for Indonesian agriculture, where the average tariff is already below the target and reducing the peaks simply drops the average.

The third column provides the level of reduction in non-peak tariffs. In the United States, for example, non-peak agricultural tariffs would be reduced by an average of 60 percent to achieve the 5 percent average target.

Rich countries would see a significant drop in the average agricultural tariff. In the advanced countries of Asia, in particular, average agricultural tariffs would fall from near 50 percent to somewhere around 10 percent—still above the target level. The United States would achieve the target, but from a more modest 11 percent initial level, whereas the European Union would see a drop in the average (extra-EU) tariff from 22 percent to just above 7 percent. Developing countries would also see significant reductions, higher on average than in rich countries. Many regions would not meet the 10 percent target because of the many tariffs higher than the 15 percent cutoff point.

In manufacturing, the average tariff rate in rich countries would decline slightly following the removal of peaks. In developing countries, the 5 percent target could be met in many regions, with Mexico and the EU-accession countries already below the target with their prevailing initial tariff rates.[11]

The "decoupling" part of the scenario is achieved by removing all domestic support in agriculture—input and output subsidies and payments to land and capital. These would be replaced by direct payments to farm households. Such lump-sum transfers, not modeled explicitly, are important in determining income distribution within each region, but they have no direct effects on the distribution of production, on income across regions, or on the results described below. Export subsidies, which have played a relatively small role recently, are also removed. The impacts of specific tariffs and TRQs in agriculture are captured in the base protection data and are modeled as part of the ad valorem equivalent tariff. The full ad valorem tariff is subject to the reductions described in table 1.8.

The scenario would yield significant gains

The scenario described and analyzed above would generate $291 billion in global economic gains—nearly 75 percent of the total potential gains from full merchandise trade reform.[12] Measured in static terms, some $159 billion[13] in additional income would be reaped by developing countries in 2015 (compared to the baseline); rich countries would gain around $132 billion (figure 1.33). The gains, which would raise income levels by 1.5 and 0.5 percent, respectively, for developing

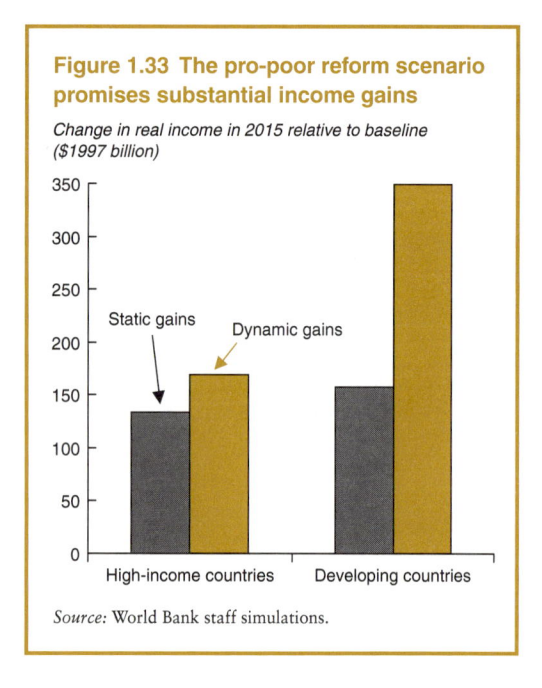

Figure 1.33 The pro-poor reform scenario promises substantial income gains

Change in real income in 2015 relative to baseline ($1997 billion)

[Bar chart showing Static gains and Dynamic gains for High-income countries (approx. 132 and 170) and Developing countries (approx. 159 and 350)]

Source: World Bank staff simulations.

and rich countries, could be much higher if dynamic effects—such as increases in productivity[14] and increasing FDI—are taken into consideration. Varying the trade model to link sectoral productivity to the export/output ratio shows that dynamic effects can indeed be substantial. In developing countries, the dynamic gains from the trade reform scenario are some 120 percent higher than the static gains. The dynamic gain for rich countries is less dramatic, because of the low GDP weight of agriculture, for which protection is strongest.

The reduction of trade barriers in agriculture and food yield $193 billion (in 2015), two-thirds of the total static gains from merchandise trade reform of $291 billion (table 1.9). More than 50 percent of these gains in agriculture and food, $101 billion, are reaped by developing countries, of which 80 percent is the result of own-reform in these two sectors. In other words, reform of agriculture and food in rich countries would lead to a gain of some $20 billion for developing countries as a whole. Manufacturing liberalization by rich countries would lead to gains of $25 billion to developing countries and could potentially even lead to a (small) loss to rich countries as increased mar-

Table 1.9 A large share of real income gains comes from lowering of barriers in agriculture and food
(real income gains in 2015 relative to the baseline in $1997 billion)

	Liberalizing region		
	Low- and middle-income countries	High-income countries	All countries
	Decomposition of static impacts		
Gains to low- and middle-income countries			
Agriculture and food	80	20	101
Manufacturing	33	25	58
All merchandise trade	114	44	159
Gains to high-income countries			
Agriculture and food	23	64	91
Manufacturing	44	−3	41
All merchandise trade	67	63	132
Global gains			
Agriculture and food	103	84	193
Manufacturing	77	22	98
All merchandise trade	181	107	291
	Decomposition of dynamic impacts		
Gains to low- and middle-income countries			
Agriculture and food	167	75	240
Manufacturing	95	9	108
All merchandise trade	265	85	349
Gains to high-income countries			
Agriculture and food	19	100	117
Manufacturing	36	13	48
All merchandise trade	55	115	169
Global gains			
Agriculture and food	185	174	358
Manufacturing	131	22	156
All merchandise trade	321	199	518

Source: World Bank staff simulations.

ket access by developing countries generates terms-of-trade losses for rich countries—losses not fully compensated by the gains in allocative efficiency. There is a degree of asymmetry in the impacts of the reforms on rich and on developing countries. The former gain significantly more from their own reforms ($114 billion of the $159 billion total), whereas the impacts for rich countries are more or less evenly spread between own-reform and developing-country reforms.

Trade would increase sharply under the scenario—particularly in the most severely protected sectors: agriculture and food (figure 1.34). Globally, merchandise trade would increase by about 10 percent (more than $800 billion), but exports from developing countries would rise by 20 percent (nearly $540 billion). The largest percentage increase in trade (nearly 50 percent) would occur in processed foods. Agricultural trade would rise by 32 percent. Developing countries should see an increase in their exports of textiles, clothing, and footwear, although its magnitude would depend on the final implementation of the Uruguay Round.

The number of poor would decline substantially under the partial reform scenario de-

GLOBAL ECONOMIC PROSPECTS 2004

Figure 1.34 Exports should rise sharply
Change in export volumes in 2015 relative to baseline ($1997 billion)

Source: World Bank staff simulations.

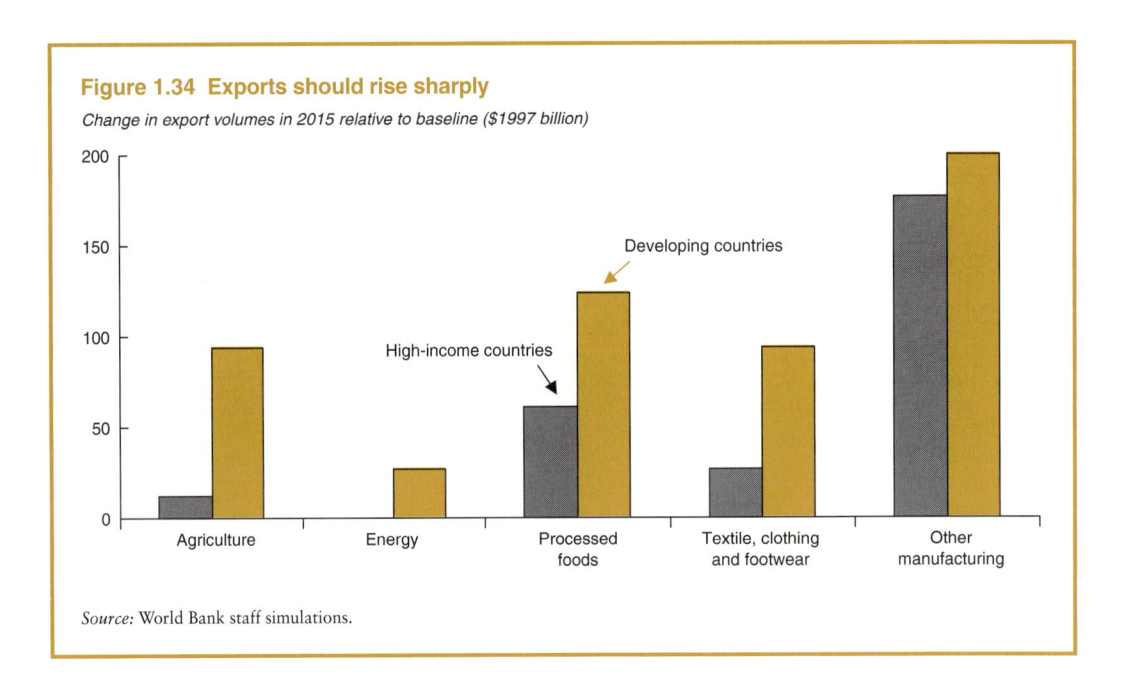

scribed here. At the world level, the number of persons living on $1/day or less would decline by 61 million, or 8 percent of the current forecast for 2015 of 734 million (figure 1.35).[15] The number living on $2/day or less would decline by 144 million. The greatest reduction in absolute terms would come in Sub-Saharan Africa. The region's unskilled workers would see the largest percentage increase in nominal wages and decreases in the cost of living. The largest percentage fall would occur in the Middle East. This region has the highest over-

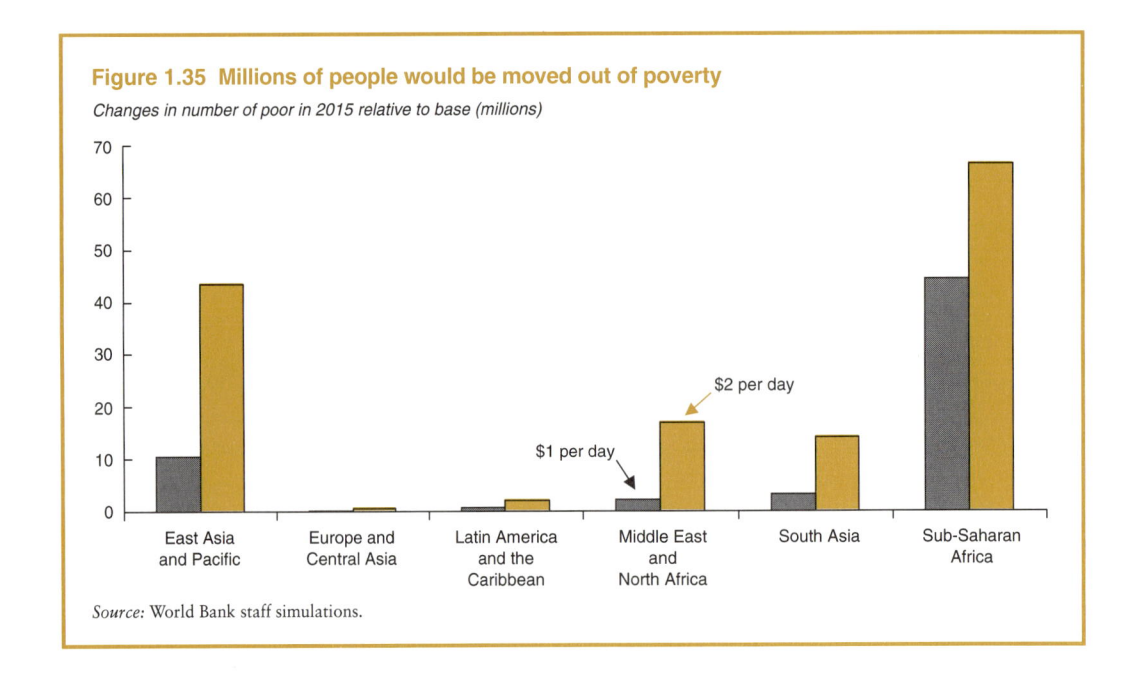

Figure 1.35 Millions of people would be moved out of poverty
Changes in number of poor in 2015 relative to base (millions)

Source: World Bank staff simulations.

52

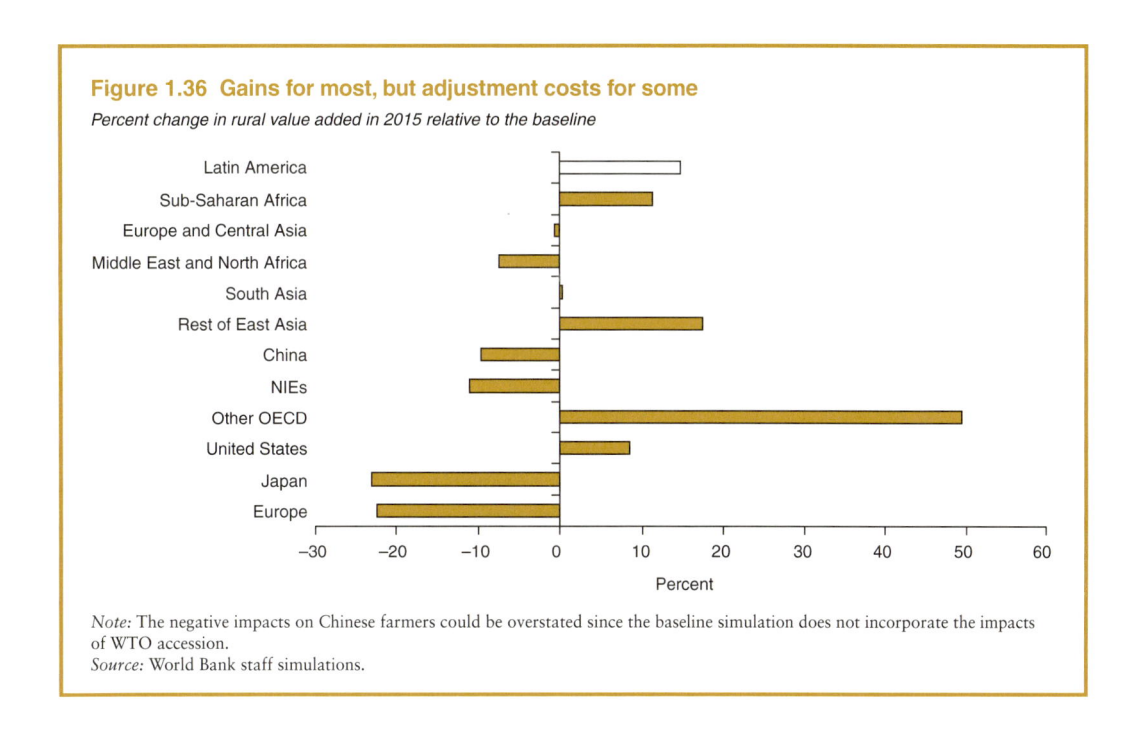

GLOBAL OUTLOOK AND THE DEVELOPING COUNTRIES

Figure 1.36 Gains for most, but adjustment costs for some

Percent change in rural value added in 2015 relative to the baseline

Note: The negative impacts on Chinese farmers could be overstated since the baseline simulation does not incorporate the impacts of WTO accession.
Source: World Bank staff simulations.

all barriers to imports and a substantial tax on consumers. However, the region has a relatively low level of poverty, particularly compared to Sub-Saharan Africa and South Asia.

The positive impact on overall growth, accompanied by a sharp boost in trade and a poverty outlook improvement leaving all regions better off in aggregate, does not signify that the reforms are without adjustment costs, even over the long term.[16] For example, given the levels of protection in the agricultural sectors, particularly in the OECD countries, farmers stand to lose the most from reductions in protection. The change in agricultural incomes needs to be put in context. First, the adjustment will occur over a 10-year period, allowing for a gradual adjustment. Second, the adjustment in most countries will be limited to a small share of GDP. In high-income countries, agricultural output is less than 3 percent of total output on average. For developing regions, agricultural output varies from a low of 7 percent for upper middle-income countries to 24 percent for low-income countries. Additionally, manufacturing will expand, and the transitional impacts will be mitigated to the extent that rural economies are diversified.

As can be seen in Figure 1.36, rural value added in Europe and in Japan could decline by more than 20 percent over the long term. And within agriculture, the distribution of the impacts is likely to be highly differentiated—across sectors within agriculture, as well as by factor ownership. For example, tenant farmers could be better off than landowners because the price of land is expected to fall in most OECD regions with the removal of protection. Farmers in some developing regions could also witness a decline in overall agricultural income—particularly in China and the Middle East and North Africa. On the other hand, farmers in Canada, Australia, and New Zealand will reap significant rewards from this reform, as will farmers in the rest of East Asia (for example in new market access for rice and vegetable oils), Latin America (grains, livestock, and sugar), and in Sub-Saharan Africa (sugar).

These adjustments will be accompanied by structural shifts in world agricultural and food output, following closely the patterns of changes

GLOBAL ECONOMIC PROSPECTS 2004

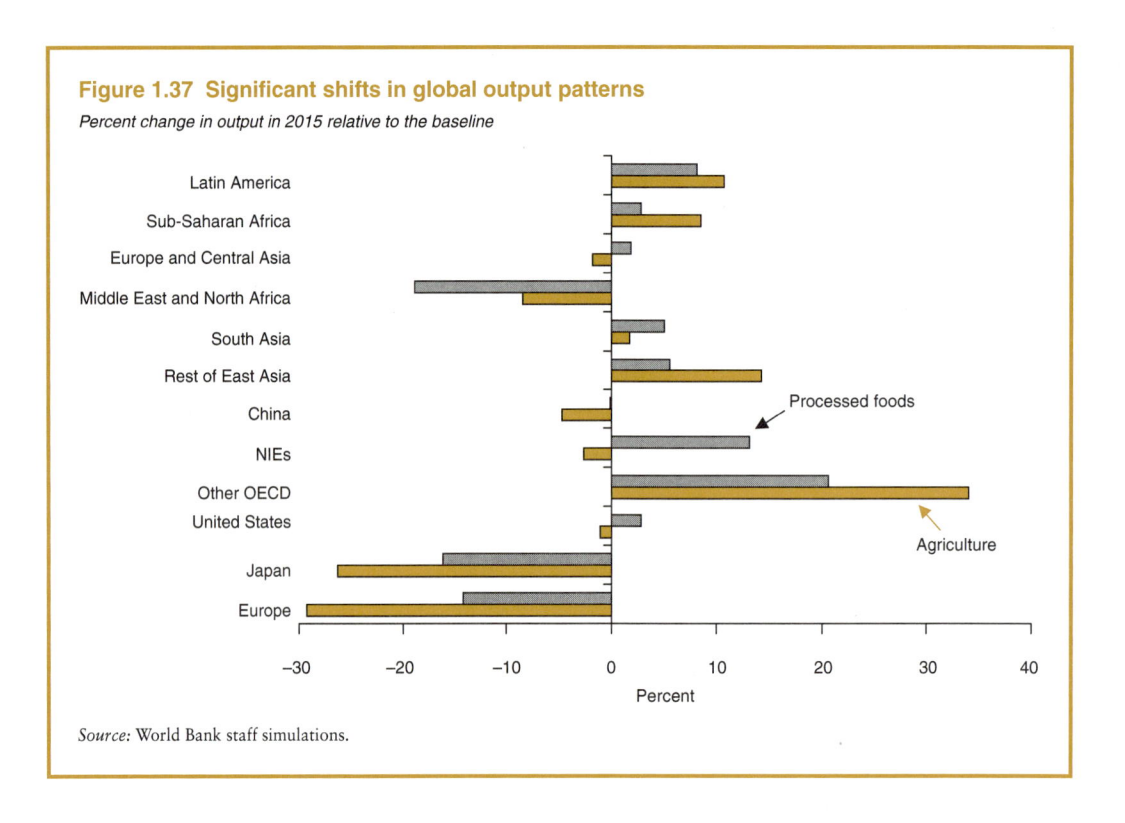

Figure 1.37 Significant shifts in global output patterns
Percent change in output in 2015 relative to the baseline

[Bar chart showing percent change in output (Processed foods and Agriculture) by region:
- Latin America: positive for both
- Sub-Saharan Africa: positive for both
- Europe and Central Asia: small changes
- Middle East and North Africa: negative for both
- South Asia: slightly positive
- Rest of East Asia: positive for both
- China: slightly negative
- NIEs: positive processed foods, slightly negative agriculture
- Other OECD: strongly positive for both
- United States: small changes
- Japan: strongly negative for both
- Europe: strongly negative for both]

Source: World Bank staff simulations.

in rural value added (figure 1.37). The changes in agricultural output tend to dominate those in processed foods, despite relatively similar levels of protection, in part because of the lower costs of inputs—that is, raw agricultural commodities—for the processing sectors. The main reductions in output occur in Europe, Japan, and the Middle East and North Africa for both agriculture and processed foods. The beneficiaries include Canada, Australia, and New Zealand among rich countries; Asia outside of China; Sub-Saharan Africa; and Latin America. The NIEs—particularly Korea and Taiwan (China)—show that they could be competitive in processed foods were they to remove agricultural protection.

Annex 1 Historical trade dynamics for developing countries

Table 1.A1 Sectoral export decomposition for developing countries[a]
Percent

	Share (percent) 1977	Share (percent) 1987	Share (percent) 1997	Average growth (percent per annum) 1977–87	Average growth (percent per annum) 1987–97	Contribution to growth (percent) 1977–87	Contribution to growth (percent) 1987–97
High income Asia excluding Japan[b]							
Agriculture	5.1	1.8	0.3	4.6	−5.9	0.9	−0.4
Oil and gas	0.6	0.1	0.1	−6.5	12.6	−0.1	0.1
Other natural resources	0.9	0.4	0.2	5.6	5.5	0.2	0.1
Processed foods	8.7	5.1	2.3	9.7	3.1	4.0	0.9
Textiles, apparel, and leather goods	30.0	25.1	13.5	13.8	4.9	23.7	7.7
Motor vehicles and parts	0.4	1.8	3.4	33.6	19.0	2.2	4.2
Electronic equipment	10.9	17.1	31.7	21.2	18.7	19.0	39.0
Other machinery	12.6	17.3	22.4	19.6	14.5	18.7	24.9
Other manufacturing	30.9	31.4	26.1	16.0	9.6	31.5	23.4
Total	100.0	100.0	100.0	15.9	11.6	100.0	100.0
East Asia and Pacific							
Agriculture	19.1	13.1	2.2	7.0	−1.8	9.9	−0.6
Oil and gas	25.3	20.7	3.6	8.9	−1.4	18.3	−0.7
Other natural resources	11.3	5.5	2.1	3.5	6.3	2.4	1.2
Processed foods	20.3	15.2	6.9	8.0	8.5	12.5	4.8
Textiles, apparel, and leather goods	5.1	14.0	22.4	23.0	23.0	18.8	24.5
Motor vehicles and parts	0.1	0.7	0.7	36.9	17.3	1.0	0.7
Electronic equipment	1.8	7.2	20.9	27.7	30.7	10.0	24.4
Other machinery	2.8	4.4	13.8	16.2	31.5	5.3	16.1
Other manufacturing	14.3	19.1	27.4	14.4	21.7	21.7	29.5
Total	100.0	100.0	100.0	11.1	17.4	100.0	100.0
South Asia							
Agriculture	27.8	22.1	5.9	5.3	−1.1	16.9	−1.0
Oil and gas	0.3	1.7	0.1	29.4	−15.9	2.9	−0.6
Other natural resources	13.4	16.9	5.2	10.3	0.4	20.1	0.3
Processed foods	19.8	12.8	10.3	3.2	10.5	6.5	9.3
Textiles, apparel, and leather goods	14.0	27.9	46.5	15.4	18.8	40.2	54.4
Motor vehicles and parts	0.9	0.6	1.2	3.9	20.6	0.4	1.4
Electronic equipment	0.3	0.4	1.2	10.5	25.0	0.5	1.6
Other machinery	5.3	4.7	4.5	6.4	12.5	4.1	4.5
Other manufacturing	18.2	13.0	25.0	4.2	20.5	8.4	30.1
Total	100.0	100.0	100.0	7.8	12.8	100.0	100.0
Latin America and the Caribbean							
Agriculture	26.0	17.8	10.0	4.3	2.8	11.1	4.1
Oil and gas	14.2	16.3	6.9	9.7	0.0	17.9	0.0
Other natural resources	7.1	5.8	4.4	6.0	6.0	4.7	3.4
Processed foods	20.1	14.1	12.0	4.5	7.1	9.1	10.4
Textiles, apparel, and leather goods	2.7	3.8	8.5	12.2	18.1	4.7	12.0
Motor vehicles and parts	1.5	3.6	8.4	18.5	18.6	5.3	12.0
Electronic equipment	1.7	3.1	5.9	14.9	16.2	4.2	7.9
Other machinery	3.6	7.6	13.3	16.7	15.1	11.0	17.5
Other manufacturing	23.1	27.9	30.6	10.4	9.9	31.9	32.6
Total	100.0	100.0	100.0	8.3	8.9	100.0	100.0

(Table continues on next page)

Table 1.A1 *(continued)*

Percent

	Share (percent)			Average growth (percent per annum)		Contribution to growth (percent)	
	1977	1987	1997	1977–87	1987–97	1977–87	1987–97
Europe and Central Asia							
Agriculture	22.8	14.7	5.2	5.2	10.6	9.6	3.8
Oil and gas	0.2	2.6	11.0	45.1	41.7	4.2	12.2
Other natural resources	18.6	9.7	4.7	3.1	14.1	4.2	3.9
Processed foods	15.0	13.4	6.3	8.7	13.8	12.4	5.2
Textiles, apparel, and leather goods	9.9	18.0	12.6	16.8	18.4	23.2	11.8
Motor vehicles and parts	1.3	1.5	3.0	11.7	31.4	1.7	3.2
Electronic equipment	0.6	0.6	2.1	10.3	38.8	0.6	2.3
Other machinery	10.1	8.5	9.3	8.1	24.0	7.5	9.5
Other manufacturing	21.6	30.9	45.9	14.0	27.7	36.8	48.1
Total	100.0	100.0	100.0	9.9	22.8	100.0	100.0
Middle East and North Africa							
Agriculture	1.8	2.4	1.9	2.5	2.1	−15.9	1.0
Oil and gas	86.2	69.4	42.4	−2.5	−0.4	586.9	−5.0
Other natural resources	1.0	2.3	2.0	8.1	3.0	−37.8	1.4
Processed foods	0.9	1.5	1.4	4.7	4.6	−16.0	1.4
Textiles, apparel, and leather goods	1.0	2.1	5.8	7.1	15.6	−31.6	12.2
Motor vehicles and parts	0.5	0.3	0.5	−5.9	11.2	6.6	0.9
Electronic equipment	0.2	0.6	2.0	13.6	18.0	−12.6	4.4
Other machinery	0.8	2.4	4.1	11.4	10.1	−47.7	6.9
Other manufacturing	7.6	19.0	39.9	9.3	12.7	−332.0	76.7
Total	100.0	100.0	100.0	−0.3	4.6	100.0	100.0
Sub-Saharan Africa							
Agriculture	23.9	20.4	13.2	1.1	0.9	8.8	2.8
Oil and gas	37.9	38.2	18.3	2.8	−2.1	39.2	−10.8
Other natural resources	13.3	12.7	12.2	2.2	4.9	10.6	11.4
Processed foods	8.9	7.0	6.5	0.3	4.5	0.9	5.6
Textiles, apparel, and leather goods	0.3	1.2	4.7	16.5	20.8	4.0	9.7
Motor vehicles and parts	0.1	0.2	0.9	9.2	25.2	0.4	2.0
Electronic equipment	0.1	0.2	0.4	12.7	13.1	0.6	0.7
Other machinery	1.0	1.7	4.1	8.6	15.1	4.0	7.6
Other manufacturing	14.4	18.4	39.8	5.3	13.8	31.5	70.9
Total	100.0	100.0	100.0	2.7	5.4	100.0	100.0
Low- and middle-income countries							
Agriculture	13.4	12.6	5.2	4.1	1.9	11.2	1.4
Oil and gas	51.6	33.5	12.0	0.4	0.5	3.3	0.8
Other natural resources	6.3	6.3	3.8	4.8	5.9	6.3	2.5
Processed foods	9.5	10.0	7.4	5.4	8.0	10.9	6.0
Textiles, apparel, and leather goods	2.6	7.1	15.5	16.1	20.3	14.8	19.8
Motor vehicles and parts	0.6	1.4	2.8	13.6	19.4	2.6	3.5
Electronic equipment	0.7	2.7	9.8	20.4	26.6	6.1	13.5
Other machinery	2.1	4.7	10.6	13.8	20.8	9.1	13.6
Other manufacturing	13.4	21.7	33.0	10.0	16.1	35.7	38.9
Total	100.0	100.0	100.0	4.8	11.3	100.0	100.0

a. The years represent three-year averages to remove some of the volatility from the data. Thus 1977 represents the average of 1975–77, 1987 is the average of 1985–87, and 1997 is the average of 1995–97. Relative caution is advised regarding Europe and Central Asia, where data prior to 1990 are not always reliable. This would have only a small impact on the total because of the region's relatively small weight.
b. High-income Asia is excluded from the low- and middle-income region in the totals. It is provided for information and includes Hong Kong (China), Republic of Korea, Singapore, and Taiwan (China).
Source: GTAP release 5.0.

Table 1.A2 Regional export decomposition for developing countries[a]
Percent

	Share (percent)			Average growth (percent per annum)		Contribution to growth (percent)	
	1977	1987	1997	1977–87	1987–97	1977–87	1987–97
High income Asia excluding Japan[b]							
Quad countries	65.6	69.4	47.0	16.5	7.4	70.5	35.9
High income Asia excluding Japan	7.8	8.6	15.1	16.9	18.1	8.8	18.3
East Asia and Pacific	8.5	9.2	25.0	16.9	23.3	9.5	32.8
South Asia	0.7	2.1	1.6	28.7	8.5	2.5	1.3
Latin America and the Caribbean	1.3	1.1	2.8	13.5	22.6	1.0	3.6
Europe and Central Asia	0.2	0.2	1.6	13.2	39.3	0.2	2.3
Middle East and North Africa	7.1	3.9	2.1	9.1	5.2	2.9	1.3
Sub-Saharan Africa	2.6	1.2	1.2	7.1	11.8	0.8	1.2
Rest of the world	6.1	4.4	3.6	12.0	9.5	3.9	3.2
World total	100.0	100.0	100.0	15.9	11.6	100.0	100.0
East Asia and Pacific							
Quad countries	66.1	58.6	54.8	9.8	16.6	54.6	53.8
High income Asia excluding Japan	18.7	26.2	26.2	15.0	17.4	30.3	26.2
East Asia and Pacific	4.8	4.9	7.1	11.4	21.7	5.0	7.6
South Asia	1.3	2.1	1.5	16.4	13.2	2.6	1.3
Latin America and the Caribbean	2.4	1.3	2.0	4.8	22.2	0.7	2.1
Europe and Central Asia	0.3	0.7	1.4	21.3	26.6	0.9	1.6
Middle East and North Africa	2.9	2.6	2.6	10.1	17.5	2.5	2.7
Sub-Saharan Africa	1.4	0.7	1.0	3.6	21.5	0.3	1.1
Rest of the world	2.1	2.8	3.4	14.2	19.8	3.1	3.6
World total	100.0	100.0	100.0	11.1	17.4	100.0	100.0
South Asia							
Quad countries	52.7	64.8	62.3	10.0	12.4	75.6	61.2
High income Asia excluding Japan	4.4	7.3	9.5	13.4	16.0	9.8	10.5
East Asia and Pacific	4.6	2.8	7.3	2.7	24.0	1.3	9.1
South Asia	4.7	4.8	3.5	8.1	9.1	5.0	2.9
Latin America and the Caribbean	0.6	0.6	1.6	7.8	24.2	0.6	2.0
Europe and Central Asia	2.0	1.2	2.9	2.7	22.9	0.5	3.5
Middle East and North Africa	22.2	12.8	7.4	2.0	6.8	4.3	5.1
Sub-Saharan Africa	4.1	2.2	2.8	1.3	15.9	0.5	3.1
Rest of the world	4.7	3.5	2.8	4.5	10.5	2.4	2.5
World total	100.0	100.0	100.0	7.8	12.8	100.0	100.0
Latin America and the Caribbean							
Quad countries	75.0	77.2	68.9	8.6	7.7	79.1	62.8
High income Asia excluding Japan	0.7	1.9	2.9	20.1	13.6	2.9	3.7
East Asia and Pacific	1.0	1.6	2.8	13.6	15.0	2.1	3.7
South Asia	0.3	0.6	0.4	15.2	5.9	0.8	0.3
Latin America and the Caribbean	15.9	12.0	20.2	5.3	14.7	8.8	26.2
Europe and Central Asia	1.0	0.7	1.0	5.2	12.5	0.5	1.2
Middle East and North Africa	3.3	2.9	1.8	6.9	4.1	2.6	1.1
Sub-Saharan Africa	1.0	1.4	0.8	11.4	2.8	1.6	0.3
Rest of the world	1.8	1.6	1.1	7.1	4.6	1.5	0.7
World total	100.0	100.0	100.0	8.3	8.9	100.0	100.0

(Table continues on next page)

GLOBAL ECONOMIC PROSPECTS 2004

Table 1.A2 *(continued)*
Percent

	Share (percent) 1977	1987	1997	Average growth (percent per annum) 1977–87	1987–97	Contribution to growth (percent) 1977–87	1987–97
Europe and Central Asia							
Quad countries	75.7	68.3	57.9	8.8	20.8	63.6	56.4
High income Asia excluding Japan	0.9	0.5	3.2	4.1	46.2	0.3	3.5
East Asia and Pacific	0.6	2.3	5.5	26.0	33.7	3.4	5.9
South Asia	1.1	1.5	0.6	13.1	11.5	1.7	0.4
Latin America and the Caribbean	2.6	1.5	1.3	4.0	21.2	0.8	1.3
Europe and Central Asia	0.9	1.9	23.5	18.7	57.5	2.6	26.7
Middle East and North Africa	10.9	19.4	3.9	16.4	4.6	24.8	1.6
Sub-Saharan Africa	1.5	0.4	0.3	−4.2	20.7	−0.3	0.3
Rest of the world	5.7	4.2	3.9	6.4	22.0	3.1	3.9
World total	100.0	100.0	100.0	9.9	22.8	100.0	100.0
Middle East and North Africa							
Quad countries	77.3	74.6	66.6	−0.7	3.4	158.5	52.4
High income Asia excluding Japan	5.1	6.5	11.3	2.2	10.6	−37.8	19.8
East Asia and Pacific	1.9	2.1	6.3	0.5	16.7	−3.1	13.6
South Asia	1.0	3.5	3.6	13.3	4.6	−75.5	3.6
Latin America and the Caribbean	6.0	3.2	1.9	−6.4	−0.7	89.1	−0.4
Europe and Central Asia	1.1	2.7	2.8	9.1	5.2	−46.0	3.1
Middle East and North Africa	4.6	4.8	4.0	0.0	2.8	0.4	2.6
Sub-Saharan Africa	0.9	0.7	1.4	−2.7	11.6	6.8	2.5
Rest of the world	2.1	1.9	2.2	−1.2	6.1	7.6	2.8
World total	100.0	100.0	100.0	−0.3	4.6	100.0	100.0
Sub Saharan Africa							
Quad countries	83.7	84.4	70.8	2.8	3.5	86.6	50.9
High income Asia excluding Japan	1.1	2.3	6.5	10.6	16.6	6.3	12.5
East Asia and Pacific	0.6	0.8	4.8	4.6	26.5	1.2	10.6
South Asia	0.5	1.0	1.9	8.7	12.9	2.3	3.3
Latin America and the Caribbean	3.3	3.9	2.9	4.4	2.5	5.7	1.6
Europe and Central Asia	0.3	0.6	1.3	11.1	14.1	1.6	2.3
Middle East and North Africa	2.0	1.4	1.7	−0.7	7.4	−0.5	2.1
Sub-Saharan Africa	3.9	4.0	7.2	3.1	11.7	4.5	11.9
Rest of the world	4.6	1.7	2.9	−7.1	11.4	−7.8	4.7
World total	100.0	100.0	100.0	2.7	5.4	100.0	100.0
Low and middle income							
Quad countries	75.5	72.1	61.7	4.3	9.6	66.5	56.2
High income Asia excluding Japan	5.1	8.9	13.5	10.8	16.0	15.3	15.9
East Asia and Pacific	2.1	2.6	5.6	7.2	20.3	3.5	7.2
South Asia	1.0	2.0	1.5	12.8	8.5	3.8	1.3
Latin America and the Caribbean	6.9	5.1	6.1	1.8	13.2	2.2	6.6
Europe and Central Asia	0.9	1.3	4.4	9.3	25.7	2.1	6.0
Middle East and North Africa	4.5	4.4	2.9	4.5	7.0	4.2	2.2
Sub-Saharan Africa	1.5	1.3	1.4	3.0	12.2	0.9	1.4
Rest of the world	2.6	2.2	2.9	3.3	14.2	1.6	3.2
World total	100.0	100.0	100.0	4.8	11.3	100.0	100.0

a. The years represent three-year averages to remove some of the volatility from the data. Thus 1977 represents the average of 1975–77, 1987 is the average of 1985–87, and 1997 is the average of 1995–97. Relative caution is advised regarding Europe and Central Asia, where data prior to 1990 are not always reliable. This would have only a small impact on the total because of the region's relatively small weight.
b. High-income Asia is excluded from the low- and middle-income region in the totals. It is provided for information and includes Hong Kong (China), Republic of Korea, Singapore, and Taiwan (China).
Source: GTAP release 5.0.

Notes

1. Technically, the non-economic component of confidence is modeled as an unobserved state variable and estimated using a Kalman filter/smoother, with data pertaining to economic conditions as exogenous controls. The model was fitted on monthly data over the period 1984–2001 (September). Then the estimate was used together with actual, observed economic data to predict confidence out of sample over the period October 2001–April 2003.

2. It was decided at the December 2002 Copenhagen Summit to invite eight transition countries to join the EU in May 2004.

3. The differences between Sub-Saharan Africa and South Asia are not limited to the higher growth rate in the latter over the last decade. The poverty gap indicator—a measure of the average distance to the poverty line for the poor—has been much higher in Sub-Saharan Africa. This implies that even at identical growth rates, poverty would have decreased more rapidly in South Asia.

4. The initial poverty estimate will also be subject to revisions in the national income and product accounts because adjustments to the survey-based consumption levels will follow adjustments to consumption derived from the national accounts.

5. A numerical example may help clarify the procedure. Say population is 1,000 in 1999 and per capita consumption growth in 2000 is 5 percent and population growth is 1 percent. If the headcount index is 40 percent in 1999, then the number of poor is 400. With a headcount elasticity of 1.5, the headcount index would improve from 40 to 37 percent (40*(1–1.5 *0.05)), assuming there is no change in the distribution of income. Total population in 2000 reaches 1,010, thus the number of poor is 374, a decline of 6.5 percent, whereas the headcount index improves by 7.5 percent. The difference is the population growth rate.

6. These comparisons are not strictly exact because last year's 1999 levels do not incorporate the new survey information nor other adjustments to the historical data.

7. The survey coverage in the Middle East and North Africa region is particularly sparse compared to most other developing regions. Per capita GDP across the region tends to be relatively high and therefore poverty rates low, so small changes to poverty levels in one or two sizeable countries with a fair number of poor—for example Egypt or Yemen—can have a disproportionate impact on the regional poverty level.

8. For example specific tariffs penalize more competitive exporters with relatively lower prices.

9. In the case of the European Union, intra-EU trade is excluded from the average tariff calculation and the reduction.

10. The formula for cutting the non-peak tariffs is given by the following expression:

$$\tau_i^1 = \chi \cdot \tau_i^0 \quad \text{for } i \in \{Agric, Manu\} \text{ where}$$

$$\chi = \frac{\tau_a^1 \sum_i M_i - \sum_{i \in \{Peak\}} \tau_p^1 M_i}{\sum_{i \in \{Peak\}} \tau_i^0 M_i}$$

The target average is τ_a^1. The import levels are given by M. All tariff peaks are reduced to τ_p^1. All other tariffs are reduced by the factor χ, given by the formula above. There is nothing preventing the adjustment factor from being above 1 (that is, initial tariffs could increase to achieve the target reduction) or below 0 (that is, non-peak tariffs would have to become negative to achieve the target). In the illustrative pro-poor scenario, the reduction factor is capped above by 1—in which case the average will be below the target, and bound below by 0 in which case the average will be above the target. This is the case of Japan in agriculture. An alternative would be to further reduce the peaks so that the target is achieved.

11. Setting the level of the maximum tariff can have some unintended consequences. In the case of developing country manufacturing tariffs, for example, setting the maximum tariff to 20 percent instead of 15 percent could actually reduce the overall average. The reason is that all tariffs in the 15 to 20 percent band in the latter (15 percent) case are bound to below 15 percent. In the former (20 percent) case those tariffs would be reduced by a certain percentage amount—perhaps even 100 percent. The difference in the average tariff will depend on the number of tariffs within the 15 to 20 percent band and the relative import weights.

12. The model is similar to that used to produce the gains from trade reform in *Global Economic Prospects 2002*. More information regarding the nature of the simulations and a more detailed description of the results is given in that report. The model documentation is available at //http://www.worldbank.org/prospects/pubs/techref.pdf. *Global Economic Prospects 2002* reported global merchandise trade reform gains of $355 billion (in the static exercise). The gains have risen modestly in this report—essentially for two reasons. We have upgraded the database from release 5.0 of the GTAP data set to release 5.3, and we have a new baseline reflecting two years of observed changes in economic performance and a (minor) reevaluation of long-term growth prospects. The current model is also based on a different regional and sectoral aggregation, which can affect the impacts of trade reform. (There are more regions and sectors and, all else being equal, one would expect this to raise the real income gains by removing some of the aggregation bias of trade policy

instruments). There have also been a few minor changes to model specification and parameters.

13. All figures, unless otherwise stated, refer to changes in 2015 compared with the baseline level. Dollar amounts are measured in real terms and are based on 1997 dollars. Figures can be converted to 2003 terms by adjusting for economic growth and inflation. The former would involve dividing a figure by $(1.03)^{(2015-2003)}$, where it is assumed that the global economy grows at 3 percent per annum in real terms between 2003 and 2015. The inflation adjustment involves multiplying a figure by $(1.025)^{(2003-1997)}$ where it is assumed that the rate of inflation is 2.5 percent per annum between 1997 and 2003. (Both growth and inflation rates are approximations.) The total adjustment factor is 81 percent, so that the global gain of $295 billion in 2015 is more or less equivalent to $235 billion in 2003 global GDP and prices.

14. Few dispute that trade openness will improve productivity. There is nonetheless great incertitude about the channels—greater domestic competitiveness, imports of technology-laden goods, FDI, export-driven competitiveness—and the magnitude. The results reported herein are intended to illustrate the potential magnitudes.

15. This compares with a reduction of 114 million persons in the case of full merchandise trade reform.

16. The positive income gains—identified in virtually all of the model's regions—imply that transitional mechanisms can be implemented, leaving everyone better off. Whether these mechanisms are designed and implemented is an important issue, but typically the decision of local governments.

References

Greener, Robert. 2002. "AIDS and Its Macroeconomic Impact." In Steven Forsythe, ed., *State of the Art: AIDS and Economics*. International AIDS and Economics Network, 49–55. Available at http://www.iaen.org/library/statepidemic/chapter7.pdf.

Moatti, J. P., I. N'Doye, S. M. Hammer, P. Hale, and M. D. Kazatchkine. 2002. "Antiretroviral Treatment for HIV-Infected Adults and Children in Developing Countries: Some Evidence in Favor of Expanded Diffusion." In Steven Forsythe, ed., *State of the Art: AIDS and Economics*. International AIDS and Economics Network, 96–117. Available at http://www.iaen.org/library/statepidemic/chapter12.pdf.

UNAIDS. 2002. Fact Sheet: Regional Roundup: Sub-Saharan Africa. July. Available at http://www.unaids.org/barcelona/presskit/factsheets/FSssafrica_en.pdf

World Bank. 2003. *Global Development Finance 2003*. Washington, D.C.: World Bank.

2

Trade Patterns and Policies: Doha Options to Promote Development

Developing countries have become major players in the global economy
Over the past two decades, developing countries have increased their share of global trade from about one-quarter to one-third. As a group, they have moved beyond their traditional specialization in agricultural and resource exports into manufactures. Countries that were low income in 1980 managed to raise exports of manufactures from roughly 20 percent of their total exports to more than 80 percent, and many have entered the ranks of today's middle-income countries. The middle-income group of 1980 also increased its manufactured share, but somewhat less rapidly, to reach nearly 70 percent. This dramatic change in trade volume and composition has given developing countries a new interest—and a powerful voice—in the ongoing Doha round.

These changes are not just due to declines in the prices of agricultural and resource commodities relative to manufactures—the strong shift in the composition of exports shows up even when price changes are removed. Further, it is not just an artifact of a few large, high-growth exporters such as China and India. The share of manufactures in the exports of developing countries other than China and India rose from one-tenth in 1980 to almost two-thirds in 2001. It increased sharply, but not equally, in all regions. The share of manufactures in merchandise exports is now between 80 and 90 percent in East Asia, Europe and Central Asia, and South Asia, but only 60 percent in Latin America. Sub-Saharan Africa and the Middle East and North Africa have yet to reach the 30 percent mark, and many countries—particularly poor countries—remain dependent on exports of agricultural and resource commodities.

The rising tide of exports did not lift all boats. Forty three countries had *no increase* on average in their merchandise exports for the 20 years after 1980. Of this group, 20 countries remained strongly dependent on oil or other natural resources, such as phosphates for Nauru or copper for Zambia. Severe conflicts undercut the performance of another 18 countries, including Rwanda and Timor Leste. Trade embargos stifled the export performance of five other countries, including Libya and Sudan. In almost all these countries, the investment climate was not sufficiently favorable—for a range of reasons, sometimes resource depletion, sometimes poor economic management—to attract the investments needed to transform the pattern of exports.

Developing countries are moving into high-value-added products
Growth in traditional labor-intensive manufactures accounts for only part of the gain in exports of manufactures. Exports of textiles and clothing from low-income countries grew at 14 percent per year between 1981 and 2001, but other commodity groups grew even faster.

Exports of electronic products, many of which did not exist in 1980, grew at 21 percent per year—fast enough to double every few years. Further, developing countries expanded their range of markets, with the share of developing-country markets growing from 15 to 35 percent over the period. The continual move to new products and new markets helped high-growth exporters like India and China to avoid sharp declines in their terms of trade, which, given the rapidity of their export growth, might otherwise have been expected.

Between 1991 and 2001, all regions improved their competitiveness in the global marketplace as measured by market share. Europe and Central Asia, Latin America, and South Asia outperformed the other regions, but all gained market share at the expense of the rich countries. This was not true in the preceding decade, when several regions lost market share, notably Europe and Central Asia, the Middle East and North Africa, and Sub-Saharan Africa.

Why did such rapid and fundamental changes in trade patterns occur?

Investments in people and in factories both played a role. Average educational levels and capital stock per worker rose sharply throughout the developing world. Also, improvements in transport and communications, in conjunction with developing-country reforms, allowed the production chain to be broken up into components, with developing countries playing a key role in global production sharing.

Policy was no less important. The dramatic liberalization of tariff and nontariff barriers in developing countries after the mid-1980s increased developing countries' competitiveness. The negative impacts of protection on all export activities declined, but more so for manufactures and processed primary products than for agriculture and natural resources. Although successive multilateral trade rounds liberalized global manufactures, rich countries continued to protect their agriculture. That pattern has been progressively emulated by developing countries over the last two decades, with the result that developing countries' agricultural exports grew more slowly than if agriculture had taken the liberalizing path of manufactures.

Now comes the hard part: reducing protection of sensitive sectors

Developing-country exports now face obstacles in the most sensitive sectors. Industrial-country tariffs on manufactures from developing countries are five times higher than they are on manufactures from other industrial countries. The barriers imposed by developing countries on other developing countries, however, are even higher. Of course, protection takes forms other than *ad valorem* tariffs—among them quotas, specific duties, and antidumping duties. As with tariffs, these measures tend to be used more frequently against the labor-intensive products from developing countries. Average antidumping duties are ten times higher than tariffs in industrial countries, and around five times higher than in developing countries. In short, both groups of countries impose substantially higher barriers on exports from developing countries.

The way in which protection is reduced will make a difference to developing countries

Several approaches—modalities—for negotiations have been proposed for reducing tariffs on agricultural and nonagricultural goods. The 146 World Trade Organization (WTO) members are now discussing formulas that provide enough discipline to bring about liberalization and address tariff peaks and escalation, while offering enough flexibility to accommodate the constraints of all members. Besides tariffs, reform of the rules on antidumping measures is a critical priority. Antidumping measures, originally intended as a response to anticompetitive behavior, are now widely regarded as being used to facilitate market cartelization and are increasingly a source of nontransparent and costly protection.

Changing patterns in developing-country exports

Historically, developing countries have been regarded as exporters of primary commodities and importers of manufactures, a theme repeated even in recent textbooks on development (Todaro 1994). The situation has changed drastically since the beginning of the 1980s, however, as developing countries have become important exporters of manufactured products (figure 2.1). Manufacturing exports have risen in importance in high-income countries, with their share in total exports rising from around 70 percent to more than 80 percent in the 20 years preceding 2001. This shift was much more marked in the middle- and low-income countries. In the middle-income group, the share of manufactures in total exports rose from 20 percent to almost 70 percent over the period. In low-income countries,

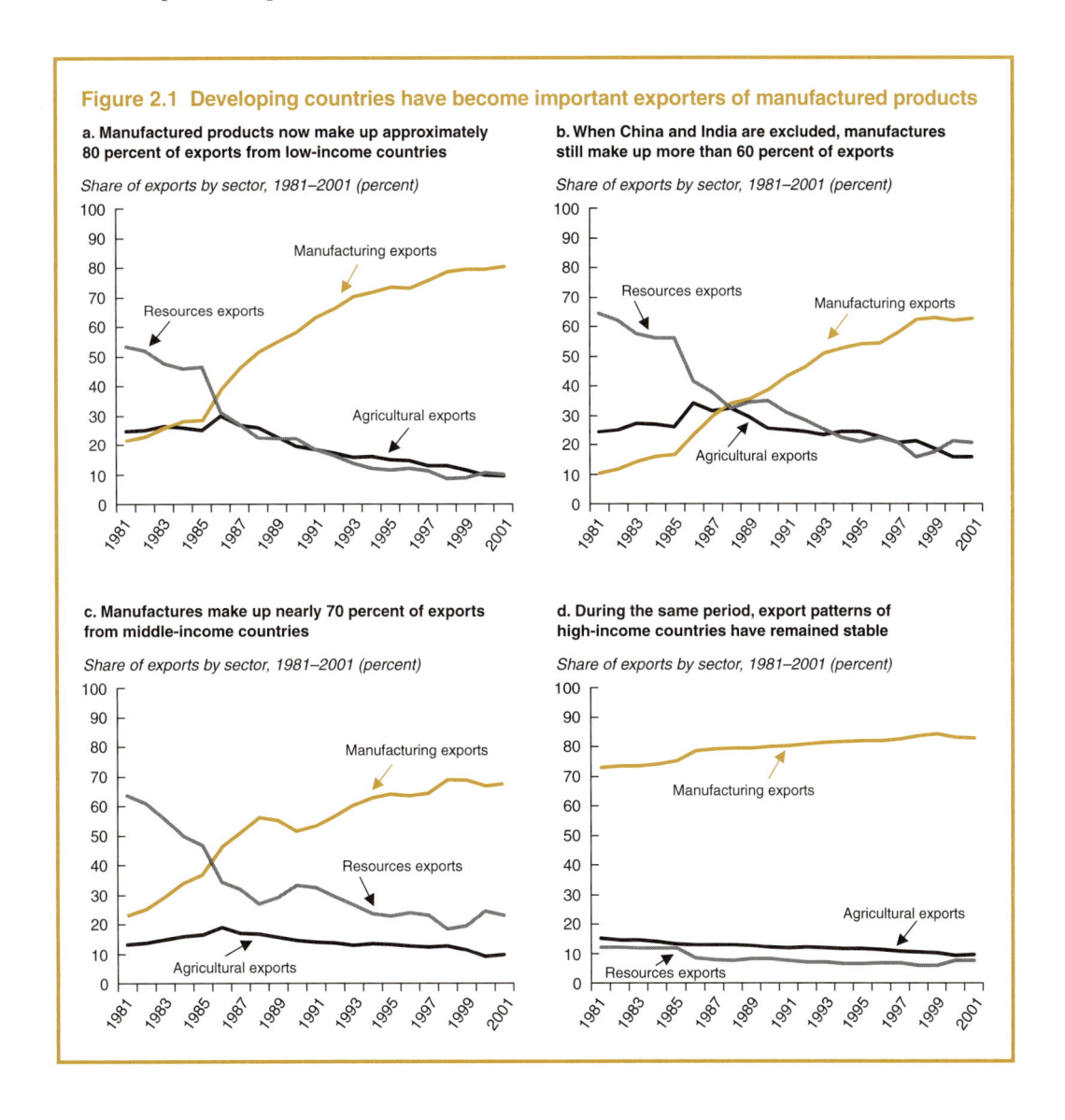

Figure 2.1 Developing countries have become important exporters of manufactured products

a. Manufactured products now make up approximately 80 percent of exports from low-income countries

b. When China and India are excluded, manufactures still make up more than 60 percent of exports

c. Manufactures make up nearly 70 percent of exports from middle-income countries

d. During the same period, export patterns of high-income countries have remained stable

the share of manufactures rose from 20 percent to more than 80 percent.

Nor are China and India the only countries driving these changes. Even when China and India are excluded, the rise in the share of manufactures is from 10 percent to more than 60 percent of total exports. Clearly, China and India are important, but much broader changes in the composition of developing-country exports are under way. If we eliminate the disproportionate effects of large exporters altogether, by considering simple average export shares, the average share of manufacturing exports rose from 25 percent to 50 percent in the unweighted low-income country group, and from 28 to 48 percent in the middle-income group.

The share of manufacturing exports in total exports has risen sharply in all regions (figure 2.2). In East Asia and the Pacific, the increase began from a high base—over 50 percent—but then increased to almost 90 percent by 2001. In Europe and Central Asia, the manufactures share began at an even higher level, over 60 percent, and rose to almost 90 percent by 2001. Because of Latin America's strong natural resource endowments (de Ferranti, Perry, Lederman, and Maloney 2002) the situation there was quite different initially, with manufactures contributing only 20 percent of total exports in 1981. That share had almost tripled by 2001—to more than 60 percent. In the Middle East and North Africa, resource exports, particularly oil, remain dominant, although their share fell from more than 90 percent to around 60 percent during the period under scrutiny, while the importance of manufacturing exports rose from close to zero to around 30 percent. In South Asia, manufacturing exports rose from around half of total exports to more than 80 percent. Resource-based exports and agricultural exports remained important in Sub-Saharan Africa, although the share of manufactures rose from 10 to 27 percent.

Clearly, agricultural and resource exports remain important for many countries and regions, particularly in Africa. However, the broad-based nature of the shift into manufacturing exports means that developing-country policymakers and others concerned about development must consider the impact of policies on trade in manufactured products.[1]

Developing countries are moving up the value-added ladder

A decomposition of the growth rates of exports from each group of countries by level of technology indicates that developing countries are gaining ground in higher-technology exports (table 2.1). The low-income group had by far the highest growth rate of total exports, at 14 percent per year—a rate sufficient to cause exports to expand 14-fold over the 20-year period considered.[2] The middle-income countries also experienced substantially higher growth rates than the high-income countries, suggesting that developing countries have been catching up with developed countries in their trade patterns—in strong contrast with the indications of divergence observed in many analyses of economic growth (Pritchett 1997).

At the product level, growth in exports of raw primary products was relatively low, at 2 percent per year globally. In processed agricultural products, such as meats, processed foods, alcoholic beverages, tobacco products, and processed woods, growth rates were substantially higher, at 6 percent globally, 7 percent for the low-income country group excluding China and India, and 12 percent for China and India.

Trade in low-technology manufactures (such as textiles and clothing), simple manufactures (toys, sporting goods), and iron and steel products grew at rates substantially above the world average rate. Exports of these products from the low-income country group grew at much higher rates than from other country groups, with export growth rates of 14 percent for textiles and 16 percent for other low-technology products.

In medium-technology manufactures, a similar pattern emerges, with global growth rates above the world average, and growth rates of exports from low- and middle-income countries greatly outstripping rates from the high-income countries. Exports of automobiles and components from low- and middle-income countries grew particularly rapidly, at more

TRADE PATTERNS AND POLICIES: DOHA OPTIONS TO PROMOTE DEVELOPMENT

Figure 2.2 Manufactures account for a growing share of exports in all regions

a. Manufactures now make up almost 90 percent of exports from East Asian developing countries

Share of exports by sector, East Asia and Pacific, 1981–2001 (percent)

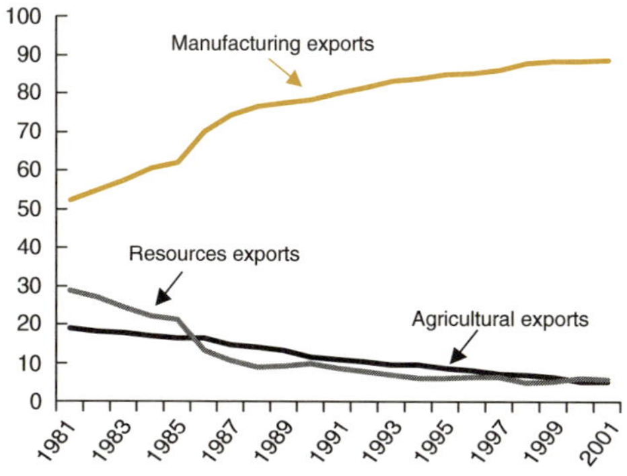

b. The same is true of the developing countries of Europe and Central Asia

Share of exports by sector, Europe and Central Asia, 1981–2001 (percent)

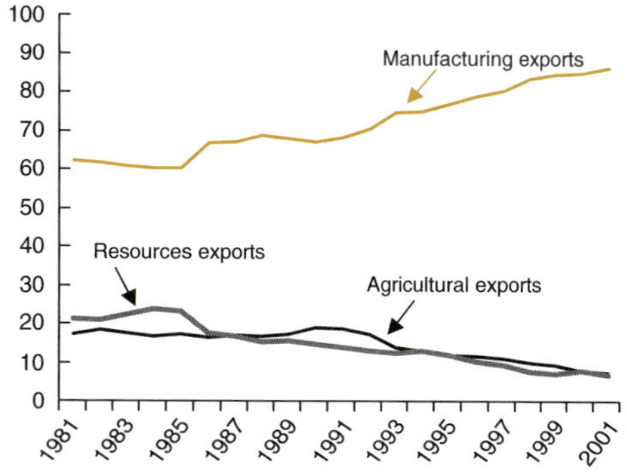

c. The share of manufactures in exports from Latin America and the Caribbean tripled in the last two decades

Share of exports by sector, Latin American and the Caribbean, 1981–2001 (percent)

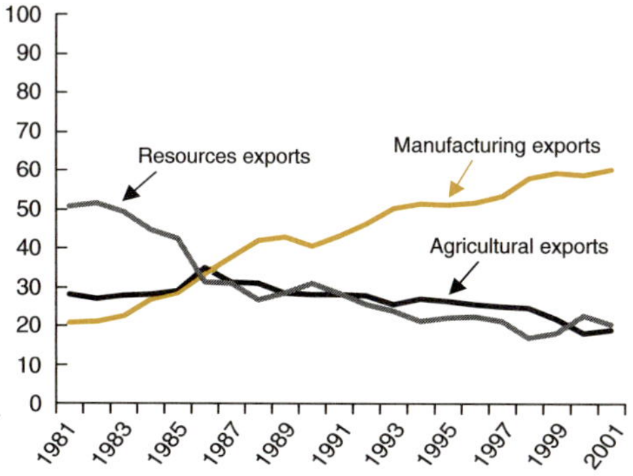

d. Manufactures grew from insignificance in exports from the Middle East and North Africa

Share of exports by sector, Middle East and North Africa, 1981–2001 (percent)

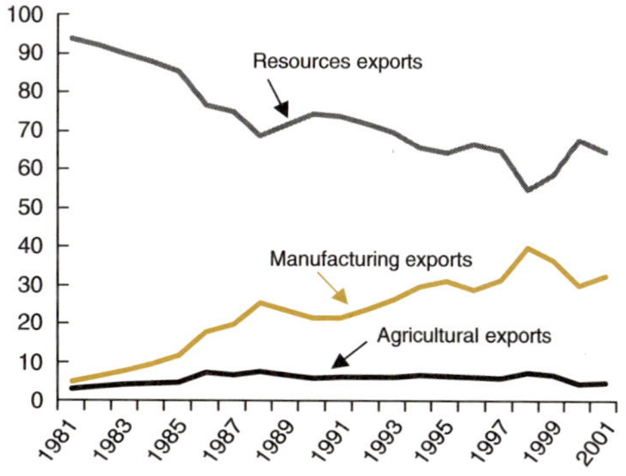

e. Manufactures grew to almost 80 percent of exports from South Asia

Share of exports by sector, South Asia, 1981–2001 (percent)

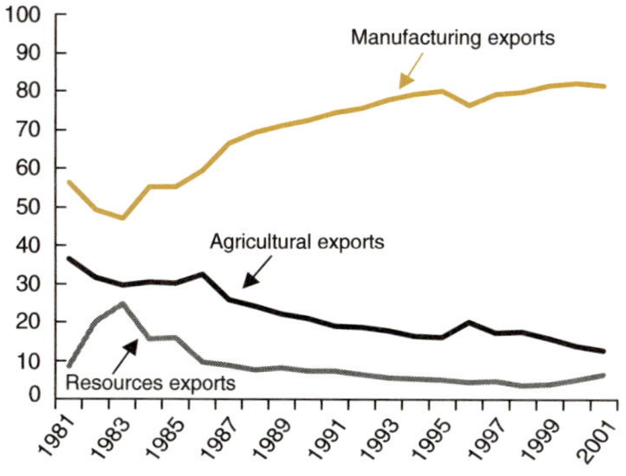

f. The share of manufactures in exports from Sub-Saharan Africa nearly tripled, but from a low baseline

Share of exports by sector, Sub-Saharan Africa, 1981–2001 (percent)

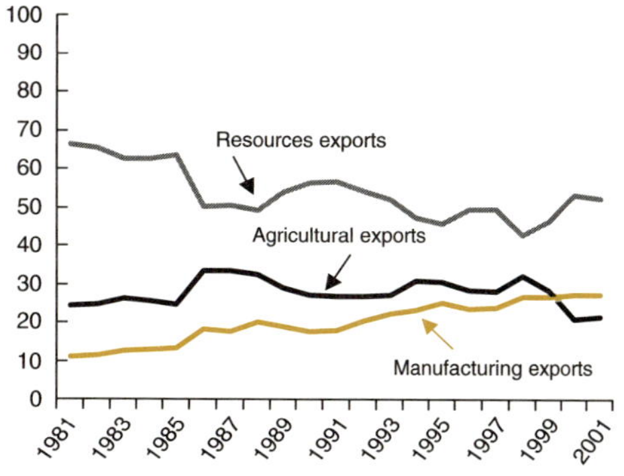

Source: COMTRADE.

GLOBAL ECONOMIC PROSPECTS 2004

Table 2.1 Developing countries are becoming exporters of high-value products
Annual growth rates (percent)

	Low income, less China and India	Low income	China and India	Middle income	High income	World
Primary products	1	2	5	1	4	2
Resource-based manufactures						
Agricultural	7	8	12	6	6	6
Other	4	7	10	5	5	5
Low-technology manufactures						
Textiles	14	15	15	7	5	8
Other	16	19	20	10	6	8
Medium-technology manufactures						
Automotive and components	22	20	19	19	7	8
Process industry products	14	13	12	11	6	7
Engineering products	21	23	24	12	7	8
High-technology manufactures						
Electronic	21	26	36	17	10	13
Other	10	16	20	12	9	9
Total	13	15	17	10	6	7

Note: Table 1 presents the annual growth rates by product group and by country groups assigned on the basis of 1981 income levels to avoid the selection bias that results when end-of-period attributes are used as the basis for selection. Product definitions are supplied by the WTO. Data analysis undertaken in World Integrated Trade Solutions (WITS) using "mirror" data from UN COMTRADE. Country groups defined by income status in 1981. While the results from this approach must be treated with some caution, because the level of technology of the process involved is frequently more important than the technology level of the product, examining the nature of the products being traded is clearly of interest.
Source: COMTRADE, WITS, WTO.

than 22 percent per year. Exports of engineering products such as engines, pumps, and instruments from low-income countries grew at close to 21 percent per year. The highest growth rates of all occurred in high-technology products—particularly electronic goods, such as computers, televisions, and components. World trade in these goods grew more than twice as fast as overall world trade. Export growth from low- and middle-income countries was much faster again, with exports of electronic products from low-income countries growing at the extraordinary rate of more than 21 percent per year—enough to expand exports almost 50-fold over the period.

Low-income countries are less reliant than before on resource-based exports

The importance of the growth rates noted above depends greatly on the share of each broad product type—resource-based, low-technology, medium-technology, and high-technology—in total exports.

Low-income countries showed the most dramatic transformation of export patterns between 1981 and 2001 (figure 2.3). In 1981, these countries depended on resource-based products for 87 percent of their exports, a share that had fallen to 25 percent by 2001. The share of low-technology manufactures rose substantially, from 13 to 38 percent, while that of medium-technology exports went from 3 to 15 percent. High-technology exports exploded from 2 to 21 percent.

The middle-income countries in 1981 were originally much more dependent than other countries on resource-based products—an important contributor to their economic success up to that point (figure 2.3b). In 1981, resource-based products accounted for 81 percent of their exports, a share that fell to a still-substantial 39 percent in 2001. The share of low-technology manufactures rose from 9 to 18 percent in the same countries, while the share of medium-technology exports more than tripled from 6 to 27 percent, and high-technology manufactures jumped from 3 to 24 percent.

The transformation of high-income countries' exports was much less dramatic than for

Box 2.1 Poor export performance in 43 countries

Not all countries participated in the otherwise positive trends for developing countries. Forty-nine countries experienced negative real growth rates over the 20-year period for merchandise exports. Six of the 49 were tourism-based economies that did poorly in merchandise trade but in fact experienced rising national incomes associated with tourism exports.

Of the 43 export-contracting countries, poor performance was attributable to combinations of excessive dependence on one or two primary products, civil conflict, and politically motivated trade embargoes—often complicated by inept governance. In 1981, these countries derived an average of 85 percent of their export earnings from primary products; 20 years later the average was 75 percent. Of the 43 countries, 20 were less-developed countries.

Twenty cases were heavily dependent on one or two primary products, such as oil (Cameroon), phosphates (Nauru), or copper (Zambia), and failed to diversify over the next two decades. Cameroon, for example, despite its richness in natural resources, relies on oil for about one-third of export revenues, and timber or cocoa for much of the rest, leaving it vulnerable to fluctuation in the prices of these commodities. The oil boom led to a significant increase in public spending and a top-heavy civil service, which makes it difficult to respond swiftly to decreases in the price of oil. To make matters worse, the lack of a clear agricultural policy transformed the country into a net importer of food, accelerating the already deteriorating trade balance.

Eighteen countries experienced severe conflicts or war—among them Comoros, Rwanda, and Timor Leste. Another five countries, including Libya and Sudan, experienced trade embargoes.

A more felicitous tale is that of Barbados, one of the tourism-based economies. In 1981 the country was highly dependent on sugar. But progressive and stable political leadership, investments in education, and public investments in infrastructure to support tourism diversified and transformed the economy. Barbados once had the same per capita income as Jamaica; today it is one of the most prosperous countries in the Caribbean, with a per capita GDP of $9,700 in 2000.

Source: World Bank staff.

---

the developing countries. The share of resource-based exports fell from 37 to 5 percent, while the share of low-technology exports remained close to 13 percent (figure 2.3c). The export share of medium-technology manufactures rose from 36 to 38 percent, while that of high-technology exports increased sharply—from 13 to 24 percent of total exports.

Global production sharing is creating new opportunities

Much of the change in developing-country export patterns, and particularly the rise in high-technology exports, is associated with the phenomenon of global production sharing (Deardorff 2001; Hummels, Ishii, and Yi 2001). Production sharing benefits rich and poor countries by allowing production to be broken into discrete stages, each performed in the countries best suited to it. Labor-intensive stages of production, for example, are typically done in labor-abundant countries. Potentially, production sharing can greatly expand the range of activities in which developing countries can participate—holding out the promise of increasing employment and reducing poverty.

Of course, breaking the once-rigid linkages among stages in the production process makes it more difficult to interpret the implications of the shift to manufactures—particularly high-technology products. In many cases, developing countries undertake only those production activities that require low-skilled labor—a low-tech part of the production of high-tech commodities. However, the buoyant demand for such commodities helps offset the relatively stagnant demand for some traditional agricul-

GLOBAL ECONOMIC PROSPECTS 2004

Figure 2.3 **Technology-laden manufactures have increased as a share of exports from each group of countries, while the share of resource-based exports has diminished**

a. Low-income countries are moving out of resource-based industries into low-technology exports

Share of exports by sector, low-income countries, 1981–2001 (percent)

b. Middle-income countries are increasing the level of technology in their exports

Share of exports by sector, middle-income countries, 1981–2001 (percent)

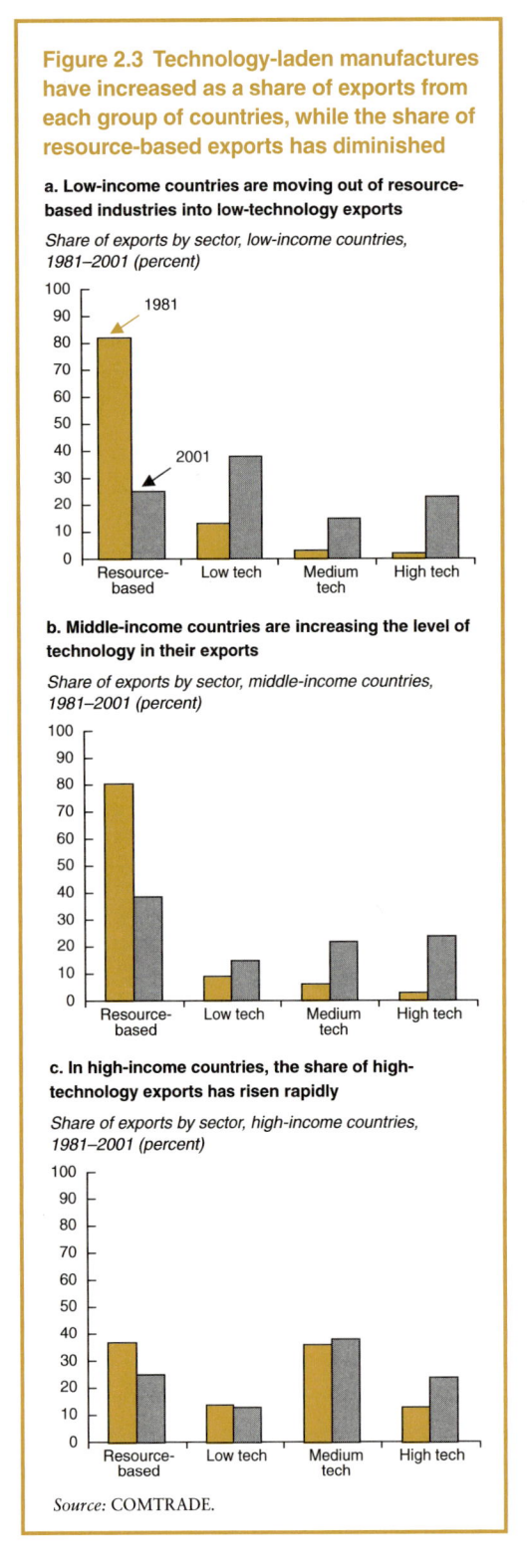

c. In high-income countries, the share of high-technology exports has risen rapidly

Share of exports by sector, high-income countries, 1981–2001 (percent)

Source: COMTRADE.

tural commodities and can create important productivity gains through learning-by-doing and the expansion of productive firms.

The move to global production sharing heightens the importance of timely, efficient, and low-cost transportation. Even quite small differences in transport costs and the timeliness of transportation services can have quite dramatic consequences for national incomes. Hummels (2001) estimates that an increase of one day in the time taken to deliver a good is equivalent to an increase of 0.8 percent in the cost, not just of transportation, but of the good itself. Redding and Venables (2001) conclude that differences in transport costs in a world of global production sharing may account for a large proportion of the observed differences in incomes among countries. In this mode of production, countries must pay transport costs to obtain their inputs and to consign their outputs. If value added is a small share of output value, as is frequently the case, then transport costs have enormous leverage on the residual returns available to pay workers and owners of capital. If value added is 20 percent of the gross output value in the absence of trade costs, for example, then a transport cost of 10 percent of output to ship products out, and an equal cost to bring in components, could wipe out returns to productive factors.

To gain an idea of the potential importance of global production sharing in developing countries, we have calculated indexes of vertical specialization of the type developed by Hummels, Ishii, and Yi (2001) for several developing countries. These indexes expose the share of imported inputs embodied in each unit of goods exported—either directly or after indirect use of imported inputs is taken into account. Although imperfect—they do not allow for differences between export- and domestically oriented sectors in their use of intermediate inputs—these measures provide a structured assessment of the extent and changes in production sharing.[3] Two sets of results are presented in figure 2.4. The lower bars estimate the share of export value accounted for by direct use of imported intermediates, whereas the

Figure 2.4 Global production sharing is increasingly important for China and India

Share of imported inputs in a unit of exports, India, 1980–1998 (percent)

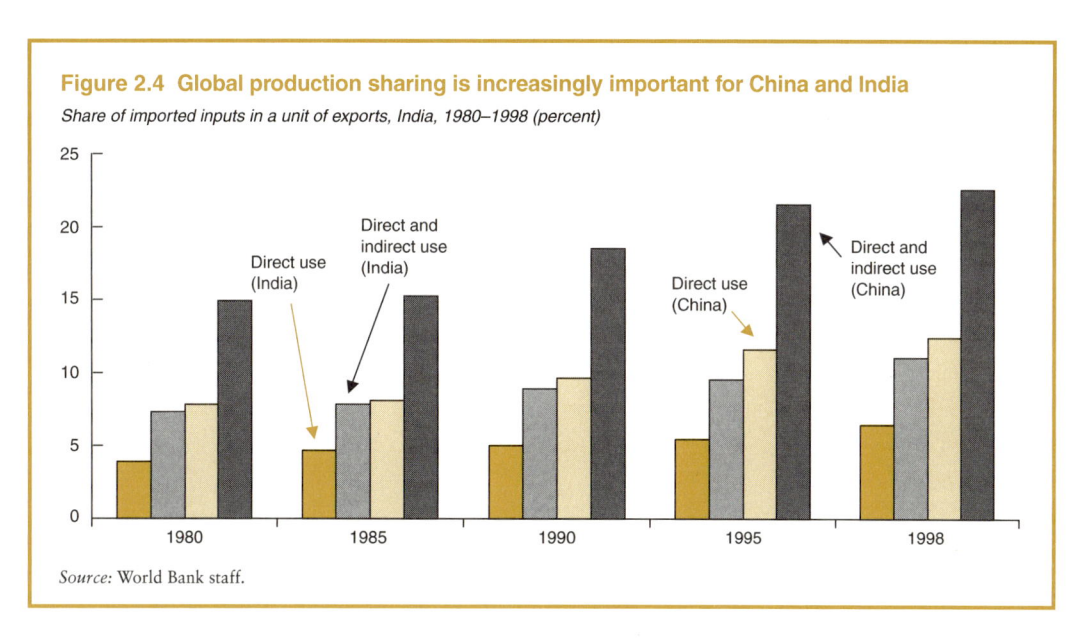

Source: World Bank staff.

higher bars represent direct plus indirect use of imported intermediates.

The importance of global production sharing in India has more than doubled since 1980. In China, even though production sharing began from a considerably higher level than in India, it almost doubled over the period, to 22 percent. Even so, the estimates understate the importance of global production sharing in China, where policy has strongly favored the use of imported inputs in labor-intensive production of manufactures (Ianchovichina 2003), and where exports based on the processing of imported intermediates account for about half of total exports. However, the graph highlights the substantial increase in the importance of the phenomenon in China over the period—particularly since 1987, when duty-free access was extended to a wide range of imported intermediates used in the production of exports.

To take several other examples, Singapore's economy is much more integrated into the world economy than is middle-income Colombia. Singapore's total vertical specialization index hovered around 60 percent of the value of its exports over the past two decades, with a direct specialization index of more than 50 percent. By contrast, in Colombia, the total index rose from 6.4 to 7.9 percent—not much more than a tenth of Singapore's. Although Colombia's larger economy would be expected to show less vertical specialization than Singapore's, the fact that it is so much less integrated than China's or India's suggests that constraints on transport and communications may be inhibiting Colombia's participation in global production sharing.[4]

China and India have tightened their integration with the world economy since 1980. Their experience suggests that successful exporters of manufactures can avoid the problems of declining terms of trade that preoccupied many thinkers in the 1950s and 1960s (Bloch and Sapsford 2000) and that remain implicit in many current models of world trade and growth. A striking feature of the expansion of exports from developing countries is that the terms of trade of countries whose exports have risen extremely rapidly have *not* deteriorated to the extent that one might predict using conventional economic models. Most of the models used by economists would predict that large increases in exports would be followed by substantial declines in export prices, as countries exported more and more of the same products.

Declines in the terms of trade of China, India, and other high-export-growth countries,

GLOBAL ECONOMIC PROSPECTS 2004

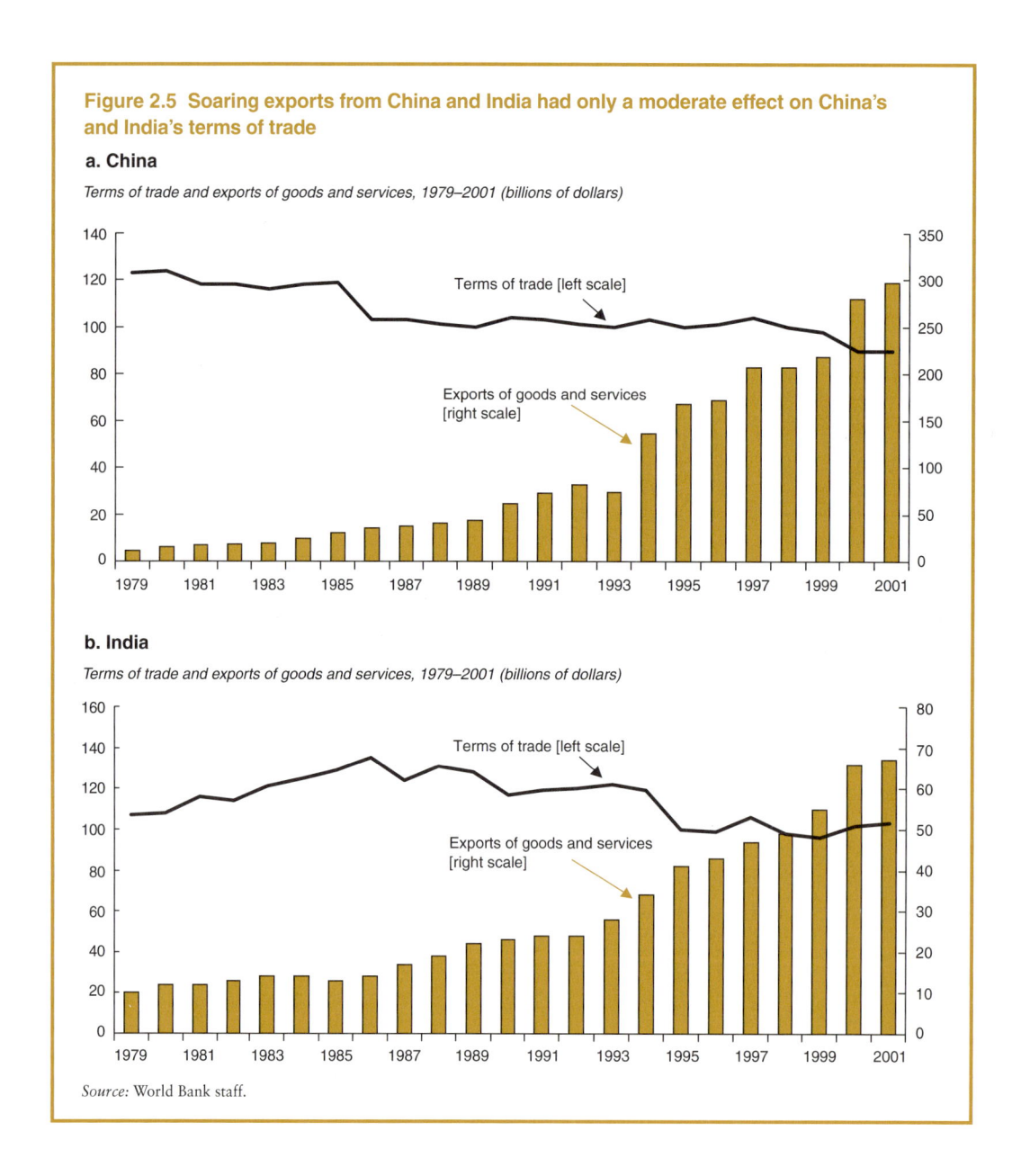

Figure 2.5 Soaring exports from China and India had only a moderate effect on China's and India's terms of trade

a. China

Terms of trade and exports of goods and services, 1979–2001 (billions of dollars)

b. India

Terms of trade and exports of goods and services, 1979–2001 (billions of dollars)

Source: World Bank staff.

however, have been much more modest than would be expected given their high rates of export expansion. China's export revenues grew almost thirty-fold (3,000 percent) in value terms between 1979 and 2001 (figure 2.5). Over the same period, the ratio of China's export prices to import prices—its terms of trade—declined by nearly 30 percent. Clearly, China's gains in export value would have been considerably greater had the terms of trade not deteriorated in this way, but the gains in growth of export value, and its purchasing power, were clearly enormous. While reaping immense benefits from its burgeoning export trade, China essentially shared some of those benefits with its trading partners in the form of improvements in *their* terms of trade. India's exports grew sevenfold during the same period, while its terms of trade deteriorated by perhaps 4 percent.

A key to the apparent discrepancy between the predictions of economic models and actual outcomes is that export growth in some developing countries appears to have been accompanied by vigorous expansion in the range of products exported and in the markets in which those exports were sold (Hummels and Klenow 2002; Kehoe and Ruhl 2002; Evenett and Venables 2003), and by increases in the quality of the goods exported (Schott 2002). These important developments mean that policymakers in developing countries can worry much less about declining terms of trade if they can focus on reform of policies—both at the border and behind it—and on competing successfully in new products and markets.

Clearly, the dramatic changes seen in developing countries' export patterns can be expected to have a major impact on their interests in the current WTO negotiations. In the early 1980s, before the Uruguay Round, developing countries relied heavily on exports of resource-based products and had relatively limited interest exports of manufactured products, which until then had been the focus of WTO negotiations on market access. Since that time, however, the interests of the middle-income countries and the many poor countries that now export high-technology products have broadened dramatically. Further, given the dramatic increase in vertical specialization in production, all countries are much more dependent on the availability of the services needed to support decentralized production—giving developing countries a much greater stake in negotiations under the General Agreement on Trade in Services (GATS).

Behind the patterns: Economic and policy determinants

What caused the transformation in world trade patterns described in the previous section? Did exports grow "passively" in response to expansion in world markets? Or did the observed growth depend on improvements in competitiveness resulting from reforms in policies, or on growth in investment and productivity?

Differences between export growth in a given region and average world growth rates can be ascribed to two key factors: (1) growth in world demand for the region's products and (2) increases in competitiveness because of lower output prices, improvements in quality, or shifts in the pattern of exports to products in greater demand.

From 1981 to 1991, the developing countries of East Asia experienced export growth of 232 percent, compared with the global average growth rate of 115 percent. The demand for the products exported from East Asia grew slightly faster than the world average, at 124 percent, but East Asian export performance was outstanding primarily because of an increase in competitiveness that raised East Asia's exports by 109 percentage points relative to overall market growth. Europe and Central Asia lost competitiveness over the same period, causing their exports to grow by 94 percent relative to growth in the market for their exports of 124 percent and to world export growth of 115 percent. The commodity-dependent exporters of the Middle East and North Africa suffered heavily from contractions in the demand for the products they produced; the world market for their exports shrank by 21 percent. In addition, they lost competitiveness within their own product markets, with the result that their exports fell by 24 percent over the period. By contrast, the product mix of South Asian exporters was helpful; the markets for their products grew by 129 percent over the period. South Asian countries also experienced substantial improvements in competitiveness, which accounted for an additional 70 percentage points of export growth, bringing their total export growth to just under 200 percent. The market for the products exported by Latin America and the Caribbean expanded by 54 percent—less than half the average for the world as a whole—but these countries managed to gain an additional 21 percent increase in their exports through increases in competitiveness.

Table 2.2 Developing countries' exports became more competitive in the 1990s
Source of export growth relative to world average growth, 1981–2001 (percent)

	1981–91			1991–2001		
	Total	Demand	Competitiveness	Total	Demand	Competitiveness
Industrial countries	133	148	−16	48	70	−22
Europe and Central Asia	94	122	−28	255	48	206
East Asia and Pacific	232	124	109	139	75	64
Latin America and Caribbean	75	54	21	137	50	87
Middle East and North Africa	−24	−21	−3	60	58	3
South Asia	199	129	70	113	36	77
Sub-Saharan Africa	10	20	−10	68	35	33
World	115	—	—	68	—	—

Source: COMTRADE.

For 1991 to 2001, export growth in all developing country regions outstripped that of the industrial countries (table 2.2). While high in East Asia and the Pacific, it was even higher in the developing countries of Europe and Central Asia, where market share responded to a dramatic improvement in competitiveness.[5] Of the developing country regions, only East Asia and the Pacific benefited from above-average growth in demand. But all regions except the Middle East and North Africa grew at or above world average growth rates through increases in competitiveness.

What explains improvements in competitiveness?
Changes in production factors used by developing countries probably improved their competitiveness. One of the most misunderstood predictions of economics is that changes in the factors employed in open economies will change the mix of goods produced and exported, rather than the prices of the input factors. Increases in the amount of capital per worker in an open economy can, for instance, be expected to increase the share of output from capital-intensive sectors, rather than depress the return on capital. Similarly, increases in the amount of education per worker can be expected to increase the share of output from knowledge-intensive activities, rather than declines in returns to education and increases in unemployment of skilled workers. In this respect, open economies are much better placed than closed economies, where growth in any factor can be expected to depress its price, as the domestic demand for the goods in which it is used intensively becomes saturated. Of course, world markets, too, are finite, and rapid increases in supply can lead to declines in world prices—as appears to have occurred in coffee markets in recent years. But world markets are much larger than those of individual countries. The problem of saturation is much less likely to become serious for trade in manufactures, because there is much more two-way trade among developing countries in these goods. For this reason, Martin (1993) found that each developing country was likely to be better off if all developing countries benefited from increases in manufacturing productivity than if it alone benefited.

Other likely influences on the structure of outputs and exports include changes in trade and investment policies; changes in the market opportunities facing developing countries; and the development of new market opportunities in which developing countries already have, or can develop, a comparative advantage. Clearly, these influences are related—increases in market opportunities and improvements in trade and investment policies are likely to stimulate investment in physical and human capital.

Increases in the importance of foreign direct investment are another contributing factor to the changes in developing countries' participation in international trade. As documented in World Bank (2002), foreign direct

Table 2.3 Investment in people and in capital grew rapidly
Percent annual changes in factor endowments, 1960–90

	Capital per worker	Education per worker	Secondary education per worker	Tertiary education per worker
Industrial	3.7	0.3	2.2	4.9
Developing				
East Asia and Pacific	5.1	4.2	9.2	3.4
Latin America and Caribbean	2.4	2.0	5.3	6.7
Middle East and North Africa	3.4	2.3	1.9	6.3
South Asia	3.2	3.3	4.3	6.4
Sub-Saharan Africa	2.1	4.2	9.7	12.6

Source: Nehru and Dhareshwar (1993); Nehru, Swanson, and Dubey (1995).

investment grew dramatically during the 1990s. Not only did it bring capital to developing countries, augmenting the total supply of capital per worker, but it brought know-how, and connections with other elements in the network of global production sharing.

One likely contributor to the observed change in the mix of developing-country exports is the rising amount of capital per worker available in some developing economies. In East Asian economies, the annual growth rates of capital per worker have been almost one and a half times those in the advanced industrial countries (Nehru and Dhareshwar 1993; Nehru, Swanson and Dubey 1995). In other regions, the average rate of growth in capital per worker has been lower than in the industrial countries, even though some developing countries outside East Asia have rates of saving and investment that match those found in East Asia. Increases in the amount of secondary and tertiary education per worker have been much higher for most developing country regions than in the industrialized world—albeit frequently from a low level.

To the extent that these resources have been effectively employed, this deepening of financial and human capital per worker can be expected to encourage a shift away from labor-intensive activities toward activities that use more capital and skills. Broad estimates of the growth rates of financial and educational capital are presented in table 2.3 for each developing country region. The first column measures the growth of capital per worker, while subsequent columns measure years of education and average years of secondary and tertiary education per worker. While these are only crude measures of the growth of these inputs per worker, they do represent an indication of the efforts that have been made in developing countries to increase the capital and skills available per worker.

The relationship between accumulation of factors of production and the export mix is likely to be quite complex, with countries first expanding their output of labor-intensive manufactures and then, beyond a certain level of capital and skills, moving into a different range of products (Schott 2003). Further, questions have arisen regarding how effectively many countries have been able to use the additional capital and human skills (Pritchett 2000, 2001). It seems highly likely, however, that the observed rapid increases in capital and skills per worker have been important in many cases of successful development and that they are vital to long-term progress. Without large increases in the availability of skilled labor, it would be difficult to explain the rapid increases in the exports of high-technology products from developing countries—especially from the low-income countries. Even where high-technology exports involve routine operations performed on sophisticated imported inputs, advanced organizational and technical skills are needed to ensure consistent and reliable supplies of high-quality exports.

Lowering protection throughout the developing world created new opportunities—

Since the mid-1980s, the large-scale liberalization of trade policies in developing countries has widened market access and lowered the implicit taxation on exports that import tariffs entail. Average tariffs in developing countries fell to around 12 percent by 2000—about one-third of their level in 1983. This large reduction was accompanied by even larger reductions in nontariff barriers and exchange-rate overvaluation—both of which strongly exacerbated the protectionist effects of tariffs in the 1980s (World Bank 2000).

Absolute reductions in protection were even larger in individual countries. India, for example, reduced its average tariff from 100 percent in 1986 to 32 percent in 1999. While some reductions in protection have occurred in industrial countries—through tariff reductions and through abolition of nontariff barriers—the changes have been quite small relative to those in developing countries. Between 1980 and 2001, the average tariff in industrial countries fell from 9.8 to 3.7 percent—a significant fall, but much smaller than that observed in developing countries, where the average tariff fell from 30 percent to 12.7 percent over the same period.

These figures, and some standard assumptions, allow us to divide up the contribution of trade reform to developing country export growth into a component due to countries' own liberalization and one due to improved market access and export demand. The tariff reductions in developing countries reduced the price of imports to domestic consumers by an average of 12 percent, while import prices in the industrial countries were reduced by 3.4 percent. The increase in the demand for exports from developing countries is determined by the reductions in import prices in their markets—both in industrial countries and in other developing countries. Over the period from 1986 to 2001, the industrial countries absorbed two-thirds, on average, of developing-country exports. Therefore, we estimate the improvement in market access by weighting the price change due to tariff cuts in industrial countries by two-thirds and the reduction in developing countries by one-third, yielding an average price reduction for developing country exports of 6.4 percent, almost exactly half the stimulus that comes from developing countries' own exports. This suggests that, in aggregate, *developing countries' own liberalization* has been the primary channel through which trade reform has expanded developing countries' export growth. Because reform in any one developing country benefits other developing countries as well, the total contribution of developing country reform can be captured by combining the "own-liberalization" effect with the market-access benefits provided by other developing countries. When we do this, we find that 88 percent of the stimulus to developing-country exports following tariff liberalization derives from developing-country liberalization.

Such large reductions in protection can be expected to have marked effects on the pattern of exports, as well as their level. Protection raises the costs of all domestic industries by increasing the costs of their inputs—including both intermediate inputs and factors.[6] However, this effect varies among sectors. Typically, manufactures are much more vulnerable to the adverse effects of protection because they are more dependent than agricultural and resource-based activities on imported intermediate inputs. Further, this vulnerability has grown over time as production has moved from regionally integrated production—the original approach taken by firms such as Ford and the large integrated steel mills in an earlier era of industrialization—to internationally integrated production networks involving many firms and countries.

Protection regimes are often erected to promote industrialization without thorough consideration of their impact on the production of manufactured goods and the structure of exports. Tariffs and other trade barriers affect exports primarily by raising the costs of production inputs. Because protection policies rarely improve the returns small developing countries can obtain from sales of their exports, their impact on exports can be judged by considering their effect on the costs of intermediate inputs—and hence on the returns available for payment to factors. This can be done simply by applying the concept of the effective rate of protection to measure the effect of protection on the value added in export production. While this approach underestimates the adverse effects of protection by ignoring indirect cost-increasing effects, it provides a simple and transparent indication of the direct effects.

—by reducing the implicit taxes on exports

The burden on exports of tariffs on intermediate input costs[7] is illustrated by the cases of Brazil, China, India, and Malawi in 1986, when estimated rates of average protection were first available for each country, and 1997, following large reductions in protection (table 2.4). The impact of protection on exports differs considerably from country to country, but two key features are evident. First, agricultural processing and manufacturing (whether labor or capital intensive) for export are much more heavily taxed than are agricultural and resource commodities. Second, the rate of taxation has generally declined substantially since the mid-1980s, while remaining substantial for industrial products.

At the levels of protection prevailing in 1986, export activities in agricultural processing and in capital- or labor-intensive manufactures were taxed at essentially prohibitive levels. In India, the taxes directly imposed by protection on agricultural processing and capital-intensive manufacturing averaged more than 60 percent. (Nontariff measures, domestic licensing requirements, and exchange-rate distortions, if computed, would have further increased the effective tax.) In Brazil, the estimated impact of tariffs on returns from exporting manufactured products and processed agricultural goods was even more sharply negative—around 70 percent. In China, the direct impacts of protection appear to have been on the same order of magnitude, with agricultural processing facing taxes of more than 70 percent and labor-intensive manufactures close to 60 percent. These problems were compounded by strong policy-driven obstacles to the expansion of state-run firms, which eventually were mitigated by the emergence of an entirely new class of firms—the township and village enterprises—not subject to the constraints of the state-run firms. The export tax rates in Malawi appear to have been much lower than in China and India, even before the reforms, perhaps because such a small and trade-dependent economy simply could not maintain the types of trade barriers found in the bigger countries.

Although a very few agricultural processing and manufacturing activities that depended less on intermediate inputs might have been able to survive at average tariff rates of 100 percent (as in India), it seems highly likely that

Table 2.4 Tariffs hurt exports—but less so in the 1990s than in the 1980s

Cost penalties on exports associated with import tariffs (percent)

	Brazil		China		India		Malawi	
	1986	1997	1986	1997	1986	1997	1986	1997
Agriculture	−43	−5	−28	−15	−14	−5	−9	−7
Agricultural processing	−83	−28	−72	−54	−64	−39	−20	−16
Resources	−45	−6	−14	−7	−9	−3	−6	−5
Labor-intensive manufacturing	−72	−17	−54	−35	−45	−23	−18	−15
Capital-intensive manufacturing	−79	−22	−46	−28	−60	−35	−11	−9
Services	−31	−3	−26	−14	−16	−6	−5	−4

Note: Effective rate of protection applying to exporters is the proportional change in returns to value-adding factors resulting from tariff protection.
Source: World Bank data.

reductions in tariffs—and nontariff barriers—of the type observed around the world between 1986 and 2001 (World Bank 2000) must have contributed to the great expansion of developing countries' manufacturing exports.

Reductions in average tariffs were complemented by the introduction of duty-exemption or drawback arrangements under which export producers obtained access to duty-free inputs for use in export production. These arrangements offer one way, legal under GATT, to reduce the burdens imposed by import duties. Some exporters, such as China, have used them successfully to develop labor-intensive exports (Ianchovichina 2003; Ianchovichina and Martin 2003).

However, such policies are an imperfect solution to the problems created by protection. Whether introduced throughout the economy or in specific free-trade zones, such arrangements are administratively demanding. In many cases, particularly in Africa, they have failed to operate successfully (Madani 1999). Further, they tend to encourage firms to concentrate on production activities that add a small amount of value to imported inputs, rather than on activities more closely integrated with domestic production. Ianchovichina (2003) found that exporting activities had become much more import-intensive than other industries as a result of the incentives created by duty exemptions. Since one of the key lessons of the new economic geography is that there may be substantial gains from activities that encourage the development of backward—as well as forward—linkages (Amiti 2003), incentives toward shallow processing activities may cause highly protected economies to miss many opportunities for growth. Reductions in overall tariffs are a much better alternative than duty exemption. Not only do they remove the incentive for unnecessarily shallow specialization, but they also reduce the price of nontraded goods and factor inputs (Corden 1997), and further increase the stimulus to production for export.

Another problem with relying on duty exemptions rather than relatively low and uniform tariff rates is that their introduction reduces the pressure for more general reductions in protection, since exporters—a potentially powerful source of pressure for reductions in tariffs—no longer suffer the direct impact of protection (Cadot, de Melo, and Olarreaga 2002).

Redressment of behind-the-border costs imposed by inadequate infrastructure and excessive, inappropriate regulation has also helped developing-country exports (Dollar, Hallward-Driemeier, and Mengistae 2003). Other behind-the-border problems include those associated with clearance through customs—excessive or arbitrary inspections or requests for documentation, demands for bribes or other informal payments, and so on. Several of these problems are dealt with in greater detail in chapters 5 and 6.

The dramatic changes in the nature of their participation in world trade have greatly changed the incentives of developing countries to participate in the world trading system. When developing countries exported goods—cocoa, rubber, coffee—that did not compete directly with those produced in developed countries, they had little incentive to participate in politically difficult exchanges of market-access concessions that characterized the multilateral trading system. At the same time, the effects on exports of their protection regimes were relatively subdued, since their primary exports—as we have seen—required fewer intermediate inputs. The shift to manufactures increases the importance of access to markets in which there is likely to be strong domestic competition. And the prices of export-oriented manufactures are, of course, very sensitive to the costs of intermediate inputs, since exporters are unable to pass these costs on without pricing themselves out of the market.

Market access for development: The agenda

Reciprocal exchanges of tariff reductions, the key element of all previous WTO negotiations, will be a critical element in the current negotiations. Tariffs, however, are not the only issue. Two additional topics central to market access for developing countries are:

- The phasing out of textile and clothing quotas, and
- Frequent recourse to antidumping measures.

Phasing out quotas on textiles and clothing is crucial

The commitment to phase out quotas on textiles and clothing was made in 1994 as part of the Uruguay Round agreement. That commitment took the form of an Agreement on Textiles and Clothing, under which quotas were to be phased out in three tranches. Products accounting for 16 percent of 1990 imports were to return to GATT disciplines immediately, with an additional 17 percent returning in 1998, and 18 percent in 2002. However, because the imports used as the baseline included products typically traded only by the industrialized countries, importing countries were able to meet their commitments without abolishing any significant quotas until the third phase of integration, beginning January 1, 2002. The delay in the abolition of quotas has meant that perhaps 85 percent of the effective quotas against developing countries remain in effect—including the most restrictive. Unless the industrial countries go back on their solemn commitments, often reaffirmed, all of the remaining quotas will be abolished on January 1, 2005.

It is difficult to predict the impact of quota abolition, since the textile industry is so heavily distorted by quota and tariff protection in both industrial and developing countries. What is clear is that some countries, such as China and India, with strong underlying comparative advantage in the production of these goods, have had their exports sharply restricted by the presence of the quotas. Other suppliers, much less severely restricted by quotas and/or tariffs, have been able to expand their exports considerably. This group includes three distinct categories:

- Exporters such as Hong Kong, China; Taiwan, China; and the Republic of Korea, for which clothing and textiles are industries that likely will be allowed to decline and "sunset"
- Exporters such as Mauritius and Cambodia, whose exports have been less tightly restricted by quotas and which have had preferential tariff access for at least some commodities
- Countries such as Mexico and Turkey that face neither quota constraints nor tariff barriers in their major markets.

Abolition of quotas will remove much of the incentive for continued production in the first group of exporting countries and reduce the margin of preference enjoyed by the free-access countries. (Their preference will drop from the margin provided by tariffs plus the export-tax equivalent of other countries' quotas, to just the margin provided by tariffs.)

Results provided by simulation models suggest that countries such as China and India, which have relatively low production costs, are likely to make substantial gains in market share following abolition of the quotas (Yang, Martin, and Yanagishima 1997; François and Spinanger 2002). These results are conditioned on the assumptions of the models, and particularly on differentials in the extent to which the quotas restrict the exports of different countries. While some countries, such as China, provide high-quality data on the extent to which the quotas restrict their exports, data for many other exporters are much less widely available. Another indicator of the underlying competitiveness of individual exporters is the share of their exports shipped to nonquota markets. The more efficient the supplier and the more restrictive the quotas it faces, the more of its exports it will tend to ship to less lucrative nonquota markets (figure 2.6).

While the share of clothing exports (using WTO categories) exported to nonquota markets is a crude index of the extent to which exports are restricted by quotas, some interesting patterns appear. The first is that some countries—Albania, Costa Rica, Mexico, Morocco, Pakistan, and Tunisia—directed almost all of

Figure 2.6 Many developing countries face an adjustment when quotas are lifted

Share of clothing exports to nonquota markets by developing-country exporters, 2001 (percent)

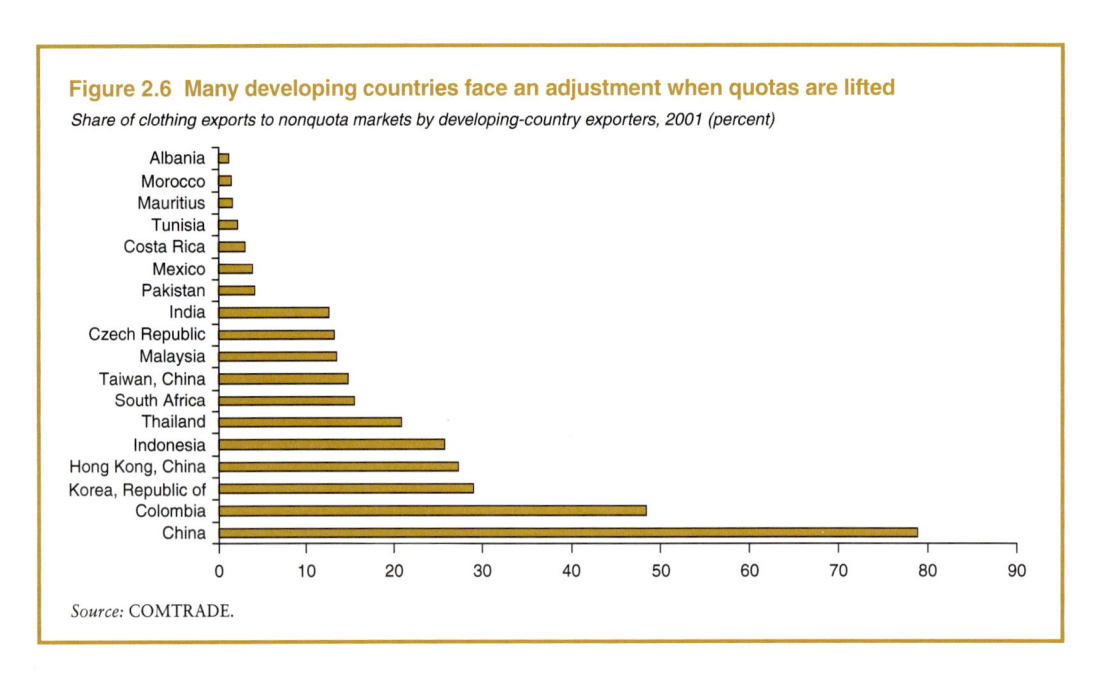

Country	Percent
Albania	~1
Morocco	~1
Mauritius	~1
Tunisia	~2
Costa Rica	~3
Mexico	~3
Pakistan	~4
India	~12
Czech Republic	~13
Malaysia	~13
Taiwan, China	~14
South Africa	~15
Thailand	~21
Indonesia	~26
Hong Kong, China	~27
Korea, Republic of	~29
Colombia	~49
China	~79

Source: COMTRADE.

their clothing exports to the quota-restricted countries, suggesting that their quotas were large enough to let them focus on these markets, or that their competitiveness did not allow them to export to less-lucrative nonquota markets. Another group of countries, such as the Czech Republic, India, Indonesia, and South Africa, exported more than 10 percent of their exports to nonquota markets—suggesting both restrictive quotas and an ability to compete at currently depressed world prices for clothing. Finally, Colombia and China exported 50 and 79 percent, respectively, of their exports to nonquota markets. Countries in this category appear likely to be highly restricted and to have strong potential for expanding their exports following abolition of the quotas.

The abolition of some restrictive quotas in January 2002 provides another source of insight into the implications of quota abolition. Because the abolished quotas covered only a small fraction of total textile and clothing trade, one would expect a disproportionate response to their disappearance, since additional resources waiting to be channeled into textiles and clothing could, for the moment, be redirected only into the products liberalized. In fact, a key feature of the adjustment to abolition of these quotas has been rapid growth in exports of these products, particularly from China.

Whether current supplying countries maintain or lose market share following quota abolition will depend on whether they undertake reforms in advance to maintain their competitiveness. The current system contains, for many countries, *disincentives* for policy reforms that lower costs, improve efficiency, and increase supply. Increases in the supply of exports from a country that has filled its quotas must be shipped to a limited range of markets not constrained by quotas, where prices are likely to decline if significant additional quantities are exported (Elbehri, Hertel, and Martin 2003). Once the quotas are abolished in the world's largest markets, however, the gains from reforms that reduce costs are likely to be much greater. If countries use the greater competition that follows the abolition of quotas as a stimulus for reforms that increase productivity, they stand to gain much more than they could have hoped to gain in the past. Bhardwaj, Kathuria, and Martin (2001) point to areas in India, for example, where such reforms are needed to allow the industry to become more competitive. Needed reforms include: eliminating policies that create disincentives for

Table 2.5 Quota abolition in China will move resources from other activities to textiles and clothing
Percent change in export volumes

Sector	Anticipated change
Apparel	125.7
Automobiles and parts	−22.8
Cotton	−8.6
Electronics	−10.6
Leather and shoes	−5.0
Metal products	−11.9
Textiles	41.9
Other manufactures	−14.1

Source: Staff results from model of Ianchovichina and Martin (2001, 2003).

factory production, eliminating reservation of particular activities for handloom production, and improving duty exemption arrangements. The specific needs for policy reform will, of course, vary across countries.

How will the phase-out of quotas on textiles and clothing affect other sectors? By inducing highly competitive producers to shift from other activities into textiles and clothing, the abolition of quotas is likely to reduce supplies of other goods, creating opportunities for other exporters. The likely response of Chinese industry, for example, to the abolition of current quotas on textiles and clothing is a shift in resources away from other goods (table 2.5). The specific results presented in table 2.5, produced using a model by Ianchovichina and Martin (2001, 2003), should not be seen as predictions of outcomes, however, since the phase-in of China's liberalization commitments under its WTO accession, and the continuing high rates of investment in physical and human capital in China, tend to stimulate the output of many activities, including some of those mentioned in the table.

But the changes anticipated by the model do suggest the importance of examining the disincentives for production of goods other than textiles and clothing. If a country has, for example, a duty-exemption arrangement covering the needs of the textile and clothing sectors and has not developed exports of other manufactured goods, it is more likely to suffer from increased competition following abolition of the textile and clothing quotas than if it had a more balanced export pattern. Thus, policy should not only seek to improve productivity in the textiles and garment sector, but also to improve productivity in other sectors, where competition may be less intense following abolition of the quotas.

How tariffs are reduced will affect the development promise of Doha

Given the mercantilist nature of international trade negotiations, developing-country policymakers contemplating the Doha Development Agenda will want to identify the export sectors in which they face the most significant trade barriers. The average tariff barriers facing exporters from each region are shown in table 2.6. Because separate negotiations on market access are being conducted for agricultural goods and nonagricultural goods, the table is divided into two sections.

Tariffs imposed by the industrial countries on imports from developing countries are typically much higher than those they levy on other industrial countries. In agriculture, the industrial countries impose an average 15 percent tariff on imports from other industrial countries, whereas the rates on imports from developing countries range from 20 percent (Latin America) to 35 percent (Europe and Central Asia). Outside of agriculture, the discrepancy is even more striking. Tariffs on imports from other industrial countries average 1 percent, while those from developing countries face tariff averages ranging from 2.1 percent (Latin America) to 8.1 percent (South Asia).

The differences in tariff averages reflect in part the presence of major trading blocs such as the European Union and the North American Free Trade Agreement (NAFTA), which include key industrial-country trade partners. In part, also, they reflect differences in the pattern of exports and the broad profile of tariffs. In the GATT trade rounds during which the greatest strides toward liberalization were made (the Kennedy and Tokyo Rounds of the

Table 2.6 Industrial countries levy higher tariffs on imports from developing countries than from other industrial countries—and some regions have high tariff walls
Protection rates facing exporters in each region, 1997 (percent)

Exporting Region	East Asia	Europe and Central Asia	Latin America	Middle East	South Asia	Sub-Saharan Africa	Industrial
Agriculture							
East Asia	31.0	30.3	15.5	45.3	38.4	19.0	30.5
Europe and Central Asia	24.2	36.4	23.8	55.3	34.2	12.7	35.1
Latin America and Caribbean	42.1	36.0	14.8	50.3	29.7	24.7	20.4
Middle East	23.0	43.4	14.9	76.4	31.8	18.9	23.4
South Asia	16.6	34.6	13.7	41.1	27.7	11.0	25.8
Sub-Saharan Africa	26.7	20.3	14.4	39.1	30.9	33.6	23.6
Industrial	33.3	43.7	20.1	65.4	16.4	24.0	15.3
Nonagriculture							
East Asia	8.2	13.8	15.1	12.2	28.1	14.5	5.1
Europe and Central Asia	6.4	6.4	11.4	8.6	25.8	12.8	5.9
Latin America and Caribbean	4.3	6.7	15.4	8.9	19.4	11.9	2.1
Middle East	5.4	11.5	8.8	11.4	33.6	11.7	6.0
South Asia	7.1	11.0	13.6	10.2	19.0	17.4	8.1
Sub-Saharan Africa	4.4	6.1	11.7	6.1	27.6	20.6	4.2
Industrial	7.4	9.6	8.5	10.4	25.2	12.2	1.0

Source: Weighted averages calculated using GTAP Version 5 Database (www.gtap.org). Most-favored-nation rate except for major free-trade blocs such as the European Union and the North American Free Trade Agreement. Does not include other preference schemes.

1960s and 1970s), developing countries were not active participants in the trading of reciprocal market-access concessions. Under the circumstances, it was more likely that their products would be omitted from the sharp reductions in tariffs made in those rounds.[8]

A reasonable objection to this interpretation is that some developing countries face substantially lower tariff rates than are presented in table 2.6 and may even benefit from access to industrial country markets at prices above world market levels. This is true for many countries and groups of countries. The countries of the African, Caribbean, and Pacific group enjoy preferences on many of their exports to the European Union. The least-developed countries receive preferences under the Union's Everything But Arms Agreement. Other countries receive preferences as members of Euro-Mediterranean agreements, the U.S.–Caribbean Basin Initiative, the U.S Africa Growth and Opportunity Act, and preferences provided to least developed countries and other developing countries under the Generalized System of Preferences.

Recent research suggests, however, that conditions such as rule-of-origin requirements reduce the benefits provided by such agreements substantially below the gains implied by the nominal preferences (Brenton 2003). Furthermore, many of these countries suffer from restrictions on their access to markets for a wide range of other products. And other countries with a large fraction of the world's poor receive no benefit at all from these preferences—in fact they are harmed by diversion of their exports to preference-receiving countries. China and India alone contain well over 500 million people living on $1 per day or less (World Bank 2003). These countries receive only minimal benefit from these preferential arrangements.

Developing countries tend to levy higher tariffs on imports from other developing countries than do the industrial countries (table 2.7). This is particularly striking in the case of agricultural products, where the tariffs levied

Table 2.7 Developing countries pay large amounts in tariffs to their neighbors
The share of the burden on each region's exports imposed by region of destination (percentage of total barriers faced by exporting region)

Exporting Region	East Asia	Europe and Central Asia	Latin America	Middle East	South Asia	Sub-Saharan Africa	Industrial	Total
Agriculture								
East Asia	32.8	0.7	0.6	5.6	4.7	2.1	53.6	100
Europe and Central Asia	1.7	19.8	0.6	13.9	0.4	1.4	62.3	100
Latin America (LAC) and Caribbean	13.7	1.6	10.8	14.8	1.4	1.9	55.6	100
Middle East and North Africa	2.1	3.0	0.6	44.4	1.6	1.0	47.3	100
South Asia	12.6	2.0	0.7	28.2	7.5	1.8	47.4	100
Sub-Saharan Africa	7.1	2.3	0.4	4.8	4.0	10.0	71.4	100
Industrial	16.1	3.2	5.0	19.1	0.6	2.7	53.3	100
Nonagriculture								
East Asia	37.4	1.5	6.3	4.8	5.9	4.2	39.9	100
Europe and Central Asia	2.8	13.5	2.1	5.8	2.0	2.9	71.0	100
Latin America and Caribbean	3.7	0.3	63.8	1.7	1.2	1.5	27.7	100
Middle East and North Africa	8.2	1.8	2.4	12.4	28.6	3.1	43.4	100
South Asia	8.8	0.6	3.1	9.7	6.8	7.9	63.0	100
Sub-Saharan Africa	9.0	0.7	4.2	1.7	7.7	40.4	36.3	100
Industrial	31.1	6.8	15.3	14.3	6.5	6.1	19.9	100

Source: Weighted averages calculated using GTAP Version 5 Database (www.gtap.org). Most-favored-nation rate except for major free-trade blocs such as the European Union and the North American Free Trade Agreement.

on developing-country exports are frequently twice as high as the already high rates levied by the industrial countries. For nonagricultural products, the differences are even greater in proportional terms. The tariffs imposed by South Asia on imports from developing countries, for instance, are frequently five times as high as the rates imposed by industrial countries. It is also notable that countries levy high tariffs on imports from other countries in their region, particularly in Sub-Saharan Africa, where the average tariff levied is higher on African products than on imports from any other region.

How important are the effects of the tariff rates discussed above? The answer depends on the size of the trade volumes to which they apply. One way to get a rough indication of the importance of tariffs in particular markets is to examine the value of the duty charged on exports to that market. This measure effectively weights each tariff rate by the value of the trade to which it applies. Although clearly flawed in cases where trade flows are strongly inhibited by high tariff rates or where much trade takes place at preferential rates, the measure does provide at least a crude adjustment for the relative importance of different markets.[9]

In agriculture, all developing regions face their most significant barriers in the industrial countries. Although the burden is greatest in Sub-Saharan Africa, where over 70 percent of the barriers faced are imposed by the industrial countries, the industrial countries account for more than 50 percent of the barriers facing all developing regions except South Asia and the Middle East and North Africa. Even there, industrial-country barriers are substantial, accounting for almost half of the total direct burden imposed on their exports. In only one region, the Middle East and North Africa—where barriers imposed by other countries of the region loom particularly large—do the barriers erected by the developing world approach the effect of those imposed by developed countries. After the developed countries, however, the most important barriers are often found in neighboring countries, as in the case of East Asia, where neighbors' barriers account for almost a third of the barriers facing exporters, and the Middle East, where they account for close to 50 percent.

In nonagricultural trade, industrial-country barriers are clearly much more important than would be implied by the relatively low tariff rates shown in table 2.7. Their importance to exporters, however, varies substantially by region. For developing countries in Europe and Central Asia, they are particularly important, accounting for over 70 percent of total levies on exports. Industrial-country barriers are also particularly important in South Asia, where they account for close to two-thirds of the tariff burden. By contrast, the industrial-country share is closer to 40 percent in East Asia, the Middle East and North Africa, and Sub-Saharan Africa, and under 30 percent in Latin America and the Caribbean. For the industrial countries themselves, barriers in other industrial countries are now relatively small, at under 20 percent of the total, a fact that undoubtedly contributes to developed countries' interest in securing trade liberalization in developing countries. These generalizations notwithstanding, the differences mask country-level patterns, obliging policymakers in each country to do their own analysis.

Use of antidumping actions to generate protection has reached an advanced stage

GATT and the WTO acknowledge the sovereign rights of member countries to impose certain new trade restrictions or to replace old ones. A number of these are "exceptions" to the general intention of providing an open international trading system, such as import restrictions that relate to national security. Others are part of the management of the trading system. These are usually described as being allowed under "GATT/WTO rules" rather than as "exceptions."

Within the GATT/WTO system the general justification for such rules is that they allow members to accommodate and at the same time isolate a powerful interest that might otherwise set back an entire liberalization program.[10] Since the Uruguay Round these trade rules—particularly antidumping—have been invoked with increasing frequency—particularly by developing economies. Moreover, WTO members increasingly treat their use as a reserved right of unilateral protection similar to the national-security exception, rather than as an instrument to manage an ongoing and multilateral process of liberalization. (See box 2.2.)

Recent data on the incidence of use of antidumping rules by broad country groups reveal several ominous patterns. The first is a tendency for both developed and developing countries to resort to antidumping measures—1,979 between 1995 and June 2002 (table 2.8). More antidumping actions were initiated by developing countries against other developing countries than by or against industrial countries.

The emergence of developing countries as major users of antidumping measures is a recent phenomenon. The use of this form of protection, which requires complex and expensive administrative processes, has traditionally been eschewed by developing countries. However, perhaps in part because WTO has become less tolerant of some other avenues for introducing discretionary protection, such as measures for balance-of-payment purposes, many developing countries have begun to make use of antidumping measures. In 1996, 767 antidumping actions were pending, of which 581 had been introduced by industrial countries. By June 2002, the number of pending actions had grown to 1,189, of which 636 had been initiated by industrial countries and 553 by developing and transition economies.

All groups of countries show a striking tendency to impose antidumping measures disproportionately against the exports of developing and transition economies. But when the actions shown in table 2.8 are divided by the dollar value of imports from each group, the result is that industrial countries impose

Box 2.2 Swimming upstream: The case of Vietnamese catfish

On July 22, 2003, the *New York Times* wrote the following editorial that illustrates well the vicissitudes of exporters in antidumping waters:

> . . . After embracing decidedly un-Marxist reforms, Vietnam became one of globalization's brightest stories in the 1990's. The nation, a onetime rice importer, transformed itself into the world's second largest rice exporter and a player in the global coffee trade. The rural poverty rate was slashed to 30 percent from 70 percent. The normalization of ties between Hanoi and Washington brought American trade missions bent on expanding Vietnamese free enterprise. One of these delegations saw in the Mekong Delta's catfish a golden export opportunity, with the region's natural conditions and cheap labor affording Vietnam a competitive advantage. Sure enough, within a few years, an estimated half-million Vietnamese were living off a catfish trade nurtured by private entrepreneurs. Vietnam captured 20 percent of the frozen catfish-fillet market in the United States, driving down prices. To the dismay of the Mississippi Farm Bureau, even some restaurants in that state—the center of the American catfish industry—were serving the Vietnamese species.
>
> Soon . . . Vietnamese farmers were caught in a nasty two-front war being waged by the Catfish Farmers of America, the trade group representing Mississippi Delta catfish farmers. The Mississippi catfish farmers are generally not huge agribusinesses, and many of them struggle to make ends meet. But that still does not explain how the United States, the international champion of free market competition, could decide to rig the catfish game to cut out the very Vietnamese farmers whose enterprise it had originally encouraged.
>
> Last year . . . the American catfish farmers managed to persuade Congress to overturn science. An amendment, improbably attached to an appropriations bill, declared that out of 2,000 catfish types, only the American-born family—named Ictaluridae—could be called 'catfish.' So the Vietnamese could market their fish in America only by using the Vietnamese terms "basa" and 'tra'. . . . Catfish Farmers of America, ran advertisements warning of a 'slippery catfish wannabe,' saying such fish were 'probably not even sporting real whiskers' and 'float around in Third World rivers nibbling on who knows what.' Not satisfied with its labeling triumph—an old trade-war trick perfected by the Europeans—the American group initiated an antidumping case against Vietnamese catfish. And for the purposes of this proceeding, Congressional taxonomy notwithstanding, the fish in question were once again regarded as catfish, not basa or tra. . . .
>
> Antidumping cases involve allegations that imports are being sold more cheaply than they are back home or below cost, practices rightly banned by trade laws. . . . In this case, the Commerce Department had no evidence that the imported fish were being sold in America more cheaply than in Vietnam, or below their cost of production. But rather than abandoning the Mississippi catfish farmers to the forces of open competition, the department simply declared Vietnam a "nonmarket" economy. The designation allowed it simply to stipulate that there must be something suspect going on somewhere—that Vietnamese farmers must not be covering all the costs they would in a functioning market economy. Tariffs ranging from 37 percent to 64 percent have been slapped by the department on Vietnamese catfish. . . .
>
> Prices along the Mekong crashed, as the exporters who buy his fish moved to protect their margins. . . . Faced with the prospect of losing their investment, [farmers] might be shocked to learn that [the] Commerce Department says they do not operate in a free market. . .

The United States International Trade Commission, an administrative agency in Washington, provided its final verdict on July 23. The verdict stated that the American catfish industry was hurt by unfair competition due to dumping by Vietnam—making the tariffs permanent.

Source: New York Times, July 22, 2003.

GLOBAL ECONOMIC PROSPECTS 2004

Table 2.8 Most antidumping actions are filed by developing countries against other developing countries
Antidumping actions initiated between 1995 and June 2002

Initiated by	Initiated against			
	Industrial economies	Developing economies	Transition economies	All economies
Industrial economies[a]	198	494	127	819
Developing economies[b]	357	649	138	1,144
Transition economies[c]	4	6	6	16
All economies	559	1,149	271	1,979

a. Australia, Canada, 15 European Union members, Iceland, Japan, New Zealand, Norway, Switzerland, and the United States.
b. All other economies excluding industrial economies and transition economies. China is included in the totals for developing economies
c. 27 transition economies, as defined by *World Development Report* 1996 (Albania, Armenia, Azerbaijan, Belarus, Bosnia-Herzegovina, Bulgaria, Croatia, Czech Republic, Estonia, Macedonia (FYR), Georgia, Hungary, Kazakhstan, Kyrgyzstan, Latvia, Lithuania, Moldova, Poland, Romania, Russian Federation).
Source: WTO Antidumping Committee Reports.

antidumping measures on developing countries more than twice as frequently as the developing countries' volume of exports would imply. Against transition countries, the statistics are even worse, with measures being applied four times as frequently as their volume of trade would imply. Developing countries are only marginally better in their treatment of developing countries, and impose antidumping measures against other developing countries 50 percent more frequently than would be suggested by the volume of imports. Industrial countries are treated relatively lightly by both industrial and developing countries, with only 43 percent as many actions imposed on them as would be implied by their value of imports.

Rates of protection being applied through antidumping measures are astonishingly high (table 2.9). Though industrial economy tariffs now average only 4 percent, their antidumping rates have been *seven to ten* times higher. This is new protection, not a temporary return to rates of protection previously negotiated down under WTO auspices. The antidumping duties imposed by developing countries also are much higher than their tariff rates, with provisional measures ranging from 84 to 126 percent.

And antidumping rates are discriminatory. Antidumping decisions often apply different rates to imports from different sources (table 2.9).[11] The same biases are found in antidumping rates as have been reported for tariffs and various nontariff forms of protection: rates applied by developing economies are higher, and the bias against imports from developing economies is even more pronounced in rates applied by developing economies than in those applied by industrial economies.

Table 2.9 Antidumping rates are much higher than tariff rates
Averages of highest and lowest rates applied in antidumping cases (percent)

	Average antidumping margins				
	Provisional measures		Definitive duties		Average tariff rates
	Low	High	Low	High	
Industrial economies	28	41	31	48	4
Developing economies	84	126	58	83	13
All economies	50	75	43	64	5

Note: Post-Uruguay Round applied tariff rates; antidumping measures in place as of December 31, 2002; ad valorem rates.
Source: Calculations based on countries' notifications to the WTO.

The scale of the antidumping duties levied varies a great deal by country within groups, with some countries imposing extraordinarily high duties and other countries relatively moderate rates—although virtually all such duties are very high relative to currently prevailing tariff rates. While some countries, such as Australia, impose duties in the same order of magnitude as current tariffs, some countries are imposing duties at truly astronomical rates, and rates that seem likely to be prohibitive under almost all circumstances. A number of Latin American countries have measures above 100 percent, and frequently substantially above this level—the rates in Argentina, Mexico, and Peru exceed 300 percent (table 2.10). Further, these rules are frequently applied to much broader groups of products in developing countries than has been the case in the past.

The large differences among countries in antidumping duty rates highlight the flexibility in the WTO rules on antidumping, flexibility that allows countries to "find" high margins of dumping, and to allow countries to impose high duties against them. It strains credulity to believe that exporters to Mexico and Argentina are 10 times as prone to dumping as exporters to the United States. Different interpretations of the same WTO rules, therefore, are leading to widely different outcomes, raising serious questions about the objectivity of the process.

Table 2.10 Antidumping duties are high
Average dumping margins for measures currently in place, by country (percent)

Average antidumping margins	Against all economies			
	Provisional measures		Definitive duty	
By country	Low	High	Low	High
Argentina	163	328	62	63
Australia	6	16	20	43
Brazil	54	64	38	47
Canada	40	41	42	42
China	28	50	27	50
Colombia	34	40	53	67
Czech Republic	n/a	n/a	29	73
Egypt	n/a	n/a	22	55
European Union (15)	33	45	32	46
India	64	91	69	105
Israel	4	10	11	26
Jamaica	256	256	104	104
Korea	47	56	31	41
Malaysia	28	65	10	25
Mexico	269	345	51	65
New Zealand	42	42	28	62
Peru	75	330	73	246
Poland	n/a	n/a	23	23
South Africa	40	63	38	53
Taiwan, China	n/a	n/a	76	116
Thailand	36	47	32	36
Trinidad and Tobago	119	119	135	135
Turkey	n/a	n/a	93	101
United States	30	49	29	50
Venezuela	116	119	123	123

n/a not applicable.
Note: Dumping margins associated with definitive measures in place as of December 31, 2002. Where applicable, numbers reflect dumping margins determined during the latest review of each case. For several countries (China, India, Peru, and Thailand), the table illustrates dumping margins related to antidumping measures in place as of June 30, 2002.
Source: Semiannual reports under Article 16.4 of Antidumping Agreement, submitted by individual WTO members to Committee on Antidumping Practices. The list of countries currently maintaining antidumping measures has been extracted from the Report (2002) of the Committee on Antidumping Practices, and from the above-mentioned Semiannual Reports of WTO members. No data were available for Indonesia or the Philippines.

Figure 2.7 Antidumping barriers by sector and by country group

Dumping margins in place, as of December 2002: target countries and sectors

[Bar chart showing average dumping margins (%) by sector for Transition economies, Developing economies, and Industrial economies, with x-axis from 0 to 140. Sectors: High Technology Manufactures, Medium Technology Manufactures, Low Technology Manufactures, Resource Based Manufactures, Primary Products.]

Source: Calculations based on countries' notifications to the WTO.

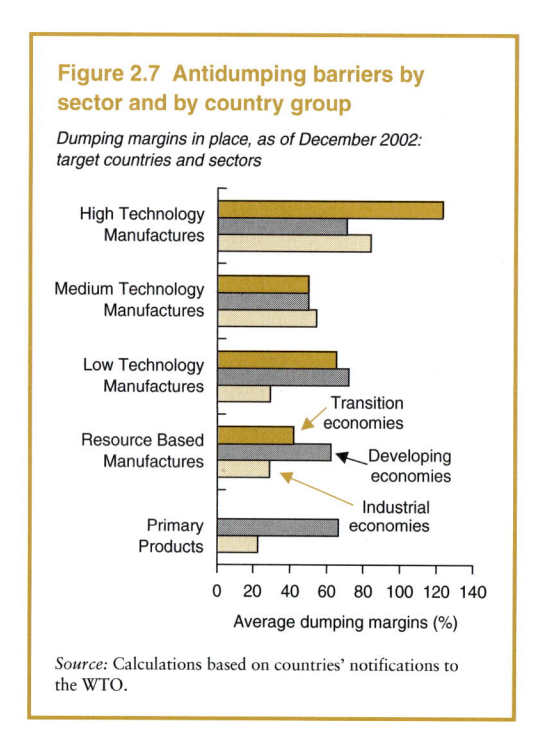

The intensity of use of antidumping measures depends heavily upon the sectors in which it is applied. Figure 2.7 shows the height of the barriers imposed against developing countries by the level of technology in their exports. It reveals that antidumping barriers are disproportionately high against their exports of primary products, resource-based manufactures, and low-technology manufactured exports. For primary products, the average antidumping duty against developing countries is three times as high, at around 60 percent, as against the industrial countries. This means that antidumping barriers are relatively lower on the most dynamic exports of developing countries, high-technology exports. However, the antidumping barriers against these exports remain very high in absolute terms, at 65 percent.

The use of antidumping actions to generate protection has reached an advanced stage. It now threatens developing countries' trade both through the damaging effects on their own economies, and through adverse impacts on their export opportunities. The Ministerial Declaration launching the Doha Development Agenda includes consideration of antidumping measures, and provides an opportunity for beneficial reform. Although reform will be difficult given the strong political support for this type of protection from industries in both developed and developing countries, the rapidly growing economic damage to all economies—those imposing these duties and those suffering from them—makes reform a high priority.

From Doha to Cancún and beyond: How should protection be reduced?

Most of the protection in world markets is imposed through barriers to market access—an essential pillar of other elements of protection regimes, such as export subsidies in agriculture. Without a supporting tariff to preclude imports, an export subsidy will become merely a subsidy on return—exports will flow out in order to collect the subsidy, but the goods exported will be replaced by imports, with no significant impact on domestic producer prices. Reducing tariffs and other barriers to market access, therefore, is the central issue in removing the protection that distorts world markets.

WTO members are negotiating, in accordance with the agenda agreed at Doha, on approaches to reduce protection on agricultural and nonagricultural goods. For nonagricultural goods, in particular, the negotiations are to include reduction or elimination of tariff peaks and tariff escalation, and to emphasize products of interest to developing countries (WTO 2001). An emphasis on reducing tariff peaks is important both because such peaks are very costly to the countries imposing such tariffs, and because they are frequently on products of particular interest to developing countries. Francois, Martin, and Manole (2003) find that approaches to trade reform that most sharply reduce peak tariffs result in larger reductions in the average tariffs facing low-income countries.

Box 2.3 The scourge of the specific

For most products, most countries impose protection through *ad valorem* tariffs. This form of protection is more transparent than other types of tariffs, such as specific or compound tariffs. A 10 percent tariff rate raises the price of an imported good by the same 10 percent whether the good is a car worth $20,000 or a bicycle valued at $50. A specific tax of $50, by contrast, has an enormously different impact on the bicycle and the car. Further, the impact of the specific tariff depends on market conditions. If bicycle prices tumble to $20, then the specific tariff of $50 will raise prices by 250 percent instead of 100 percent.

Specific tariffs, which are very common on agricultural products, also are important on a number of industrial products of interest to developing countries, particularly textiles, clothing, and footwear. Recent research by Schott (2001) has revealed a striking tendency for poorer countries to export versions of many manufactured products with lower unit values than those exported by higher-income countries. As countries develop, they frequently upgrade their products, using more capital and skill to produce a better version of the same product. Schott finds that the unit value of a shirt from Japan, for instance, is 20 times that of the same good from the Philippines. In this situation, specific tariffs are likely to be much more of a burden on poorer developing countries than on industrial countries.

Ad valorem equivalents of specific tariffs are usually higher on imports from developing countries than from high-income countries

a. Ad valorem equivalent (AVE) protection on overcoat exports to the United States
Ad valorem equivalents of U.S. specific tariffs on overcoats (percent)

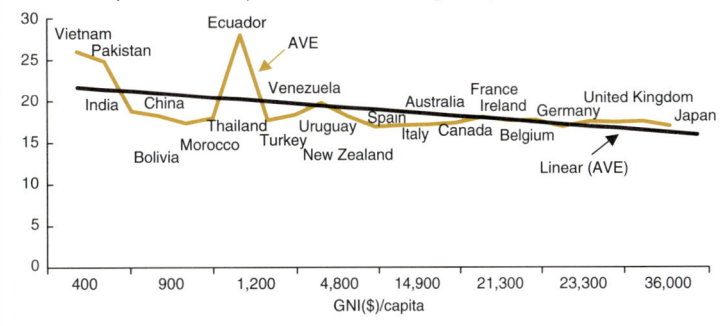

b. AVE tariffs on exports of leather shoes from Pakistan to Japan
Ad valorem equivalents of EU specific tariffs on leather shoes (percent)

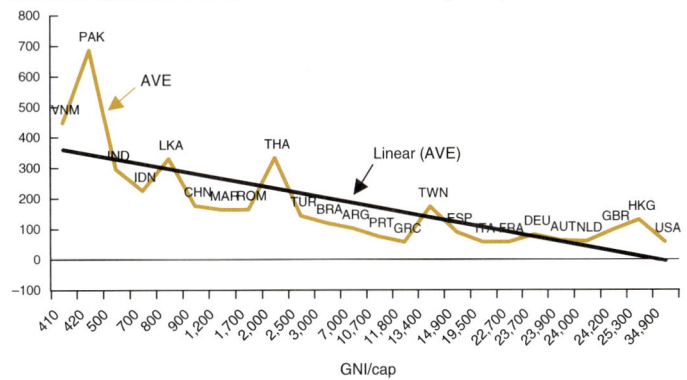

c. Ad valorem equivalent (AVE) protection on starch exports to the European Union
Ad valorem equivalents of EU specific tariffs on starch (percent)

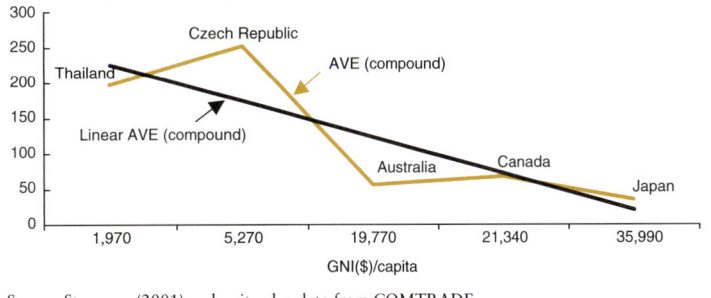

Source: Stawowy (2001) and unit value data from COMTRADE.

(Box continues on next page)

Box 2.3 (continued)

We draw on a detailed analysis of *ad valorem* equivalents undertaken at UNCTAD (Stawowy 2001) to compare these burdens across countries.

We find many cases where the *ad valorem* equivalents of specific tariffs are sharply higher on poor than on rich countries. The top figure shows, for instance, that Vietnam and Ecuador face tariffs on overcoats twice as high as Japan does—a type of discrimination covered up by the specific tariff. Exports of leather shoes from Pakistan to Japan feel the boot strongly—they are subject to tariffs of around 700 percent, while exports from the advanced industrial countries are taxed at less than 100 percent.

Also in the EU market, Japan pays less than 50 percent, while Thailand and the Czech Republic pay over 100 percent on their exports of starch—surely enough to stiffen resistance to this form of protection once the facts are known.

The nontransparency of specific tariffs, and the fact that they can discriminate so strongly against lower-income countries, are two good reasons for supporting proposals (WTO 2003a, Annex I) to eliminate specific tariffs under the Doha Development Agenda. The proposals for the elimination of specific tariffs clearly deserve strong support from everyone concerned about the welfare of the poor.

Using a formula is important

A key choice in multilateral market-access negotiations is whether to proceed using a "request-and-offer" approach or a formula approach. Under a request-and-offer approach, countries with major supply-and-demand interests in a particular area agree on bilateral tariff "concessions" that are then generalized to all other members on a most-favored-nation basis. As noted by Baldwin (1987), this approach was successful in achieving substantial reductions in protection under the GATT only in the initial Geneva Round of negotiations in 1947. The request-and-offer approach made disappointingly slow progress in the four following rounds of negotiations.[12] Only with the introduction of a comprehensive formula approach during the Kennedy Round (1963–67) was it again possible to cut protection substantially—35 percent versus an average of 2.5 percent in the previous four negotiations. The next round, the Tokyo Round (1974–79), used a more sophisticated formula, the so-called Swiss formula. It achieved a 30 percent reduction in average tariffs and brought down the higher tariffs by much more than the lower ones. Unfortunately, however, many products of particular interest to developing countries were excluded, partly because developing countries were not active *demandeurs* in these negotiations.

The Uruguay Round (1986–94) used a simpler approach for nonagricultural tariffs that involved setting broad tariff-reduction goals, such as a 30 percent reduction on industrial products, but left the distribution of the cut across sectors up to negotiations between trading partners. This approach was successful in achieving substantial tariff reductions. It was not, however, successful in achieving higher proportional cuts in higher tariff rates and thereby in reducing tariff escalation. Abreu (1996) observes that manufactured goods with higher tariff rates typically had smaller proportional tariff cuts.

In the Doha negotiations, there appears to be a broad consensus that some sort of formula will be required to obtain reductions in protection sufficiently broad-based to achieve increases in market access. The increase in the number of active participants seeking to use the WTO to achieve increases in market access—and to lock in reductions in tariffs—would make the one-on-one, request-and-offer procedures even less likely to succeed than they have in past GATT negotiations.

Some formulas are more prodevelopment than others

Even with a broad agreement to employ a formula, much needs to be done to bridge the gap among alternative approaches. Many different approaches have been proposed, and not all can be considered in this study, but examination of a few key proposals is instructive. In agriculture, the United States and the Cairns Group have proposed a Swiss-formula approach that would reduce all tariffs below 25 percent, regardless of their initial level. At the other end of the spectrum, Europe and Japan have proposed an approach involving a "headline" reduction of 36 percent that could easily be evaded, and only a 15 percent required reduction in individual tariffs. This would allow protection for Japanese rice, for example, to remain at close to 600 percent.

In nonagricultural market access, China, India, and Korea all have made proposals for formulas that would sharply reduce tariffs and reduce high tariffs relative to average tariffs. The European Union has advocated an approach involving different tiers for tariffs, an approach that would facilitate larger reductions in high tariffs relative to lower rates. Japan has proposed a formula that would give countries flexibility with individual tariffs but that would require larger reductions in average tariffs on high-tariff goods.

Adopting a formula that limits tariff peaks relative to average tariffs is important for developing countries. Some countries have proposed "flexible" approaches allowing retention of peak tariffs, while others have proposed approaches that sharply reduce peaks relative to other tariffs. Politically, it is frequently attractive to retain high tariffs on sensitive products where political support for protection is strong. This political convenience needs to be weighed against the adverse implications for the country itself, and for its trading partners, if high protection is retained in some sectors. Retaining high levels of protection in some sectors is likely to be costly to the importing economy because high rates of protection mean large distortions in production and consumption patterns. The economic costs of these distortions rise with the square of the tariff, so the costs of a tariff twice as high as the average are four times those of an average tariff. Further, high tariffs are inefficient in raising tariff revenues because the volume of imports across these tariff barriers is likely to be small.

From the point of view of developing-country exporters, approaches that allow countries to retain tariff peaks—and especially approaches that would allow the industrial countries to retain high peaks—are likely to be problematic for another reason. The tariff structures of most industrial countries involve quite low average tariffs as a result of the eight previous rounds of GATT/WTO negotiations. But they continue to contain many high peaks on products of particular interest to developing countries (Hoekman and Olarreaga 2002). The coefficient variation of industrial country tariffs—the variation relative to the average level—is now much higher in these countries than it is in developing countries, where the wave of tariff reductions during the 1980s and 1990s cut higher tariffs in line with average tariffs.

There is a particular concern with approaches that allow the retention of high peaks—such as the average-cut approach proposed by a number of high-protection countries in the negotiations on agricultural market access.[13] Such an approach, based on a meaningless measure, provides scope for evasion of countries' commitments in the Doha Development Agenda to reduce protection and to provide special and differential treatment in favor of developing countries.

A wide range of formulas is available, the effects of which depend upon a combination of factors, including the extent to which the formulas would reduce average rates of protection, as well as the variability of tariffs around that average (see box 2.4). An important issue to understand is the extent to which changing the dispersion of overall protection, for a given average cut in tariffs, affects the average reduction in protection facing developing coun-

Box 2.4 "Average cuts," the cut you have when you're not having a cut

Years ago, as concern grew about the impacts of drunk driving, the venerable Clayton's Nonalcoholic Tonic repositioned its advertising with the slogan "Clayton's, the drink you have when you're not having a drink." Macho individuals could still exhibit the bravado of having one or two "for the road" while avoiding the sharply increased penalties associated with drunk driving. Today, as concern builds about the adverse impacts of agricultural policy distortions for world trade, and particularly for developing country farmers, the notion of an average cut in tariffs takes on a similar tone. With this device, policymakers can commit to sharp cuts in agricultural protection without actually doing anything at all.

To see how this paradox arises, consider a putative agreement to cut agricultural protection by 50 percent in a country with just two agricultural tariffs—one of 1 percent and one of 100 percent. A cut of 100 percent in the 1 percent tariff, and of zero in the 100 percent tariff, yields the necessary 50 percent average cut in tariffs—great for the headlines.

But in reality, virtually nothing has been done. The average tariff has fallen by half of 1 percent, from 50.5 percent to 50 percent. Of course, policymakers could load the cuts onto the high tariff, taking the average tariff from 50.5 percent to 0.5 percent. It is unlikely that they would do this, however. The 100 percent tariff is high because it is supported by strong interest groups, which would surely oppose their industry being "sacrificed." The fundamental problem with the average-cut approach is that it provides no reward for cutting a high tariff rather than a low one, and hence allows policymakers to avoid the agreed goal of achieving substantial improvements in market access.

As we have seen, the "average-cut" approach provides little or no guidance on the effects of liberalization. It can be totally deceptive in its suggestion that sizable reductions in protection are required. Even when it is built into a tiered reduction in protection, such as the three-band system of tariff cuts with higher cuts in higher tariffs proposed in the Harbinson draft (WTO 2003c), the use of the average-cut approach makes the average cuts specified in each group almost meaningless, by providing an incentive to reduce the highest tariffs in each band by the smallest possible amount.

The proponents of the average-cut approach argue that more specific formulas are not acceptable because they do not provide the flexibility needed to reduce their agricultural tariffs. But, as we have seen, the average-cut approach provides complete flexibility to do nothing (or anything), and none of the discipline that is the *sine qua non* of world trade rules. To provide some discipline, proponents of the average-cut approach allow for a minimum cut in each tariff line. But this approach is extremely rigid unless the minimum cut is very low, in which case there is no discipline.

If the desire for flexibility made by the proponents of average cuts were accepted, what could be done to provide some discipline? Fortunately, there is a simple and nondeceptive alternative. A rule that specifies a "cut in average tariffs" would allow for flexibility while ensuring that protection was reduced on average, while providing some reward for cutting high tariffs, rather than low tariffs. The simple, but not purely semantic, move to a requirement for a cut in the average—rather than an average-cut—would preserve flexibility, while introducing some discipline.

Source: World Bank staff.

---

tries. Approaches that attack tariff peaks more aggressively will be more beneficial to developing countries, since developing countries face disproportionately high tariffs. Francois and Martin (2003) derive a flexible Swiss formula that allows higher tariffs to be addressed more or less aggressively for any given reduction in average tariffs. Francois, Martin, and Manole (2003) show that approaches that are more aggressive in reducing high rates of protection will result in larger cuts in average rates of protection faced by developing countries. Such approaches also reduce variation in tariffs, which is a major source of cost to the importing

Box 2.5 The implications of five tariff-cutting proposals

As is evident from the table, the proposal by China uses a Swiss-formula approach, but with a ceiling for each country based on the average level of its own tariffs (see Annex table 2A.1). After the application of the formula, all tariffs will be below the original average, and countries with higher average tariffs have tariff reductions that are, in percentage points, larger than those in countries with lower tariffs. Countries with more variable tariffs will, in general, face larger percentage reductions in tariffs, because the tariff peaks that give rise to variability are reduced very sharply. In industrial countries, the formula is applied to countries' applied tariff rates. In developing countries, the formula is generally applied to the average of applied and bound tariffs.

The proposal by the European Union seeks to compress the distribution of tariffs by dividing tariffs up into bands and applying higher proportional cuts on tariffs in higher bands. Tariffs below some threshold to be negotiated, such as 2 percent, are to be set to zero. A specific proposal to set the bands is offered in an addendum to the proposal, and it is that specific proposal that we analyzed.

The proposal by India involves making a proportional cut, of a magnitude to be negotiated, in all tariffs. The proportional cut in developing-country tariffs would be two-thirds of that in developed countries. After application of the formula, tariffs above three times the average would be reduced to three times the average after application of the formula. Bound tariff rates are to be used as the base rates, with unbound tariffs for each product to be replaced initially with the higher of the highest bound rate in its schedule, or the applied rate for that product. For illustrative purposes, we set the proportional cut at 50 percent.

The U.S. approach involves reducing to zero all tariffs of 5 percent or less. Then, a Swiss formula with a ceiling parameter of 0.08 is applied to all other tariffs. Applied rates, rather than bound rates, are generally used as the base. This approach is to be implemented by 2010, with all tariffs being reduced to zero by 2015.

The proposal by the chair of the Market Access Committee involves use of a Swiss formula with the ceiling parameter equal to each country's average tariff, scaled up or down by a parameter, B, to be negotiated. The base rate is to be the bound rate, unless the tariff line is unbound, in which case it is to be twice the applied rate. In addition, the proposal calls for reductions of tariffs to zero in a range of sectors, including electronics, fish, footwear, leather goods, motor vehicle parts, and textiles and clothing. In this initial assessment of the effects of the proposals, these elements—whose inclusion is still to be negotiated—have not been included.

Source: World Bank staff.

---

country (Martin, Van der Mensbrugghe, and Manole 2003).

A much wider range of approaches has been offered in the negotiations on nonagricultural market access than in agriculture (see chapter 3). We examine five proposals on market access for nonagricultural products that are sufficiently specific to allow analysis of their implications for tariffs—those from China, the European Union, India, the United States, and from the chair of the WTO's Market Access Committee. The implications of any of these formulas (box 2.5) depend heavily upon the base tariff rates to be cut, the approach taken to cutting, the treatment of tariffs that are initially unbound, and whether any supplementary provisions call for eliminating tariffs on particular groups of products. To gain some idea of the consequences of these measures, we examine their implications for tariffs facing low-income countries in four major markets—Brazil, the European Union, India, and the United States.

One key issue in any of the formulas is the selection of the base tariff rates. Traditionally, the GATT/WTO system has used bound rates as the basis for subsequent negotiations. As well as having the advantage of familiarity, this approach has an important dynamic advantage. If countries believe that bound rates will be the basis for future negotiations, they will feel free to reduce applied rates when they are convinced that this is in their economic interests. Negotiations based on bound rates embody a pure, one-for-one form of credit for such autonomous liberalization.[14] If a country chooses to reduce its applied rates below the bound level, then reductions in applied rates flowing from any future agreements to cut bound rates by a particular percentage will be smaller since any given cut in bound rates will require a correspondingly smaller reduction in applied rates. Use of applied rates as the base for tariff reductions creates potential incentives to increase applied rates and is certainly likely to have a chilling effect on future autonomous liberalization.

In examining the implications of the different formulas, we build on the analysis of WTO (2003b), which examines the implications of tariff reduction formulas for a hypothetical schedule of tariff bindings. We apply the tariff reduction formulas to the specified base tariffs (bound, applied, or a combination), and then examine the implications for applied rates by comparing the resulting tariff bindings with applied rates prior to the analysis. If the new binding is below the prior applied rate, then the new applied rate is reduced to the new bound rate. Table 2.11 presents weighted average tariffs for each of the four focus economies under each of the five proposals.

A striking feature of the results is just how sharply all five formula approaches reduce tariffs in the industrial-country markets considered. Average tariffs facing the low-income countries in the United States, for example, are reduced from 4.3 percent to 1.4 percent by the Chinese formula and 1.3 percent by the U.S. formula. All of the formulas also would substantially reduce the standard deviation of tariffs in the industrial countries—indicating that they would reduce tariff peaks sharply.

The situation in developing-country markets is considerably different, however. There, tariff reductions are much smaller as a proportion of the initial tariff rates—although not necessarily in percentage points of tariff, since the initial tariff rates are much higher. The smaller reductions as a percentage of initial tariffs are a reflection in large measure of the "tariff binding overhang"—the situation where tariff bindings are substantially above applied rates. They also reflect the smaller percentage reductions for developing countries inherent in India's formula, as well as India's proposal to allow unbound tariffs to be set at the highest binding in the schedule, or at the applied rate for the commodity being liberalized, whichever is higher. The U.S. formula would lead to substantial reductions in applied tariffs in India and Brazil, with tariffs facing low-income exporters falling to 6 percent in India and 5 percent in Brazil. The EU formula also would result in large cuts in applied rates in developing countries, with tariffs facing low-income exporters falling to 10.8 in India and just over 8 percent in Brazil, a striking finding given that this approach is based on bound tariff rates.

A key issue is whether the reductions in tariffs are to be measured using percentage cuts in tariffs or alternative measures, such as the percentage-point reduction in tariffs or the percentage-point reduction in the price of imports brought about by the tariff reduction.[15] As noted above, only the U.S. formula and, to a lesser extent, the European formula, bring about large percentage-point reductions in tariffs in India or Brazil. If however, progress is measured in terms of the percentage-point cut in tariffs or the percentage-point cut in import prices, then the reductions in India and Brazil look much more substantial, even under the Indian formula or the Chinese formula, where the percentage cut in tariffs is relatively small. Clearly, much patient analysis will be required to assess the consequences of the proposed reforms for individual countries—and a lot of hard bargaining before WTO members are likely to agree on a specific package of re-

Table 2.11 Competing formulas make a big difference for tariffs
Weighted average on tariffs (percent) for Brazil, European Union, India, and the United States under various proposed formulas

Affected area	Formula	Applied tariff, average	Applied tariffs, weighted average, low-income countries	Applied tariffs, weighted average, middle-income countries	Standard deviation
Brazil	Initial tariff	15.95	14.55	14.00	5.96
	Chinese formula	12.34	11.47	10.17	3.49
	European formula	10.11	9.66	8.14	2.51
	Indian formula	15.50	14.20	12.28	5.83
	U.S. formula	5.04	4.71	4.00	1.20
	Chairman's formula B=2	15.60	14.20	12.37	5.68
	Chairman's formula B=1	13.33	12.17	10.64	4.08
European Union	Initial tariff	4.18	5.28	3.76	3.72
	Chinese formula	1.85	1.99	1.45	1.14
	European formula	2.06	2.67	1.87	2.02
	Indian formula	1.94	2.49	1.78	1.77
	U.S. formula	1.29	1.73	1.23	1.87
	Chairman's formula B=2	2.18	2.52	1.80	1.64
	Chairman's formula B=1	1.56	1.74	1.25	1.08
India	Initial tariff	32.99	28.12	26.71	8.57
	Chinese formula	28.19	24.09	21.98	8.48
	European formula	11.98	11.24	10.82	1.90
	Indian formula	28.30	24.23	21.96	8.67
	U.S. formula	6.31	5.93	5.71	0.73
	Chairman's formula B=2	29.40	25.15	22.96	8.14
	Chairman's formula B=1	23.78	20.99	19.36	5.82
United States	Initial tariff	3.70	4.26	3.23	4.53
	Chinese formula	1.40	1.35	1.11	1.14
	European formula	1.76	2.10	1.56	2.20
	Indian formula	1.50	1.69	1.25	1.67
	U.S. formula	1.00	1.31	0.82	1.80
	Chairman's formula B=2	1.63	1.75	1.37	1.59
	Chairman's formula B=1	1.13	1.17	0.95	1.03

Source: World Bank staff.

forms. We hope that the analysis presented here will make an important contribution to clarifying the issues and tradeoffs involved in these choices.

Putting development into the Doha Development Agenda requires serious liberalization

Although trade policy reform has contributed to an unprecedented shift in export composition and trade growth, the next steps will be difficult. Today's protection remains heavily concentrated in the most politically sensitive areas—textiles, clothing, and other labor-intensive manufactures, as well as agriculture—in both rich and poor countries. In nonagricultural goods, three efforts are particularly crucial:

- First, the progressive phase-out of quotas under the Agreement on Textiles and Clothing, now lagging, is critical to providing market access for developing countries. Reforms in current quota-holding countries may be necessary to ensure a smooth adjustment.

- Second, efforts to cut back antidumping measures that create a patchwork of ad hoc protection are essential if market access granted by the right hand, through quota elimination and tariff reductions, is not to be withdrawn by the left hand of new access-restricting antidumping suits.
- Third, moving forward in nonfarm trade requires a Swiss-formula, or related top-down approach, that will require disproportionately greater reductions in high tariffs so as to mitigate antidevelopment policy embedded in trade regimes around the world. The choice of the formula, and of its coefficients of reduction, is important.

Much must be done behind the border to ensure that countries that have missed out during the current wave of international integration will be able to take advantage of the opportunities provided by a more streamlined and development-friendly trading system. If these measures are adopted—along with others associated with agricultural trade, labor mobility, and the special treatment some developing countries enjoy—then the promise of the Doha Development Agenda may be realized.

Table 2A.1 The various liberalization proposals have very different features

Features of trade liberalization proposals advanced by China, the European Union, India, the United States, and the Chair of the WTO Market Access Committee

Proposal	Base rate (T_0)	Unbound tariff	Sectoral tariff elimination	Formula
China	Developed: applied rate Developing: simple average of applied and bound rate			$T_1 = \left(\dfrac{(A + B \times P) \times T_0}{(A + P^2) + T_0} \right)$ A: Simple average of T_0 $P = T_0/A$ B=3 for 2010, B=1 for 2015
European Union	Bound rate	Applied duty, November 14, 2001		$T_1 = B_1^L + (T_0 - B_0^L) \times \left[\dfrac{B_1^U - B_1^L}{B_0^U - B_0^L} \right]$ B_0^L and B_0^U are lower and upper limits in the base bracket B_1^L and B_1^U in the new bracket
India	Bound rate	Higher of maximum bound rate and applied rate on cut-off date		Step 1. $T_1 = (1 - (A \times Y / 100)) \times T_0$ A=1 for developed countries A=0.67 for developing countries Step 2. Minimum of T_1 and three times the average of results from Step 1
United States	Lesser of applied rate and bound rate		Wood products; non-ferrous metals; bicycle parts; soda ash; photographic film; electronics; fish and fishery products; scientific equipment; environmental goods; Information Technology Agreement (ITA) products and goods covered by the Agreement on Trade in Civil Aircraft, Uruguay Round zero-for-zero sectors	Step 1. Period to 2010. $T_1 = 0 \quad\quad\quad\quad\;\, if\ T_0 \leq 5\%$ $T_1 = \dfrac{8 \times T_0}{8 + T_0} \quad if\ T_0 > 5\%$ Step 2. From 2015, all tariffs go to zero.
Chair, WTO Market Access Committee	Bound rate	Two times the MFN applied rate (2001). If MFN applied rate is zero, then 5 percent.	Electronics and electrical goods; fish and fish products; footwear; leather goods; motor vehicle parts and components; stones, gems, and precious metals; and textiles and clothing	$T_1 = \dfrac{B \times T_a \times T_0}{B \times T_a + T_0}$ T_a is the initial average tariff B is a coefficient to be determined

Source: WTO.

Notes

1. One potential concern with any measure of the share of particular exports is the impact of price changes. If, for instance, changes in the observed shares of exports reflect primarily changes in prices over the sample, then they might be reversed by subsequent price changes. It is difficult to fully adjust for price changes, but at least a crude indication was obtained by deflating each component of exports by a suitable deflator and comparing the result with undeflated export shares. It appears that the changes in shares have primarily been the result of changes in the volume of exports. This implies that they are much more likely to be sustained than changes resulting only from changes in the prices of particular export goods. Increases in the prices of resources—and particularly oil—have caused increases in the importance of exports of these goods in the past, but these have been reversed by subsequent price declines.

2. The use of categories defined by income status at the beginning of the sample period makes an enormous difference. If we define our low-income sample by income status at the end of the period, the trade growth rate of the low-income group is below average.

3. This analysis was undertaken using the 1997 input-output data from the Global Trade Analysis Project (GTAP), input-output information for 1997, and the GTAP time series database of trade and trade patterns. See Hummels, Ishii, and Yi (2001) for precise definitions of these measures.

4. While the resistances to integration graphically captured in the book "Why the Emperor's New Clothes Are Not Made in Colombia" (Morawetz 1981) have certainly abated, the continuing low level of integration suggests the continued existence of considerable resistance to the level of integration associated with global production sharing.

5. The growth performance of this region is biased upward because of large-scale under-reporting of trade prior to 1990.

6. The rise in the price of factor inputs and the prices of nontraded goods is frequently identified as the real exchange rate appreciation associated with protection policies.

7. This is an underestimate of the costs imposed by protection on exporters. In addition, tariffs raise costs by raising the costs of nontraded goods and nontraded factors of protection. This adverse impact, the so-called real exchange rate effect, should also be taken into account.

8. Baldwin (1987) estimates that the average tariff reductions by the industrial countries were 35 percent in the Kennedy Round and 30 percent in the Tokyo Round.

9. Details on the barriers faced by individual countries on individual products in particular markets can be obtained using the WITS software (see www.wits.worldbank.org).

10. Another justification might be that such rules guide members toward good policy actions—actions that advance the national economic interest of the members that apply them. This historically is not the rationale for their inclusion in the GATT/WTO. Empirically, extensive research has shown that antidumping actions are not "good" protection, they are ordinary protection with a good public relations program.

11. The average of rates actually applied is thus at least as high as the lower figure, no higher than the higher figure.

12. A simple formula was first tried out in the Dillon Round (Ernest Preeg, personal communication).

13. This approach focuses on achieving specified average tariff cuts, rather than cuts in the average. Unfortunately, a given average cut can likely be achieved with minimum political impact by imposing large cuts in the lowest tariffs, rather than the large cuts in the highest tariffs that are economically desirable.

14. Approaches that use historical applied rates, such as applied rates at the end of the Uruguay Round, would also have this feature of providing credit for subsequent, autonomous liberalization.

15. This measure, which involves measuring the change in the tariff rate divided by one plus the tariff rate, is widely used in analytical work, and reported extensively in Finger, Ingco, and Reincke (1996).

References

Abreu, M. 1996. "Trade in Manufactures, the Outcome of the Uruguay Round, and Developing Country Interests." In Will Martin and L. Alan Winters, eds., *The Uruguay Round and the Developing Countries*. Cambridge: Cambridge University Press.

Amiti, M. 2003. "How the Sequence of Trade Liberalization Affects Industrial Location." Mimeo, January 17. World Bank, Washington, D.C.

Baldwin, R. E. 1987. "Multilateral Liberalization." In J. Michael Finger and A. Olechowski, eds., *The Uruguay Round: a Handbook for the Multilateral Trade Negotiations*. World Bank, Washington D.C.

Bhardwaj, A., S. Kathuria, and Will Martin. 2001. "Implications for South Asian Countries of Abolishing the Multifibre Arrangement." Policy Research Working Paper 2721. World Bank, Washington, D.C.

Bloch, H., and D. Sapsford. 2000. "Whither the Terms of Trade: an Elaboration of the Prebisch/Singer

Hypothesis." *Cambridge Journal of Economics* 24: 461–81.
Brenton, Paul. 2003. "Integrating the Least Developed Countries into the World Trading System: The Current Impact of EU Preferences under Everything But Arms." Policy Research Working Paper 3018. World Bank, Washington, D.C.
Cadot, O., J. de Melo, and Marcelo Olarreaga. 2002. "The Protectionist Bias of Duty Drawbacks: Evidence from Mercosur." *Journal of Development Economics* 59 (1): 161–82.
Corden, M. 1997. *Trade Policy and Economic Welfare, 2nd edition.* Oxford: Oxford University Press.
Deardorff, A. 2001. "International Provision of Trade Services, Trade and Fragmentation." *Review of International Economics* 9 (2): 233–48.
de Ferranti, D., G. Perry, D. Lederman, and W. Maloney. 2002. *From Natural Resources to the Knowledge Economy: Trade and Job Quality.* Latin America and Caribbean Studies, World Bank, Washington, D.C.
Dollar, D., M. Hallward-Driemeier, and T. Mengistae. 2003. "Investment Climate and Firm Performance in Developing Economies." Mimeo, March 5. World Bank, Washington, D.C.
Elbehri, A., T. Hertel, and Will Martin. 2003. "Estimating the Impact of WTO and Domestic Reforms on the Indian Cotton Industry." *Review of Development Economics* 7 (3):343–59.
Evenett, Simon J., and A. Venables. 2003. "Export Growth by Developing Countries: Market Entry and Bilateral Trade." Mimeo. World Trade Institute, Berne, Switzerland.
Finger, J. Michael, Ingco M.D., and U. Reincke. 1996. "The Uruguay Round: Statistics on Tariff Concessions Given and Received." World Bank, Washington, D.C.
François, J., and Will Martin. 2003. "Formula Approaches for Market Access Negotiations." *World Economy* 26 (1):1–28.
François, J., Will Martin, and V. Manole. 2003. "Choosing Formulas for Market Access Negotiations." Revised version of paper prepared for *Festschrift* conference for Professor Peter Lloyd, Melbourne.
François, J., and D. Spinanger. 2002. "China Accession, ATC Phaseout, and Market Access in Textiles and Clothing." Mimeo. Erasmus University, Rotterdam.
Hoekman, B. and M. Olarreaga. 2002. "Une proposition pour l'OMC: La « Super » clause de Nation Plus Favorisée." *Reflets et Perspectives de la Vie Economique*, XLI, 2.
Hummels, D. 2001. "Time as a Trade Barrier." Mimeo. Krannert School of Management, Purdue University, West Lafayette, Ind.

Hummels, D., and P. Klenow. 2002. "The Variety and Quality of a Nation's Trade." Working Paper 8712. National Bureau of Economic Research, Cambridge, Mass.
Hummels, D., J. Ishii, and K.M. Yi. 2001. "The Nature and Growth of Vertical Specialization in World Trade." *Journal of International Economics* 54:75–96.
Ianchovichina, E. 2003. "GTAP-DD: A Model for Analyzing Trade Reforms in the Presence of Duty Drawbacks." GTAP Technical Paper 21, Center for Global Trade Analysis, Department of Agricultural Economics, Purdue University, Layfayette, Ind. [www.gtap.org.]
Ianchovichina, E., and Will Martin. 2001. "Trade Liberalization in China's Accession to the WTO." *Journal of Economic Integration* 16 (4): 421–45.
———. 2003. "Economic Impacts of China's Accession to the WTO." World Bank, Washington, D.C. [www.worldbank.org/trade]
Kehoe, T., and K. Ruhl. 2002. "How Important is the New Goods Margin in International Trade?" Mimeo. University of Minnesota, Minn.
Madani, D. 1999. "A Review of the Role and Impact of Export Processing Zones." Policy Research Working Paper 2238. World Bank, Washington, D.C.
Martin, Will. 1993. "The Fallacy of Composition and Developing Country Exports of Manufactures." *World Economy* 16 (2): 159–72.
Martin, W., van der Mensbrugghe D., and V. Manole. 2003. "Is the devil in the details?: Assessing the Welfare Implications of Agricultural and Nonagricultural Trade Reform." World Bank Working Paper forthcoming, World Bank, Washington, D.C.
Morawetz, D. 1981. Why the Emperor's New Clothes are not Made in Colombia: a Case Study in Latin American and East Asian Exports. Washington, D.C.: Oxford University Press for the World Bank.
Nehru, V., and A. Dhareshwar. 1993. "A New Database on Physical Capital Stock: Sources, Methodology, and Results." *Revisita de Análisís Económico* 8 (1): 37–59.
Nehru, V., E. Swanson, and A. Dubey. 1995. "A New Database on Human Capital Stock in Developing and Industrial Countries: Sources, Methodology, and Results." *Journal of Development Economics* 46: 379–401.
OECD (Organisation for Economic Co-operation and Development). 2002. *Monitoring and Outlook Report.* Paris.
Pritchett, L. 1997. "Divergence, Big Time." *Journal of Economic Perspectives* 11 (3): 3–17.

_____. 2000. "The Tyranny of Concepts: CUDIE (Cumulated, Depreciated Investment Effort) Is Not Capital." *Journal of Economic Growth* 5: 361–84.

_____. 2001. "Where Has All the Education Gone?" *World Bank Economic Review* 15 (3): 367–91.

Redding, Stephen, and Anthony Venables. 2001. "Economic Geography and International Inequality." CEP Working Paper 495. London School of Economics, London.

Schott, P. 2001. "Do Rich and Poor Countries Specialize in a Different Mix of Goods? Evidence from Product-Level U.S. Trade Data." Working Paper 8492. National Bureau of Economic Research, Cambridge, Mass.

_____. 2002. "Across-Product Versions Within-Product Specialization in International Trade." Mimeo. Yale School of Management, New Haven, Conn.

_____. 2003. "One Size Fits All? Heckscher-Ohlin Specialization in Global Production." *American Economic Review* 93(3): 686–708.

Stawowy, Wojciech. 2001. "Calculation of *Ad Valorem* Equivalents of Non-*Ad Valorem* Tariffs." Mimeo, UNCTAD, October.

Todaro, M. 1994. *Economic Development*. New York: Longman.

World Bank. 2000. *Global Economic Prospects 2001*. Washington, D.C.

World Bank. 2002. *Global Economic Prospects 2003*. Washington, D.C.

World Bank. 2003. *World Development Indicators*. Washington, D.C.

WTO. 2001. "Ministerial Declaration." Document WT/MIN(01)/DEC/1, November 20.

WTO. 2003a. "Draft Elements of Modalities for Negotiations on Non-Agricultural Products." World Trade Organization, Negotiating Group on Market Access, TN/MA/W/35, Geneva.

WTO. 2003b. Formula Approaches to Tariff Negotiations: Note by the Secretariat." Document TN/MA/S/Rev 2, April 11.

WTO. 2003c. "Negotiations on Agriculture: First Draft of Modalities for the Further Comments." Document TN/AG/W/1/Rev. 1, March 18.

Yang, Y., W. Martin, and K. Yanagishima. 1997. "Evaluating the Benefits of Abolishing the MFA in the Uruguay Round Package." In T. Herteb, ed., *Global Trade Analysis: Modeling and Applications*. Cambridge, Mass.: Cambridge University Press.

3

Agricultural Policies and Trade

Trade in agriculture is important to the world's poor—
Agriculture is the largest employer in low-income countries, accounting for about 60 percent of the labor force and producing about 25 percent of GDP. Even in middle-income countries, where agriculture's share of GDP is only about 15 percent, the sector still accounts for more than 25 percent of employment. When coupled with agro-related industries and food-related services, its share, even among middle-income countries, is typically 25 to 40 percent of GDP. About 73 percent of the poor in developing countries live in rural areas. Rural development, therefore, is central to alleviating poverty.

Government policy has heavily distorted agricultural performance in both developing and developed countries. Until the 1990s, industrial countries generally protected agriculture, whereas developing countries generally taxed it (Schiff and Valdes 1992). Industrial countries supported their agricultural sectors through subsidies to producers, high tariffs, and other nontariff measures such as import restrictions and quotas.

—but agricultural policies have often worked to the detriment of the poor
Most of the developing countries generated the bulk of their agricultural GDP in lower-efficiency production for the domestic market, supplying the world market with tropical commodities that could not easily be produced in the industrial countries. In products for which they competed with industrial countries, such as sugar and beef, some countries could export limited amounts under preferential-access programs. In an effort to generate public revenues from commercialized export activities, governments levied export taxes on agricultural products while protecting manufacturing through high import tariffs and other import restrictions. Even for agricultural products that were not exported, price controls, exchange rate policies, and other restrictions kept prices low for urban consumption.

In the last decade, developing countries shifted from taxing agriculture to protecting it. Import restrictions on manufactured products have declined dramatically, exchange rates have been devalued, multiple-exchange-rate systems penalizing agriculture have been abandoned, and export taxes have effectively disappeared (World Bank 2000; Jansen, Robinson, and Tarp 2002; Quiroz and Opazo 2000). Meanwhile, reforms in most industrial countries, including many of the successful middle-income countries, have been modest—despite the inclusion of agriculture under the World Trade Organization (WTO) in the Uruguay Round of international trade negotiations. The result of these policies has been overproduction and price declines in many commodities, reducing opportunities for many developing countries to expand exports and penalizing the world's poor.

Consequently, although developing countries have almost doubled their share of world trade in manufactures over the last two decades, their share in agricultural trade has been stuck at around 30 percent. During the 1990s, the growth of developing-country agricultural exports to industrial countries slowed as exports to other developing countries accelerated. During this period, 56 percent of the growth of developing-country agricultural trade was accounted for by sales to other developing countries and 44 percent by sales to industrial countries. The middle-income countries have managed to increase global market share, principally by entering into other developing countries' markets and by aggressively diversifying into nontraditional exports, such as seafood products, fruits, vegetables, cut flowers, and processed foods. Growth of these nontraditional exports has outpaced growth of traditional commodities by three to one. Meanwhile, many low-income countries, except for China, have had less success—their share of world agricultural trade has declined.

High border protection in rich countries frustrates development

These patterns reflect—among other things—the structure of global protection. Border protection in rich countries continues to be high, nontransparent, and antidevelopment. Average agricultural tariffs in industrial countries, when they can be measured, are two to four times higher than manufacturing tariffs. In addition, about 28 percent of domestic production in countries belonging to the Organisation for Economic Co-operation and Development (OECD) is protected by tariff rate quotas (TRQs). More than 40 percent of the tariff lines in the European Union (EU) and United States contain specific duties, which make it difficult to calculate average tariffs and obscure actual levels of protection. Tariff peaks as high as 500 percent confront imports from developing countries. Tariffs also increase by degree of processing, creating a highly escalating tariff structure that limits access for processed foods. Preferences do not compensate for these high levels. In the United States, only 34 percent of agricultural imports from countries covered by the Generalized System of Preferences (GSP) were eligible for preferences, and 26 percent of imports received them. Developing countries, too, have maintained high border protection and, on average, have higher agricultural tariffs than industrial countries. However, direct comparisons are difficult because of the complex nature of protection in industrial countries.

Within OECD countries, budget subsidies and transfers from consumers (from high tariffs and quantitative restrictions on domestic production of selected commodities) amounted to about $250 billion in 1999–2001. This protection decreased from 62 percent of farm revenues in 1986–88 to 49 percent in 1999–2001—still a very high percentage. Of this support, 70 percent came from consumers via higher prices associated with border protection and 30 percent from direct subsidies. In developing countries, almost all support is generated by border barriers. A silver lining to this dark cloud is that some developed-country subsidies have been at least partially delinked from levels of production, lowering the incentive to overproduce. These partially decoupled subsidies increased from 9 percent of total subsidies in 1996–98 to more than 20 percent in 1999–01.

Although official export subsidies may be small and shrinking, *effective* export subsidies created by domestic support are increasing, lending unfair advantage to industrial country producers. Currently, cotton is not classified as receiving export subsidies. Its domestic and export prices in the United States and the European Union are the same—and those prices are less than half the cost of production. Similar differences exist in many other products, a gap that will increase as industrial countries move from protection through border barriers to support through coupled or partially decoupled subsidies.

Success in the Doha Round requires reductions in agricultural protection

To be meaningful for the world's poor, the Doha Round must bring reductions in agricultural protection around the world. The benefits of global liberalization in agriculture—elimination of all border barriers and subsidies—are estimated to be very large for industrial and developing countries alike, topping $350 billion for the world. With liberalization, agricultural production would marginally shift from North to South, and the highly depressed world prices for many commodities would increase: 10–20 percent for cotton, 20–40 percent for dairy products, 10–20 percent for groundnuts, 33–90 percent for rice, and 20–40 percent for sugar (Beghin and Aksoy 2003). The impact of these price changes on low-income net importers would be small and manageable. To date, however, many of the proposals designed to elicit consensus on agricultural reform are modest. The average applied tariffs in the Quad countries would be halved at best under such proposals. Tariff peaks would remain above 100 percent for many countries. The outcomes for developing countries are even less significant. For most of them, the cuts required by one prominent proposal would leave their bound tariffs above their current applied rates, and tariff escalation and peaks would still be very high.

A serious agreement to reduce border protections would produce benefits for the world's poor that far exceed those that can be anticipated from present levels of development assistance. A first order of business is to create a more transparent and simpler trade regime in all countries by converting specific tariffs to ad valorem tariffs, eliminating minimum price regulations, cutting peak tariffs, changing the structure of TRQs so they increase over time, and introducing a transparent system of reallocation to more efficient producers. Rich countries should phase out export subsidies and subsidies that encourage overproduction, both of which are directly prejudicial to poor farmers around the world.

These reforms would also make the agriculture in industrial countries more efficient, environmentally sustainable, and more supportive of the small family farms. The experience of New Zealand, the only OECD country to reform fully, clearly demonstrates that agriculture without support can be more dynamic and efficient.

Finally, along with greater market access, low-income countries need help in eliminating behind-the-border barriers, especially the segmentation of their rural markets. Those markets should be linked to wider markets at home and abroad (box 3.1).

Poverty, rural households, and trade in agriculture

Agriculture is the livelihood of the world's poor

Growth in agriculture has a disproportionate effect on poverty because more than half of the population in developing countries resides in rural areas.[1] Some 57 percent of the developing world's rural population live in lower-middle-income countries; 15 percent in the least developed countries (LDCs).[2] Although most of the world's poor countries are in Sub-Saharan Africa, they account for about only 12 percent of developing world's rural population, whereas Asia accounts for 65 percent.

Using the $1-a-day measure of poverty, most of the world's poor live in India, China, and other lower-middle-income countries (table 3.1). National poverty data—which allow separation of rural and urban household information but are not available for all countries—yield results that are very similar to those obtained using the $1-a-day measure. They show that four countries—India, Bangladesh, China, and Indonesia—account for 75 percent of the world's rural poor. It is in Asia, therefore, that rural income growth will have the greatest impact on rural poverty.

Poverty is more common in rural areas

In countries for which separate rural and urban income data are available, 63 percent of the population, and 73 percent of the poor, live in rural areas. This is true for all regions.

A high incidence of rural poverty is found in all developing countries, whatever their level of income. More of the population is poor in low-

GLOBAL ECONOMIC PROSPECTS 2004

Box 3.1 The impact of national trade integration and reform on poverty

Poverty in rural areas of low-income countries is closely correlated with distance to local and national markets. In addition to geographic distance, the concept of distance to market includes various costs of moving goods to and from markets.

Case studies in Armenia, Malawi, and Nepal show that reductions in transportation costs bring strong gains in household welfare for individual farmers. Among these households, the poorer ones benefit disproportionately because transportation costs make up a larger percentage of their household expenditures.

Case studies in Ethiopia and Guinea reveal that many of the poor will be left behind by trade reform if no improvements are made in domestic markets. In Ethiopia, for example, 80 percent of the poor would benefit from freer trade under conditions of full market participation and price transmission, but only 55 percent would benefit without these conditions. Without improvements in the functioning of local and national markets, economic gains for the poor may reach only one-fourth of their potential.

A case study in Madagascar illustrates that improvements in trade policies may not be sufficient to restore sustained growth in the agricultural sector without better transport infrastructure and other reforms. In Madagascar, where poverty is closely related to remoteness, defined to include lack of infrastructure and access to basic services, integrating the poor into regional markets and the national economy will make a real contribution to increasing their incomes. In the absence of integration, economic growth will tend to benefit those who are already favored.

Source: Kudat, Ajwad, and Sivri (2003).

income countries, however, and in the LDCs the poverty rate for rural households reaches almost 82 percent (table 3.2). The rural share of the total number of poor households is declining with urbanization. Still, with current trends, the rural share of the global number of poor will not fall below 50 percent before 2035 (Ravallion 2000).

Most poor countries are very dependent on agriculture for household income. In Ethiopia and Malawi, for example, about three-quarters of household income is derived from agricultural activities, mainly subsistence farming. But cash income is also crucial (table 3.3). Whether derived from cash (export) crops or other sources, cash income allows farmers to

Table 3.1 Most of the world's poor live in rural areas outside the least developed countries
Distribution of poor in developing countries (1999)

	Population in millions (2001)			Percent rural	Percentage of world's rural population	Poverty headcount, under $1/day in 1999	
	National	Rural	Urban			(percent)	(millions)
Least developed countries	596	443	153	74	15	49	292
Other low income	839	501	338	60	17	26	218
Middle income[a]	1,435	478	957	33	16	8	114
China	1,272	805	467	63	27	18	226
India	1,032	745	288	72	25	35	358
Total	5,175	2,972	2,203	57	100	23	1,209

a. Excluding China and India.
Source: World Bank data.

AGRICULTURAL POLICIES AND TRADE

Table 3.2 Rural poverty is higher in poorer countries
Share of national population and of poor living in rural areas (percent)

	Sample[a] Rural dwellers	Sample[a] Share of rural dwellers who are poor	All developing countries Rural dwellers
Upper middle income	19	37	22
Lower middle income	64	72	61
Low income	65	74	60
Least developed	76	82	68
All developing countries	63	73	56

a. Sample consists of 52 countries for which separate rural and urban income data are available.
Source: World Bank data.

Table 3.3 Even in subsistence economies, cash is important
Percentage of total household income derived from various sources in rural areas, 1990s

	Ethiopia	Malawi	Mexico
Total agricultural income	77	76	24
Agricultural cash income	18	16	21
Subsistence farming	59	60	3
Transfers	16	7	13
Wages	3	8	42
Other	4	9	21
Total	100	100	100

Source: World Bank household data.

buy inputs—such as fertilizers—that increase food-crop yields, lowering the incidence of poverty and malnutrition.

The share of nonfarm income in rural households increases with a country's level of development. In Mexico, for example, the share of farm income in total rural income is much lower than in Ethiopia and Malawi. Incomes from farming are complemented by other sources, so that the direct impact of agricultural price and output variations have a much smaller impact on rural households. In industrial countries, when a broad definition of farm households is adopted, the share of farm income declines even further. Other sources of income include salaries and wages from other activities; investment income such as interest, dividends, and rents; and social transfers from health, pension, unemployment, and child-allowance schemes.

Farmers in industrial countries earn above-average incomes

In many industrial countries, the average incomes of farmers are higher than the national average, reaching almost 250 percent of average income for the Netherlands, 175 percent for Denmark, 160 percent for France, and 110 percent for the United States and Japan. In most other countries, the level of income is either equal to or marginally lower than the average income (OECD 2002d). In lower income OECD countries such as Greece, Korea, and Turkey, rural incomes are lower—around 75–80 percent of urban incomes.

As countries become wealthier, the share of rural household income from nonfarm sources rises. Off-farm income for major field crops in the United States, for example, is more than ten times greater than farm income and eight times greater than government payments (table 3.4) Government payments exceed what U.S. farmers make from the market in farming. In fact, most farms lose money from farming alone.[3]

Of agricultural subsidies, only half reaches farmers, and most goes to the richest

Agricultural protection in industrial countries helps the relatively better-off rural households—and it does so very inefficiently.[4] Ac-

Table 3.4 U.S. farmers earn less from farming than from other sources
Shares of U.S. farmers' income from various sources (billions of dollars)

Income source	Value
Farming	11.6
Government payments	14.7
Off-farm activities	122.7

Source: USDA, "Agricultural Income and Finance Outlook," September 26, 2002.

107

cording to OECD estimates, agricultural support policies deliver additional income to farm households at a rate of 50 percent *or less* of the amounts transferred from consumers and taxpayers for support purposes (OECD 2002e). In the case of market price support and deficiency payments, the share is one-fourth or less; for input subsidies, less than one-fifth. Only one-quarter of every dollar of producer support actually finds its way into the producer's pocket—the rest goes to input suppliers and owners of other factors of production (OECD 1999, De Gorter 2003). The most important outcome of these programs is that they lead to much higher land prices.

The largest farm operations, which generally are also the most profitable and the wealthiest, receive most of the benefits of support systems. In the United States, the largest 25 percent of farms have average gross farm receipts of more than $275,000 and average farm net worth of more than $780,000. They receive 89 percent of all support—in part because they produce a similar share of output. The remaining 1.6 million U.S. farms on average receive little support. Through the lens of household income surveys, the story is similar: At one extreme, farm households with an average income of $275,000 received payments averaging $32,000. At the other end of the spectrum, farm households with incomes averaging $13,000 received $2,200 in program payments.

In the European Union, where farm numbers and structures differ somewhat, the distribution of support is not markedly different. The largest 25 percent of farms have average gross farm receipts of more than €180,000 and average farm net worth of almost €500,000. They produce 73 percent of farm output and receive 70 percent of support. Farms of the next largest size have much smaller gross farm receipts, averaging just over €43,000, and average farm net worth of about €230,000. They produce 17 percent of output and receive 19 percent of support payments. The remaining 2 million EU farms produce little, receive little support, but have a sizeable average farm net worth. In Japan and Canada, the largest 25 percent of farms receive 68 percent and 70 percent of support payments, respectively.

In short, the subsidy programs prominent in current food and agriculture policy are not targeted to keeping small, struggling family farms in business but instead provide hefty rents to large farmers. Nor are current production-based policies effective in achieving their various other objectives (such as environmental sustainability and rural development). By increasing land prices they also lead to the creation of larger farms and the elimination of small family farms. Meanwhile, their unintended spillover effects on global markets, and on other countries, are large and negative.

At the most general level, it is probable that agricultural protection in rich countries worsens global income distribution. First, farmers in the North earn more on average than their own national averages. Second, the lion's share of farm aid goes to the largest and wealthiest farmers. At the other end of the global distribution spectrum, more of the poor tend to live in rural areas, and protection in rich countries tends to depress prices and demand for their goods.

International markets are important to sustained income growth in developing countries

When subsidies depress prices the impacts in poor countries can be severe. To illustrate the impact of commodity price changes, Minot and Daniels (2002) used household income data to estimate the potential impact of cotton price declines in Benin and tobacco price declines in Malawi, the major export crops of those two countries. Cotton prices have declined by almost 40 percent over the last few years. In Benin, a poor country, the impact of this decline in world cotton prices, if it were fully passed on to farmers, would reduce overall welfare in rural areas by 6–7 percent and that of cotton farmers by about 19 percent. The richest quintile of households, meanwhile, would experience a decline in income of 4 per-

AGRICULTURAL POLICIES AND TRADE

cent. Thus this price change alone would increase the poverty rate in Benin by up to 8 percentage points (depending on the simulations), from 40 percent to 48 percent.

Tobacco constitutes about 80 percent of Malawi's exports. A 30 percent decrease in world tobacco prices over the last few years has reduced the income of small growers by an average of 8 percent. The poorest quintile has lost about 13 percent, the richest 7 percent. For a typical farmer, the annual net returns from tobacco, the country's most profitable crop, declined from $108 to $26 (Integrated Framework 2003). These rough estimates understate the overall impact of the price declines, however, because cash incomes allow farmers to purchase inputs, such as fertilizer and pesticides, that increase the yields for their subsistence crops and have a significant impact on their levels of poverty and malnutrition.

The importance of the global market goes beyond price changes. For countries with a relatively small urban population, agricultural exports can produce faster growth than can domestic market demand—however fast domestic demand might be growing. In such cases, the international market provides growth opportunities without the constraint of sharply lower prices, which often accompany an increase in agricultural production. Although food production for home consumption and the domestic market accounts for most agricultural production in the developing world, agricultural exports and domestic food production are closely related. Export growth contributes significantly to the growth of nonexport agriculture by providing cash income that can be used to modernize farming practices. For those leaving the farm, growth and modernization of agriculture create jobs in agricultural processing and marketing.

On balance, cash-crop income complements and enhances food production, particularly in poorer countries where opportunities to earn nonfarm income are more limited (figure 3.1) (Watkins 2003; Von Braun and Kennedy 1994; Minot and others 2000).

Figure 3.1 Countries that produce more cash crops also produce more food

Annual growth rates of food and cash crop production in 25 countries having agricultural output equal to at least 15 percent of GNP, 1980–2001 (percent)

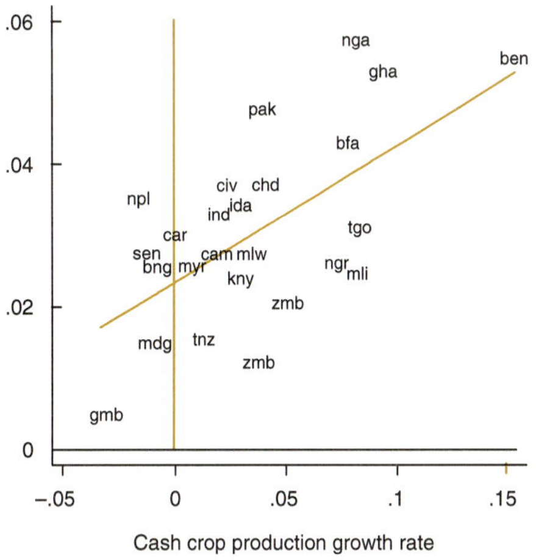

Trade and export growth in agriculture

The last two decades were periods of very rapid growth in exports from developing countries to other developing countries and to the industrialized world (table 3.5). Growth in the world economy accounts for some of this export growth, but lower trade barriers, improved supply capabilities, and increases in specialization are more important. The rapid growth in exports was true both in manufacturing, where levels of protection have been reduced significantly, and in agriculture, where significant protection remains. Nevertheless, manufacturing export growth rates were much higher.

Agricultural trade makes up a growing share of trade among developing countries, but agricultural export shares to rich countries are stable

Although developing countries' exports accelerated during the 1990s, agricultural exports

109

Table 3.5 Manufacturing exports grew much faster than agricultural exports
Export growth rates (percent)

| | World export growth rates || Developing countries' export growth rates ||||||
| | 1980–81 to 1990–91 | 1990–91 to 2000–01 | Total || Developing to developing || Developing to industrialized ||
			1980–81 to 1990–91	1990–91 to 2000–01	1980–81 to 1990–91	1990–91 to 2000–01	1980–81 to 1990–91	1990–91 to 2000–01
Agriculture	4.3	3.6	3.4	4.8	3.6	7.8	3.4	3.3
Manufacturing	5.9	4.8	7.6	8.9	7.3	10.0	7.8	8.3

Note: Manufacturing exports are deflated by the U.S. purchasing parity index (PPI) for finished goods less food and energy. Agriculture exports are deflated by the U.S. PPI for farm products.
Source: COMTRADE.

Table 3.6 South-South exports in agriculture are rising as South-North export shares fall
Share of global agricultural and manufacturing exports by source and destination, 1980–2001 (percent)

| | Developing countries ||| Industrialized countries |||
	1980–81	1990–91	2000–01	1980–81	1990–91	2000–01
Agriculture exports	35.9	32.9	36.9	64.1	67.1	63.1
To developing	9.9	9.2	13.7	15.3	11.9	14.7
To industrialized	26.0	23.7	23.2	48.8	55.3	48.4
Manufacturing exports	19.3	22.7	33.4	80.7	77.3	66.6
To developing	6.6	7.5	12.3	21.7	15.2	19.0
To industrialized	12.7	15.2	21.1	59.0	62.1	47.6

Source: COMTRADE.

did not keep pace with manufactured exports, largely because agricultural export growth accelerated only to the other developing countries (table 3.6).[5]

Developing countries increased their share of global manufacturing exports from 19 percent in 1980–81 to 33 percent in 2000–01. Expanding trade among developing countries contributed to the gain in share, but higher exports to industrial countries also played a significant part. In agriculture, by contrast, the developing countries maintained, but did not expand, their one-third share of world agricultural trade over the last two decades. The steady decline in the developing countries' share of agricultural exports to industrial countries over the period was counterbalanced by an increase in their share of exports to other developing countries. In other words, the significant deceleration of nominal import growth in industrial countries, from 5.4 percent annually during the 1980s to 1.9 percent in the 1990s, was offset by the increase in import growth in developing countries, which increased from 3 percent annually to 6 percent.

Product trends differ
What accounts for the shift in markets for the agricultural exports of developing countries? Price changes alone do not appear to explain it (box 3.2). Static markets in industrial countries for traditional developing-country products such as coffee and tea probably contributed to declining import growth rates, as did the decline in GDP growth rates, combined with low elasticity of demand.[6]

To explore the phenomenon further, we separated agricultural exports into four subgroups. The first consists of mostly tropical, developing-country products such as coffee,

Box 3.2 Did agricultural exports slow down solely because of falling prices?

In nominal terms, export growth in agricultural products decelerated significantly during the 1990s. Can the slowdown be attributed to the price declines observed in the late 1990s? The existing price series for agricultural commodities have certain limitations. Most of the standard series are based on raw commodities that constitute a much smaller percentage of the global trade flows. In most cases they exclude seafood, fruits, and vegetables—now the largest trade items. For the purposes of this chapter the authors tried several alternatives to compensate for these limitations. The unit-value indices from trade data gave inconsistent results and were eliminated, leaving three series, one from the U.S. purchasing parity index (PPI) series for farm products, which includes all products, and two from raw commodity indices. One of the latter uses world trade weights; the other, developing-country export weights. The behavior of the three indices over the last two decades is shown in the table below.

	1980–81 to 1990–91	1990–91 to 2000–01
U.S. farm products PPI	4.7	−6.8
Raw commodities (world trade weights)	−8.3	−6.6
Raw commodities (developing countries' weights)	−22.7	−15.2

If the U.S. PPI is used, a small fraction of the nominal changes in trade flows in the 1990s can be attributed to price declines in the 1990s. Raw commodity indices show that the price declines were greater in the 1980s, and if they are used to deflate the nominal exports, the deceleration would be accentuated. For that reason, the U.S. food products PPI was used to deflate aggregate exports.

---

cocoa, tea, nuts, spices, textile fibers, and sugar and confectionary products. The second is made up of temperate products highly protected in industrial countries—meats, milk and products, grains, animal feed, and edible oil and oilseeds. The third category is the dynamic nontraditional products: seafood, fruits, vegetables, and cut flowers. The last category includes other processed agricultural products, such as tobacco and cigarettes, beverages, and other processed foods.

Import growth rates in industrial countries declined across all groups, while the opposite occurred in developing countries (figure 3.2). But changes in demand are only part of the picture.

In attributing causes to differential growth rates, it is important to consider the relative roles of demand growth and market-share gains in export growth. When growth in exports of manufactures (including processed food) to industrial countries is decomposed between demand and market share, only 21 percent of developing countries' export growth appears to have been caused by demand increases. The other 79 percent was caused by changes in market share (box 3.3). Limited raw-commodity information collected by OECD does not show any significant change in import-penetration ratios in OECD countries over the last decade (OECD 2001). Meanwhile, the developing countries gained market share in every manufacturing subsector—except food processing. The protection rates for food processing in industrial countries are extremely high—far above those of any other manufacturing subsector.

GLOBAL ECONOMIC PROSPECTS 2004

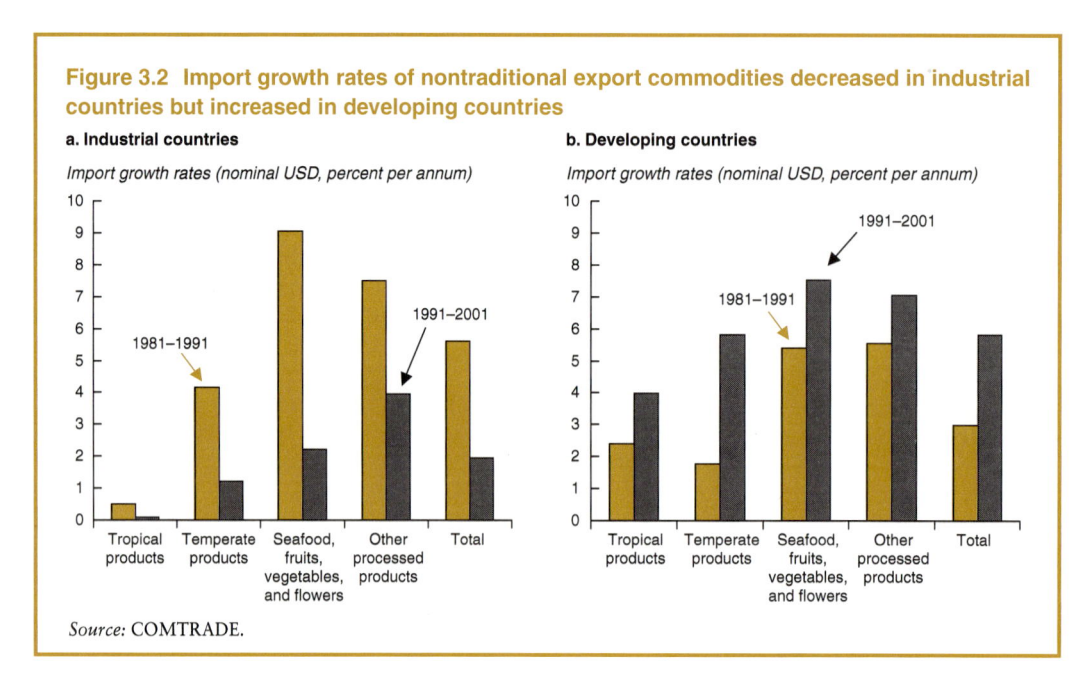

Figure 3.2 Import growth rates of nontraditional export commodities decreased in industrial countries but increased in developing countries

a. Industrial countries
Import growth rates (nominal USD, percent per annum)

b. Developing countries
Import growth rates (nominal USD, percent per annum)

Source: COMTRADE.

The evolving structure of trade: toward nontraditional products with lower rates of protection

World trade has moved away from traditional export commodities to other categories of goods. This is true of both developing and industrial countries. The product groups that gained significantly between 1980–81 and 2000–01 are fruits, vegetables, and cut flowers (19 percent); fish and seafood (12.4 percent); and alcoholic and nonalcoholic drinks (8.7 percent). Although products in these categories tend to have high income elasticities, they also enjoy lower rates of protection in industrial and large developing countries. Product groups that showed significant declines during the period were grains (14.3 to 9.5 percent); coffee, cocoa, and tea; sugar and sugar products; and textile fibers—all of which are among the traditional exports of developing countries. The declines were caused by a combination of price declines, low demand elasticities, and—in the case of sugar, grains, meats, and milk—high rates of protection and expanded production in industrial countries.

While moving away from traditional exports and into expanding subsectors, developing countries also have marginally expanded their exports of temperate products (grains, meats, and milk)—but mostly to other developing rather than industrial countries. These important developments will require changes in how developing countries' agricultural trade is conceived and analyzed (figure 3.3).

Their trade gains have brought more developing countries up against rising food safety standards in the developed world. Meeting such standards has a cost—not just in compliance, but also in documenting that compliance. This cost can be repaid in the form of higher trade. Various mechanisms exist to help developing countries rise to the standards (box 3.4).

Industrial-country export structures also have changed. Exports of protected products have declined, whereas those of beverages, fruits, and vegetables have grown. These changes are discernible despite the fact that intra-EU trade is included in the global export data. One cause of the change is that greater domestic production of protected products has made many industrial countries more self-sufficient in those products, reducing trade.

As a group, developing countries lost export market share during the 1980s, but

Box 3.3 Decomposing export growth in manufacturing

Most market-share analysis has not looked into the shares of exports from developing countries in the consumption of industrial countries. Below are estimates of developing-country exports in the domestic consumption and production of Canada, Germany, Japan, and the United States, which together absorb about 70 percent of developing countries' manufactured exports to industrial countries.

The table below shows the shares of exports from developing countries in the four countries' total absorption (demand) and the growth of exports from developing countries. Absorption is estimated as gross production minus exports, plus imports.

Gross production data in the three non-U.S. countries have been converted to U.S. dollars at current exchange rates. Because the U.S. dollar appreciated significantly against the currencies of the other three countries in the late 1990s, this conversion underestimates domestic production and demand growth. It also overestimates the share of imports, which are denominated in U.S. dollars.

Demand change is estimated assuming a constant share of exports in domestic demand between the two time periods; that is, market shares do not change. The market share changes are then estimated as the difference between the actual export growth and the export growth under a constant market share.

Developing countries increased their share of industrial countries' manufacturing imports—largely by increasing their market share, 1991–99 (percent)

| | Share of developing countries' exports in domestic demand || | Export growth due to ||
	1991	1999	Growth in exports from developing countries	Change in demand	Change in market share
Canada	4.51	7.64	117.25	28.16	89.08
Japan	2.24	4.38	95.04	−0.25	95.29
United States	5.10	9.04	169.42	51.99	117.43
Germany	7.44	8.91	18.31	−1.22	19.53
Total	4.46	7.63	110.90	23.38	87.52

Sources: UNIDO, COMTRADE. Using UNIDO and COMTRADE data, UNCTAD estimated these ratios until 1995. UNIDO's coverage in terms of gross production has become more limited since 1995.

The relationship between domestic demand growth in industrial countries and export growth from developing countries is relatively weak. Market share gains caused by the restructuring of global production are a much more powerful factor.

Between 1991 and 1999, exports of manufactures from developing countries to these four countries increased by about 139 percent, compared to about 60 percent for world trade, while the total increase in domestic demand was only 29 percent. The rest of the export growth was a result of the increases in market shares of developing country exports in industrial-country markets. A change of one percentage point in absorption shares during the decade would increase exports from developing countries by approximately 28 percentage points, equal to the total absorption growth over the decade.

The same conclusion holds true for the 15 three-digit ISIC subsectors that range from very capital intensive (rubber and glass) to very labor intensive (garments and footwear).

The only subsector in which demand growth was greater than the market share gains, and in which the developing countries lost market share, was food processing. In that subsector, the market share of developing countries declined from 2.42 percent in 1991 to 2.40 percent in 1999. Why? Food processing enjoyed the greatest protection of any subsector, and protection did not decline over the last decade. Because a large portion of agricultural exports are classified under food processing, protection of the subsector explains part of the deceleration of agricultural exports from developing to industrial countries during the 1990s.

Source: Aksoy, Ersel, and Sivri (2003).

GLOBAL ECONOMIC PROSPECTS 2004

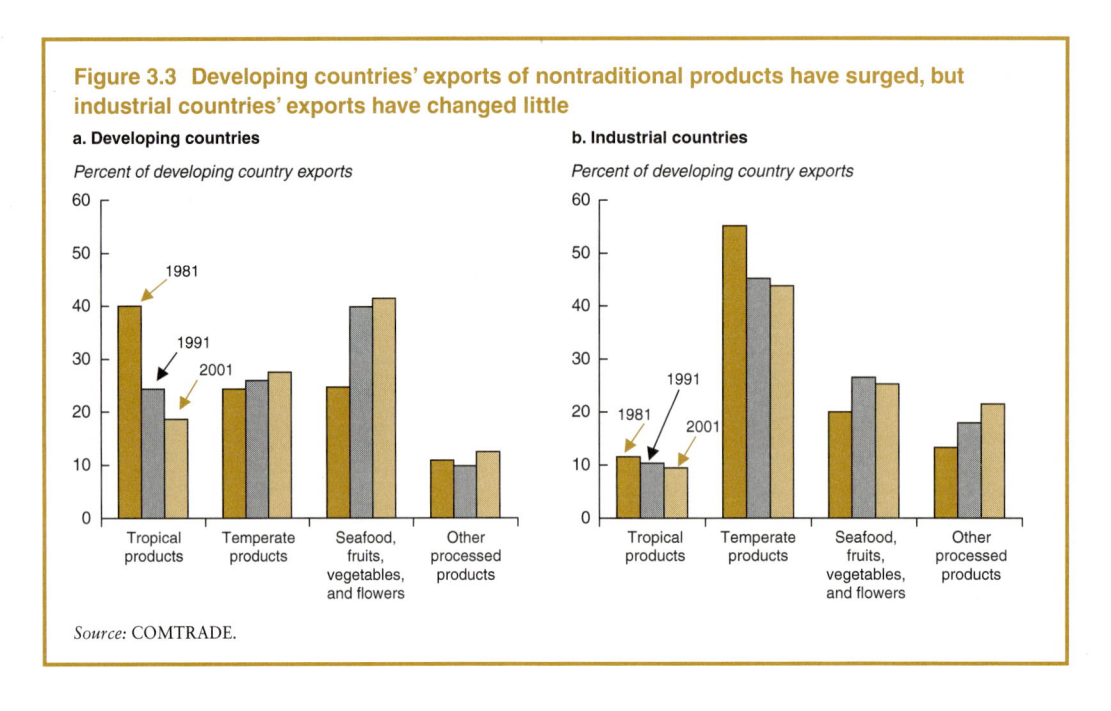

Figure 3.3 Developing countries' exports of nontraditional products have surged, but industrial countries' exports have changed little

a. Developing countries
Percent of developing country exports

b. Industrial countries
Percent of developing country exports

Source: COMTRADE.

reversed that trend in the 1990s (table 3.7). Modest expansion in the 1990s brought them back to where they had been in the early 1980s. Global gains were made by middle- and low-income countries, mostly to other developing countries. China is an exception to this trend, having increased its export shares in all markets. Even in the 1990s low-income countries continued to lose market share in their exports to industrial countries, making up the loss by expanding their export shares in developing-country markets. In tropical products, where global shares declined, low-income countries increased their shares to the other developing countries.

The LDCs lost export market share in both markets during both decades. Unlike other developing countries, they have not been able to make up their market-share losses in tropical products by expanding their shares in the growing subsectors: seafood and fruits and vegetables. Their only gains have come in seafood, and much of the expansion has come from industrial-country vessels fishing in their waters. In highly protected products, South-South trade has expanded, possibly as a result of regional trading arrangements.

Global agricultural protection: The bias against development

Progress in the Uruguay Round was more formal than real

Since the 1980s, two important developments have occurred in agricultural trade policy. First, most developing and a few industrial countries have made major reforms in their protection regimes involving unilateral and regional reductions in tariffs and quotas. For example, unilateral reforms in the 1990s effectively eliminated export taxation in most developing countries. Average tariffs have declined rapidly, while other import restrictions, such as foreign exchange allocations for imports, have effectively disappeared (World Bank 2001). Manufacturing tariffs dropped more than agricultural tariffs. In at least one way, agricultural protection expanded: Many middle-income countries began subsidizing their agricultural products.

Second, the Uruguay Round Agreement on Agriculture brought agricultural trade into WTO disciplines. Before Uruguay, agricultural products had no bound tariffs, and tariffs often were supplemented by nontariff measures such

Box 3.4 Food safety standards: From barriers to opportunities

Agricultural trade is shifting toward high-value, perishable commodities such as fresh fruits, vegetables, meats, and fish. With this change have come consumer concerns over food safety. In response, governments and private companies have developed a growing array of rules, regulations, and standards. Some fear that these standards will be used by high-income countries as a tool of trade protection.

Some developing countries have risen to the higher standards. Kenya's exporters send fresh vegetables and salad greens by air freight to major European supermarket chains. In that industry, food safety standards have accelerated the adoption of modern supply-management techniques and stimulated public-private collaboration (Jaffee 2003). Many developing-country suppliers, however, will not be able to meet the more stringent standards without technical advice, upgraded production and processing facilities, better enforcement of standards, and closer working relationships with importers in high-income countries.

Nearly all of the cases of allegedly protectionist use of food safety measures brought before the WTO have involved trade between developed countries over issues such as hormone residues in meat and genetically modified foods. Although some food-import bans have been heavily publicized, their application against developing countries is quite rare and typically has involved complementary rather than competitive products. However, some evidence suggests that developing countries employ safety regulations as a protectionist measure against other developing countries.

The available evidence suggests that most food-safety-related problems that developing-country exporters encounter are well within their capacities to resolve. According to data from the U.S. Food and Drug Administration, most detentions of developing-country food products involve labeling violations or very basic problems of food hygiene—and thus of quality assurance (see table). No firm can operate long without addressing such problems.

Detentions by U.S. Food and Drug Administration of imports from developing countries 1997 and 2001 (percent)

Reasons for contravention	Latin America and the Caribbean 1996–97	Asia 1996–97	India 2001
Food additives	1.4	7.4	7.4
Pesticide residues	20.6	0.4	1.9
Heavy metals	10.7	1.5	0.6
Mold	11.9	0.8	0.4
Microbiological contamination	6.2	15.5	15.3
Decomposition	5.2	11.5	0.3
Filth	31.4	35.2	26.4
Low acid canned food	3.6	14.3	4.1
Labeling	5.0	10.8	15.7
Other	1.7	2.6	27.8
Total	100.0	100.0	100.0
Total number	3,985	5,784	2,148

Source: USFDA.

Even for more complex food safety issues, developing countries have room to maneuver. An array of strategies exists to help them meet product and process standards for international markets. Especially in middle-income countries, the *good manufacturing practices* and *good agricultural practices* long demanded by overseas customers and consumers are now being demanded by discerning domestic consumers as well. They are well within producers' reach.

The European Union lays down harmonized hygiene requirements governing the catching, pro-

(Continues on next page)

Box 3.4 *(continued)*

cessing, transportation, and storage of fish and fishery products. Processing facilities must be inspected and approved by a specified authority in the country of origin. Countries whose local requirements have been found by the Commission to be at least as stringent as those in the European Union and for which specific import requirements have been established are placed on "List I" and enjoy reduced physical inspection at the border.

Between 1997 and October 2002, the number of countries achieving List 1 status increased from 27 to 72. More than half are low-income or lower middle-income countries; half of these are low-income African countries. Another 35 countries are on List II, including the United States (Henson and Mitullah 2003).

Food safety compliance costs can include the cost of adjusting production and processing facilities; the recurrent costs to implement food safety management systems; and the costs of certification, monitoring, and enforcement. Relatively few estimates are available on the magnitude of these costs. When a country is already exporting high-valued foods, compliance may require only incremental production changes and public-sector oversight. However, for other suppliers the costs of reaching internationally competitive levels may be high. The Bangladeshi shrimp industry invested an estimated $18 million in the latter half of the 1990s to upgrade fish-processing facilities and product-testing laboratories, and to make other changes in response to repeated quality and safety detentions on exports to the European Union and the United States. However, these expenditures have been rewarded with rapidly increasing (and better priced) shrimp exports—which totaled $296 million in 2000 (Cato and others 2000).

Standards can also be a barrier to trade. Consider the case of camel milk cheese exports to the EU. Tiviski SARL, a dairy processor in Nouakchott, Mauritania, developed a technology to produce "pate molle" cheese from camel milk. It obtained the milk from nomad milk producers who were very poor. In return, Tiviski provided the producers with cheap access to credit and vaccinated their animals to ensure a supply of healthy milk. The camel cheese, after transport and production costs, was priced at $10 per kilogram in the EU. After winning a prize at a trade fair, the cheese soon found its way into elite stores like Harrods in London and Fauchon in Paris. However, it proved to be difficult to find the correct tariff line for the product, and grouping it with "other dairy, cheese" exposed it to a much higher tariff than regular cheese. To make matters worse, the EU soon decided to abolish imports of camel cheese from Mauritania, arguing that the presence of "hoof and mouth" disease in Mauritania could be transmitted from camels to other livestock, even though there is no real evidence that camels are capable of spreading the disease. The EU then imposed another restriction: camel cheese could indeed be imported—but only if mechanical methods were used to obtain milk used in its production—an unworkable proposal for the low-income milk producers who were located miles away from major ports. Mauritania did not dispute this case at the WTO because of the sheer costs involved—costs that were not justified for exports of $3 million to $5 million worth of cheese per year. Catfish producers in Vietnam have had similar difficulties accessing the American market, initially because of labeling rulings (and then later because of anti-dumping judgments; see box in Chapter 2).

The emerging set of international and developed-country food safety standards present challenges for many exporters in developing countries. Concerted efforts to address basic hygiene and quality-assurance requirements and to provide relatively simple training for farmers could go a long way in ensuring compliance with most official food safety standards. In circumstances where compliance requires greater investment—both by the public and private sectors—partnerships between developed and developing countries and among developing countries may fill the bill. Beyond this, the public has to remain vigilant that standards do not become misused as instruments of protection.

Source: World Bank staff.

Table 3.7 Developing countries have shared unequally in export market gains
Export shares of food and agricultural products by income level (as percentage of total world trade)

Income level	Exports to industrial countries 1980–81	1990–91	2000–01	Exports to developing countries 1980–81	1990–91	2000–01	Total exports 1980–81	1990–91	2000–01
Industrial	48.8	55.3	48.4	15.3	11.9	14.7	64.1	67.1	63.1
Middle-income*	19.6	18.4	17.0	7.3	6.4	9.8	26.9	24.8	26.8
Low-income	5.2	3.4	3.4	1.4	1.3	2.0	6.5	4.8	5.4
of which LDCs	1.6	0.8	0.7	0.7	0.4	0.5	2.3	1.3	1.1
China	0.7	1.3	2.1	0.9	1.2	1.4	1.7	2.5	3.5
India	0.5	0.5	0.6	0.3	0.3	0.5	0.8	0.8	1.1
Total	74.9	78.9	71.6	25.1	21.1	28.4	100.0	100.0	100.0

* Excluding India and China.
Source: COMTRADE.

as import quotas or bans, quantitative restrictions, variable levies, and monopoly purchasing by state-owned or other companies. Import barriers were coupled with the widespread use of production-related subsidies, such as price supports, which often led (and still leads) to increases in production above the level of market equilibrium. Excess production had to be stockpiled or exported, sometimes with the help of further subsidies. With the intention of aligning agricultural trade rules with those applying to trade in other goods, the Uruguay Round negotiators agreed that all import barriers, other than those in place for health and safety reasons, should take the form of transparent tariffs. Before agreeing on tariff reductions, all border measures had to be converted into their tariff equivalents—a process known as "tariffication."

The conversion of nontariff measures into tariffs was generally done using the price-gap method—the gap being the difference between domestic and world market prices. After establishing the tariff equivalent of an import restriction, reductions were applied from bound tariffs. Developed countries reduced their tariffs by an average of 36 percent and a minimum of 15 percent over six years; developing countries by an average of 20 percent and a minimum of 10 percent over ten years. The agreed reductions were simple averages, not weighted for the volume of trade, so some countries made large reductions in tariffs that were already low—for example, achieving a 50 percent reduction by dropping a tariff from 2 percent to 1 percent—or in areas of low sensitivity, while making only the minimum reduction in sensitive product areas. The Round offered limited opportunities to make minimum import commitments for certain products instead of adopting tariffs on them. The minimum import option was taken by Japan, Korea, and the Philippines for rice, and by Israel for certain sheep and dairy products. (Japan has since tariffied rice imports.)

Once a tariff was established, bindings and reductions were negotiated. In cases where tariffs were high, or where quotas had been allowed in some imports, minimum and current market-access opportunities were also negotiated. The typical result was the establishment of a minimal tariff rate for a limited volume of imports—called a tariff rate quota (TRQ).

With the removal of nontariff measures, some countries worried that they would not be able to prevent surges in import volumes or falling import prices. To allay these concerns, negotiators agreed that a special agricultural safeguard could be applied to certain products.

The Uruguay Round yielded no meaningful reduction in protection in industrial countries. In many cases, in fact, protection may have increased as a result of so-called dirty tariffication (Nogues 2002, Ingco 1997). Continued protection has led to greater import substitution, while the geographical restructuring of production that occurred in manufacturing did not occur—at least not to the same degree—in agriculture. Review of the experience to date with the new rules on market access, export subsidies, and domestic support indicates that the effects of implementation of the Uruguay Round Agricultural Agreement have been modest. The reasons include weaknesses in specific aspects of the agreement, such as high baseline support levels from which reductions were made. In some countries, including the United States, reforms undertaken before the negotiations were adequate to fulfill the new rules on reducing domestic support (OECD 2001).

Today, protection in agriculture takes different forms—tariff protection, subsidies, tariff peaks, TRQs, tariff escalation, and opaque tariffs. In reviewing these forms, the following section makes two fundamental points:

- First, the various forms of protection are often linked. For example, goods produced behind high tariff walls and with production subsidies often require export subsidies to be sold in the world market. That said, border barriers are more important than subsidies.
- Second, virtually the entire interlinked system of protection, even when used by other developing countries, is heavily biased against developing countries—and against the world's poor.

Import barriers are the most important instrument of protection

Although the conversion of nontariff barriers to tariffs during the Uruguay Round was an important step forward, average agricultural tariffs in most industrial and developing countries were and remain much higher than tariffs for nonagricultural products.

This section evaluates the agricultural trade regimes of the Quad countries (Canada, European Union, Japan, United States) and 25 developing countries in light of the Uruguay Round's objectives. Eight of the developing countries in the sample are large middle-income countries with significant agricultural sectors. Eight more middle-income countries are included to ensure regional balance. Eight lower-income countries round out the sample. Emphasis has been placed on the nature of tariffs because a key objective of the Uruguay Round was to lower tariffs and make them more transparent.

The tariff data in table 3.8 underestimate actual border protection. First, specific duties, which generally are higher than ad valorem rates, are not fully reflected in the simple av-

Table 3.8 **Agricultural tariffs are higher than manufacturing tariffs in both rich and poor countries**
Most-favored-nation, applied, ad valorem, out-of-quota duties (percent)

	Agriculture	Manufacturing	Percentage of lines covered in agriculture
Quad countries	10.7	4.0	86.7
Canada (2001)	3.8	3.6	76.0
European Union (1999)	19.0	4.2	85.9
Japan (2001)	10.3	3.7	85.5
United States (2001)	9.5	4.6	99.3
Large middle-income countries[a]	26.6	13.1	91.3
Other middle-income countries[b]	35.4	12.7	97.7
Lower-income countries[c]	16.6	13.2	99.8

a. Brazil (2001), China (2001), India (2000), Korea (2001), Mexico (2001), Russian Federation (2001), South Africa (2001), and Turkey (2001).
b. Bulgaria (2001), Costa Rica (2001), Hungary (2001), Jordan (2000), Malaysia (2001), Morocco (1997), Philippines (2001), and Romania (1999).
c. Bangladesh (1999), Guatemala (1999), Indonesia (1999), Kenya (2001), Malawi (2000), Togo (2001), Uganda (2001), and Zimbabwe (2001).
Source: WTO Integrated Database.

erages. Second, many products are subject to nontariff restrictions.

Because ad valorem equivalents of specific and other duties, where available, are much higher than the ad valorem rates, and assuming that the same tariff structure applies to Canada and Japan, which use non–ad valorem (NAV) rates on 25 percent and 15 percent of their tariff lines, the average tariffs for the two countries are seriously underestimated, lowering the Quad average. To show the degree of bias, the third column in tables 3.8 and 3.9 shows the proportion of tariff lines to which the averages apply.[7]

Excluding Canada, which has a large proportion of agricultural NAV tariffs without equivalents, average tariffs in agriculture are much higher than in manufacturing. The difference is especially pronounced in the European Union—19 percent in agriculture versus only 4.2 percent in manufacturing. Among the developing countries, the results are very similar, with a few exceptions, such as Brazil and Malaysia, where manufacturing tariffs are higher.

The developing countries in the sample have higher tariffs than the industrial countries, the highest being Morocco (64 percent), Korea (42 percent), and Turkey (49.5 percent). Indonesia (8.5 percent) and Malaysia (2.8 percent) have

Figure 3.4 Developing countries lowered tariffs on manufactured products more than on agricultural products

Average applied tariffs for agricultural and manufacturing products in developing countries, 1990, 1995, and 2000 (percent)

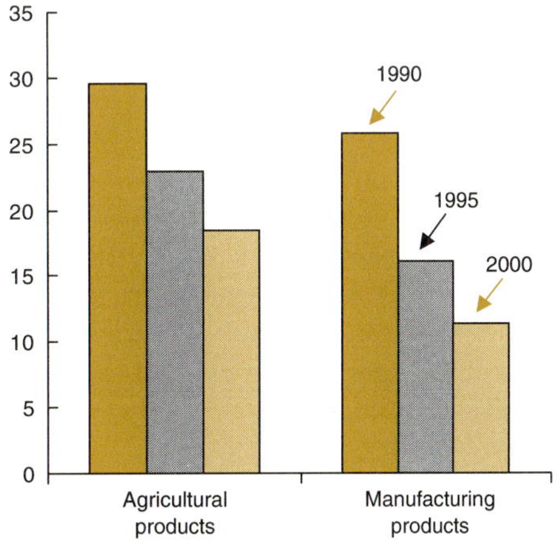

Source: TRAINS.

the lowest. Again, the average tariffs of countries that have a high percentage of NAV lines (Bulgaria, Russian Federation, South Africa, and Turkey) are seriously underestimated.

Tariffs are widely dispersed and have very high peaks. Industrial-country tariffs, although lower on average than those of developing countries, show significant tariff peaks, indicating high protection for specific products. The peaks reach almost 1,000 percent in the Republic of Korea, 506 percent in the European Union, and 350 percent in the United States.[8] Tariffs in many low-income countries have lower peaks and show less variance than those in many of the middle-income countries.

Compared to the slow reform in OECD countries, the changes in protection in developing countries were significant in the 1990s (figure 3.4). The average agricultural tariff declined from almost 30 percent in 1990 to about 18 percent in 2000, a decline of 35 percent. (The rates shown in the figure are simple averages of the average tariffs of about 50 developing countries.) Those reductions were complemented by the elimination of most ex-

Table 3.9 Agricultural tariffs: High peaks and deep valleys

Tariff peaks and variance in selected countries; MFN, out of quota, applied duties (percent and standard deviation)

	Average tariff	Maximum tariff	Standard deviation	Percentage of lines covered
Canada	3.8	238.0	12.9	76.0
European Union	19.0	506.3	27.3	85.9
Japan	10.3	50.0	10.0	85.5
United States	9.5	350.0	26.2	99.3
Korea, Rep. of	42.2	917.0	119.2	98.0
Brazil	12.4	55.0	5.9	100.0
Costa Rica	13.2	154.0	17.4	100.0
Indonesia	8.5	170.0	24.1	100.0
Malawi	15.3	25.0	9.1	100.0
Morocco	63.9	376.5	68.2	100.0
Togo	14.7	20.0	6.5	99.9
Uganda	12.9	15.0	3.7	100.0

Source: WTO Integrated Database.

port taxes as well as import licensing and many other quantitative restrictions (World Bank 2001). Average tariffs in agriculture remain much higher than those in manufacturing, however, indicating that the general tendency in the 1980s—to protect the industrial sector—no longer holds. In their study of 15 developing countries, Jensen, Robinson, and Tarp (2002) concluded that the bias against agriculture in the 1980s no longer exists. The economy-wide system of indirect taxes, including tariffs and export taxes, significantly discriminated against agriculture in only one country. It was largely neutral in five, provided a moderate subsidy to agriculture in four, and strongly favored agriculture in five.

Subsidies underpin the system of border protection

An extensive network of subsidies has evolved to support agriculture, particularly in the rich countries. Protection takes three major forms.

- Border barriers such as tariffs and quantitative restrictions, designed to support prices in domestic markets, account for about 70 percent of total protection in the OECD countries.
- Production-related subsidies given to farmers under different schemes, called "direct support," usually take the form of direct budget transfers.
- General support for agriculture—through research, training, marketing, and infrastructure programs—usually is not included in the estimates of producer supports.

In addition, many countries have subsidies for their consumers, but generally these do not affect production and thus are not included in producer-support estimates.

The support accorded to OECD-country producers through higher domestic prices and direct production subsidies was $248 billion in 1999–2001 (table 3.10). Some two-thirds of the total—$160 billion—came from the border barriers described above or from market price support mechanisms. The remainder came in the form of direct subsidies to farmers. Another $80 billion in subsidies came from

Table 3.10 Most subsidies go to producers—and come from border protection
Agricultural support in the OECD countries, 1999–2001 (billions of dollars)

	United States	European Union	Japan	Emerging supporters[a]	European Union accession countries[b]	Other OECD countries	Total OECD
Where total support goes							
Consumers	21.4	3.8	0.1	0.7	0.0	0.2	26.2
General services	22.8	9.6	12.7	7.1	0.6	2.3	55.1
Producers	51.3	99.3	52.0	30.4	3.0	12.3	248.3
Total	95.5	112.7	64.8	38.2	3.6	14.9	329.6
Where producer support goes							
Corn	8.3	2.7	N[c]	1.7	−0.1	0.2	12.9
Meat[c]	2.6	34.0	4.1	3.4	0.5	2.8	47.3
Milk	12.4	16.7	4.9	2.7	0.7	4.7	42.1
Rice	0.7	0.2	18.0	7.6	N[c]	−0.2	26.4
Wheat	4.9	9.5	0.8	0.9	0.3	0.9	17.3
Other	22.3	36.2	24.1	14.1	1.9	3.6	102.2
Where producer support comes from							
Domestic measures[d]	32.6	38.5	5.0	4.4	1.4	6.3	88.2
Border measures[e]	18.7	60.9	47.0	26.0	2.0	5.7	160.1

a. Includes Korea, Turkey, and Mexico.
b. Includes Czech Republic, Hungary, Poland, and Slovak Republic.
c. Beef and pork.
d. Direct payments to producers.
e. Tariffs and tariff equivalents of other border measures.
Sources: OECD (2002) and authors' calculations.

Table 3.11 Subsidies account for a large share of farmers' revenues
Percentage of farm-gate prices attributable to border protection and direct subsidies, 1986–2001

Area	Market price support (border protection)[a] 1986–88	1995–97	1999–2001	Direct subsidies[a] 1986–88	1995–97	1999–2001	Total producer support (estimate)[a] 1986–88	1995–97	1999–2001
OECD	48.2	28.2	31.3	14.3	13.3	17.2	62.5	41.5	48.5
European Union	65.3	28.3	34.3	10.5	20.4	21.7	75.8	48.8	56.0
Japan	145.4	131.7	138.1	16.8	13.0	14.7	162.1	144.7	152.9
United States	16.0	7.5	10.8	18.3	7.4	18.8	34.3	14.9	29.6
Eastern Europe	45.2	8.7	10.4	18.3	4.8	7.5	63.6	13.5	17.9
Australia and New Zealand	4.2	2.8	0.6	6.4	3.9	3.4	10.6	6.8	4.0
Other countries	53.1	42.6	46.3	11.1	12.8	12.2	64.2	55.4	58.5
Other industrial[b]	165.9	108.1	113.0	72.2	81.9	106.7	238.1	190.0	219.7
Other developing[c]	31.4	38.1	42.9	6.4	8.0	7.3	37.8	46.1	50.2

a. The denominator is total value of production at farm gate less market price support (both estimated at world prices).
b. Includes Norway, Switzerland, and Iceland.
c. Includes Korea, Turkey, and Mexico.
Source: OECD.

programs (such as food stamps) that directly benefit consumers ($26 billion) and from general services to agriculture ($55 billion), such as public investments in agricultural research and extension.

Of the subsidies, the share linked to income rather than production (known as "partially decoupled subsidies") increased from approximately 9 percent of total protection in 1986–88 to 21 percent in 2001. Major products that account for the bulk of support are grains, meats, milk, and sugar.

Protection rates for producers in the OECD decreased from 62.5 percent in 1986–88 to 49 percent in 1999–01, measured as a percentage of gross agricultural output at world prices. The contribution of border barriers to total protection fell from 77 percent in 1986–88 to about 65 percent in 1999–01. After decreasing rapidly from 1986, overall protection rose again after 1997 in response to declines in world agricultural prices. Support to agricultural producers from border protection and direct subsidies increased farm-gate revenues in the OECD countries by almost 50 percent in 1999–2001 (table 3.11). But the persistence of high tariffs reduces the incentives to eliminate production subsidies and various inefficiencies globally.

Agricultural support tends to be countercyclical in rich countries, pushing price adjustments into the global market and accentuating price drops. The countercyclical movement of protection reflects the specific duties and TRQs that are triggered when prices fall.

The European Union and United States have reduced their overall levels of agricultural support. For example, in the European Union farmers' prices were 65 percent higher than international prices in 1986–88; this ratio decreased to 34 percent in 1999–01. During the same period, however, direct production-related payments to farmers increased from 10.5 percent to 21.7 percent, partially compensating for the decline in border barriers. Similarly, in the United States, domestic prices, relative to international prices, declined from 16 percent to 10.8 percent.

Aggregate support levels vary significantly among the OECD countries. Some (Iceland, Norway, and Switzerland) have very high levels of support. Australia and New Zealand have very low support levels. The European Union (on the high end) and Canada (on the low end) fall between these extremes.

The Eastern European countries made the most significant reductions in protection between 1986 and 2001—from 63.6 percent to 17.9 percent. Korea's protection levels have remained very high, with small variations. Mexico and Turkey, which started with low protection, increased it over this period, mainly through higher border protection.

The high domestic price differentials in table 3.11 indicate that domestic production is protected much more significantly than the unweighted average tariff rates shown in table 3.8 would imply. In Japan, for example, border protection raises market prices by some 138 percent, whereas the average tariff is just 10 percent and the maximum ad valorem tariff is only 50 percent. The difference can only be attributed to specific duties and TRQs, which are not included in the data set. For the European Union, the situation is similar. Border protection raises prices by more than 34 percent, well above the average tariff of 19 percent. In both areas, tariffs on many local specialties are very high. For example, in the European Union the average tariffs for grains, meats, and milk and milk products are 34.6 percent, 32.5 percent, and 54.6 percent respectively.

Specific duties produce hidden tariff increases in downturns

The Uruguay Round objective of providing greater transparency of protection levels through tariffication has not been fully realized, especially in the key industrial and some middle-income countries. First, many agricultural tariffs are still specific, compound, or mixed. In such cases it is almost impossible to estimate the real level of protection because it may change over time and with the relative price of imports. Even more important are the cyclical implications of such tariff structures: protection from specific duties rises as prices decline in the world markets; protection will be higher for lower-priced products from the developing countries.[9]

The proportion of agricultural tariff lines that carry specific, compound, and mixed duties is much higher in rich countries than in developing countries (figure 3.5).[10] This means, among other things, that the transparency of agricultural tariffs in developing countries is higher than in industrial countries—and significantly higher than in manufacturing. Of the 24 developing countries included in this sample, 11 have no NAV rates, 5 have them in fewer than 1 percent of their tariff lines, and 4 in fewer than 5 percent of tariff lines. Only 4 countries, all middle income, have a higher proportion of tariff lines with NAV rates. Within the Quad, Japan has specific, compound, or mixed rates in 15 percent of its tariff lines; Canada in 24 percent; the United States in 40 percent; and the European Union in 44 percent. The United States and European Union also have duties that vary according to the content of the products in 1 percent and 4 percent, respectively, of their tariff lines. Thus the difference in the transparency of tariff rates is consistent for most developing and industrial countries, and the biggest problem with nontransparency lies with the industrial and a few middle-income countries.[11]

Within the Quad, tariff structures show some differences. In the United States, almost all categories of products have NAV rates between 30 and 60 percent. In the European Union, certain product groups—such as beverages, grains, milk and milk products, and sugar and sugar products—have more than 90 percent of tariff lines under NAV. In many developing countries, NAV rates are clustered within a few product

Figure 3.5 Rich countries use non–ad valorem tariffs more often than do developing countries

Tariff lines containing specific, compound, or mixed duties, for agriculture and manufacturing by class of country (as percentage of all lines)

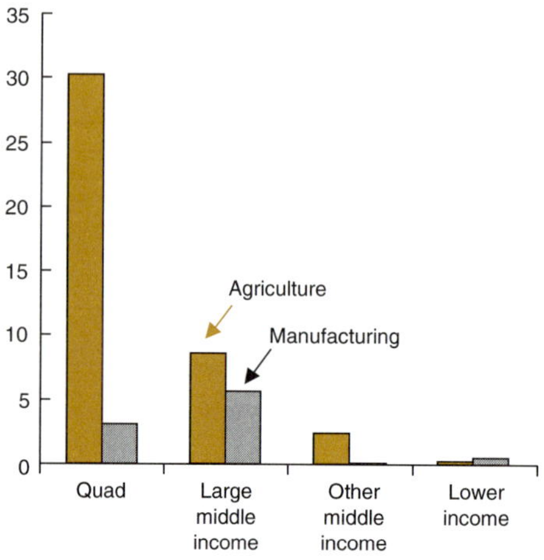

Source: WTO IDB.

AGRICULTURAL POLICIES AND TRADE

Table 3.12 Specific tariffs are higher than ad valorem rates
Average applied, out-of quota, ad valorem and ad valorem equivalents of non–ad valorem tariffs in areas for which equivalents are reported (percent)

	Average ad valorem tariff	Average ad valorem equivalent of NAV rates	Percentage of lines containing NAV rates
Australia	1.2	5.0	0.9
European Union	10.6	35.2	43.6
Jordan	21.6	58.0	0.8
United States	8.1	11.7	40.4

Source: WTO Integrated Database (IDB).

groups. For example, in Malaysia NAV rates apply to tobacco and alcohol products; in Mexico on chocolate and confectionary products; and in Korea on nuts, spices, and sugar.

Only four countries in the sample report the ad valorem equivalents of their NAV rates (table 3.12). For those four, the average equivalents are much higher than the average ad valorem rates, suggesting that average duties for countries with a large proportion of NAV duties are seriously underestimated.

The specific duties are being used primarily as an instrument of disguised protection. First, as shown in table 3.12, the ad valorem equivalents of specific duties, where known, are higher than the ad valorem rates. Second, the proportion of specific duties increases with the degree of processing (figure 3.6). They are found most frequently in lines covering final products—those classified under food processing.

Tariff escalation is particularly harmful to development

Tariff codes that apply higher tariffs to semi-processed and fully processed raw materials are strikingly antidevelopment. By hindering

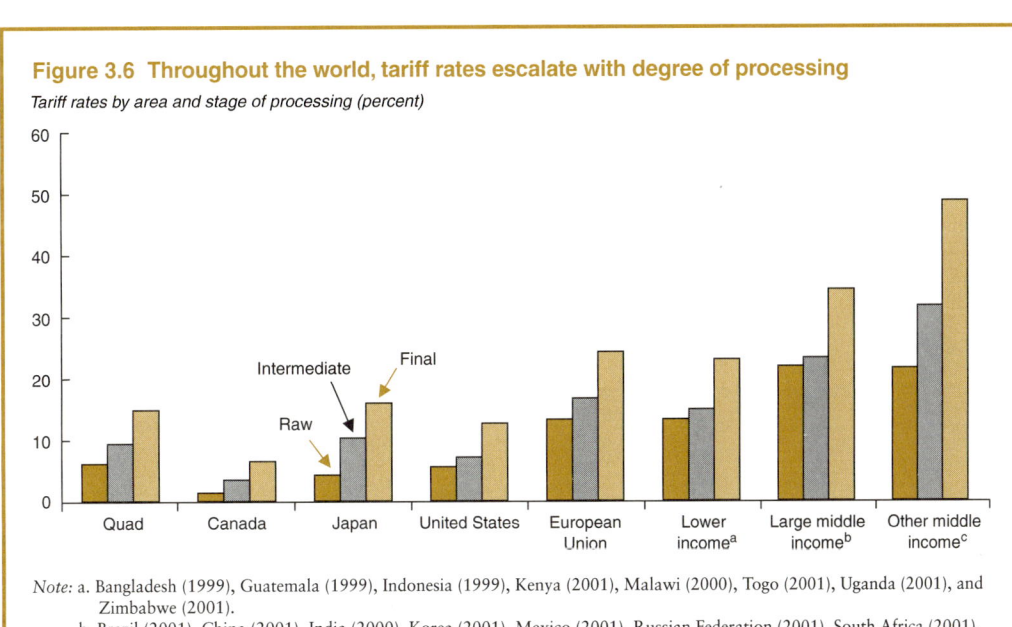

Figure 3.6 Throughout the world, tariff rates escalate with degree of processing
Tariff rates by area and stage of processing (percent)

Area	Raw	Intermediate	Final
Quad	6	9	15
Canada	2	4	7
Japan	5	10	16
United States	6	8	13
European Union	14	17	25
Lower income[a]	14	15	23
Large middle income[b]	22	24	35
Other middle income[c]	22	32	49

Note: a. Bangladesh (1999), Guatemala (1999), Indonesia (1999), Kenya (2001), Malawi (2000), Togo (2001), Uganda (2001), and Zimbabwe (2001).
b. Brazil (2001), China (2001), India (2000), Korea (2001), Mexico (2001), Russian Federation (2001), South Africa (2001), and Turkey (2001).
c. Bulgaria (2001), Costa Rica (2001), Hungary (2001), Jordan (2000), Malaysia (2001), Morocco (1997), Philippines (2001), and Romania (1999).

Source: WTO Integrated Database (IDB).

Table 3.13 Tariffs rise with level of processing
Tariff escalations in selected product groups (percent)

	European Union	United States	Korea	Japan
Tropical products				
Coffee				
Raw	7.3	0.1	5.2	6.0
Final	12.1	10.1	8.0	18.8
Cocoa				
Raw	0.5	0.0	5.0	0.0
Intermediate	9.7	0.2	5.0	7.0
Final	30.6	15.3	12.3	21.7
Sugar				
Raw	18.9	2.0	a	25.5
Intermediate	30.4	13.8	19.3	11.6[b]
Final	36.4	20.1	50.0	a
Expanding commodities				
Fruits				
Raw	9.2	4.6	49.6	8.7
Intermediate	13.3	5.5	30.0	13.2
Final	22.5	10.2	41.9	16.7
Vegetables				
Raw	9.9	4.4	135.4	5.0
Intermediate	18.5	4.4	52.2	10.6
Final	18.0	6.5	34.1	11.6
Seafood				
Raw	11.5	0.6	15.6	4.9
Intermediate	5.1	3.2	5.8	4.3
Final	16.2	3.5	20.0	9.1

a. All lines are specific.
b. 56 percent of lines are specific.
Source: WTO Integrated Database.

diversification into value-added and processed products, areas in which trade is expanding rapidly, such escalation directly penalizes investors in developing countries who seek to add value to production for export.

Tariff escalation has long been a feature of agricultural and food-processing trade and continues to be so (Golub and Finger 1979, Lindland 1997, and Gallezot 2003). Protection escalates with the level of processing in almost all countries and across all products (table 3.13). Almost all groups of countries have highly escalating tariffs (see figure 3.6), and the manufacturing component of agriculture and food processing has very high protection, explaining the developing countries' lack of penetration in food processing in industrial countries. Developing economies also apply systematic tariff escalation and high tariffs to the final stage of processing, suggesting potentially large gains if escalation were removed by developing economies (Rae and Josling 2003).

Tariff escalation is common in both traditional and new products. For traditional products (except sugar), raw stages are accorded extremely low tariffs, whereas extremely high tariffs apply to the final stages. A similar pattern appears in fruits and vegetables, for which the developing countries have found expanding markets and trade barriers are generally lower. The averages reported in table 3.13 mask very high peaks on individual products. In the United States, for example, the maximum tariff on final fruit products is 136 percent; on cocoa products it is 186 percent. In the European Union the maximum rates on processed fruits and vegetables are 98 percent and 146 percent; on cocoa products, 63 percent.

AGRICULTURAL POLICIES AND TRADE

Figure 3.7 The proportion of tariff lines containing non–ad valorem duties increases with degree of processing

Tariff lines containing specific, compound, or mixed duties, by stage of processing (as percentage of all lines)

[Bar chart showing Raw, Intermediate, Final stages for: Norway (~42, 59, 69), European Union (~22, 45, 58), United States (~38, 43, 42), Canada (~17, 23, 30), Russia (~12, 10, 54), Turkey ([zero], ~6, 13)]

Source: WTO IDB.

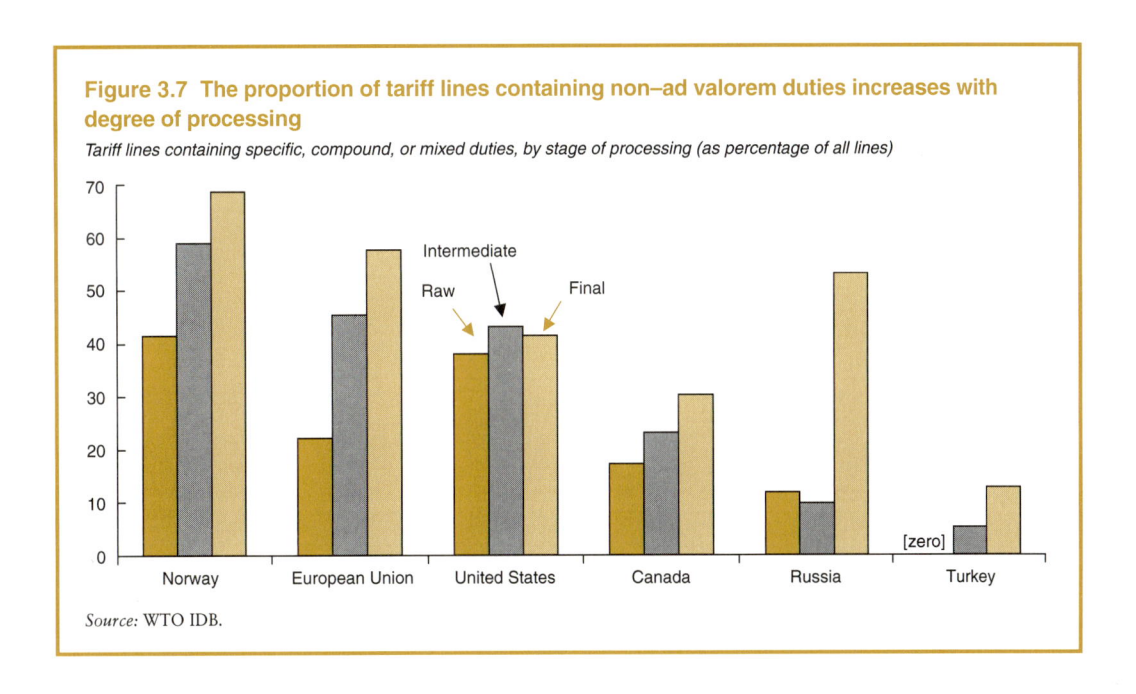

Specific duties are applied more frequently to goods with higher degrees of processing. For example, in Canada and the European Union, the share of specific duties is 17 percent and 22 percent for raw materials but 30 percent and 58 percent, respectively, for final products. Among developing countries, the Russian Federation applies specific duties in 12 percent of its tariff lines for raw materials versus 53 percent of lines covering final products (figure 3.7).

Tariff rate quotas allow a little in— and then add a tariff bite

TRQs, designed to maintain some market access, have resulted in more complex tariff regimes. Although the number of tariff lines under TRQs is small, TRQs cover some of the main commodities produced in the OECD countries (figure 3.8). According to OECD data, almost 28 percent of domestic agricultural production is protected by TRQs. Rates range from a high of 68 percent in Hungary to 0 percent in Australia and New Zealand. The European Union and United States have 38 percent and 26 percent of their production protected by the TRQs.

Export subsidies directly depress global prices

International trade rules have prohibited export subsidies on nonagricultural products since 1955. Export subsidies are still allowed in agricultural products, although these subsidies were capped and subjected to reduction commitments in the Uruguay Round. During 1995–98, WTO members used 42 percent of the budgetary expenditure and 64 percent of the volume allowed for export subsidies, with the European Union accounting for 90 percent of all OECD export subsidies.

Although their use has been reduced, export subsidies continue to distort world markets.[12] The Uruguay Round placed limits on export subsidies for individual commodities, but allowed some flexibility. Early in the implementation period, when world prices were high, usage was low and several countries carried forward their unused export subsidy credits to be used at a later date. At the same time, lower tariffs and the move toward direct production subsidies has and will continue to reduce the need for official export subsidies.

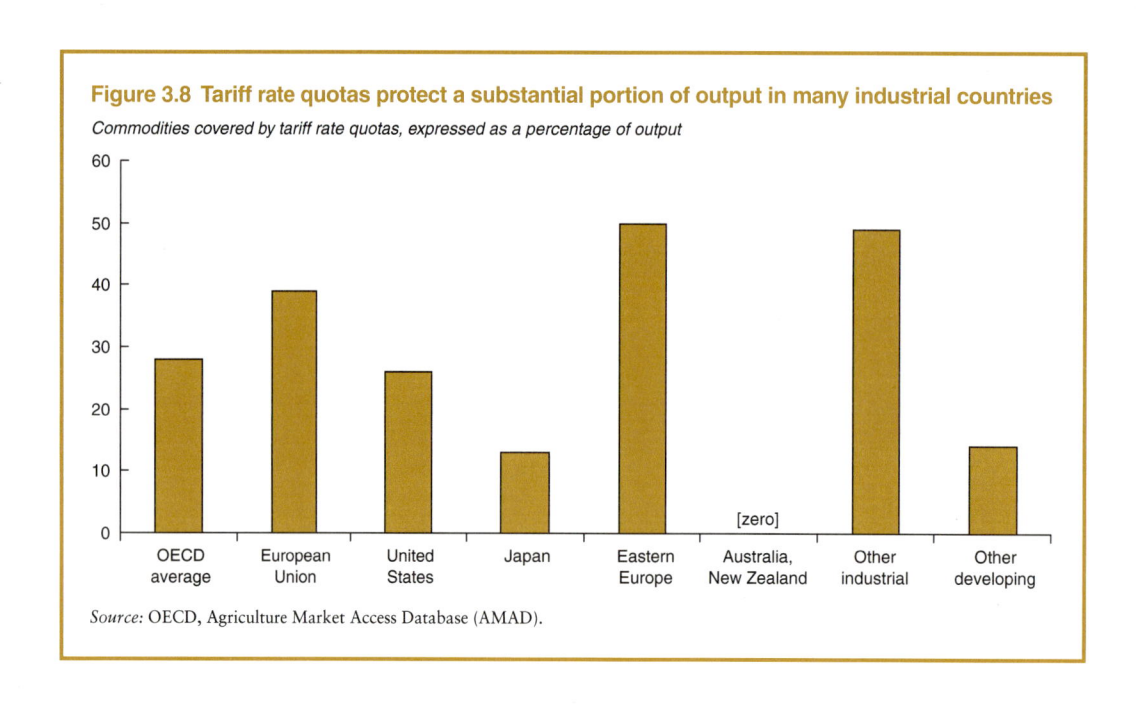

Figure 3.8 Tariff rate quotas protect a substantial portion of output in many industrial countries

Commodities covered by tariff rate quotas, expressed as a percentage of output

Region	Percentage
OECD average	28
European Union	39
United States	26
Japan	13
Eastern Europe	50
Australia, New Zealand	[zero]
Other industrial	49
Other developing	14

Source: OECD, Agriculture Market Access Database (AMAD).

Even if tariffs were eliminated altogether, current production subsidies for agriculture would cause the domestic and export price of many commodities to remain lower than their costs of production in industrial countries. By lowering production costs, production subsidies favor industrial-country farmers over developing-country producers, who do not receive direct subsidies. Cotton subsidies in the European Union and the United States are a clear case in point. Tariffs are zero, and domestic prices are the same as world or export prices (Baffes 2003, Watkins 2003). Yet in the United States in 2001 production subsidies effectively increased the prices farmers received (or reduced their costs of production) by 51 percent, leading to increased production and depressing the global price. At the same time, export prices for U.S. wheat, corn, and rice were 58, 67, and 77 percent of their costs of production (Watkins 2003).

Decoupling subsidies from production would reduce such distortions. To fully decouple subsidy payments, the definition of decoupling must make it clear that the payments are independent of production decisions (box 3.5).

The development tale of five commodities: sugar, wheat, cotton, peanuts, and rice

The development consequences of high protection in industrial countries can be traced through the story of key commodities. Although the stories are different, they share common plots: high protection, regressive subsidies, and low prices that hurt poor producers all over the world (Beghin and Aksoy 2003).

Sugar is one of the most policy-distorted commodities in the world. The European Union, Japan, and the United States account for the bulk of OECD-zone support to sugar producers, which, at $6.4 billion, is approximately equal to developing-country exports. But other countries (Mexico, Turkey, Poland, and all almost all temperate-zone sugar beet producers) also provide significant support to their producers. High border barriers in combination with the subsidies keep domestic prices in the United States and the European Union about twice as high as the world market price.

High domestic sugar prices in the European Union, Japan, and the United States have encouraged high-cost, inefficient domestic pro-

Box 3.5 Decoupling agricultural support from production decisions

Decoupling subsidies from production is designed to support producers not on the basis of current output, input use, or prices, but on historical measures, thereby limiting distortion to production and trade. Debated since 1945, decoupling became a serious option with the passage of the U.S. Food Security Act of 1985, which reduced set-asides of farm land, public stockholding, and yield payments. The European Union restructured its Common Agricultural Policy in 1992, replacing some price supports with direct payments. Mexico reformed its price-support policies along similar lines with the introduction of the Programa de Apoyos Directos al Campo (PROCAMPO) in 1994. The United States then went a step further in the 1996 Farm Bill, replacing "deficiency payments" with decoupled support based on historical data. Turkey introduced a direct income-support program in 2001, aided in part by a World Bank adjustment lending operation.

Following a sharp decline in commodity prices in the late 1990s, the United States reintroduced deficiency payments in 1999—initially as emergency assistance and subsequently as countercyclical payments legitimized in the 2002 Farm Bill. Responding to the U.S. reversal, Mexico reintroduced price supports in 2002 by setting target prices similar to those in the United States.

The move to decoupled support is a step in the right direction. However, if governments wish to help farmers adjust to free markets—the avowed purpose of decoupling—a simple and minimally distorting way to do that would be to make a one-time unconditional payment to everyone engaged in farming or deemed in need of compensation. Short of that, decoupling mechanisms should exhibit the following characteristics:

No constraints on input use. Support to specific sectors should be in the form of taxpayer-funded payments and should not require production. Neither land, labor, nor any other input should be required to be in "agricultural use."

Government credibility. Eligibility rules should be clearly defined and not allowed to change. The time period on which payments are based should not change. Payments should not be increased. New sectors should not be added to the program. Updating baselines and adding crops results in a government credibility problem, making the decoupling policy inconsistent over time. As market conditions change, governments have discretion to change eligibility criteria and payment levels, leaving them unable to make and hold to a binding commitment. As farmers change their production decisions and apply pressure for changes in supposedly decoupled support programs, decoupling is in effect preempted.

Other programs. Every decoupling program instituted to date has left other support programs in place. Coupled programs tend to interact with the decoupled program, adding incentives to overproduce.

Time limit. Payments must not extend beyond a maximum number of years. The European Union and Turkey have no limit; the United States had one (at least implicitly) but violated it; Mexico's remains in effect. A time limit ensures that payments are transitory and for adjustment purposes only.

Reform within WTO. The level of payments in aggregate and per farm, and the terms described above, should be bound in the WTO so that governments can make credible commitments without backsliding.

Source: Baffes and de Gorter (2003).

---

duction of sugar and sugar substitutes. At the same time, they have reduced overall consumption and gradually transformed these countries from net buyers of about half of the world's exports during the 1970s into net sellers in international markets in the 1990s. Meanwhile, the production and consumption of sugar substitutes (such as high-fructose corn syrups) increased to displace 10 million tons of sugar consumption—equivalent to one-third of world exports—since 1970 (Mitchell 2003). Consequently, the world prices of sugar today are below the costs of production of some of the most efficient producers. Many producers manage to keep exporting, either because they enjoy limited preferential access at high prices in

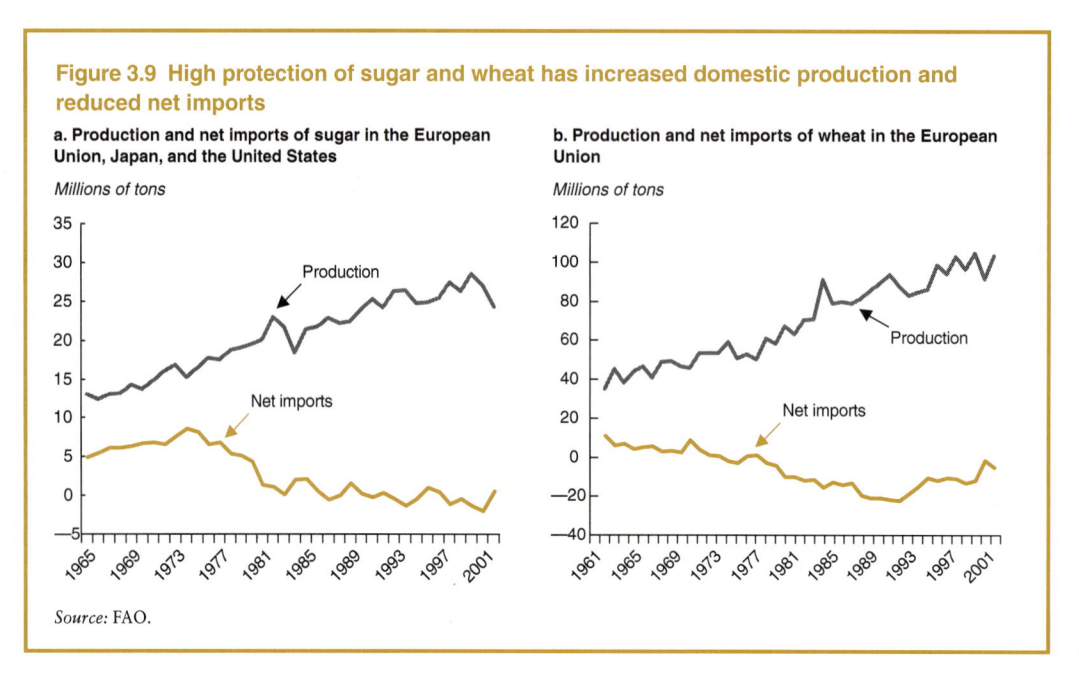

Figure 3.9 High protection of sugar and wheat has increased domestic production and reduced net imports

a. Production and net imports of sugar in the European Union, Japan, and the United States

b. Production and net imports of wheat in the European Union

Source: FAO.

industrial-country markets or because they subsidize their exports by selling at higher prices in their domestic markets. The world market has shrunk to a trade residual, with an estimated 80 percent of world production being sold in high-priced, protected markets (figure 3.9).

The benefits of sugar policy reform are substantial—particularly with multilateral reform. Presently, developed countries are protecting their sugar producers at great cost to themselves and to developing countries with export potential. A recent study of the global sugar and sweetener markets estimated that removing all trade protection and support would bring annual global welfare gains of $4.7 billion. In countries with the highest protection—Europe, Indonesia, Japan, and the United States—net imports would increase by 15 million tons per year. World sugar prices would rise about 40 percent, while prices in heavily protected countries would decline: in Japan by 65 percent, in Western Europe by 40 percent, and in the United States by 25 percent. Brazilian producers would gain the most from liberalization—about $2.6 billion per year—but this gain would be partially offset by higher consumer prices. Japan's net gain from lower consumer prices would more than offset lower producer prices on the 40 percent of sugar that is domestically produced. In the United States, producer losses would be some $200 million greater than consumer gains. Western Europe would show a net gain of $1.5 billion, with consumer gains of $4.3 billion exceeding producer losses of $3.3 billion. Exporting countries that presently enjoy preferential access to the European Union and the United States now collect some $800 million by selling into protected markets at high prices. However, the value of this preferential access is less than it appears, because many of these producers have high production costs and would not produce at all at world-market prices. The rise of world sugar prices following full liberalization would partially offset the loss of preferences and allow some preferred producers to compete. The net loss to preferred producers from full liberalization is estimated to total about $450 million per year (Borrell and Pearce 1999, Sheales and others 1999).

A similar situation occurred in EU *wheat* markets as high domestic prices encouraged production and reduced net imports from about 5 million tons in the 1970s to net exports of 20 million tons in the early 1990s, before policy reforms reduced net exports. Subsidized wheat exports from the European Union continue to depress world prices. Wheat is one of the most protected products in the European Union; total production support averaged almost $10 billion annually during 1999–2001, corresponding to a protection rate of almost 50 percent.

World trade in *cotton* shows severe policy distortions, but, unlike sugar, the distortions come through producer support rather than from border measures such as tariffs and quotas (Baffes 2003). The United States provides the greatest support to its producers—$3 billion annually. The European Union provides about $0.6 billion each year to its producers. Producer prices in the United States were 91 percent higher than the world-market price in 2001–02. In Greece they were 144 percent higher; in Spain, 184 percent higher. High-producer support encouraged U.S. cotton production to grow about 25 percent faster than world production after 1970, and EU production accelerated once Greece and Spain joined the (then) European Community in 1981 and 1986. While the United States and European Union were maintaining high support, several cotton-producing developing countries (especially those in Sub-Saharan Africa) undertook substantial policy reform to increase the efficiency of their cotton sectors. Price and export prospects of developing-country exporters—especially in Sub-Saharan Africa—would be greatly improved if support in developed countries were reduced or eliminated.

Removal of protection and support would cause a drop in production in the United States and European Union and thus boost prices. Simulations show that with full liberalization in the cotton sector—removal of trade barriers and production support, along with liberalization in all other commodity sectors—cotton prices would increase over the next 10 years by an average of 13 percent over the price that would have prevailed in the absence of reforms. World cotton trade would increase by 6 percent. Africa's cotton exports would increase by 13 percent. Uzbekistan would increase its exports by 5.8 percent and Australia by 2.7 percent, while exports from the United States would decline by 3.5 percent. Cotton production in the United States would decline by 6.7 percent; in the European Union, by 70.5 percent. In effect, cotton production in the European Union would fall back to levels that existed prior to the Common Agricultural Policy.

Groundnuts (peanuts) are one of the world's main oilseed crops. Widely cultivated in developed and developing countries, they provide livelihood and cash income to many poor farmers in the developing world, especially in Sub-Saharan Africa and Asia. In Senegal, for example, an estimated one million people (one-tenth of the population) are involved in groundnut production and processing. Groundnuts account for about 2 percent of GDP and 9 percent of exports. China is the world's largest exporter of groundnuts, followed by the United States and Argentina. Sub-Saharan Africa (where the major producers are The Gambia, Malawi, Nigeria, Senegal, South Africa, and Sudan) has lost ground in world edible groundnut markets, accounting for only 5 percent of the world market in 2001, compared to 17 percent in 1976. In the oil segment of the market, Senegal is the world's largest exporter. Governments in Sub-Saharan Africa taxed production until the early 1990s. These taxes, borne by domestic groundnut users and taxpayers, had an important domestic cost (Diop and others 2003).

Historically, world groundnut markets have been distorted by heavy government intervention designed to stimulate production through subsidies and price supports or to protect producers by controlling imports. China and India have price-control schemes and impose very high tariffs on imports. Since the mid-1990s, all major exporters have gradually liberalized their groundnut sectors, in part to fulfill their commitments under WTO agreements. Results are mixed, however, and trade in groundnuts remains heavily distorted. Both China and India have removed some import restrictions and allowed wider private-sector participation in importing groundnuts. But tariffs on groundnut products remain very high in both countries; the removal of trade distortions by China and India is essential to successful reform of groundnut markets.

The U.S. groundnut policy, highly distorted by large subsidies and prohibitive tariffs between 1930 and 2001, was recently reformed, but with high and redundant tariffs still in place. The 2002 Farm Bill eliminated some unsustainable features of previous legislation (high support prices and production quotas) but introduced new distortions that have the potential to depress world market prices and subsidize producers (for example, through countercyclical payments and a price floor mechanism that becomes effective when world prices are low). Prohibitive tariffs of almost 150 percent remain.

Full trade liberalization would raise market prices by about 19 percent for groundnuts, 18 percent for meal, and 17 percent for oil. Because the current U.S. peanut program is mostly a domestic affair, liberalization of the U.S. market would not have a far-reaching effect on world prices or on exports of the poorest developing countries. As a bloc, the OECD countries would experience welfare losses after trade liberalization—moderate gains in the United States offset by losses in Canada, the European Union, and Mexico, which would lose from trade liberalization because, with few policy distortions in these markets, they would be penalized by higher world prices after liberalization.

Although the net world welfare gains of liberalizing groundnut markets are moderate, they are still significant for small agrarian economies such as Malawi and other West African countries. In China and India, gains to consumers would be partially offset by losses to producers under full trade liberalization. Specifically, buyers in India and southern China, where groundnuts and groundnut oil are heavily used in food, would reap significant gains from liberalization.

Liberalization of the value-added markets—oil and meal—would result in even larger welfare gains in African countries. The African countries modeled in our analysis (The Gambia, Malawi, Nigeria, Senegal, and South Africa) would experience aggregate net welfare gains of $72 million, with Senegal and Nigeria gaining most. The increase in world prices after trade liberalization would lead to a total gain for African groundnut producers of some $124 million in profits. These figures are sizable for small African economies. The rest of the world would experience a net welfare loss because consumers would face higher prices for groundnut oil.

Rice is the most important food grain in the world. Production and consumption are concentrated in China, India, and Indonesia. Consumers in low-income, food-deficit countries get 28 percent of their calorie intake from rice. The rice market is a mature market, with static demand in the North and demand in developing economies growing with demographics rather than income. Prospects for growth in trade therefore rely on policy reforms.

Tariff and related border protection is very high, averaging about 40 percent globally and rising to 200 percent in some markets. Total OECD-zone support is more than $26 billion, and in Japan support is a staggering 700 percent of production cost (at world prices). Tariff escalation is prevalent (from paddy to milled rice) in many countries, including the European Union, where the tariff on milled rice is prohibitive, except for small preferential import quotas granted to a few countries. For example, the tariff on milled rice imports into the European Union is 80 percent, compared to 46 percent for brown rice. In Mexico, paddy rice enters with a 10 percent tariff, whereas brown and milled rice enter with a 20 percent tariff. This pattern of protection depresses world prices for high-quality, milled long-grain rice and discriminates against the milling sectors of exporting nations such as Thailand, the United States, and Vietnam (Wailes 2003).

Global reforms—elimination of all border barriers and support—would lead to average price increases of about 33 percent, rising to 90 percent for medium- and short-grain rice. Producers in Cambodia, China, and Vietnam would be the main beneficiaries, along with consumers in most of high-income Asia. Since most production is by small farmers in these countries, the gains would be very pro-poor as well. Following trade liberalization, net rice importers could be negatively affected by the resulting world price increase wherever the consumer prices rise following reform; that is, wherever the current ad valorem tariffs are lower than the potential world price increase. Estimates show that in Indonesia, Nigeria, and the Philippines, three large rice importers, consumer prices would fall after the reforms.

The tale of these five commodities has an important moral for those who would promote development. Cutting back on subsidies and other protection that primarily benefit relatively wealthy farmers in rich-country markets (and in some cases middle-income country markets) can open up opportunities for poor farmers in Africa, Asia, and Latin America. The effects on incomes in poor countries would be strong and immediate. In many cases the gains would be a substantial order of magnitude greater than development assistance to these same countries.

Proposals for reforms in the Doha Round

The potential gains for developing countries are large

One way to evaluate reform proposals is to compare their likely results with the potential gains from full removal of all barriers, which would yield global welfare gains of $400–900 billion, more than half of which would go to developing countries. If all trade barriers were dismantled, agriculture and food would account for 70 percent of these gains. A major share—60 percent—would derive from reforms in developing countries. The largest gains are to be had from tariff reforms in agriculture undertaken in a context of a global reform program.

Can agriculture adjust to new prices? The experience of New Zealand, which implemented the most far-reaching reforms of any industrial country, suggest that the answer is yes. New Zealand has almost no tariffs or subsidies in agriculture. Its reforms have led to higher productivity and growth rates, no changes in rural population, and a much more dynamic and environmentally sustainable agricultural sector (box 3.6). Particularly noteworthy is the fact that New Zealand farmers are able to compete effectively on world markets, expanding their share of world trade in dairy products from 6.7 percent in 1985 to 9.5 percent in 2001.

Harbinson splits the difference

Despite the large potential gains from liberalization, many of the proposals for the Doha Round are modest. Proposals range from the Japanese suggestion to impose an "average cut," which can be predicted to have little effect, to the more ambitious proposal of the Cairns Group.

The Harbinson proposal, named for Stuart Harbinson, the chairman of the WTO negotiating group on agriculture, takes the middle ground (DRIFE 2003).[13] For industrial countries, it proposes average tariff cuts of 60 percent on bound tariffs above 90 percent, a 50 percent cut on bound tariffs between 15 and 90 percent, and a 40 percent cut on bound tariffs below 15 percent.[14] For the developing countries and for products not considered strategic, it proposes average tariff cuts from bound rates of 40 percent for tariffs above 120 percent, a cut of 35 percent for tariffs between 60 percent and 120 percent, a cut of 30 percent for tariffs between 20 percent and 60 percent, and an average reduction of 25 percent in tariffs below 20 percent. These cuts would be implemented by industrial countries in equal installments over five years and over ten years for developing ones (WTO 2003). The Harbinson cuts look significant—some groups have called them radical—but their impact, depending on how they are interpreted, would not be as significant as first appears.

For the industrial world, the results would depend on whether countries achieve the average cuts by reducing lower tariffs by greater percentages (which would have relatively little effect) or cut all tariffs at the average rate. The "average cuts" called for under the Uruguay Round were interpreted loosely, with many

Box 3.6 Fewer subsidies, stronger agricultural sector

There is a strong belief among policymakers in OECD countries that trade reform in agriculture would destroy their rural communities and the agricultural sector. Yet, as the experience of one OECD country shows, protection and subsidies are not a necessary condition for the continued growth of the farm sector. Indeed, the removal of protection can be accompanied by faster agricultural growth and increases in productivity, achieved without a significant decline in the farming population or its standard of living.

Today, New Zealand has the lowest level of farm support among OECD countries—its producer support, estimated to be around 1 percent of the value of agricultural production, is primarily dedicated to research funding. This was not always the case. Producer support reached 33 percent of output in 1983, when almost 40 percent of the income of an average sheep or cattle farmer came from government subsidies. Yet, these policies were clearly unsustainable, as the loss of preferential access to the British market and an escalating inflation spiral led the government to abandon most payments to agricultural producers.

Government deregulation was quick and substantial. Nearly all subsidies were removed in 1984. The sectors involved included wheat, egg, milk, potatoes, honey, raspberries, hops, tobacco, apples, poultry, pork, and other meats. Altogether, almost 30 different production subsidies and export incentives were abolished (Bell and Elliott 1993). The government made only limited efforts to soften the impact on farmers; those who decided to exit the agricultural sector received a one-time "exit grant" of approximately two-thirds of annual income.

At the time, estimates pointed to 8,000 farms (10 percent of total) going out of business, prompting widespread opposition to the government's plan. However, only 800 farms exited the market, and those that remained became more dynamic. Since 1986–87, output of the agricultural sector has grown by more than 40 percent in constant terms. The share of farming in GDP rose from 14.2 percent in 1986–87 to 16.6 percent in 1999–2000, and growth in the farming sector has outpaced economic growth of New Zealand as a whole. The reform also prompted greater competition and lower input costs among suppliers, and brought environmental benefits through reduced waste. Although land values fell during late 1980s and early 1990s, they recovered during the later part of the decade. The share of rural population has remained constant since the abolition of subsidies.

Some of the most impressive effects of subsidy removal have been the changes in agricultural productivity. Since 1986, the annual average rate of productivity growth in agriculture has reached 5.9 percent, compared with 1 percent prior to subsidy abolition. The fact that total lamb production has increased while the number of sheep has declined by 29 percent attests to the increased efficiency of the sector. However, some studies, such as Morrison Paul, Johnston, and Frengley (2000), have questioned the positive effects of the reforms on productivity. The latter, using an unbalanced panel of 32 farms between 1969 and 1991, found that agricultural reform caused changes in the composition of output—a shift out of wool and lamb and into beef and deer—but did not affect technical efficiency. On the other hand, work using aggregate data, such as Kalaitzandonakes and Bredahl (1994), has confirmed improvements in technical efficiency following the reforms.

Overall, the removal of support did not have a grave effect on New Zealand's farmers. Instead, the policy of liberalization created a more vibrant, diversified, and sustainable rural economy in New Zealand.

Source: World Bank staff.

---

countries reducing already-low tariffs by high percentages to avoid cutting higher tariffs significantly (see chapter 2, box 2.2).

For the developing countries, the key issue is reductions from the bound, not the applied, rates. Most developing countries have bound their tariffs at relatively high rates, but reduced applied rates to much lower levels.[15] If cuts were applied to the bound rates, such countries would get credit for past unilateral reforms, but the reductions would not lead to significant tariff reductions.

The Harbinson proposals would imply substantial tariff cuts in the United States and Eu-

Table 3.14 The Harbinson proposals could greatly reduce applied tariffs in the European Union and the United States

Tariffs in the European Union and United States before and after average reduction from applied tariffs (percent)

	United States				European Union			
	Before Harbinson		After Harbinson		Before Harbinson		After Harbinson	
	Average	Peaks	Average	Peaks	Average	Peaks	Average	Peaks
Raw	5.5	350.0	2.7	140.0	13.2	131.8	6.9	52.7
Intermediate	7.1	159.3	3.8	63.8	16.6	284.8	8.3	113.9
Final	11.7	180.8	6.2	72.3	26.8	506.3	13.1	202.5
Overall	8.8	350.0	4.6	140.0	19.7	506.3	9.9	202.5

Note: The analysis excludes cigarettes and alcoholic drinks.
Source: WTO Integrated Database.

Table 3.15 The Harbinson proposals would not significantly reduce protection in the developing world—if reductions were taken from bound rates

Tariffs in selected areas before and after average reductions from bound rates (percent)

	Costa Rica		India		Jordan		Korea	
Bound rates	Average	Peak	Average	Peak	Average	Peak	Average	Peak
Before Harbinson	49.0	245.0	115.3	300.0	21.5	180.0	50.8	917.0
After Harbinson	33.8	147.0	72.3	180.0	14.9	108.0	33.2	550.2
Current applied rates	13.1	154.0	36.7	115.0	18.5	120.0	42.7	917.0

Note: The analysis excludes cigarettes and alcoholic drinks.
Source: WTO Integrated Database.

ropean Union at the end of the program under an optimistic scenario in which all tariffs were cut by the average rate from the applied rates (table 3.14).[16]

Under this optimistic scenario, the average effective tariffs in the European Union and the United States would be halved by the end of the reform process. EU tariffs would come down to about 10 percent from 20 percent, while U.S. tariffs would fall below 5 percent from 9 percent. Even so, the average agricultural tariffs in both areas would remain significantly higher than manufacturing tariffs—which stand at 4.2 and 4.6 percent respectively. Tariff peaks would remain above 140 percent in the United States and above 200 percent in the European Union.

For the developing countries, the optimistic scenario reduced the bound rates by the average cut. Four country examples are given in table 3.15 above. Cuts from bound rates do not significantly lower protection in most developing countries. In India and Costa Rica, at the end of 10 years, the Harbinson reform would leave bound tariffs significantly above applied rates. For Jordan and Korea, bound rates after 10 years would be marginally below the current applied rates. Because these results would hold for most developing countries, existing levels of protection in the developing world would not be significantly reduced under the Harbinson proposals.

Cushioning adjustment: The impact of reforms on net food importers

Serious reforms in global trade policies would lead to price increases for many products now protected. These price changes could lead to balance-of-payments problems for low-income developing countries that are net agricultural importers. Currently, the developing countries as a group—low- and middle-income alike—enjoy a trade surplus in agriculture. But many countries are net importers, and they could be negatively affected. Of 58

Box 3.7 The potential impact of real preferences

Given the high level of agricultural protection in many industrial countries, the value of preferences should be very high and should lead to high rates of export expansion in the countries that receive them. After Spain and Portugal joined the European Union, and after Mexico joined NAFTA, exports rose dramatically, especially in highly protected milk products (see figures below).

Milk and milk products are the most protected of all commodities, and, at $42 billion, they have the highest level of OECD support. However, this highly protected subsector responds similarly to other protected sectors such as grains and meat products. Joining NAFTA or the European Union implies more than simple preferential access—for example, membership in a trade bloc offers a more secure and predictable environment for investment than is usually provided by unilateral preferences—but the experiences of Mexico, Portugal, and Spain illustrate the potential response of many developing countries if they were given free access with few other restrictions.

Source: COMTRADE.

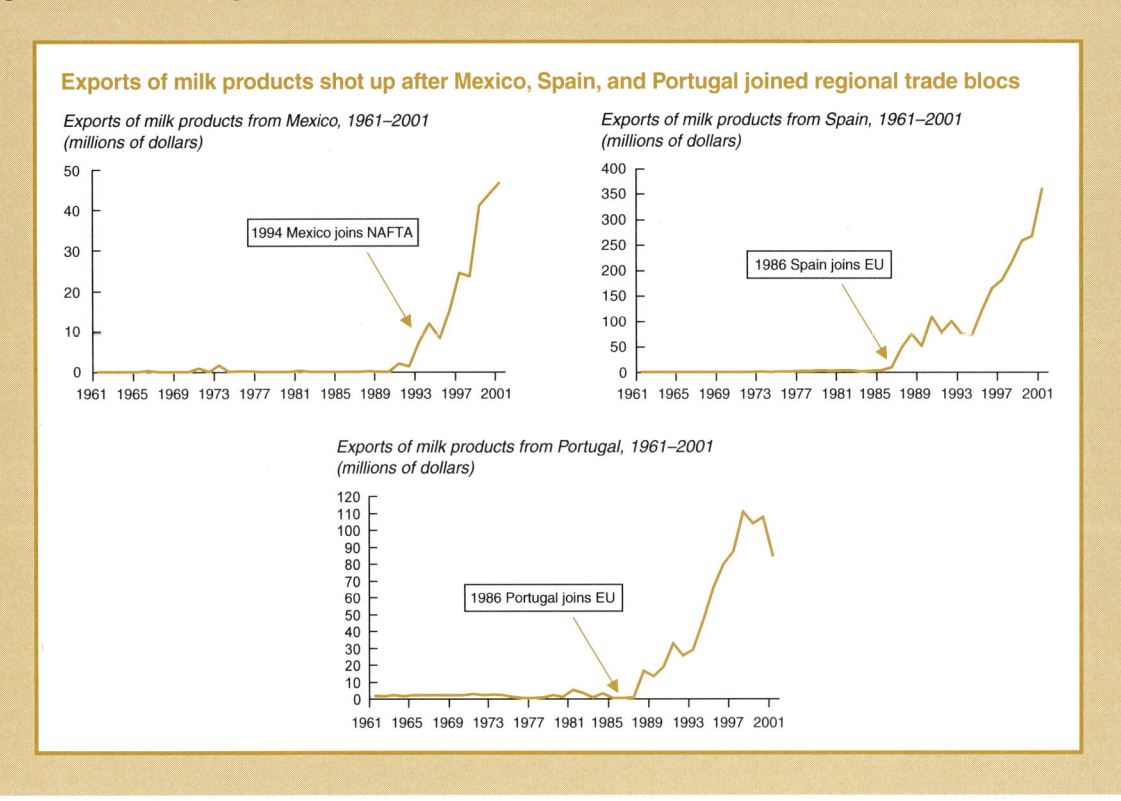

Exports of milk products shot up after Mexico, Spain, and Portugal joined regional trade blocs

Exports of milk products from Mexico, 1961–2001 (millions of dollars) — 1994 Mexico joins NAFTA

Exports of milk products from Spain, 1961–2001 (millions of dollars) — 1986 Spain joins EU

Exports of milk products from Portugal, 1961–2001 (millions of dollars) — 1986 Portugal joins EU

countries classified as low income in 2000–01, 29 were net importers; of 89 classified as middle-income, 51 were net importers.

Among the middle-income countries, the total net imports of the net importers were almost $56 billion; 46 percent of the imports went to high-income, industrialized developing countries such as Hong Kong (China), Republic of Korea, Singapore, and Taiwan (China). Another 35 percent went to the oil exporting countries—Algeria, Saudi Arabia, and the United Arab Emirates. Excluding these and small island states, Egypt and Oman account for 57 percent of remaining imports. Thus the impact of agricultural price increases on the middle-income countries would be limited, particularly as a proportion of their trade.

Among low-income countries, oil-producing Angola, Nigeria, and Yemen account for almost 32 percent of the total deficit. Twelve countries in conflict account for another 21 percent. Only 14 low-income countries are real net food importers; their total net imports were only $2.8 billion in 2000–01. In this group, three countries account for 80 percent of the net imports: Bangladesh, Pakistan, and the Democratic Republic of Korea. The rest of the low-income countries have a deficit of just $565 million, a small percentage of their trade. These countries would gain from price increases, because their exports are also predominantly agricultural, as well as from other aspects of a multilateral trade negotiation. Nonetheless, the international community should be prepared to provide assistance to countries to help them adjust to and take advantage of new trade opportunities.

Can tariff preferences substitute for reform?

Some have argued that the poor are not harmed by the protection practices of rich countries because the Quad countries are generous in granting trade preferences. To be sure, the levels of protection in industrial countries are moderated by tariff and quota preferences. However, as we saw earlier in this chapter, most of the poor live not in the least developed countries, which get deep preferences, but in Asia, which gets fewer preferences, if any. Thus deep preferences do not reach the majority of the world's poor living on less than $1 day. Aside from the LDCs, many of the countries that enjoy preferences are not among the world's poorest. For example, a significant portion of the EU's low-tariff sugar quota benefits Mauritius, the richest country in Sub-Saharan Africa. Half of the countries that benefit from U.S. sugar quotas are net sugar importers. Rules governing preferences are typically complex and cumbersome, preventing many producers from taking advantage of them (see chapter 6).

The United States is the only country that collects data on the effect and degree of use of preferences. Agricultural exports from all developing countries total about $25 billion; of that total, approximately $15 billion, representing mainly tropical products not produced in the United States, enters the country duty-free—here preferences have no effect. Of products in the GSP, most agricultural products with nonzero tariffs are not eligible for preferences—only 34 percent of imports covered by the GSP were eligible for preferences; only 26 percent received them.

Preferences are more generous in other, mainly regional, programs. U.S. preferences for Mexico and the LDCs are much more extensive than for the rest of the world, and the eligibility ratio is almost 100 percent. However, this measure reveals little about the actual coverage of these schemes because it records only products actually exported and not those that would have been exported if granted preferences or lower tariffs. For example, the total exports of agricultural products with nonzero rates from the 64 GSP countries come to no more than the exports of Mexico, which receives almost full preferences (table 3.16).

Tighter rules of origin also complicate preferences. For example, seafood imports under Europe's Everything But Arms preference scheme for least developed countries have stricter rules of origin than do its other preference programs, the GSP and Cotonou agreements. Similarly, the NAFTA agreement, the world's most extensive preferential trade regime, is associated with very detailed and product-specific rules of origin (box 3.8).

Although preferences may help some very poor countries, they are no substitute for multilateral reform that will benefit all the world's poor.

Summary: A pro-poor agenda for policy change

Realizing the development promise of the Doha Agenda will require the international community to tackle some of the most difficult problems of agricultural trade. Agriculture remains one of the most distorted areas of international trade, and those distortions impede development. A pro-poor program of trade reform would contain several important elements:

A reduction in the use of specific duties and greater transparency is necessary to bring

Table 3.16 U.S. trade preferences—a plethora of programs
U.S. trade preferences for agricultural products, 2002 (millions of dollars)

Country group (number of countries in group)	Total value (a)	Share of (a) for which duty is greater than zero (b)	Share of (b) for which no preference is available (c)	Share of (b) eligible for preference (d=b−c)	Eligible but not requesting preference (e)	Preference received (f=d−e)
ATPA (Andean) (4)	2,242.6	870.2	106.7	763.4	256.4	507.0
U.S. LDCs (40)	369.0	65.6	0.0	65.6	12.2	53.3
Non-LDC AGOA (15)	600.5	168.9	0.4	168.5	20.0	148.5
Non-LDC CBI (19)	3,005.3	1,391.3	0.7	1,390.6	10.8	1379.8
Jordan	1.2	1.0	0.1	0.9	0.1	0.8
Mexico	6,319.6	3,866.9	0.0	3,866.9	13.8	3,853.1
Other GSP countries (64)	9,769.6	3,662.0	2,408.5	1,253.6	300.6	952.9
Non-GSP developing	2,906.5	939.9	855.8	84.1	0.7	83.5
Total developing	25,214.3	10,965.7	3,372.1	7,593.5	614.6	6,979.0

Source: U.S. International Trade Commission.

Box 3.8 Rules of origin in preferential schemes are complicated—and often contradictory

Rules of origin are a key element in determining the extent to which countries are able to use the preferences available to them. EU rules of origin are product-specific and sometimes complex. For some products a change of tariff heading is required. Others must meet a value-added requirement. Still others are subject to a specific manufacturing-process requirement. In some cases these requirements are combined. For certain industrial products, alternative methods of conferring origin are specified—for example, change of tariff heading or satisfaction of a value-added requirement. Although clearly more flexible, such an approach is not available for any agricultural products. For many products the EU rules require a change of chapter, which is even more restrictive than a change of heading. In certain cases the EU rules provide for a negative application of the change of tariff classification by proscribing the use of certain imported inputs. For example, the rule of origin for bread, pastry, cakes, biscuits, and so on requires a change of tariff heading *except* from any heading in chapter 11 (products of the milling industry). Hence, bakery products cannot use imported flour and still qualify for the preferential rates.

Although the European Union has sought to harmonize the processing requirements for each product, some of the general rules vary substantially, particularly with regard to the nature and extent of "cumulation" and the "tolerance rule." In this regard the rules of origin for the Everything But Arms scheme differ from those of the Cotonou Agreement—and also from those of other free-trade agreements. The Cotonou Agreement, for example, provides for full cumulation—inputs from other Cotonou countries can be freely used. The GSP allows more limited diagonal cumulation, which may occur only *within* four regional groupings: ASEAN, CACM, the Andean Community, and SAARC. The EU agreement with South Africa contains a general tolerance rule of 15 percent, whereas those with Mexico and Chile allow only 10 percent.

The rules of origin for the U.S. GSP scheme define a 35 percent value-added criterion that is common across all included products. In later bilateral trade agreements, such as the NAFTA and the recently signed free-trade agreement with Singapore, the United States has stipulated extensive and often very complicated product-by-product rules of origin which run to several hundred pages. In any event, the common rule applied in the GSP is that sensitive products are excluded from preferences.

Source: World Bank staff.

agricultural protection regimes closer to the tariff structures used for manufacturing. All specific, mixed, composite, and seasonal tariffs should be replaced with transparent ad valorem duties. Not only will this make the protection clear, but also it will eliminate discrimination against lower-priced exports from developing countries. Since tariff peaks are very high—and will stay high under the existing reform proposal—the peaks must be capped, with some arrangement for reducing tariff escalation on agricultural products.

The combination of tariff walls and domestic subsidies that annually channel some $248 billion to producers in the industrial countries must be dismantled, as must the high levels of protection in developing countries. Export subsidies must be further reduced and ideally eliminated. Discipline should also extend to food aid (see box 3.9). Finally, border barriers

Box 3.9 Food aid principles

Food aid recipients constitute a special group of low-income, food-importing countries with urgent needs arising from natural disasters, disease, and civil conflict. In June 2003, FAO identified 37 countries requiring food assistance, most of them in Sub-Saharan Africa, but others in Asia, the Middle East, Europe and Central Asia, and Central America and the Caribbean.[17] Overall, food aid accounts for a relatively small proportion of world trade, around 2 to 4 percent of traded cereal volumes during the period 1995–2000.[18]

Though needed and effective immediately after disasters, food aid raises development and trade concerns when extended for longer periods or driven by supply. From a commercial standpoint, food aid may disguise export subsidies, or it may be used for developing commercial export markets or promoting strategic objectives. Furthermore, it may alleviate pressure on governments to reform policies and promote self-sufficiency.

When given in kind, food aid may be detrimental to local producers by lowering prices and by altering traditional dietary preferences. When distributed outside of normal indigenous commercial channels, as is usually the case, in-kind food aid also undermines the development of those channels and disrupts movement of food to the deficit areas from surplus regions in the country and neighboring countries. These events can then increase the likelihood and severity of future famine situations.

The trade aspects of food aid are regulated by many agreements and conventions. The Uruguay Round Agreement on Agriculture (URAA, Section 10.4) requires that food aid not be tied to commercial exports of agricultural products, that it accord with the FAO Principles of Surplus Disposal and Consultative Obligations, and that it be given under genuinely concessional terms. Nevertheless, the distinction between legitimate food aid and commercial interests is difficult to make. Thus, although the actual food aid budgets of the five largest donors in 1998 were $2.9 billion, Trueblood and Shapouri (2002) estimate the annual cost of an insurance scheme to provide food security for 67 needy countries would have cost less than $450 million per year from 1988 to 1999.[19]

Any WTO agreement should tighten the URAA provisions to facilitate genuine food aid while preventing the abuse of aid to circumvent export subsidy restrictions. Proposals include limiting food aid to grants only or to in-kind provision only in response to appeals from the United Nations or other appropriate international bodies. Donations in cash or channeled through international agencies would be most desirable.[20] Several principles, some beyond the purview of the WTO, should govern the provision of food aid:

- Food aid should be in the form of full grants and provided only for needs of well-defined vulnerable groups or in response to an emergency as determined by the United Nations.
- Cash aid should be provided unless in-kind food aid is a more appropriate response to the crisis (for example, because marketing channels are not functioning, in-kind aid can be better targeted).
- Food aid should never be used as surplus disposal by industrial countries.
- An impact assessment on marketing and local incentives should be undertaken when food aid is provided, and designs should be altered or mitigation should be undertaken if significant negative impacts are observed.

Source: World Bank staff.

against processed foods, which constitute the expanding part of agricultural and food trade, must be brought explicitly into the negotiations. Policies governing such products should be aligned with those governing other manufactured products. Reform of these policies will yield immense global benefits, especially in developing countries.

Decoupling subsidies can be positive. Reducing subsidies without lowering border barriers will have only marginal effects. Similarly, decoupling subsidies from direct production will have no effect if border barriers are not slashed. However, if border protection is reduced and subsidies decoupled from production requirements, the effects would be positive. To succeed, the decoupling programs must have characteristics that most past efforts have lacked (see box 3.5).

A global effort should be made on particular commodities with large development consequences. Certain individual commodities can have important effects on both developing and industrial countries. Sugar, cotton, wheat, and groundnuts all illustrate ways in which policy regimes—particularly in the OECD countries—can adversely affect developing countries when allowed to operate over long periods of time.

A program of development assistance to manage the adjustment to reform—particularly in food-importing countries—is a priority. The effects of tariff and subsidy reform are unlikely to affect most countries adversely, but the risk that a handful of countries may experience a net terms-of-trade loss cannot be treated lightly. Adjustment is not likely to be costly. Careful analysis shows that most net food importers are either high-income industrialized countries or major oil exporters. Many of the remaining net food importers have high tariff walls, so that reducing the tariffs could offset all or most of the increase in the global price. Nonetheless, such countries would lose the revenues associated with the high tariffs and so would experience some dislocation. Development assistance can also help countries take advantage of new trading opportunities that arise with trade liberalization.

Notes

1. Global poverty rates have been estimated on a consistent basis at $1 a day. Unfortunately, the poverty data are not separated for rural and urban populations. The only source of data where the poverty rates can be separated between rural and urban households is based on the national poverty rates that vary across countries, and the country coverage of these surveys is limited. Data used here cover the surveys for 52 country household surveys conducted between 1990 and 2001. The sample has a higher share of rural population than the overall average and both ratios are given in the tables for reference.

2. A comprehensive analysis of (a) protection indicators (tariff protection, nontariff barriers, and trade-distorting domestic policies such as market price supports and export subsidies), and (b) performance indicators (export structure and output) requires consistent information that is available only for the OECD countries and then only for some product groups.

Even for the OECD, the focus of data is more the protection of selected commodities than the overall trade regime. Thus, the measures covered by OECD data systems and the tariff data from the WTO are not fully consistent. Definitions of the agricultural sector also vary. The OECD database focuses on key raw commodities that have high protection; others exclude fisheries, which have become the biggest food trade item. Many agricultural items are covered under food processing and thus are classified under manufacturing rather than agriculture. Because processed foods constitute a growing share of consumption and trade, their absence from the data seriously understates trade in agricultural products. Finally, trade regimes in agriculture include complicated duty structures, extensive use of quotas and other restrictions, and complicated and changing subsidy schemes, all of which make it impossible to devise simple measures of protection and distortions.

Information for the developing countries is more limited and is only partially consistent. In the analysis presented in this chapter, partial data will be patched together to give a picture of agricultural trade regimes and export performance in industrial and developing countries.

For the purposes of this study, the agricultural sector is defined broadly to include fisheries and processed food products in all subgroups. For example, the seafood and seafood products subgroup includes raw, frozen, and processed seafood. This classification allows us to include all stages of processing and to construct data series that are economically consistent. See annex I for the details of the coverage and definition of subgroups.

3. Of 20 categories of farms tracked by the U.S. Department of Agriculture, 12 lose money from farming alone. Most of the money-losing categories consist of smaller farms. USDA, Agricultural Income and Finance Outlook, September 26, 2002.

4. OECD (2002) The Incidence and Income Transfer Efficiency of Farm Support Measures.

5. From the trade data, it is very difficult to separate out food processing from raw agricultural trade. The definition used here treats food processing within agriculture and manufacturing excludes food processing.

6. Annual GDP growth in industrial countries slowed from 3.0 percent in the 1980s to 2.3 percent in the 1990s. In the developing countries, during the same period, annual GDP growth accelerated from 3.1 percent to 3.7 percent. Unless there was a significant change in income elasticities between the 1980s and 1990s, the changes in GDP growth rates are not large enough to cause the shift in import growth rates. But faster liberalization in developing countries can explain some of the shift.

7. Annex 2 Table 4 shows the ad valorem and non-ad valorem rates separately, as well as the proportion of the tariff lines to which the average applies.

8. In the European Union and United States, very high tariffs are all specific. The variance and peaks for Canada and Japan probably do not reflect the real peaks because specific duties are excluded.

9. For example, in the European Union the duties on wine are 13 Euros per hectoliter, which corresponds to about 12 cents per bottle. For wines that come from developing countries such as Bulgaria and Moldova, CIF prices per bottle are less than $1, which gives a tariff rate of about 12 percent, a high rate. For a $10 dollar bottle from California, the tariff rate would be just 1.2 percent, a very low one.

10. Individual country details are given in annex 2.

11. A recent OECD publication argues that the administration of ad valorem rates could cause difficulties for the customs administration; the developing countries have been administering such rates with much lower administrative capacity (OECD 2002a).

12. Additional distortion is produced by circumvention, possibly through the subsidy elements in export credits, export restrictions, and revenue-pooling arrangements in major products.

13. The Harbinson proposal presents the current status of agricultural negotiations on establishing numeric targets, formulas, and other 'modalities' for countries' commitments to increase market access, decrease export subsidies, and reduce distorting domestic support as mandated by the Uruguay Round Agreement on Agriculture. The proposal also spells out propositions on special and differential treatment and the role of nontrade-concerns.

14. These are average cuts, so the actual cuts in each line could be lower.

15. This is also true of many industrial countries but the difference between the bound, and applied rates is much smaller.

16. The European Union and United States were selected because there are tariff equivalents for the specific duties. The data for the European Union is for 1999, the last year for which the tariff equivalents were available.

17. http://www.fao.org/docrep/005/y9643e/y9643e04.htm

18. http://www.foodgrainsbank.ca/downloads/fjfa_foodaid.pdf

19. Trueblood, Michael, and Shahla Shapouri. 2002. "Safety Nets: An Issue in Global Agricultural Trade Liberalization." *Agricultural Outlook* (Economic Research Service/U.S. Department of Agriculture). March. http://www.ers.usda.gov/publications/agoutlook/Mar2002/ao289f.pdf

20. WTO, Committee on Agriculture Special Session. 2002. "Negotiations on Agriculture: Overview." TN/AG/6. Pages 58–61. December 18, 2002. http://www.wto.org/english/tratop_e/agric_e/negoti_modoverview_e.pdf

References

Aksoy, M. Ataman, Z. Ersel, and B. Sivri. 2003. "Demand Growth versus Market Share Gains: Decomposing Export Growth in the 1990s." Mimeo. World Bank, Washington, D.C.

Baffes, John. 2003. "Cotton Market Setting Policies, Issues, and Facts." Mimeo. World Bank, Washington, D.C. March.

Baffes, John, and Harry de Gorter. 2003. "Decoupling Support to Agriculture: An Economic Analysis and Recent Experience." *Annual World Bank Conference on Development Economics*. Paris, May 15–16.

Beghin, John, and M. Ataman Aksoy. 2003. "Agricultural Trade and the Doha Round. Lessons from Commodities Studies." *Annual World Bank Conference on Development Economics*. Paris, May 15–16.

Bell, B., and R. Elliott. 1993. "Aspects of New Zealand's Experience in Agricultural Reform Since 1984," Ministry of Agriculture and Forestry, Auckland, New Zealand.

Borrell, Brent, and David Pearce. 1999. "Sugar: the Taste Test of Trade Liberalization." Center for International Economics, Canberra and Sydney, Australia, September.

Cato, James C., and C. A. L. Dos Santos. 2000. "Costs to Upgrade the Bangladesh Frozen Shrimp Processing Sector to Adequate Technical and Sanitary Standards." In L. J. Unnevehr, ed., *The Economics of HACCP*. Saint Paul, Minn.: Eagan Press.

DRIFE (Danish Research Institute of Food Economics). 2003. "Note on the Harbinson Draft on Modalities in the WTO Agriculture Negotiations." Agricultural Policy Research Division, Frederiksberg, Denmark.

De Gorter, H. 2003. "Agricultural Support Programs and Farm Household Incomes." Mimeo. World Bank, Washington, D.C.

Diop, Ndiame, John Beghin, and Mirvat Sewadeh. 2003. "Groundnut Policies, Global Trade Dynamics, and the Impact of Trade Liberalization." Mimeo. World Bank, Washington, D.C. March.

Federated Farmers of New Zealand. 2002. "Life after Subsidies: The New Zealand Farming Experience 15 Years Later." Wellington, New Zealand.

Gallezot, J. 2003. "La progressivité tarifaire de l'UE vis à vis des produits agricoles et agroalimentaires." Mimeo. Institut National de Recherche Agronomique, Unité Mixte de Recherche Économie Publique, Paris-Grignon. January.

Golub, S., and J. Michael Finger. 1979. "The Processing of Primary Commodities: Effects of Developed-country Tariff Escalation and Developing Country Export Taxes." *Journal of Political Economy* 83 (3): 559–77.

Henson, Spencer, Ann-Marie Brouder, and Winnie Mitullah. 2000. "Food Safety Requirements and Food Exports from Developing Countries: The Case of Fish Exports from Kenya to the European Union." *American Journal of Agricultural Economics*, No. 5.

Hoekman, Bernard, Francis Ng, and Marcelo Olarreaga. 2002. "Reducing Agricultural Tariffs versus Domestic Support: What's More Important for Developing Countries?" Mimeo. World Bank, Washington, D.C. September.

Ingco, M. 1997. "Has Agricultural Trade Liberalization Improved Welfare in the Least-Developed Countries? Yes." Policy Research Working Paper 1748. World Bank, Washington, D.C.

Integrated Framework. 2003. "Malawi Diagnostic Integration Study, Integrated Framework Diagnostic." Trade Integration Studies, Washington, D.C., May.

Jaffee, Steven. 2003. "From Challenge to Opportunity: The Transformation of Kenyan Vegetable Trade in the Context of Emerging Food Safety and Other Standards." Mimeo. World Bank, Washington, D.C.

Jansen, H. Tarp, Sherman Robinson, and Finn Tarp. 2002. "General Equilibrium Measures of Agricultural Policy Bias in Fifteen Developing Countries." TMD Discussion Paper 105. International Food Policy Research Institute, Washington, D.C.

Kalaitzandonakes, N. G., and M. E. Bredahl. 1994. "Protectionism, Efficiency, and Productivity Growth." In M. Hartmann, P. M. Schmitz, and H. von Witzke, eds., *Agricultural Trade and Economic Integration in Europe and in North America*. Kiel, Germany: Wissenschaftsverlag Vauk Kiel KG.

Kudat A., M. I. Ajwad, and B. Sivri. 2003. "A Synthesis of Trade and Poverty Country Studies in Diagnostic Trade Integration Studies." Mimeo. World Bank, Washington, D.C.

Lindland, J. 1997. "The Impact of the Uruguay Round on Tariff Escalation in Agricultural Products." *Food Policy* 22: 487–500.

Minot, Nicholas, and Lisa Daniels. 2002. "Impact of Global Cotton Markets on Rural Poverty in Benin." International Food Policy Research Institute, Washington, D.C. November.

Minot, Nicholas, M. Kherallah, and P. Berry. 2000. "Fertilizer Market Reform and the Determinants of Fertilizer Use in Benin and Malawi." MSSD Discussion Paper 40. International Food Policy Research Institute, Washington, D.C. October.

Mitchell, Donald. 2003. "Sugar Policies: Opportunity for Change." Mimeo. World Bank, Washington, D.C. March.

Morrison Paul, Catherine J., Warren Johnston, and Gerald Frengley. 2000. "Efficiency in New Zealand Sheep and Beef Farming: The Impacts of Regulatory Reform." *Review of Economics and Statistics* 82 (2): 325–37.

Nogues, Julio J. 2002. "Comment to 'Trade, Growth, and Poverty—A Selective Survey,' by Andrew Berg and Anne Krueger, and 'Doha and the World Poverty Target,' by L. Alan Winters." Commentary presented at the Annual World Bank Conference on Development Economics, May.

Nogues, Julio J. 2003. "Agricultural Exports in a Protectionist World: Assessing Trade Strategies for MERCOSUR." Paper prepared for the Trade and Integration Division of the Inter-American Development Bank.

OECD (Organisation for Economic Co-operation and Development). 1999. "Distributional Effect of Agricultural Support in Selected OECD Countries." Directorate for Food, Agriculture, and Fisheries, Committee for Agriculture, Paris.

_____. 2001. "The Uruguay Round Agreement on Agriculture: an Evaluation of Its Implementation in OECD Countries." Paris.

_____. 2002a. "A Positive Agenda." Directorate for Food, Agriculture, and Fisheries, Committee for Agriculture. Paris.

_____. 2002b. "Methodology for the Measurement of Support and Use in Policy Evaluation." Paris.

_____. 2002c. "Agricultural Policies in OECD Countries: Monitoring and Evaluation." Paris.

_____. 2002d. "Farm Household Income Issues in OECD Countries: A Synthesis Report." Directorate for Food, Agriculture, and Fisheries, Committee for Agriculture. Paris.

_____. 2002e. "The Incidence and Income Transfer Efficiency of Farm Support Measures." Directorate for Food, Agriculture, and Fisheries, Committee for Agriculture. Paris.

Quiroz, J., and L. Opazo. 2000. "The Krueger-Schiff-Valdés Study 10 Years Later: A Latin American Perspective." *Economic Development and Cultural Change* 49 (1): 181–96.

Rae, A., and T. Josling. 2003. "Processed Food Trade and Developing Countries: Protection and Trade Liberalization." *Food Policy* 28: 147–66.

Ravallion, Martin. 2000. "On the Urbanization of Poverty." Mimeo. World Bank, Washington, D.C.

Rosengrant, M. W., and S. Meijer. 2002. "Agricultural Trade Liberalization to 2020: Impact on Trade, Price, and Economics Benefits." International Food Policy Research Institute, Washington, D.C. September.

Schiff, Maurice, and Alberto Valdés. 1992. *The Political Economy of Agricultural Pricing Policy.* Volume 4 of *A Synthesis of the Economics in Developing Countries.* Baltimore: Johns Hopkins University Press.

Sheales, T., S. Gordon, A. Hafi, and C. Toyne. 1999. "Sugar International Policies Affecting Market Expansion." ABARE Research Report 99.14. Australian Bureau of Agricultural and Resource Economics, Canberra, Australia. November.

USDA (U.S. Department of Agriculture). 2002. "Agricultural Income and Finance Outlook." Washington, D.C. September 26.

Von Braun J., and E. Kennedy. 1994. *Agricultural Commercialization, Economic Development, and Nutrition.* Baltimore: Johns Hopkins University Press.

Wailes, Eric. J. 2003. "Global Trade and Protection Regimes in Rice Trade." Mimeo. University of Arkansas, Fayetteville. April.

Watkins, Kevin. 2003. "Northern Agricultural Policies and World Poverty: Will the Doha 'Development Round' Make a Difference?" *Annual World Bank Conference on Development Economics.* Paris, May 15–16.

World Bank. 2000. *Global Economic Prospects and the Developing Countries 2001.* Washington, D.C.: World Bank.

_____. 2001. *Global Economic Prospects and the Developing Countries 2002.* Washington, D.C.

WTO (World Trade Organization). 2003. "Negotiations on Agriculture First Draft of Modalities for the Further Commitments." WTO Document No: TN/AG/W/1/Rev.1. Geneva.

4

Labor Mobility and the WTO: Liberalizing Temporary Movement

Globalization is driving the movement of people across borders
With globalization—the dramatic expansion of cross-border trade and investment—has come an upsurge in international labor mobility. Falling costs of transportation and communication have reduced the distances between peoples, and the drive for better lives has motivated workers to move to areas where jobs are more plentiful and pay is better. Foreign-born persons now account for 10 percent of the total population in the United States, 5 percent in Europe, and 1 percent in Japan. In Canada and Australia, foreign-born persons represent 17 and 24 percent of the total population, respectively.[1]

Even so, today's movement of people is still well below levels experienced in the late nineteenth century, and migration rates, now hampered by restrictive policies, are well below cross-border flow of goods and investment. By 2000, according to the United Nations, 175 million persons were living outside their country of birth—about 3 percent of the world's population. By contrast, global exports of goods reached almost a third of GDP, and financial flows were well above 10 percent (OECD 2001c; World Bank 2003; United Nations 2000).

While long term and settlement migration are still predominant in most developed countries, migrant flows are now more diverse and complex, with migrants moving back and forth more readily and rapidly. Temporary movement, in particular by highly skilled workers, has seen the largest growth in the past decade.

Both rich and poor countries can benefit
Both developed and developing countries have much to gain from an increased flow of workers. Rich countries benefit because they gain workers whose skills are in short supply. Also, as demographics drive up the average age in rich countries, migration allows an influx of younger workers who contribute to pension systems that would otherwise be actuarially unviable. Poor countries gain from higher wages as well as from the remittances that accrue from migration. In 2001, worker remittances alone provided some $70 billion to developing countries, nearly 40 percent more than all development assistance and significantly more than net debt flows to developing countries. Returning workers also often bring new skills back to the sending country. To be sure, there are costs to both receiving and sending countries: labor markets and social services may be strained in the rich countries, and developing countries may lose skilled workers who have been educated with public resources. Nonetheless, if a temporary visa system were introduced in rich countries permitting movement of labor up to 3 percent of the total labor force, world incomes would rise by nearly $160 billion (Walmsley and Winters 2002).

The GATS could facilitate temporary movements

Temporary movement of certain types of workers—service suppliers—is included under the World Trade Organization (WTO) General Agreement on Trade in Services. This is designed to facilitate the movement of people in a way analogous to the movement of goods and capital. This type of temporary movement—called Mode 4 in the GATS—is treated as other services in the global negotiations. They allow countries to negotiate fixed limits accorded to all foreign workers on a most-favored-nation (MFN) basis. Some developing countries see temporary movement under GATS Mode 4 as their key interest in services trade and are expecting real progress in the context of the Doha Development Agenda negotiations.

However, progress has been minimal because of policy restrictions

To date, however, even judging by the relatively limited liberalization of trade in services during the Uruguay Round, little has been done to loosen conditions governing the temporary movement of natural persons supplying services (Mode 4). Mode 4 today accounts for less than 2 percent of the total value of services trade. Present commitments refer almost exclusively to higher level personnel. More than 40 percent of Mode 4 commitments are for intracorporate transferees whose mobility is intimately related to foreign direct investment; another 50 percent of commitments cover executives, managers and specialists, and business visitors. All this means that the Mode 4 liberalization achieved to date has been of limited significance for developing countries whose comparative advantage lies in the export of medium- and low-skilled, labor-intensive services.

Two fundamental tensions hamper progress on Mode 4 labor mobility. The first is that governments are reluctant to undertake permanent commitments when employment demand varies with cyclical conditions, and when several OECD countries are facing difficulties in integrating existing immigrant communities into their labor market and societies. Wanting to maintain immigration and labor market policy flexibility, countries have made GATS commitments far below the degree of TMNP access already afforded under domestic laws and regulations. An important corollary of this tension is that the extent of TMNP liberalization for some sectors and categories of workers where labor demand routinely exceeds supply (for example, in tourism, information technology, and medical-related services) may be significantly greater than in other categories of labor, particularly unskilled labor.

A second tension stems from the fact that the strong regional character of migration patterns creates domestic political support for programs that favor neighboring countries, while Mode 4 commitments necessarily are open to all countries on an MFN basis. Preferential migration schemes are commonly negotiated at the bilateral and regional levels, and MFN-based liberalization would undermine these. Because the many bilateral labor agreements are usually untied to trade policy or other agreements, they afford governments a greater degree of flexibility to adjust programs to evolving migration trends and labor market needs.

While the potential gains from increasing temporary labor mobility, including for service suppliers under GATS Mode 4, could be sizeable, the analysis presented in this chapter cautions that expectations of far-reaching forward movement need to be tempered because of the political sensitivity of such trade in receiving countries. That sensitivity has become more pronounced in the context of decelerating worldwide economic growth and heightened security concerns.

Expanding Mode 4 requires changes to realize its modest potential

Tensions notwithstanding, present levels of Mode 4 access fall far short of even its relatively modest potential. One possible response is for developing countries to actively expand their requests and offers in the Doha Round. Also, WTO members could adopt rules that would provide greater clarity and predictability. And to help regularize entry and exit while ensuring improved security, countries could adopt a GATS visa system that would facilitate national visas for up to one year, subject to appropriate checks and strict rules of administration.

The bigger picture: Global migration and remittance trends

Although on an upward trend over the last two decades, migration is still far below its historic peak. The greatest migratory flows took place between the middle of the nineteenth century and the onset of World War I, when an estimated 10 percent of the world's labor force relocated permanently across borders (World Bank 2001). Mass migration was a major factor in equalizing incomes across countries throughout this period, by some estimates exerting a greater influence than either trade or capital movements (Lindert and Williamson 2001).

Since World War II, globalization has led to more unrestricted movement of both goods and capital, while international policies toward migration have become more restrictive. As a result, the overall scale of labor migration remains relatively smaller than that of capital or trade flows. Only 3 percent of the world's population—some 175 million people—live outside their country of citizenship, and the number of permanent legal immigrants to the United States is less today than it was in 1914, both in absolute terms—850,000 vs. 1.2 million—and as a percentage of the total population—0.35 percent vs. 1.5 percent. By contrast, global exports of goods represent almost one-third of world GDP (World Bank 2003; OECD 2001c).

While South-North migratory flows receive the most attention, much cross-border labor mobility—representing roughly half of the total number of migrants—takes place between developing countries. While poorly measured and less well understood than flows into the North, some patterns are evident: South Asians typically travel to the Middle East and East Asia, while South Africa, Nigeria, and Côte d'Ivoire together have accounted until recently for up to half of Africa's migratory flow. Almost everywhere, most migrants tend to stay within their regions, reflecting the importance of culture and language and the lower costs associated with geographical proximity.

Around the world, migration is on the rise
Five forces have governed world migration since the mid-nineteenth century:

- Wage and opportunity gaps between rich and poor countries
- Regional conflicts and political instability in developing countries
- The relative share of young adults in the populations of sending and receiving countries
- Numbers of migrant stock residing in receiving countries
- Reductions in the cost and inconvenience of travel.

These forces are still driving South-North, and South-South, migration. Successful development and poverty eradication in the developing world almost certainly will release part of the poverty constraint on potential emigrants while simultaneously reducing the motivation of many to move. In regions where development has been slower and poverty more obstinate, rising populations, dwindling opportunities, and lower travel costs will combine to impel emigration. The shrinking share of young adults in the developed countries, particularly in Japan and Western Europe, and the rising share of young people in South Asia, Africa, and other parts of the world are complementary drivers of labor movement. Growing numbers of young people in the developing world have acquired the education and training needed to assume skilled positions in developed economies. And as the numbers of the foreign-born grow in developed countries, their presence makes it easier and more attractive for newcomers to join them (Hutton and Williamson 2002).

Wage differentials remain high. The average hourly wage in manufacturing is about $30 in

Germany, while in some parts of China and India it is only 30 cents. Between the United States or France and newly emerging countries such as Thailand or Malaysia the gap is tenfold. Meanwhile, the supply of labor is swelling in developing countries—particularly in South Asia and Africa, where poverty is concentrated. Each year 83 million people are added to the world's population, 82 million of them in the developing world (World Bank 2001).

The continuing demographic transition in industrial countries adds to these pressures. As their populations age and average levels of training and education rise, developed countries face a declining ratio of workers to retirees and an increasing scarcity of lower-skilled labor (box 4.1). In some service occupations, particularly those most directly related to population aging (medical care and associated personal care services), where there is no substitute for human labor, the demand for—and benefits of—movement of lower-skilled labor are likely to continue to increase (Winters 2003).

The foreign and foreign-born make up a growing share of the population of most major industrial countries, rising over the last decade from 4.6 to 5.4 percent in the European Economic Area, and from 7.9 to 10.4 percent in the United States (table 4.1) Because the population of developing countries is about five times greater than that of devel-

Box 4.1 Population aging and migration

The combined demographic effects of the baby boom that marked the immediate post-war period, the fall in fertility rates that began in OECD countries in the late 1960s, and longer life expectancy have led to a striking acceleration in population aging in virtually all advanced industrial societies.

Population aging is much more marked in Europe and Japan than in North America, but all three regions will be affected. According to demographic projections by the United Nations, the populations of the European Union and Japan are expected to fall by 10 percent and 14 percent, respectively, between 2000 and 2050, representing a decline of some 55 million in all. In both Japan and the European Union, the dependency ratio (defined as the ratio of pensioners to workers) is expected to decline from five to one today to three to one in 2015. For the United States, projections still point to an increased total population over the same period, but the dependency ratio also rises.

Recent research has considered the economic and fiscal impact of these demographic trends in the OECD area (OECD 2000, 2001c, 2002; Visco 2000). Without offsetting measures, the growing dependency could place enormous strains on social security, Medicare, and pensions systems. Far-reaching decisions are required over the medium and long term to meet shifting labor demands and to safeguard balance and equity in the systems of social protection—decisions related to the length of working life, levels of contributions and benefits, and productivity advances.

One solution receiving increased consideration in several countries is to increase levels of permanent immigration to modify population structures and mitigate the social and economic costs of aging. Immigration has advantages. It can quickly increase the economically active population because new immigrants tend to be younger and more mobile. Also, fertility rates among immigrant women are often relatively high, which can help boost population growth. This has only a limited impact in the short run, however.

Immigration alone cannot provide the answer to population aging, as demonstrated by simulations produced by the United Nations (2000). The simulations show that maintaining steady dependency ratios until 2050 would require an enormous increase in migration flows—for the United States and the European Union, migration balances would have to be at least 10 times the annual averages of the 1990s. Such scenarios seem implausible by historical standards, and in light of the likely political reactions.

─────────

Source: OECD (2001f).

Table 4.1 Migration is rising in many OECD countries
Migration flows and stocks of foreign and foreign-born population in OECD countries, annual averages, 1990–2000 (thousands, except where otherwise noted)

	1990–94	1995–99	2000
Immigration			
Australia			
Permanent	99	87	92
Temporary	104	154	224
Canada			
Permanent	236	204	227
Temporary workers[a]	64	69	86
European economic area[b]	1,614	1,352	1,426
Japan	244	251	346
United States			
Permanent	1,209	747	850
Temporary[c]	1,357	1,893	2,741
Net migration per thousand inhabitants			
Australia	4.3	5.1	5.4
Canada[d]	..	5.4	5.1
European economic area[e]	3.1	1.7	2.5
Japan	−0.03	−0.04	0.3
United States	3.3	3.3	3.1
Asylum seekers			
Australia	9	9	12
Canada	30	26	36
Central and Eastern Europe	3	13	26
European economic area	516	326	427
United States	136	105	57
Acquisitions of nationality			
Australia	107	102	80
Canada	130	160	205
European economic area[f]	460	690	720
Japan	12	16	18
United States	315	680	900

	1990 (percent)	2000 (percent)	2000 (thousands)
Stock of foreign population			
European economic area[g]	4.6	5.4	20,381
Japan	0.9	1.3	1,686
Stock of foreign-born population			
Australia	22.8	23.6	4,517
Canada[h]	16.1	17.4	4,971
United States	7.9	10.4	28,400

.. negligible
a. Inflows of foreign workers entering Canada to work temporarily (excluding seasonal workers) provided by initial entry.
b. Includes Austria, Greece, Italy, and Spain. No 2000 data for Denmark available; 1999 data substituted.
c. Excluding visitors, transit migrants, foreign government officials, and students.
d. Fiscal years (July to June).
e. Data relate to 1999–2000 average instead of 2000.
f. Excluding Greece and Ireland.
g. Excluding Greece. No 2000 data available for France; 1999 data substituted.
h. Data are for 1991 instead of 1990 and for 1996 instead of 2000.
Source: OECD (2002f).

oped countries, migrants comprise a larger share of the total population in rich countries (6 percent) than in poor countries (1 percent).

The uneven composition of immigration flows reflects differing policy objectives and historical and institutional backgrounds in various countries. Some countries, such as Australia, Switzerland, and the United Kingdom, explicitly give priority to foreign workers, so that this group accounts for around half of all immigration. Other OECD countries, because they tend to restrict work-related migration, implicitly give priority to nonselective migration arising from family reunification (which accounts for approximately 80 percent of flows into the United States and France, for example) or requests for asylum (approximately half in the Nordic countries) (OECD 2002f).

Because legal immigration is restricted, illegal migration has risen noticeably in recent years, as have trafficking in human beings and expenditures to combat both phenomena. Illegal migration into the European Union soared tenfold in the 1990s, reaching half a million people annually by the end of the decade. In the United States, an estimated net inflow of 300,000 undocumented workers occurs each year, although this could well underestimate the actual scale of illegal migration.

Newer factors are compounding the more familiar drivers of migration. The developing world's rising share of educated workers—those who have completed secondary education—has jumped from one-third to nearly one-half over the past three decades. Increasingly, the growing pool of skilled developing-country labor is meeting industrial-country shortages, as the marketplace for skills widens to encompass the entire globe. Meanwhile, continued declines in transportation and communication costs and thus greater access to information on migration opportunities via global media, the Internet, and diaspora networks in receiving countries are breaking down barriers to migration (Nielson 2002).

Remittances by migrants are an important source of income for many developing countries

Remittances from foreign workers, both permanent and temporary, are the second-largest source of external funding for developing countries, after foreign direct investment (FDI). In 2001, workers' remittances to developing countries stood at $72.3 billion, considerably higher than total official development assistance and private non-FDI flows, and 42 percent of total FDI flows to developing countries that year (table 4.2). For most of the 1990s, remittance receipts exceeded official development assistance (World Bank 2003).

As with actual movements of people, the data on payments are susceptible to measurement problems—not all flows, even from legal migration, are captured in the balance of payments accounts, and in situations where substantial illegal migration occurs, the bulk of the international resource flows also may be missed. Such difficulties notwithstanding, initial estimates of these flows can be derived

Table 4.2 **Workers' remittances are the second-largest source of external funding for developing countries**

Remittance receipts and payments by developing countries in 2001 (billions of dollars)

	All developing	Low income	Lower middle income	Upper middle income
Total remittance receipts	72.3	19.2	35.9	17.3
As percentage of GDP	1.3	1.9	1.4	0.8
As percentage of imports	3.9	6.2	5.1	2.7
As percentage of domestic investment	5.7	9.6	5.0	4.9
As percentage of FDI inflows	42.4	213.5	43.7	21.7
As percentage of total private capital inflows	42.9	666.1	44.9	20.2
As percentage of official development assistance	260.1	120.6	361.7	867.9
Other current transfers[a]	27.2	6.1	14.0	7.1
Remittances and other current transfers	99.5	25.3	49.9	24.4
Total remittance payments	22.0	1.2	1.7	19.1
Excluding Saudi Arabia	6.9	1.2	1.7	4.0

a. Other current transfers include gifts, donations to charities, pensions received by currently retired expatriate workers, and so on. They also may include personal transfers by migrant workers to families back home.
Source: World Bank (2003).

Figure 4.1 Workers' remittances are an important source of income for many developing countries

Top developing-country recipients of workers' remittances, 2001 (billions of dollars and percent of GDP)

Left panel (billions of dollars, scale 0–12):
- India
- Mexico
- Philippines
- Morocco
- Egypt, Arab Rep.
- Turkey
- Lebanon
- Bangladesh
- Jordan
- Dominican Republic
- El Salvador
- Colombia
- Yemen, Rep.
- Pakistan
- Brazil
- Ecuador
- Yugoslavia, FR (Serb./Mont.)
- Thailand
- China
- Sri Lanka

Right panel (percent of GDP, scale 0–30):
- Lesotho
- Jordan
- Albania
- Nicaragua
- Yemen, Rep.
- Moldova
- Lebanon
- El Salvador
- Cape Verde
- Jamaica
- Yugoslavia, FR (Serb./Mont.)
- Morocco
- Dominican Republic
- Vanuatu
- Philippines
- Honduras
- Uganda
- Ecuador
- Sri Lanka

Source: World Bank (2003).

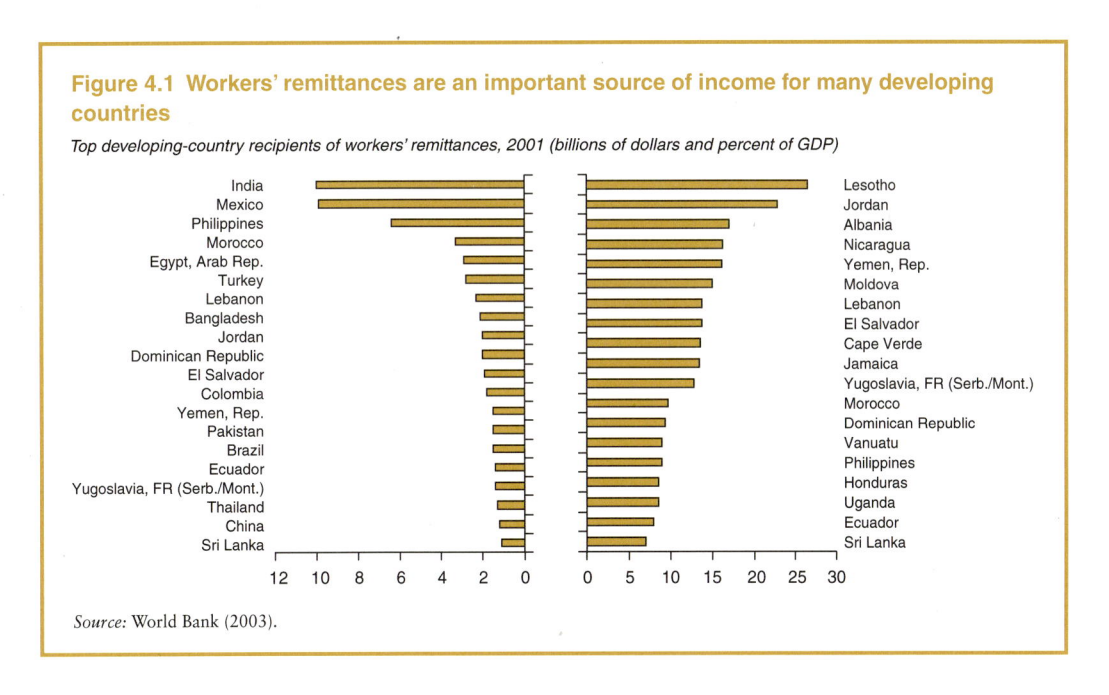

from balance of payments statistics by combining workers' *compensation* (transfers relating to work abroad of less than one year) and workers' *remittances* (transfers made by workers whose stay abroad exceeds one year) (World Bank 2003).

In nominal terms, the top recipients of remittances included several large developing economies—India, Mexico, and the Philippines—although as a share of GDP, remittances were larger in other low-income countries in 2001 (figure 4.1). Broken down along regional lines, countries in Latin America and the Caribbean were the largest recipient of remittances in nominal terms in 2001, but relative to the size of GDP, South Asia was the largest recipient, with remittances of nearly 2.5 percent of GDP. Remittance flows to countries in Sub-Saharan Africa also were significant, accounting for 1.3 percent of GDP (table 4.3).

Workers' remittances are spread more evenly among developing countries than are capital flows—the top 10 recipient countries in 2001 received 60 percent of total remittances to developing countries as compared with a top 10 share of 68 percent of GDP, 72 percent

Table 4.3 Remittances are a significant source of income in all regions of the developing world

Workers' remittances received by developing countries, by region, 1999–2002 (in billions of dollars and as percentage of GDP)

(billions of dollars)	1999 $ billions	1999 % GDP	2000 $ billions	2000 % GDP	2001 $ billions	2001 % GDP	2002 $ billions	2002 % GDP
Total	67	1.2	66	1.1	72	1.3	80	1.3
East Asia and Pacific	11	0.7	10	0.7	10	0.6	11	0.6
Europe and Central Asia	8	0.9	9	0.9	9	0.9	10	1.0
Latin America and Caribbean	17	1.0	19	1.0	23	1.2	25	1.5
Middle East and North Africa	12	2.2	11	1.9	14	2.3	14	2.2
South Asia	15	2.6	13	2.3	14	2.3	16	2.5
Sub-Saharan Africa	4	1.3	3	0.8	3	1.0	4	1.3

Sources: IMF, *Balance of Payments Yearbook;* World Bank, *World Development Indicators* (2001).

of exports, and 74 percent of FDI. Remittances also are more stable than private capital flows, which tend to move in a pro-cyclical manner.

Temporary movement of workers

Many people move only temporarily—students, tourists, business visitors exploring or conducting trade and investment activities, and people working abroad under a range of schemes. People working or conducting business are thus a subset of temporary movement, and GATS Mode 4, temporary movement of natural persons as service suppliers, is a further subset of this group.

Most of the developed economies experienced significant growth in certain types of temporary migration during the 1990s (table 4.4). In the United States, for example, the average number of temporary immigrants per year doubled between 1990–94 and 2000, at which point the total was more than three times larger than permanent immigrants (see table 4.1).

The absence of global figures on temporary foreign workers and the limitations of existing migration data[2] make analysis difficult and definitive conclusions impossible. However, according to the OECD (2001), some trends have begun to emerge.

Although available statistics are insufficient to identify conclusively the primary traders in temporary mobility, the picture is not a simple one. Developed countries are major exporters, as well as importers, of labor. Similarly, some developing countries are significant importers. By some value indicators—for example, compensation of employees—developed countries account for most of the flow in both directions. On the other hand, developing countries are the major receivers of remittances (see figure 4.1). Temporary movement is by no means unidirectional. Relative to the overall size of labor markets, the number of temporary foreign workers remains small for most countries, except for the Arab states of the Persian Gulf. The areas of highest growth are short-term movements (from three to six months) (OECD 2001b). Movements of both skilled and unskilled workers appear to be concentrated in the service sectors of major receiving countries, notably in construction, commerce, catering, education, health care, services to households, and other services. In developing countries, foreign workers tend to be concentrated in primary activities (agriculture, fishing, and mining) as well as in manufacturing, although the share in services (particularly tourism-related) is rising in several countries (UNCTAD 2001).

Although the volume of global trade represented by temporary foreign workers remains small compared to overall trade in goods and services, it is very important for some industries and for some countries. Indeed, exports

Table 4.4 Temporary movement is rising in rich countries
Entries of temporary foreign workers in selected OECD countries, 1992–2000 (thousands)

	1992	1993	1994	1995	1996	1997	1998	1999	2000
Australia	40.5	14.9	14.2	14.3	55.7	81.7	92.9	99.7	115.7
Canada	70.4	65.4	67.5	69.5	71.5	75.4	79.5	85.4	93.7
France	18.1	—	—	—	13.6	12.9	11.8	13.4	15.4
Germany	332.6	69.1	53.9	61.7	271.0	267.7	244.0	274.1	331.6
Italy	—	—	—	—	—	—	—	18.7	24.52
Japan	—	—	—	—	124.1	143.5	151.7	156.0	183.9
Korea, Rep. of	8.3	12.4	33.6	47.0	81.4	105.0	75.4	111.0	122.5
Sweden	—	—	—	—	—	—	—	15.0	19.4
Switzerland	127.8	—	—	—	63.4	47.4	40.3	46.1	50.3
United Kingdom	57.6	25.9	26.3	32.9	78.7	89.7	98.8	107.9	134.1
United States	143.0	112.5	130.7	147.5	191.2	—	342.7	422.5	505.1

— Not available.
Note: Definitions vary among countries and the figures are not strictly comparable.
Source: OECD (2002f).

Box 4.2 Temporary labor movement and the East Asian crisis of 1997–98

Increased labor migration, particularly the temporary movement of unskilled labor, was an important dimension of structural change and globalization within much of Northeast and Southeast Asia in the 1980s and 1990s. Conservative estimates suggest that the number of migrants doubled or even tripled in most net labor importing countries from the early 1980s to the onset of the financial crisis in 1997 (Athukorala and Manning 1999). By the onset of the crisis, some 2 million overseas migrant workers were employed in Northeast Asian economies outside China, and an even larger number—some 3 to 4 million—worked in Southeast Asia.

The Asian financial crisis changed the context within which those labor movements occurred, posing a major threat to economic growth. International capital flows reversed, many firms went bankrupt, and unemployment rates rose steeply in the crisis-affected countries (World Bank 2000). Demand for labor plummeted in the modern sectors of labor-receiving countries. Yet a recent examination of labor mobility patterns before and after the financial crisis suggests that the economic turmoil did not alter the fundamental conditions underpinning high levels of intraregional migration, especially of unskilled contract workers (Manning 2002)—a widening wage gap and imbalances between supply and demand for labor across East Asia.

Countries in the region—especially the net labor importers: Hong Kong (China), Malaysia, Republic of Korea, and Thailand—have continued to rely on inflows of migrant workers. Many such migrants are unskilled. Indeed, the willingness of migrant workers to undertake so-called 3-D jobs (difficult, dirty, and dangerous) shunned by nationals in export-oriented industries has helped economic recovery. The large real gains to workers who migrate to more developed countries were documented in a recent study: unskilled Indonesian workers can earn $2 or more per day in neighboring Malaysia compared to 28 cents per day at home (World Bank 2001).

The migration of skilled and professional workers also was an important part of the internationalization of East Asian labor markets during the 1990s. FDI and associated trade flows resulted in significant skilled migration from developed to developing countries—as well as considerable out-migration of skilled and professional migrants from countries in the region. Workers from the Philippines dominated the latter flows, reflecting both slower rates of FDI and economic growth domestically, and a modern sector incapable of absorbing enough graduates from the well-developed education sector.

Several countries have sought to develop a more coherent migration policy in light of the social effects of the cutback in labor demand and unemployment that accompanied the crisis. This may be good news for many migrant workers who need protection against exploitation. In-migration of unskilled overseas workers, meanwhile, can be expected to continue to support production in both tradable and nontradable industries in the more affluent East Asian economies.

Source: World Bank staff.

---

of labor services in many developing countries account for a substantial share of output and trade. In several developing countries (mainly lower income), such flows dwarf the value of total services exports (OECD 2001b). Moreover, migration flows are resilient—for example, they were much more stable than capital flows in the wake of the recent Asian financial crisis (box 4.2).

Burgeoning cross-border investment—horizontally through mergers or joint ventures and vertically through relocation or so-called greenfield investments—accounts for much new temporary movement, helped along by advances in transportation, communications, logistics, and organization that have altered all phases of the business process. Today's companies not only can but must respond quickly to emerging opportunities by forming specialized task teams, regardless of where the personnel are based. Business functions previously handled by expatriate staff, resident representa-

Table 4.5 Foreign-born workers meet skill shortages in rich countries
Percentage of foreign workers in selected sectors, 2001

	Education	Information technology	Health professions (except nurses)
Austria	3.0	28.3	6.3
Belgium	3.3	6.0	4.0
France	2.8	4.2	1.7
Germany	2.8	5.7	4.4
Italy	0.3	0.4	1.0
Netherlands	1.6	2.8	1.4
Norway	4.3	4.3	5.7
Switzerland	13.0	19.3	16.5
United Kingdom	5.9	6.4	7.8
United States (foreign-born)	8.3	18.3	13.2

Source: OECD (2002f).

tives, or correspondent firms now may be accomplished by expert personnel on temporary assignments. Shorter product lifecycles, higher customer expectations, and stiffer competition force companies to be ready to send expert personnel abroad on short notice—or to bring them to the firm's home country for specialized tasks in engineering, production, and marketing. Companies entering new markets often wish to bring experienced staff from other locations to assist with the establishment phase (OECD 2001b). Indeed, among those temporary foreign workers who would fall under GATS Mode 4, the mobility of intracompany transferees—key personnel involved in the establishment or operation of enterprises abroad—has shown the fastest growth.

Investment liberalization can also create a demand for exports of skilled labor from the host country. Foreign firms in India, for example, have become aware of the skills available in India and are now meeting demand for various services in their home countries with supply from India (OECD 2001b). The growing importance of South-South FDI is an important vector of more highly skilled temporary labor movement between developing countries (World Bank 2003).

Temporary labor is used to meet skills shortages in developed countries, particularly in information and communication technology, but also in education and health-related services, which cannot be met quickly enough by domestic training programs and institutions (OECD 2001b) (table 4.5). Recent growth in the movement of highly skilled workers has been supported by specific programs designed to address key national shortages (box 4.3).

Bilateral and regional approaches to labor mobility

Regional trade agreements, which include provisions on labor mobility, range from a few that provide no-cost movement of all types of workers and service providers—although with caveats that allow exclusions from certain public services and restrictions based on public health and safety—to others, the majority, that target only intracorporate transferees and business visitors.[3] Some—such as the EU, EEA, and CARICOM—allow a relatively high degree of freedom of movement with few special procedures. Others, notably the North American Free Trade Association (NAFTA), allow for some regulated mobility and involve relatively detailed special procedures implemented among a few parties. Still others (such as APEC) are aimed at facilitating existing mobility, adding some special procedures, but retaining maximum flexibility to continue existing national practices (OECD 2002b) (box 4.4).

The differing approaches to labor mobility in regional trade agreements reflect a range of factors, including the degree of geographical proximity of the parties and the extent of similarities in their levels of development, as well as other cultural and historical ties. Agreements among countries enjoying geographic proximity and similar levels of development generally adopt a more liberal approach to labor mobility (EU, EFTA, EEA, Trans-Tasman Travel Arrangement) as compared to agreements among geographically distant members of differing levels of development (APEC, U.S.-Jordan). But this is not always the case (MERCOSUR, SAARC) (OECD 2002b).

The range of special provisions found in various regional trade agreements, but not in the

Box 4.3 Recent initiatives to facilitate temporary movement of highly skilled workers

Australia has established a number of business-sponsored temporary entry programs, supported by business service centers for employers seeking skilled foreign workers. Canada initiated a pilot program related to software development workers under which Human Resources Development Canada pre-identified a general need within the labor market for such workers. This enabled suitably qualified applicants with a job offer from a Canadian employer and any necessary visa (depending upon country of origin) to be automatically validated (that is, not subjected to labor market needs tests). Under a pilot project, spouses of "highly skilled foreign workers" who are admitted to Canada for at least six months also are permitted employment authorizations without being subjected to labor market testing.

France published a decree in 1998 permitting companies to hire foreign workers skilled in computer science if the company can demonstrate its inability to fill the post with a local candidate. Germany offered 20,000 employment permits ("green cards") for up to five years to computer and information technology specialists recruited outside the European Union. By August 2000, 13,000 green cards had been issued.

Japan announced a plan in November 2000 to recruit 30,000 skilled IT engineers and researchers from overseas by 2005. In the United Kingdom high-volume nonimmigrant visa employers with a proven track record receive streamlined and fast-tracked visa approval. Simplified fast-track procedures are now applied for issuing work permits for certain occupations, and the list of occupations susceptible to labor shortages has been extended. The maximum length of a work permit also has been extended from four to five years. The United States raised the annual quota of H-1B visas for professional and skilled workers by nearly 70 percent in 2000, providing temporary admission for 195,000 people over the next three fiscal years. The 7 percent ceiling on the proportion of visas going to nationals of any given country also was dropped. Faced with adverse cyclical developments in its labor market, the United States recently set the annual quota of H-1B visas at 65,000, the level set prior to the dot com boom of the late 1990s.

Source: OECD (2001b, 2002f).

---

general GATS provisions related to the temporary movement of service suppliers, includes:

- Access to the labor market (EU, EFTA, EEA, Trans-Tasman Travel Arrangement)
- Full national treatment and market access for service suppliers (ANZCERTA)
- Commitments on visas (NAFTA; U.S.-Jordan, which extends the commitment beyond service providers)
- Special market access or facilitated access for service providers and others (APEC, Canada-Chile, CARICOM, Europe Agreements, NAFTA)
- Separate chapters dealing with all temporary movement, including movement related to investment (Japan-Singapore) or to trade in goods or investment (Group of Three)
- Specific reference to key personnel in relation to investment (EU-Mexico, FTAA)
- Extension of WTO treatment to non-WTO members (AFTA); and nondiscriminatory conditions for workers, extending beyond service suppliers (Euro-Med) (OECD 2002b).

To assess the degree of liberalization offered in a regional trade agreement, provisions related to labor mobility should be considered in conjunction with provisions in the same agreements related to supply of services. Generally, the right to labor mobility does not automatically entail the right to practice a certain pro-

Box 4.4 A trade facilitation approach to labor mobility: NAFTA and APEC

For professionals, "Trade NAFTA" (TN) visas are available to citizens of Canada or Mexico for entry into the United States, provided that the profession is on the NAFTA Chapter 16 list, the candidate meets the specific criteria for that profession (typically a university degree in a relevant field of study), the prospective position requires someone in that capacity, and the candidate is going to work for a United States employer.[4] TN status lasts for one year and is renewable. The requirements for entry to the United States differ, however, for Mexican and Canadian nationals. Canadians are not required to have a visa or prior approval, but can receive TN status at the port of entry. The candidate must have a letter from a U.S. employer offering a job, or requesting an intracompany transfer, with a job description. For Mexicans, the employer must file a labor condition application (I-29 Petition for Non-Immigrant Workers), and the candidate must apply for a visa at the U.S. Embassy in Mexico.

Anecdotal evidence suggests that industry experience with TN visas has been positive, with evidence of difficulties confined to some confusion among border officials as to how the TN operates and the need for a regularly updated NAFTA professions list.

The APEC Business Travel Card offers accredited business travelers visa-free travel and expedited airport processing for travelers visiting participating economies. After an initial pilot, the scheme was made permanent in March 1999. Current participants include Australia, Chile, China, Chinese Taipei, Hong Kong (China), Indonesia, Republic of Korea, Malaysia, New Zealand, and the Philippines. Brunei Darussalam, Peru, and Thailand have signed the Operating Framework but are yet to issue cards.

The scheme allows considerable flexibility for individual economies. Its Operating Framework is not binding, with members committed to implementing it on a best-effort basis. Each government pre-clears applicants (a process that can be customized by each country, such as requiring formal sponsorship by a business organization). Once home authorities have provided clearance, details of the candidate are sent to all participating economies, which must offer a response within two weeks. Economies can refuse clearance for an individual without providing reason, but this will only restrict travel to that particular economy rather than vetoing the entire application. Following responses from other economies, the card is issued by the home economy authorities (who also have the sole right to cancel the card). Fees can be charged for issuance of the card and can vary among participating economies.

The card is valid for three years from the date of issue and provides multiple short-term business entries, stays of two or three months on each arrival, and access to special immigration processing counters on arrival and departure. The cards are the size of a credit card, are manual or machine-readable, and must contain the signature and photograph of the cardholder as well as the list of countries for which entry has been approved. Cardholders are still required to present their passports. Separate applications for visas and work permits are not required. Additionally, all economies retain the right to refuse entry to cardholders at the border.

Some 3,400 cards had been issued by mid-2002, with initial assessments indicating that the scheme is working effectively, with strong support from the business community and only a small percentage of applicants refused. There is no limit on the number of cards that can be issued.

Source: OECD (2001b).

---

fession. National regulations regarding licensing and recognition of qualifications are still applied and candidates must meet all criteria and conditions (OECD 2002c).[5]

Few agreements provide immigration rights or supersede national immigration practices. In most agreements, the signatories retain broad discretion in matters of residency and visas. Some agreements specify that the agreement cannot be invoked to challenge national decisions to refuse entry (Euro-Med), or provide remedies only where a pattern of restrictive practice can be proved (Canada-Chile, NAFTA) (OECD 2002c).

Overall, progress in facilitating movement of less-skilled temporary foreign workers has not been extensive at the regional level. Indeed, regional trade agreements tend to replicate the two key biases found in GATS favoring highly skilled (mostly professional) workers and the close links between investment and the specialized skills such investments require.

Additionally, bilateral foreign worker programs, which have been designed to fill both skilled and unskilled labor shortages, have existed in a number of countries for some time. Such agreements often cover seasonal workers in agriculture and tourism; project workers in construction; and various other employment-specific workers.

Understanding the impact of temporary foreign workers

What are the determinants of migration?

Economic models of migration tend to focus on the economic incentives facing migrants. In the absence of legal restrictions on immigration, cross-border labor mobility is often assumed to depend on the size of the gap in labor and income that existed between industrialized and developing countries (wages, working conditions, social security arrangements), and on the extent of information on that gap available to potential migrants. Migration would increase when the gap widened or when more information on the gap became available. Accordingly, it is not rare to see migration described in terms of a pent-up flood: if the tap is opened a little bit, more immigrants will come in; if it is closed, fewer will come. Yet there are strong reasons, rooted in observed trends in international migration, to believe that such a characterization is not fully accurate.

Labor mobility tends to be more complex than either trade or capital mobility. Even very large differences in economic returns (measured by wages) are not sufficient to induce migration in most people. Demographic, educational, and labor market conditions in both the source and destination countries affect migration decisions, as well as laws and policies in both countries, information and information flows, chain migration effects (among family members or those from the same origin area), transport and transaction costs, capital constraints (which may influence potential migrants' ability or willingness to incur these costs), and "exogenous" factors such as civil unrest and climate. There may well be substantial "disutility" costs associated with relocation from one's social-cultural-linguistic context into an alien one. These costs can in fact be among the most important factors in cross-border migration. The fact that the world's poorest countries supply a very small share of internationally mobile workers lends credence to the oft-observed notion that binding poverty constrains out-migration.

Moreover, migration decisions often are depicted as essentially on-off and unidirectional in nature when in practice people migrate for a host of economic and non-economic reasons. They initially may intend to stay temporarily and then return or move on to a third country, or they may intend to settle. Globalization increases the number and complexity of these flows. For this reason, some analysts prefer to talk about migration and migrants rather than immigration and immigrants (Home Office 2001).

Economic analysis of the temporary movement of foreign workers straddles the two worlds of trade and migration. This is in light of significant differences in the nature and skill profile of worker categories concerned and by the sharply differing lengths of time such workers can spend in foreign labor markets. Thus a business visitor going abroad to assess future opportunities or to conclude contract negotiations may stay only a few days. Such a transaction is largely akin to cross-border trade in services (so-called Mode 1 trade under GATS) and differs little from goods trade to the extent that it does not involve lasting factor movement. Not so for revolving teams of contract-based workers in construction services or for intracompany transferees, who may be deployed abroad for several years (and yet may constitute a transaction for the purposes of the GATS). In the latter cases, such "trade" in services has more in common with the economics of migration, as migrating workers reduce the supply of labor in the sending country while adding to it in receiving countries. Furthermore, the temporary movement of labor is often tied to longer-term flows of capital (in the form of foreign direct investment).

The essence of international trade lies in securing the gains from cross-country differences in costs, prices, endowments, or tastes. The larger such differences, the greater the potential gains from removing obstacles to such trade. The disparity between the abundance of labor in developing countries and its scarcity in the developed world suggests that significant pro-development returns—potentially greater than those stemming from the full liberalization of trade in goods—could be had if medium- and less-skilled workers in developing countries were allowed to provide their services temporarily in developed countries.

What are the gains from temporary movement?

Although labor remains far less mobile than goods and capital, the increasing diversity of migrants' nationalities and the migration channels used, as well as the growing share of temporary and skilled workers in total migration flows, does indicate a growing prominence for migration in the broader context of economic globalization.[6] Links between labor mobility and the liberalization of trade and investment have gained in visibility, as modern trade agreements have proliferated and broadened at both the regional and multilateral levels. Such developments have sparked an interest within the research community in measuring the potential effects of liberalizing labor flows.

Several recent studies have drawn attention to the potential benefits arising from a progressive relaxation of barriers to labor mobility (table 4.6). Winters (2003a) suggested that if developed countries were to raise to 3 percent of their labor force their quotas on the inward movements of temporary workers from developing countries, they would realize an overall gain of $150 billion each year. His work concludes that the gains from such liberalization would be shared equally by developed and developing countries. Most important, from a development perspective, these findings suggest that the largest benefits (to both sending and receiving countries) would come from the movement of lower-skilled workers, as those workers are spread more evenly over the economy, benefiting more sectors, than highly skilled ones (OECD 2002a).

Winters and Walmsley (2002) recognize that adjusting wage levels in response to competition from low-skilled developing country workers could entail high social costs. Such findings underscore the long-term importance of enhancing the educational levels and human capital of lower-skilled individuals to ensure that fewer developed country nationals are competing directly with unskilled workers from poorer countries. To manage the complex political economy that TMNP liberalization could entail and to minimize adverse (or excessively concentrated) distributional effects for vulnerable workers in receiving countries, the authors suggest that the liberalization process should be incremental, with the most sensitive sectors exempted. Affected workers may be helped through adjustment schemes similar to the U.S. Trade Adjustment Assistance Act, the assistance provisions of NAFTA, Canada's General Adjustment Assistance Programme, and Australia's Special Adjustment Assistance (Borjas 2000; Borjas, Freeman, and Katz 1997; OECD 2002a).

Because liberalization of merchandise trade has reduced price differentials between developed and developing countries to a ratio of two to one—whereas service prices and wage differentials continue to differ by a factor of ten or more—the gains from liberalizing cross-

Table 4.6 The distribution of costs and benefits associated with Mode 4 trade

| Sending countries || Receiving countries ||
Benefits	Costs	Benefits	Costs
In a situation of saturated labor markets, departure of workers exerts a downward pressure on unemployment, and an upward pressure on (low) wages. Once abroad, workers proceed to income transfers (compensation of employees and remittances), which are a major source of capital inflows and investment for many developing countries. Upon return of the workers, global human capital of the country is increased.	In a situation of labor shortages, departure of workers exerts only an upward pressure on (high) wages. The effects of temporarily losing human capital and public investment (education and training expenses) depend on the scarcity of the workers' skills (see cost of removing a doctor v. a low-skilled worker). Replacement of scarce resources could generate high costs. In a situation of saturated labor markets, return of workers exerts an upward pressure on unemployment, and a downward pressure on wages.	Temporary admission of foreign workers is a response to labor needs (shortages in some sectors or geographic areas). Entry of foreign service providers results in increased competition (wider choice of better services at lower price) at lower cost (activity stays in the country). Temporary admission of workers is a partial substitute for permanent immigration (less sensitive and lesser use of public infrastructure and services).	Temporary admission of foreign workers could delay the structural adjustment of the economy. In a situation of saturated labor markets, arrival of workers exerts an upward pressure on unemployment and a downward pressure on wages. Departure of workers generates a replacement cost and a loss of human capital and investment (training).
Maximizing benefits		**Maximizing benefits**	
Provide adequate infrastructure and career opportunities to maximize the use of competence acquired abroad once the worker is back. Create incentives for return. Negotiate commitments from other members in sectors where the national labor market is saturated. Adopt structural adjustments in sectors of labor shortages to prevent outflows of workers.		Create a possibility for workers to change visa status (become permanent resident) to avoid departure of the most useful ones. Facilitate temporary admission of workers and create incentives to attract workers in specific sectors or geographic areas (where shortages exist). Adjust the national economy to new competitive conditions.	
Overall benefits			
For business: a source of increased flexibility, profitability, and competitiveness; an instrument for facilitating trade and penetrating new markets For individuals: acquisition of vocational skills and know-how, including the learning of a foreign language; improved quality of life while abroad (compensation for expatriation); increased employment opportunities upon return			

Source: OECD (2001, 2002a).

border labor movements and other trade in services could be much greater than from further liberalizing trade in goods. Rodrik (2002) proposes a scheme under which skilled and unskilled workers from developing countries could apply for temporary visas entitling them to work in developed countries for three to five years, after which they would return to their home countries. The author suggests that if admissions were capped at 3 percent of the developed countries' labor force, the scheme could generate direct income gains of as much as $200 billion annually. Returnees' investments and the transfer of their experience would produce further gains for sending countries (OECD 2002d).

The source of the gains identified in the studies discussed above is a narrowing of wage differentials between rich and poor countries—a politically sensitive subject. In the regulated labor markets of many WTO member countries, domestic legislation limits or opposes downward pressure on wages. Moreover, many recipient (developed) countries require equality of treatment for temporary workers (equal wages and social protection parity requirements) with nationals at comparable levels of skill and experience (OECD 2002d). For these and other reasons, most models assume no more than a halving of differentials. To the extent that national provisions sustain domestic wages, the overall gains of Mode 4 liberalization may be lower, but in such cases adjustment costs will be concomitantly lower as well.

Other factors that may affect the overall gains of greater mobility of temporary labor are the cost of creating or scaling up temporary visa schemes[7] and the possibility that temporary workers might join the ranks of the unemployed in the developed countries. Overshadowing such technical factors, however, are the doubts and fears arising from the recent rise in legal and illegal migration in the OECD area. The bursting of the dot-com bubble of the late 1990s and the security implications of the ongoing war against terrorism have compounded those fears, making significant liberalization of temporary movement less probable than was believed possible a few years ago.

And the costs?

Temporary movement may help address several concerns often associated with the political debate over more permanent migration in both developing and developed countries (see table 4.6). One such concern revolves around the possible impact on developing countries of a "brain drain," and its longer-term consequences for capital accumulation and growth in the developing world. Indeed, if the pattern of trade growth reduces the demand for skilled labor in skill-scarce developing countries while increasing the demand for skilled labor in skill-abundant developed countries, the result could be a widening of the gap in labor income of skilled workers between the North and the South while narrowing the gap in labor income of unskilled workers. Ghose (2002) concludes that "in a world without restrictions on labor mobility, increased trade worsens the brain drain from developing countries but has uncertain effects on overall migration. Trade and flows of skilled labor are complements while trade and flows of unskilled labor are substitutes." Under such circumstances, measures to increase the mobility of skilled workers can reinforce the initial comparative advantage of the trading countries, so that skill-abundant countries become ever more skill abundant, while labor-abundant countries become ever more (low-skill) labor abundant. Trade expansion combined with the unrestricted mobility of skilled workers could conceivably put the accumulation of human capital beyond the reach of many developing countries.[8]

Much of the existing literature on brain drain focuses on the short-term costs in sending countries. Indeed, such costs can be substantial—higher education is subsidized heavily in developing countries and skilled migrants carry away scarce human capital built through public investments. But some of the purported disadvantages associated with the migration of skilled workers from developing to developed countries can be partially mitigated if the movement is temporary. Temporary migrants may generate sizeable remittance flows which, along with the accumulation and subsequent repatriation of embodied knowledge and global experience when workers return, could substantially increase the benefits associated with greater temporary movement. Key to achieving this outcome are changes in the design of both trade and immigration policies in receiving countries and stepped-up efforts on the part of sending countries to increase *return migration* of skilled workers while pursuing enhanced temporary movement of lower-skilled workers in developed country markets. Doing so would help to ensure that the growth of trade does not exacerbate developing country skill shortages.

For sending countries, TMNP has risks and rewards[9]

The impact of the temporary movement of workers on the sending country can be considered at three levels. First, there are economic effects of removing the worker from the labor market (*departure*). Next, during the *stay abroad*, the worker will maintain contacts with the home country, remitting funds to family or making direct investments. Finally, there is the economic impact of the migrant's *return* to the home country. Each of these effects is considered in turn.

Departure: Temporary migration and domestic labor markets. A genuine risk associated with sending workers abroad is that scarce resources, such as human capital, will be lost—often at a substantial public cost in education and training investments.[10] Workers who go abroad are generally young, highly motivated, well educated, and not easy to replace, especially in developing countries, where wages are lower, career paths are limited, and working conditions less satisfactory than abroad (PSI/EI 1999, OECD 2002d). An important corollary of the "brain drain" is indeed the risk that developing countries will indirectly subsidize industrial country R&D by exporting the human capital embedded in locally trained workers. Indeed, the cost of providing university education to professionals who then move to wealthier countries for increased opportunities may represent a net resource loss for developing nations. Tax policy can be used to recover some of the loss—for example, by requiring students who choose to leave the country to repay their education expenses before departing.

Further, because highly skilled workers earn more, consume more, pay more taxes, and are more productive than the unskilled, their departure, even if temporary, can have a significant impact on a developing country's economy and impede its development (WTO 1998, Devan and Tewari 2001). Moreover, because skilled migrants are often from relatively affluent households that do not require regular income support, they may be less likely than unskilled migrants to send back remittances (Ghose 2002). As long as the movement of such workers remains temporary, however, it is certainly preferable to the more lasting brain drain caused by permanent emigration (WTO 1998, OECD 2002d).

Temporary movement of workers can help to ease the strain on domestic labor markets—work abroad can be an escape route from unemployment, and can reduce a country's overall unemployment rate (Werner 1996). This is most often the case for unskilled workers, although in some countries the number of people trained for certain occupations exceeds the absorptive capacity or needs of the local market—as is the case for Indian engineers, for example.[11] Whether out-migration sustains wages in the sending country (Ghosh 1998) or exacerbates an existing skills shortage (Werner 1996), its effect will be less if the migration is temporary than if it were permanent—thereby reducing not only the potential risk but also the potential reward of temporary mobility as a policy tool (OECD 2002d).

Receiving countries can play a part in preventing particularly harmful shortages of skilled personnel in developing countries. For example, the British government has published a code of conduct for trusts under the National Health Service (NHS) that prohibits the recruitment of nurses from countries where they are in short supply, such as in South Africa or the West Indies. The code is not legally binding (OECD 2002d).

Through appropriate policies and incentives, sending countries can encourage skilled migrants to return (box 4.5). To date, incentive policies have a mixed record, often failing to address the real reasons behind workers' decisions to settle abroad permanently—acculturation, better career opportunities, and access to and integration within personal and

Box 4.5 Initiatives to encourage return migration

Up to one-third of R&D professionals from the developing world reside in the OECD area. Foreign studies constitute a major channel for migration, especially in science and technology—79 percent of 1990–91 PhD graduates in science and technology from India and 88 percent of those from China were still working in the United States in 1995, compared to only 11 percent of Koreans and 15 percent of Japanese. The migration of skills can be slowed through the return of expatriates to their country of origin. Returnees contribute to economic development through their valuable management experience, entrepreneurial skills, and access to global networks. The Ministry of Science and Technology in China, for example, estimates that most of China's Internet-based ventures were started by returning overseas students.

Taiwan (China), the Republic of Korea, and Singapore have been successful in fostering return migration by opening up their economies and employing policies to foster domestic investments in innovation and R&D. Korea has focused on upgrading its research institutions, such as the Korea Institute for Science and Technology, as a way of attracting returnees (UNDP 2001). The government of Taiwan (China) likewise played an important role in drawing back American-trained scientists and engineers, who have subsequently helped to develop the country's information technology sector. A National Youth Commission has been established there as a clearinghouse for potential employers and returning scholars seeking employment, and an airfare subsidy is granted to the graduating student, spouse, and up to two children, if they decide to return to Taiwan (China). The Commission also has established channels of communication with overseas scholars to simplify recruitment when the need arises (Cultural Division of Taipei 1998).

Opportunities for research, innovation, and entrepreneurship at home are needed to stimulate returns of migrants and capital. Developing countries such as India, for example, have the capacity to invest in R&D and human infrastructure, and thus are more able to draw migrants back. China recently launched a project to develop 100 universities into world-class institutions that not only provide higher education, but also academic employment and research opportunities. An alternative for less-developed countries is to create a good communication network among expatriates by linking them to counterparts in their county of origin. Scientific diaspora and other expatriate knowledge networks can help sending countries reap benefits and know-how from emigrants overseas. Forty-one expatriate knowledge networks have been identified around the world. The FORS Foundation, for example, seeks to involve Romanian scientists in Romania and abroad in contributing to economic reform in Romania. Grassroots initiatives in South Africa and Latin America have been developed to connect researchers abroad to networks in their home countries.

The worldwide network of Indian professionals has been investing in skill development at home to raise endowments and bolster the finances of some of India's institutions of higher education. The Indian government also has contributed to the emergence of private networks among Indian professionals abroad through legislative and tax rules that encourage remittances and investment. The Return of Qualified African Nationals Program, conducted by the International Organization for Migration, has attempted to encourage the return of qualified nationals and helped them to reintegrate. Even Switzerland has promoted networking and contact among Swiss scientists in the United States through Swiss-List.com, an online network. France has a similar network.

Source: World Bank staff.

professional networks. Chinese Taipei addressed those reasons by investing heavily in research and education. More than half of the enterprises in Chinese Taipei's Hsinchu Science Park were created by engineers who had worked for a time in California's Silicon Valley. Today the park accounts for nearly 10 percent of Chinese Taipei's gross national product (Devan and Tewari 2001). The Hsinchu example illustrates the positive economic impact that workers can have upon their return from a temporary stay abroad (OECD 2002d).

Staying in touch: Temporary migration as a source of increased financial inflows. Because banning temporary movement by workers is neither feasible nor desirable, sending governments have an interest in optimizing the benefits of such movement, for example, by offering incentives for the repatriation of foreign earnings (OECD 2002d).

The economic impact of remittances and associated labor receipts depends significantly on the use to which the funds are put in the sending country. They may be consumed, invested, or saved. Moreover, if they are consumed, the impact will differ again depending on the nature (consumer or capital goods) and origin (local or imported) of the goods consumed (Werner 1996). An ILO study on Indonesia shows that income from temporary work abroad was applied by workers and their families to pay off debts, sustain consumption, raise savings, and finance investments, in that order (ILO 1996). In India, expatriate engineers working either permanently or temporarily in Silicon Valley have accounted for most of the investments made in the cities of Bangalore and Hyderabad, which have become new poles of growth for the country, establishing India as an export powerhouse in software design and IT-outsourcing industries (Devan and Tewari 2001, OECD 2002d). The current Mexican administration has reshaped the government's attitude toward migrants to the U.S., including greater advocacy on their behalf with the U.S. government. The Ecuadorian government has a program designed to increase the earnings of its citizens working abroad, whose remittances are the country's largest source of foreign exchange after petroleum.

An important feature of TMNP is the observed tendency for workers to retain closer links with their home country if the length of their stay abroad is relatively short and predetermined. Remittances seem to be greatest when a worker expects to return at a fixed date (Galor and Stark 1991). Temporary migration may thus do more to encourage remittances than permanent migration. Many visa regimes require proof of a fixed-term contract (pre-established and limited duration); it could be argued that this type of regulation may therefore have benefits for sending and receiving countries alike (OECD 2002d).

Returning: Returning migrants as a source of increased human capital. Where labor mobility is only temporary, the net benefits of departure may be partially offset by the effects on return. Yet the balance need not be zero, as the country's stock of human capital will have grown between the time of departure and the time of return (OECD 2002d).

The additional skills (languages, experience, know-how) acquired by temporary workers can be put to work upon their return, thereby contributing to economic growth and development. Indeed, as endogenous growth theories suggest, increases in human capital can yield significant positive externalities and durably affect the long-term growth prospects of developing countries. In particular, the accumulation of human capital can be instrumental in helping developing countries to move into more skill-intensive production. Yet just as with firms, taking advantage of such capital requires a suitable enabling environment. In particular, the home country must be able to provide the infrastructure and career opportunities necessary to meet the aspirations workers may have developed during their stay abroad (OECD 2002d).

Temporary movement may be an important vector for enhancing two-way trade and investment flows between sending and receiving countries. The Indian experience confirms such linkages, for while India may have exported a number of its skilled workers in recent years, the flow has not been one-way; the country saw its IT exports increase from $150 million in 1990 to $4 billion in 2000. The recent surge in FDI directed toward India's high-tech centers is similarly related to the presence abroad of a large group of scientists, engineers, and entrepreneurs (Nielson 2002).

For receiving countries, temporary movement is politically sensitive but usually beneficial

While the temporary movement of workers is not likely to unduly disrupt the sending country's labor market, the potential effects of such mobility on segments of the receiving country's labor market may at times be more significant. There, the concern arises that mobile foreign workers may be in direct competition with nationals of the host country working permanently in the same occupations. Even if the migrant's stay is temporary, the growing number of foreign workers and the continuous influx of workers over different time horizons under contract-based flows could increase competition in the labor market (OECD 2002d).

From this angle it is easy to see why immigration can be controversial in receiving countries. There is evidence that unskilled migration reduces the relative wages of unskilled workers in industrial countries (Borjas, Freeman, and Katz 1997). An inflow of unskilled workers from the South will benefit highly skilled workers in the North. Their jobs are not threatened by the latter, and the presence of immigrants will lower prices for many goods and services consumed by the skilled workers. But the same inflow will reduce real wages of unskilled northern workers (World Bank 2001), and over time contribute to a deterioration in income distribution. Against this latter trend, however, demographic and educational trends in affluent countries will combine in the coming decades to raise the relative wages of unskilled labor in the absence of migration (see box 4.1). As these demographic effects will likely be large, scope may therefore exist for increased flows of unskilled labor in an environment of relative wage stability.

Despite the acknowledged benefits of temporary migration, the norm in receiving countries is to continue to impede the movement of low-skilled or unskilled workers through various restrictions. Such restrictions can contribute to the recent sharp rise observed in undocumented low-skilled workers throughout the OECD area. The stricter border controls enacted to contain such flows may inhibit the ability of undocumented workers to maintain closer two-way links with sending countries (in part because of a reluctance to incur the high costs and attendant risk of illegal reentry) through formal temporary migration channels. As a result, undocumented workers become particularly vulnerable to various forms of work-related abuse and often become caught in a poverty trap (Papademetriou 2001).

Impact on the receiving country labor market. Migrants, especially workers involved in temporary movement, tend to concentrate in sectors and regions characterized by labor shortages at both the high and low end of the skills spectrum. It may thus be less likely for them to compete directly with native workers than is commonly assumed.[12] In the majority of receiving countries, temporary foreign workers are found mainly in the following five sectors: (a) health (especially doctors and nurses; doctors are more likely to practice in remote/rural areas); (b) education, particularly higher education (that is, academic and research staff); (c) information technology; (d) catering; and (e) agricultural labor.

It is important, however, to understand why migrants (including temporary migrants) are concentrated in these sectors. In health and education, wages in most countries are set by policy or collective bargaining, and relatively clear procedures for recognizing foreign credentials are in place. Migration in these sectors benefits the public sector—and hence the general public—as workers become taxpayers and consumers of public services. In IT and other private sector professions prone to labor shortages, wages are more likely market-determined. But supply is constrained by lags in training home-country specialists. In the absence of migration, firms would bid up wages and after a lag, supply would respond. But with flexible work permit systems, firms can import migrants, especially on temporary contracts. In low-paying sectors such as catering and domestic services, unskilled local workers are typically unwilling or unable to fill the available jobs. The effect of temporary foreign workers in these sectors again is to benefit firms, but it is not likely that workers in receiving countries will be significantly disadvantaged: if migrants do not fill these jobs, they simply tend to go unfilled or are not created in the first place (Home Office 2001).

In all three cases, the receiving country tends to benefit overall from filling labor market gaps through migration/temporary movement. The result of such mobility is likely to include reduced inflationary pressures and an increase in the overall efficiency of firms. Expansion of such temporary schemes has thus become a preferred means of responding to labor shortages in receiving countries, whether these are seasonal, cyclical, regional, sectoral, or skills-related (Werner 1996). From an economic viewpoint, the ability to bring in foreign labor is essential, since human capital limitations can depress investment and create significant income transfers to the most highly qualified workers at the expense of the rest of the workforce and of the country's consumers (Hodge 1999, OECD 2002d). However, the impact of temporary workers on the workforce in receiving countries is the subject of significant debate, in particular with regard to wages and working conditions (box 4.6).

Temporary foreign workers may also bring more direct benefits. Intracompany transferees consume the bulk of their income in the host country (housing, food, clothing) and make use of that country's services (banks, transportation, communications). Their income therefore generates wealth to the host country, which would not be the case if the services were provided remotely across borders (under online outsourcing, for example), or if consumers required such services abroad. The presence of the temporary foreign worker's employer in the host country is itself a source

Box 4.6 Wages and conditions

The basic question is whether temporary workers should receive the same wages and conditions as nationals employed in the same industry. In many countries (particularly OECD countries), this is a legal obligation—and 50 WTO members have included this stipulation in their Mode 4 commitments. But some developing-country advocates contend that such requirements undermine the comparative advantage upon which Mode 4 trade should be based—the relatively inexpensive labor of sending countries.

Such arguments are met with fierce resistance from unions in developed countries, which fear that cheaper temporary foreign workers could undermine the hard-won gains of workers in developed countries. To prevent foreign "strike breakers," 22 WTO members also have reserved the right to suspend Mode 4 commitments in the event of labor-management disputes. Even where foreign workers may not actually be paid less, their presence may act as an impediment to reform. For example, some claim that the temporary employment of foreign nurses has allowed governments to ignore the root causes of their nursing shortages—the need for better wages and working conditions (OECD 2002f).

Proponents of wage parity argue that because a temporary foreign worker in an OECD country faces living costs in that country, there is no justification for paying lower wages. Moreover, temporary foreign workers, particularly women in domestic services and other lower-skilled activities, can be highly vulnerable to exploitation if not fully subjected to local labor laws.

Equal treatment, however, does not always result in equitable outcomes. In many countries, temporary workers are required to contribute to social security programs in the receiving country from which they receive no, or minimal, benefits. One alternative in this regard could be for social security charges from temporary migrant workers to be paid into separate funds and reimbursed upon workers' return to their home country.

———————
Source: Nielson (2002) and OECD (2001b).

> **Box 4.7 E-commerce and temporary movement**
>
> Some WTO members, in particular developing countries, have expressed concern that the growth of trade in services via information and communications technologies will become a substitute for trade via temporary movement of service suppliers (Mode 4). In some cases, services are now delivered over the Internet that previously required physical presence. This tends to be more common in knowledge-intensive fields of activity and can be attractive to companies wishing to pay developing-country wages rather than local (developed country) wages, as is generally required for workers temporarily relocated. Still, the Internet is not always a good substitute. Security and confidentiality requirements may limit its use, and in some countries the infrastructure is not yet capable of fulfilling contracts remotely.
>
> Trade in services over the Internet can offer service suppliers from developing countries the opportunity to participate in global trade, notwithstanding their lack of commercial presence in foreign markets. While some of this trade may be in knowledge-intensive areas, primarily benefiting those developing countries with a large pool of skilled labor, a range of lower skilled "back-office" services are now traded over the Internet—among them basic data entry and customer call centers.
>
> Technological developments may be changing the nature of temporary movement, rather than removing the need for it, with increasing numbers of employees managing their international responsibilities through a combination of regular communication link-ups and frequent, shorter business trips to the local operations, referred to as "virtual assignments." Replacing longer-term assignments with more frequent shorter ones, in addition to virtual working, helps companies manage the costs of international responsibilities. ICT also may play a role in encouraging employees to accept longer-term assignments by reducing the sense of isolation from friends, family, and cultural context.
>
> *Source:* OECD (2001b).

of wealth (jobs preserved, intermediate consumption of goods and services, business taxes, and so on) (OECD 2002d).

In fact, by focusing on the physical mobility of temporary movement of foreign workers critics may miss a key point: A country cannot restrain international competition in hopes of preserving the market share of domestic producers simply by blocking the entry of temporary foreign workers. For example, India is widely recognized for expertise in computer services, thus explaining the heavy flow of Indian computer specialists to more advanced countries. It is likely that if those countries were to refuse temporary visas to these workers or introduce stricter limitations on their issuance, the work could still be outsourced to India over electronic networks via Modes 1 and 2 (Chadah 2000, OECD 2002d). Indeed, some developing countries point to outsourcing of work, including over the Internet, as an alternative to sending qualified personnel abroad (box 4.7).

Temporary movement as a first step toward permanent migration. Temporary movement can be a first step to permanent residence, either legally (by changing visa categories) or illegally (overstaying). Overstaying is a risk with all forms of temporary entry, including for tourists. Administered schemes for temporary movement arguably could help discourage employers from using undocumented workers by making available legal temporary foreign workers for seasonal activities. Where temporary workers are permitted to apply for permanent-resident status, their temporary stay may serve as a useful preselection of candidates for future migration (OECD 2002a, Nielson 2002).

Available data show little evidence of large-scale transfer of workers from temporary to

> **Box 4.8   Boosting intra-EU labor mobility**
>
> The Treaty of Rome recognizes the principle of free movement for nationals of EU countries wishing to reside or work within the area formed by the signatory states. More recently, measures have been taken to facilitate intra-European mobility. These include a directive on free movement of nonworkers, students, and retired persons, and a series of directives on mutual recognition of skills and access to certain public service jobs previously reserved for nationals.
>
> Nevertheless, intra-European mobility remains very low, involving less than 0.2 percent of the total population of the Union, a level seven times lower than movements among the nine major census areas in the United States. The low mobility within Europe is partly attributable to linguistic and cultural barriers, but it is also a result of structural rigidities in the labor markets of individual member states.
>
> In 2002, the European Commission launched an action plan for mobility and skills with a view to facilitating geographic mobility in the period up to 2005 by removing remaining administrative and legal barriers, increasing the portability of supplementary pension rights of migrant workers, and improving existing regimes of skills recognition in the regulated professions.
>
> *Source:* OECD (2002f).

permanent status. The U.K. work permit system allows employees to apply for permanent settlement after four years of continuous employment, but in practice, a relatively small proportion seem to settle permanently (in 1998, 3,160 work permit holders settled in the United Kingdom against approximately 70,000–80,000 work permits approved each year). Indeed, even where all, or most, barriers have been removed, floods of foreign workers generally have failed to materialize, as intra-EU labor flows show in the context of a single labor market (OECD 2001b) (box 4.8).

Security concerns. Any attempt to facilitate individual mobility must confront today's increased concerns about national security. While all countries ultimately share such concerns, they tend to pose a greater challenge for policy officials in major receiving countries. Brought into sharper focus since September 11, 2001, security considerations are changing the balance between the facilitation and enforcement aspects of immigration controls, with measures to facilitate the entry of foreign workers increasingly scrutinized to ensure they do not become conduits for entry by illegal or undesirable individuals. There can be little doubt that tightening immigration controls because of heightened concerns over national security is likely to have a chilling effect on TMNP liberalization. Meaningful expansion of temporary worker programs requires that security clearance be quick and reliable. The challenge politically is to separate the security arguments from labor market or service export considerations, and to strike an acceptable balance between economic efficiency and national security (Mattoo 2003).

It estimated that up to 250,000 information-technology professionals from India work in the United States, some on temporary visas and others on work permits. But with almost all visa applications taking longer to process, Indian technology companies are taking steps to adapt to the increasingly limiting conditions. For example, Infosys, a leading provider of software services, is ensuring that the bulk of its outsourcing activities are undertaken on site in India rather than in the United States or Europe. The spectacular recent growth of IT outsourcing in developing countries, while minimizing the need for labor movement, is nonetheless proving controversial, with fears of an exodus of white-collar jobs in service industries. A case in point is the recent set of legislative measures passed by the states of Connecticut, Maryland, New Jersey, and Washington, restricting outsourcing of state government services. Similar concerns, and calls for similar policy responses, have been voiced in Europe.

Besides restricting the movement of workers, delays in travel can harm the competitiveness of firms. There is evidence that the competitiveness of subsidiaries of U.S. companies established in China has been adversely affected as tightened security has hampered the ability of U.S. companies to obtain visas for Chinese nationals to conclude deals, undertake training, and even attend strategic seminars and meetings in the United States. Parent companies in the United States are complaining about lost contracts and the move of Chinese clients to European companies that can offer faster and more predictable issuance of visas.

While recognizing the importance of border security in an environment of heightened risk, care must be taken that the granting of visas and work permits does not become a disguised barrier to trade. India's minister for trade and commerce recently termed the denial of visas and restrictions on the movement of natural persons as an indirect method by developed nations of denying market access to developing nations. Care also must be taken to reconcile the need for increased security at entry points with that of allowing commerce to flow as freely as possible. This includes recourse to new technologies, notably biometrics, a system of fingerprint and retinal recognition, and more traditional methods such as permanent resident cards.

Mode 4 and the WTO

As noted above, some types of temporary foreign workers—service suppliers—are covered under the WTO General Agreement on Trade in Services (GATS). Greater freedom for the temporary movement of individual service suppliers is being negotiated under the GATS, as part of the multilateral negotiations set in process following the WTO meetings in Doha in November 2002.

These discussions go by the label of "Mode 4" negotiations, in reference to the classification of the modes of service delivery in the GATS agreement. Mode 1, or "cross-border supply," is analogous to trade in goods; Mode 2 is "consumption abroad" (for example, tourism or study abroad); Mode 3 is "commercial presence" (as in the supply of a service through a subsidiary or branch in another country); and Mode 4 is "temporary movement of individual service suppliers."[13] WTO members can elect to commit to providing market access and/or national treatment for each mode of supply for any number of around 160 possible services sectors and sub-sectors.

Mode 4 is defined as the supply of a service by a service supplier of one WTO member, through presence of natural persons of a member in the territory of another member on a temporary basis. While there is some debate about what exactly this means, Mode 4 service suppliers generally:

- Gain entry for a specific purpose (for example, to fulfill a service contract as self-employed or as an employee of a service supplier);
- Are confined to one sector (as opposed to workers who enter under general migration or asylum programs who can move among sectors);
- Are temporary (that is, they are neither migrating on a permanent basis nor seeking entry to the labor market). "Temporary" is not defined under the GATS, but permanent migration is explicitly excluded, and thus this issue is left to the discretion of each country. In practice, the time frames set out in WTO members' commitments on Mode 4 range from several weeks to up to three to five years, varying among countries, sectors, and professions. Thus, for example, Japan allows foreign business travelers to stay for a maximum of 90 days, but certain cate-

gories of intracorporate transferees can stay as long as five years.
- Are service suppliers. Being a services agreement, GATS Mode 4 only covers service suppliers—there are no parallel WTO rules covering movement of people related to agriculture or manufacturing.[14]
- Are service suppliers at all skill levels, although in practice WTO members' commitments are limited to the higher skilled (see below) (Nielson 2002).

Measurement of Mode 4 trade suffers from poor data, tepid commitments, and a range of barriers

There are two ways to measure Mode 4 trade: by value or by number of service suppliers (see box 4.9). Services trade statistics face a number of conceptual and practical problems and, despite progress, reliable figures are some way off. Nonetheless, available estimates—and they are very rough—suggest that, in terms of the monetary value of trade, Mode 4 is the

Box 4.9 Measuring Mode 4 is still imprecise

Value of trade: Balance-of-payments statistics
Balance-of-payments statistics capture some labor-related flows of relevance to the estimation of trade under Mode 4:

"Compensation of employees" (wages, salaries, and other compensation received by individuals working abroad for less than one year). This measures both overestimates (includes workers other than service providers) and underestimates (excludes business visitors and individuals staying more than a year abroad) trade under Mode 4.

"Workers' remittances" (transfers from workers who stay abroad for a year or longer). This measure overestimates (covers all expatriates, regardless of the sector in which they work) and underestimates (only a residual income after expenditure and savings in the host country, and many such remittances are not effected through official channels) trade under Mode 4.

Statistics on trade in services are available only for some services sectors and traditionally have not been broken down by modes. Figures for Mode 4 are likely to be significantly underestimated.

The number of people: Migration and labor statistics
Statistics on the number of people moving under Mode 4 are scarce and highly imprecise. Statistics are available for temporary foreign workers for several countries, but they are not an exact match to GATS Mode 4. Main problems include:

- Business visitors may be excluded or hidden under tourist visas (a significant part of Mode 4 trade).
- Migration statistics consider "temporary" to be 12 months or less; under the GATS it is undefined but in practice can be up to 6 years.
- Migration categories generally do not distinguish between service and non-service activities.
- It is not always possible to judge whether the activities covered by some visa categories are commercial and would qualify as the supply of a service under the GATS (for example, occupational trainees, professional exchange programs).
- Some visa categories include persons both consuming and supplying services (for example, exchange visitors encompass exchange students and visiting lecturers).

Neither of these sources—value of trade and numbers of people—capture the dynamic effects of Mode 4 and its essential role in facilitating trade under other modes (for example, Mode 3, commercial presence; Mode 1, cross-border supply).

Some national figures for entries under specific visa programs may closely correspond with Mode 4 (for example, temporary medical practitioner visas), but because of the above problems, no aggregate figures are available for all entrants falling under Mode 4 at the national level. Additionally, given the absence of detailed temporary entry visa regimes in many countries, aggregate global estimates of the number of people moving to supply services under Mode 4 are not possible.

Source: OECD (2001b) and Nielson and Cattaneo (2003).

Table 4.7 **TMNP is the smallest of the four modes of international service supply**
Service exports by mode of supply, 2001 (billions of dollars and percentage of total)

Mode of international service supply	1997 Value	1997 Percentage of total	2001 Estimate	2001 Percentage of total	Proxy
1 Cross-border supply	890	41.0	1,000	28.2	BOP: commercial services minus travel
2 Consumption abroad	430	19.8	500	14.1	BOP: travel exports
3 Commercial presence	820	37.8	2,000	56.3	FATS statistics turnover
4 Movement of natural persons	30	1.4	50	1.4	BOP: compensation of employees
Total	2,170	100.0	3,550	100.0	

BOP is balance of payments. FATS is Foreign Affiliate Trade in Services.
Source: IMF, *Balance of Payments Yearbook.*

smallest of the four modes of services supply (table 4.7).

Negotiations on Mode 4 first took place during the Uruguay Round of trade talks held from 1986 to 1993, but they were not particularly successful—in fact, they served primarily to facilitate exploratory business visits and the movement of high-level personnel within multinational corporations. While the Uruguay Round negotiations were formally concluded in December 1993, negotiations in several areas—basic telecommunications, financial services, maritime transport services, and the movement of natural persons—were extended beyond the end of the Round because of widespread dissatisfaction with the level of liberalization achieved in those areas. Further negotiations on Mode 4, concluded on June 30, 1995, produced no major breakthrough. Only Australia; Canada; the European Communities; and its member states, India, Norway, and Switzerland improved on the commitments they made in the Uruguay Round, and these improvements were annexed to the Third Protocol to the GATS. The improvements mainly concern access opportunities for additional categories of services suppliers, usually independent foreign professionals in a number of business sectors, or the extension of such professionals' permitted duration of stay.

A look at members' current GATS schedules shows that levels of commitments vary strongly across modes of supply. Within a given sector, trade conditions for Mode 4 tend to be significantly more restrictive than conditions for other modes. No developed country has scheduled a "none" entry (signifying unfettered access) for its Mode 4 commitments, and only 1 percent of market-access commitments undertaken by developing countries are fully liberal. This compares with one out of two entries for Mode 2 (consumption abroad) being full commitments.[15]

Many schedules have established links across modes of supply. Members' schedules are mostly biased in favor of intracorporate transferees, hence making the economic value of such commitments dependent on access conditions for Mode 3 (table 4.8). Such commitments are of limited interest to WTO members which, given their level of economic development, are not significant foreign investors. Schedules are also more open for highly skilled labor, where developing countries tend to be net importers, since their comparative advantage lies with relatively unskilled labor-intensive services.

As of April 2002, an overview of members' horizontal commitments shows that the majority of the entries scheduled—nearly 280 out of a total of 400—concern executives, man-

Table 4.8 Most Mode 4 commitments by WTO members are in management categories

Entries by WTO members that have made Mode 4 commitments in the horizontal section of their GATS schedules as of April 2002, by type of natural person

	Number of entries	Percentage of entries
Intracorporate transferees, of which	168	42
Executives	56	
Managers	55	
Specialists	56	
Others	1	
Executives	24	28
Managers	42	
Specialists	44	
Business visitors, of which	93	23
Commercial presence	41	
Sales negotiations	52	
Contract suppliers	12	3
Other	17	4
Total	400	100

Source: Mattoo and Carzaniga (2003).

the commitments scheduled by developed and developing countries. Both groups seem to have been equally hesitant in undertaking very liberal commitments for Mode 4 (box 4.10).[16]

The periods for which entry may be permitted have not always been indicated. This is surprising because it might be expected that, in the absence of a definition of "temporary" in the GATS, members would provide more precision in their schedules. Where time limits have been specified, the relevant periods are shorter for business visitors than for executives, managers, and specialists. The focus of existing commitments on employed persons is reflected also in members' frequent use of employment links as an entry criterion: "Pre-employment," usually of one year, is one of the most recurrent restrictions. Numerical quotas and economic needs tests rank next in terms of frequency of limitations. While most of the quotas relate to the total staff of a company, some members also have reserved the right to operate quotas based on parameters, such as senior staff or wages. Significant administrative discretion results from the frequent scheduling of economic needs tests without indication of the criteria on which they are operated; with such entries, the relevant government agency grants access to

agers, and specialists. Of these, some 170 entries explicitly relate to intracorporate transferees. Only 17 percent of all horizontal entries may cover low-skilled persons as well ("business sellers" and "other"). It is also revealing that few significant differences exist between

---

Box 4.10 Key impediments to Mode 4 trade

Five policy impediments discourage Mode 4 trade.

- Quantitative restrictions on the movement of natural persons with a view to protecting local labor markets.
- Economic needs tests and labor certification requirements, whereby prospective employers must certify that no domestic workers were available prior to hiring a foreign worker. Particularly troublesome is the lack of transparency and the high degree of administrative discretion applied to such tests, which reduces the predictability of trading conditions. The administration of such tests also may cause significant delays in hiring procedures.
- Issuance and renewal of visas and work permits may be cumbersome, expensive, stringent, and lack transparency.
- Social security contributions (lack of tax credits in the home country), double taxation burdens placed on foreign workers, non-portability of pension and other social contributions.
- Lack of recognition of qualifications, educational degrees, training, and experience, especially in regulated professions.

Source: Mattoo (2003).

foreign natural persons provided that unspecified economic conditions are met.

What's on the table in the current negotiations?

Proposals related to Mode 4 in the current services negotiations by both developed and developing countries address many of the issues identified above.[17] Six proposals relate specifically to Mode 4; others raise Mode 4 in the context of sectoral proposals. Some propose ways to expand existing market access, either through the development of sectoral commitments or by expanding access available to one group (such as intracorporate transferees) or the categories of personnel that benefit from favorable Mode 4 access. Other proposals seek to improve the level of access by removing obstacles to existing commitments, such as lack of information or cumbersome and inappropriate administrative procedures. Some make links to the development of broader regulatory disciplines under GATS Article VI.4, or raise specific barriers such as economic needs tests or recognition of qualifications.

The negotiating proposals on Mode 4 tabled by WTO members pursue two core objectives. One class of proposals, favored by developing countries, focuses on widening market access. Another, preferred by developed countries, aims at increasing the effectiveness of existing market-access commitments (Nielson 2002). Together, such proposals provide a useful roadmap of what an improved and more equitable outcome on Mode 4 trade could comprise within the framework of the Doha Development Agenda. Key issues under discussion include:

Greater clarity and predictability in WTO members' commitments. Common definitions for main personnel categories are included in many WTO members' commitments. Many members refer to "executives, managers, specialists," but there is no common understanding of who is covered by these categories; use of a worker category nomenclature developed by the ILO could be useful in this regard.

Providing clearer information on economic needs tests (where entry of foreigners is subject to an assessment of needs in the domestic market), such as criteria used, responsible authorities, likely timeframe for determinations, and record of recent decisions (Nielson 2002).

Greater transparency. Existing access is not always used because service suppliers lack information on the necessary requirements and procedures. WTO members could provide one-stop information on all relevant procedures and requirements via a dedicated website covering all WTO members, through notifications to the WTO, or by creating a one-stop contact point at the national level. Other suggestions include prior consultation on regulatory changes, timely responses to applications, and the right of appeal (Nielson 2002).

Adoption of a GATS visa. This would facilitate entry of Mode 4 workers, including avoidance of the detailed visa procedures currently required in many countries (often not separated from permanent migration). India has put forward the idea of a GATS visa, which would be issued rapidly, be time-limited, cover both independent service suppliers and intracorporate transferees, feature rights of appeal, and be backed up by a bond, with sanctions for abuse. The main idea behind the proposal is to distinguish between temporary and permanent flows of migrants in the administration of entry procedures.[18] The key elements of a GATS visa scheme are presented in box 4.11 (Nielson 2002).

Enhanced market access commitments. There are several additional areas where expanded market access for specific groups would substantially increase the scope for developing countries' Mode 4 entry:

- Commitments for particular service sectors in high demand (such as ICT, professional services) rather than the current blanket treatment for Mode 4 entry across all sectors;

Box 4.11 Elements of a possible GATS visa/permit regime

Coverage: Either all categories of service providers covered by sectoral and horizontal commitments under Modes 3 and 4 (visas), or only intracorporate transferees (including at trainee level) and key personnel providing services pursuant to a contract between two businesses (permits).

Duration of stay: Less than 12 months; no single visit to exceed 365 days; 3 years for intracorporate transferees. Stays of less than 3 months (but possibly multiple entries over the course of a year) would not require a visa.

Procedure: A separate body dealing with GATS visas as contact point within the overall immigration framework; a one-source availability of all relevant rules and regulations; information on the status of applications to be available upon request; authorities required to provide notification of delays; expedited security checks; consultation mechanism for any changes to the rules.

Time for issuance: 2 to 4 weeks from filing of application to issuance of visa, but with procedures for issuance in one day or at port of entry under special circumstances.

Conditions: For intracorporate transferees, proof of employment with current employer for a defined period (6 months) and performance bonds; demonstrated experience of performing services at senior level; proof of qualifications for some senior levels of personnel; contracts above a certain value not subject to economic needs tests.

Role of companies: A company-specific GATS visa for personnel working for well-known and reputable companies. Following certification by immigration authorities, companies could self-administer transfers.

Appeal rights: Appeal against rejection, with a decision within one month.

Renewal: Simple procedures with fees reflecting administrative costs.

Prevention of abuse: Declaration of intention not to establish a permanent residence; inability to change to another visa category during life of the GATS visa; payment of bonds by sponsoring company to local embassy or consulate; imposition of special safeguard of one year's duration against any WTO member whose companies have a pattern of visa abuse.

Sources: OECD (2001), drawing on Chanda (1999), Zutshi (2000), and European Services Forum (2001).

- Better access for some groups, in particular intracorporate transferees, via "blanket" applications by companies or by charging companies for streamlined processing (including via a GATS visa);
- More access for other types of skilled, but not necessarily highly skilled, personnel such as "technical support personnel," "nonprofessional essential personnel," and trainees (future executives) (Nielson 2002);
- Progressively reducing the range of admissible worker categories subject to labor market/economic needs tests, with no economic needs tests applied to intracompany transferees or to certain professional service providers working on a contract basis.

Of the six proposals tabled specifically on Mode 4 by WTO members to date, four are by developed countries—Canada, the European Union, Japan, and the United States—whereas only two are from developing countries—Colombia and India. The fact that so few developing country members of the WTO have articulated negotiating proposals in an area of obvious export interest is somewhat surprising. This lack of interest may connote a preference for the guaranteed access afforded to sending countries by bilateral guest worker programs (an outcome that appears to mirror the tendency for some developing countries to pursue preferential bilateral trade agreements rather than multilateral agreements). It also may reflect the difficulties many developing countries have faced in identifying their export interests in services trade, an area of high demand in trade-related capacity building. The dearth of negotiating proposals need not, however, imply that individual developing countries are not formulating specific requests for greater access for their workers to developed-country markets in the context of ongoing bilateral request-offer negotiations under the GATS.

Discovering mutual interests is essential not only for the success of Mode 4 negotiations but also for the GATS as a whole

The success of the GATS negotiations may depend on progress on Mode 4 trade. As Mattoo (2003) notes, liberalizing advances in the multilateral trading system have always derived from the reciprocal exchange of market-access concessions. It is important that developing countries understand the potential of, and press for, enhanced access in an area of natural comparative advantage. Such an understanding, if not opposed by the OECD countries, should enable developing countries to engage more effectively in the GATS negotiations.

Furthermore, there is reason to believe that reduced barriers to the temporary movement of service providers will produce substantial global benefits. Significant gains already are being realized, for example, in the software industry—some 60 percent of India's burgeoning exports are provided through the movement of software engineers to the site of the consumer. And with greater liberalization of barriers to the movement of people, many more developing countries could "export" at least the significant labor component of services such as construction, professional services, environmental services, and transport. A benefit of the temporary nature of such movement is the potential for both the host country and the home country to gain. For exporting countries the financial and knowledge benefits would be greatest if service suppliers return home after a certain period abroad, and for importing countries the temporary movement would create fewer domestic problems than immigration.

However, there are a number of significant issues and concerns to be addressed. Experience with bilateral or regional temporary worker schemes might highlight some of the practical means of tackling policy challenges and concerns associated with temporary movement—issues such as the operation of bonding requirements, avoidance of double taxation of temporary workers, repatriating social security and pension contributions to the sending country, ensuring that the temporary nature of entry not be abused, and on-site inspections of work sites employing TMNP workers.[19]

None of these issues are insurmountable—but they require a new level of policy dialogue and coordination among trade, labor, and migration authorities, both at the national and international level, to find workable solutions (Nielson 2002).

Notes

1. Two definitions of migrants are used: Europe and Japan usually refer to country of citizenship in defining "foreign," whereas in the United States, Australia, and Canada country of birth is the relevant definition.

2. Available statistics are incomplete and not readily comparable between countries. While most migration systems distinguish between temporary and foreign migration, the definition varies among countries. To a certain extent, statistics on highly skilled workers tend to be better, because data on such workers are collected in connection with their temporary visas. Work permits and visas are valuable sources of data (OECD 2001b). The situation is even more difficult for statistics on those temporary foreign workers falling under GATS Mode 4—for example, Mode 4 entrants usually cannot be separated from broader groups, and even when migration data provide occupations—such as "managers"—they are not disaggregated by sector. Further, many business visitors may enter under tourist visas and not appear in employment-related figures, particularly where no short-term business visitor visa exists. Industry surveys can be a useful, but limited, source of data for Mode 4 (Nielson and Cattaneo 2003).

3. This section draws heavily upon the chapter on labor mobility prepared by Julia Nielson of the OECD Secretariat in the study "Regional Trade Agreements and the Multilateral Trading System" prepared for the Trade Committee of the OECD (OECD 2002c).

4. H-1B visas are also available for professionals entering the United States. Some main differences between H-1B and TN visas include: H-1B visas include requirements to show that temporary hires will not adversely affect U.S. workers; TNs are granted for one year, but renewals are unlimited, whereas H-1B visas have a three-year duration with one renewal (up to six years). Similar conditions to TNs are applied to traders and investors and intracompany transferees under E1/E2 and L1 visas, respectively (OECD 2001b, citing Globerman 2000).

5. Provisions facilitating mutual recognition are included in some agreements (for example, EFTA), and others have complementary arrangements. For example, the ANZCERTA Services Protocol, the Trans-Tasman Travel Arrangement, and the Trans-Tasman Mutual Recognition Arrangement together provide that persons registered to practice an occupation in one country can practice an equivalent profession in another (OECD 2002e).

6. This section of the chapter relies heavily on "Service providers on the move: economic impact of Mode 4" prepared by Olivier Cattaneo and Julia Nielson of the OECD Secretariat for the Trade Committee of the OECD (OECD 2002d).

7. With the exception of the "settlement countries" (Australia, Canada, New Zealand, United States), or others with significant migration (Germany, United Kingdom), many WTO members do not currently have specialized regimes in place to deal with temporary entrants as service providers (OECD 2002d).

8. Not everyone agrees that permitting workers to move abroad temporarily, or indeed to emigrate permanently, reduces the sending country's welfare. Stark and Wang (2001) suggest that emigration can have the opposite effect—that is, improve the welfare of those left behind. They argue that migration opportunities create a strong incentive to acquire greater skills through education. Only a portion of graduates will emigrate, while many will remain behind, better educated than they would have been if immigration opportunities had not been provided (Winters 2003b). Such effects thus can generate spillover benefits in sending countries, effects that are likely to be felt intergenerationally (Commander, Kangasniemi, and Winters 2002).

9. This section of the chapter draws heavily on "Service providers on the move: economic impact of Mode 4" prepared by Olivier Cattaneo and Julia Nielson of the OECD Secretariat for the Trade Committee of the OECD (OECD 2002d).

10. In health services, the World Health Organization has suggested offsetting earnings generated by migrant service workers against (1) reduced domestic access to these services, (2) loss in the quality of services, and (3) loss of public investment (Scholtz 1999).

11. Circumstances may even induce a deliberate policy of encouraging migration as a way of combating unemployment (Abella and Abrerar-Mangahas 1997). The effectiveness of such a strategy may be limited by the reluctance of workers to accept a job abroad as a substitute for one at home (OECD 2002d).

12. Borjas (2000) suggests that immigration may contribute to improving domestic-factor use by compensating for the reluctance of native workers to move from areas of relative labor surplus to areas of shortage. Such findings hold especially in health-related professions, with obvious social benefits for populations in more geographically remote areas.

13. Mode 4 is defined in Article I:2(d) as entailing "the supply of a service . . . by a service supplier of one Member, through presence of natural persons of a Member in the territory of any other Member." The Annex on Movement of Natural Persons Supplying Services under the Agreement (hereinafter the Annex) specifies that two categories of measures are covered: those affecting natural persons who are "service suppliers of a Member"; that is, self-employed suppliers who obtain their remuneration directly from customers; and those affecting natural persons of a Member who are "employed by a service supplier of a Member in respect of the supply of a service." These natural persons can be employed either in their home country and be present in the host market to supply a service, or employed by a service supplier in the host country.

The Annex clarifies that the GATS does not apply to measures affecting individuals seeking access to the employment market of a member, or to measures regarding citizenship, residence, or permanent employment. There is no specified timeframe in the GATS of what constitutes "temporary" movement; this is defined negatively, through the explicit exclusion of permanent presence. A cursory look at members' schedules shows that the maximum length of stay permitted under Mode 4 varies with the underlying purpose. Thus, while business visitors generally are allowed to stay up to 90 days, the presence of intracorporate transferees, another frequently scheduled category, tends to be limited to periods of between two and five years. The Annex does provide for the possibility that commitments, and therefore access conditions, may be scheduled by "categories of natural persons," thereby introducing an additional element of flexibility.

The Annex also clarifies that, regardless of their obligations under the Agreement, members are free to regulate the entry and stay of individuals in their territory, including through measures necessary to protect the integrity of their borders and to ensure the orderly movement of natural persons across those borders, provided that the measures concerned "are not applied in such a manner as to nullify or impair the benefits accruing to any Member under the terms of a specific commitment." The operation of visa requirements only for natural persons of certain members, but not for others, is not per se regarded as nullifying or impairing such benefits.

14. This is a strange distinction—are temporary foreign workers engaged in picking apples temporary agricultural workers or suppliers of fruit-picking services? Is an employee of General Electric's consumer credit arm engaged in service or manufacturing activities? (Nielson 2002)

15. Calculated on a sample of 37 sectors deemed representative for various services areas. (See document S/C/W/99, March 2, 1999). The shallow level of commitments for Mode 4 is to a certain extent also reflected in the pattern of horizontal limitations, which apply across all sectors: there are five times as many limitations scheduled for Mode 4 than for Mode 2. In turn, this reflects many members' basic method to scheduling Mode 4 entries. Contrasted with other modes, the "negative list" approach to scheduling limitations has been turned upside down: schedules start with a general "unbound" which is then qualified by liberalization commitments, mostly limited to specified types of persons (for example, managers), movements (intracorporate), and stays (up to four years).

Commitments are often exclusively governed by what is inscribed in the horizontal part of the schedule, so that identical access conditions apply to all scheduled sectors. Commitments usually are based on functional or hierarchical criteria, related either to the type of person involved (executive, manager, specialist) or to the purpose of their movement (for example, to establish business contacts, negotiate sales, set up a commercial presence). Besides, no generally agreed definitions or precise descriptions exist of the types of natural persons to which access is granted, which can detract from the predictability of entry conditions.

16. Access conditions scheduled by countries acceding to the WTO after 1995 also are substantially identical to the ones scheduled by Uruguay Round participants. This contrasts with the situation in the three other modes of supply, for which recently acceded members have generally undertaken deeper commitments. The only detectable difference with regard to Mode 4 is a relatively higher number of commitments scheduled by recent WTO members for "contract suppliers"—that is, employees of a foreign enterprise who have completed a contract to supply a service in a country but does not have a commercial presence in that market.

17. This section of the chapter relies heavily on Nielson (2002) and OECD (2001b).

18. Although the Indian proposal for the adoption of a GATS visa has helped to broaden the scope of Mode 4 discussions among trade and immigration officials, the odds of seeing such a scheme adopted in the DDA seem remote. Indeed, the sobering experience emerging from attempts to implement the APEC Business Travel Card, epitomized by the reluctance of three key APEC Members (Canada, Japan, and the United States) to implement the scheme, suggests a long road ahead in liberalizing TMNP at the multilateral level (OECD 2001b). It should be noted that from the point of view of migration authorities, TMNP represents a small proportion of those crossing borders every day. The additional resources required to create special treatment for such persons—which a GATS visa would entail—are hard to justify in the face of other priorities, notably in border security, arising for larger groups of migrants. Such resources also could be well beyond the administrative capacities of many developing country WTO members (Nielson 2002). See OECD (2001b) for more discussion of the potential impact of a GATS visa scheme.

19. Winters and others (2002, pp. 43–50) provide a useful summary of such programs and the means to enforce them in France, Germany, the United Kingdom, and the United States.

References

Abella, Manolo I., and M. A. Abrera-Mangahas. 1997. *Sending Workers Abroad: A Manual for Low- and Middle-Income Countries.* Geneva: International Labor Office.

Athukorala, P., and C. Manning. 1999. *Structural Change and International Migration in East Asia.* Melbourne: Oxford University Press.

Borjas, George J. 2000. *Labour Economics,* 2nd ed. Boston: McGraw Hill.

Borjas, George, Richard B. Freeman, and Lawrence F. Katz. 1997. "How Do Immigration and Trade Affect Labour Market Outcomes?" In *Brookings Papers on Economic Activity*, pp. 1–67.

Chadah, Rajesh. 2000. GATS Negotiations and Developing Countries: A Case Study of India. Mimeo. Washington, D.C.: The World Bank.

Chanda, R. 1999. "Movement of Natural Persons and Trade in Services: Liberalising Temporary Movement of Labour under the GATS." New Delhi: Indian Council for Research on International Economic Relations. Available at www.icrier.res.in.

Chanda, Rupa. 2002. "Movement of Natural Persons and the GATS: Major Trade Policy Impediments." In Bernard Hoekman, Aaditya Mattoo, and Philip English, eds., *Development, Trade, and the WTO*. Washington, D.C.: World Bank.

Commander, S., M. Kangasniemi, and L. Alan Winters. 2002. "The Brain Drain: Curse or Boon? A Survey of the Literature." Paper prepared for International Seminar on International Trade, May, Stockholm.

Devan, J., and P. S. Tewari. 2001. "Brains Abroad." *The McKinsey Quarterly*, No. 4.

European Services Forum. 2001. "Draft Model Schedule Covering the Temporary Entry of Natural Persons under the General Agreement on Trade in Services." July 20. Brussels: European Science Foundation.

Galor, O., and O. Stark. 1991. "The Probability of Return Migration, Migrants' Work Effect, and Migrants' Performance." *Journal of Development Economics*, No. 35.

Ghose, Ajit K. 2002. "Trade and International Labor Mobility." Employment Paper 2002/33. International Labor Office, Geneva.

Ghosh, Bimal. 1998. Gains from Global Linkages: Trade in Services and Movements of Persons. New York: St. Martins' Press.

Globerman, Steve. 2000. *Trade Liberalisation and the Migration of Skilled Professionals and Managers: The North American Experience*. London: Blackwell Publishers.

Hodge, James. 1999. "Examining the Cost of Services Protection in a Developing Country: the Case of South Africa." Paper presented at the World Services Congress, November, Atlanta.

Home Office. 2001. "Migration: an Economic and Social Analysis." RDS Occasional Paper 67. London: Home Office.

Hutton, T., and J. G. Williamson. 2002. "What Fundamentals Drive World Migration?" NBER Working Paper 9159. National Bureau of Economic Research, Cambridge, Mass. September.

International Labor Office (ILO). 1996. *Emigration Pressures and Structural Change: Case Study of Indonesia*. Geneva.

Lindert, Peter H., and Jeffrey G. Williamson. 2001. "Does Globalization Make the World More Unequal?" National Bureau of Economic Research (NBER) Paper 8228. Cambridge, Mass.

Manning, Chris. 2002. "Structural Change, Economic Crisis, and International Labor Migration in East Asia." *The World Economy* 25(3): 359–85.

Mattoo, Aaditya. 2003. "Introduction and Overview." In Aaditya Mattoo and Antonia Carzaniga, eds., *Moving People to Deliver Services*. New York and Washington, D.C.: Oxford University Press and World Bank.

Mattoo, Aaditya, and Antonia Carzaniga, eds. 2003. *Moving People to Deliver Services*. New York and Washington, D.C.: Oxford University Press and World Bank.

Nielson, Julia. 2002. "Service Providers on the Move." Evian Group Compendium, Lausanne: Evian Group.

OECD (Organisation for Economic Co-operation and Development). 1998. *Migration, Free Trade, and Regional Integration in North America*. Paris.

———. 2000. *Globalisation, Migration, and Development*. Paris.

———. 2001a. *Migration Policies and EU Enlargement: The Case of Central and Eastern Europe*. Paris.

———. 2001b. "Service Providers on the Move: A Closer Look at Labor Mobility and the GATS." TD/TC/WP/Final. Paris.

———. 2001c. *Trends in International Migration*. 2001 SOPEMI Report. Paris.

———. 2002a. *International Mobility of the Highly Skilled*. Paris.

———. 2002b. "Labor Mobility in Regional Trade Agreements." TD/TC/WP/Final. Paris.

———. 2002c. *Migration and the Labour Market in Asia: Recent Trends and Policies*. Paris.

———. 2002d. "Service Providers on the Move: The Economic Impact of Mode 4." TD/TC/WP/Final. Paris.

———. 2002e. "Service Providers on the Move: Mutual Recognition Agreements," TD/TC/WP/48. Paris.

———. 2002f. *Trends in International Migration*. 2002 SOPEMI Report. Paris.

Papademetriou, Demetrios G. 2000. "Labor Mobility and Human Resources Development Policies." *Globalisation, Migration, and Development*. Paris: OECD.

PSI (Public Services International). 1999. "The WTO and the GATS: What Is at Stake for Public Health?" *Common Concerns for Workers in Education and the Public Sector Series*. Brussels. June.

Rodrik, Dani. "Feasible Globalisations." NBER Working Paper W9129. National Bureau of Economic Research, Cambridge, Mass. August.

Scholtz, Peter. 1999. "International Trade Agreement and Public Health: WHO's Role." Paper prepared for conference on Increasing Access to Essential Drugs in a Globalized Economy, Geneva, World Health Organization, April 11–12.

Stark, Oded, and Yong Wang. 2001. *Inducing Human Capital Formation: Migration as a Substitute for Subsidies*. Reihe Okonomie Economics Series 100. Vienna: Institute for Advanced Studies.

UNCTAD (United Nations Commission on Trade and Development). 2001. "Movement of Natural Persons under the GATS: Perspectives for the New Negotiations." Mimeo. Geneva.

United Nations. 2000. "Replacement Migration: Is it a Solution to Declining and Ageing Populations?" Population Division, Department of Economic and Social Affairs, New York: United Nations.

Visco, Ignazio. 2000. "Immigration, the Labour Market, and Development." Paper presented at conference on Migration Scenarios for the 21st Century, Rome, July.

Werner, Heinz. 1996. *Temporary Migration for Employment and Training Purposes, Social Cohesion, and Quality of Life*. Brussels: Council of Europe.

Winters, Alan. 2001. "Assessing the Efficiency Gain from Further Liberalisation: A Comment." In Roger Porter, Pierre Sauve, Arvind Subramaniam, and Americo Beviglia-Zampetti, eds., *Efficiency, Equity and Legitimacy: The Multilateral Trading System at the Millennium*. Washington, D.C.: Brookings Institution Press.

Winters, Alan. 2003a. "The Economic Implications of Liberalising Mode 4 Trade." In Aaditya Mattoo and Antonia Carzaniga, eds., *Moving People to Deliver Services*. New York and Washington, D.C.: Oxford University Press and World Bank.

———. 2003b. "GATS Mode 4: The Temporary Movement of Natural Persons." Mimeo. Brighton: University of Sussex.

Winters, Alan O., and Terrie L. Walmsley. 2002. "Relaxing the Restrictions on the Temporary Movement of Natural Persons." Mimeo. Brighton: University of Sussex.

Winters, Alan, T. L. Walmsley, Z. K. Wang, and R. Grynberg. 2002. "Liberalising Labor Mobility under the GATS." Economics Discussion Paper 87, University of Sussex, Brighton, U.K. October.

World Bank. 1995. *World Development Report 1995: Workers in an Integrating World*. Washington, D.C.

World Bank. 2000. *East Asia: Recovery and Beyond*. Washington, D.C.: The World Bank.

———. 2001. *Globalization, Growth, and Poverty: Building an Inclusive World Economy*. Washington, D.C.

———. 2001. *Global Economic Prospects and the Developing Countries 2002: Making Trade Work for the World's Poor*. Washington, D.C.

———. 2002. *Global Economic Prospects and the Developing Countries 2003: Investing to Unlock Global Opportunities*. Washington, D.C.

———. 2003. *Global Development Finance 2003: Striving for Stability in Development Finance*. Washington, D.C.

WTO (World Trade Organization). 1998. "Presence of Natural Persons (Mode 4)." Background note by the Secretariat, S/C/W/75, Council for Trade in Services. Geneva. December 8.

Zutshi, B.K. 2000. "Liberalisation of Temporary Mobility of Natural Persons." Intervention before the European Services Forum International Conference on GATS 2000 negotiations, Brussels, November 27.

5

Reducing Trading Costs in a New Era of Security

Security measures can drive up transport costs
In the wake of September 11 and worldwide worries about terrorism, governments everywhere have enacted security measures that could, if not managed properly, drive up trade costs and shut out exports from developing countries. This action has focused attention on the search for greater efficiency in international transportation, the need for cooperation in adopting collective measures to promote transport security, and the imperative of improving customs regimes, port facilities, and logistics management.

The cost of moving goods between destinations and across international borders is often as important as formal trade barriers in determining the cost of landed goods—and ultimately of market share. The costs of transport among many points are as significant as tariffs. Other delays are equally costly. One study estimates that every day spent in customs adds nearly 1 percent to the cost of goods. In developing countries, transit costs are routinely two to four times higher than in rich countries.

But they hold out the promise of facilitating and securing trade
A study of the trade effects of September 11 estimated that world welfare declined by $75 billion per year for each 1 percent increase in costs to trade from programs to tighten border security. Developing countries are particularly vulnerable to cost increases related to security threats. Limited budget resources, dependence on foreign trade and investment, and outdated infrastructure and technology present serious challenges for these countries.

Fortunately, new security protocols being deployed at ports, customs offices, and border posts around the world have the potential to streamline trade transactions as well as promote safety and security. However, a global framework must be established to ensure that the needs of developing countries are addressed as security regimes take shape. The G-8 and developing-country partners should take the lead in drafting such a framework.

Regulations hamper competition in international transport systems and raise costs
Anticompetitive regulations and private commercial practices inflate trade costs by restricting international air and maritime transport services to developing countries. The share of trade shipped by air has grown to 30 percent for U.S. imports in 1998, but international air transport is one of the service sectors that is most heavily shielded from international competition. By denying entry to efficient outside carriers, bilateral air service agreements increase export costs for developing countries. Though international airline alliances increase network efficiency, they can be harmful if they impede effective competition. City-pair routes

on which more than two passenger airlines or dedicated freight airlines operate can cut costs by an average of more than 10 percent.

Maritime transport is often subject to practices such as cargo reservation schemes and limitations on port services that protect inefficient service providers. Such competition-restricting practices among shipping lines and port operators can increase freight rates up to 25 percent on some routes. Rising concentration in the market for port terminal services has increased the risk that private firms may capture the benefits of government reforms. Abusive practices by private operators are of special concern in developing countries, where traffic volumes are lower and competitive forces inherently more limited.

Investments in improving ports, customs, and trade-related institutions can have a substantial payoff

Building capacity in trade-related services can provide the great gains in this new environment. If the countries now below the world average in trade-facilitation capacity could be raised halfway to the average, trade among 75 countries would increase by $377 billion annually, according to new analyses outlined in this chapter. Facilitating trade to improve export-led growth therefore depends on policy reform, technical assistance, and modernization of infrastructure. All trading partners can benefit when barriers are removed and capacity is strengthened—with many of the benefits of reform and modernization flowing directly to developing countries.

Domestic policy reform is now even more important—

Domestic policy reform is needed to ensure that the benefits of modernized customs, port facilities, and related investments in information technology are realized. Streamlining regulations to remove technical barriers and liberalizing transport and telecommunications can promote domestic competition and significantly lower transport costs while expanding the availability and choice of services in many developing countries. In particular, appropriate legal and regulatory frameworks are needed to ensure competition. Developing countries need to address such domestic reform to take advantage of the opportunities offered by a liberalized trading system.

—and new multilateral efforts could prove beneficial

Multilateral efforts to reduce transport frictions could include revamping competition-restricting regulations in air and maritime transport. Such an effort might include revisiting antiquated exemptions of transport from OECD antitrust legislation. Involving developing countries more centrally in global security planning, together with a program of appropriate technical assistance, would help developing countries mitigate security-driven cost increases that would otherwise reduce their participation in the global market. A commitment to multilateral efforts on trade facilitation would also have a high payoff—the World Customs Organization (WCO), the multilateral development banks, bilateral donors, and private groups are all important players. The leadership of the G-8 should join multilateral and other development institutions in a plan to facilitate and expand trade, strengthen security, and promote domestic development.

Broad trade facilitation goals do not fit neatly into the disciplines of the World Trade Organization (WTO). In contrast to stroke-of-the-pen tariff reductions, improving ports, customs, and logistics involves a continuing process of institutional changes that move countries toward best practice. The lion's share of the agenda requires national action, supported by multilateral development agencies to promote—and in some cases finance—institutional changes. However, if the Doha Round propels the WTO into a supporting role in the broader trade-facilitation agenda, negotiations on simplified and harmonized trade procedures could advance best practice in administering fees and formalities in trade and in reducing the costs and uncertainty of transit trade, especially for land-locked countries.

Most importantly, obligations undertaken by developing countries should be carefully tailored to long-term implementation capacity. Any new agreement should include innovative procedures for settling disputes before they move toward WTO-sanctioned action.

Why transport, trade facilitation, and logistics matter

The costs of transporting developing-country exports to foreign markets are a much greater hindrance to trade than are tariffs. A comparison of countries' "transport cost incidence" (the share of international shipping costs in the value of trade) and their tariff incidence (the trade-weighted ad valorem duty actually paid) shows that for 168 out of 216 U.S. trading partners, transport cost barriers outweigh tariff barriers. For the majority of Sub-Saharan African countries, the tariff incidence was relatively insignificant, at less than 2 percent, while their transport cost incidence exceeded 10 percent (World Bank 2001). A doubling of shipping costs is associated with slowdowns in annual growth equivalent to more than one-half of a percentage point.

Trade-related transaction costs—freight charges as well as other logistical expenses—are a crucial determinant of a country's ability to participate in the global economy. Transport costs determine potential access to foreign markets, which in turn explains up to 70 percent of the variance in countries' GDP per capita. Among the problems that add to the costs of trade are:

- Frequent reloading of goods
- Port congestion affecting turnaround time for feeder vessels
- Complicated customs-clearance procedures
- Complex and nontransparent administrative requirements, often pertaining to documentation
- Limited use of automation leading to high costs for processing information
- Uncertainty about the enforceability of legal trade documents such as bills of lading or letters of credit.

Policies to remove nontariff barriers and accelerate the flow of goods and services across borders—in short, to facilitate trade—are thus at the forefront of today's trade-policy debate.[1] Cross-country evidence suggests that high transport costs tax growth in countries with underdeveloped transport links (World Bank 2001). Inefficient internal transport systems can widen income inequalities within countries by separating the hinterland regions from the global marketplace.

Box 5.1 The evolving definition of trade facilitation

OECD: "Simplification and standardization of procedures and associated information flows required to move goods internationally from seller to buyer and to *pass payments* in the other direction."

UN/ECE: A *"comprehensive and integrated approach* to reducing the complexity and cost of the trade transactions process, and ensuring that all these activities can take place in an efficient, *transparent, and predictable manner,* based on internationally accepted norms, standards, and best practices."

APEC: "Trade facilitation generally refers to the simplification, harmonization, *use of new technologies,* and other measures to address procedural and administrative impediments to trade."

APEC: "The use of technologies and techniques which will help members to *build up expertise,* reduce costs and lead to better movement of goods and services."

Source: Wilson and others (2002), citing various institutional sources.

The new international security dimension in trade

The terror and tragedy of September 11, 2001, have emphasized the need for reforms in border and transport infrastructure. Terrorist attacks can seriously disrupt the passage of people, goods, and modes of transport across borders. Measures designed to stop terrorism can add certainty and stability to the global economy, raise investor confidence, and facilitate trade. Secure trade is now as important as free trade—and the two need not be mutually exclusive.[2]

Since the September 11 attacks, billions of dollars have been spent to enhance port security, install airport security equipment, strengthen customs authorities, and bolster border security. While much attention has been devoted to new security protocols in the United States, security plans in other parts of the world also have been revised and strengthened.[3] The G-8 has committed itself to increasing security for all transport modes and to promoting policy coherence and coordination among international organizations such as the International Civil Aviation Organization (ICAO), International Maritime Organization (IMO), and WCO.

The bombing of the *VLCC Limburg* off the coast of Yemen in 2002 was a stark reminder of weaknesses in global maritime systems, which handle 95 percent of world trade. The event alarmed the shipping world and prompted sweeping new security proposals, several of which are outlined below.

The security of maritime transport has been strengthened, but the costs and benefits of the new security programs have yet to be assessed

A series of measures aimed at strengthening maritime security and suppressing acts of terrorism was adopted by the IMO at its diplomatic conference in December 2002. These included changes to the 1974 Safety of Life at Sea Convention (SOLAS), which covers 98 percent of the world's fleets. The International Ship and Port Facility Security Code, which will go into force on July 1, 2004, for vessels in international trade, contains detailed security-related requirements for shipping companies, port authorities, and governments, together with guidelines on meeting the requirements. The new rules cover security plans, security officers, and certain security equipment.

In the United States, the Maritime Transportation Security Act of 2002 (MTSA), signed by President Bush in November 2002, is intended to improve safeguards at the country's 361 sea and river ports and to improve intelligence on cargo and personnel entering U.S. ports. Many of the requirements imposed by the IMO protocol also are mandated by the MTSA. Port-security efforts have been extended with the introduction of the Anti-Terrorism and Port Security Act of 2003.

In April 2002, the trade community and the U.S. Customs Service (USCS) launched the Customs-Trade Partnership Against Terrorism (C-TPAT) to improve security along the entire transport chain. The initiative encompasses manufacturers, warehouse operators, and shipping lines. Participation in the voluntary scheme is open to all importers, airfreight consolidators, carriers, and non-vessel-owning common carriers that agree to comply with the supply-chain security profile. Under the program, importers or carriers provide USCS with documentation relating to security measures at each step along the route of goods—from the factory to the warehouse, the port, and the ocean carrier.[4]

The United States has imposed new controls to increase the screening of freight containers arriving at and leaving ports with goods bound for the United States. Almost 90 percent of all freight is transported in containers, 244 million of which move annually among the world's seaports. The Container Security Initiative (CSI), introduced in January 2002 by the USCS, is designed to prevent terrorists from concealing personnel or weapons of mass destruction in U.S.-bound cargo. Participating countries agree to help the USCS identify and screen high-risk containers at the earliest stage. Beginning with the world's 20 busiest ports,

CSI initiative will be extended until 100 percent of containerized cargo is covered.[5]

The bilateral agreements that underpin the CSI may discriminate against ports not covered by CSI. The European Commission, concerned that the United States had approached only some large European ports, argued that the CSI could divert trade to Rotterdam, for example, and create competitive distortions among ports in the European Union—violating EU fair trade rules. Although the top nine northwest European ports handle 80–90 percent of Europe's containerized cargo bound for the United States, the other 11 that also export to the United States would be affected. In a recent development, the European Union has given the European Commission the power to negotiate a maritime security agreement with the United States to replace the bilateral deals with eight EU countries. In return, the Commission has decided to drop legal action against EU members that signed deals with Washington.[6]

The CSI measure is especially important for countries that send a substantial share of their exports to the United States—for example, 20 percent of Malaysian exports are to the United States. By not joining the CSI, Malaysian goods could lose competitiveness in the global market—a risk not many nations are willing to take. Countries that do not implement the required procedures would have a competitive disadvantage because their shipments would undergo more complex examinations and thus be cleared more slowly.

The WCO passed a resolution on Security and Facilitation of the International Trade Supply Chain in June 2002 to enable ports in all 161 member nations to develop programs similar to the CSI and consider adopting stricter security measures. These measures are intended to enhance security and improve facilitation through a comprehensive reform of customs. With nations seeking reciprocal inspection rights, Japanese officers have been positioned at the ports of Los Angeles and Long Beach to screen high-risk cargo containers bound for Japan. Canadian customs inspectors also have been posted at Newark, New Jersey, and Seattle.

Under the USCS's 24-Hour Advance Cargo Manifest Rule, which took effect on February 2, 2003, carriers must provide cargo manifests electronically via the Automated Manifest System (AMS) 24 hours before loading a container bound for a U.S. port. USCS will use the information to identify containers that pose a potential risk and determine whether containers can be cleared for loading. Ships unable to meet the requirements risk receiving "no load" orders and thus being detained at the port of origin. Failure by a shipper to comply with the notification requirement carries a fine and the possibility of seizure and forfeiture of the cargo. Even freight not bound for the United States—a shipment from Hong Kong to Canada via the United States, for example—must meet the requirements. Canada's Customs and Revenue Agency adopted a similar manifest rule for marine cargo imports in April 2003.

The U.S. Food and Drug Administration (FDA) has proposed registration of an estimated 400,000 domestic and foreign food facilities to prevent a threat to the U.S. food supply as mandated by the Bioterrorism Act of 2002. Starting December 12, 2003, importers must file advance notice of food shipments with the FDA. Estimates by the FDA suggest that the U.S. food industry could lose as much as $6.5 million in perishable imports if the rule for importers is adopted.[7] Many agricultural commodities such as bananas and broccoli are still growing on the stalk, vine, or tree the day before loading, and in some cases as few as six hours before.[8] Such cargo may spoil if shipments are held up because of documentation requirements. In the highly competitive market for agricultural commodities, this risk could prompt importers in other countries to move away from U.S. suppliers. The Bioterrorism Act may also be harmful to Indonesia's small and medium enterprises, which are big exporters of food and agricultural products.

The USCS intends to extend the advance electronic cargo reporting requirement to imports and exports transported by air and on land. Final rules are expected by October 1, 2003. Since September 11, airlines have spent

$43 billion on security measures—among them more thorough baggage checks, greater in-flight inspection, and new regulations for secure cockpit doors.[9] A new passenger data collection system, the Advance Passenger Information System (APIS), was recently introduced by the United States; already it has raised ethical questions about a passenger's right to privacy.[10] With regard to air cargo, new security proposals are expected this year from the U.S. Transport Security Administration. Road and rail transport operators also have also been the subject of new measures to forestall attacks.[11]

Canada has tightened security at airports, ports, and border crossings to prevent shipments to the United States from being delayed. The Canadian government will spend $112.7 million over the next five years to improve security at maritime borders. Canada's Customs Self-Assessment and Partners in Protection programs, like C-TPAT in the United States, are based on the hypothesis that if companies adopt secure practices, inspectors will be free to focus on shipments from companies whose practices are uncertain. With respect to air transport, the Canadian Air Transport Security Association has improved luggage screening by installing explosive-detection equipment at many large airports in Canada.[12] In May 2003, the EU adopted a brief that suggested high security standards on maritime transport to be applied across the member states, new requirements on passenger ships on domestic voyages, and heightened security of the entire maritime transport security chain.

Accounting for nearly 60 percent of world GDP and half of all trade, the 21 countries of the Asia Pacific Economic Cooperation group (APEC) have had to adopt new technologies to strengthen security without impeding trade. At a recent meeting in Bangkok, APEC adopted Secure Trade in the APEC Region (STAR)—a set of measures to protect cargo, ships making international voyages, international aviation, and people in transit. Ports in the APEC region now must upgrade security to meet STAR standards. At a meeting in February 2003 in Thailand, APEC announced its commitment to protect cargo through programs of container security, container risk assessment, and advance electronic information on container content. The group also will endeavor to introduce more effective baggage screening in airports in the region, improve coordination among immigration officials, establish new cyber-security standards, develop an advanced passenger information system, and devise systems for tracking and monitoring potential threats. APEC's new counterterrorism task force will coordinate these activities.[13]

Developing countries may have a hard time meeting new security requirements

Balancing new security priorities with economic and trade objectives is complicated. Security proposals can affect global supply chains by requiring costly changes in business practices, process redesigns, and new equipment. Critics fear that developing nations could be squeezed out of the global trading system because of their limited capacity to implement the new international initiatives. High transport costs, poor infrastructure, and the high costs of border clearance already pose a large obstacle to their development. Customs services in many less-developed countries lack qualified personnel to operate advanced security equipment and the ability to execute the necessary reforms in their domestic administration. In response to new security demands, for example, shippers are adding extra cycle time to their supply chain rather than risk delays or fines.[14]

The USCS 24-hour rule has affected ports that accept cargo as few as six hours before departure, dealers in perishable commodities that are harvested and loaded within 24 hours, and shipments of emergency replacement parts and medical supplies. Holding additional inventories to hedge against delays and disruptions requires more storage space and more operating capital.

The 24-hour rule also has introduced extra costs for Indian exporters. Almost 35 percent of outbound trade from India is headed to the United States, including 600,000 containers. Exporters must now pay additional costs to local agencies that help them with documentation. While large manufacturers can provide detailed commodity descriptions, the small-scale and cottage industry units, which are big exporters, may be unable to provide the correct description that is required at a level consistent with the Harmonized Tariff Schedule (HTS) codes of USCS.

Descriptions such as "freight of all kinds" are no longer acceptable. If officials are uncertain about their contents, containers may miss their scheduled carrier sailing dates. Electronic filing and paperless clearance are additional challenges. Most transactions handled by ocean carriers are still conducted by fax or phone. Many shippers in India still use manual typewriters—obviously hindering their ability to provide data in electronic form. Many governments may be unaware of the potentially negative trade-related repercussions from inaction on security.

Despite limited finances and capacity to facilitate trade, some developing countries such as Sri Lanka have adopted cargo security measures that are on par with ports in many developed countries. The same applies to Bangladeshi facilities that boast advanced detection devices. These measures, however, are focused on imports into the country, emphasizing the need to enhance inspection of exports.

Airlines and airports throughout Asia are working toward the goal of screening all checked baggage. The Agency for Air Transport Security in Africa (ASECNA) is investing $27 million to modernize member states' airport security infrastructure.[15]

Security-driven improvements can benefit trade

New programs to combat terrorism and corruption clearly will involve investment in new technology and infrastructure—possibly raising the costs of trade in the short to medium term. At the same time, the prospect of reducing future threats through technology-intensive customs inspections should be viewed as an investment in greater trade efficiency.[16] Automated technology—such as bar codes, wireless communications, radio frequency ID tags, tamper-proof seals for containers with global positioning technology, and other electronic measures—could accelerate global trade while improving security (Reddy 2002). Sharing information among terminal operators, shippers, and customs brokers can help expedite the movement of freight through terminals without any new physical investment. By reducing delays in container clearance through customs, the need for shippers to pay "tea money"[17] to officials would be diminished—contributing to port efficiency (figure 5.1). In addition, simplification of customs procedures can increase the chances of detection of fraud and criminal activities.

Figure 5.1 Customs clearance takes longer in the developing world than in the OECD, lowering the competitiveness of developing-country trade

Average days required for customs clearance by sea, by region

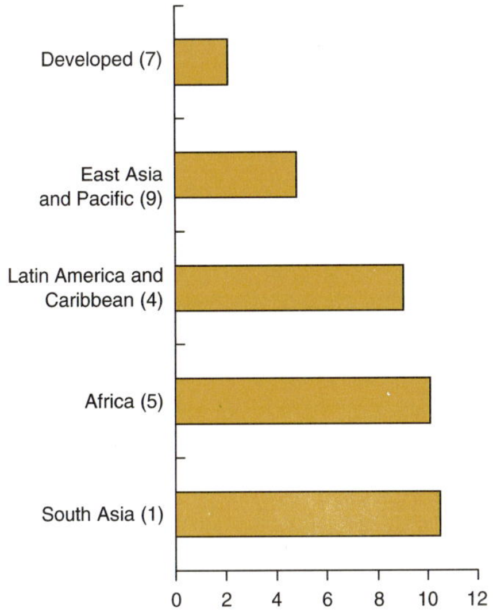

- Developed (7): ~2
- East Asia and Pacific (9): ~5
- Latin America and Caribbean (4): ~9
- Africa (5): ~10
- South Asia (1): ~11

Note: The number in parenthesis indicates the number of countries selected from each region to calculate the average. Developed includes France, Germany, Greece, Netherlands, Spain, Sweden, United States; East Asia and Pacific includes China, Hong Kong (China), Indonesia, Malaysia, Philippines, Singapore, Taiwan (China), Thailand, Vietnam; Latin America and Caribbean includes Argentina, Brazil, Chile, Mexico; Africa includes Mozambique, South Africa, Egypt, Guinea Bissau, Angola; South Asia includes India.
Source: International Exhibition Logistics Associates (http://www.iela.org).

GLOBAL ECONOMIC PROSPECTS 2004

Security-inspired modernization can bring about overdue improvements to ocean shipping. The USCS Automated Commercial Environment (ACE) project, which replaces paper documents with electronic methods of identifying high-risk containers, is expected to save U.S. importers $22.2 billion and the U.S. government $4.4 billion in administrative costs over 20 years. Hong Kong recently launched electronic filing for cargo manifests for all modes, which will enhance the efficiency and accuracy in submitting these documents. Pakistan has introduced electronic filing of a single shipping document at Port Qasim as part of an effort by its customs service to streamline clearance and reduce transaction costs. According to recent research, automated customs can lower the direct costs of customs clearance by the equivalent of 0.2 percent of the value of traded goods. By accounting for the indirect benefits of reduced delays, costs are reduced by 1 percent of merchandise value. (Hertel, Walmsley, and Ikatura 2001).

Implementation of these measures, which involve important changes throughout the supply chain, may prove a difficult task for many developing countries. But if the costs of complying with new security-inspired measures can be recovered later through greater efficiencies in the supply chain, the end result will be a global trading system that works better for everyone—securing trade and smoothening trade flows simultaneously.

Can the impact of security measures be quantified?

The recent introduction of the new security protocols and their even more recent implementation make it difficult to quantify their impact on trade. Leonard (2001) estimated the new security-related costs at 1–3 percent of the value of traded goods, while analysis by the OECD (2002a, 2002b) suggests a more modest impact.[18]

Security-driven frictional costs of transport, handling, insurance, and customs can affect trade even in the medium and long run. Walkenhorst and Dihel's 2002 study of the effects of September 11 on international trade indicates that even countries not directly involved in a terrorist event may expect their income to decline by $75 billion per year as a result of a 1 percent ad valorem increase in frictional costs to trade.[19] While Western Europe and North America suffer the greatest loss in absolute terms, other regions, such as South Asia, North Africa, and the Middle East, are the main losers when income losses are related to the size of the economies (figure 5.2).[20] A one-percentage-point increase in trade costs would cost South Asia $6 billion, more than one-half of one percentage point when expressed as a percentage of GDP. Regions with high trade-to-GDP ratios and sectors with elastic import demand incur the greatest trade and income losses in relative terms.

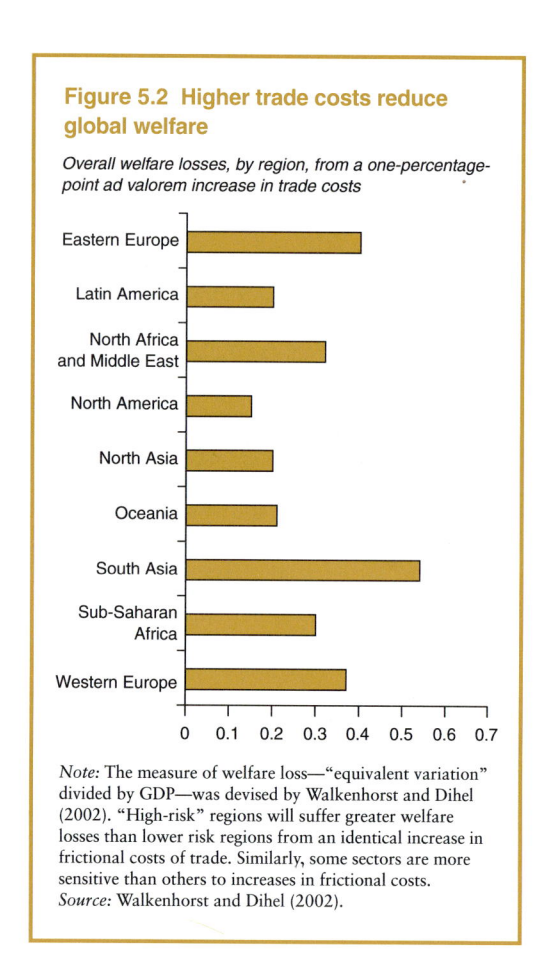

Figure 5.2 Higher trade costs reduce global welfare

Overall welfare losses, by region, from a one-percentage-point ad valorem increase in trade costs

Note: The measure of welfare loss—"equivalent variation" divided by GDP—was devised by Walkenhorst and Dihel (2002). "High-risk" regions will suffer greater welfare losses than lower risk regions from an identical increase in frictional costs of trade. Similarly, some sectors are more sensitive than others to increases in frictional costs.
Source: Walkenhorst and Dihel (2002).

The threat of terrorism is not the only source of frictional costs. War and epidemic disease, too, call for extraordinary measures that often disrupt trade. The 2003 war in Iraq imposed significant costs on manufacturers, shippers, wholesalers, and retailers stemming from supply-chain disruptions, blockages of vital sea routes, and delays in shipments. This was especially true for manufactures linking factories in Asia with markets in North America and Europe. New protocols at seaports and airports have been implemented this year to prevent the spread of severe acute respiratory syndrome, or SARS, a virus that has swept large parts of Asia. The outbreak has sharply reduced passenger travel to, from, and within Asia, especially Hong Kong and China. Tourism has fallen sharply.[21]

A coordinated action plan on trade and security is clearly needed

Even though the costs of compliance could be large and disproportionate for smaller countries, all participants in the global trading system have an incentive to invest in counterterrorism efforts. As noted above, the initial costs of new security procedures will pay off in the long run through efficiency gains, better management of information, and greater use of electronic commerce. It is easy to square enhanced security with improved trade facilitation at a theoretical level, however; it may well be more difficult in practice.

The importance of *partnerships* at various levels in the global security campaign is clear. The IMO, ICAO, and other organizations should step up their technical cooperation activities to help developing countries improve their capacity to bolster security and trade. Assistance should be coordinated so as to ensure absorption and nonduplication of capacity-building initiatives provided by the developed world. The WCO has conducted a survey of members' capacity-building needs to ensure that security measures do not impede development. Initiated by the World Bank in 1999, the Global Facilitation Partnership for Transportation and Trade, which includes several international, private, and professional organizations, has focused on facilitating trade—with security one of its themes.

Development institutions, in partnership with national governments, have a role to play in risk assessment, training, development of human capital, and improving customs administration and infrastructure in their client countries. They also can help track international initiatives and assess implications for developing countries.

Because containers travel by sea, road, and rail, their regulation is especially problematic. The container may be subject to IMO regulations when on ship, but on land national governments may impose a different set of legislations. The interdependence and linkages among different transport modes call for a *coordinated security approach* among sectors and modes. A ship may be owned by a company in one country, crewed by national of a second country, and carry the cargo of a third to a port of a fourth. Regional and bilateral partner-ships among countries and stakeholders can strengthen information exchange, cooperation in training, and sharing of best practices, resulting in mutual enhancement of security efforts.[22] The United Nations International Drug Control Program (UNDCP) container security project and the United Nations Economic Commission for Europe (UNECE) supply chain model are particularly promising in this regard.

The APEC STAR initiative has stressed greater cooperation between governments and private business to protect the global economy.[23] Sustained *dialogue* between governments and industry is needed to implement measures to protect supply chains against security threats. The private sector needs to be directly involved with governments in crafting the most efficient ways of complying with the requirements and to ensure the integrity of trade from the point of manufacture to the port of delivery. In October 2001, for example, a joint venture plan between Boeing and Israel's El Al airline was aimed at integrating airlines' security concerns into the early stages of the aircraft production process, with a view to providing a higher level of security at a lower cost (OECD 2002a).

A *risk-assessment template* should be developed to ensure that high-risk areas are targeted for special security programs. The measures adopted should be those that distort trade the least and provide the greatest benefits, especially for exports from developing nations. Since it is impossible to screen and inspect all containers, procedures to identify high-risk containers—by detecting irregularities in shipping patterns—could be deployed. Emphasis on detecting corrupt practices such as bribery will be needed to prevent controls from being evaded.

A formula for *cost-sharing* that is optimal for all also must be developed. The Hong Kong Shippers Council (HKSC) and the ASEAN Federation of Forwarders Associations (AFFA) have urged USCS to subsidize the cost of its new requirements and U.S. importers to share with Asian exporters the burden of providing information.

Caution must be exercised to ensure that security barriers do not become trade barriers. One possible solution may be a new intergovernmental program with the mandate to plan coordinated and comprehensive trade-related security programs. Such a program could ensure the win-win outcome that is achievable in security and trade, while recognizing the special needs of developing countries. The G-8, in cooperation with developing countries, is one logical forum for development of a coordinated "Action Plan for Security and Trade."

The anticompetitive effects of international transport regulations

Costs rise and fall with public policies and private practices. For a long time, many transport services came under the aegis of public monopolies, and state-owned enterprises exerted a powerful force in the transport sectors of many countries. Such public monopolies are becoming increasingly difficult to jusify. Private entry and competitive market structures have proved viable for almost all transport modes and generally have brought greater efficiency and lower prices for consumers. However, public and private barriers remain pervasive in air and maritime transport—restricting competition and increasing costs. In general, they should be replaced with systems that rely on private provision of services.

International air transport services are heavily protected

Efficient air transportation is an important determinant of an economy's export competitiveness. This is especially true for high-value, nonbulky manufactures, perishable horticultural and agricultural products, and time-sensitive intermediate inputs traded within international production networks. Efficient air cargo services play a critical role in attracting investment—including foreign direct investment (FDI)—in these sectors, which can be an important source of employment and economic growth.

The share of world trade shipped by air has grown continuously over the past decades—for example, from 7 percent of U.S. imports in 1965 to 30 percent in 1998. In terms of ton-miles shipped worldwide, air cargo has grown by almost 10 percent annually from 1970 to 1996, while ocean shipping grew only 2.6 percent per year over the same period (World Bank 2001). More than 20 percent of African exports enter the United States by air, and, for a quarter of all product groups, the share of air-shipped exports exceeds 50 percent.[24]

For many developing countries, the cost of air transportation often far exceeds the costs observed on developed-country routes. Amjadi and Yeats (1995) found, for example, that air transport costs made up between 10 and 50 percent of the value of African exports to the United States, a much higher proportion than for U.S. imports from non-African countries.

High air freight rates on developing-country routes are primarily due to two factors. First, the *cost* of serving developing countries may be higher. Developing countries are farther from the world's economic centers, increasing the cost of operating aircraft. And overall trade volumes tend to be smaller on routes serving less-developed countries, preventing operators from reaping economics of scale and scope. Thin traffic densities also may adversely affect the *quality* of air transportation, as services may be offered less frequently. Second, different degrees of *competition* in the provision of air services may affect the markup that air cargo operators may be able to charge on a particular route. The extent of competition among cargo carriers again depends on traffic volumes—as economies of scale and scope limit the number of providers that can be sustained on a particular route. Competition also may be influenced by government policies—in particular, restrictive market-access agreements for the provision of air transport.

In an econometric investigation conducted for this report, we attempted to quantify the determinants of air transport costs using a sample of 139 randomly selected city-pair routes in the Western Hemisphere. Preliminary results suggest that distance is a key determinant of international air cargo freight rates—most likely due to the cost of fuel and the capital cost of operating aircraft. Across the sample, a one-percentage-point increase in city-pair distance leads to a 0.72 percent increase in prices—a higher distance elasticity than that typically found for maritime transport. Countries located far from economic centers are therefore at a disadvantage.

Moreover, the investigation confirms that there are sizeable *economies of scale* in the provision of air transport. On average, a 10 percent increase in city-pair traffic volumes leads to a drop of slightly more than 1 percent in the observed freight rate. In view of the wide variance in freight traffic volumes, the scale effect can be quite large—and in most cases it works against poorer nations. Finally, *competition* among airlines is found to exert downward pressure on freight rates. City-pair routes on which more than two passenger airlines or dedicated freight airlines operate enjoy, on average, 10.7 percent lower prices.

Liberalizing air services can help reduce costs—
What are the implications of these findings for public policy? First, there remain significant policy-induced barriers to competition in air cargo services. The complex system of air service agreements (ASAs) still governs the market for international air cargo services. ASAs are typically negotiated bilaterally, although recent years have seen the emergence of regional arrangements. Among other things, they designate the airlines allowed to operate on city-pair routes and the number and frequency of flights they can operate.

Over time, ASAs have become increasingly liberal. For example, the so-called Bermuda-type agreements do not regulate capacity on each route but allow the designated airlines to negotiate the number and frequency of flights. "Open skies" agreements are even less restrictive, allowing all airlines to fly on all routes between two countries without any *ex ante* controls on capacity.

More liberal ASAs can be a way of promoting competition and thus lowering air cargo freight rates. Moreover, greater freedom in designing air transport networks could allow air service operators to reap greater economies of scale and scope, offering additional cost savings. Indeed, it is thought that liberalization in protected air service markets may lead to consolidation among airlines, as operators seek to generate larger scale and network economies. Consolidation may not necessarily be associated with lessened competition, as fewer operators may compete on a larger number of routes. But it does suggest that liberalization needs to be accompanied by competition policies that ensure a review of mergers, acquisitions, and other forms of private cooperation on economic efficiency grounds (World Bank 2001).

—but important challenges remain
Notwithstanding the benefits of air-service liberalization, thin traffic densities and the associated lack of economies of scale are likely to remain a key obstacle to substantially lowering air cargo freight rates in the developing

world. Moreover, liberalization may lead airlines to foster the adoption of hub-and-spoke networks, which may lower prices on well-connected hub routes but could actually raise freight rates on thin spoke routes.

Overcoming these challenges may call for broader policy reforms. Countries have long recognized the need for universal service policies in a variety of service sectors to ensure that remote and poor regions are offered services at affordable prices. These policies include special service obligations imposed on operators, universal service funds, and various forms of subsidies. The universal service concept could be extended by international action to remote and poor countries within continents. The necessary action could come in the form of tax breaks offered by developed countries on air cargo service provided to certain developing country locations or through the establishment of an international fund for the provision of universal air services.

Regulations in maritime transport also restrict competition

Various trade barriers have been imposed on international maritime transport that protect inefficient service providers and hamper effective competition. Public policy restrictions include cargo reservation schemes that require part of the cargo carried in trade with other states to be transported only by ships carrying a national flag (or other ships deemed national by other criteria). Cargo sharing with trading partners can be done unilaterally, or on the basis of bilateral and multilateral agreements. Although more and more countries have phased out such requirements, countries ranging from Benin to India still have in place reservation policies that at least nominally restrict the scope of trade.

Cooperative agreements among maritime carriers on technical or commercial matters are another type of practice that restrains competition. For example, liner conference agreements set uniform freight tariff rates and conditions of service, often employing exclusive contracts and other loyalty-inducing instruments to prevent the entry of outside shipping lines. Private cooperation can improve network coordination, generate economies of scope, and provide a wider range of services to consumers of shipping lines. But a recent study of the impact of price-fixing and cooperative working agreements on liner freight rates for U.S. imports, found that liberalization of certain port services would lead to an average price reduction of 8 percent and cost savings of up to $850 million (Fink and others 2002a). Private practices continue to have a strong impact on liner freight rates; breaking up carrier agreements could cause prices to decline further by 20 percent, with additional cost savings of $2 billion (table 5.1).

Seaport services have recently witnessed a trend toward increased private-sector partici

Table 5.1 Elimination of anticompetitive private practices can cut costs drastically

	Liberalization of port services	Breakup of cooperative working agreements	Breakup of price-fixing agreements	Cumulative effect of the breakup of private carrier agreements	Cumulative total effect
Average percentage price reduction	8.3	5.3	15.7	20.0	26.4
Projected total savings for all U.S. imports (in millions of dollars)	850.4	544.1	1618.4	2063.0	2712.5

Note: The average percentage price reductions are computed from the sample of 59 countries included in the study, while the projected total savings apply to all U.S trading partners. Given the functional form of the underlying regression equation, the individual effects do not sum to the cumulative effects. See Fink and others (2001) for additional explanatory notes.
Source: World Bank (2001).

pation and greater competition within and among ports. Different ownership and operation structures have emerged with respect to port management, provision of infrastructure, and the supply of services. With the emergence of large global port operators, there is now a greater risk of abuse of market power—abuse that could reduce the benefits gained from port liberalization. Creating regulatory capacity and strengthening institutions is necessary for the success of port reforms.

Trade facilitation

To be effective, trade-facilitation measures must include or be accompanied by improvements in domestic regulatory procedures and institutional structures. Above all, they must include development assistance to raise trade-related capacity—individual, institutional, and social—in developing nations. One example of the need for capacity building and technical assistance in the trade-facilitation agenda relates to the technology required for expediting cargo clearance. International commerce depends increasingly on information technology—most basically for the electronic transmission of trade information. Modern customs methods of profiling consignments or traders based on risk-assessment techniques can help expedite cargo clearance. Compiling a unique set of computerized information for each shipment enables data to be processed before cargo arrives, thus expediting clearance and speeding delivery.

Measures to speed the flow of goods and services across international borders have played a critical role in the expansion of global trade over the past decades. Cross-border trade in raw materials, components, and intermediate goods by multinationals with integrated production and distribution facilities now constitutes more than one-third of world trade. This expansion would not have been possible without precisely timed maritime container services, express door-to-door delivery of air freight, new information and communications technologies, and other services. All parties to a transaction gain from fast, easy, and low-cost trading conditions.[25]

High logistic costs affect competitiveness

Although the incidence of logistics costs varies, with some developing countries more efficient than others in providing trade services, a study by the United Nations Commission on Trade and Development (UNCTAD) estimates that average customs transactions in developing countries involve 20 to 30 parties; 40 documents; and 200 data elements, 30 of which had to be repeated at least 30 times. Subramanian and Arnold (2001) broke down the cost of international shipment into five categories: ocean freight, inland transport cost, and three indicators of logistics costs—custom inspection, cargo handling and transfer, and processing of trade documentation. Their analysis shows that logistics accounted for no less than a third of the cost of door-to-door shipment of containerized carpets from Nepal to Germany and teabags from India to the United Kingdom. Using a similar methodology, a World Bank (1997) study of the performance of Brazilian ports reported that per-container costs for administrative procedures and customs clearance could be reduced by more than 20 percent (from $1,727 to $1,320) if international best practices were followed.

For small economies, higher logistics costs translate directly into higher import and export prices. To remain competitive in industries where profit margins are thin, exporters must either pay lower wages to workers, accept lower returns on capital, or enhance productivity. The pressure on factory prices and productivity is even higher for countries exporting products that have a high import content, such as domestic export-oriented firms producing garments or electronic final goods using imported materials—as is the case with many developing countries. In these cases, where small differences in transaction costs can determine whether the export venture is commercially viable or not, logistical efficiency can mean greater retention of the value-added benefits of trade-led growth. Particularly in labor-intensive

Box 5.2 The logistics needs of a German car part manufacturer in Tunisia

As the subsidiary of a large German car part supplier, Leoni Tunisie S.A. produces cable and electronic components for Daimler Chrysler and other European car manufacturers. The just-in-time supply chains in the car industry put high demands in the logistics system. Leoni has outsourced all logistics needs to an international forwarder that has a legal subsidiary in Tunisia.

A full production and logistics cycle lasts about nine days. Raw materials and intermediate products are sourced from across Europe, Asia, and the United States. They are consolidated at Leoni's headquarters in Germany and shipped to about a dozen factories in various countries. Several trucks leave Germany for Tunisia each week. The trailers are cleared and sealed by German customs on the firm's premises, where they are picked up by the logistics provider. The forwarder drives the trailers to Genoa or Marseilles (2–2.5 days), places them without a driver on RoRo ferries (20–24 hours by sea), claims them at Rades's port, and delivers them to a factory in Sousse (2–3 hours by land). Once assembled, the finished components are cleared by a Tunisian customs officer on the premises before they are sent on their return journey. Eight trucks carrying approximately 350 tons of finished parts leave Tunisia each week. The company considers the chain to be efficient and reliable.

Even so, the just-in-time demands of the industry are posing a threat to Tunisia as a production base—more and more clients require six-day cycles. Because internal production processes have been streamlined, further time savings depend on logistics efficiency. Leoni Tunisie recently lost an internal company competition for a new factory with a potential for 1,700 jobs to Leoni's Romanian subsidiary. The reasons cited for the loss were not wage competitiveness or the investment environment—the company regards Tunisia as very competitive—but Eastern Europe's logistics advantage. The land journey between Romania and Germany takes one day less in each direction. According to the CEO of Leoni Tunisie, Tunisia will need to economize on logistics costs (including better air cargo connections or high-speed ferries to Europe) if it is to retain its competitive advantage in time-sensitive industries.

Source: Mueller-Jentsch (2002).

---

industries in developing countries, high transport costs may preclude wage growth, thus affecting the standard of living of workers.

A study that examined the effect of higher shipping and port charges in the garment industry of Bangladesh estimated that exports could rise by 30 percent, raising hard-currency earnings by 125 percent, if port inefficiencies were reduced. One recent estimate, based on comparisons between air and ocean freight rates for U.S imports, puts the per-day cost for shipping delays at 0.8 percent of the value of trade for manufactured goods—with only a small fraction attributable to the capital costs of the goods while on the ship (box 5.2).

Minimizing transit time is particularly important in modern commerce, given the trend toward just-in-time production systems that enable firms to outsource stages of production to geographically dispersed locations. Research by Hummels (2001) showed that delivery times had a pronounced effect on imports of intermediate products, suggesting that rapid delivery of goods is crucial for the maintenance of multinational vertical product chains. Hummels found that each day saved in shipping time due to a faster transport mode and faster customs clearance was worth almost one percent, ad valorem, for manufactured goods. Uncertain order-to-delivery times impose implicit production costs as well. If logistics services are unreliable and infrequent, firms are likely to maintain higher inventory holdings at every stage of the production chain, requiring additional working capital. Forgone earnings can be significant for firms in countries with high real interest rates. Gausch and Kogan (2001) found that inventory holdings in the manufacturing sector in many developing countries are two to five times higher than in the United States. Their estimates further show that developing countries could reduce the unit cost of production by as much as 20 percent by reducing inventory holdings by half.

Better measures of trade facilitation are yielding some positive results
With increased attention to the benefits of reducing nontransport barriers to trade, efforts have been made to assess the importance of trade facilitation. Because empirical measures of trade facilitation are lacking, however, progress has been limited.

Several recent studies quantify the benefits of improved trade facilitation, modeled as a reduction in the costs of international trade or as an improvement in the productivity of the international transportation sector. UNCTAD (2001) considers trade facilitation in the broader context of creating an environment conducive to developing e-commerce usage and applications. The results show that a reduction of one percentage point in the cost of maritime and air transport services could increase Asian GDP by $3.3 billion.[26] If trade facilitation is expanded to include improvements in wholesale and retail trade services, an additional $3.6 billion could be gained by a one-percentage-point improvement in the productivity of that sector. APEC (1999) found that the shock-derived reduction in trade costs ranged from 1 percent of import prices for industrial countries and the Republic of Korea, Taiwan, and Singapore, to 2 percent for developing countries.[27] The study estimated that APEC merchandise exports would increase by 3.3 percent from trade-facilitation efforts.

Empirical studies of the impact of enhanced e-commerce and telecommunication access, improved customs procedures, and harmonized or improved standards also demonstrate the benefits of trade facilitation in specific fields. Freund and Weinhold (2000) found that a 10-percentage-point increase in the relative number of web hosts in one country would have increased trade flows by 1 percent in 1998 and 1999. Fink, Mattoo, and Neagu (2002b) found that a 10 percent decrease in the bilateral calling price was associated with an 8 percent increase in bilateral trade.

Moenius (2000) estimated the effect of bilaterally shared and country-specific standards on goods trade, finding that shared standards generally promoted trade. Hertel, Walmsley, and Itakura (2001) quantified the impact on trade of greater harmonization of e-business standards and of automating customs procedures between Japan and Singapore, concluding that such reforms would increase trade flows between these countries as well as with the rest of the world. In agricultural trade, Wilson and Otsuki (2003) find that the major exporters of nuts and cereals would gain $38.8 billion if divergent national food-safety standards relating to aflatoxins were replaced by the Codex international standard.

Those results show clearly that when trade is facilitated, trade volumes rise
In their study of APEC manufacturing trade, Wilson, Mann, and Otsuki (2003a) incorporate indicators linked to multiple categories of trade facilitation into a single model, thus allowing a synthetic analysis that prioritizes areas for reform. The authors estimate the relationship among four indicators and trade flows using a gravity model.[28] Wilson, Mann, and Otsuki (2003b) expand the scope of the analysis to include 75 countries worldwide, including 52 developing countries. The indicators in the analysis are:

- Port efficiency (through measurements of port infrastructure)
- Customs environment (including nontariff fees)
- Regulatory environment (including transparency of government policy and control on corruption)

- Use of e-commerce by businesses, a proxy for the service-sector infrastructure necessary to implement e-business.

The study estimates the potential increase in trade following improvements in each trade-facilitation area. The authors examine a scenario in which trade-facilitation capacity in *below-average* countries is raised *halfway* to the average for the entire set of countries. This approach recognizes that in some countries trade is already being facilitated at levels approaching the global best, leaving little room for improvement, whereas in others a standardized improvement of, say, 10 percent in trade facilitation would be quite difficult, requiring additional capacity-building assistance. Figure 5.3 illustrates the projected gain, by trade-facilitation indicator, for the 75 countries examined.

Preliminary findings suggest that better trade facilitation would increase trade among the 75 countries by approximately $377 billion dollars—an increase of about 9.7 percent. About $33 billion (0.8 percent) of the gain would come from improved customs regimes, and about $107 billion (2.8 percent) from more efficient ports. But the largest gain—$154 billion, or 4.0 percent—would come from enhancing infrastructure in the services sector (figure 5.3). Reforms and improvements affecting exports would have a greater effect on trade growth than would changes affecting imports, suggesting that the export-promotion effect of trade facilitation should not be underestimated in designing capacity-building efforts.

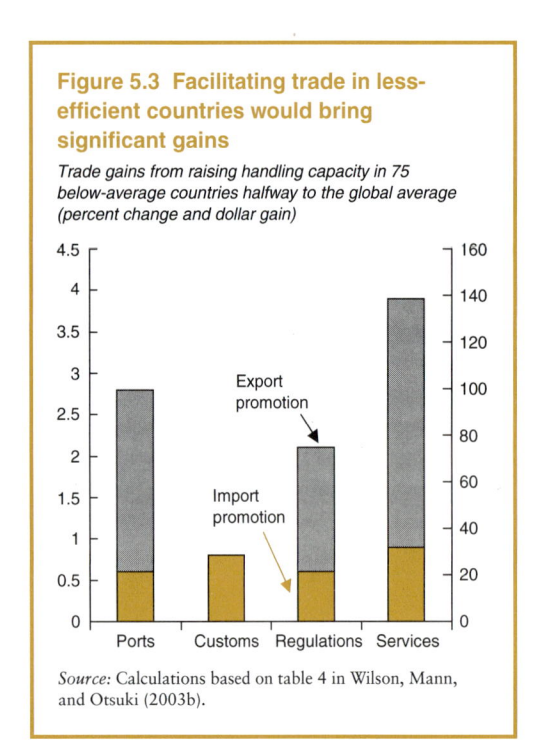

The impact of individual trade-facilitation measures differs significantly from region to region, but improvements in service-sector infrastructure would provide the largest gain in sum of imports and exports in all regions—particularly in South Asia (figure 5.4). The potential gains from improvements in port efficiency also are great—again, particularly in South Asia.

The gains to be expected from domestic reform alone (figure 5.5) show similar patterns to those projected for global reforms, implying that priority areas for domestic reform are consistent with reforms to raise capacity globally. In assigning priorities for capacity building, enhancing port efficiency and improving service-sector infrastructure appear to be most important for domestic and global action.

Reforming domestic policies is indispensable

The benefits from investment in modern customs, port facilities, and new technology, however, can only be realized if an appropriate regulatory framework is in place. In this regard, domestic reforms have an important role to play, by making better use of existing resources and improving the efficiency of services. Liberalization of transport and telecommunication networks can help encourage domestic competition and produce substantial cost reductions. Liberalization also offers the added advantage of widening the availability and choice of services in many developing countries. As discussed earlier, the prevalence of anticompetitive practices by transport service providers

Figure 5.3 Facilitating trade in less-efficient countries would bring significant gains

Trade gains from raising handling capacity in 75 below-average countries halfway to the global average (percent change and dollar gain)

Source: Calculations based on table 4 in Wilson, Mann, and Otsuki (2003b).

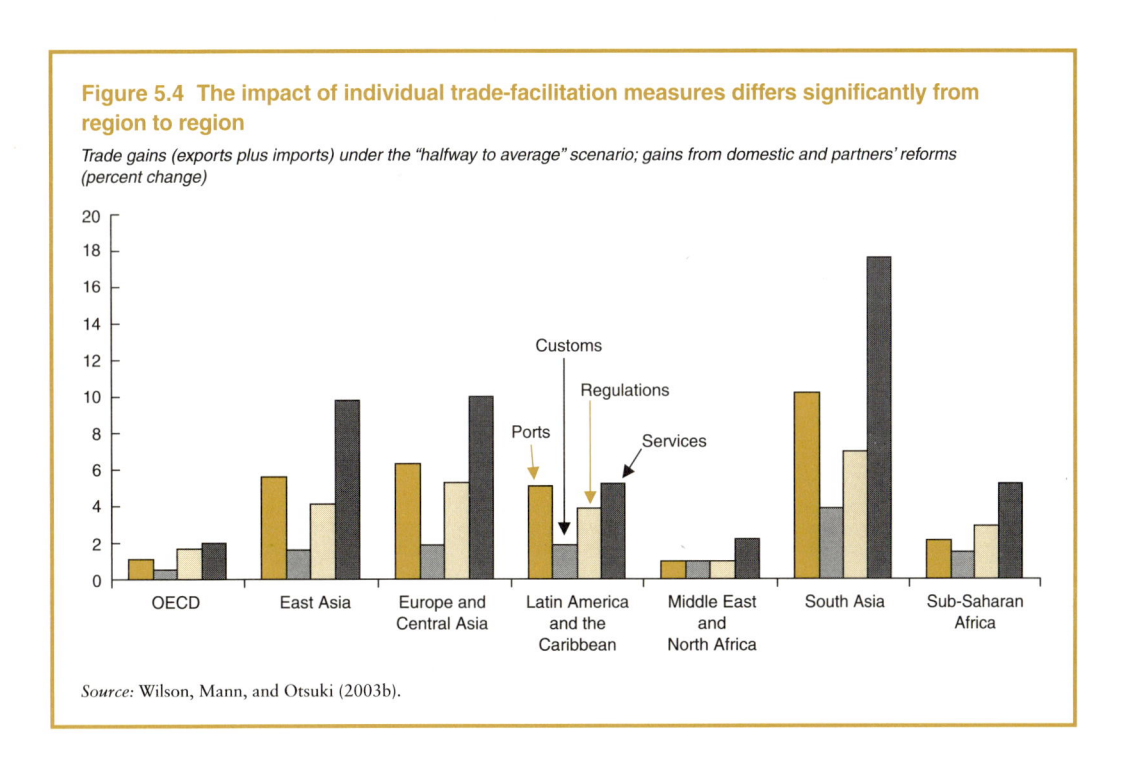

Figure 5.4 The impact of individual trade-facilitation measures differs significantly from region to region

Trade gains (exports plus imports) under the "halfway to average" scenario; gains from domestic and partners' reforms (percent change)

[Bar chart showing trade gains across regions: OECD, East Asia, Europe and Central Asia, Latin America and the Caribbean, Middle East and North Africa, South Asia, Sub-Saharan Africa. Four bars per region representing Ports, Customs, Regulations, and Services.]

Source: Wilson, Mann, and Otsuki (2003b).

calls for the development of efficiency-oriented competition policies. Replacement of inefficient public monopolies in international transport systems with private operators can thus increase competition.

Cross-country comparisons provided in Wilson, Mann, and Otsuki (2003b) reveal significant difference in countries' potential for gains from trade facilitation. Guatemala, for example, has great potential to reap trade gains by reforming its service-sector infrastructure. In contrast, the potential importance of regulatory reform predominates in Indonesia. In Nigeria, reform of the customs system would have the most productive outcome. In all countries, domestic reform would have greater impact on total trade than would reforms by trading partners.

Trade facilitation and the WTO agenda

The Singapore Ministerial Declaration in 1996 empowered the WTO for the first time to look at trade facilitation in a compre-hensive fashion.[29] Exploratory work on the trade-facilitation agenda centered on ways to simplify trade procedures, to harmonize them to conform to a rule-based multilateral framework, and to integrate the work of other international organizations involved in trade-facilitation into the WTO framework. But progress on trade facilitation at WTO's next two ministerial conferences was limited.[30]

The Doha Declaration raised the issue of negotiations on trade facilitation

The Doha ministerial raised the possibility of launching multilateral negotiations on trade facilitation at the Cancun ministerial meeting in September 2003.[31] The "Doha agenda" on trade facilitation referenced simplifying trade procedures, enhancing technical assistance and capacity building, and recognizing limitations in capacity associated with a country's level of development. The Doha ministerial declaration was explicit in recognizing the need to increase trade-related capacity in developing countries and address the issue of implementation costs associated with capacity building,

GLOBAL ECONOMIC PROSPECTS 2004

Figure 5.5 Domestic reforms alone would produce many of the same gains as global reform

Trade gains (exports plus imports) under the "halfway to average" scenario; gains from domestic reforms only (percent change)

[Bar chart showing Ports, Customs, Regulations, and Services gains across OECD, East Asia, Europe and Central Asia, Latin America and the Caribbean, Middle East and North Africa, South Asia, and Sub-Saharan Africa]

Source: Wilson, Mann, and Otsuki (2003b).

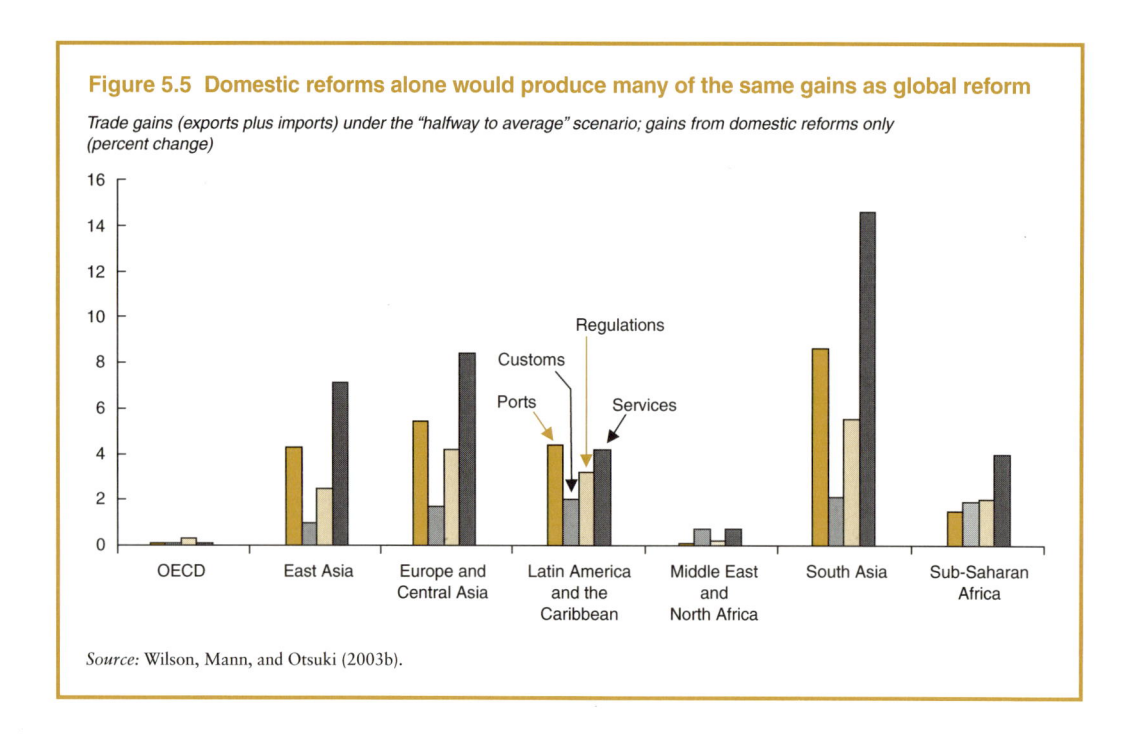

particularly in developing and least-developed countries.

Some proposals under discussion envisage either building new or strengthening existing rules and principles of transparency, simplification, efficiency, proportionality, nondiscrimination, and due process within the country for independent litigations involving trade disputes, as well as recourse to the WTO Dispute Settlement Undertaking, if need be, to ensure nondiscriminatory treatment of traders in member countries.

Not everyone agrees that trade facilitation measures should be on the agenda at Cancun. Proposals advanced by the proponents of a rules-based approach to trade facilitation focus on the role and importance of the WTO. Are national governments free, they ask, to follow the recommendations of the WCO's revised Kyoto convention on customs procedures? Are they likely to do so? Or should these recommendations be a reference point for WTO rules?[32] The WTO has many more members than WCO, the proponents point out, and the revised recommendations of the Kyoto convention have not been ratified by all WCO member countries. To the proponents, a binding framework would help establish effective compliance with the recommendations of the revised Kyoto convention.

The challenges to negotiations on trade facilitation center on two concerns. First, it is not clear that binding multilateral rules on customs and border-crossing procedures are actually needed; implementing institutional changes requires country ownership and voluntary actions. Second, it is not clear that any new rules could be enforced through conventional dispute-settlement proceedings and penalties, since violations of those rules often stem from the limited capacity of governments to meet their obligations. Rules alone are not likely to produce the desired reforms or modernizations. Those depend on capacity building, and capacity building depends on resources—financial and other.

Simplifying administrative and procedural requirements in customs and border-crossing procedures—unlike negotiations on tariff cuts, for example—depends directly on improvements in physical infrastructure, institutional reform, and other complex development objectives that typically involve large commitments of resources for training and capital equipment. In an environment of constrained resources, expenditures on such improvements must be made in accordance with the priorities of the national development strategies.

The trade-facilitation agenda requires a broad multilateral effort

Trade facilitation necessarily involves both infrastructure investments and revisions in legal frameworks, technology training, and other measures. A little capacity building could go a long way. Expediting customs clearance procedures by providing transparent and clear guidelines, for example, reduces the discretionary power of customs officials, thereby reducing the scope for corruption by establishing a right of independent judicial appeal (box 5.3). Assistance to modernize customs procedures by upgrading information technology and applying risk-based criteria in reviews of documentation and cargo, allowing for self-assessment and audit-based (as opposed to transactions-based) release of goods can also have high payoffs (box 5.4).

Because behind-the-border policies affect cross-border trade, trade-related capacity building must have a broad scope. The procedural and administrative burdens on traders are often aggravated by overlapping and duplicative informational requirements from several ministries, departments, or agencies. New ways of minimizing such requirements include the single-window concept: official controls are administered by a single agency. This and other innovations often require coordination of several government agencies, as well as changes in domestic regulatory procedures and institutional structures.

Multilateral agreement on standards of transparency and acceptable fees as well as new ways to publish and disseminate applicable trade laws, rules, fees, and schedules—perhaps through a new information clearinghouse or inquiry center for WTO members—could help countries facilitate trade. Discussions also could include development of harmonized and quantifiable measures of "timely release of goods." Consideration of wider use of the "supplier's declaration of conformity" with technical regulations for low-risk goods—along with a parallel program to expand information technology systems and databases—could decrease and simplify documentation requirements. Strengthening the provisions of GATT Article V (Freedom of Transit) could be particularly beneficial to land-locked countries.

Box 5.3   Tackling corruption in customs: Peru

Eliminating customs corruption in Peru required changes in laws, regulations, and human-resources policy.

After firing corrupt employees, the Peruvian customs service established a uniform code of conduct and contracted with a university to develop tests of employee competence. Continued employment was contingent on passing the tests. Although substantial pressure was exerted on the customs service to rehire discharged employees, it was able to resist the pressure with support from government allies. As a result of these efforts, employee corruption decreased, while competence levels improved. Salaries of retained personnel were increased by nearly 10 times the previous salaries.

To increase the competence of customs officers, hiring for professional positions was limited to university graduates. The service established a training academy, offering up to one year of training to new and incumbent employees. In addition to these efforts, customs embarked on a program to bring new skills and knowledge to the organization through external recruitment of mid-career professionals—economists, auditors, statisticians, and information technology experts.

Source: Wilson et. al (2002).

Box 5.4 Customs reform in Lebanon

Lebanon's ongoing customs reform project is part of a fiscal reform project under the sponsorship of the United Nations Development Programme and the World Bank. An inefficient customs service has long been a major logistical bottleneck in Lebanon. Procedures were nontransparent and time-consuming. Most of the 7–12 days needed for container delivery were due to customs delays. Such deficiencies not only imposed unnecessary economic costs but also bred corruption.

Under the reform project, customs clearance was reduced from 13 to 5 basic steps—entry and acceptance of declaration, inspection of goods for verification of declared information, assessment of information, automatic calculation of taxes, and payment of taxes. Clearance procedures were then aligned with international procedures, with UN and EU standards translated into Arabic for the first time. A one-page administrative document replaced 26 complex and outdated forms. These reforms enabled the clearance process to be computerized, with a new software program monitoring the days required for clearance. The computerization process was accompanied by staff training and a restructuring of work procedures. Clearance operations were set up on the shop floors of some of the main importers and exporters, with inspectors using risk-assessment criteria to conduct selective inspections. To inform users of their rights and responsibilities and to further streamline the inspection process, the customs service published a summary of its border regulations.

Preliminary results of the ongoing reform indicate that although the percentage of consignments cleared without inspection had quadrupled between 1997 and 1999 (from 10 to 40 percent) and the average days needed for clearance had declined from six to four as a result of more selective testing, the average rate of tariff collection remained constant.

Source: Mueller-Jentsch (2002).

Any negotiation on trade-facilitation measures, however, must carefully consider how the WTO's dispute-settlement provisions could be tailored to ensure that the capacity constraints of developing countries are taken into account when enforcing commitments undertaken by governments. Important capacity-building work done by several institutions outside the WTO framework provides a model for a future multilateral agenda to raise trade-facilitation capacity in developing countries. It is difficult to see how this level of institutional change and assistance coordination could be "enforced" through dispute settlement mechanisms.

Lowering transport costs, increasing security, and facilitating trade

The costs of moving goods across international borders are a crucial determinant of a country's export competitiveness. Every day spent in customs adds almost 1 percent to the costs of goods. High costs also result from regulations and practices that impede effective competition in international transport systems.

Open skies and universal service can lower international transport costs for developing countries

Improving competition in air transport will require revisions in air service agreements to reduce barriers to entry into markets. Moving progressively toward "open skies" agreements would allow all airlines to fly on all routes between two countries without any *ex ante* controls on capacity. This would lower air cargo freight rates and could allow air service operators to obtain greater economies of scale and scope, offering additional cost savings. It may well be that liberalization in protected air service markets may lead to consolidation among airlines, as operators seek to generate larger scale and network economies. (Consolidation may not necessarily reduce competition, however, as fewer operators may compete on a larger number of routes.) Even with open entry, thin traffic densities and the associated lack of economies of scale are likely to remain key obstacles to lowering air freight rates in the developing world. If liberalization leads airlines to adopt hub-and-spoke networks, prices could fall on well-connected hub routes, while rising on some spoke routes. To reduce this risk by cross-subsidizing transport to remote and poor areas within continents, the concept of universal service should be embraced internationally. Rich countries could offer tax breaks on air cargo service provided to certain developing country locations. Alternatively, an international fund for the provision of universal air services could be established.

For maritime transport, one avenue to improvement would be to subject the industry to MFN treatment in routes as part of the larger GATS discussion on services. Doing so would undermine the competition-restricting liner codes that prevent new entries in designated shipping routes. Another avenue would be to review exemptions in U.S. and EU antitrust law for maritime transport.

Security can be increased without jeopardizing trade flows from developing countries

Even though the costs of compliance with new security measures could be large and disproportionate for smaller countries, all participants in the global trading system have an incentive to invest in counterterrorism. Such investments are likely to pay off in the long run through efficiency gains, better management of information, and greater use of electronic commerce. To ensure that they do, several steps must be taken.

First, technical assistance must be increased. The IMO, ICAO, and other organizations should step up their technical cooperation efforts to provide more training in risk assessment, customs administration, and infrastructure planning in their client countries.

Second, nations must coordinate trade-related actions not only with other countries, but also with their own private sectors. The interdependence and linkages among different transport modes call for a coordinated approach to security among sectors and modes. Regional and bilateral partnerships among countries can strengthen channels for information exchange and cooperation in training and sharing of best practices, resulting in mutual enhancement of security efforts. Other regions could follow APEC's lead by looking for ways to design collaborative programs with the private sector to implement security measures.

Third, a risk-assessment template would ensure that high-risk areas are targeted for special security programs. The measures adopted should be those that distort trade the least and provide the greatest benefits, especially for exports from developing nations.

Fourth, a formula for cost-sharing must be developed. The Hong Kong Shippers Council (HKSC) and the ASEAN Federation of Forwarders Associations (AFFA) have urged the USCS to subsidize the cost of its new requirements and U.S. importers to share with Asian exporters the burden of providing information.

Trade facilitation depends on capacity building and development assistance

Capacity building and development assistance are necessary if countries are to make the most of trade-facilitation measures—whether those measures stem from security imperatives or multilateral trade talks. Attempts to build trade capacity may require several elements—from building basic transport infrastructure to making legislative changes and training regulators. Some developing countries may require only technical assistance to expedite cargo clearance through electronic trade documentation. Others will need much more help. No single package will meet the needs of all countries.

Whether or not trade facilitation becomes part of multilateral trade negotiations, measures that lower transport costs, remove barriers to goods and services moving across borders, and build capacity in trade facilitation must be pursued. Success will depend first on governments and the private sector in developing countries, but also on the G-8, UN agencies, the WCO, the World Bank, and other international development institutions. Multilateral efforts to support domestic policy reform and institutional improvements in developing countries are particularly important if investments in trade facilitation are to yield their full potential—a potential that is great indeed.

Notes

1. These sections draw on Wilson and others (2002), among other sources.

2. A study of the effect of security on private investment and growth by Poirson (1998) spanning 53 developing countries from 1984–95 indicates that enhanced security fosters private investment and growth in developing economies. Private investment in the short run increased by 0.5 to 1 percentage point of GDP, in relatively insecure countries that adopted security measures to the levels in "best practice" regions. Moreover, economic growth received a boost by 0.5 to 1.25 percentage points per year in the long term.

3. The newly created Department of Homeland Security includes Customs, Immigration and Naturalization Services (INS), Border Patrol, and the federal Agricultural Inspection Service. The Department provided $170 million in port security grants in June 2003. Under discussion is a plan that would include an additional $1 billion for the Transportation Security Administration, $200 million to $700 million more for the Coast Guard, and an increase in federal grants to local police and fire departments for counterterrorism training.

4. Some overseas suppliers are covered under the C-TPAT because they are subsidiaries of U.S. companies enrolled in the initiative.

5. The Swedish port of Goteborg has become the twelfth to join the Container Security Initiative (as of May 2003). Those already participating include: Rotterdam, LeHavre, Bremerhaven, Hamburg, and Antwerp in Europe; Singapore, Hong Kong, and Yokohama in Asia; and Vancouver, Montreal, and Halifax in Canada. These ports are at different stages of implementation of the CSI framework. CSI is now moving into its second phase, which will include Turkey, Dubai, and about 20 other nations in Asia, Latin America, Europe, and Africa.

6. On a related note, Europe's largest air cargo carriers, which are calling for a level playing field among the United States, Europe, and the rest of the world as far as security and its costs are concerned, criticized U.S. government aid of $10 billion to its airlines to conform to increased security measures. European carriers believe that the aid has helped U.S. carriers slash rates on very competitive North Atlantic routes.

7. Another proposal under consideration is the filing of a bill of lading by U.S. Agricultural exporters 24 hours before loading the containerized freight.

8. The Agricultural Ocean Transport Coalition has urged Customs to require no more than 12 hours advance notice for agricultural products and 6 hours for perishable products.

9. U.S. VISIT, a new entry-exit system to be installed in U.S. airports and seaports by January 1, 2004, will be based on visas that include biometric features such as fingerprints and photographs to identify foreign visitors. The EU has also earmarked Euro 140 million to fund biometric identification technology for visas.

10. A U.S.-EU dilemma arose over reservation records demanded by the United States that violated EU's data privacy rules. An interim agreement was reached, after the United States assured the European airlines of "appropriate handling" of the records, which include not only names but also the passenger's itinerary, contact phone number, and other details, such as credit card numbers.

11. The United States has initiated "smart border" programs with Canada and Mexico, that use modern technology to enhance security and expedite movement across borders.

12. Canada levied a C$24 (US$15) Air Traveller's Security Charge on all round-trip tickets in April 2002, to finance the increased airport security measures. The tax—the highest security tax in the world—contributed to a 10.2 percent decline in passenger traffic across Canada since the beginning of 2002, and resulted in a steep fall of 50 percent on some short routes.

13. Recognizing the lack of resources to buy new technology, the United States intends to provide financing to developing countries with transportation security projects. Two security experts from the United States have arrived in Indonesia to assist in upgrading cargo security and assess the implementation of security measures at the country's seaports and airports. The United States announced a joint initiative with Thailand to transform Laem Chabang port into a safe transportation port.

14. Given that a ship carries thousands of containers at any time, inspection of the cargo could cause delays. While the scanning process is quite fast, the problem lies with the turnaround time of the containers targeted for scanning. It would take time to transport the container to and from the scanning area, and con-

tainers that are late for loading would tie up hauling equipment and reduce stowage efficiency.

15. In other developments:
- The Japanese Ministry of Land, Infrastructure, and Transport (MLIT) is set to introduce antiterrorist legislation that will prevent foreign ships from entering Japanese ports unless they have a security crew on board and can provide identification.
- Hong Kong's customs authorities have created a terrorist response system, acquiring mobile x-ray machines and a radiation detector to scan cargo and beefing up its intelligence capabilities with more staff and equipment.
- The ICAO has adopted resolutions designed to assure the safety of passengers, ground crew personnel, and the public. Its Regulated Agent Regime requires parties in the flight chain to implement measures to strengthen air-cargo security.
- The Australian government's Aviation Transport Security Bill aims to provide screening of all baggage checked on international flights. A $100 million federal plan to protect the nation's maritime gateways also has been enacted.
- The New Zealand government will be allocating $5.9 million next year and $1.9 million in future years to the Ministry of Foreign Affairs and Trade, for security.

16. A recent online survey by BDP International indicated by a three to two margin that exporters believed the implementation of the 24-hour rule would enhance security. About 23 percent of those surveyed said that the impact was extreme, 30 percent reported moderate to significant costs of compliance, half did not know how to recover costs, and 42 percent plan to absorb expenses. With respect to implementation of the advance manifest filing rule, USCS has issued less than 400 "No-Load" directives for violations of cargo description requirements in its first three months of enforcement.

17. Tea money refers to the use of illegal or unfair means, such as bribery to gain an advantage in business. Ports and airports all over the world are places where tea money comes in handy to expedite deliveries and shipments.

18. Estimates by Leonard were made soon after the events and could reflect the major disruptions faced during the period.

19. This figure is comparable to the estimates of $30–58 billion losses for the insurance industry by the OECD (2002b).

20. The authors employ four alternative scenarios to quantify the trade and welfare impacts, in which all frictional costs are increased by 1 percent ad valorem. However, assumptions are made regarding such increases as varying across regions and sectors according to exposure to terrorism risks following the September 11 attacks. For example, high-risk regions (North America, Middle East, North Africa) are assumed to experience increases in frictional costs that are two and a half times as high as cost increases in low risk regions. The figure shows only the uniform increase in frictional costs to trade.

21. Since a large part of the airfreight is transported in the bellies of passenger planes, a cutback in passenger flights has an impact on cargo.

22. Australia and New Zealand are strengthening their Pacific regions border control relationship by cooperating and exchanging information regarding smuggling, air and sea cargo security approaches, SARS, and general border protection issues.

23. In its "Cargo Security White Paper," the National Customs Brokers and Forwarders Association of America (NCBFAA) has outlined ways for the trading industry to assess risks, build information links to help government officials, and use technology to improve cargo security. It recommends building a "chain of custody dataset" to verify people connected to a shipment and assess cargo security throughout the supply chain.

24. See Amjadi and Yeats (1995).

25. This part draws extensively from the WTO (1999).

26. See UNCTAD 2001, table 8, page 33.

27. APEC (1999).

28. See Global Competitiveness Report 2001–2002, World Competitiveness Yearbook 2001–2002, and Kaufmann, Kraay, and Zoido-Lobaton (2002), for the list of countries in the dataset.

29. The ICC, a nongovernmental organization that has long advocated trade facilitation, promoted the subject on the WTO agenda at the Singapore ministerial meeting.

30. The Ministerial conference in Geneva (1998) concentrated on the perceived threat to the global economy due to the ensuing Asian financial crisis. Although there were several proposals in favor of and against launching trade negotiations in the period prior to the Singapore ministerial meeting in 1999, trade facilitation was overshadowed by other events at the Seattle ministerial (Woo 2002).

31. The Doha declaration states: "Recognizing the case for further expediting the movement, release, and clearance of goods, including goods in transit, and the need for enhanced technical assistance and capacity building in this area, we agree that negotiations will take place after the fifth session of the ministerial on the basis of a decision to be taken, by explicit consen-

sus, at the session on the modalities of the negotiations. In the period until the fifth session, the Council for Trade in Goods shall review and, as appropriate, clarify and improve relevant aspects of Articles V, VIII, and X of the GATT 1994 and identify the trade-facilitation needs and priorities of members, in particular developing and least-developed economies. We commit ourselves to ensuring adequate technical assistance and support capacity building in this area." WTO (2001).

32. See WTO (2002) and Messerlin and Zarrouk (2000).

References

Amjadi and Yeats. 1995. "Have Transportation Costs Contributed to the Relative Decline of Sub-Saharan African Exports? Some Preliminary Evidence." World Bank Working Paper 1559.

APEC (Asia Pacific Economic Cooperation). 1999. "Assessing APEC Trade Liberalization and Facilitation." Update, Economic Committee. September.

Fink, Carsten, Aaditya Mattoo, and Ileana Cristina Neagu. 2002a. "Trade in International Maritime Services: How Much Does Policy Matter?" *World Bank Economic Review* 16(1): 81–108.

———. 2002b. "Assessing the Impact of Communication Cost on International Trade." World Bank Working Paper 2929.

Freund and Weinhold. 2000. "On the Effect of the Internet on International Trade." Board of Governors of the Federal Reserve System International Discussion Paper 693.

Gausch and Kogan. 2001. "Inventories in Developing Countries: Levels and Determinants, a Red Flag on Competitiveness and Growth." World Bank Working Paper 2552.

Hertel, T., T. Walmsley, and K. Ikatura. 2001. "Dynamic Effects of the 'New Age' Free Trade Agreement between Japan and Singapore." *Journal of Economic Integration* 24: 1019–49.

Hummels, D. 2001. "Time as a Trade Barrier." Unpublished. Department of Economics, Purdue University, West Lafayette, Ind.

Kaufmann, Kraay, and Zoido-Lobaton. 2002. "Governance Matters II: Updated Indicators for 2000–01." World Bank Working Paper 2772.

Leonard, J. 2001. "Impact of the September 11, 2001, Terrorist Attacks on North American Trade Flows." E – Alert, Manufacturers Alliance, Arlington, Virginia.

Messerlin, Patrick A., and Jamel Zarrouk. 2000. "Trade Facilitation: Technical Regulations and Customs Procedures." *The World Economy* 23 (4): 577–593.

Mueller-Jentsch, Daniel. 2002. *Transport Policies for the Euro-Mediterranean Free-Trade Area. An Agenda for Multi-modal Transport Reform in the Southern Mediterranean.* World Bank Technical Paper 527. Washington, D.C.

Moenius, Johannes. 2000. "Three Essays on Trade Barriers and Trade Volumes." Ph.D. dissertation. University of California, San Diego.

OECD (Organisation for Economic Development and Co-operation). 2002a. "The Impact of the Terrorist Attacks of 11 September 2001 on International Trading and Transport Activities." Unclassified Document TD/TC/WP (2002)9/Final. Paris.

———. 2002b. "Economic Consequences of Terrorism." *OECD Economic Outlook* 71: 117–40. Paris.

Poirson. 1998. "Economic Security, Private Investment and Growth in Developing Countries." IMF Working Paper WP/98/04.

Reddy, R. 2002. "Friction over Security Gaps," *Intelligent Enterprise.* October 8 (Available at http://www.intelligententerprise.com/021008/516 infosc1-1.shtml)

Subramanian U., and J. Arnold. 2001. *Forging Subregional Links in Transportation and Logistics in South Asia.* World Bank, Washington, D.C.

UNCTAD (United Nations Commission on Trade and Development). 2001. E-Commerce and Development Report.

Walkenhorst, Peter, and Nora Dihel. 2002. "Trade Impacts of the Terrorist Attacks of 11 September 2001: A Quantitative Assessment." Paper prepared for the Workshop on The Economic Consequences of Global Terrorism. Berlin, June 12–13.

Wilson, John S., and Tsunehiro Otsuki. 2003. "Food Safety and Trade: Winners and Losers in a Non-harmonized World." *Journal of Economic Integration* 18 (2): 266–87.

Wilson, John S., Catherine L. Mann, and Tsunehiro Otsuki. 2003a. "Trade Facilitation and Economic Development: Measuring the Impact." Working Paper 2933. World Bank, Washington, D.C.

———. 2003b. "Trade Facilitation and Capacity Building: Global Perspective." Unpublished. World Bank, Washington, D.C.

Wilson, John S., Catherine L. Mann, Yuen Pau Woo, Nizar Assanie, and Inbom Choi. 2002. *Trade Facilitation: A Development Perspective in the Asia-Pacific Region.* Singapore: APEC Secretariat.

Woo, Yuen Pau. 2002. "Trade Facilitation in the WTO: Singapore to Doha and Beyond." In Will Martin and Mari Pangestu, eds., *Options for the Next Trade Round: View from East Asia.* Cambridge, U.K.: Cambridge University Press.

World Bank. 1997. "Multilateral Freight Transport: Selected Regulatory Issues." Report 16361-BR.

———. 2001. *Global Economic Prospects 2002: Making Trade Work for the World's Poor.* Washington, D.C.

WTO (World Trade Organization). 1999. "Development Aspects of Trade Facilitation." WT/COMTD/W/57. Geneva.

———. 2001. "Doha WTO Ministerial Declaration." WT/MIN(01)/DEC/1. Geneva. November.

———. 2002. "Compendium of WCO Capacity Building Tools." G/C/W/445. Geneva.

6

Development and the Doha Agenda

The challenges confronting developing countries seeking to expand their international trade are primarily domestic. Countries that have expanded their share of global markets have generally shared certain conditions: a progressively more open domestic trade regime; a supportive investment climate; and complementary policies relating to education, health, and infrastructure. Most of this agenda is *national* and requires domestic policies to deal with prevailing constraints to increasing trade. The World Trade Organization (WTO) negotiating agenda is necessarily limited to a narrow subset of issues that overlaps only partially with priority development concerns for most countries (Finger 2001).

In this sense, the WTO is not a comprehensive development institution. It is a negotiating forum in which governments make trade policy commitments that improve access to each others' markets and establish rules governing trade. Developing countries can gain from both functions: first, because trade openness, growth, and poverty reduction are mutually reinforcing; and, second, because a rules-based world trading system protects small players that have little ability to influence the policies of large countries. Rules can reduce uncertainty by placing mutually agreed limits on the policies that governments may adopt—thus potentially helping to increase domestic investment and lower risks.

Historically, many WTO rules evolved to reflect the perceived interests of developed countries in an era when the participation of developing countries was limited. Many rules reflect the status quo practices that have already been adopted in industrial countries. The wider latitude accorded agricultural subsidization reflects the use of such support policies in many developed countries. The same is true for the permissive approach historically taken toward the use of import quotas on textile products—in principle prohibited by General Agreement on Tariffs and Trade (GATT) rules. New disciplines adopted in the WTO often mirror regulatory practices of rich countries. For example, the recent inclusion of rules on the protection of intellectual property rights has led to the perception that the WTO contract demands regulatory changes in developing countries without any corresponding changes in regulatory policies in industrial countries.[1]

As developing countries have become more actively involved in the WTO, the challenge is to design rules that promote development. Meeting that challenge means evaluating the implications of various ways to achieve this objective. Rarely is this a straightforward process, especially when it comes to the "behind-the-border" regulatory policies that are increasingly the subject of multilateral discussions. Negotiating pro-development rules in such a context requires the active engagement of developing countries.

The developing countries' traditional approach has been to seek differential treatment. "Special and differential treatment" (SDT) provisions in the WTO span three core areas: *preferential access* to developed-country markets, typically without reciprocal commitments from developing countries; *exemptions* or deferrals from some WTO rules; and *technical assistance* to help implement WTO mandates. What constitutes a developing country is not defined in the WTO—a country's status is a matter of self-declaration. All in all, the current system has not worked especially well, and many countries are seeking a new approach.

Trade preferences have been disappointing in delivering market access: the dilemma

Developed countries grant preferences voluntarily rather than as part of a binding multilateral negotiation. Those preferences often come laden with restrictions, product exclusions, and administrative rules. Preference programs often cover only a share of exports from developing countries, and among those eligible countries and products, only a fraction of preferences are actually utilized. Products and countries with export potential often do not receive preferences, whereas eligible countries and product categories often lack export capacity.

Another problem is that preferences, even when effective, are likely to divert trade away from other excluded developing countries because the exports of developing countries tend to overlap more with each other than with those of developed countries.

Finally, preferences do little to help the majority of the world's poor. Most of those living on less than $1 per day live in countries like China, India, Pakistan, and Association of Southeast Asian Nations (ASEAN) member countries, which receive limited preferences in products in which they have a comparative advantage. Meanwhile, many middle-income countries justify relatively high barriers to trade on SDT grounds, to the detriment of poorer developing countries whose access is impeded.

Nondiscriminatory trade liberalization for poor countries—and poor people— is critical

Recent initiatives by developed countries to extend duty- and quota-free market access for the least developed countries (LDCs) could, if fully implemented, make preferences more effective. But because offering deep, unilateral preferences to larger countries is not politically feasible, preferences can do little for the majority of the poor in non-LDCs. Providing opportunity for all of the world's poor, therefore, requires multilateral, nondiscriminatory liberalization of trade, so that all developing countries can develop their comparative advantage. Most of the gains from trade liberalization result from a country's own reforms. As reciprocity in the exchange of liberalization commitments is the engine of the WTO process, both low- and middle-income countries should harness reciprocity to gain market access.

Elements of a development-supportive trade regime would include a binding commitment by developed countries to abolish export subsidies, decouple agricultural support, and significantly reduce—or eliminate—tariffs on products of export interest to developing countries. Negotiations should target tariff peaks, specific tariffs, and tariff quotas, while aiming for a significant overall reduction in the average level of applied tariffs. The pursuit of these objectives would be more supportive of development than one that continues to emphasize nonreciprocal preferential access to markets.

Negotiating WTO rules that support development is a major challenge

Trade-policy disciplines that can be implemented through a stroke of pen, such as tariff reductions, are fundamentally different from regulatory disciplines and administrative rules that require institutional changes. In contrast to tariff reforms, administrative rules may require substantial resources to establish or strengthen implementing institutions. Domestic rules and regulations must be customized to local circumstances. Thus, rules relating to regulatory practices are unlikely to be a development priority for *every* country, nor are the benefits to global partners likely to be proportional in all countries. The experience after the Uruguay Round with implementation of agreements by developing countries has demonstrated that limiting recognition of differential capacities and levels of development to uniform transition periods is inadequate, as are nonbinding offers of technical assistance. Allowing for greater differentiation among developing countries in determining the reach of WTO rules is important.

Aid for trade must be complemented by action in developing countries

Development assistance must play an important role in helping to expand and improve the trade capacity needed for countries to benefit from better access to markets. Low-income countries confront many challenges in identifying and addressing trade-related policy and public investment priorities. Those priorities should be made explicit in the form of a national development strategy. That strategy, not a WTO agenda, should drive technical and financial assistance. Diagnostic trade-integration studies completed for several LDCs reveal that action is required in areas lying far beyond the scope of WTO agreements. Trade facilitation and logistics are especially important. Additional development assistance could help low-income countries address such priorities. Such assistance should also help countries adjust and adapt to a gradual reduction in trade preferences and address the effects of possible increases in world food prices.

Special and differential treatment and the WTO

The idea that developing countries should receive SDT has a long history in the GATT/WTO system. It has three related dimensions. First, for certain products, developing countries are granted access to developed-country markets at tariffs lower than the most-favored-nation (MFN) rates through policies such as the Generalized System of Preferences (GSP). Second, they may be temporarily exempted from certain disciplines or granted greater discretion to apply restrictive trade policies. Third, they may request technical assistance from high-income countries to implement trade rules and related reforms.

The intellectual foundation of SDT was laid in the 1960s by Raoul Prebisch and Hans Singer, who argued that developing-country exports were concentrated mainly in commodities with volatile and declining terms of trade. They called for import-substitution policies, supported by protection of infant industries at home, and preferential access to export markets. Although the rationale for these policies remains controversial (see, for example, Bhagwati 1988), in 1968 the Generalized System of Preferences (GSP) was launched under United Nations Conference on Trade and Development (UNCTAD) auspices. This called on developed countries to provide preferential access to developing-country exports on a voluntary basis.[2] Because GSP programs violate the GATT's MFN rule, GATT contracting parties waived the MFN requirement in 1971 for 10 years, thereby placing GSP within the GATT framework. In 1979, at the conclusion of the Tokyo Round, permanent legal cover for the GSP was obtained through the so-called Enabling Clause,[3] which called for preferential market access for developing countries and limited reciprocity in GATT negotiating rounds to levels "consistent with development needs." It also confirmed that developing countries should have greater freedom to use restrictive trade policies. An important feature of the Enabling Clause was that SDT was to be phased out when countries reached a certain level of development. That level was never defined, however, leaving eligibility for trade preferences to the discretion of preference-granting countries.

The existence of the GSP and limited reciprocity in GATT negotiations affected the patterns of MFN trade liberalization in both the Kennedy (1964–67) and Tokyo Rounds (1973–79) (see chapters 2 and 3). The end result was larger tariff reductions in goods primarily of export interest to industrialized economies.[4] Average levels of trade protection in developing countries were reduced relatively little. Lack of engagement by developing countries also facilitated the emergence of restrictive quota regimes for textiles under the Multi-fiber Arrangement (MFA) and the effective removal of GATT disciplines on agriculture-related trade policies (Hudec 1987).

Under the pre-WTO trade regime, new rules extending the original GATT treaty were applied on a voluntary basis. Extensions were called "codes," whose disciplines bound only the contracting parties that signed them (Hoekman and Kostecki 2001). This approach to rule extension was removed with the creation of the WTO. In contrast to the GATT, all WTO agreements and disciplines, with the exception of rules on government procurement and trade in civil aircraft, apply to all members regardless of level of development—although in many cases transition periods apply to developing countries. A consequence of this so-called Single Undertaking and the expansion in the coverage of multilateral rules to new areas, such as intellectual property and trade in services, was that developing-country governments were confronted with a significant implementation agenda as well as new policy constraints.[5]

In the runup to WTO's 1999 Seattle ministerial meeting, SDT and implementation concerns figured prominently. The 2001 Doha Ministerial Declaration emphasized the importance of SDT, stating that "provisions for special and differential treatment are an integral part of the WTO agreements." Paragraph 44 called for a review of SDT provisions with a view to "strengthening them and making them more precise, effective, and operational." On the basis of this mandate, developing countries made over 85 suggestions to strengthen SDT language in various WTO agreements. The proposals included calls for improved preferential access to industrialized countries, further exemptions from specific WTO rules, and binding commitments on developed countries to provide technical assistance to help implement multilateral rules. Despite intensive talks during 2002, no agreement on these proposals emerged. One reason was that many of the proposals sought to convert nonbinding, "best endeavors" language into obligations binding on developed countries. Another was disagreement over what types of provisions would promote development. The latter issue is fundamental, of course, but it was never the focus of explicit analysis and discussion in the relevant WTO committee (Keck and Low 2003).

Market access for development

International trade helps raise and sustain growth—a fundamental requirement for reducing poverty—by giving firms and households access to world markets for goods, services, and knowledge; lowering prices and increasing the quality and variety of consumption goods; and fostering specialization of economic activity in areas where countries have a comparative advantage. Through the diffusion and absorption of technology, trade fosters the investment and positive externalities that are associated with learning. Policies that shelter economic agents from the world market impede these benefits and dynamic gains. While adjustment costs and measures to safeguard the interests of poor households should not be neglected in the design of policies, openness to trade is associated with higher incomes (Irwin 2002). Moving toward an open trade policy and identifying the needed complementary domestic policies should consequently figure centrally in the design of national poverty-reduction strategies. Many developing countries have pursued unilateral liberalization of their trade regimes in the last two decades. They have also concentrated on obtaining preferential access to rich-country markets.

Preferences result in limited market access and are uncertain

Trade preferences granted by developed countries are voluntary. They are not WTO obligations. Donor countries determine eligibility criteria, product coverage, the size of preference margins, and the duration of the preference. Developed-country governments rarely have granted deep preferences in sectors where developing countries had the largest export potential. Indeed, preferences tend to be the most limited for products protected by tariff peaks (Hoekman, Ng, and Olarreaga 2002).

Developing countries often obtain only limited preferences in sectors where they have a comparative advantage (table 6.1).[6] In some cases, developing countries face higher average tariffs because of the composition of their exports. Some subcategories include tariff peaks that further restrict access for developing countries. The primary reason for this pattern of protection is that in some sectors there is strong domestic opposition to liberalization in developed countries. However, it is also partly a consequence of the limited engagement by developing countries in reciprocal negotiations.

Benefits are often limited by design. Market share or value thresholds limit the extent to which recipients can export on preferential terms. In the United States, for example, a country's GSP eligibility for a given product may be removed if annual exports of that product reach $100 million[7] or if there is significant damage to domestic industry. In the European Union, products classified as "sensitive" only benefit from a 3.5-percentage-point reduction of the MFN tariff rate, except for clothing, for which the reduction is 20 percent.[8] Most chemicals, almost all agricultural and food products, and all textiles, apparel, and leather goods are classified as "sensitive."[9] The European Union also excludes from GSP eligibility certain products from large countries—regardless of their per capita income. Examples include Brazil, China, India, and Indonesia. Finally, the European Union has a safeguard clause allowing preferences to be suspended if imports "cause or threaten to cause serious difficulties to a Community producer."

In numerous instances, products or countries have been removed from GSP eligibility, either as the result of specific criteria having been satisfied (see above) or because of lobbying by domestic interest groups in importing countries. The resulting uncertainty can only have a negative impact on incentives to invest in export sectors. Binding multilateral liberalization commitments under the WTO are more secure. The uncertainty of unilateral preferences also arises from conditions that may be attached

Table 6.1 Developing countries rarely receive significant preferences in sectors in which they would have a comparative advantage

Import revenues, market shares, and tariff rates for key products without GSP preferences in the European Union and United States in 2001 (percent, except where otherwise noted)

	Total imports (billions of dollars) EU	Total imports (billions of dollars) U.S.	GSP recipients' market share EU	GSP recipients' market share U.S.	LDC market share EU	LDC market share U.S.	Average tariff rate EU	Average tariff rate U.S.	Average tariff rate faced by GSP recipients EU	Average tariff rate faced by GSP recipients U.S.
Dairy products	1.4	1.2	15	11	1	1	9.9	13.4	15.9	19.7
Textiles and yarn	15.3	9.6	42	21	3	1	5.4	7.8	4.6	7.2
Apparel and clothing	48.7	60.8	54	47	8	7	10.2	15.3	8.8	15.9
Leather products	6.1	7.6	74	24	1	1	2.3	10.4	1.9	11.5
Footwear	6.5	16.1	67	18	1	1	7.5	10.6	7.4	10.0
Ceramics and glassware	6.2	8.7	27	13	1	1	5.1	6.3	3.8	8.2

Note: GSP countries only; LDCs may obtain deeper preferential treatment. China is included under EU GSP but excluded by the United States.
Source: World Integrated Trade Solution.

Table 6.2 Utilization rates for preference-eligible products with high MFN tariffs are low

Preference use by GSP recipients in the U.S. market, 2001 (percent, except where otherwise noted)

Category	Total imports (billions of dollars)	Imports from GSP recipients (billions of dollars)	Share imported under GSP	Share under all preference programs	Average applied tariffs on all imports
Cut flowers	0.72	0.43	3	95	6
Prepared fish	0.72	0.47	7	13	9
Cane or beet sugar	0.56	0.41	29	77	6
Fruit, nuts	0.78	0.34	20	33	15
Unmanufactured tobacco	0.75	0.58	3	7	68
Acrylic alcohols	1.56	0.73	55	94	5
Ethers, ether-alcohols	1.78	0.34	84	84	5
Carboxylic acids	1.64	0.73	4	4	5
Trunks, suitcases	4.59	1.17	0	6	10
Articles of leather	2.68	0.52	18	21	8
Plywood and panels	1.10	0.46	18	22	5
Footwear	13.87	2.39	0	1	11
Apparel, knitted	25.00	11.50	0	25	14
Apparel, not knitted	35.10	15.90	1	15	14
Hats, headgear	0.96	0.33	0	2	7
Articles of jewelry	5.40	2.10	54	70	6

Note: Table reports data on imports (at the 4-digit HS classification) of products on which the United States applied tariffs that exceeded 4 percent in 2001, and where GSP recipient countries had significant exports to the United States.
Source: U.S. International Trade Commission.

to eligibility. Such conditions often relate to worker protection, human rights, intellectual property, and the environment.[10]

Recent initiatives by the European Union, the United States, and several other industrialized countries to provide either full or much increased duty- and quota-free access to their markets for exports from LDCs clearly improves the situation. However, excessively restrictive rules of origin remain an important impediment to full use of these deeper preferences, which, moreover, do not extend to many poor countries with substantial trade capacity.

The use of preferences is limited

All preferential programs, whether unilateral or reciprocal (under free-trade agreements), impose significant administrative costs related to enforcement of rules of origin.[11] These rules are imposed to prevent transshipment—that is, reexport of products produced in noneligible countries. Rule-of-origin requirements and related inspection procedures can be quite costly. They also may be explicitly protectionist in intent. An example is the so-called triple transformation rule in textiles, which requires imported clothing to be made from textiles produced with yarn spun in either the preference-granting or the beneficiary country. Although rules of origin are necessary for preferences to work and are beneficial in ensuring that value is added and employment created in the recipient country, it is important to ensure that rules of origin are not intentionally or inadvertently protectionist.

Rules of origin and associated paperwork and administrative requirements are likely to be a major reason that many eligible products do not enter developed-country markets under preference provisions—instead exporters pay the applicable MFN tariff. Except for certain alcohols, sugar, flowers, and jewelry, less than one-third of eligible exports from beneficiary countries entered the United States under any preference program in 2001 (table 6.2). An indicator of the restrictiveness of these rules is that only 65 percent of eligible apparel exports from the Caribbean and Central America enter the United States under all preference programs, despite a preference margin of more than 14 percent.

Limited use of preference programs is also observed in other countries. Sapir (1997) showed that in 1994, only one-half of Euro-

DEVELOPMENT AND THE DOHA AGENDA

Table 6.3 Actual use of preference programs is declining
Quad country imports from GSP beneficiaries (billions of dollars) and ratio of use of available preferences (percent), 1994–2001

Year	Total imports	Dutiable imports	Eligible for preference	Receiving preference	Rate of use of preferences (percent)
1994	448	283	162	83	51.1
1995	539	331	195	108	55.1
1996	585	351	178	100	56.0
1997	575	346	200	100	50.1
1998	543	311	183	74	40.6
1999	548	290	166	68	40.7
2000	623	308	171	72	42.0
2001	588	296	184	71	38.9

Source: Inama (2003).

pean imports that could potentially benefit from GSP entered under this preferential regime, reflecting the combined effect of rules of origin and tariff quotas. In 2001, imports by the Quad (Canada, the European Union, Japan, and the United States) from GSP beneficiaries totaled $588 billion, of which $296 billion were subject to duties and $184 billion were covered under various preferential programs (table 6.3). Only $71 billion of the eligible exports actually received preferential treatment (approximately 39 percent of eligible exports). The share for LDCs, however, is higher at approximately 60 percent (Inama 2003), reflecting less restrictive treatment.

Who benefits from preferences?

A relatively small number of mostly middle-income countries are the main beneficiaries of preference programs. These countries have the capacity to exploit the opportunities offered by meeting the administrative requirements. In 2001, 10 of the 130 eligible countries accounted for 77 percent of U.S. non-oil imports under GSP provisions (figure 6.1). The same countries accounted for only 49 percent of all imports from GSP-eligible countries. However, some small countries have benefited significantly from preferential access to markets where high tariffs, subsidies, or other policies are used to drive the domestic price of the product to levels well above the world market price. An example is Mauritius, which has preferential access to the EU market for sugar and has been granted a relatively large quota (Mitchell 2003). Such benefits are obtained at high cost to EU taxpayers and consumers, and to other excluded developing countries.

There also is evidence that GSP programs are associated with success stories in countries with the capacity to benefit from access opportunities. Ozden and Reinhardt (2003b) compare the export performances of U.S. GSP beneficiaries with those of countries removed from eligibility (those said to have "graduated"). Their results suggest that countries removed

Figure 6.1 The benefits of U.S. trade preferences are distributed unequally
Top 10 beneficiaries of U.S. generalized system of preferences, 2001 (percentage of total GSP benefits)

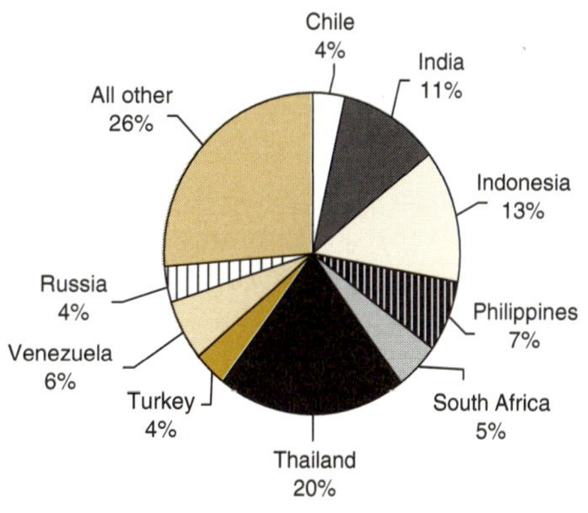

- Chile 4%
- India 11%
- Indonesia 13%
- Philippines 7%
- South Africa 5%
- Thailand 20%
- Turkey 4%
- Venezuela 6%
- Russia 4%
- All other 26%

Source: USITC Dataweb.

211

Figure 6.2 Countries "graduating" from U.S. generalized system of preferences have better export performance than those still in program

Export performance of countries dropped from U.S. GSP program in 1976–2000 vs. those remaining in program (percent)

Source: Ozden and Reinhardt (2003b).

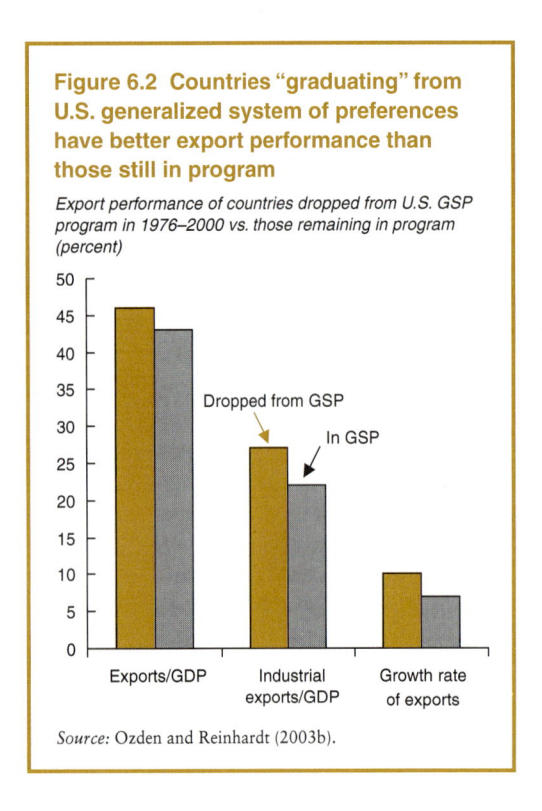

from the GSP outperform those remaining eligible for GSP treatment (figure 6.2). Countries that are not on GSP tend to have higher ratios of exports to GDP, as well as higher export growth rates. This could be interpreted as evidence that for some countries—the successful ones—GSP played a role in generating the initial export expansion. While great care is required in attributing causality—clearly many other factors will be important in determining export performance—one reason for the better performance of countries that were removed from GSP is probably their own trade policies. Because import protection is equivalent to taxation of exports, liberalization is a precondition for substantially expanding exports.

Preferences have a hierarchy

The foregoing discussion has focused primarily on GSP. In practice, unilateral preferences granted by the European Union and the United States are implemented under many different programs (box 6.1). The differences among these programs in product coverage, eligibility criteria, and administrative rules (especially rules of origin) have important implications, not only for the countries who benefit from them, but also for those excluded.

The United States, for example, has implemented the African Growth and Opportunity Act, the Caribbean Basin Initiative, and the Andean Trade Promotion Act, as well as several reciprocal free-trade agreements (with Israel, Jordan, and Mexico). Major EU programs include the Cotonou convention covering the African, Caribbean, and Pacific (ACP) countries, and the Everything-But-Arms initiative, which covers LDCs. The European Union also has concluded a large number of preferential trade agreements with neighboring countries in Europe, North Africa, and the Middle East (Schiff and Winters 2003).

These unilateral and reciprocal programs differ in several important respects from the GSP. First, they include sectors excluded by standard GSP programs—for example, apparel and food products. Thus, by 2009 Everything But Arms will cover all exports of beneficiary countries (the 49 LDCs) without exception—all duties and quotas will have been removed. Similarly, the Caribbean, Andean, and African programs of the United States include apparel, in contrast to its GSP program. Second, the administrative requirements of these deeper preferential schemes tend to be more relaxed regarding rules of origin and competitive needs tests (USTR 2002).

Notwithstanding these improvements, the overall impact of these programs has not yet been very significant, with the exception of apparel exports to the United States from certain African countries (more on this below). The share of LDCs in total imports of the United States and the European Union has not increased significantly in recent years (figure 6.3). In the case of Everything But Arms, this may reflect, in part, that the products that matter most to a number of LDCs—bananas, rice, sugar—will be liberalized only in 2006 or 2009. Most of the products exported by LDCs already were eligible for duty-free entry

Box 6.1 EU and U.S. preference programs

United States
Generalized System of Preferences (GSP): The U.S. GSP program has existed since 1976. Criteria for eligibility include not aiding international terrorists and complying with international environmental, labor, and intellectual property laws. Unlike the European GSP (see below), the U.S. program grants complete duty- and quota-free access to eligible products from eligible countries. China and several "graduated" countries are not eligible—among them Hong Kong (China), Republic of Korea, Malaysia, Singapore, Taiwan (China), and Malaysia.

Textiles and apparel, footwear, and many agricultural products are not eligible for the GSP. Certain products from certain countries can be excluded if the total exports pass the "competitive needs limit"—$100 million per tariff line or $13 million if the exporting country has more than a 50 percent share of U.S. imports. Total imports to the United States under GSP provision totaled $14.5 billion in 2001, or 1.5 percent of total U.S. non-oil imports and 13 percent of all non-oil exports to the United States from GSP recipients. In most eligible sectors where the MFN tariff rate is above 5 percent, the share of exports entering under the program from eligible countries is only 30–40 percent, in part as a result of rules-of-origin requirements.

Caribbean Trade Preferences: The Caribbean Basin Economic Recovery Act (CBERA), commonly known as the Caribbean Basin Initiative (CBI), was enacted in 1984 and modified in 1990. Twenty-four countries are eligible. Duty-free treatment is granted on all products other than textiles and apparel, certain footwear, handbags, luggage, petroleum and related products, certain leather products, and canned tuna. In 1998, only 18 percent of exports from beneficiary countries were in eligible product categories. The 2000 Caribbean Basin Trade Partnership Act (CBTPA), provides NAFTA-equivalent treatment for certain items (mainly apparel) excluded from duty-free treatment under the CBI program.

Andean Trade Preferences: The Andean Trade Preferences Act (ATPA) extends preferences to Bolivia, Colombia, Ecuador, and Peru. Enacted in 1991 as part of U.S. efforts to reduce narcotic production and trafficking, it was modeled after the CBI and has similar eligibility requirements and product coverage. Duty-free treatment is granted on all products except textiles and apparel, certain footwear, petroleum and related products, certain leather products, canned tuna, rum and sugar, syrup, and molasses. The main differences with GSP are that the Andean scheme covers more products, has more liberal qualifying rules, and is not subject to competitive need limits. ATPA rules of origin permit inputs from CBERA beneficiaries. ATPA was renewed in 2002 as the Andean Trade Promotion and Drug Eradication Act (ATPDEA) and expanded to include tuna, leather and footwear products, petroleum products, and apparel—subject, however, to restrictive rules of origin. For example, if apparel is assembled from U.S. fabrics, no quotas or duties apply, but if local inputs are used, duty-free imports are subject to a cap of 2 percent of total U.S. imports (increasing to 5 percent in equal annual installments).

African Trade Preferences: The African Growth and Opportunity Act (AGOA), passed in 2000, offers beneficiary Sub-Saharan African countries duty-free and quota-free market access for essentially all products. AGOA excludes textiles but extends to duty- and quota-free treatment for apparel made in Africa from U.S. yarn and fabric. If regional fabric and yarn are used, there is a cap of 1.5 percent of U.S. imports, increasing to 3.5 percent over eight years. African LDCs are exempt from all rules of origin for a limited period of time, helping to significantly expand apparel exports from countries such as Lesotho.

European Union
Generalized System of Preferences: Preferences under GSP are available to all developing countries, including China. Overall, 36 percent of tariff lines are eligible for reduced tariffs, and 32 percent are eligible for duty-free access. Twelve percent of tariff lines (mostly agricultural) are excluded and subject to full MFN duty. Excluded products include meat, dairy products, cereals, sugar, wine, and products for which the European Union sets minimum import prices. Approximately 36 percent of all products are classified as "sensitive"—often those with the highest MFN tariffs (Panagariya 2002). Sensitive products

(Continues on next page)

Box 6.1 (continued)

are subject to a flat 3.5-percentage point-reduction in the MFN tariff, implying that the higher the duty, the smaller the proportionate impact of the preference. Specific duties are reduced by 30 percent; if a product is subject to both ad valorem and specific duties, the specific duty is not reduced.

Additional tariff reductions are available under special incentive schemes for the protection of labor rights (an additional 5-percentage-point reduction), the environment (an additional 5 percentage points), and for countries that combat drug production and trafficking (duty-free access for certain products). Currently only one country, Moldova, has requested and satisfied the requirement relating to labor rights (but not the environment). A group of Latin American countries and Pakistan benefit from arrangements relating to drugs.

Countries can be excluded from the GSP (based on their development level) or from particular product categories. Sectoral exclusions are determined by specific criteria based on shares of EU imports from GSP-beneficiary countries and certain indicators of development and specialization.[a] For example, Argentina is excluded from preferences for live animals and for edible products of animal origin, while Thailand is excluded from preferences for fishery products.

ACP countries (Cotonou Agreement): ACP countries are granted preferences that often exceed those available under the GSP. Most industrial products are duty and quota free. Preferences are less comprehensive for agricultural products. In 2000 duties were still applied to 856 tariff lines (837 of which were agricultural products). Of these, 116 lines were excluded from the Cotonou Agreement, although specific protocols govern access for sugar and bananas on a country-specific basis. An additional 301 tariff lines were eligible for reduced duties, subject to specific quantitative limits (tariff quotas) set for the ACP countries as a group. The remaining 439 products were eligible for reduced duties without limits on exported quantities.

Everything But Arms: Introduced in March 2001, this program grants duty-free access to imports of all products from the LDCs, with the exception of arms and munitions, without any quantitative restrictions. Liberalization was immediate except for three major products: fresh bananas, rice, and sugar. Tariffs on these three items will be reduced gradually to zero (in 2006 for bananas; in 2009 for rice and sugar), while tariff quotas for rice and sugar will be increased annually. Access to the EU market is governed by the rules of its GSP scheme. A key feature of the program is that in contrast to the GSP, preferences for the LDCs are granted for an unlimited period and are not subject to periodic review.

---

a. Some ad hoc exclusions are applied to China, the CIS countries, and South Africa in the fisheries and iron and steel sectors.

---

under GSP or Cotonou provisions. As a result, Everything But Arms had no immediate impact (Brenton 2003). In the case of the United States, export market shares of countries eligible under the three primary deep preference programs have not increased (figure 6.4).[12]

The primary exception is apparel, which shows remarkable export growth, especially in the case of AGOA. Total exports of apparel since 1996 increased by more than 200 percent for AGOA countries, and approximately 60 percent for Caribbean and Andean countries. As a result, in 2002, apparel exports to the United States from AGOA countries were approximately $1.1 billion, compared to $750 million from Andean countries and $9.5 billion from Caribbean countries. These countries accounted for some 20 percent of the $58 billion U.S. apparel import market. This growth is mainly a result of exemptions from quotas and tariffs imposed on other exporters. In the case of AGOA, rules of origin are removed temporarily for some countries for a limited period, providing an extra advantage. A crucial issue is how these regions will fare when remaining quotas (mostly faced by countries in South and East Asia) are phased out at the end of 2004, as required by the WTO

Figure 6.3 Preferences have not increased the share of the least developed countries in imports into the European Union and the United States

Share of LDCs in total imports of European Union and United States, 1966–2002 (percent)

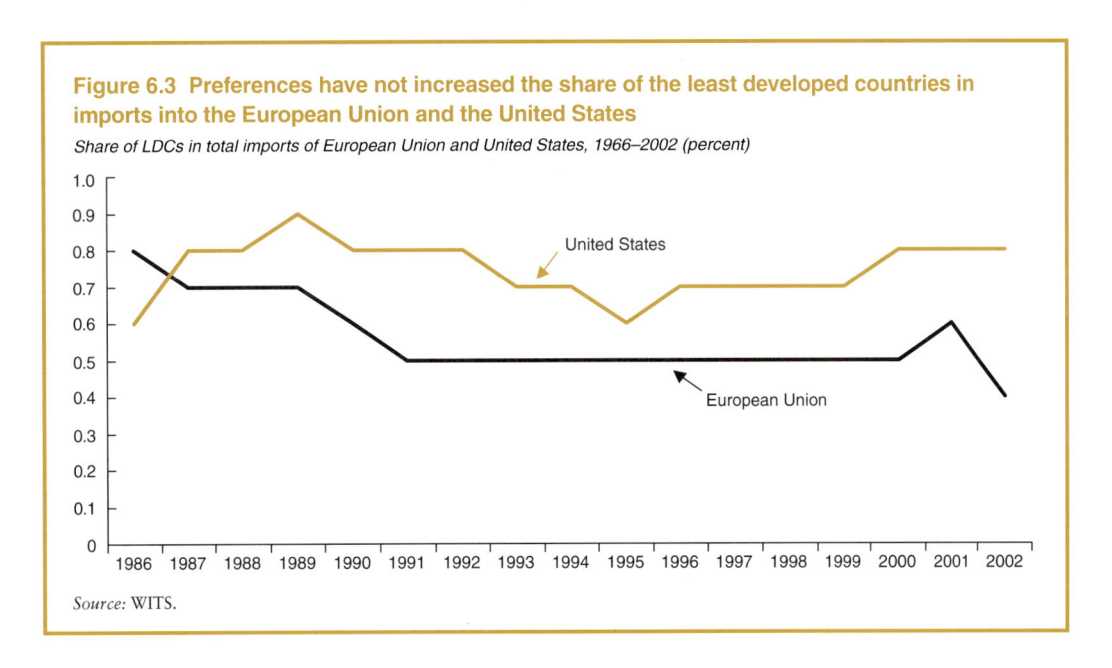

Source: WITS.

Agreement on Textiles and Clothing. This is also the time when liberal rules of origin under AGOA are set to expire. Competitive pressures are likely to increase substantially, giving rise to a need for adjustment and for investment programs to improve productivity and diversification of the export base. Extending the liberal rules of origin under AGOA would help reduce the impact of the abolition of the remaining import quotas on textiles and clothing.

The available evidence suggests that preferences by industrialized countries have the greatest effect on developing-country exports if they are granted on a reciprocal basis as part of a deep regional free-trade agreement. Spanish exports to the European Union and Mexican exports to the United States rose dramatically following accession to the European Union and NAFTA, respectively (figure 6.6). This supply response is not just the result of removing import barriers by northern partners, but also of the "regime change" that occurred in these countries and the consequent change in risk premiums, uncertainty, and investment incentives. A large part of the regime change involved changes in investment, regulatory, and administrative policies, not just preferential trade liberalization. These data therefore suggest that a reciprocal liberalization strategy supported by complementary domestic policies may have a much larger impact than unilateral preferences.

Figure 6.4 Market shares of countries eligible for three U.S. "deep preference" programs have not increased

Shares of AGOA, Andean, and CBI countries in U.S. imports (excluding oil and previous metals), 1996–2002 (percent)

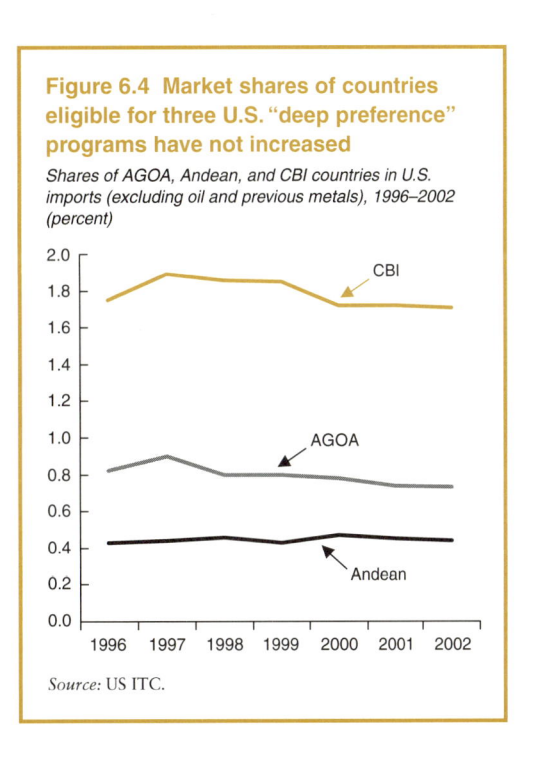

Source: US ITC.

215

Figure 6.5 Preferred countries' apparel exports to the United States have risen
Growth of apparel exports to United States, 1996–2002 (percent)

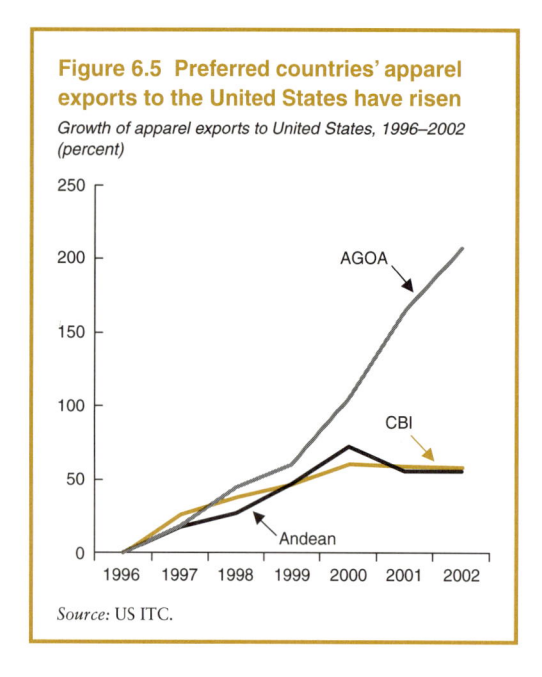

Source: US ITC.

Preferences have unintended consequences

Numerous side effects of unilateral preferences also must be considered when assessing the case for them. Preferences can lead to more protectionist trade policies in recipient countries. Ozden and Reinhardt (2003b) show that U.S. GSP recipients implement more protectionist trade policies than countries removed from the GSP program (figure 6.7). Although their finding does not prove causality, preferences can decrease the incentives for domestic exporters to mobilize in favor of more liberal trade policies. Because domestic trade policies affect developing countries' growth prospects more than barriers in their export markets, the perverse-incentive effect of unilateral preferences may be quite damaging. Similarly, preferential market access may lower the incentives for developing countries to participate actively in multilateral negotiations, in part because they believe that they will not receive any further concessions in the multilateral process or because of concerns about erosion of preferences. The latter may create conflicts of interest between preferred and nonpreferred developing countries. To the extent that countries specialize in similar product categories and sell at low margins in competitive markets, even small preferences in certain categories could make a difference for some countries, fueling those conflicts of interest.

As an example, 36 countries in Sub-Saharan Africa are eligible to export apparel products into the United States without any tariffs or quantitative restrictions under AGOA. These countries risk losing preference margins if MFN protection is reduced in the United States. Many of these countries temporarily face no rules of origin requirements. Twenty-four countries in the Caribbean and Central America enjoy similar privileges under the CBPTA. Through bilateral NAFTA preferences and unilateral Caribbean and African preferences, beneficiary countries managed to increase their share of U.S. apparel imports to around 32 percent (figure 6.8). Such countries may be concerned about the erosion of their preferences if MFN protection is reduced.

Sugar is a product for which preference erosion will have important consequences for several countries. Quota allocations in protected markets, such as the European Union, are currently very concentrated in a few countries that tend to have high costs relative to other producers. For example, Mauritius has 38 percent of EU quotas (Mitchell 2003). Given the extension by 2009 of duty- and quota-free access to the EU market for all LDCs, Mauritius will confront much greater competition in the EU market.

Most of the academic research on preference programs has concluded not only that they generally yield modest export increases (at best), but also that a significant portion of these gains is because of trade diversion from nonbeneficiaries. Multilateral liberalization would reduce some of the detrimental effects of preferential access to highly distorted markets. For example, moving to free trade in sugar markets not only would result in estimated global welfare gains (the sum of producer, consumer surpluses, and tax revenues) of $4.7 billion, but also would yield a 38 percent increase in world sugar prices and boost sugar trade by about 20 percent. Brazil alone

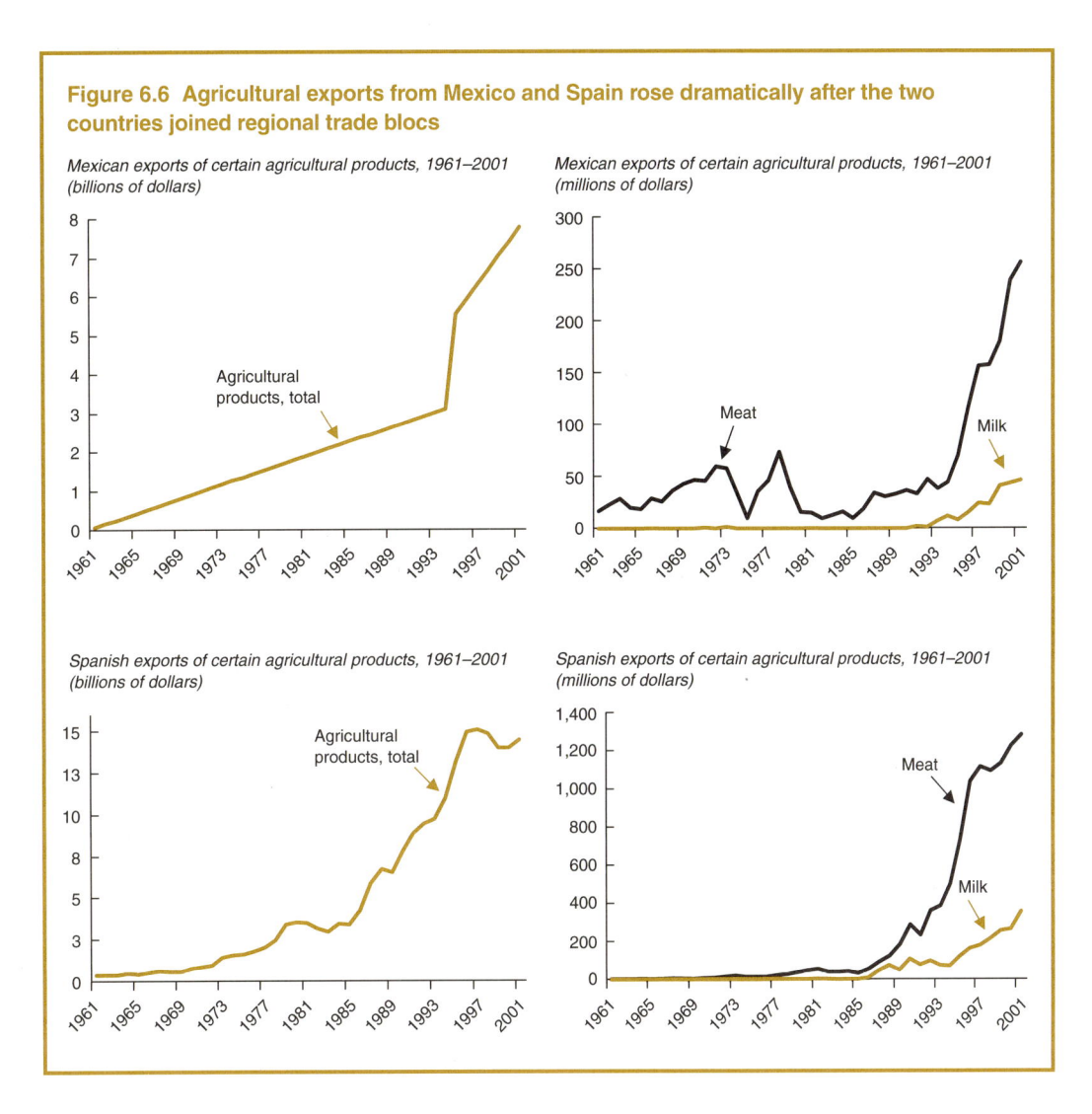

Figure 6.6 Agricultural exports from Mexico and Spain rose dramatically after the two countries joined regional trade blocs

Mexican exports of certain agricultural products, 1961–2001 (billions of dollars)

Mexican exports of certain agricultural products, 1961–2001 (millions of dollars)

Spanish exports of certain agricultural products, 1961–2001 (billions of dollars)

Spanish exports of certain agricultural products, 1961–2001 (millions of dollars)

would experience a real income gain of some $1.6 billion. Although countries such as Mauritius could lose significantly, coordinated global liberalization across all products would offset some of the lost rents. World sugar price increases alone would offset about one-half of the lost quota rents for countries that currently have preferential access. Moreover, the loss in preference rents would be much less than is commonly expected, because many of the beneficiaries are high-cost producers. Indeed, the cost to the European Union and United States of providing each $1 of preferential access has been estimated to be more than $5—a very inefficient way to provide development assistance (Beghin and Aksoy 2003).

How much preferences are likely to be eroded as a result of further multilateral trade liberalization will depend both on the benefits countries currently obtain from preference programs and the speed with which preferences are eroded. The foregoing discussion suggests that the overall benefits of unilateral market access preferences are limited by exclusions for sensitive products, rules of origin, and limited supply capacity. The fact that a substantial share of total exports from eligible countries under AGOA and Everything But Arms preferences

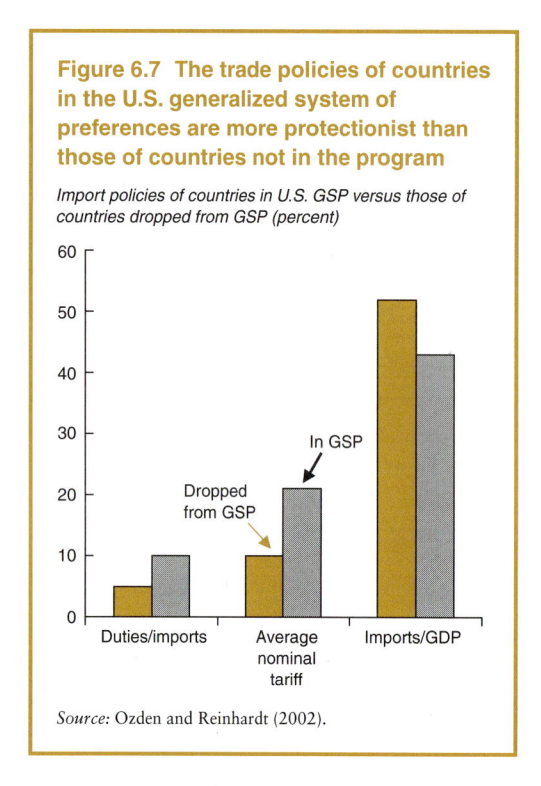

Figure 6.7 The trade policies of countries in the U.S. generalized system of preferences are more protectionist than those of countries not in the program

Import policies of countries in U.S. GSP versus those of countries dropped from GSP (percent)

Source: Ozden and Reinhardt (2002).

do not enter duty free (Inama 2003, Brenton 2003) is one illustration.

One way of obtaining a sense of the magnitude of possible preference erosion is first to assume that LDCs obtain full preferential access to Quad markets and then to assess the impact of a reduction in MFN tariffs. A recent exercise along these lines suggests that the aggregate impact of a 40 percent reduction in average MFN tariffs would lower LDC exports by about $440 million, or 1.6 percent of total exports (IMF 2002). This estimate does not take into account terms-of-trade changes from the MFN tariff reductions, which on average can be expected to be positive for exporting countries, reducing the losses from preference erosion. Moreover, in practice, it is likely that part of the rents from preferences accrues to the importing countries, and especially to intermediaries (Tangermann 2002). Account also should be taken of the benefits to countries with preferences of the erosion in preferential access of other countries—especially members of free-trade agreements—and, as noted earlier, of the impact of rules of origin. As MFN tariffs are by definition not associated with rules of origin, such liberalization may well result in export gains for countries in products that in principle benefit from preferences. Thus, it may be more beneficial for developing countries to obtain more secure MFN reductions on their key exports than to seek to preserve preference margins on products with relatively high MFN tariffs (Laird, Safadi, and Turini 2003).

The available evidence and analysis suggests that preference erosion is unlikely to be a major issue for many countries, given that automatic compensation will result from broad-based multilateral liberalization of market access. However, specific developing countries and sectors in these countries may be hurt, and resources for adjustment need to be mobilized and allocated. Governments should prepare by determining where adjustment needs are likely to be most significant, so that technical and financial assistance can be provided. Actions of the type discussed in chapters 2 and 5 to facilitate trade, complemented by the adoption of more liberal rules of origin, will help to attenuate the impact of preference erosion.

The low share of exports entering under preferences, and the recent research suggesting that rules of origin play a role in that low share, suggest that the rules used to determine origin should be simplified. The recent experience under AGOA, under which several beneficiary countries significantly expanded apparel exports to the United States after origin restrictions were relaxed, illustrates this point. The WTO includes an Agreement on Rules of Origin that aims to foster the harmonization of the rules used by members. The agreement calls for a work program to be undertaken by a Technical Committee, in conjunction with the World Customs Organization, to develop a classification system regarding changes in tariff subheadings based on the Harmonized System (Hoekman and Kostecki 2001). The harmonization program provides a potential

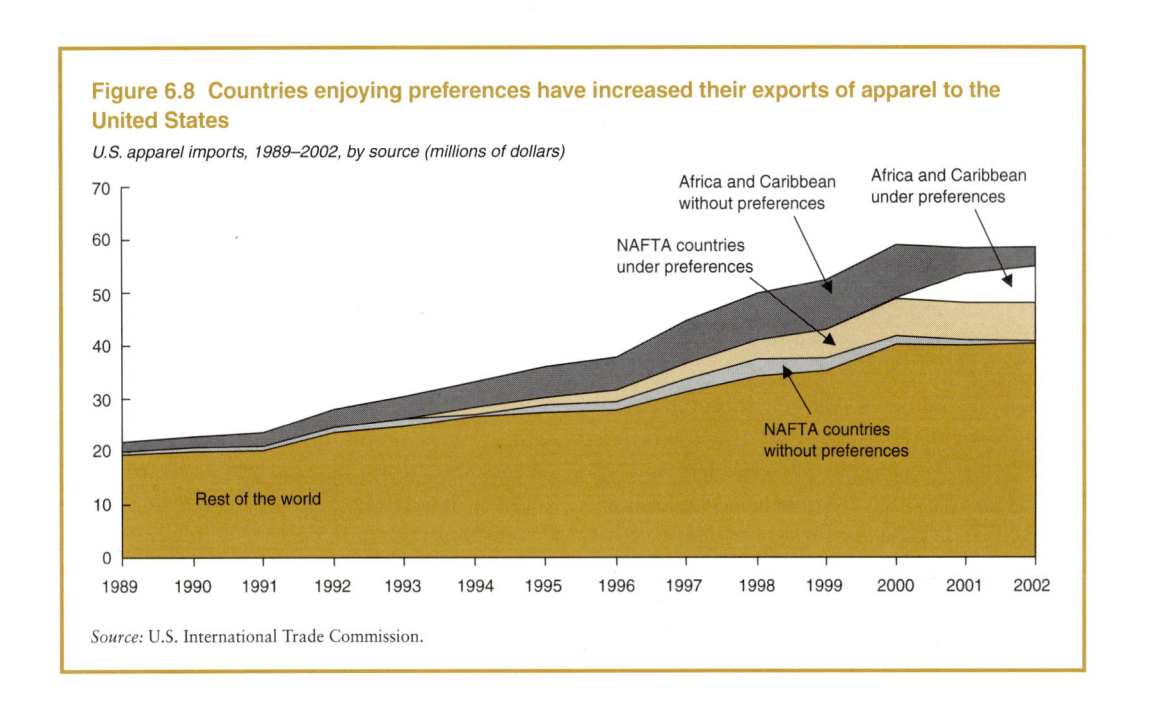

Figure 6.8 Countries enjoying preferences have increased their exports of apparel to the United States

U.S. apparel imports, 1989–2002, by source (millions of dollars)

Source: U.S. International Trade Commission.

solution to rules-of-origin problems. While the harmonized rules are intended to be applied in cases of nonpreferential commercial policy—tariffs, import licensing, antidumping—they could be applied to preferential trade as well. A recent proposal by Canada to use a common value-added criterion and to allow for comprehensive cumulation (extending to major players such as China) is an alternative approach. Yet another option is to emulate the "visa" procedure for textile products used under AGOA—this could help to substantially reduce uncertainty for traders. Indeed, minimizing uncertainty is a critical feature of making preferential regimes effective.[13]

The ultimate goal is MFN-based, reciprocal liberalization

MFN-based market access will have the greatest beneficial impact on development.[14] One reason is that it implies that elements of "reverse SDT"—special opt-outs and exemptions that benefit interest groups in industrialized countries at the expense of developing countries—will be removed. Eliminating agricultural subsidy programs, high protection for textile and apparel products, tariff peaks, and tariff escalation would not only be beneficial to developing countries (and developed-country consumers), but also would facilitate further trade reforms in developing countries.

Developed *and* developing countries alike could affirm their commitment to poverty alleviation by accepting an ambitious program of liberalization that would include the abolition of export subsidies, substantial decoupling of agricultural support, and significant reduction of MFN tariffs on labor-intensive products of export interest to developing countries. The program must include significant trade liberalization by developing countries, a major source of the total potential gains. MFN liberalization should extend to middle-income countries, which are among the most dynamic markets in the world and where trade barriers are often substantially higher than in developed countries, and would usefully extend to LDCs as well.

In defining negotiating modalities to pursue desired MFN liberalization, WTO members should set a concrete timetable and agree on specific benchmarks for product coverage and maximum tariffs. The challenge is to identify reciprocal commitments that make economic sense and support development. The overuse of nonreciprocity in past market-access negotiations has excluded developing countries from the major source of gains from trade liberalization—namely the reform of their *own* policies. Nonreciprocity is also a reason why tariff peaks today are largely on goods produced in developing countries. A willingness to pursue liberalization at home is critical to increase developing countries' participation in global trade, particularly South-South trade, which is subject to significant barriers (see chapter 3).[15]

Services are of great importance to development—it is difficult for firms to be competitive in the absence of efficient services sectors. Substantial opportunities exist to expand developing-country services exports and to liberalize further access to developing-country markets. While the latter would bring the greatest gains, temporary access to service markets (particularly labor markets) in developed countries also would generate large gains for developing countries (see chapter 4). In addition, binding the current set of liberal policies applied to cross-border trade (GATS Modes 1 and 2) would assist governments in pursuing domestic reforms. Many developing countries have begun to exploit opportunities offered by the Internet and telecommunication networks to provide services through cross-border trade. Currently such trade is generally free of restrictions, but that freedom is not locked in through the GATS (Mattoo 2003).

Toward a new regime for WTO rules

Several WTO agreements offer developing countries some latitude to pursue restrictive trade policies and provide transition periods and technical assistance to help in implementing agreements (box 6.2).[16]

Should trade rules apply to all developing countries? If so, should account be taken of differences in national capacities to implement and benefit from multilateral rules? In answering these questions, it is helpful to distinguish between (a) agreements and disciplines that pertain to the core business of the WTO—traditional trade policies such as tariffs, quotas, and export subsidies—and (b) rules whose implementation requires significant resources or the existence of well-functioning complementary institutions. With respect to the first category, developing countries would benefit from abiding by the same trade-policy disciplines that apply to developed countries. The overwhelming conclusion in the economic literature is that traditional trade-policy instruments should not be used in pursuit of development objectives.[17]

A country's trade policy is a key link in the transmission of price signals from the world market to the national economy. Undistorted price signals from world markets, in combination with an exchange rate that reflects macroeconomic conditions, encourages efficient resource allocation consistent with comparative advantage. An open trade regime gives consumers and firms access to a greater variety of goods and services, including capital and intermediate goods, and contributes to productivity growth through access to global technology and by forcing domestic firms to become more efficient.

Although numerous arguments have been developed that potentially provide a rationale for intervention to protect infant industries—most of which revolve around some type of market failure or externality—trade policy is rarely if ever an appropriate instrument. Moreover, well-known political economy problems are associated with protection of infant industries. The prospect of protection can give rise to unproductive rent-seeking behavior with associated scope for (legal) lobbying and (illegal) corruption (Bhagwati 1988). Moral hazard problems can easily arise because the reward for an industry doing well is the removal of protection, which can generate perverse incentives for firms to underperform so as to retain protection.

Economic first principles suggest that a subsidy-type policy generally will be less distorting (more efficient) than trade policy in offsetting

> ## Box 6.2 Major WTO provisions allowing developing countries greater freedom to use restrictive trade policies
>
> *Infant industry protection.* GATT Articles XVIII:a and XVIII:c allow for removal of tariff concessions or use of quotas if necessary to establish an industry in a developing country. Compensation must be offered to countries that would be negatively affected.
>
> *Balance-of-payments protection.* Article XVIII:b allows a nation to impose trade measures to safeguard its balance of payments. In contrast to Articles XVIII:a and c, surveillance and approval procedures are less burdensome, and compensation need not be offered to affected countries. Not surprisingly, no country has invoked the infant industry provisions of the GATT since 1967, but numerous countries have made use of Article XVIII:b. In the Uruguay Round, Article XVIII:b was revised and surveillance procedures were tightened. WTO members must now publicly announce time schedules for the removal of restrictive import measures taken for balance of payments purposes and must, in principle, use price-based measures (such as tariffs).
>
> *Subsidies:* The WTO Agreement on Subsidies and Countervailing Measures (ASCM) attempts to distinguish between subsidies (defined as financial contributions by government) that can be justified on the grounds of market failure, or on noneconomic grounds, and those that distort the incentive to trade in a major way. Nonspecific subsidies (defined as those for which access is general or eligibility automatic on the basis of clear, objective criteria) are permitted and cannot be countervailed. Subsidies contingent on export performance or on the use of domestic rather than imported goods are generally prohibited. Permitted measures that create "serious prejudice"—defined to exist if the total ad valorem subsidization of a product exceeds 5 percent, if subsidies are used to cover operating losses of a firm or industry, or if debt relief is granted for government-held liabilities—can be countervailed or disputed. Subsidies that can be shown to have had a negative effect on a partner's exports likewise may be countervailed or disputed. LDCs and countries with GNP per capita below $1,000 are exempted from the prohibition on export subsidies. Developing countries that have become competitive in a product—defined as having a global market share of 3.25 percent—must phase out any export subsidies over a two-year period.
>
> ---
>
> *Source:* Hoekman and Kostecki (2001).

an externality. From an economic viewpoint, the drafters of the GATT were therefore justified in placing relatively stringent constraints on the use of trade policy, and in particular, on the use of quantitative restrictions and local content requirements. Moreover, in cases in which import competition proves too fierce, the WTO allows for safeguards—emergency protection through safeguards. However, WTO safeguard provisions impose conditions that enhance certainty and help ensure that interventions are made only for good cause.

The foregoing does not imply that developing countries should be forced to sign away their ability to use trade policies—all countries have the right under the WTO to impose tariffs or export taxes if they so desire. Committing to abide by the same rules on the use of traditional trade polices that pertain to developed countries, however, will benefit consumers and enhance welfare in developing countries.

The WTO does not identify or constrain what governments can do in the realm of nontrade policy to maximize the benefits of trade. As emphasized by Stern (2002), any credible poverty reduction strategy must rest on two pillars: a good investment climate to propel growth, and empowerment of poor people through participation in decisions that shape their lives. Although a sound trade policy is a major element of any successful development strategy, other factors are equally important. Institutions to manage the distributional implications of trade reforms and to ensure that consumers, enterprises, and farmers have access to competitive markets for goods and services are critical to harnessing greater trade for development.

Nor does the WTO constrain the ability of governments to address market failures through subsidies or taxes. In many cases the intervention required to address an externality will be horizontal (general), not sector- or industry-specific, and thus be nonactionable. For example, food subsidies, household energy subsidies, and health and education programs are not vulnerable to WTO action. Similarly, factor-use subsidies—for example, for the wages of workers taken directly off the unemployment rolls—are permissible unless they are configured in such as way as to make them *de facto* subsidies to specific sectors. Overall, therefore, the sorts of subsidies of most use in fighting poverty and offsetting market failures are not constrained by WTO disciplines (McCulloch, Winters, and Cirera 2001).

Several policy options are open for future rules and regulations

Some developing countries and many civil society groups have charged that some WTO agreements do not support development. In such cases, the appropriate solution may be to reopen (renegotiate) agreements where members perceive the rules to be unbalanced or detrimental to their interests. This has been the approach taken by some proponents of the so-called Development Box in the Agreement on Agriculture (box 6.3). It is also the approach that has been suggested by the chair of the WTO General Council to address several proposals made by developing countries on SDT. In addition to the Agreement on Agriculture, an agreement often viewed as unbalanced is the Agreement on Trade-Related Aspects of Intellectual Property Rights (TRIPS).[18]

One lesson that emerged from the Uruguay Round is that it is important but difficult to assess what makes sense from a development perspective. In large part this is a reflection of the absence of strong trade interests and stakeholders in developing countries who might inform their governments of their preferences and clarify the implications of various proposals (Finger 2001; Hoekman 2002). As a result, the "trade-related" aspects of international issues are often identified by constituencies in major trading powers and may not have much relevance for development.

Because countries differ widely in their domestic priorities and in their capacities to implement change, it is as important as it is difficult to identify how and where development will be promoted by proposals to expand the reach of the WTO into (new) regulatory areas.

With respect to behind-the-border policies affecting trade, it is difficult to design generic rules that apply to all. Even if negotiators get the economics right, there is a danger that good policies may be resisted. Dealing with these types of issues in the context of negotiation may also induce a predominant focus on costs, as reforms will be seen as concessions to foreign interests, as opposed to being in the national interest (Finger 2002). Given their complexities and the limited negotiating resources available in most low-income countries, such issues may be best left off the negotiating table (Winters 2002). However, if negotiations are launched on these topics, it will be important to recognize that for many countries they may not have a high priority.

Differential interests and capacities must be recognized

As noted previously, the challenge is to get the rules right from a development perspective. Even if this is done, in the sense that constituencies in developing countries are enthusiastic about what has been negotiated and governments regard implementation as being in the national interest, other issues may constitute a higher priority for investment of scarce administrative and financial resources.

These observations suggest the need for differentiation among developing countries in determining the reach of WTO rules that are resource intensive; that is, those that require

Box 6.3 A "development box" for the Agreement on Agriculture?

The primary focus of the Uruguay Round Agreement on Agriculture was to bring this sector back into the trading system—that is, to reimpose multilateral disciplines on trade-distorting domestic support policies. A major feature of the agreement was to distinguish between permitted subsidies (the "green box") and subsidies subject to reduced commitments and disciplines. Because the objective of negotiators in the Uruguay Round was to reduce distorting types of support, it does not cover the types of market imperfections likely to be found in developing countries, nor does it recognize their need to pursue "second-best" policies where they do not have the institutional capacity to pursue the most efficient policies to combat poverty. As a result, several countries have sought to introduce a "development box" into the agreement, which would identify a set of measures to enhance food security, stimulate agricultural production, and reduce rural poverty in developing countries. Examples of such proposals:

- Direct and indirect investment and input subsidies or other supports to households below the national poverty level to encourage agricultural and rural development. Such supports could be product-specific as well as general, as long as they are effectively targeted to the rural poor.
- Programs supporting product diversification in small, low-income developing countries currently dependent on limited commodities for their exports, including programs involving government assistance for risk management.
- Domestic foodstuffs at subsidized prices in targeted programs aimed at meeting food requirements of the poor, whether urban or rural, as part of an overall effort to enhance food security.
- Transportation subsidies for agricultural products and farm inputs to poor remote areas.
- Programs involving government assistance for establishment of agricultural cooperatives or other institutions that promote marketing, quality control, or otherwise strengthen the competitiveness of poor farmers.
- A "special" safeguard provision, available only to developing countries, to provide rapid, time-limited protection against import surges that hurt poor producers, especially dumped imports of subsidized goods.
- Acceptance that some products—especially key staple commodities critical to food security—would not be subject to liberalization commitments.

While often defended as examples of needed preferences, proposals for a development box effectively involve changing the terms of the Agreement on Agriculture. Many of the provisions have been included in the "Harbinson" draft, which suggests approaches for future liberalization commitments in the Doha negotiations on agriculture (WTO 2003). The draft also contains a large number of provisions permitting developing countries far greater leeway in protecting agriculture through border measures such as tariffs and tariff quotas than would be the case for developed countries. Such policies may be justified because low-income developing countries do not have the fiscal capacity to support agriculture through less trade-distorting direct-income supports, but they may lead to the same inefficiencies that have undermined competitiveness of many industries nurtured behind high protective barriers. While getting the economics right is important and requires careful analysis, the efforts to alter the terms of the Agreement on Agriculture is arguably the most appropriate method of addressing rules that are not perceived to support development.

Sources: Ruffer, Jones, and Akroyd (2002); Hoekman, Michalopoulos, and Winters (2003).

significant complementary legal, administrative, and institutional investments or capacity or that will result in large transfers from developing countries. The basic rationale for differentiation is that certain agreements may not be development priorities for some countries or may require that other preconditions be satisfied before implementation can be beneficial. Such preconditions can be proxied by the attainment of a minimum level of per capita income, institutional capacity, and economic scale (size). Some WTO disciplines may not be appropriate for very small countries, for example, in that the regulatory institutions required may be unduly costly.[19]

Several options could be considered to take country differences into account in WTO agreements.[20] Options include:

- Adopting a rule of thumb that makes a group of countries eligible to opt out of provisions that entail substantial implementation costs until specific criteria or benchmarks have been met. This rule would require renegotiating the current set of country groups recognized in the WTO (the LDCs, all developing countries, and developed countries). It would also require establishing criteria to identify which agreements are affected.
- Establishing an agreement-specific approach under which application of rules to any given country is determined by agreement-specific criteria, possibly linked to availability of technical assistance and an action plan for implementation.
- Adopting a country-specific aproach that places trade-reform priorities in the context of national development plans as defined in Poverty Reduction Strategy Papers, and relying on multilateral monitoring to establish a cooperative framework under which countries may be assisted in gradually adopting WTO norms.

A common feature of these possibilities is that they require a narrower definition of eligibility for temporary exemptions from WTO rules. Country classification is inevitably a sensitive issue, as is the question of determining the "coherence" of WTO rules with national development priorities and identifying the implications of different types of WTO rules. What constitutes "resource intensive," for example? And what agreements would give rise to large implementation costs? These questions will require analysis. Determining implementation criteria would require input from relevant development institutions, national and international, to strengthen policy coherence at both levels. One advantage of an agreement-specific "implementation audit mechanism" is that it could avoid explicit country classifications, giving rise instead to a monitoring process to support developing countries in managing trade reforms and implementing WTO agreements by recognizing competing demands on scarce resources.

Involving development agencies may reduce the risk of inducing countries to adopt and pursue a program of trade and regulatory reform that may not, in fact, be suited to the country. During the Uruguay Round many countries were concerned about avoiding possible "cross-conditionality" between WTO and international financial institutions; this led to a ministerial declaration on "coherence" to call for "avoiding the imposition on governments of cross-conditionality or additional conditions" resulting from cooperation between the WTO and the international financial institutions.[21] Indeed, care would be required to avoid "cross-conditionality."

Several alternative options may therefore be feasible in recognizing differences in the ability to benefit from implementation of resource-intensive rules. Deciding on the best approach will require considerable thought and discussion. What matters most at this point is that WTO members acknowledge the issue. It might be expeditious to make a decision in Cancun to consider alternative approaches along the lines sketched out above. Given the steady expansion of the WTO into regulatory areas, doing so would help make development relevance more than a slogan.

WTO commitments must be enforced through monitoring and dispute settlement

While getting rules right is important, so is enforcement and accountability. Two aspects of enforcement of commitments are particularly important. The first is regular information on implementation of agreements and complementary actions being pursued in other forums and organizations. The second concerns the ability of developing countries to use WTO dispute-settlement mechanisms in instances in which partners have not respected the terms of an agreement. Developing countries may be at a disadvantage in using such mechanisms because of resource constraints and lack of retaliatory power. Proposals to address such biases are discussed below.

Strengthened assessment and monitoring

Strengthening mechanisms for regular monitoring of implementation of agreements and performance of both developed and developing countries would help improve transparency and accountability. This should extend to the provision of information on national trade-related priorities by developing countries, the funding and investment requirements these priorities involve, and the extent to which international and bilateral donors have provided assistance. A first step in compiling information on assistance provided was taken in 2002 by the WTO and the Development Assistance Committee of the Organisation for Economic Co-operation and Development (OECD), building on a database of bilateral and multilateral development projects. The WTO's *Trade Policy Reviews* provide a potential mechanism for bolstering monitoring, although the publication schedule of reports would need to be increased for timely information to be made available to WTO members. The type of mechanisms to put in place would depend in part on the approach taken to determine the reach of resource-intensive rules.

The weaker social safety nets and insurance mechanisms in the developing world, as well as higher rates of poverty and vulnerability to external shocks, suggest that more attention and resources should be devoted to costing out the implementation requirements of proposed rules and to calculating their costs and benefits. The multiagency Integrated Framework for Trade-Related Technical Assistance could be used to support this objective in LDCs. Developing-country think tanks and policy research networks—for example, the Global Development Network—also have an important role to play in assisting governments with the required assessments at the national level, supported by bilateral and multilateral development institutions.

Dispute settlement

Whatever agreements eventually emerge from the Doha Round, enforcement will be important. But how well can low-income countries defend their rights in the WTO? During 1995–2002, 305 bilateral disputes were brought to the WTO, entailing over 1,800 "grievances"—specific allegations of violation of a WTO provision (Horn and Mavroidis 2003). Developing countries brought 123 of the 305 disputes, about one-third. Most of these complainants were middle-income economies. Low-income countries (defined by Horn and Mavroidis as those with a per capita income below $800) were complainants in only 18 cases and respondents in only 21. LDCs did not participate at all—they never acted as complainant or respondent. Thus, well over half of the WTO membership does not participate in WTO dispute settlement.[22]

That many developing countries have not participated in WTO dispute settlement reflects the manifold challenges of such participation. A first challenge to defending rights through the WTO is obtaining knowledge that a WTO provision may have been violated by a partner government. A second is convincing the government to bring the case forward—enterprises alone have no legal standing before the WTO. A third is expectation of a positive payoff from bringing a case—a function of the remedy available and the likelihood that the trading partner will actually implement it.

Small countries cannot credibly threaten retaliation—the ultimate threat that can be made against a member that does not comply with a WTO panel recommendation—because raising import barriers will have little impact on the target market, while being costly in welfare terms.[23] Thus, pressure to comply with panel rulings is largely moral. In practice, the system has worked rather well, in that recourse to retaliation has rarely been required to enforce multilateral dispute-settlement decisions. This is a reflection of the repeated nature of WTO interactions and the resulting value that governments attach to maintaining a good reputation. Nonetheless, asymmetry in enforcement ability can affect incentives to use the system. The classic recommendation by economists to address the problem is to change the rules so that nonimplementation of panel recommendations would be punished by withdrawal of market-access commitments by *all* WTO members. But suggestions to this effect have always been resisted (Hudec 1987, 2002).

Retaliation involves raising barriers to trade, which is generally detrimental to all parties. The power of retaliation may also be captured by protectionist interests in an importing country. A superior approach would be to strengthen compensation provisions. Developing countries have proposed, for example, that WTO panels should be authorized to recommend payment of financial compensation in cases where a developing country loses its trade in a product as a result of actions by a developed country that are inconsistent with WTO norms.[24] Such suggestions have a long history (Hudec 2002).[25] Mexico recently suggested allowing countries that have won a dispute but where implementation has not occurred to auction off the resulting retaliation rights.[26]

While compensation or fines would be less distorting than trade sanctions, they may not be very effective in inducing compliance, as the costs would disperse among all taxpayers. Other options should therefore be considered, including stronger surveillance mechanisms and greater opportunities for interested parties to bring cases in national forums. Whatever is done, it is important to halt the emerging trend toward escalating retaliation and the use of trade sanctions.

Aid for trade: addressing national priorities

Trade capacity is critical in ensuring that low-income countries are able to benefit from trade opportunities. Numerous studies—most recently the Diagnostic Trade Integration Studies undertaken in LDCs under the auspices of the Integrated Framework initiative—have identified institutional weaknesses and an adverse investment climate as a major source of comparative disadvantage.[27]

The reports reveal that many countries remain largely without the appropriate institutional frameworks and systems to manage their trade policy and that trade costs severely limit the competitiveness of developing-country firms in export markets. Transport costs are often the single most important component of cost for exporters in several of the countries. The transport sectors (air, ports, trucking) are often plagued by a lack of domestic competition (see chapter 5).

These anticompetitive conditions impinge directly on the welfare of the poor. In most LDCs, the majority of poor households derive their income from agriculture and agro-processing. Agricultural trade integration can therefore increase both productivity and rural incomes by providing better access to modern inputs and technologies and by encouraging exports.[28] In addition to the fragmentation of markets and the remoteness of many farming communities, binding constraints include transportation bottlenecks that, combined with numerous informal fees and internal checkpoints, lead to high transaction costs (in Ethiopia, Guinea, and Nepal), lack of basic post-harvest marketing infrastructure (in Ethiopia, Guinea, Malawi, Mauritania, and Yemen), lack of water control infrastructure (in Ethiopia and Senegal), and a pervasive degradation of natural resources (Tsikata 2003). To improve competitiveness and extend the benefits of trade to the poorer segments of the population, better domestic market integration should be a key policy objective in many LDCs.

Development assistance can play an important role in bolstering trade capacity, thereby allowing countries to benefit from liberalized access to international markets. Additional funds are needed to address both policy and public-investment priorities, to help low-income countries adapt to a reduction in trade preferences following further nondiscriminatory trade liberalization, and to assist poor net-importing countries to deal with the potential detrimental effects of a significant increase in world food prices, should these materialize. The world community made general commitments to this effect at the International Conference on Financing for Development in Monterrey in March 2002—the need now is to translate the "Monterrey consensus" into identification and financing of trade-related investment priorities.

Although more "aid for trade" would be beneficial, it is important to avoid a situation in which a desire by donor countries to see developing countries implement certain WTO agreements diverts assistance away from recipients' own development priorities. This is one of the risks of suggestions to make technical assistance a requirement of new WTO rules and to link implementation of WTO agreements to the provision of such assistance. Ideally, identification and delivery of trade-related technical assistance should be embedded in the national policy-setting processes used by governments and the donor community—for example, the Poverty Reduction Strategy Papers. This would ensure that trade priorities are considered for funding along with other development priorities.

Putting development into the Doha agenda

utting development into the Doha agenda requires actions by developing and developed countries alike. Interests and priorities differ from country to country, but improved access to markets in agriculture, manufactures, and services would be most beneficial.

In fact, liberalized market access on an MFN basis has the greatest potential payoff, in terms of development and poverty reduction, of any issue on the Doha agenda.

Because duty- and quota-free access to major markets can help to offset the many disadvantages that confront firms in poor countries, developed countries should continue to grant trade preferences to LDCs and similarly disadvantaged countries, emulating Europe's Everything But Arms initiative. To maximize the benefits of such deep preferences, concerted action should be taken to minimize the trade-restricting effect of rules of origin and related administrative requirements.

But preferences are best viewed as a transitional instrument. What matters most in any effort to expand exports on a sustained basis is a good investment climate, including openness to trade. Indeed, most of the potential gains from trade reform could be realized by *unilateral* liberalization.

Traditional forms of preferential treatment cannot be the primary instruments to enhance the development-relevance of the WTO. Instead, countries must commit to engage in the reciprocal exchange of market-access concessions. Continuing to exempt developing countries from trade-policy disciplines is not likely to achieve development goals.

With regard to behind-the-border regulation, the same principle should apply as with trade-policy disciplines: ensuring that the rules support development.[29] Getting the rules right requires each country to think hard about what is in its national interest. Even where the potential benefit of an agreement may be clear, poor countries may not have the resources required to implement it immediately, perhaps because other issues command higher priority or because complementary policies and institutions must be put in place before implementation will be beneficial. In this regard, a new concept of special and differential treatment, one that would establish clear criteria and mechanisms to link implementation to development priorities and capacities, could be most fruitful.

Promoting the trade and development prospects of low-income countries requires action on many fronts. The key needs—to establish priorities for reforming domestic policy and enhancing trade-related capacity—grow more acute as MFN trade barriers are reduced, and the value of preferences is eroded. A precondition for effective use of additional development assistance—whether in the form of grants or development loans—is that the necessary priorities are determined appropriately. In many low-income countries much more should be done to integrate trade priorities into national development strategies and investment allocation decisions.

It should be possible to move rapidly toward providing greater access for all countries to others' markets in goods and services. As far as rule-making is concerned, agreement on an approach that recognizes the significant differences among countries will give development a much more solid place in the WTO. Most important is to address what is by far the most urgent challenge of expanding trade for development—identifying and dealing with trade constraints *within* countries, whether those constraints derive from policies, poor infrastructure, or limitations in capacity.

Notes

1. See World Bank (2002), Finger and Schuler (2000), and Hoekman and Kostecki (2001) for a discussion and references to the literature.

2. Hudec (1987) and Finger (1991) review the background in some depth, noting that SDT was heavily influenced by foreign policy considerations, especially the Cold War.

3. The full name is Decision on Differential and More Favorable Treatment, Reciprocity and Fuller Participation of Developing Countries. See Hudec (1987) for further discussion of the history.

4. This was first documented by Finger (1974, 1976).

5. Because WTO rules are often based on those prevailing in OECD countries, implementation costs are asymmetrically distributed. Post-Uruguay Round research—for example, Finger and Schuler (2000) and Finger (2001)—revealed that the costs associated with complying with certain WTO disciplines can be significant. This is in part because of the rules themselves, but mostly because of the ancillary investments that are required to allow the rule to be applied.

6. Note that China and Mexico are included in the European Union's GSP recipients' list while they are excluded from the U.S. list. The United States has a free trade area agreement (FTA) with Mexico and does not grant GSP status to China. On the other hand, South Africa, Turkey, and Eastern European countries have FTAs with the European Union and, hence, are excluded from its GSP while they receive GSP status from the United States.

7. The limit is $13 million if the exporting country has more than 50 percent market share.

8. For most textile and clothing products, the 20 percent reduction is less than 3.5 percentage points.

9. According to EU Council regulation 2501/2001, there are some nonsensitive agricultural and food products. According to Annex IV, these are artichokes, castor oil, frogs' legs, grapefruit, green tea, inactive yeasts, licorice extract, malt beer, papayas, pepper, and sweet potatoes.

10. U.S. intellectual property advocacy groups have used GSP eligibility as an instrument to induce a number of countries (including El Salvador, Honduras, Panama, Paraguay, Poland, and Turkey) to take actions in such areas.

11. Rules of origin are intended to prevent trade deflection and to determine where a good originates for duty purposes when two or more countries are involved in the production of a product. The general rule is that the origin of a product is the one in which the last substantial transformation took place, that is, the country in which significant manufacturing or processing occurred most recently. Significant or substantial is defined as the level of transformation sufficient to give the product its essential character. Various criteria can be used to determine if a substantial transformation occurred. These include a change in tariff heading (as when, as a result of whatever processing was performed the good is classified under another category of the Harmonized System), the use of specific processing operations, tests based on the value of additional materials embodied in the transformed product, or the amount of value added in the last country where the good was transformed.

12. These categories make up around 65–75 percent of the exports of the AGOA and Andean Program beneficiaries and tend to dominate general patterns with their volatile prices.

13. A major benefit of Everything But Arms is that the preferences are not time-limited.

14. This was the approach used in the GATT before the creation of the GSP. See Hudec (1987) and Finger (1991).

15. Given that many developing countries either have not bound tariffs at all or have high tariff bindings, this will automatically imply that credit will be given for past reductions in applied tariffs and—provided formulas are used—that autonomous liberalization (reduction in applied tariff rates) will not prejudice future WTO negotiations. See Francois and Martin (2003) for an in-depth analysis of alternative formula-based approaches.

16. This section draws in part on Hoekman, Michalopoulos, and Winters (2003).

17. See, for example, Hoekman, Michalopoulos, and Winters (2003), Noland and Pack (2003), Irwin (2001, 2003), and Hausmann and Rodrik (2002).

18. Research on the effects of TRIPS suggests that net transfers from low- to high-income countries could be substantial (World Bank 2001).

19. For example, despite remarkable reductions in customs clearance times that have been achieved by some LDCs (sometimes from weeks to days or hours, as in Senegal), the customs regimes in many participating countries are characterized by long clearance times, a plethora of informal fees, and inadequate performance monitoring indicators (see chapter 5). Many countries are struggling to implement the Agreement on Customs Valuation and to work with and reform other institutions whose actions impinge on customs efficiency such as security and enforcement.

20. These options are discussed further in Stevens (2002), Prowse (2002), Wang and Winters (1999), and Hoekman, Michalopoulos, and Winters (2003).

21. Declaration on the Contribution of the World Trade Organization to Achieving Greater Coherence in Global Economic Policymaking, December 15, 1993.

22. Busch and Reinhardt (2002) found that developing countries accounted for around 30 percent of complaints under both GATT and WTO, but that the share of cases against developing countries had risen from 8 percent to 37 percent during the period covered by their study. This suggests that the shift to the WTO—with the associated expansion of disciplines on developing countries—has given rise to a significant increase in the probability of engaging in dispute settlement. However, Holmes, Rollo, and Young (2002) concluded that the simple hypothesis that disputes will be proportionate to trade shares is not borne out by the data. They also found that income per head or measures of openness did not help to explain the incidence of disputes, suggesting that there is no significant bias between small and large countries, or between richer and poorer countries, in terms of participation in the system as complainants or respondents. Horn, Mavroidis, and Nordström (1999) similarly conclude that the evidence for "bias" is not particularly strong once one controls for the fact that disputes should be correlated with the number of incompatible measures a country's exporters encounter and the volume of trade, and takes into account that there is likely to be a threshold below which it is not worth bringing a case.

23. See Bown (2002) for a recent analysis and references to the relevant literature.

24. WT/GC/W/162

25. For a discussion of a proposal by Brazil and Uruguay to reform the dispute settlement system to include financial compensation, see Dam (1970, 368–73).

26. In their analysis of this proposal, Bagwell, Staiger, and Mavroidis (2003) conclude that the probability of the winning country being compensated is highest if such rights extend to the losing party.

27. The Diagnostic Trade Integration Study (DTIS) is an analytical tool developed to reexamine the policy and institutional constraints to trade for LDCs, and to identify technical assistance needs for the purpose of enhancing LDCs' integration into the global economy. As of July 2003, DTIS reports had been completed for Burundi, Cambodia, Ethiopia, Guinea, Lesotho, Madagascar, Malawi, Mali, Mauritania, Nepal, Senegal, and Yemen. See www.worldbank.org/trade.

28. Increasing productivity in agriculture is critical for the transformation of these economies. Reducing the price of food products increases the real income of the whole population and allows higher household spending in nonagricultural products, thus favoring diversification.

29. The GATT/WTO may have it right when it comes to rules on the use of trade policy; for example, the ban on the use of quotas and the focus on binding tariffs. This is much less clear when it comes to other agreements, such as TRIPS. The solution in such cases is to reopen existing agreements, something that can readily be done. Many of the agreements are already subject to ongoing negotiations.

References

Bagwell, K., R. Staiger, and Petros C. Mavroidis. 2003. "The Case for Auctioning Countermeasures in the WTO." Mimeo, Columbia University, New York.

Beghin, John, and M. Ataman Aksoy. 2003. "Agricultural Trade and the Doha Round: Preliminary Lessons from Commodity Studies." Mimeo. World Bank, Washington, D.C.

Bhagwati, Jagdish. 1988. *Protectionism*. Cambridge, Mass.: MIT Press.

Bown, Chad. 2002. "The Economics of Trade Disputes, the GATT's Article XXIII and the WTO's Dispute Settlement Understanding." *Economics and Politics* 14: 283–323.

Brenton, Paul. 2003. "Integrating the Least Developed Countries into the World Trading System: The

Current Impact of EU Preferences under Everything But Arms." Policy Research Working Paper 3018. World Bank, Washington, D.C.

Brenton, Paul, and M. Manchin. 2002. "Making EU Trade Agreements Work: The Role of Rules of Origin." CEPS Working Document 183. Brussels.

Busch, M., and E. Reinhardt. 2003. "Developing Countries and GATT/WTO Dispute Settlement." Mimeo. Emory University, Atlanta, Georgia.

Dam, Kenneth. 1970. *The GATT: Law and the International Economic Organization.* Chicago: University of Chicago Press.

Evenett, Simon. Editor. 2003. *The Singapore Issues and the World Trading System.* Berne: State Secretariat for Economic Affairs.

Finger, J. Michael. 1974. "GATT Tariff Concessions and the Exports of Developing Countries: United States Concessions at the Dillon Round." *Economic Journal* 84 (335).

———. 1976. "Effects of the Kennedy Round Tariff Concessions on the Exports of Developing Countries." *Economic Journal* 86 (341).

———. 1991. "Development Economics and the General Agreement on Tariffs and Trade." In J. de Melo and André Sapir, eds., *Trade Theory and Economic Reform: North, South, and East.* Oxford, U.K.: Basil Blackwell.

———. 2001. "Implementing the Uruguay Round Agreements: Problems for Developing Countries." *The World Economy* 24 (9): 1097–1108.

Finger, J. M. 2002. "The Doha Agenda and Development: A View From the Uruguay Round," Manila: Asian Development Bank.

Finger, J. Michael, and Philip Schuler. 2000. "Implementation of Uruguay Round Commitments: The Development Challenge." *The World Economy* 23: 511–25.

Francois, J., and Will Martin. 2003. "Formula Approaches for Market Access Negotiations." *The World Economy* 26: 1–28.

Hausmann, R., and Dani Rodrik. 2002. "Economic Development as Self-Discovery." CEPR Discussion Paper 3356, Center for Economic Policy Research, London.

Hoekman, Bernard. 2002. "Strengthening the Global Trade Architecture for Development." *World Trade Review* 1: 23–46.

Hoekman, Bernard, and Michel Kostecki. 2001. *The Political Economy of the World Trading System.* Oxford, U.K.: Oxford University Press.

Hoekman, Bernard, Aaditya Mattoo, and Philip English, eds. 2002. *Development, Trade and the WTO: A Handbook.* Washington D.C.: World Bank.

Hoekman, Bernard, Constantine Michalopoulos, and L. Alan Winters. 2003. "Development and More Favorable and Differential Treatment of Developing Countries." Mimeo, Development Research Group, World Bank, Washington, D.C.

Hoekman, Bernard, Francis Ng, and Marcelo Olarreaga. 2002. "Tariff Peaks in the Quad and Least Developed Country Exports." *World Bank Economic Review* 16: 1–22.

Holmes, P., J. Rollo, and A. Young. 2002. "Emerging Trends in WTO Dispute Settlement: Back to the GATT?" Mimeo. University of Sussex, U.K.

Horn, Henrik, and Petros C. Mavroidis. 2003. "Which WTO Provisions are Invoked by and Against Developing Countries?" Mimeo. Institute for International Economics, Stockholm.

Horn, Henrik, Petros C. Mavroidis, and Hakan Nordström. 1999. "Is the Use of the WTO Dispute Settlement System Biased?" CEPR Discussion Paper, Center for Economic Policy Research, London.

Hudec, Robert. 1987. *Developing Countries in the GATT Legal System.* London: Trade Policy Research Centre.

———. 2002. "The Adequacy of WTO Dispute Settlement Remedies: A Developing Country Perspective." In Bernard Hoekman, Aaditya Mattoo, and Philip English, eds., *Development, Trade, and the WTO: A Handbook.* Washington, D.C.: World Bank.

IMF (International Monetary Fund). 2002. "Financing of Losses Due to Preference Erosion." Washington, D.C. Mimeo.

Inama, Stefano. 2003. "Trade Preferences and the WTO Negotiations on Market Access." Mimeo. United Nations Commission on Trade and Development (UNCTAD), Geneva.

Irwin, Douglas. 2002. *Free Trade Under Fire.* Princeton: Princeton University Press.

———. 2003. "Interpreting the Tariff-Growth Correlation of the Late Nineteenth Century." *American Economic Review* 91 (May 2002): 165–69.

Keck, Alexander, and Patrick Low. 2003. "Special and Differential Treatment." Mimeo. World Trade Institute, Berne.

Laird, Sam, Raed Safadi, and Alessandro Turini. 2003. "The WTO and Development." Mimeo. United Nations Commission on Trade and Development (UNCTAD), Geneva.

Mattoo, Aaditya. 2003. "Shaping Future Rules for Trade in Services: Lessons from the GATS." In Takatoshi Ito and Anne O. Krueger, eds., *Trade in Services in the Asia Pacific Region.* NBER. Chicago: University of Chicago Press.

Mitchell, Donald. 2003. "Sugar Policies: Opportunity for Change." Mimeo. World Bank, Washington, D.C.

McCulloch, N., L. Alan Winters, and Xavier Cirera. 2001. *Trade Liberalization and Poverty: A Handbook*. London: Center for Economic Policy Research.

Noland, Marcus, and Howard Pack. 2003. *Industrial Policy in an Era of Globalization: Lessons from Asia*. Washington, D.C.: Institute of International Economics.

Ozden, Caglar, and E. Reinhardt. 2003a. "The Perversity of Preferences." Policy Research Working Paper 2955, World Bank, Washington, D.C.

———. 2003b. "First Do No Harm: GSP and the Effect of Trade Preferences on Developing Country Exports." Mimeo. World Bank, Washington, D.C.

Panagariya, A. 2002. "EU Preferential Trade Policies and Developing Countries." *The World Economy* 25 (10): 1415–32.

Prowse, Susan. 2002. "The Role of International and National Agencies in Trade-Related Capacity Building." *The World Economy* (9): 1235–61.

Rodrik, Dani, ed. 2003. *In Search of Prosperity: Analytic Narratives on Economic Growth*. Princeton, N.J.: Princeton University Press.

Ruffer, Tim, S. Jones, and S. Akroyd. 2002. "Development Box Proposals and Their Potential Effect on Developing Countries." Mimeo. Report for U.K. Department for International Development, London.

Sapir, André. 1997. "The Political Economy of EC Regionalism." *European Economic Review* 42: 717–32.

Schiff, M., and L. Alan Winters. 2003. *Regional Integration and Development*. Oxford, U.K.: Oxford University Press and Washington, D.C.: World Bank.

Stern, Nicholas. 2002. *A Strategy for Development*. Washington D.C.: World Bank.

Stevens, Christopher. 2002. "The Future of SDT for Developing Countries in the WTO." Mimeo. Institute of Development Studies, University of Sussex, U.K. May.

Tangermann, S. 2002. "The Future of Preferential Trade Arrangements for Developing Countries and the Current Round of WTO Negotiations on Agriculture." Food and Agriculture Organization, Rome.

Tarr, David. 2002. "Arguments For and Against Uniform Tariffs." In Bernard Hoekman, Aaditya Mattoo, and Philip English, eds., *Development, Trade, and the WTO: A Handbook*. Washington, D.C.: World Bank.

Tsikata, Yvonne. 2003. "Integrating into the Global Economy: Challenges, Experiences and Policy Lessons from the Integrated Framework." Mimeo. World Bank.

USTR (United States Trade Representative). 2002. "Report on U.S. Trade and Investment Policy Toward Sub-Saharan Africa and Implementation of the African Growth and Opportunity Act." Report Submitted by the President to the Congress, Washington, D.C.

Wang, Z. K., and L. Alan Winters. 2000. "Putting 'Humpty' Together Again: Including Developing Countries in a Consensus for the WTO." CEPR Policy Paper 4. London. March.

Winters, L. Alan. 2002. "Doha and the World Poverty Targets." Paper presented at the Annual Bank Conference on Development Economics, World Bank, Washington, D.C. April.

World Bank. 2001. *Global Economic Prospects and the Developing Countries 2002: Making Trade Work for the Poor*. Washington, D.C.: World Bank.

World Bank. 2002. *Global Economic Prospects and the Developing Countries 2003: Investing to Unlock Opportunities*. Washington, D.C.: World Bank.

Appendix 1
Regional Economic Prospects

East Asia and Pacific

Recent developments

THE YEAR 2002 was one of solid recovery in much of East Asia. GDP growth in developing East Asia rose from 5.5 percent in 2001 to 6.7 percent in 2002. However, the renewed economic slowdown in the developed world, relatively high oil prices in the first part of 2003, and the SARS outbreak in the region, dampened the pace of the regional recovery in the first half of 2003. However, East Asian growth is expected to rebound progressively, as economies get beyond the short-run impact of SARS, oil prices wane, and global growth revives.

A smart rebound in exports was one important driver in the regional recovery in 2002—regional exports rose nearly 14 percent in dollar terms, after having been flat in 2001 as a result of the global slowdown and the deep recession in world high-tech demand. Intraregional exports were especially strong, in particular to China, which is emerging as a major hub for regional production and trade networks. Robust household consumption provided further support for the recovery, and, in several cases, the year saw the start of a stronger trend in fixed investment as well. But the regional picture was not uniformly upbeat, with more modest growth rates, or even continued outright recession in some of the smaller or lower-income economies.

As has been the case for some years, growth in 2002 was strongest in the transition economies, China and Vietnam, where sustained strength in exports, consumption, and investment pushed 2002 GDP growth to 8 percent and 7 percent, respectively. But growth also strengthened in several of the countries that had been hardest hit by 2001's fall in world-trade growth and high-tech demand, exceeding 6 percent in Korea, 5 percent in Thailand, and 4 percent in both Malaysia and the Philippines. Prompt policy action helped mute the impact of the Bali terrorist attack on Indonesia's economy, which nevertheless managed only 3–4 percent growth for a second year. Overall, the robust performance supported continued reductions in poverty.

The strong growth momentum of 2002 became more diffused in the first quarter of 2003, continuing in some countries, waning in others, and falling sharply in yet others. The strongest performances were in China and Thailand, where year-on-year first-quarter growth reached 9.9 percent and 6.7 percent, respectively, supported by both domestic demand and export growth. First-quarter growth was 4.5 percent in the Philippines—at the higher end of expectations. However, some signs of a downshift were already emerging in Malaysia, where first-quarter growth dipped to 4 percent from over 5 percent in the latter part of 2002, while in Indonesia growth continued at a modest 3.4 percent pace (figure A1.1).

Figure A1.1 Some slowing of growth into the first quarter of 2003

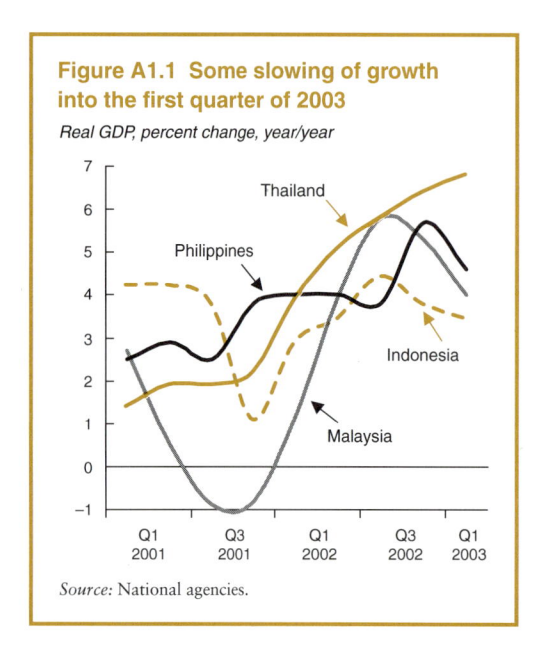

Real GDP, percent change, year/year

Source: National agencies.

Second-quarter data for China, at 6.7 percent growth, shows the domestic effects of SARS quite clearly. An increased deceleration was observed in the high-income or newly industrializing economies (NIEs) of the region. GDP in the first quarter fell by 1–2 percent in Korea and Hong Kong (at a quarter-on-quarter seasonally adjusted annual rate), while it rose at only 0.7 percent in Singapore (on the same basis). In Korea, policy efforts to restrict excessive growth in consumer borrowing and the impact of security concerns with regard to North Korea, contributed to a fall in consumer spending and machinery and equipment investment. Exports also slowed from the end of 2002, though they increased strongly year-on-year in dollar terms. The weaker trends in GDP growth and trade for the NIEs continued into the second quarter.

Among the factors contributing to slower East Asian growth in 2003 was the downturn in growth in most parts of the developed world in the last quarter of 2002 and early 2003. The still hesitant and uncertain pace of recovery in the global high-tech industry, to which East Asia is a key supplier, has been another factor affecting exports. World semiconductor sales, which had slumped 31 percent in 2001, inched forward by about 1 percent in dollar terms for 2002 as a whole, despite a strong rebound on a quarter-to-quarter basis during much of 2002. However, global semiconductor sales peaked in the three months prior to November 2002, and trended lower in December and early 2003. These erratic developments in global and sectoral demand have had some impact in slowing East Asian export growth in the first part of 2003. Exports for East Asia as a whole started the year strongly, up 20 percent over year ago (oya) in the first quarter in dollar terms, but by April–May dollar export growth rates had slowed to below 10 percent in the majority of cases, or even below 5 percent in some. China and Thailand were the only countries where dollar exports continued to grow at rates of over 30 percent and 20 percent, respectively.

The World Health Organization's March alert about SARS sparked extraordinary public concern throughout East Asia and around the world. The number of cases worldwide rose from very few in mid-March to 8,360 by the end of May (most of which were in China and Hong Kong, with smaller numbers in Taiwan, China, and Singapore), and then leveled off at around 8,465 by mid-June, indicating that the outbreak had been brought under control, at least for the time being. Most of the economic impacts of the outbreak were the result of public perceptions and fears *about* the disease, and from precautions taken against it, rather than from the disease itself. The principal way SARS appears to spread is through droplet transmission, and so worst affected were service industries, which depend on face-to-face interaction between service providers and customers, especially tourism, and related sectors such as restaurants and hotels, retail sales, business travel, and transportation.

April tourist arrivals in Hong Kong and Singapore were down by 65–70 percent from year-earlier levels, for example, while passenger traffic in all Asia-Pacific air carriers fell by 45 percent in that month. With fears about SARS being at their height in April and May, before easing substantially in June, the economic im-

REGIONAL ECONOMIC PROSPECTS

pacts will likely be concentrated in the second quarter, especially in economies with large tourism sectors, such as Hong Kong (China), Singapore, Thailand, and Malaysia. As noted, there was a significant impact in China, which had the largest number of SARS cases, though growth there is still expected to reach 7–8 percent for the year as a whole, because of the very strong momentum of the economy going into 2003, and the relatively small role of tourism.

Short-run outlook

Developing East Asian growth is expected to dip to around 6.1 percent in 2003 from 6.7 percent in 2002, before picking up pace in 2004 and later years. That is, the impacts of SARS and the global slowdown are expected to be modest. Several factors should support regional activity in the near term. For one thing, China is an increasingly important market for other East Asian countries, and continued growth there should provide some support for other East Asian economies' exports, despite the disruption caused by SARS. Chinese imports were still rising at a 30–40 percent year-on-year dollar rate in April-May.

Exports in several Southeast Asian countries have been boosted by higher prices for agricultural primary commodities such as rice, rubber, palm oil, coconut products, and lumber from late 2001 on. International capital markets had been afflicted by high levels of volatility and risk aversion through much of 2002, but were showing intriguing signs of a turnaround late in 2002 and early 2003. Spreads on emerging market and high-yield corporate debt fell sharply, while flows to emerging market funds began to increase. Of course many East Asian countries already had achieved low spreads because of the dramatic increase in their foreign reserves and the large fall in their net foreign indebtedness in recent years. However, the improvement in general emerging market sentiment will be good news for countries such as the Philippines and Indonesia, which tend to face higher spreads because of their more precarious fiscal positions.

At the level of domestic policy, low inflation, a shift to greater exchange rate flexibility, and a marked improvement in external balance sheets have all enhanced the ability of central banks to implement supportive monetary policies in many East Asian countries. Real interest rates have fallen to historically low levels in recent years and this should provide an environment conducive to growth. Most regional stock

Table A1.1 East Asia and Pacific forecast summary

Growth rates/ratios (percent)	1991–2000	2001	2002	2003	2004	2005	2006–15
Real GDP growth	7.7	5.5	6.7	6.1	6.7	6.6	6.2
Consumption per capita	5.5	4.1	6.1	5.3	6.5	6.5	5.8
GDP per capita	6.4	4.5	5.8	5.2	5.8	5.7	5.4
population	1.2	0.9	0.9	0.9	0.9	0.8	0.8
Gross Domestic Investment/GDP[a]	28.8	30.5	33.0	33.7	34.4	35.2	30.4
Inflation[b]	6.8	2.6	3.3	3.7	4.6	2.8	
General gvt. budget balance/GDP	−0.9	−3.3	−3.4	−3.4	−3.2	−2.9	
Export Market Growth[c]	8.3	−2.2	3.9	6.9	8.2	8.1	
Export volume[d]	11.5	2.7	15.7	14.6	13.7	11.3	
Terms of trade/GDP[e]	−0.1	0.1	−0.1	0.6	−0.7	−1.1	
Current account/GDP	0.4	2.7	3.2	1.9	2.1	1.2	
Memorandum items							
East Asia excluding China	4.6	2.3	4.4	3.9	5.0	5.4	4.9

a. Fixed investment, measured in real terms.
b. Local currency GDP deflator, median.
c. Weighted average growth of import demand in export markets.
d. Goods and non-factor services.
e. Change in terms of trade, measured as a proportion of GDP (percentage).
Source: World Bank baseline forecast July 2003.

markets rebounded quite sharply between late March (precisely when the SARS crisis was starting) and June, indicating that financial markets were looking beyond the near-term disruptions while currencies in most flexible exchange rate economies have also appreciated against the dollar. In several countries governments also felt able to undertake small programs of fiscal stimulus to bolster economic activity during the temporary SARS shock, in particular in Malaysia, Hong Kong, Singapore, and Korea.

Long-term outlook

The years since the 1997 financial crisis have been ones of extraordinary volatility and uncertainty in the world economy. East Asian economies have actually come through this period reasonably well. Simple average growth in the five crisis countries was 4.6 percent in 1999–2002, while including China and Vietnam it reached 5.1 percent. Contributing to this reasonably positive experience has been a broad array of efforts at policy reform—albeit often gradual and incomplete—accompanied by a gradual strengthening of domestic demand. Robust household consumer spending helped underpin growth during 2001's export slowdown, and it also continued to bolster the regional recovery through much of 2002. Efforts to recapitalize and restructure the financial sector have been successful enough for banks to foster the emergence of new consumer credit markets, a positive development from a long-run standpoint, although bank management and regulators will need to ensure it does not become a source of vulnerability.

Investment spending has been strong in China and Vietnam, but in general it has remained erratic and, on the whole, still relatively weak in the crisis countries. But even here, there were some signs of an emerging pickup in 2002, for example in housing construction. A number of factors should support a stronger investment revival in due course, including continued domestic economic growth, improvement in corporate profitability and reduction in corporate indebtedness, the running down of overcapacity, and continued macroeconomic stability. And structural and institutional reform efforts to improve the investment climate will also be important. These include reducing barriers to foreign direct investment in services; strengthening infrastructure and the provision of other public services important for business; and improving the regulatory, legal, and judicial frameworks. Also important will be continued financial and corporate sector restructuring and reform, including reforms to improve financial supervision and regulation, and strengthen corporate governance.

While some governments have undertaken counter-cyclical fiscal policies in 2003, given the significant public debt built up after the crisis, policy attention in the medium term is becoming more focused on the need for fiscal consolidation, and also, to some extent, on better addressing the risks of implicit or contingent liabilities. Looking forward, there is scope to focus on better public administration and financial accountability, improve public service delivery, and address questions of governance more broadly—that is, to provide growing volumes of critical public goods while maintaining sound fiscal positions. Developing East Asia is expected to achieve per capita growth of close to 5.5 percent in the medium to longer term, given continued steady efforts to improve structural policies and the quality of institutions.

South Asia

Recent developments

GDP GROWTH in the South Asia region declined to 4.2 percent in 2002 from 4.9 percent in 2001, a downward revision from our previous estimate of an acceleration of growth as published in *Global Development Finance—2003*. The slowdown largely reflects adverse weather conditions and a decline in agricultural output in India, Nepal, and near stagnation in Bangladesh. Additionally, Nepal experienced a plunge in

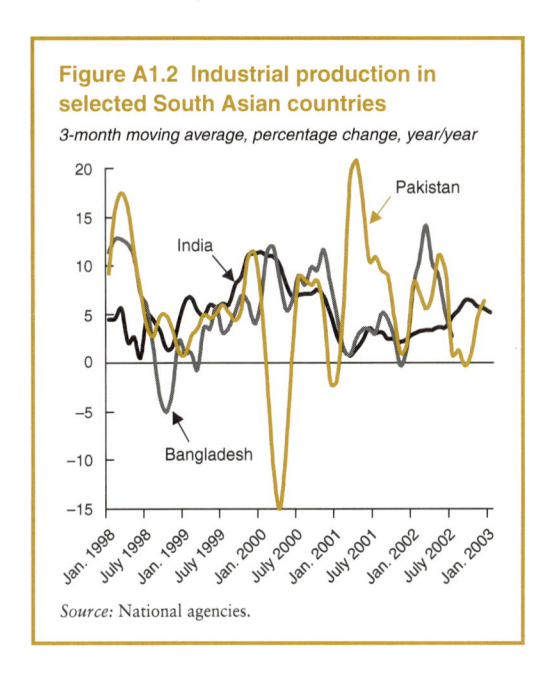

Figure A1.2 Industrial production in selected South Asian countries
3-month moving average, percentage change, year/year

Source: National agencies.

tourism receipts and a sharp decline in manufacturing output, as the domestic insurgency intensified. Pakistan and Sri Lanka both enjoyed a rise in growth rates in 2002 over 2001, because of strong government consumption in Pakistan and a recovery in the services sector—along with improved political stability tied to progress on peace talks and a yearlong cease-fire—in Sri Lanka.

Industrial production in the main economies continued to register gains of 5–10 percent entering 2003 (figure A1.2). Driven largely by a recovery in India's exports, export volume growth accelerated for the region on average—despite sluggish external demand—thus reducing the region's net trade deficit. Current account balances in the two largest economies, India and Pakistan, posted surpluses, and the region's aggregate external balance strengthened. But exports from Nepal declined significantly, because of weak external demand and heightened competition.

A number of regional economies experienced a significant increase in remittances during 2002 over 2001, notably Bangladesh, India, Nepal, Pakistan, and Sri Lanka. In Bangladesh, the reported increase in inflows of remittances is a reflection of incentives introduced by the government to channel remittances through official sources. In Pakistan and Sri Lanka, increases in remittances are largely attributed to the improvements in their domestic security situations and to progress in macroeconomic stabilization. High interest rate differentials in India may have contributed to a rise in banking transfers there. While net FDI inflows to Pakistan rose markedly in 2002, attracted by increased macroeconomic stabilization and progress in reforms, net inflows to India declined. In Bangladesh, FDI inflows fell by over 60 percent, mainly reflecting the determination of an absence of export markets (gas exploration) and the lack of progress in reforms of the infrastructure sector, such as in ports, power, and telecommunications.

India's and Pakistan's nominal exchange rates appreciated relative to the U.S. dollar during 2002, while the exchange rates of Bangladesh and Sri Lanka remained relatively flat. Nepal's exchange rate is pegged to the Indian rupee. Throughout much of South Asia, inflation remained broadly stable, as feed-through effects of higher oil prices were offset by easing price pressures tied to generally weaker domestic demand conditions. In Sri Lanka, inflationary pressures were reduced from 2001, but remained close to 10 percent on average in 2002.

There was some progress in the consolidation of persistent fiscal deficits, which are prevalent throughout the region (in large part because of weak revenue collection). By containing outlays and raising revenues, Bangladesh reduced its budget deficit to 4.7 percent of GDP in 2002 from just below 6 percent of GDP in 2001. It improved its financing profile by reducing its reliance on more expensive domestic financial markets and increasing its reliance on external financing sources. Sri Lanka also achieved a two-point reduction in its budget deficit, from 10.8 percent of GDP in 2001 to 8.8 percent in 2002, and was able to shift the composition of its financing to longer-term instruments. Pakistan brought its underlying

GLOBAL ECONOMIC PROSPECTS

budget deficit down slightly to 5.1 percent of GDP. India's general government fiscal deficit was little changed from 11 percent of GDP (including both central and state deficits), despite increased revenue collection.

Near-term outlook

Growth is forecast to accelerate throughout the region in 2003, up to an average of 5.4 percent, assuming a return to trend agricultural production, a recovery in external demand, and continued improvements in political stability and regional security. Domestic demand, especially private consumption and fixed investment, is expected to accelerate, spurred by recovery in agricultural incomes. Growth in government spending is expected to accelerate less strongly. A projection of higher growth in India underpins this forecast, as it represents nearly 80 percent of the region's aggregate GDP. Aside from a recovery in agricultural output, growth in India is likely to be supported by continued strong expansion in the services sector especially in information technologies now burgeoning in the Bangalore area. A continued recovery in Pakistan's gross fixed investment rates, coupled with a forecasted acceleration of private consumption growth, is projected to support growth in 2003. With higher domestic demand, import volume growth is forecast to accelerate on aggregate for the region in 2003, leading to a narrowing of the current account surplus.

Medium-term prospects

South Asian growth is expected to maintain an average of close to 5.4 percent over the medium term, assuming normal weather conditions—leading to recovery and acceleration of agricultural output—and a continued recovery in external demand. Declining oil prices, both in nominal and real terms, should reduce pressures on current account balances for the region, which is overwhelmingly a net energy importer. India should benefit from a recovery in domestic demand (particularly in the manufacturing sector) and firming export volume growth. Bangladesh is expected to witness strengthening domestic demand and recovering exports, and on the supply side, a strong performance of SMEs and export-oriented manufacturing units (provided proposed structural reforms are carried out). Both Pak-

Table A1.2 South Asia forecast summary

Growth rates/ratios (percent)	1991–2000	2001	2002	2003	2004	2005	2006–15
Real GDP growth	5.2	4.9	4.2	5.4	5.4	5.4	5.4
Consumption per capita	2.0	3.5	1.5	2.9	3.3	3.5	3.3
GDP per capita	3.3	3.1	2.5	3.7	3.7	3.8	4.1
population	1.9	1.7	1.7	1.6	1.6	1.5	1.3
Gross Domestic Investment/GDP[a]	21.3	22.0	22.8	22.7	22.5	22.3	25.0
Inflation[b]	7.8	3.0	1.8	5.1	5.8	4.7	
General gvt. budget balance/GDP	−10.5	−8.3	−9.8	−9.7	−9.3	−8.5	
Export Market Growth[c]	7.7	0.2	2.9	6.0	7.5	7.3	
Export volume[d]	11.5	9.1	3.5	5.9	7.4	8.0	
Terms of trade/GDP[e]	−0.1	0.0	0.5	0.7	0.4	0.1	
Current account/GDP	−1.5	−0.5	0.5	0.4	0.2	−0.1	
Memorandum items							
GDP growth: South Asia excluding India	4.4	3.2	3.6	4.8	5.3	5.6	5.2

a. Fixed investment, measured in real terms.
b. Local currency GDP deflator, median.
c. Weighted average growth of import demand in export markets.
d. Goods and non-factor services.
e. Change in terms of trade, measured as a proportion of GDP (percentage).
Source: World Bank baseline forecast July 2003.

istan and Sri Lanka are projected to benefit from continued macroeconomic stability and an associated acceleration of growth. The peace process is expected to yield significant economic gains in Sri Lanka. Similarly, Nepal is likely to experience strengthening growth, assuming continued improvement in the security situation there, with a recovery in domestic demand, exports, and in tourism receipts. Further, recent steps toward improving relations between India and Pakistan may lead to greater stability in the sub-region, paving the way for increased business confidence and stability. Throughout the region, growth should be underpinned by continued firm expansion in services and industrial production.

Recovery in external demand and a gradual return to lower oil prices is likely to be more than offset by generally firming import demand, which is expected to lead to a moderate decrease in the region's aggregate current account surplus to an average balance near zero as a share of GDP over the medium term (2004–05). At the individual country level, India and Pakistan's projected current account surpluses are expected to roughly balance the projected deficits in Bangladesh, Nepal, and Sri Lanka.

The fiscal positions of the South Asian economies are forecast to improve moderately, assuming some progress in raising budget revenues and in the management of government expenditures. Inflation is projected to increase somewhat, albeit still at generally moderate levels, because of the assumed pick-up in growth and assumptions of a more accommodative monetary stance in a number of countries, though falling oil prices are expected to partially offset these factors.

Long-term outlook

Long-term growth in South Asia is forecast to average about 5.4 percent, in line with the GEP 2003 growth forecast. This forecast is somewhat higher than the 5.2 percent average real growth posted during the 1990s. The higher projected growth over the coming decade through 2015 reflects a number of underlying assumptions, not least of which is a larger contribution to growth by the private sector. This in turn reflects the expectation of progress with fiscal consolidation and continued structural reforms, including reforms in trade, banking, privatization, and infrastructure. These factors, combined with the improvement in human capital indicators in recent years—such as rising literacy rates and school enrollments and declining infant mortality rates—will lead to an increase in productivity. Despite a projection of declining infant mortality rates, overall the South Asian population growth rate is projected to decelerate as birth rates are expected to decline at faster rates. Lower population growth in the coming decade, along with the forecast growth rates, implies that per capita GDP growth will be close to 4.0 percent per year.

Risks

There are a number of risks to the forecast. Persistent fiscal deficits continue to be a risk in a number of the region's economies, India in particular, as they can undermine fiscal sustainability, contribute to a growing debt-to-GDP ratio, and lead to higher interest rates, thereby crowding out private investment and diverging public outlays from investment to interest payments and limiting the scope for both fiscal and monetary policies. Fiscal consolidation is required, which would not only mitigate such vulnerabilities, but also provide for broader scope of action in macroeconomic policies to pursue sustained higher growth. The forthcoming phase-out of the Multi-Fibre Arrangement (MFA) in 2005 will imply greater competition for the region's textile exporters. While India and Pakistan appear to be gearing up for the impending increase in competition, the impact of the MFA phase-out on other South Asian regional economies is more uncertain, particularly in Bangladesh, Nepal, and Sri Lanka (where garment exports represent about 75 percent, 25 percent, and just over 50 percent of total merchandise exports, respectively). Given the importance of the agricultural sector to the region, the threat of severe weather conditions and associated poor harvests remain a significant risk to growth outcomes. Political risks and uncertainties also remain a concern, because of both internal and external factors. Heightened domestic and regional instability could undermine growth prospects and slow the pace of economic reforms. Remittances could be affected by increased instability in the Middle East. And significantly higher-than-forecast energy prices would pose an additional burden on current account positions.

Latin America and the Caribbean

Recent developments

The Latin American region has begun to recover from last year's recession. The upturn this year reflects the tentative recovery in Argentina and Uruguay as well as calming of pre-election jitters in Brazil at the end of 2002. As a result, regional growth in 2003 is projected to reach 1.8 percent, compared to last year's contraction of 0.8 percent. Although the region is on a favorable recovery path, its growth rate remains well below potential and below that of other regions. In addition to Argentina and Uruguay, Chile, Mexico, Colombia, and Brazil, countries with generally stronger policy frameworks, registered a somewhat improved growth performance.

The fact that the 2002 recession was relatively short reflects both domestic structural policy, renewed confidence, and external factors. Domestic macropolicies have improved significantly: the region managed to reduce inflation to single-digit figures (for 2003–Q1, the regional inflation rate was 8.3 percent), proving that the commitment of central banks to low inflation is, although not universal, quite widespread across the region. Similarly, balanced fiscal policies have been applied and the expected 2003 regional public deficit should be about 2 percent of GDP. For example, the new president of Brazil has reiterated the country's commitment to balanced macropolicies, and this has rapidly thwarted negative expectations for the future.

A second domestic factor explaining the region's enhanced resilience to crisis is found in the substitution of inward-oriented development policies (through the maintenance of high trade barriers and other perverse price incentives) by more liberal trade and market-friendly policies. This shift has helped the economies to diversify and has broadened the regional export base while diminishing its dependency on a narrow set of commodity prices. As shown in figure A1.3a, during the 1970s, exports of agricultural products, oil and other natural resources for the region as a whole, accounted for about one-quarter and one-fifth, respectively, of total exports; two decades later, both sectors accounted for about one-tenth of total exports, and manufacturing has become an important source of foreign exchange.

Additional important elements contributing to the success of this outward-oriented development strategy have been the NAFTA agreement—that directly benefited Mexico, but generated spillovers to other countries—and increased intraregional integration. Indeed, the revamping of *Mercosur* and other sub-regional integration arrangements are being discussed in Latin America, together with the plans for a hemispheric free-trade area. Chile and Mexico suffered least from the 2001–2 economic downturn, thanks to their effective integration in the global economy and good macroeconomic policies. Chile recently signed an FTA with the United States that is anticipated to be ratified by the two governments by end-2003, and become operational in 2004: the FTA grants free access to 87 percent of Chilean exports to U.S. markets.

A final factor is the achievement of healthier current account positions. The Latin American region has witnessed a drop of more than 3.5 points in the ratio of the current account balance to GDP (from −4.4 percent in 1998 to −0.8 percent in 2002) resulting from a reduction of the region's borrowing needs and the

REGIONAL ECONOMIC PROSPECTS

Figure A1.3a Sectoral export shares (selected countries)

Agriculture

Shares in percent of total exports

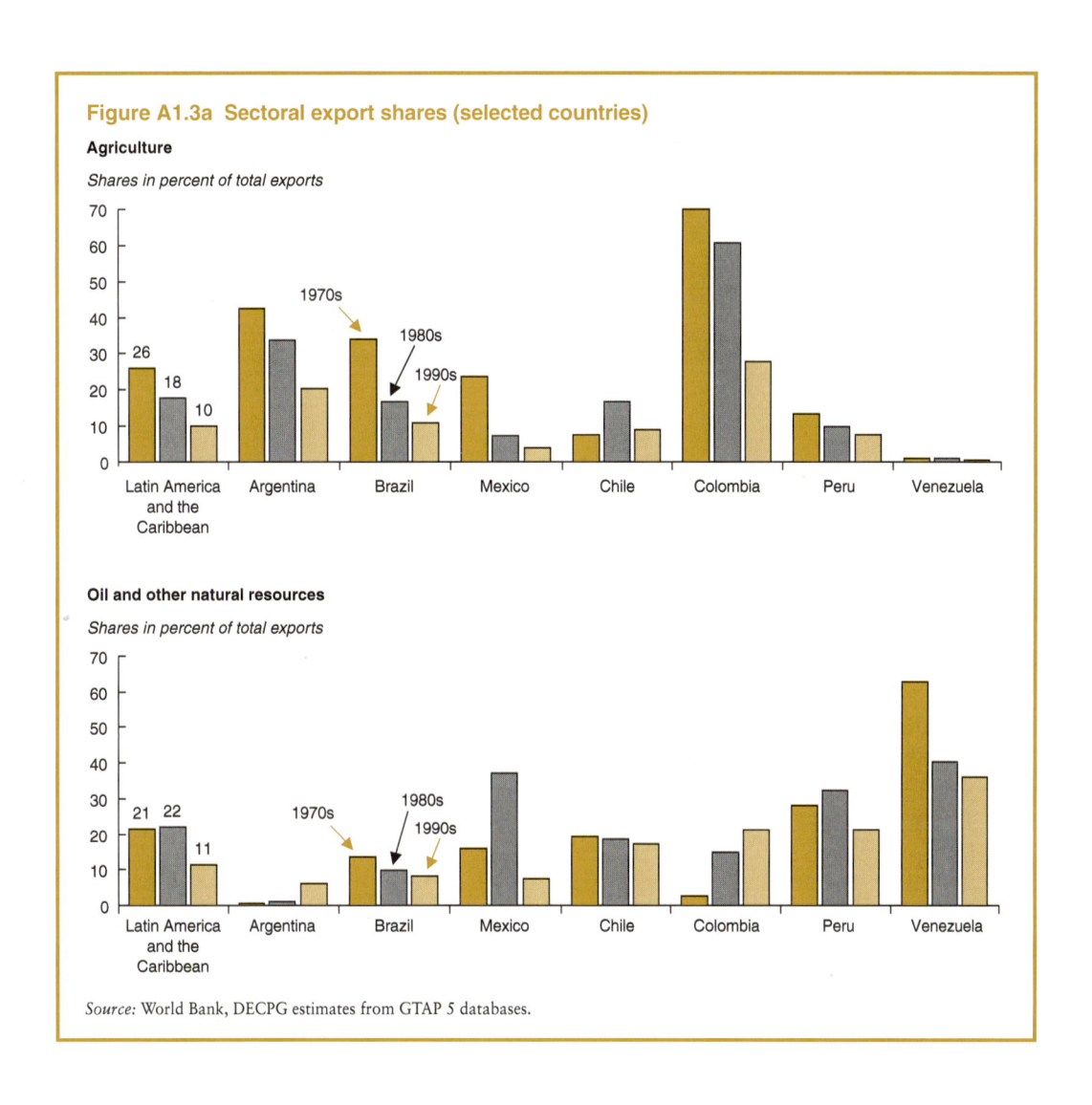

reluctance of global investors to enter emerging markets. The adoption of more flexible exchange rate regimes is probably an important structural change. Anticipated increases in GDP growth are not expected to directly translate into large unsustainable current account deficits.

Despite the sluggish global economy, some specific improvements in the external environment are also contributing to recovery in the region. A weaker U.S. dollar is the first of these improvements: servicing the region's dollar-denominated external debt becomes less onerous, net oil importers suffer less from oil price surges, and usually non-oil commodity prices surge with a falling dollar. Moreover, the weakening of the dollar against the euro should help manufacturing exporters with currencies following the dollar by raising the competitiveness of their goods in the euro zone and enabling their share of exports to the EU to rise.

The recent dramatic reduction of spreads on yields of foreign sovereign debt for the region is another favorable global financial development. The reduction in spreads—highlighted in figure A1.3b (in Brazil spreads narrowed from

241

Figure A1.3b Latin American yield spreads

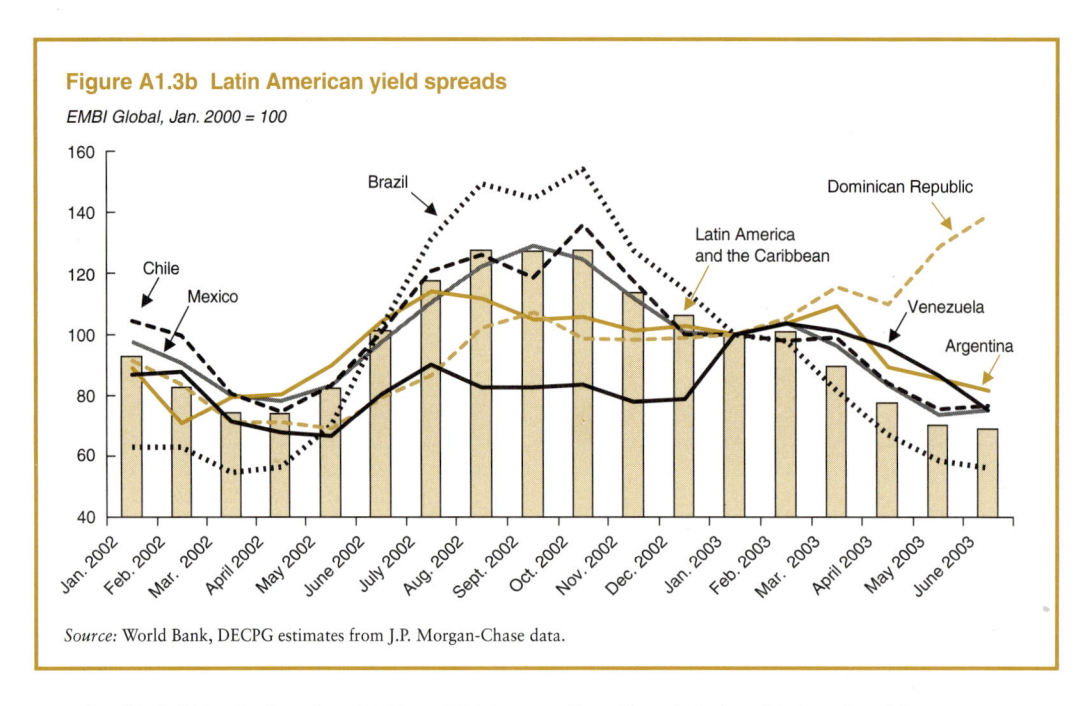

EMBI Global, Jan. 2000 = 100

Source: World Bank, DECPG estimates from J.P. Morgan-Chase data.

a peak of 2,067 bp in October 2002 to 754 bp in April 2003, Mexican spreads have reached an all-time low, those of Peru and Colombia are at their lowest levels since 1998 and 2000, respectively)—has not yet been accompanied by large capital inflows. For Latin America, average monthly flows during the first half of 2003 registered $5.3 billion, modestly above the $4.3 billion average of the same period in 2002. In fact the bond price rally may be tied to an excess of global investors' demand for higher yield instruments over the supply of new issues by borrowers. However, it should be mentioned that Mexico has been quite active in international capital markets and that even Brazil has already been able to place issues twice this year.

Near-term outlook

Improving world trade growth coupled with increased OECD economic growth led by the United States should further boost the export-led recovery of Latin America in 2004–05. Also, by 2004, the region's largest economies will have surpassed the worst of their crises (Argentina and Uruguay) or potential for crises (Brazil and Colombia) and, with some exceptions, all countries should experience a recovery of domestic demand and record positive rates of growth. The regional average growth rate should climb to 3.7 percent in 2004 and to 3.8 percent in 2005. Even if current account deficits increase in most of the expanding economies of the region, low world interest rates, lower perceived risks for Latin American assets (bonds, equities, or direct investments), the continuation of fiscal prudence in the region, and flexible exchange rates should maintain a cap on these incipient deficits. Even though the 2003 –0.5 percent ratio of current account deficit to GDP for the region is unlikely to be maintained, external deficit ratios are not foreseen anywhere near the 1995–99 average of more than 3 percent, but rather a modest –0.7 percent for 2004 and –1 percent for 2005.

Clearly some uncertainty remains, given that these projections assume that no (domestic or external) adverse development reverses the easing of financial pressure on the region's most vulnerable countries. High levels of debt still burden fiscal authorities and tight monetary policies required to keep inflation under control may limit expansion. This is especially true for Brazil; however, thanks to its enhanced credibility, the central bank in this country may be able to ease its stance in the near future.

Furthermore, some country risks persist. Several challenges await Argentina: a) restructuring the banking system to reactivate credit (which is still contracting); b) replacing inefficient taxes, including on export and savings, with new efficient taxes; c) building a solid regulatory and institutional framework to protect property rights and deal with other governance issues; d) renegotiating public utilities tariffs that have been held well below the rate of inflation; and e) eventual restructuring of the defaulted debt. The Republica Bolivariana de Venezuela started to export oil again, but its political crisis is not over and macroeconomic instability, price controls, and other distortions need to be addressed. Recently, the government endorsed an Economic Stability agreement that pledges to make every effort to improve its external accounts by reestablishing the level of oil income and implementing the necessary adjustments to the currency control regime; however, previous similar attempts have failed.

The Caribbean countries, and this also applies to some small Central American countries, are still facing the difficult transition from being tropical agriculture export-oriented economies to becoming more diversified. Their preferential trade agreements are expiring or are severely eroded, and their successful attempts at diversifying toward tourism and financial services received a severe set-back in 2002 from which they have not yet recovered.

Long-term prospects
In the longer term, Latin American countries could achieve higher growth rates if they overcome several critical structural constraints (table A1.3). On the external front, a number of countries rely heavily on the United States as a source of imports, as a destination for exports, and as a source of external finance. As shown in figure A1.3c, the United States has become the region's major export market destination, increasing from 36 percent of total exports in the 1970s to almost 50 percent in the 1990s.

Given the lackluster growth forecasts for the Euro zone, a stronger link to the United States may be considered positive; however, geographical diversification may reduce risks. In particular, European markets have lost importance for Latin American exporters and this may be corrected by pushing for more bilateral agreements and a more comprehensive lift of European restrictions to market access.

The rising share of intraregional trade is a positive sign and may help Latin American countries negotiate trade and other integration agreements as a block, vis-à-vis OECD countries. In fact, trade integration should be a priority among the long-term development policies—Latin America, compared to East Asia, shows much lower trade-to-GDP ratios—and deeper trade integration agreements bring additional benefits in terms of increased foreign investment and also boost credibility to sound macro policies.

On the internal front, some of the major impediments of the past, such as large fiscal imbalances and perverse price incentives, have been removed (though not consistently in all countries). However, smaller fiscal deficits have been obtained mainly through expenditure restraints, with potential long-term issues on infrastructure development and poverty eradication, and most countries still have relatively (with respect to more developed countries) low tax revenues to GDP ratios. Low tax revenues result from a strong reduction of international trade duties (in itself a positive development), inefficient collection, evasion, and other governance issues. Low revenues have been compensated by recurring to unstable non-tax revenues (oil royalties or other natural resources form of taxation, privatiza-

GLOBAL ECONOMIC PROSPECTS

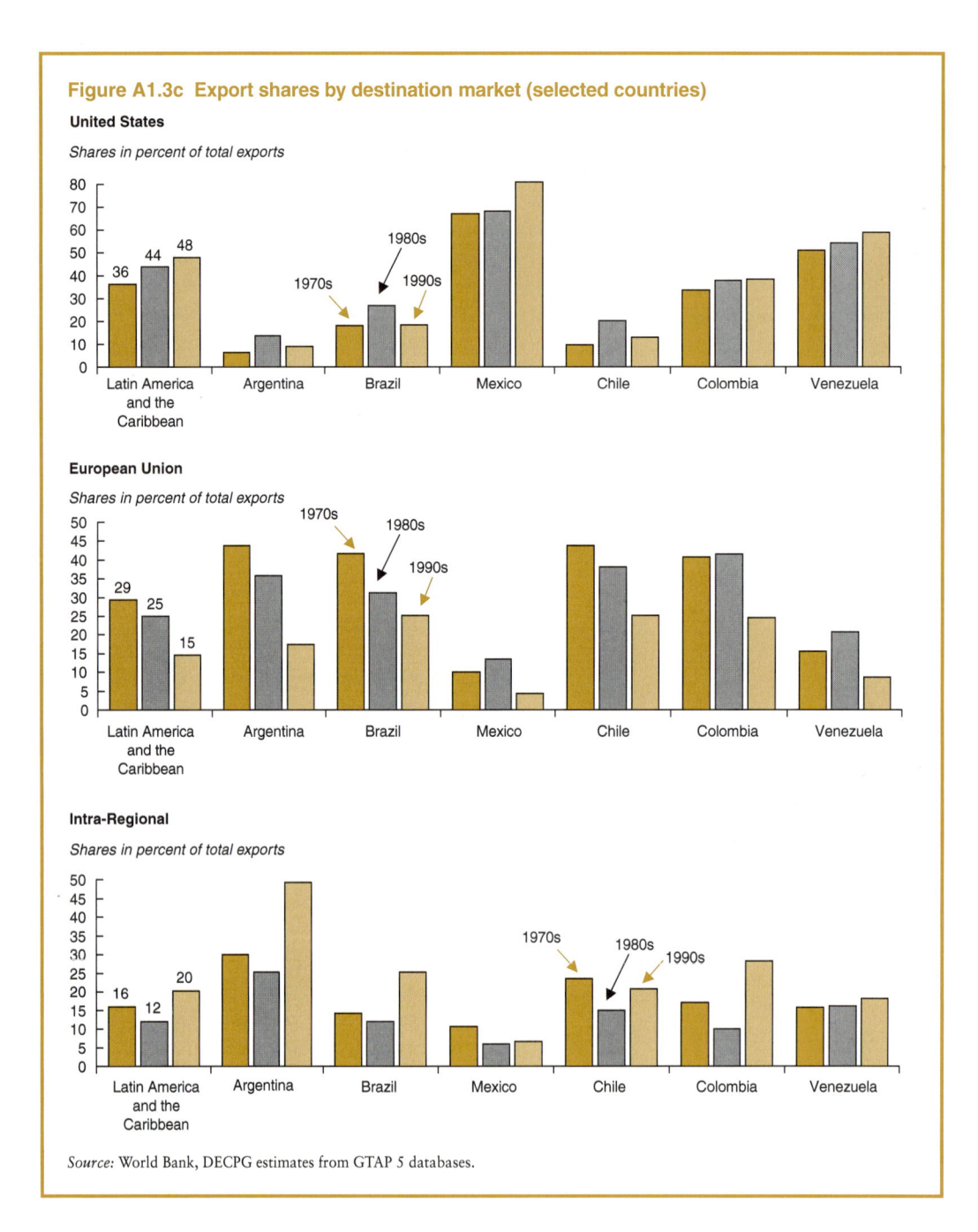

Figure A1.3c Export shares by destination market (selected countries)

United States
Shares in percent of total exports

European Union
Shares in percent of total exports

Intra-Regional
Shares in percent of total exports

Source: World Bank, DECPG estimates from GTAP 5 databases.

tion), generating a situation of inadequate and volatile government income.

In the long term, beyond macroeconomic stability and commitment to sound fiscal and monetary policies, LAC countries will have to tackle governance issues, attempt to correct a skewed income distribution, and develop mature financial markets necessary to generate enough resources to become less dependent on foreign finance, allowing important investments in physical infrastructure and human capital to be financed domestically.

Table A1.3 Latin America and the Caribbean forecast summary

Growth rates/ratios (percent)	1991–2000	2001	2002	2003	2004	2005	2006–15
Real GDP growth	3.4	0.3	–0.8	1.8	3.7	3.8	3.8
Consumption per capita	2.4	–0.9	–3.5	–0.1	1.8	1.9	2.3
GDP per capita	1.7	–1.2	–2.3	0.4	2.3	2.5	2.5
population	1.7	1.6	1.5	1.4	1.4	1.3	1.2
Gross Domestic Investment[a]	19.8	19.1	18.0	17.6	18.4	18.4	22.6
Inflation[b]	12.0	5.5	4.7	4.1	4.0	4.0	
General gvt. budget balance/GDP	–3.0	–1.8	–2.9	–2.0	–1.0	–0.6	
Export Market Growth[c]	9.4	–1.2	0.5	5.0	8.6	7.2	
Export volume[d]	8.7	1.0	2.2	9.2	11.2	10.2	
Terms of trade/GDP[e]	1.7	–0.2	0.1	–0.4	0.1	–0.7	
Current account/GDP	–2.7	–2.7	–0.8	–0.5	–0.7	–1.0	
Memorandum items							
GDP growth: LAC excluding							
Argentina	3.2	1.2	1.0	1.5	3.6	3.9	
Central America	4.4	1.5	1.9	2.4	3.1	3.8	
Caribbean	4.0	3.1	3.0	0.9	2.4	4.1	

a. Fixed investment, measured in real terms.
b. Local currency GDP deflator, median.
c. Weighted average growth of import demand in export markets.
d. Goods and non-factor services.
e. Change in terms of trade, measured as a proportion of GDP (percentage).
Source: World Bank baseline forecast July 2003.

Eastern Europe and Central Asia

Recent developments

GDP IS NOW estimated to have expanded by 4.6 percent in 2002 for ECA, an upward revision from the 4.1 percent projected in the last forecast presented in *Global Development Finance 2003* (World Bank 2003). Growth prospects proved to be more resilient than previously anticipated, primarily because of the strength of domestic demand, which was more than able to offset lackluster growth in the region's main export markets. The firming of ECA regional economic growth in 2002—over the 2.2 percent growth posted in 2001—was driven by the huge 15 percentage point swing in Turkey's performance (from a contraction of 7.4 percent in 2001, following the financial crisis, to an upswing of 7.8 percent in 2002). The ECA average growth excluding Turkey registered a slowing to 3.9 percent in 2002, contrasted with 4.5 percent in 2001. This latter trend largely reflected the aggregate slowdown in the CIS region.

Growth in the Central and Eastern European Countries (CEECs), excluding Turkey, was unchanged in 2002 relative to 2001 at 2.9 percent. Including Turkey, GDP growth averaged 4.5 percent for the group, swinging up sharply from a 0.8 percent contraction posted in 2001. Regional growth was underpinned by expanding domestic demand, often spurred by fiscal policy (Hungary, Czech Republic, Poland, Slovenia, Slovakia) and/or easing monetary policies (Czech Republic, Latvia, Lithuania, Romania). Furthermore, despite tepid external demand, export growth remained firm in many of the CEECs.

In the Commonwealth of Independent States (CIS), GDP growth continued to slow to an average of 4.7 percent in 2002, down from 5.8 percent in 2001, and following the spike in CIS average growth of 8.4 percent posted in 2000. The slowdown largely reflects a deceleration of growth in Russia, as the effects of the devaluation of the 1998 crisis and the rents from high energy prices eroded. Diminished import demand from Russia—representing an important export market for the remaining CIS countries—contributed to the easing of growth in the rest of the region. In addition, growth decelerated in Turkmenistan, because of a poor cotton harvest and slower growth of natural gas exports (the result of pipeline constraints), and suffered a decline in Kyrgyz Republic, tied to an accident at its largest gold mine and a temporary decline in exports. The South Caucasus countries (Armenia, Azerbaijan, and Georgia) and Belarus, however, experienced an acceleration of growth.

Near-term outlook

ECA aggregate growth is forecast to slow moderately to 4.3 percent in 2003. This projected growth rate for 2003 is higher than anticipated in GDF 2003, and reflects stronger than expected growth in a number of countries, particularly in Russia, which has exhibited firming domestic demand during the first quarter of 2003 (figure A1.4). The deceleration of ECA aggregate growth between 2002 and 2003 is primarily because of a projected moderation of growth in Turkey following the sharp upswing in 2002.

Growth in Turkey is projected to decelerate largely because of base effects following the strong recovery in 2002. Other factors affecting Turkey's near-term outlook include the continued required fiscal consolidation, the expected slowdown in inventory building, weaker tourism revenues because of the Iraq conflict, and limited foreign investment. The current account deficit has been rising rapidly, driven by rising imports, the recovery in domestic demand, and higher oil prices. Export growth has remained relatively robust despite the recent real appreciation of the lira and weak external demand. As of end-April, the Turkish government appeared on track for the Fund's program, but the pace of reforms will need to accelerate to sustain growth.

In the CEECs, excluding Turkey, growth in 2003 is projected to accelerate moderately (by 0.5 percentage points) because of continued penetration in new export markets and an expected boost to consumer confidence because of progress in the EU accession process.[1] In particular, growth is projected to accelerate moderately in Albania, the Czech Republic, Poland (which represents 13 percent of the region's GDP), and Slovenia. Growth in the remaining economies is forecast to either remain flat or decelerate moderately.

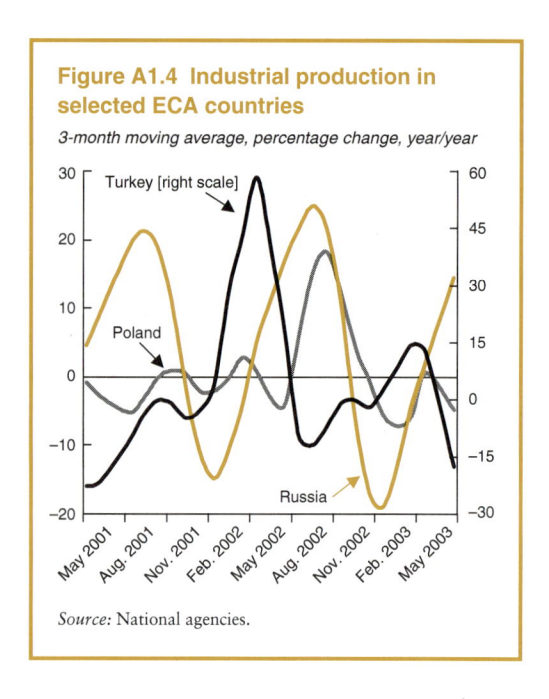

Figure A1.4 Industrial production in selected ECA countries
3-month moving average, percentage change, year/year

Source: National agencies.

In the CIS, growth is projected to strengthen in 2003, as domestic demand has begun to accelerate in Russia, underpinning growth there, which in turn should support growth in other CIS countries dependent on Russia's import demand. First-quarter data for 2003 show strong growth in energy exports and industrial activity in Russia, spurring stronger investment, especially in the energy sector. This, coupled with an increase in private consumption—boosted by strong growth in real incomes and falling unemployment—is leading to higher output. Further, the recent appreciation of the euro against the dollar has led to increased import prices for Russian imports from Europe, relative to US dollar-denominated oil export revenues, which in turn is stimulating increased demand for cheaper domestic products. While oil prices have declined in recent months, they are still high relative to the average over the last few years and are projected to average $26.5/bbl in 2003 (given the spike during the first quarter), up from $24.9/bbl in 2002 (and well above the $21/bbl reference price used for the Russian budget). The southern-tier energy exporters of Kazakhstan and Azerbaijan are expected to continue to post high growth rates, driven by the ongoing oil sector investment boom, and supported by strong FDI inflows. Manufacturing and services related to investment in the oil sector are expected to continue to expand as well. GDP growth in most other CIS economies is anticipated to either remain flat or decelerate in 2003, with the exceptions of Georgia, where a rise in investment is projected, linked to the construction of oil and gas transit pipelines, and the Kyrgyz Republic, which is anticipated to benefit from a revival in its gold production.

Medium-term prospects

ECA regional growth is expected to first accelerate to 4.5 percent in 2004, and then to decelerate to 4.1 percent in 2005, reflecting divergent trends at the sub-regional levels: accelerating growth in the CEECs and slowing activity in the CIS.

Growth in the CEECs (including Turkey) is projected to accelerate from 3.5 percent in 2003 to 4.3 and 4.7 percent in 2004 and 2005, respectively, in part because of a gradual buildup in external demand. The first round of new EU members, in particular, is expected to continue to receive significant inflows of FDI (in addition to EU transfers)—which will remain an important source of external finance and support for long-term growth. Sustained growth in Turkey assumes the country will remain committed to the Fund's program, and that structural reforms will contribute to a correction in internal and external balances. These factors, along with the assumption of declining interest rates, are expected to help spur domestic demand in Turkey.

Growth is expected to slow in the CIS from 5.3 percent in 2003 to 4.6 and 3.4 percent in 2004 and 2005, respectively, assuming significant decline in oil price in both 2004 and 2005—from $26.5/bbl in 2003 to $22/bbl and $20/bbl in 2004 and 2005, respectively—and a corresponding decline in the growth impetus through fiscal linkages.

Long-term prospects

Higher investment rates and ongoing restructuring of the capital base are expected to contribute to stronger growth in the CEE countries during the second decade of transition than posted during the previous decade. Further, continued improvements in the policy environment, including greater macroeconomic stability, are expected to underpin the projected higher growth rates. The EU accession process and coming membership will continue to act as an anchor for structural reforms and will help attract significant inflows of FDI. While structural reforms are being pursued in many CIS countries, in general, implementation is not as advanced or as widespread as in the CEE sub-region's economies, and in some cases there is significant resistance to structural reforms. This implies lower long-run growth in comparison. The recent boom in hydrocarbon rents has provided an impetus to growth, facilitating the introduction of a number of reforms to oil-exporting countries, and contributing to an increase in investment outlays (particularly in the energy sector). However, given the volatility of energy market prices, these economies will not be able to sustain recently achieved higher growth rates until diversification from energy becomes more broadly based. Given the degree of energy dependence in many of the CIS economies, particularly Russia, the projected softening of oil prices—to an average nominal price of about $19 per barrel for the 2005–10 period, in the underlying forecast—implies a ratcheting down of the sub-region's growth from recent high rates.

Risks

There are three main risks to the forecast:

- *Global trade and growth prospects:* More sluggish than anticipated world growth prospects, and/or a delayed re-

Table A1.4 Europe and Central Asia forecast summary

Growth rates/ratios (percent)	1991–2000	2001	2002	2003	2004	2005	2006–15
Real GDP growth	−1.6	2.2	4.6	4.3	4.5	4.1	3.4
Consumption per capita	0.0	3.2	5.4	5.1	4.8	4.5	3.1
GDP per capita	−1.8	2.0	4.5	4.3	4.4	4.0	3.3
Population	0.2	0.1	0.1	0.1	0.1	0.1	0.1
Gross Domestic Investment/GDP[a]	24.6	21.7	20.8	21.1	21.5	22.0	28.8
Inflation[b]	76.0	6.1	4.0	5.8	6.5	2.7	
General gvt. budget balance/GDP	−4.0	−8.4	−9.3	−8.4	−7.1	−6.2	
Export Market Growth[c]	6.6	4.6	2.4	8.2	7.2	7.4	
Export volume[d]	10.0	5.5	6.7	8.1	8.5	8.4	
Terms of trade/GDP[e]	0.8	0.9	−1.6	1.7	0.0	−0.3	
Current account/GDP	−2.5	−1.4	1.1	0.6	0.1	−0.5	
Memorandum items							
GDP growth: transition countries[f]	−2.5	4.5	3.9	4.5	4.4	3.8	
Central and Eastern Europe[f]	0.6	2.9	2.9	3.4	4.2	4.4	
CIS	−4.4	5.8	4.7	5.3	4.6	3.4	

a. Fixed investment, measured in real terms.
b. Local currency GDP deflator, median.
c. Weighted average growth of import demand in export markets.
d. Goods and non-factor services.
e. Change in terms of trade, measured as a proportion of GDP (percentage).
f. Excluding Turkey.
Source: World Bank baseline forecast July 2003.

covery, especially in the EU, could undermine or reduce the export led component of growth, especially for the CEECs;
- *Domestic policies and investor confidence*: Delays in fiscal consolidation in countries with large budget deficits (Turkey, Hungary, Poland, Czech Republic), which would risk diminished use of automatic stabilizers; skewed fiscal and monetary policies (as witnessed in Poland, for example); crowding out of private investment; and a slowdown of structural reforms. In Turkey, failure to achieve substantial decline in real interest rates would result in significantly lower growth outturns. For the EU accession candidate countries with large fiscal deficits, overall fiscal consolidation as well as public expenditure restructuring will be necessary to join the European exchange rate mechanism and to absorb EU transfers, which require national co-financing; the growth outlook will also partly depend on a recovery in external demand, which could cushion the adjustment process. Countries with large twin fiscal and external deficits (Turkey, Croatia, etc.) could undermine confidence of foreign investors and result in difficulties in maintaining access to financing;
- *Energy prices:* A sharper decline in oil price (induced, for example, by low world growth outcomes), could translate into a marked deceleration in growth for both CIS energy exporters and countries dependent on Russia's consumer markets. For the ECA region's energy exporters, effective management of large government oil revenues and continued structural reforms are required to pave the way for sustained long-term growth, economic diversification, and employment creation. Medium- and long-term prospects depend largely on rapid diversification of the production base and exports.

Sub-Saharan Africa

Recent developments

A SUBDUED EXTERNAL environment, together with poor weather and homegrown problems of governance and civil strife, held real growth in Sub-Saharan

REGIONAL ECONOMIC PROSPECTS

Africa (SSA) to 2.8 percent in 2002, down from 3.2 percent in 2001. Faced with Europe's faltering economy and rising geopolitical uncertainty, real export growth slumped to just 0.7 percent, the worst outcome in a decade, while net exports contributed –0.8 percent to GDP growth. Meanwhile, domestic absorption was flat at 3.6 percent. Notably, investment spending was relatively resilient, especially in South Africa and a number of oil exporters. Early indications from the first half of 2003 are that performance will be similar in the current year and growth in SSA is expected to remain at 2.8–3 percent.

In domestic economies, adverse weather compounded by civil strife has seriously disrupted food production for more than half the region's population, and as many as 40 million persons are facing acute hunger.[2] Drought has been particularly severe in the horn of Africa, comprising Ethiopia and Eritrea and parts of the Sudan, leaving over 15 million urgently in need of food aid. But disruptions have occurred in numerous other countries as well because of weather or civil strife, including Angola, Burundi, Democratic Republic of Congo, the Gambia, Malawi, Mauritania, Senegal, and Zimbabwe. Apart from the humanitarian crises, with agriculture representing nearly one-fifth of GDP—over one-quarter excluding South Africa—the macroeconomic impact is to reduce household incomes and expenditure. On average, consumption grew by just 2.4 percent in 2002 (0.1 percent per capita), down from 3.1 percent in 2001.

For the region as a whole, the terms of trade strengthened in 2002, thanks both to gains in export prices and a decline in the cost of manufactured imports. Oil prices were up 2.4 percent over 2001 which, with net energy exports accounting for some 8 percent of GDP, contributed 0.2 percent to incomes. Non-energy commodities are also enjoying a significant rebound, albeit from very low levels after the dizzying declines of the late 1990s. This rebound is primarily the result of supply constraints rather than growth in demand. Compared to low points reached since 2000, the price of gold in 2002 was up 14 percent, copper up 13 percent, cotton up 24 percent, and cocoa up a sharp 107 percent. Year over year, agricultural export prices gained an average of 20.5 percent and though metals and minerals declined a further 2.3 percent, the export-weighted average price of non-energy commodities for the region was up 13.5 percent, while non-oil exporters' terms of trade strengthened by 4.2 percent. Moreover, higher frequency data on metals indicate signs of recent strength as well. No sustained upward trend is anticipated given highly competitive new suppliers coming on stream, but at least key export markets appear to be stabilizing around present levels (figure A1.5a).

Tourism has been affected not only by weak income growth in the OECD, especially Europe, but also by security concerns arising from the September 2001 terrorist attacks and the run-up to the Iraq war. If the rest of the world needed a reminder that travel to the region is risky, it came in the form of a terrorist attack in Kenya in November 2002 that left fifteen dead, including three Israeli tourists. Barring further negative shocks, the low point for tourism was likely reached at the time of the Iraq war when travel to SSA was down by nearly one-quarter compared to the year before. Nevertheless, that virtually guarantees a

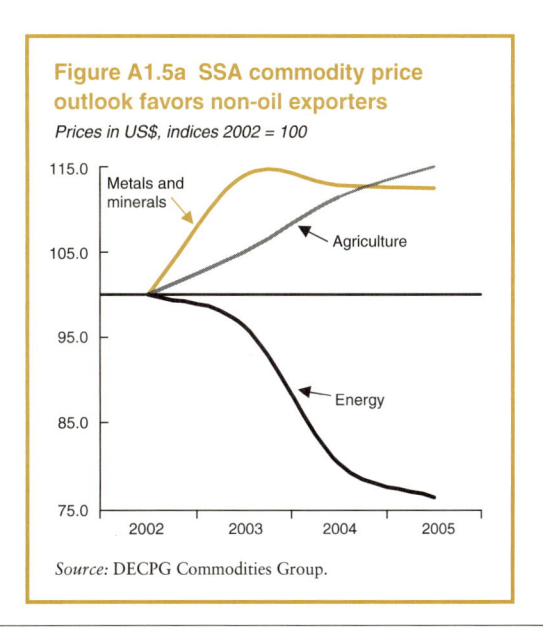

Figure A1.5a SSA commodity price outlook favors non-oil exporters
Prices in US$, indices 2002 = 100

Source: DECPG Commodities Group.

249

mediocre year at best and the World Travel and Tourism Council (WTTC) forecasts a slight decline of 0.2 percent in GDP and employment in the tourism sector in 2003. At the same time, however, South Africa was the world's fastest growing tourist destination in 2002, with 20 percent growth in arrivals over the year before, and the momentum continued into 2003, though the pace is likely to slow with the stronger rand. Thus, superimposed on the overall pattern of growth has been a southward shift in the industry's center of gravity. Whether this will be reversed remains to be seen.

In spite of the overall disappointing results, there were some positive developments. Average per capita income rose for a fourth successive year in 2002, which is the longest sustained increase in over two decades. Moreover, the slowdown was largely attributable to a small group of poor performers. In Nigeria, a lower OPEC quota and budget gridlock offset much of the potential gain from higher oil prices, Ethiopia and Eritrea suffered through another year of increasingly savage drought, and deepening political crises paralyzed Côte d'Ivoire and Zimbabwe. For this group of countries—representing around one-third of the region's population and GDP—growth fell by two-thirds, from 1.7 percent to 0.6 percent in the year. This same group also contributed to most of the retrenchment in exports. By contrast, elsewhere in the region, GDP growth slowed only marginally. As usual, politics played an overarching role and countries in conflict or experiencing civil disruption were at the bottom of the league. Even here there is a glimmer of hope, though, in the growing institutional strength of initiatives such as the African Union, NEPAD, and the East African Community.

Also encouraging is further evidence of Africa's potential competitiveness, given the right incentives and opportunities. An impressive recent example is the growth of nontraditional exports under the U.S. African Growth and Opportunity Act (AGOA), which extends preferential access to imports from a growing list of eligible countries. So far, there have been relatively few beneficiaries—Nigeria, South Africa, Gabon, Lesotho, and Kenya account for nearly 93 percent of U.S. imports under AGOA preferences—and three-quarters of the total consists of oil. But non-oil exports grew rapidly in 2002. Despite a slump in the U.S. economy that led to an overall decline of nearly 16 percent in AGOA exports, nontraditional exports were sharply higher—textiles and apparel more than doubled from 2001, while transportation equipment and agricultural products were up 80 percent and 38 percent respectively.[3]

In South Africa, the sharp fall of the rand beginning in 2000 provided a strong stimulus to growth, but much of that was reversed through 2002 and into 2003 as the currency bounced back because of tight money and the unwinding of the Reserve Bank's net open forward position which had unnerved investors. Growth in 2002 was a still-robust 3.0 percent, though the contribution to growth from trade declined to negative territory, while domestic demand soared by 4.1 percent. Though the domestic economy slowed in the first quarter of 2003, growth remained relatively strong at 3.5 percent (saar), particularly investment, which was up an impressive 8 percent. Given the momentum evident in the first quarter, domestic demand should remain relatively strong, though with the rand remaining firm, net exports will be a drag on growth and GDP is expected to grow only around 2.8 percent. Especially worthy of note is an auspicious turnaround in the labor market in 2002, with formal sector payrolls increasing after seven straight years of decline, even though the increase of 70,000 jobs is small compared to the official estimate of 4.8 million unemployed.

In Nigeria, slower growth in 2002 reflected OPEC production constraints and the impact of budget gridlock that limited spillovers from oil production to the rest of the economy in spite of strong prices. Hydrocarbons constitute almost all Nigerian exports, but gas is taking an increasing share, and in 2002 a one-third increase in liquid natural gas (LNG) production partially offset a 6 percent fall in oil. Production in the first quarter of 2003 was up around 5 percent from 2002, somewhat below the average increase for OPEC as a whole.[4] Nigeria would like an increase in its quota from the current level of 2.1mb/d that is well below capacity. But a significant rise in the near term is unlikely, as slow growth in the industrial economies will constrain the global sector. Nevertheless, higher production in 2003 in addition to further growth in LNG and continuing price strength, will underpin a stronger performance this year. The most encouraging recent news from Nigeria concerned the presidential election which has strengthened the fragile political process. But, equally important, meaningful progress on economic reform has been frustratingly slow. On balance, growth this year and in the medium term is likely to be only moderate.

Near-term outlook

Though the forecast calls for world economic growth to accelerate in the second half of 2003, the pace of recovery is expected to remain sluggish, especially in Europe where the economy stalled in the first quarter and the risk of outright recession has risen. Even with a pickup in momentum going into the second half, the EU is expected to grow by only 0.9 percent in 2003 and 1.9 percent in 2004. SSA should benefit from a more rapid expansion of European imports thanks to the appreciation of the euro, but the 4.1 percent increase in EU import demand anticipated over the next two years is barely half the pace of the late 1990s. Moreover, travel and tourism will continue to reflect security concerns, fanned recently by the UK government's decision in May (since retracted) to ban commercial flights to Kenya, though, as noted, there will be differences within the region. However, for SSA overall the external environment will provide only modest support for growth in the current year, with exports rising 2.9 percent. A further acceleration to 4.9 percent is expected in 2004 as the recovery continues to build.

The forecast anticipates stronger growth for both energy and non-energy exporters in the medium term as the global recovery consolidates. Energy sectors are expected to contribute significantly to regional growth, especially with a moderate rebound in Nigeria from a weak performance in 2002. But, more generally, West Africa is emerging as an energy hot spot, with mainly offshore exploration and development activities underway from Angola through the Gulf of Guinea, and extending to nontraditional energy producers from São Tomé and Principe, to Mauritania. Major energy-related infrastructure projects including the West African Gas Pipeline and Nigeria's plan to end gas flaring by 2004 will also have a direct impact on investment and incomes. Though linkages to non-energy sectors are generally weak, increased fiscal revenues will permit relatively expansionary fiscal policies. Overall, oil exporters' growth is expected to reach 3.6 percent in 2003 and accelerate further to 3.9 percent by 2005. Despite some retrenchment in non-oil commodity prices in the second quarter, non-oil exporters will benefit from better terms of trade in the current year and relative stability after that. Policy improvements are expected to have a cumulative impact on competitiveness and will help attract investment. Realistically, though, this is a slow process and many of the benefits will be realized only in the longer term (figure A1.5b).

Long-term prospects

In the longer run, SSA will continue to face formidable obstacles to growth from low savings and investment rates, limited quantity and quality of infrastructure and human capital, and especially HIV/AIDS. As a result of the growing severity of the HIV/AIDS epidemic, population growth for the region has been revised downward by 0.3 percent to 1.9 percent per annum. Total GDP growth has been lowered by the same amount. The expectation is that per capita GDP growth will remain at 1.6 percent. This expectation may be optimistic given the long-run performance of the region, but even so it is barely half of what is needed to achieve the MDGs. There is little doubt that SSA will continue to lag behind

GLOBAL ECONOMIC PROSPECTS

Figure A1.5b Non-oil exporters increasingly drive SSA growth

GDP growth, percent

Note: RSA = Republic of South Africa.
Source: World Bank staff simulations.

ing governance and policymaking in general. For the region as a whole, real per capita income in absolute terms peaked in 1974, declining since then at an average annual rate of 0.7 percent. Yet differences across the region are striking. The worst performances have inevitably been associated with failed states and civil conflict, including Sierra Leone where growth has averaged –3.0 percent over the period, Democratic Republic of Congo at –5.6 percent, and Liberia at –5.8 percent. But, at the other end of the spectrum, long-term growth averaged 4.4 percent in Mauritius and 5.6 percent in Botswana. In between, there are success stories of spectacular turnarounds. Mozambique, after a protracted civil war and average growth of –1.8 percent during the 1980s, averaged 5.6 percent from 1992–2001. Already Mozambique, and other countries such as Uganda and Tanzania, have made substantial progress and have results to show for it, while many others are at an earlier stage of the process. By early 2003 almost all countries in the region were participating in the PRSP process, with 15 having completed PRSPs and

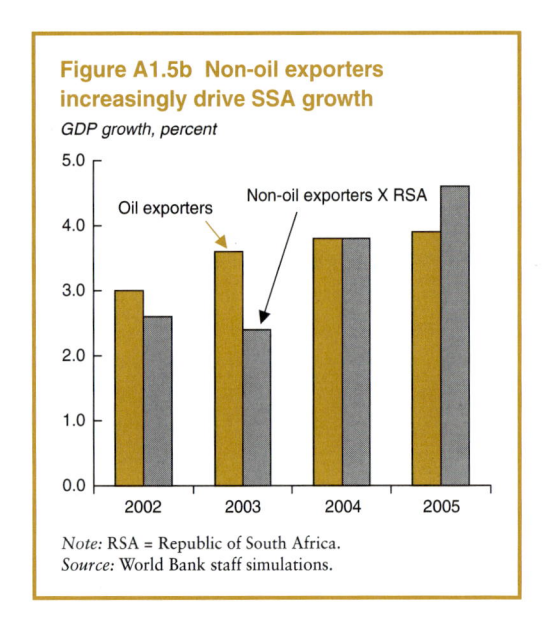

other developing regions over the forecast period, with outcomes well behind best practice in other regions.

The expectation of a reversal of SSA's lengthy downward spiral hinges on strong assumptions about ending conflicts and improv-

Table A1.5 Sub-Saharan Africa forecast summary

Growth rates/ratios (percent)	1991–2000	2001	2002	2003	2004	2005	2006–15
Real GDP growth	2.3	3.2	2.8	2.8	3.5	3.8	3.5
Consumption per capita	–0.3	0.6	0.1	0.5	0.8	1.1	1.2
GDP per capita	–0.3	0.8	0.5	0.5	1.3	1.6	1.6
Population	2.6	2.4	2.3	2.3	2.2	2.2	1.9
Gross Domestic Investment/GDP[a]	17.4	19.3	19.8	20.2	20.0	20.1	20.8
Inflation[b]	10.5	5.8	4.2	3.7	4.2	4.7	
General gvt. budget balance/GDP	–4.5	–1.6	–1.0	–1.6	–1.6	–1.7	
Export Market Growth[c]	7.3	0.4	2.0	5.0	7.3	7.1	
Export volume[d]	4.5	3.8	0.7	2.9	4.9	5.4	
Terms of trade/GDP[e]	0.1	–1.5	0.5	–0.4	–0.8	–0.5	
Current account/GDP	–2.0	–2.2	–2.2	–2.7	–2.5	–2.6	
Memorandum items							
GDP growth: SSA excluding South Africa	2.9	3.6	2.7	2.8	3.8	4.3	
Oil exporters	2.6	4.3	3.0	3.6	3.8	3.9	
CFA countries	2.6	3.1	1.9	2.2	3.1	3.5	

a. Fixed investment, measured in real terms.
b. Local currency GDP deflator, median.
c. Weighted average growth of import demand in export markets.
d. Goods and non-factor services.
e. Change in terms of trade, measured as a proportion of GDP (percentage).
Source: World Bank baseline forecast July 2003.
SSA is Sub–Saharan Africa. CFA is Communaute Financiere Africaine.

another 25 having I-PRSPs. Meanwhile, regional initiatives are enhancing the credibility of governments and strengthening intraregional cooperation. At the same time, however, deep-seated conflicts in West and Central Africa remain to be resolved and in many areas political processes remain fragile.

In principle, higher standards of governance and improved policies will encourage higher savings and investment, and raise productivity and growth. Yet, at the same time it will remain a struggle to overcome low levels of human and physical capital, poor infrastructure, HIV/AIDS, and negative perceptions of international investors. Moreover, the region remains highly dependent on primary commodity exports, hence exposed to high external volatility. While these factors indicate downside risks to the projections, achieving the moderate improvement in performance envisaged by the forecast seems a plausible baseline expectation.

Middle East and North Africa

Recent developments

THE OVERARCHING event in the Middle East and North Africa in 2002–03 was the buildup toward the war in Iraq, provoking continued high oil prices, further shocks to the tourism sector, and declining confidence in the private sector. Uncertainty before the war had an even larger impact than the war itself. However, the economic shocks resulting from the conflict highlighted several weaknesses in regional economies—the slackening of the investment climate, weakness in the private sector, and the relatively poor prospects for new foreign direct investment.

In the rise of uncertainty surrounding the situation in the Gulf in 2002 and early 2003, oil prices surged and oil exporters lifted oil production. Combined with fiscal expansion programs, it led to an acceleration of output growth to 3.2 percent in oil-exporting countries in 2002. High oil prices helped to keep current account balances in surplus in 2002 for oil exporters at $20 billion, 4.8 percent of GDP. Algeria continued expenditures under the PSRE (*Programme de soutien a la relance économique*), boosting the construction and services sectors and offsetting weakness in the agricultural sector, which was affected by a severe drought, particularly devastating for cereal crops. Private sector growth in Saudi Arabia and several Gulf countries is expected to remain weak as a result of the disruption caused by the war in Iraq, but companies from Saudi Arabia and Kuwait will benefit from subcontracting work associated with the reconstruction of Iraqi infrastructure. In Iran, the lifting of import restrictions in the past year has allowed the non-oil industrial and manufacturing sector to raise production, and domestic demand has been a strong driver for growth.

Developments were more adverse for diversified exporters, particularly those in the Middle East. The prospects for war in Iraq led to continued stagnation of tourism, which had not fully recovered from the events of September 11. These factors and the waning of external demand, particularly in Europe in late 2002, drought conditions in several countries, and a weak investment climate in several North Africa countries all contributed to a fall in growth from 3.8 percent in 2001 to 2.8 percent in 2002. Growth in Egypt appeared set for recovery in late 2002 with a recovery in tourist arrivals and increasing business confidence, but tourist arrivals fell in the first half of 2003. The Egyptian exchange rate was floated in January 2003, but the central bank is maintaining higher interest rates to prevent further depreciation of the pound, curbing private investment. Production in Jordan plummeted over late 2002 and into early 2003 (figure A1.6). Contraction in the agricultural sector was caused by drought conditions in Tunisia, the fourth consecutive year of drought. Exports, particularly from the manufacturing sector, were adversely affected by the waning of demand from the European Union in late 2002. A tighter fiscal stance, in the face of a widening current account deficit, also con-

GLOBAL ECONOMIC PROSPECTS

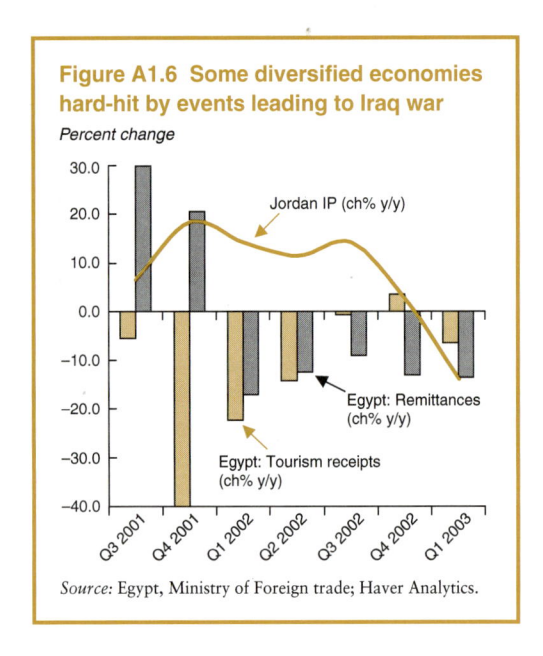

Figure A1.6 Some diversified economies hard-hit by events leading to Iraq war

Source: Egypt, Ministry of Foreign trade; Haver Analytics.

strained growth. However, Tunisia continued to pursue reforms in the financial sector and continued to attract FDI in 2002 thanks to the award of a second GSM license when global flows to developing countries were shrinking. Conversely, Morocco had positive agricultural growth in 2002, but the industrial modernization program under the Euro-Med Association Agreement and the privatization programs have tended to stagnate. The exception to this generally gloomy picture is Jordan, with buoyant GDP and export growth despite a slowdown in export market growth and a stagnating tourism sector.

Short-term prospects

Prospects in 2003–04 will be shaped by the path of oil prices and public expenditures in oil-exporting countries; the recovery of external demand; the speed of recovery in the tourism, trade, and transportation sectors in the Middle East post-war; weather conditions; and the policy response to slackening of the investment climate in the diversified exporters. Growth in the region is expected to rise slightly in 2003 to 3.3 percent as oil exporters increase production and exports and diversified exporters recover from the adverse impacts of slowing external demand and drought conditions. The diversified exporters should begin to recover in 2004 as external demand improves and as growth in oil exporters is buoyed by further fiscal expansion, somewhat offsetting the impacts of lower oil prices and production.

Most of the acceleration in 2003 will occur in the oil-exporting countries, which are expected to grow more quickly in 2003 as a result of fiscal pump-priming and increased oil production quotas. GDP growth in oil exporters should reach 3.9 percent in 2003–04. Oil production levels for the oil exporters in 2003 will be higher than 2002, ensuring that the oil sector will make large, positive contributions to GDP volume growth. High profitability in oil, and in services sectors, such as telecommunications and banking, has led to surges in stock markets in Iran and Saudi Arabia, particularly as a result of thin markets. Firms in the Gulf Cooperation Council (GCC) countries are expected to benefit from contracting agreements as the reconstruction of Iraq gets underway in the second half of 2003, helping to boost the weak private sector. Evidence is also emerging that citizens of oil-exporting countries, particularly in the Gulf, are traveling less and boosting domestic consumption.

Saudi Arabia and Iran have begun to push through needed reforms in several sectors such as mining, capital markets, and insurance, as well as privatizing state concerns to encourage foreign investment in the oil sector. But Algeria has abandoned proposed hydrocarbons reforms. Moving into 2004, the impetus to growth from the oil sector should wane in these countries as oil prices and production fall, but continued fiscal stimulus and a rebound in private sector activity should maintain GDP growth. Growth in Algeria will be supported in 2004 by the online debut of a major gas project, but fiscal stimulus under the PSRE is being absorbed more slowly than expected.

Growth in the diversified exporters is forecast to remain sluggish in 2003 at 2.4 percent, caused by stagnation in tourism in the first half of the year because of the Iraq war. The agricultural sector in Tunisia will expand in the wake of good rains, and agricultural expansion will continue in Morocco, but slow import demand in Europe will keep the manufacturing sectors depressed. The countries most affected by the Iraq war were border nations Syria and Jordan. Both countries have extensive trade links with Iraq, and Jordan sourced its oil from Iraq at concessional rates. Prior to the war, Jordan's exports to Iraq were growing strongly. The disruption to oil supplies from Iraq and to haulage routes through Iraq has meant that output growth in the first half of 2003 in these countries was adversely affected. The Jordanian government has decreased fuel subsidies and broadened the tax base to ease the impact on the fiscal accounts of higher oil prices, affecting the current balance. Jordanian exports to other destinations, particularly to the United States through the "Qualified Industrial Zones," are unaffected by the disruption caused by the conflict, but uncertainty in the private sector has decreased confidence.

In response to this range of negative growth factors, central banks in several countries (Jordan, Morocco, Tunisia) have reduced interest rates to stimulate domestic demand. Growth conditions should improve later in 2003 and into 2004 as confidence returns to the tourism market, the European economy rebounds, and the effects of lower interest rates filter through to domestic investment. Diversified economies are expected to grow 3.7 percent in 2004. This is below the average of the diversified exporters during the 1990s, where GDP growth achieved annual growth of 4.2 percent. The lackluster investment climate in these countries requires further attention in the reform process.

Long-term prospects

Reducing unemployment through higher GDP growth remains the key challenge for the region, particularly given the very high rates of growth expected in the labor force, as the age structure of the population shifts to reduce the dependency ratio, constituting a "demographic gift." The region has achieved macroeconomic stability for the most part, with low inflation and stable external debt positions, but growth in the region is not reaching its potential, with many countries still stuck with per capita GDP growth of around 1.5 percent. Prospects for growth and sustainable employment can be improved through reforms in trade regimes and a strengthened investment climate. Traditional trade liberalization, such as lowering tariff and non-tariff barriers, is vital considering that the Middle East and North African (MENA) region is one of the more highly protected developing regions. While MENA's export products (excluding oil) are not highly integrated into global trade markets, the region has strong potential for non-energy exports. The Mediterranean countries are well on the way to trade reforms through their commitments over the coming decade to the Euro-Med agreements, bilateral trade agreements, and WTO membership. But trade reforms must also include 'behind the border' reforms (trade facilitation, services liberalization, and improved competitiveness) designed to increase productive efficiency.

Reform of the investment climate is needed to ensure sustainable employment growth, because trade reforms increase growth only when they stimulate new investment. Much of the impetus to growth in recent years in many countries has come from the public sector, and much of the FDI flowing into the region is targeted to extractive industries or parastatals that have been privatized. To capture greater benefits from trade and financial market integration, policy-makers in the region should focus on structural and microeconomic impediments to efficient resource allocation and to improve competition. Policy reforms are required to ensure a sound regulatory environment in product and factor markets. Improving governance, improving the quality of public institutions,

Table A1.6 Middle East and North Africa forecast summary

Growth rates/ratios (percent)	1991–2000	2001	2002	2003	2004	2005	2006–15
Real GDP growth	3.4	3.2	3.1	3.3	3.9	3.5	4.3
Consumption per capita	0.2	4.8	1.8	1.0	1.3	1.3	2.3
GDP per capita	1.2	1.3	1.1	1.3	1.9	1.5	2.5
Population	2.2	1.9	1.9	1.9	1.9	1.9	1.7
Gross Domestic Investment/GDP[a]	21.4	21.3	21.6	21.8	22.0	22.1	26.2
Inflation[b]	7.5	2.6	3.8	4.0	4.0	4.0	
General gvt. budget balance/GDP	−1.2	−0.8	−3.0	−2.3	−3.2	−2.2	
Export Market Growth[c]	7.5	−1.1	2.2	8.3	8.1	7.9	
Export volume[d]	5.7	3.6	1.2	4.2	5.5	5.2	
Terms of trade/GDP[e]	0.3	−1.8	0.1	−2.2	−1.7	−1.1	
Current account/GDP	−1.9	4.2	3.5	0.3	−1.5	−2.6	
Memorandum items							
GDP growth: Oil exporters	3.0	2.9	3.2	3.9	3.9	3.3	
Diversified exporters	4.2	3.8	2.8	2.4	3.7	3.8	

a. Fixed investment, measured in real terms.
b. Local currency GDP deflator, median.
c. Weighted average growth of import demand in export markets.
d. Goods and non-factor services.
e. Change in terms of trade, measured as a proportion of GDP (percentage).
Source: World Bank baseline forecast July 2003.

and enforcing public accountability are necessary if a vibrant public sector is to evolve. Combating bureaucratic delays and inefficiency, improving the quality of infrastructure services, and fighting corruption are also essential elements of a better investment climate.

With only one-third of the labor force active today, women represent a huge untapped resource in the region. Experience from around the world suggests that women, particularly the young and well-educated, can reap gains from trade and investment climate reforms. These gains are already evident in the garment and textile industry in Egypt, Jordan, Morocco, and Tunisia. Provided that economic and social barriers to women are dismantled, women can more widely participate in economic life, thereby boosting economic growth and productivity in the region.

Notes

1. In April 2003, eight transition countries signed the accession treaty to join the EU in May 2004, along with Malta and Cyprus.

2. The UN's FAO's Global Information and Early Warning System identifies 25 countries representing 56 percent of total Sub-Saharan population where agricultural production has been seriously disrupted. (ftp://ftp.fao.org/docrep/fao/005/y9304e/y9304e00.pdf) According to the UN WFP, 40 million persons in SSA are facing acute hunger because of drought, disease, and conflict (http://www.wfp.org/index.asp?section=3).

3. http://www.agoa.gov/resources/TRDPROFL03.pdf. AGOA rules of origin are to be tightened in 2004 and it remains to be seen how long lasting the benefits will be.

4. According to data from the Energy Information Agency of the US Department of Energy. See http://www.eia.doe.gov/emeu/ipsr/t11a.xls.

Appendix 2
Global Commodity Price Prospects

Commodity prices increased significantly from the lows reached shortly after the terrorist attacks on September 11, 2001 (figure A2.1). Crude oil prices rose 78 percent from the December 2001 lows to the highs in February 2003, just prior to the start of the war in Iraq, but have since declined. Agricultural prices were up 29 percent from the lows to recent monthly highs, while metals and minerals prices rose 15 percent. The decline of the dollar since early 2002 (10 percent on a real-trade weighted basis) contributed to the rise in commodity prices. Petroleum and most agricultural prices are now expected to decline on rising supplies, while metals and minerals prices are expected to continue their recovery because of higher demand in the foreseen economic recovery.

The increase in crude oil prices resulted from strong OPEC production discipline, extremely low inventories, cold winter weather, and supply disruptions in Venezuela, Iraq, and Nigeria. Higher output from other OPEC members leading up to the war in Iraq prevented prices from spiking sharply higher, and use of strategic stocks was not required. Crude oil stocks remain low and the return of Iraqi exports has been delayed, thus prices are likely to remain relatively firm for the balance of 2003. The return of Iraqi exports and rising capacity in both OPEC and non-OPEC countries is expected to lead to lower prices in 2004 and beyond. Large increases in production are expected in a number of regions in the coming years, in particular the Caspian, Russia, West Africa, and several deepwater locations. Much of the moderate growth in world oil demand is expected to be captured by non-OPEC producers, thus rising supply competition, both inside and outside OPEC, is expected to lead to lower prices.

The rise in agricultural prices since October 2001 was caused mostly by reduced supplies from earlier low prices and severe El Niño-related droughts in 2002 (in Australia, Canada, the Middle East, and the U.S.), which reduced grain and oilseed production. Cocoa supplies were disrupted by conflict in Côte d'Ivoire, while production was reduced for natural rubber, robusta coffee, cotton, and vegetable oils because of earlier low prices.

Most of the sharp agricultural price increases in 2002 and 2003 are expected to be reversed as surplus production capacity once again results from higher prices. More rapid economic growth would strengthen demand somewhat and moderate the price declines. However, income elasticities for most agricultural commodities are low, and with weak demand growth agricultural prices are expected to decrease.

Fertilizer prices generally increased in 2003 along with the recovery in agricultural commodity prices. Higher prices for natural gas—a key input in nitrogen fertilizer production—caused nitrogen fertilizer prices to rise sharply. In addition, production capacity utilization in the fertilizer industry increased to five-year highs and further contributed to the price in-

Figure A2.1 Commodity price trends
Index, January 2000 = 100

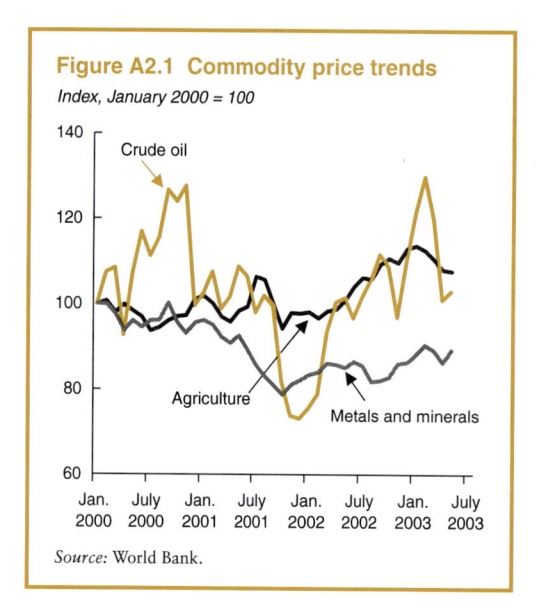

Source: World Bank.

creases. The recent downturn in agricultural commodity prices is expected to be reflected in lower fertilizer prices in 2004 and 2005.

The modest recovery in metals and minerals prices resulted from production cuts beginning in 2001, and weakening of the U.S. dollar. Demand growth has been weak, and stocks of most metals remain high. The one exception is nickel, where strong demand for stainless steel, low inventories, and tight supplies, caused prices to almost double since the lows in 2001. A recovery in metals demand is expected to send most metals markets into deficit and allow prices to increase over the next several years. If global economic growth accelerates more quickly than projected, metals and minerals prices would increase more rapidly in the near term. Over the longer term, real prices are expected to decline as production costs continue to fall because of new technologies and improved managerial practices. There is also little constraint on primary resource availability.

Real commodity prices declined significantly from 1980 to 2002, with the World Bank's index of agricultural prices down 47 percent, crude oil prices down 43 percent, and metals and minerals prices down 35 percent (figure A2.2). Such declines in commodity prices relative to manufactures prices pose real challenges for developing countries that depend on primary commodities for a substantial share of their export revenues. For example, 57 percent of merchandise exports from Sub-Saharan Africa in 2000 came from primary commodities and fuels. The situation is not expected to improve, with real non-oil commodity prices expected to increase only modestly through 2015 and crude oil prices expected to decline by 23 percent from 2002 levels. Multilateral trade negotiations could lead to higher agricultural prices if reforms reduce production subsidies and tariffs in major consuming and producing countries; however, little progress on reforms has thus far been achieved. (Specific commodity prices and price indices forecasts for 2003, 2004, 2005, 2010, and 2015 in current and constant dollars are given in appendix tables A2.14–16. The forecasts do not reflect the effects of a multilateral trade agreement because of the uncertainty of such an agreement.)

Beverages

The World Bank's index of beverage prices (composed of coffee, cocoa, and tea prices) is

Figure A2.2 Real commodity prices
Index, 1990 = 100

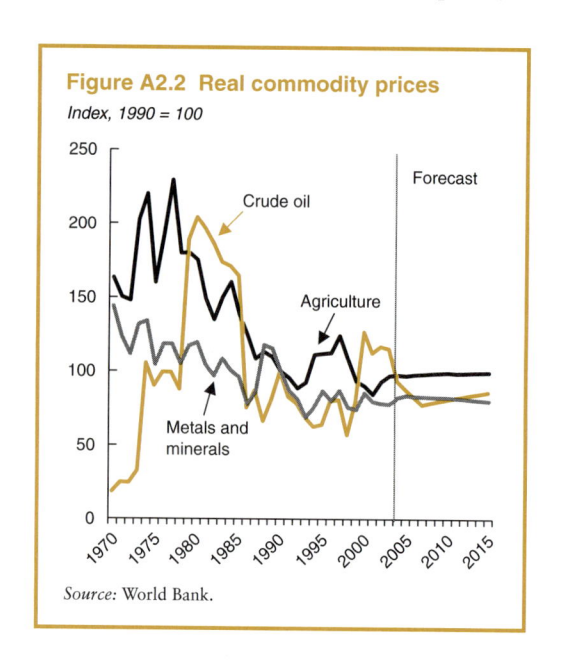

Source: World Bank.

Figure A2.3 Beverage prices
US cents per kilogram

Sources: International Coffee Organization, International Cocoa Organization, International Tea Committee.

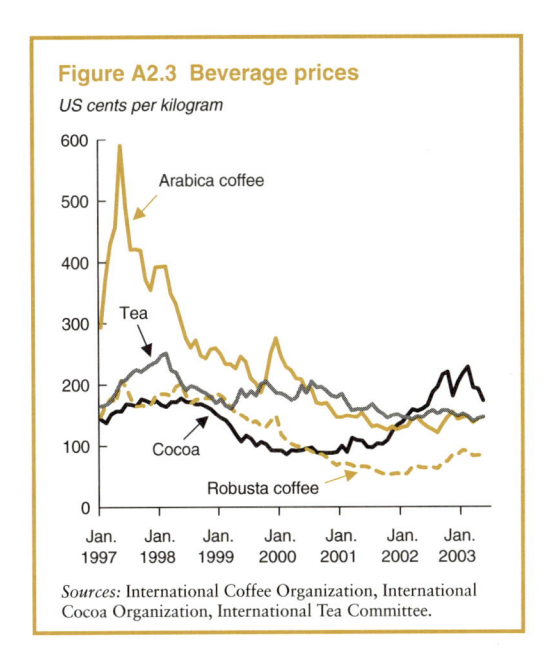

expected to increase by about 6 percent in 2003, largely reflecting coffee price increases (arabica up 7 percent and robusta up 33 percent) in response to reduced output from Brazil (figure A2.3). Cocoa prices, which have been (and are likely to be) extremely volatile because of the political unrest in Côte d'Ivoire, are expected to remain unchanged. Fears that tea prices might suffer a major setback resulting from the military conflict in Iraq did not materialize and the three-auction average for 2003 is expected to remain at its 2002 level.

Coffee. Despite the increase in coffee prices expected in 2003, (robusta up US$0.22 to US$0.88/kg and arabica up US$0.10 to US$1.46/kg) prices will remain near historical lows—at about one-third of their 1960 real levels. Low coffee prices reflect both the surge in supplies and weak demand. During the past five seasons, global coffee production has averaged 114 million 60 kg bags, compared to 99 million bags during the five prior seasons when coffee prices peaked. Per capita consumption in the major importing countries has been stagnant at 4.6 kgs of green coffee equivalent during the past ten years.

Surpluses over the past four seasons have kept the coffee market depressed, and this situation has often been referred to as the "coffee crisis" by the popular press. Attempts to deal with the surpluses have either been largely unsuccessful or abandoned. The Association of Coffee Producing Countries (ACPC), which urged coffee-producing countries to join its export retention scheme, ceased operating last year. The International Coffee Organization (ICO), in an effort to reduce coffee availability and thus push prices higher, called for the removal of low-quality coffee beans. This plan too has met resistance because there is no well-defined compensation mechanism in place. In addition, improved roasting methods have made it easier to remove the harsh taste of natural arabicas and robustas, enabling roasters to produce the same coffee quality with lower-quality green beans, thus putting into question ICO's proposal.

Global coffee production during the 2003–04 season is expected to be about 107 million bags, down from last season's 123 million bags (table A2.1). Almost all of the reduction is because of reduced Brazilian output (from 52 million bags in 2002 to 34 million bags in 2003), which is partly because of less favorable weather conditions and partly because of the strength of the Brazilian currency. Still, Brazil will account for one-third of global coffee output while Colombia and Vietnam are expected to reach 12 and 11 million bags, respectively, and be the second and third largest coffee suppliers of arabica and robusta, respectively.

Coffee prices are projected to increase in 2004, with arabica up 9 percent and robusta up 5 percent. Over the longer term, real coffee prices are expected to increase relative to the 2002 depressed levels but remain well below the historical highs of the 1970s and more recent highs of the mid-1990s. By 2015, real arabica and robusta prices are projected to increase about 50 and 70 percent, respectively, over their 2002 levels. Prices would still be only about half of their 1990s peaks.

Table A2.1 Coffee production in selected countries
(million bags)

	1998	1999	2000	2001	2002	2003
Brazil	35.6	30.8	34.1	35.1	51.6	33.6
Colombia	10.9	9.5	10.5	12.0	10.9	11.8
Vietnam	7.5	11.0	15.3	12.3	10.3	10.8
Indonesia	7.0	6.7	6.5	6.2	6.0	6.1
México	5.0	6.2	4.8	4.2	4.4	4.7
Guatemala	4.3	4.4	4.6	3.5	3.8	3.8
Ethiopia	3.9	3.8	3.7	3.8	3.0	3.3
Uganda	3.6	3.1	3.2	3.5	3.1	3.2
World	108.4	113.4	116.6	110.1	122.8	107.1

Note: Years refer to crop years beginning in April.
Source: U.S. Department of Agriculture.

Cocoa. Cocoa prices have staged a remarkable recovery, going from a 30-year low of US$0.86/kg in February 2000 to a 16-year high of US$2.28/kg in February 2003. Prices have been extremely volatile, especially during the last two years, with month-to-month price changes often exceeding 10 percentage points. While the recovery in prices is a result of the return to normal supply levels, the volatility is a reflection of the political instability in Côte d'Ivoire, the world's dominant supplier.

Global cocoa production is expected to reach 3 million tons during the marketing season ending in September 2003, up from last season's 2.85 million tons (table A2.2). All of the increase is expected to come from Ghana, the world's second-largest cocoa supplier (from 341 to 450 thousand tons). Côte d'Ivoire's share is expected to remain largely unchanged at 1.26 million tons. Cocoa prices for 2003 are expected to remain at their 2002 levels, but a small decline is expected in 2004 as production continues to increase, an assessment which is based on the assumption that the strong prices enjoyed during the last two seasons will provide further incentives to cocoa growers to maintain their trees and increase production. The degree of volatility in cocoa prices is likely to remain high until the political unrest in Côte d'Ivoire is settled.

Table A2.2 Beverages global balances

	1970	1980	1990	1999	2000	2001	1970–80	1980–90	1990–00
Coffee *(Thousand bags)*									
Production	64,161	86,174	100,181	116,581	110,104	122,759	2.1	1.4	1.2
Consumption	71,536	79,100	96,300	106,343	108,186	110,750	1.0	2.0	0.2
Exports	54,186	60,996	76,163	90,394	86,823	88,974	0.8	2.4	1.7
Cocoa *(Thousand tons)*									
Production	1,554	1,695	2,506	2,812	2,850	2,996	0.5	4.6	1.2
Grindings	1,418	1,556	2,335	3,014	2,858	2,976	0.2	4.5	2.6
Stocks	497	675	1,791	1,111	1,137	1,127	2.4	13.9	–4.7
Tea *(Thousand tons)*									
Production	1,286	1,848	2,516	2,895	3,021	3,000	4.1	2.9	1.5
Exports	752	859	1,132	1,330	1,391	1,419	24	2.4	1.6

Notes: Time reference for coffee (production and exports) and cocoa are based on crop years (October to September for cocoa and April to March for coffee). For coffee consumption and tea time is calendar year.
Sources: US Department of Agriculture, International Coffee Organization, International Cocoa Organization, International Tea Committee, and World Bank.

Tea. The three-auction average tea price is expected to remain largely unchanged in 2003 vs. 2002 at about US$1.50/kg and therefore not to recover from the 20 percent decline between 2000 and 2002. The weakness in tea prices is expected to persist because of oversupply and a trend of slow growth of consumption. Production in 2002 was about the same as in 2001, but production is expected to increase in 2003. The rapid increase in production in Vietnam has contributed to already ample supplies and threatens to depress prices. Vietnam has doubled production since 1990.

Tea prices have been volatile because of the uncertainties associated with the war in Iraq and concerns that imports would be disrupted. In addition, excessive rains in Sri Lanka, the largest exporter, disrupted supplies. By 2015 real tea prices are expected to be slightly lower than in 2002.

Food

The World Bank's food price index is expected to rise 4.3 percent in 2003 and be up 11.2 percent from the low in 2000. However, the index is still well below highs reached in 1997 (figure A2.4). Following recent increases, the index is expected to decline 2.4 percent in 2004 and an additional 2.1 percent in 2005 as grain and oilseed prices decline from recent highs. Grains prices have increased almost 15 percent from the lows in 2001 and fats and oils prices have increased 26 percent. Over the longer term, real food prices are projected to decline 2.7 percent from 2003 to 2015.

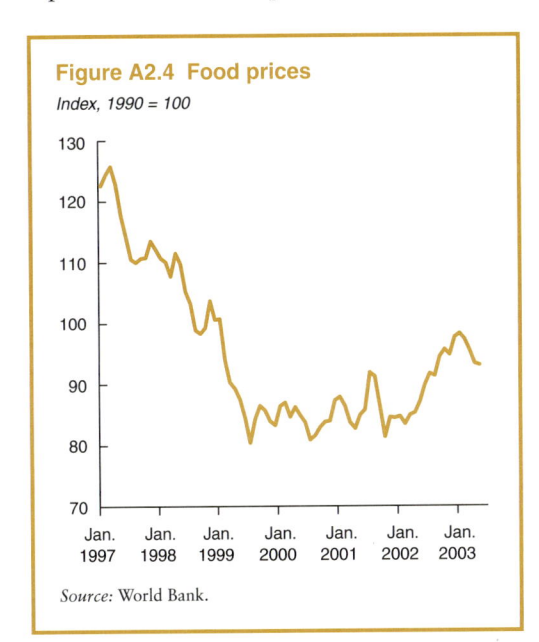

Fats and oils. Prices of fats and oils are expected to increase almost 7 percent in 2003, which gives a cumulative increase of 20 percent since 2001. However, prices have recovered less than half of the decline experienced from 1997 to 2001. The price increase is expected to be greatest in groundnut oil (up 60 percent). Price increases are expected to be less in the two major oilseed crops, soybean and palm, with soybean oil up 16 percent and palm oil up 9 percent.

Global production of the 17 major fats and oils is expected to increase by 1.4 percent in the season starting October 2003, following last season's increase of 2.5 percent. Demand in 2003–04, to be fueled by increased imports by China and India, is projected to outpace production by at least 1 percentage point.

Global soybean production has increased by more than 5 percent per year since 1990, with the most rapid increase in Brazil and Argentina (table A2.3). Argentina and Brazil have been increasing production at nearly 10 percent per year since 1990.

Global palm oil production has doubled every eight years during the past three decades with the largest increases coming from Indonesia and Malaysia (table A2.4).

Figure A2.4 Food prices
Index, 1990 = 100

Source: World Bank.

Table A2.3 Soybean production
(millions of tons)

Year	Argentina	Brazil	United States	World
1990	11.5	15.8	52.4	104.1
1995	12.4	24.2	59.2	124.9
2000	27.8	39.0	75.1	175.1
2001	30.0	43.5	78.7	184.3
2002	35.0	51.0	74.3	194.0

Note: Argentina, Brazil, and the U.S. account for about 83 percent of global production.
Source: USDA.

Table A2.4 Palm oil production
(million tons)

Year	Indonesia	Malaysia	Nigeria	World
1980	0.69	2.58	0.43	4.59
1985	1.24	4.13	0.39	7.04
1990	2.41	6.10	0.58	11.03
1995	4.22	7.81	0.66	15.22
2000	7.05	10.8	0.74	21.87
2001	8.03	11.8	0.77	23.92
2002	9.02	11.9	0.78	25.03
2003	9.60	12.7	0.79	26.59

Source: Oil World.

Grains. Global grain stocks, relative to use, are expected to recover slightly from last year's lows (excluding China where data is very uncertain). However, stocks remain low and there is still a risk that prices could rise sharply if yields in the coming crop year are significantly below trends. If yields are near trend, then prices should decline and stocks should continue to rebuild.

Maize prices are projected to rise 6.7 percent in 2003 and then decline 5.7 percent in 2004 as production increases and stocks rebuild (table A2.5). Production in the U.S., the major producer with 40 percent of world production, is projected to increase 12 percent in 2003–04 compared to the previous year. Real prices are projected to decline about 4 percent from 2003 to 2015 as yields continue to grow faster than consumption, as was the case during the 1990s.

Rice prices are projected to rise about 4 percent in 2003 and an additional 3.0 percent by 2005. Rice prices are well below historical norms relative to other food grains, and this should increase import demand for rice relative to wheat. Lower Indian exports this year because of drought will also contribute to the price increases. Global rice stocks are low and prices could increase significantly if a poor crop reduces stocks further. Over the longer term, real rice prices are projected to rise 4.6 percent by 2015 vs. 2003, while most other grains prices are projected to decline.

Wheat prices are expected to decline in 2003–05 as production recovers from severe drought. Prices increased from US$112/ton in 1999 to US$148/ton in 2002, but are expected to decline to US$133/ton by 2005. Production in the major exporters (U.S., EU, Canada, Australia, and Argentina) is expected to increase 20 percent in the 2003–04 crop year and stocks are expected to increase 17 percent. However, global wheat stocks remain low (table A2.5) and there is a substantial risk that prices could rise if the drought persists.

Sugar. Sugar prices averaged 15.2 cents/kilogram in 2002 (figure A2.5). They are ex-

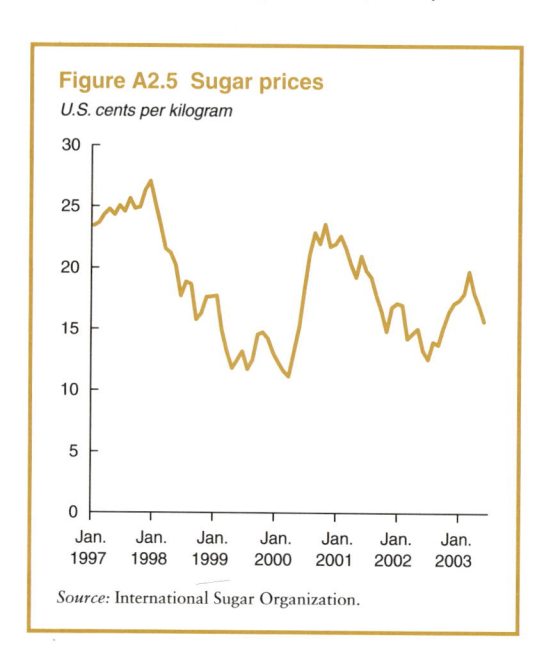

Table A2.5 Global grain stocks-to-use
percentages (excluding China)

	Maize	Rice	Wheat	Total grains
1997–98	10.1	9.3	16.5	13.0
1998–99	11.5	10.2	18.0	14.0
1999–00	11.4	11.8	17.1	13.6
2000–01	11.6	13.6	18.6	14.4
2001–02	10.4	13.1	20.4	14.9
2002–03	6.3	10.0	15.8	12.0
2003–04	8.9	10.2	16.9	12.5
90s Low	6.1	8.6	13.9	9.8

Note: Data for 2003–04 is the USDA's May 2003 estimate for wheat and maize and World Bank estimate for rice.
Source: USDA.

Figure A2.5 Sugar prices
U.S. cents per kilogram

Source: International Sugar Organization.

Table A2.6 Foods global balances
(million tons)

	1970	1980	1990	2000	2001	2002	1970–80	1980–90	1990–00
Grains									
Production	1,079	1,430	1,769	1,839	1,872	1,807	2.88	1.55	1.04
Consumption	1,114	1,451	1,717	1,862	1,902	1,906	2.58	1.78	1.02
Exports	119	212	206	233	237	237	6.35	0.13	0.94
Stocks	193	309	490	536	506	407	7.24	3.83	–0.56
Soybeans									
Production	42.1	62.2	104.1	175.1	184.3	194.0	6.84	1.87	5.08
Consumption	46.0	68.1	104.3	172.2	182.3	194.2	6.53	2.04	4.99
Exports	12.3	20.8	25.4	55.5	55.1	63.2	5.24	0.80	2.88
Stocks	3.4	10.3	20.6	30.6	32.0	31.0	13.83	–0.66	0.20
Sugar *(raw equivalent)*									
Production	70.9	84.7	109.4	130.4	134.7	143.3	2.80	1.59	3.26
Consumption	65.4	91.1	106.8	130.3	134.9	136.6	3.30	1.40	3.00
Exports	21.9	27.6	34.1	37.7	40.7	46.6	3.26	0.83	3.12
Stocks	19.6	19.5	19.3	37.3	34.0	32.2	3.96	–0.77	4.52
Fats and oils									
Production	39.8	58.1	80.8	117.2	120.1	121.8	3.68	3.54	3.70
Consumption	39.8	56.8	80.9	116.8	120.9	123.8	3.55	3.69	3.64
Exports	8.8	17.8	26.9	38.3	41.0	42.2	7.05	4.19	3.39
Stocks	5.2	9.3	12.2	14.8	13.6	12.1	7.09	2.44	0.69

Notes: Time references for grains, soybeans and sugar are based on marketing years, shown under the year in which production began, and vary by country; for fats and oils, crop years begin in September. Fats and oils includes the 17 major fats and oils.
Sources: USDA and Oil World.

pected to increase slightly in 2003 and 2004 as supplies are curtailed and stocks reduced. High crude oil prices have contributed to the price increase by diverting sugar cane production to ethanol production in Brazil for use as vehicle fuel. Prices are projected to average about US$0.16/kg in 2003 and 2004, and rise slightly in 2005. The longer-term price prospects are not encouraging for producers unless global policy reforms are agreed in the current round of multilateral trade negotiations. Without reforms, nominal prices are expected to remain low except when supplies are reduced by drought in a major producing country.

Brazil, the world's lowest cost and largest sugar exporter, with about one-third of world sugar exports, has increased production and exports dramatically since 1990 and is expected to continue expanding. This has put downward pressure on prices, as Brazilian exports have increased from 1.3 million tons in 1990–91 to 14.2 million tons in 2002–03.

Global consumption grew by 3.0 percent per annum during the 1990s (table A2.6).

Raw Materials

The index of agricultural raw materials prices (composed of tropical hardwoods, cotton, and natural rubber) declined sharply during the Asia crisis and then stabilized before declining again as supplies of commodities continued to increase (figure A2.6). Prices reached a low in 2001 and have since recovered because of higher cotton and natural rubber prices. Nominal prices are projected to increase an additional 6 percent by 2005 from 2003 levels, while real prices are projected to rise 10 percent from 2003 to 2015.

Cotton. Cotton prices are expected to increase 28 percent in 2003, following declines in the two previous years that took prices to 30-year lows. The price recovery is due mostly to an 11 percent reduction in supplies in the

GLOBAL ECONOMIC PROSPECTS

Figure A2.6 Raw materials
Index, 1990 = 100

Source: World Bank.

The A Index cotton price is expected to average US$1.30/kg during 2003 and remain at approximately the same level during the next two seasons, as the market appears to have reached a balance. By 2015, real prices are projected to increase 30 percent relative to 2002 levels.

Natural Rubber. Rubber prices are expected to increase 23 percent in 2003, after falling to historical lows in 2001 following the Asian financial crisis. The recent strength in rubber prices reflects increased demand as well as supply controls by Thailand and Indonesia, the dominant natural rubber suppliers with a combined 60 percent of global output. Consumption in 2002 increased 3.6 percent over 2001 and preliminary figures for 2003 indicate that it will stay strong. China, the world's dominant natural rubber consumer, has been the major source of increased demand (table A2.8). In the 12-month period ending May 2003, Chinese rubber demand increased 7 percent. Strong demand was also present by other main buyers, notably the U.S., Japan, and Germany. The demand for natural rubber has also been aided by lower demand for synthetic rubber, whose prices increased considerably because of high crude oil prices (crude oil is a major cost component of synthetic rubber).

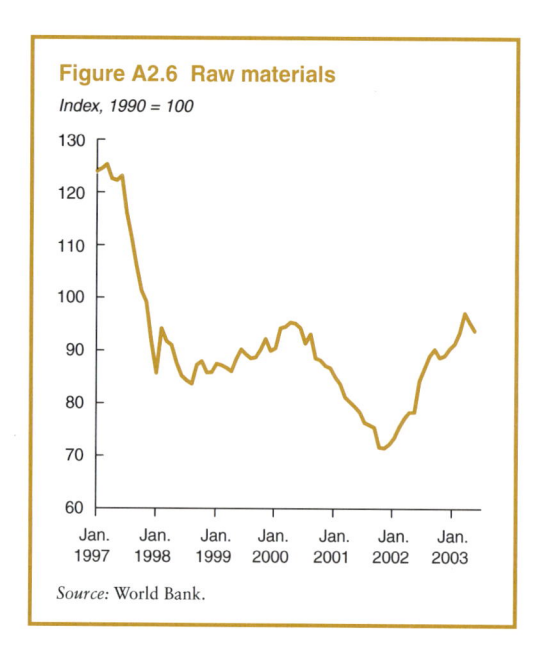

2002–03 marketing season (table A2.7). Most of the reduction came from China and the U.S., the world's two dominant cotton suppliers, which account for over 40 percent of global output.

The 2003 increase in cotton prices is expected to lead to a strong supply response, according to the International Cotton Advisory Committee. They estimate the 2003–04 global cotton production will be 9 percent higher than this season's crop. Most of the increase is expected to come from China (almost 1 million tons). Global consumption is expected to stay slightly higher than production, causing stocks to fall for a second consecutive season.

Natural rubber prices are expected to remain above US$0.90/kg for the next two to three years. Over the longer term, real prices are projected to increase slightly over the 2002 levels.

Table A2.7 Cotton production in selected countries
(million tons)

	1998	1999	2000	2001	2002	2003
China	4.50	3.83	4.42	5.32	4.92	5.80
United States	3.03	3.69	3.74	4.42	3.75	3.71
India	2.71	2.65	2.38	2.69	2.35	2.68
Pakistan	1.48	1.91	1.82	1.80	1.70	1.80
Uzbekistan	1.00	1.13	0.98	1.06	1.03	0.99
Franc Zone	0.90	0.93	0.70	1.03	0.93	0.95
World	18.55	19.09	19.46	21.51	19.20	20.96

Notes: Years refer to crop years that begin in August.
Source: International Cotton Advisory Committee.

Table A2.8 Natural rubber consumption
(thousand tons)

	1999	2000	2001	2002
China	997	1,123	1,224	1,332
United States	1,116	1,142	1,010	1,046
Japan	733	753	729	774
India	617	638	631	675
Korea, Rep. of	325	331	327	321
Germany	226	250	245	254
France	253	262	262	241
World	6,771	7,129	6,973	7,223

Sources: LMC International, International Rubber Study Group.

Tropical Timber. Tropical timber prices recovered in 2002 and 2003 from sharp declines in 2001, with nominal prices up 9 percent in 2002 and expected to be up an additional 5 percent in 2003. The initial price increases were supported by the decline of the dollar vs. the Yen and Euro, but the price recovery appears to have stalled in 2003 as demand has weakened in Asia and Europe. China has become the largest tropical log importer, displacing Japan, and has become a significant plywood producer and exporter. The partial ban on log exports from Asian and African exporters, intended to increase domestic processing, has raised the prices of logs, and somewhat restricted supplies, while depressing prices of sawnwood and plywood relative to logs. However, the bans have not been totally effective and illegal exports continue. Tropical timber prices are expected to continue to recover, up 3 percent in 2004 and up 7 percent in 2005, with demand in China, Japan, and Europe important factors determining the rate of price increase. Real tropical timber prices are projected to increase 28 percent from 2003 to 2015, but stay below the highs of the 1990s as new technology allows better utilization of timber.

Fertilizers

Fertilizer prices generally increased in 2003 as demand increased because of the rise in agricultural commodity prices. Among the

Table A2.9 Raw materials global balances

	1970	1980	1990	2000	2001	2002	1970–80	1980–90	1990–00
Cotton *(thousand tons)*									
Production	11,740	13,832	18,970	19,461	21,510	19,200	1.2	3.1	0.8
Consumption	12,173	14,215	18,576	19,886	20,194	21,000	1.1	3.1	0.2
Exports	3,875	4,414	5,081	5,857	6,496	6,500	0.9	2.8	0.5
Stocks	4,605	4,895	6,645	9,637	10,585	8,780	1.7	2.8	1.4
Natural rubber *(thousand tons)*									
Production	3,140	3,820	5,080	6,730	7,190	7,110	1.8	3.2	3.1
Consumption	3,090	3,770	5,190	7,340	7,080	7,390	1.6	3.2	3.3
Net Exports	2,820	3,280	3,950	4,930	5,140	5,040	1.3	2.1	1.8
Stocks	1,440	1,1480	1,500	1,930	2,040	1,760	0.6	0.2	3.7
Tropical timber *(thousand cubic meters)*									
Logs, production	210	262	300	279.5	283.3	n.a.	1.5	1.7	0.5
Logs, imports	36.1	42.2	25.1	18.6	17.9	n.a.	0.2	5.1	5.4
Sawnwood, production	98.5	115.8	131.8	109.1	106.2	n.a.	1.2	1.7	2.0
Sawnwood, imports	7.1	13.2	16.1	23.1	22.5	n.a.	5.0	2.6	3.3
Plywood, production	33.4	39.4	48.2	58.1	55.5	n.a.	1.2	2.0	0.5
Plywood, imports	4.9	6.0	14.9	19.0	19.2	n.a.	0.7	9.1	3.6

Annual growth rates (percent) shown in last three columns.

n.a. = Not available.
Notes: Time reference for cotton is based on crop year beginning in August; for natural rubber and tropical timber, time refers to calendar year.
Sources: International Cotton Advisory Committee, International Study Rubber Group, FAO, and World Bank.

Figure A2.7 Fertilizer prices
US$s per ton

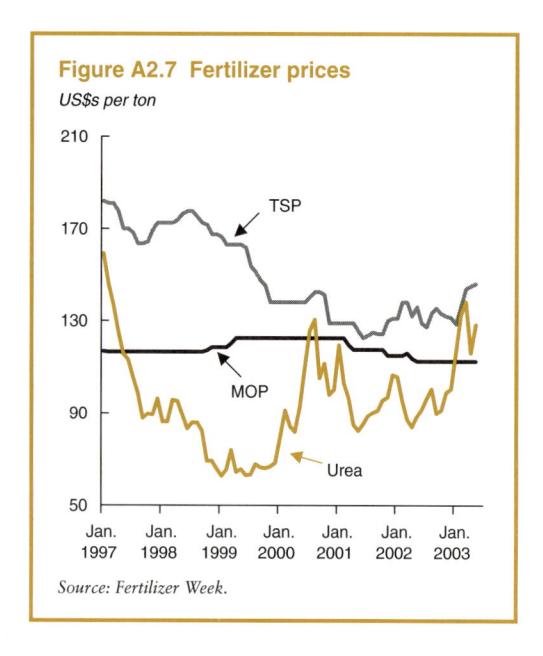

Source: Fertilizer Week.

three major types of fertilizer, nitrogen prices (as represented by urea) increased most rapidly because of higher prices of natural gas used in production in addition to demand increases. Phosphate fertilizer prices, as represented by triple super phosphate (TSP), increased after falling for several years as demand increased and production capacity utilization increased.

Potash prices, as represented by muriate of potash (MOP), remained constant because prices are set by annual contracts, and have not kept up with changed market fundamentals. Fertilizer demand is expected to fall in 2004 and 2005 in response to the recent downturn in agricultural prices and this should cause most fertilizer prices to weaken.

Urea prices rose about 38 percent in 2003 due partly to higher prices for natural gas. Demand increased by an estimated 4 percent resulting from higher planted crop area and higher application rates. Nitrogen production capacity utilization increased to about 85 percent in 2002 from about 81 percent in 2001, and is at the highest level in several years. In response to higher prices and demand, global production and exports both increased about 4 percent in 2002 after declining in the previous year. Prices are expected to decline about 4 percent per year in 2004 and 2005 as demand weakens and natural gas prices begin to decline resulting from lower crude oil prices. By 2015, real urea prices are expected to fall 9.5 percent from 2003 levels as the industry expands production capacity more rapidly than demand.

MOP prices remained unchanged in 2003, but new contract prices are likely to increase in

Table A2.10 Fertilizers global balances
(million tons)

	1970	1980	1990	1999	2000	Est. 2001	1970–80	1980–90	1990–00
Nitrogen									
Production	33.30	62.78	82.28	87.75	84.62	82.3	6.53	3.12	0.28
Consumption	31.76	60.78	77.18	84.95	81.62	n.a.	6.86	2.60	0.56
Exports	6.77	13.15	19.59	23.94	24.70	24.6	7.23	5.10	2.34
Phosphate									
Production	22.04	34.51	39.18	32.51	31.70	30.7	3.72	1.70	−2.10
Consumption	21.12	31.70	35.90	33.46	32.65	n.a.	3.85	1.39	−0.90
Exports	2.92	7.51	10.50	12.70	12.11	n.a.	8.37	5.01	1.44
Potash									
Production	17.59	27.46	26.82	25.01	25.54	25.9	3.97	−0.03	−0.49
Consumption	16.43	24.24	24.68	22.12	22.16	n.a.	3.93	0.05	−1.07
Exports	9.45	16.72	19.82	22.65	23.41	23.2	4.89	0.73	1.68

n.a. = Not available.
Notes: All data are in marketing years.
Source: FAO. The data for 2001 are estimated by World Bank staff from industry sources.

2004 in response to improved demand and the highest capacity utilization rates in five years. Production rose about 3 percent in 2002, with most of the increase coming from Canada, which accounts for 40 percent of world exports and one-third of production. Prices are expected to increase by about 3 percent in 2004 and remain at the higher level in 2005. Increased domestic production in China, along with large surplus global production capacity, is expected to keep price increases small. By 2015, real prices are projected to fall 3.5 percent compared to 2003.

TSP prices increased 7 percent in 2003 after falling 23 percent from 1998 to 2001 and increasing 6 percent in 2002. Production increased by about 7 percent in 2002, with production in the U.S.—the world's largest producer with a 30 percent share—increasing by 13 percent, according to industry sources. Exports declined because of a sharp drop in Chinese imports, which were replaced by increased domestic production. TSP prices are expected to decrease marginally in 2004 and 2005 as demand weakens; however, surplus production capacity is smaller than for other major fertilizers and is expected to remain tight over the next several years. Thus real prices are projected to remain about constant between 2003 and 2015.

Metals and Minerals

Metals and minerals prices have rallied a number of times since the lows of October 2001, often on investor expectations that a global economic recovery would lead to higher demand for metals. However, prospects for a strong economic recovery have kept being pushed back and the price rallies have been short-lived. Yet the index for metals and minerals is up 13 percent since October 2001 on improving fundamentals—notably producer cutbacks, some modest reduction of inventories, and weakening of the U.S. dollar.

As major producers and consumers do not have their currencies linked to the dollar, the metal prices in dollars fluctuate with the value

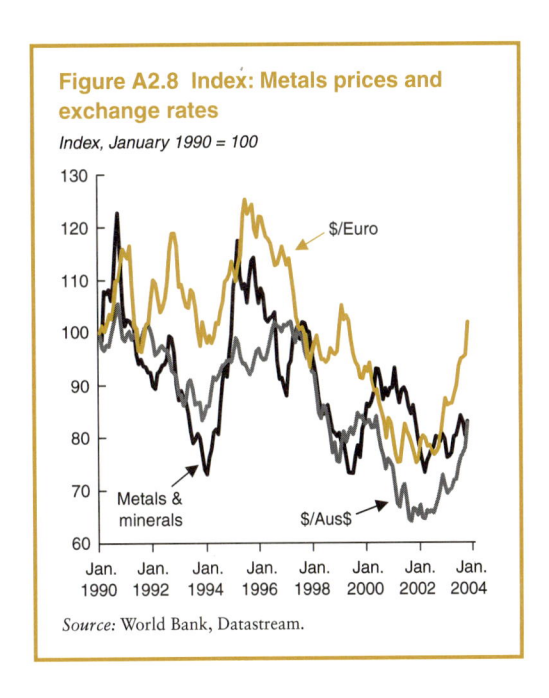

Figure A2.8 Index: Metals prices and exchange rates

Index, January 1990 = 100

Source: World Bank, Datastream.

of the U.S. dollar, rising when the Euro or Australian dollar appreciate and falling in the opposite case (figure A2.8).

Most metals markets are expected to remain in surplus or a balanced position in 2003, and slip into deficit in 2004 as demand recovers. During the upturn of the next economic cycle metals prices could rise significantly, as is typical during a recovery. However, higher prices will induce development of new capacity and the restart of idle facilities, and prices will eventually recede. Real prices are expected to decline in the longer term (figure A2.9), as production costs continue to fall from new technologies and improved managerial practices, and there is little constraint on primary resource availability. The one exception is nickel, where new supply prospects over the next few years are quite limited, which could lead to much higher prices.

Aluminum

Aluminum prices have been relatively steady the past year (figure A2.10), despite extremely high inventories and a market in surplus. Three main factors have limited an expected widening surplus and supported prices. First,

GLOBAL ECONOMIC PROSPECTS

Figure A2.9 Index: Metals and minerals

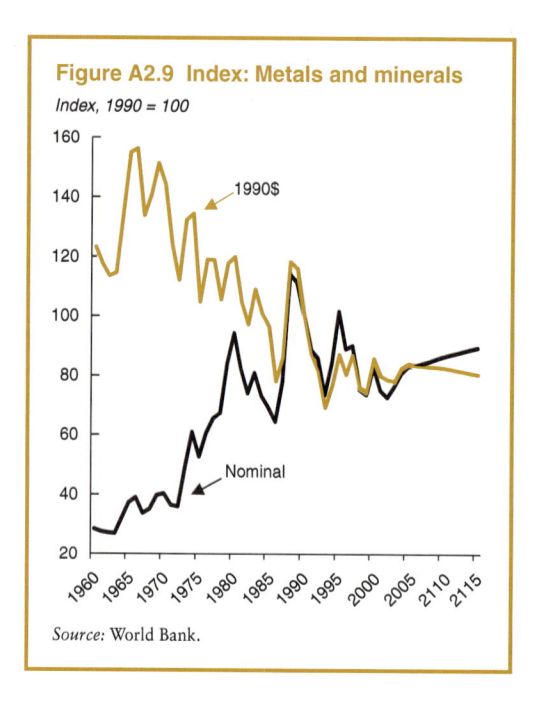

Index, 1990 = 100

Source: World Bank.

minum production growth—where much of the recent increase has occurred—as it is a large importer of alumina. Finally, tightness in scrap supplies has generated higher demand for primary aluminum.

If these conditions continue into 2004, the large surplus that had been forecast may not occur. This may limit the price declines that some had forecast. However, world aluminum production in May was the highest on record, with Chinese production up 29 percent for the first five months of this year. There is also the possibility that shut-in capacity could be restarted.

The aluminum market is expected to move into deficit in 2005, but there are a number of uncertainties in the near term, e.g., the extent of demand growth, reactivation of idle capacity, and the size of Chinese net exports. Real prices for primary aluminum are expected to slightly decline in the long term following a modest recovery during the next economic cycle. New low-cost capacity in a number of countries, e.g. Canada and the Middle East, is expected to meet the relatively strong growth in demand, although new investment will continue to require low-cost power supplies. There is not expected to be any constraint on *alumina* supply over the forecast period, and several new alumina capacity expansions are underway, e.g., Australia and Brazil.

several production cuts have occurred in North America and elsewhere because of electric power-related difficulties. Second, tightness in alumina supplies has resulted in high alumina prices, which may slow Chinese alu-

Figure A2.10 Aluminum price and LME stocks

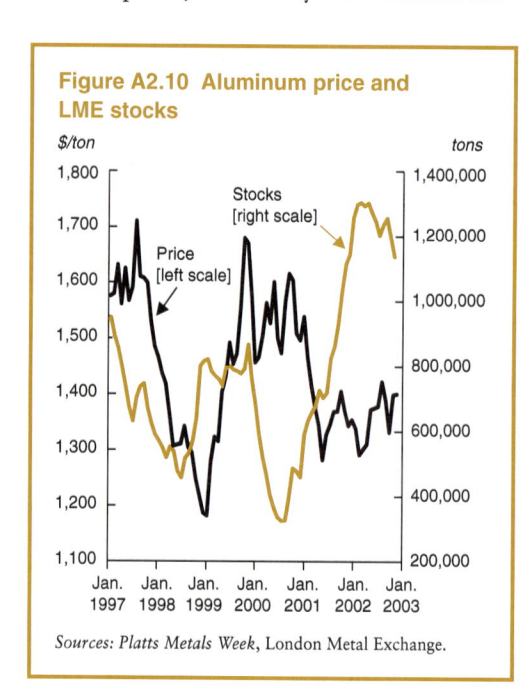

Sources: Platts Metals Week, London Metal Exchange.

Copper

Copper prices have risen more than 20 percent from the lows of October 2001, largely because of a number of production cutbacks and curtailments that began in 2001. This has helped reduce the large surplus that emerged in 2001, and LME copper stocks have fallen about 30 percent from the peak in 2001—yet they remain relatively high (figure A2.11). In the first quarter of 2003, the global copper market moved into deficit according to the *International Copper Study Group*, because of lower world production and relatively strong demand, particularly in China where consumption rose more than 20 percent from a year earlier.

Figure A2.11 Copper price and LME stocks

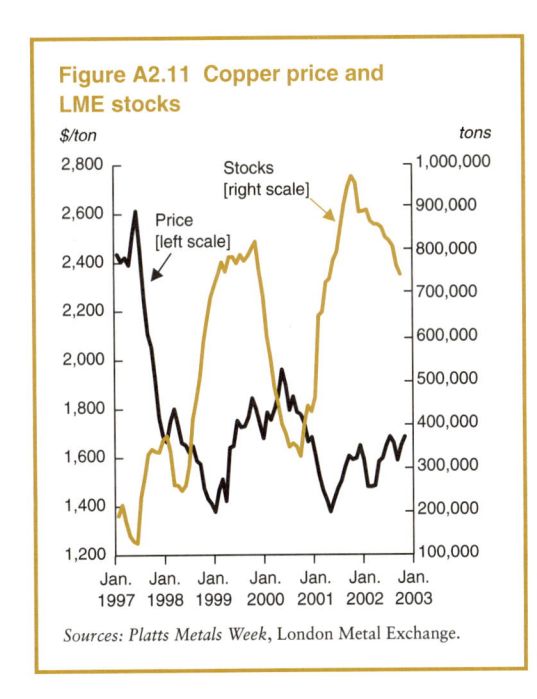

Sources: Platts Metals Week, London Metal Exchange.

Demand outside of China and neighboring Asian countries remains relatively weak, and the market could remain in surplus in 2003. Much will depend on the extent of the economic recovery and continuation of production cuts in Latin America and the U.S. The market is expected to move into deficit in 2004 as demand recovers, which will put upward pressure on prices. However, the restart of idled capacity in Chile and the U.S. could prevent prices from moving sharply higher.

In the medium term, the market is expected to return to balance as new capacity is expected to meet the projected growth in global consumption of around 3.5 percent per year, which will be mainly driven by strong growth in China and other Asian countries. Over the longer term, increases in new low-cost capacity are expected to result in a continued decline of real prices. A major uncertainty over the forecast period will be the volume of Chinese imports.

Nickel

Nickel prices have risen about 75 percent from October 2001 (figure A2.12), because of low stocks, strong demand for stainless steel, and tight supplies. A strike at Inco's operations in Sudbury, Canada, on June 1, 2003, briefly sent prices above US$9,500/ton, but prices receded after Russia's Norilsk agreed to release 24,000 tons from inventory. This followed an announcement by the company in April to release 16,000 tons.

Demand for nickel rose 6 percent in 2002 because of strong growth of stainless steel production, led by China, which increased stainless steel output by around 20 percent. Growth for both stainless steel and nickel is expected to weaken slightly this year, mainly because of the slowdown in Europe, before strengthening in 2004. The nickel market is expected to slip into deficit this year and remain so in 2004 and 2005, mainly because of a dearth of major new projects to come on stream over this period.

Nickel producers have had a number of setbacks with pressure acid leach (PAL) technology at new laterite deposits (a high proportion of potential new developments have this type of ore-body). Technical problems and substantial cost overruns have significantly

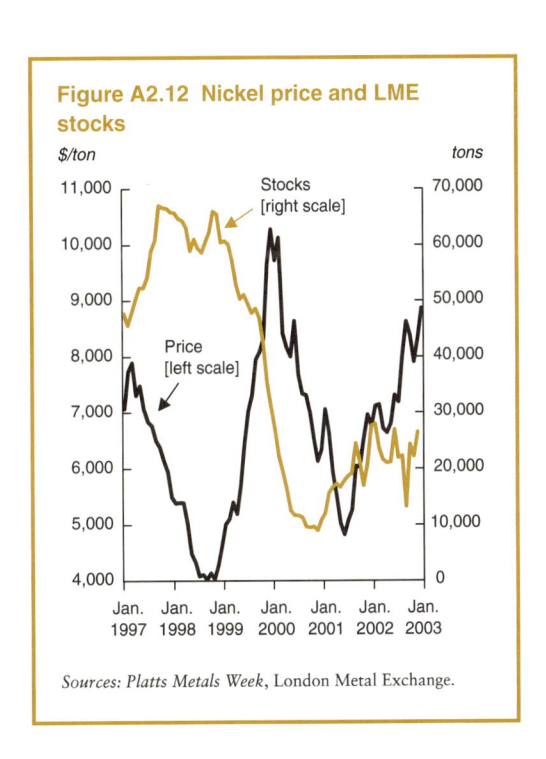

Figure A2.12 Nickel price and LME stocks

Sources: Platts Metals Week, London Metal Exchange.

Table A2.11 Metals and minerals global balances
(thousand tons)

	1970	1980	1990	2000	2001	2002	Annual growth rates (%) 1970–80	1980–90	1990–00
Aluminum									
Production	10,257	16,027	19,362	24,485	24,477	26,099	3.2	1.9	2.4
Consumption	9,996	14,771	19,244	24,903	23,561	24,944	3.2	1.8	2.6
LME Ending Stocks	n.a.	68	311	322	821	1241	n.a.	–0.3	0.3
Copper									
Production	7,583	9,242	10,809	14,820	15,889	15,336	1.9	1.1	3.2
Consumption	7,294	9,400	10,780	15,176	14,876	14,963	2.5	1	3.5
LME Ending Stocks	72	123	179	357	799	856	7.4	–5.6	7.1
Nickel									
Production	n.a.	717	842	1,107	1,145	1,177	n.a.	1.6	2.8
Consumption	n.a.	742	858	1,172	1,178	1,206	n.a.	1.5	3.2
LME Ending Stocks	2	5	4	10	19	22	n.a.	–0.5	9.6

n.a. = Not available.
Sources: World Bureau of Metal Statistics, London Metal Exchange, and World Bank.

limited the expected ramp-up of production at new projects in Australia. In addition, Inco has temporarily suspended some construction work at its US$1.4 billion Goro project in New Caledonia, after costs escalated by 30–45 percent. The company's current review of the project may delay start-up of production into 2006. These difficulties at laterite projects will likely impact development of forthcoming PAL operations. Cost estimates for future developments are being raised, which will likely result in higher long-term nickel prices.

With no new major greenfield projects on the immediate horizon, nickel prices could jump significantly over the next couple of years before new supplies bring the market back into balance. Over the longer term, large new projects are planned for development, and a new generation of technology and operational practices may help to reduce costs. In addition to the risks of higher costs, a major uncertainty for the nickel market is the pace of demand growth in China.

Gold

In 2002, gold prices climbed above their four-year trading range of roughly US$250–$300/toz, largely because of the buyback of hedged positions by gold producers (referred to as dehedging). In addition, increased investment demand resulting from declining equity markets and the U.S. dollar helped support prices. More recently, much of the movement in gold prices seems to have been largely currency related (figure A2.13).

Producer dehedging totaled about 4.5 million ounces in the first quarter of 2003 (6 per-

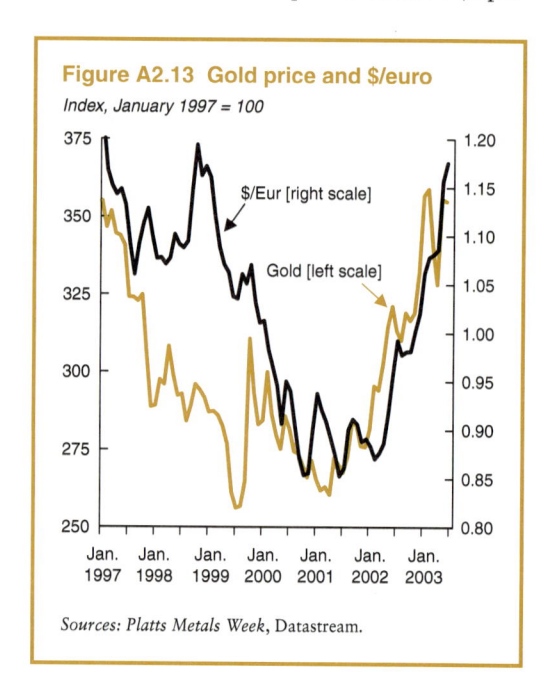

Figure A2.13 Gold price and $/euro
Index, January 1997 = 100

Sources: Platts Metals Week, Datastream.

Table A2.12 Gold global balance
(tons)

	2001	2002	2002 (% y/y.)	1Q02	2Q02	3Q03	4Q04	1Q03	1Q03 (% y/y.)
Jewelry	3,037	2,688	−11.5	655	638	657	738	586	−10.5
Other Fabrication	476	485	1.9	125	117	117	126	151	20.8
Bar Hoarding	248	252	1.6	80	53	61	58	35	−56.3
Net Producer Hedging	151	423	180.1	31	104	149	139	145	367.7
Implied Net Investment	–	130	n.a.	40	48	24	17	64	60.0
Total Demand	3,912	3,978	1.7	931	960	1,008	1,078	970	4.2
Mine Production	2,623	2,587	−1.4	570	637	727	653	572	0.4
Official Sector Sales	529	556	5.1	163	118	83	191	151	−7.4
Old Gold Scrap	708	835	17.9	198	205	198	234	248	25.3
Implied Net Disinvestment	52	–	n.a.	–	–	–	–	–	
Total Supply	3,912	3,978	1.7	931	960	1008	1078	970	4.2

n.a. = Not available.
Sources: Gold Field Minerals Service and World Bank.

cent of producer hedges), about the same level of reduction that occurred in each of the third and fourth quarters of 2002, according to *Gold Field Mineral Services*. Many companies have indicated a desire to further reduce their hedges, and shareholder sentiment generally appears to be against hedging. This was evidenced in the first quarter of 2003 when, despite high prices, little new hedging took place. However, hedging of gold is unattractive at current low interest rates.

It is expected that producer dehedging will slow in the second half of this year and in 2004, and remove much of the support under gold prices. And at some point, higher interest rates may trigger another bout of hedging.

Higher gold prices have had a negative impact on consumer demand. In the first quarter of 2003, jewelry demand fell by more than 10 percent (table A2.12), with declines in both developing and developed regions. In the largest consuming country, India, demand fell 13 percent, following a 20 percent drop in 2002. High prices will continue to weaken the price-sensitive jewelry demand market, and stimulate investment in new production, and from scrap. Over the medium term prices are expected to fall below US$300/toz as supplies from all sources exceed demand. Even below US$300/toz, mine production is expected to continue to increase moderately as new low-cost operations come on stream.

Finally, official central bank sales continue to take place. An important determinant of medium-term prices will be the decision by central banks whether to further stem official gold sales when the Washington Agreement expires in 2004 (the European Central Bank and 14 European central banks agreed in September 1999 to sell only 400 tons of gold per year, and not more than 2,000 tons in total, for the subsequent five years).

Petroleum

Since late 1999, the average oil price (for Brent, Dubai, and WTI) has generally been above US$25/bbl, with the exception of the slump following the September 11, 2001, attacks (figure A2.14). Excluding the slump, oil prices averaged about US$27.1/bbl, compared to US$17.6/bbl over the 1986–99 period. The higher prices are mainly because of strong production discipline by OPEC, but have also been supported by periods of low stocks, supply disruptions, and cold weather.

Following the collapse of prices in 1998, OPEC began adjusting production quotas as required to maintain prices within a band of US$22–$28/bbl for its basket of crudes. By and large the organization has been successful, though its market share has slowly eroded. For OPEC-10 (excluding Iraq), its *crude oil* production as a share of total world oil supply fell

GLOBAL ECONOMIC PROSPECTS

Figure A2.14 Oil price and OECD stocks

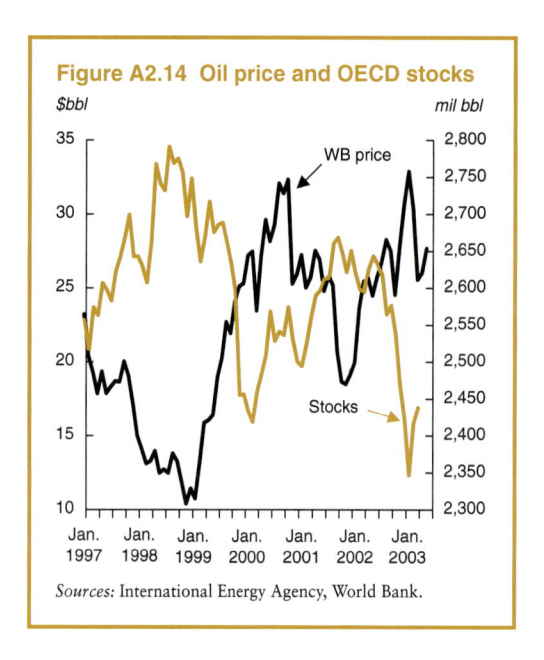

Sources: International Energy Agency, World Bank.

from 35 percent in 1996–97 to 30 percent in 2002.

The escalation of prices in 2002 resulted from large OPEC production cuts (figure A2.15), augmented by expectations of supply disruption as the U.S.-led coalition prepared for war in Iraq. The physical market tightened in the second half of 2002 from lower OPEC output, and then oil inventories fell precipitously after Venezuela's oil exports ceased in December because of strikes, and as cold weather raised peak-winter demand. At end-winter 2003, oil inventories were near historic lows.

With the loss of Venezuela's production and impending loss of Iraq's exports, other OPEC producers raised production significantly, particularly from the Gulf. Saudi Arabia's production rose from 7.7 mb/d in the fourth quarter of 2002 to more than 9.0 mb/d by March 2003, and the rest of OPEC (excluding Venezuela and Iraq) added more than 1 mb/d over this period, with the largest increases from Kuwait, UAE, and Algeria. At the same time, Venezuela's production began to recover, although it appears that some 0.4 mb/d of capacity was permanently lost as a result of the strikes.

The disruption to oil supplies from the war in Iraq was limited to Iraqi exports of about 2 mb/d. Higher output from other OPEC members was sufficient to prevent a sharp spike in prices, and emergency stocks in consuming countries were not withdrawn. Oil prices peaked in early March just before the conflict commenced at US$34.2/bbl.

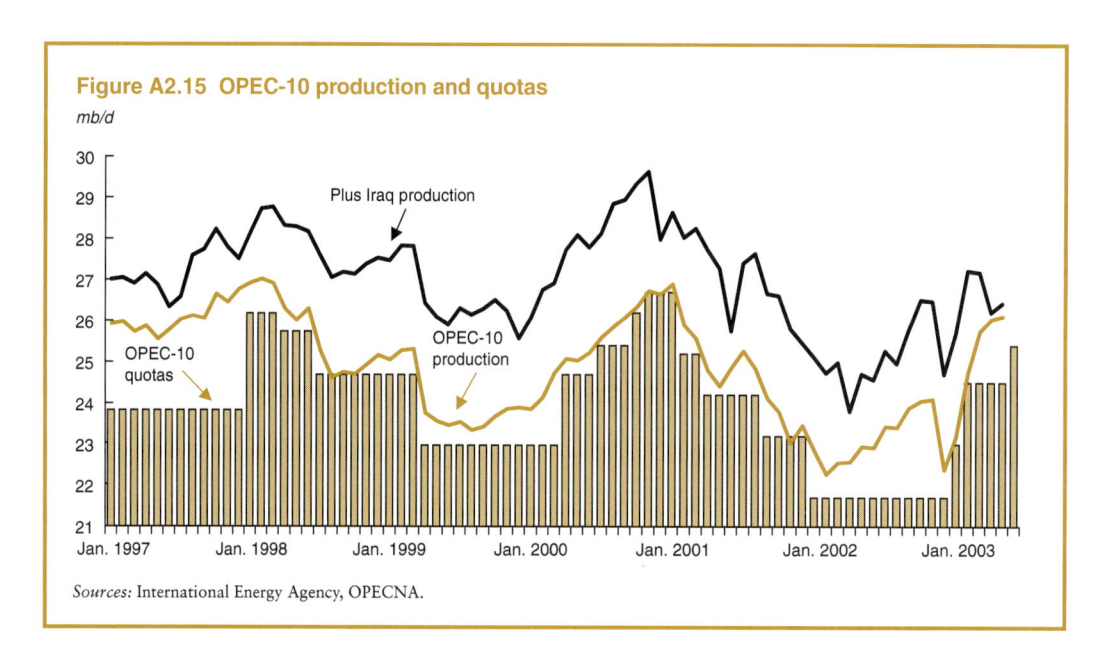

Figure A2.15 OPEC-10 production and quotas

Sources: International Energy Agency, OPECNA.

Iraq's exports did not restart soon after the war ended because of widespread looting and problems with pumping facilities and pipelines. Because of broader problems with electricity, water, and other facilities that service the oil sector, it is unlikely that Iraq's pre-war production of around 2.5 mb/d will be reached this year.

The delay in resumption of Iraqi exports and the low level of oil inventories eases the task for OPEC this year of maintaining prices within its band. However, the difficulty managing oil prices is expected to deepen in 2004, as Iraq oil exports exceed pre-war levels. OPEC will have to absorb Iraq back into its quota system at some point, and quotas for all members may need to be adjusted. A number of OPEC members are raising capacity and will likely request higher quotas, e.g., Algeria and Nigeria. The expansion of OPEC capacity will occur when non-OPEC producers are expected to capture virtually all of the growth in world oil demand. Consequently, oil prices are expected to fall to the lower end of OPEC's price band in 2004.

Downward pressures on oil prices are expected to continue in subsequent years, as much of the moderate growth in world oil demand, about 1.5 mb/d, will be captured by strong gains in non-OPEC supply of more than 1 mb/d per year. Large increases are expected from Russia, the Caspian Sea, West Africa, and the Western Hemisphere, including the U.S. because of significant developments in the deepwater Gulf of Mexico. BP reports that between 2002 and 2007, 5 mb/d of new supply are likely to come on stream from these regions alone.

This will leave little room for growth in OPEC production. With the build-up of new capacity in many OPEC countries, including Iraq, oil prices are expected to decline. By 2006–07, oil prices are expected to fall to US$18/bbl (figure A2.16) as significant volumes of new production begin from the Caspian, and as production and export capacity increase more broadly from the FSU, West Africa, and other regions.

A risk to the forecast is that OPEC will maintain strong production discipline over the next few years to keep prices at or above US$25/bbl. If successful, it would further impact oil demand growth and stimulate even greater supplies from competing sources. It is felt that OPEC would only prolong a decline in oil prices that is expected by mid-decade.

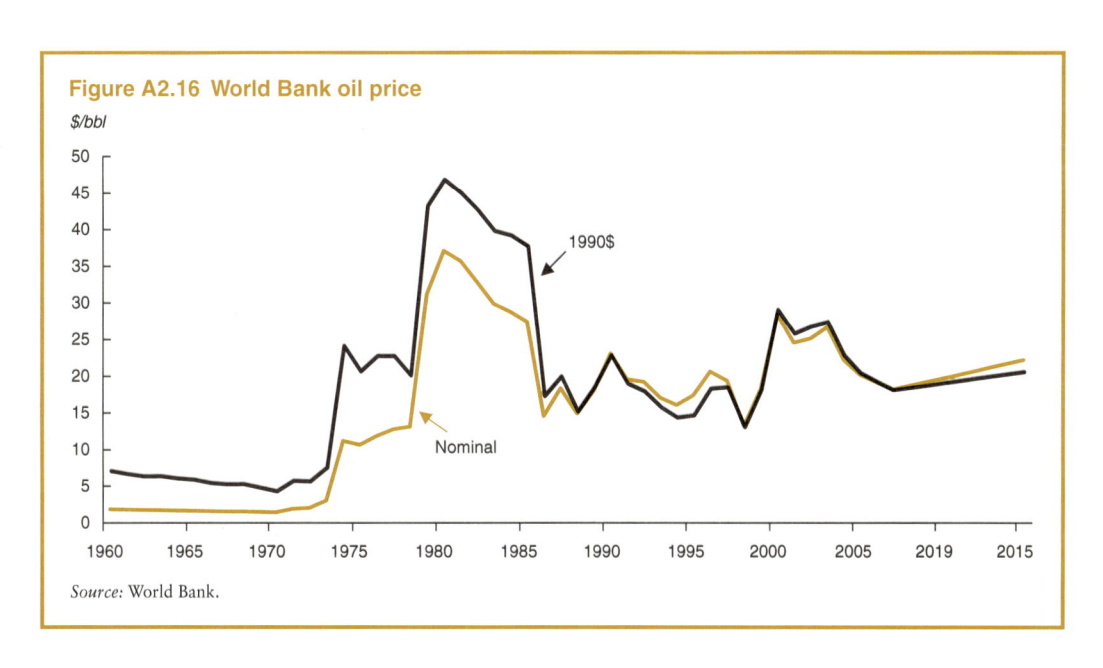

Figure A2.16 World Bank oil price

Source: World Bank.

Table A2.13 Petroleum global balance
(million barrels per day)

	\multicolumn{6}{c	}{Million barrels per day}	\multicolumn{3}{c}{Annual growth rates (%)}
	1970	1980	1990	2000	2002	2003	1970–80	1980–90	1990–00
Consumption									
OECD	34.0	41.5	41.5	47.8	47.6	48.2	2.0	0.0	1.3
FSU	5.0	8.9	8.4	3.6	3.7	3.8	5.9	–0.6	–7.2
Other non-OECD	6.8	12.3	16.1	24.8	25.6	25.9	6.1	2.7	4.1
Total	45.7	62.6	66.0	76.2	76.9	77.9	3.2	0.5	1.3
Production									
OPEC	23.5	27.2	24.5	30.7	28.6	29.8	1.5	–1.0	1.9
FSU	7.1	12.1	11.5	7.9	9.4	10.2	5.4	–0.5	–2.6
Other non-OPEC	17.4	24.6	30.9	38.0	38.6	39.1	3.5	2.3	1.9
Total	48.0	63.9	66.9	76.6	76.5	79.1	2.9	0.5	1.3
Stock Change, Misc.	2.3	1.3	0.9	0.4	–0.3	1.2			

Sources: British Petroleum, International Energy Agency, and World Bank.

In the longer term, demand growth will only be moderate, as it has been the past two decades (table A2.13), but new technologies, environmental pressures, and government policies could further reduce this growth. Prices below US$20/bbl are sufficiently high to generate ample development of conventional and non-conventional oil supplies, and there are no apparent resource constraints far into the future. In addition, new areas continue to be developed (e.g., deep water offshore), and development costs are expected to continue to fall from new technologies (shifting supply curves outward). In addition, OPEC countries are increasing capacity, and will add to the supply competition in coming years. Consequently, real oil prices are expected to continue their long-term decline.

Table A2.14 Commodity prices and price projections in current dollars

Commodity	Unit	Actual 1970	Actual 1980	Actual 1990	Actual 2000	Actual 2002	Projections 2003	Projections 2004	Projections 2005	Projections 2010	Projections 2015
Energy											
Coal, Australia	$/mt	n.a.	n.a.	39.67	26.25	27.06	26.00	26.50	27.00	29.50	32.00
Crude oil, average	$/bbl	1.21	36.87	22.88	28.23	24.93	26.50	22.00	20.00	19.50	22.00
Natural gas, Europe	$/mmbtu	n.a.	3.40	2.55	3.86	3.05	3.75	3.00	2.65	2.75	3.00
Natural gas, US	$/mmbtu	0.17	1.55	1.70	4.31	3.35	5.25	3.75	3.50	3.25	3.50
Non-Energy Commodities											
Agriculture											
Beverages											
Cocoa	c/kg	67.5	260.4	126.7	90.6	177.8	177.0	172.0	167.0	160.0	150.0
Coffee, other milds	c/kg	114.7	346.6	197.2	192.0	135.7	145.5	158.7	165.4	210.1	230.4
Coffee, robusta	c/kg	91.4	324.3	118.2	91.3	66.2	88.2	92.6	92.6	104.7	125.0
Tea, auctions (3) average	c/kg	83.5	165.9	205.8	187.6	150.6	150.0	155.0	160.0	170.0	170.0
Food											
Fats and oils											
Coconut oil	$/mt	397.2	673.8	336.5	450.3	421.0	442.0	460.0	470.0	500.0	530.0
Copra	$/mt	224.8	452.7	230.7	304.8	266.3	305.0	380.0	420.0	450.0	475.0
Groundnut oil	$/mt	378.6	858.8	963.7	713.7	687.1	1100.0	1000.0	890.0	795.0	796.0
Palm oil	$/mt	260.1	583.7	289.8	310.3	390.3	425.0	415.0	415.0	420.0	445.0
Soybean meal	$/mt	102.6	262.4	200.2	189.2	175.2	193.0	183.0	175.0	185.0	195.0
Soybean oil	$/mt	286.3	597.6	447.3	338.1	454.3	527.0	485.0	450.0	460.0	480.0
Soybeans	$/mt	116.9	296.2	246.8	211.8	212.7	241.0	225.0	210.0	225.0	235.0
Grains											
Maize	$/mt	58.4	125.3	109.3	88.5	99.3	106.0	100.0	95.0	105.0	112.0
Rice, Thailand, 5%	$/mt	126.3	410.7	270.9	202.4	191.9	199.0	202.0	205.0	220.0	230.0
Sorghum	$/mt	51.8	128.9	103.9	88.0	101.7	106.0	100.0	95.0	105.0	112.0
Wheat, US, HRW	$/mt	54.9	172.7	135.5	114.1	148.1	143.0	135.0	130.0	145.0	155.0
Other food											
Bananas, US	$/mt	166.1	377.3	540.9	424.0	528.6	410.0	425.0	440.0	530.0	555.0
Beef, US	c/kg	130.4	276.0	256.3	193.2	212.7	211.6	218.2	220.5	222.0	220.0
Oranges	$/mt	168.0	400.2	531.1	363.2	555.0	645.0	550.0	500.0	510.0	530.0
Shrimp, Mexico	c/kg	n.a.	1,152	1,069	1,513	1,052	1,200	1,275	1,350	1,550	1,650
Sugar, world	c/kg	8.2	63.16	27.67	18.04	15.18	16.00	15.40	15.00	19.00	21.00
Agricultural raw materials											
Timber											
Logs, Cameroon	$/cum	43.0	251.7	343.5	275.4	n.a.	275.0	280.0	285.0	320.0	350.0
Logs, Malaysia	$/cum	43.1	195.5	177.2	190.0	163.4	185.0	188.0	205.0	245.0	265.0
Sawnwood, Malaysia	$/cum	175.0	396.0	533.0	594.7	526.5	550.0	570.0	610.0	700.0	780.0
Other raw materials											
Cotton	c/kg	67.6	206.2	181.9	130.2	101.9	130.1	129.0	132.3	141.1	143.3
Rubber, RSS1, Malaysia	c/kg	40.7	142.5	86.5	69.1	77.1	95.0	90.0	94.8	88.2	90.4
Tobacco	$/mt	1,076	2,276	3,392	2,976	2,740	2,700	2,750	2,800	2,950	3,000
Fertilizers											
DAP	$/mt	54.0	222.2	171.4	154.2	157.5	177.0	175.0	170.0	170.0	175.0
Phosphate rock	$/mt	11.00	46.71	40.50	43.75	40.38	38.00	38.00	38.00	40.00	42.00
Potassium chloride	$/mt	32.0	115.7	98.1	122.5	113.3	112.5	115.0	116.0	118.0	120.0
TSP	$/mt	43.0	180.3	131.8	137.7	133.1	142.0	140.0	140.0	146.0	154.0
Urea, E. Europe, bagged	$/mt	n.a.	n.a.	119.3	101.1	94.4	130.0	128.0	126.7	125.0	130.0
Metals and minerals											
Aluminum	$/mt	556	1,456	1,639	1,549	1,350	1,390	1,425	1,500	1,600	1,700
Copper	$/mt	1,416	2,182	2,661	1,813	1,559	1,650	1,800	1,900	2,000	2,050
Gold	$/toz	35.9	607.9	383.5	279.0	310.0	330.0	300.0	280.0	300.0	300.0
Iron ore, Carajas	c/dmtu	9.84	28.09	32.50	28.79	29.31	31.95	32.00	31.00	32.00	32.50
Lead	c/kg	30.3	90.6	81.1	45.4	45.3	47.0	51.0	55.0	60.0	62.5
Nickel	$/mt	2,846	6,519	8,864	8,638	6,772	8,200	8,500	8,000	6,700	6,800
Silver	c/toz	177.0	2,064	482.0	499.9	462.5	460.0	480.0	500.0	525.0	550.0
Tin	c/kg	367.3	1,677	608.5	543.6	406.1	470.0	500.0	525.0	540.0	550.0
Zinc	c/kg	29.6	76.1	151.4	112.8	77.9	80.0	92.0	100.0	105.0	110.0

n.a. = Not available.
Note: Projections as of June 24, 2003
Source: World Bank, Development Prospects Group.

Table A2.15 Commodity prices and price projections in constant 1990 dollars

Commodity	Unit	Actual 1970	1980	1990	2000	2002	Projections 2003	2004	2005	2010	2015
Energy											
Coal, Australia	$/mt	n.a.	n.a.	39.67	26.97	28.06	26.87	27.49	27.59	28.84	29.93
Crude oil, average	$/bbl	4.31	46.80	22.88	29.01	25.84	27.39	22.82	20.44	19.06	20.58
Natural gas, Europe	$/mmbtu	n.a.	4.32	2.55	3.96	3.16	3.88	3.11	2.71	2.69	2.81
Natural gas, US	$/mmbtu	0.61	1.97	1.70	4.43	3.48	5.43	3.89	3.58	3.18	3.27
Non-Energy Commodities											
Agriculture											
Beverages											
Cocoa	c/kg	240.6	330.5	126.7	93.1	184.3	183.0	178.4	170.6	156.4	140.3
Coffee, other milds	c/kg	408.8	440.0	197.2	197.3	140.7	150.4	164.7	169.0	205.4	215.5
Coffee, robusta	c/kg	325.7	411.7	118.2	93.8	68.6	91.2	96.1	94.6	102.4	116.9
Tea, auctions (3) average	c/kg	297.7	210.6	205.8	192.8	156.1	155.0	160.8	163.5	166.2	159.0
Food											
Fats and oils											
Coconut oil	$/mt	1416.0	855.3	336.5	462.7	436.5	456.9	477.2	480.2	488.8	495.7
Copra	$/mt	801.6	574.7	230.7	313.1	276.1	315.3	394.2	429.1	439.9	444.3
Groundnut oil	$/mt	1349.5	1090.1	963.7	733.3	712.4	1137.0	1037.5	909.4	777.1	744.6
Palm oil	$/mt	927.1	740.9	289.8	318.8	404.6	439.3	430.5	424.0	410.6	416.2
Soybean meal	$/mt	365.7	333.1	200.2	194.4	181.6	199.5	189.9	178.8	180.8	182.4
Soybean oil	$/mt	1020.8	758.6	447.3	347.4	471.0	544.7	503.2	459.8	449.7	449.0
Soybeans	$/mt	416.8	376.0	246.8	217.7	220.5	249.1	233.4	214.6	219.9	219.8
Grains											
Maize	$/mt	208.2	159.0	109.3	91.0	102.9	109.6	103.8	97.1	102.6	104.8
Rice, Thailand, 5%	$/mt	450.3	521.4	270.9	208.0	198.9	205.7	209.6	209.5	215.1	215.1
Sorghum	$/mt	184.7	163.6	103.9	90.4	105.5	109.6	103.8	97.1	102.6	104.8
Wheat, US, HRW	$/mt	195.7	219.3	135.5	117.2	153.5	147.8	140.1	132.8	141.7	145.0
Other food											
Bananas, US	$/mt	592.1	478.9	540.9	435.7	548.0	423.8	440.9	449.6	518.1	519.1
Beef, US	c/kg	465.0	350.3	256.3	198.5	220.6	218.7	226.4	225.3	217.0	205.8
Oranges	$/mt	599.1	508.0	531.1	373.2	575.5	666.7	570.6	510.9	498.5	495.7
Shrimp, Mexico	c/kg	n.a.	1,462	1,069	1,554	1,090	1,240	1,323	1,379	1,515	1,543
Sugar, world	c/kg	29.32	80.17	27.67	18.5	15.7	16.5	16.0	15.3	18.6	19.6
Agricultural raw materials											
Timber											
Logs, Cameroon	$/cum	153.3	319.5	343.5	283.0	n.a.	284.2	290.5	291.2	312.8	327.4
Logs, Malaysia	$/cum	153.8	248.2	177.2	195.2	169.4	191.2	195.0	209.5	239.5	247.9
Sawnwood, Malaysia	$/cum	623.9	502.7	533.0	611.1	545.9	568.5	591.4	623.3	684.3	729.6
Other raw materials											
Cotton	c/kg	241.1	261.7	181.9	133.8	105.7	134.4	133.8	135.2	137.9	134.0
Rubber, RSS1, Malaysia	c/kg	145.2	180.8	86.5	71.0	79.9	98.2	93.4	96.9	86.2	84.6
Tobacco	$/mt	3,836	2,889	3,392	3,058	2,841	2,791	2,853	2,861	2,884	2,806
Fertilizers											
DAP	$/mt	192.5	282.1	171.4	158.5	163.3	183.0	181.6	173.7	166.2	163.7
Phosphate rock	$/mt	39.2	59.3	40.5	45.0	41.9	39.3	39.4	38.8	39.1	39.3
Potassium chloride	$/mt	114.1	146.9	98.1	125.9	117.5	116.3	119.3	118.5	115.4	112.2
TSP	$/mt	153.3	228.8	131.8	141.5	138.0	146.8	145.2	143.1	142.7	144.1
Urea, E. Europe, bulk	$/mt	n.a.	n.a.	119.3	103.9	97.8	134.4	132.8	129.5	122.2	121.6
Metals and minerals											
Aluminum	$/mt	1,982	1,848	1,639	1,592	1,400	1,437	1,478	1,533	1,564	1,590
Copper	$/mt	5,047	2,770	2,661	1,863	1,617	1,705	1,867	1,941	1,955	1,918
Gold	$/toz	128.1	771.6	383.5	286.7	321.4	341.1	311.2	286.1	293.3	280.6
Iron ore	c/dmtu	35.1	35.7	32.5	29.6	30.4	33.0	33.2	31.7	31.3	30.4
Lead	c/kg	108.0	115.0	81.1	46.6	46.9	48.6	52.9	56.2	58.7	58.5
Nickel	$/mt	10,147	8,275	8,864	8,876	7,021	8,475	8,818	8,174	6,549	6,360
Silver	c/toz	631.0	2619.4	482.0	513.7	479.5	475.5	498.0	510.9	513.2	514.5
Tin	c/kg	1309.6	2129.3	608.5	558.5	421.0	485.8	518.7	536.4	527.9	514.5
Zinc	c/kg	105.5	96.6	151.4	115.9	80.7	82.7	95.5	102.2	102.6	102.9

n.a. = Not available.
Note: Projections as of June 24, 2003
Source: World Bank, Development Prospects Group.

Table A2.16 Weighted indices of commodity prices and inflation

	Actual					Projections[a]				
Index	1970	1980	1990	2000	2002	2003	2004	2005	2010	2015
Current dollars										
Petroleum	5.3	161.2	100.0	123.4	109.0	115.8	96.2	87.4	85.2	96.2
Non-energy commodities[b]	43.8	125.5	100.0	86.9	83.0	88.8	89.7	91.1	97.7	102.6
Agriculture	45.8	138.1	100.0	87.7	86.5	92.7	92.6	93.7	102.0	107.6
Beverages	56.9	181.4	100.0	88.4	84.6	89.1	92.4	93.6	106.1	111.6
Food	46.7	139.3	100.0	84.5	90.1	94.0	91.7	89.8	96.5	101.1
Fats and oils	64.4	148.7	100.0	96.2	101.2	112.4	107.7	104.2	108.4	114.1
Grains	46.7	134.3	100.0	79.5	88.1	89.8	87.0	85.0	93.2	98.8
Other food	32.2	134.3	100.0	77.7	82.2	81.2	81.2	80.8	88.7	91.8
Raw materials	36.4	104.6	100.0	91.4	83.2	93.6	93.8	98.8	106.1	113.0
Timber	31.8	79.0	100.0	111.0	98.1	103.3	106.8	114.6	132.2	146.7
Other Raw Materials	39.6	122.0	100.0	78.0	73.1	86.9	84.9	88.0	88.3	90.0
Fertilizers	30.4	128.9	100.0	105.8	100.5	100.5	102.6	101.7	105.4	110.9
Metals and minerals	40.4	94.2	100.0	83.0	72.8	78.1	81.6	83.6	86.4	89.5
Constant 1990 dollars[c]										
Petroleum	18.9	204.5	100.0	127.0	117.2	119.7	99.8	89.3	83.3	89.9
Non-energy commodities	156.3	159.2	100.0	89.4	89.3	91.7	93.1	93.1	95.5	96.0
Agriculture	163.3	175.2	100.0	90.3	93.0	95.8	96.0	95.8	99.7	100.7
Beverages	202.8	230.2	100.0	90.9	91.0	92.1	95.9	95.7	103.7	104.4
Food	166.5	176.7	100.0	87.0	96.9	97.2	95.1	91.8	94.4	94.6
Fats and oils	229.5	188.6	100.0	99.0	108.8	116.2	111.7	106.4	105.9	106.7
Grains	166.6	170.4	100.0	81.8	94.7	92.8	90.2	86.9	91.1	92.4
Other food	114.9	170.5	100.0	80.0	88.4	84.0	84.2	82.5	86.7	85.9
Raw materials	129.8	132.7	100.0	94.0	89.5	96.7	97.3	100.9	103.7	105.7
Timber	113.3	100.3	100.0	114.2	105.5	106.8	110.8	117.1	129.2	137.3
Other Raw Materials	141.1	154.8	100.0	80.2	78.6	89.8	88.1	89.9	86.3	84.2
Fertilizers	108.3	163.6	100.0	108.9	108.1	103.9	106.5	103.9	103.0	103.7
Metals and minerals	143.9	119.5	100.0	85.4	78.3	80.7	84.6	85.5	84.5	83.7
Inflation indices, 1990=100[d]										
MUV index[e]	28.05	78.81	100.00	97.17	92.99	96.75	96.39	97.87	102.30	106.91
% change per annum		10.88	2.41	−0.29	−2.18	4.05	−0.37	1.53	0.89	0.88
US GDP deflator	33.59	65.93	100.00	123.56	127.91	129.96	132.69	135.87	152.83	172.07
% change per annum		6.98	4.25	2.14	1.75	1.60	2.10	2.40	2.38	2.40

a. Commodity price projections as of June 24, 2003.
b. The World Bank primary commodity price indices are computed based on 1987–89 export values in US dollars for low- and middle-income economies, rebased to 1990. Weights for the sub-group indices expressed as ratios to the non-energy index are as follows in percent: agriculture 69.1, fertilizers 2.7, metals and minerals 28.2; beverages 16.9, food 29.4, raw materials 22.8; fats and oils 10.1, grains 6.9, other food 12.4; timber 9.3 and other raw mterials 13.6.
c. Computed from unrounded data and deflated by the MUV index
d. Inflation indices for 2002–2015 are projections as of June 10, 2003. MUV for 2001 is an estimate. Growth rates for years 1980, 1990, 2000, 2002, 2005, 2010 and 2015 refer to compound annual rate of change between adjacent end-point years; all others are annual growth rates from the previous year.
e. Unit value index in US dollar terms of manufactures exported from the G-5 countries (France, Germany, Japan, UK, and US) weighted proportionally to the countries' exports to the developing countries
Source: World Bank, Development Prospects Group. Historical US GDP deflator: US Department of Commerce.

Appendix 3
Global Economic Indicators

GLOBAL ECONOMIC PROSPECTS

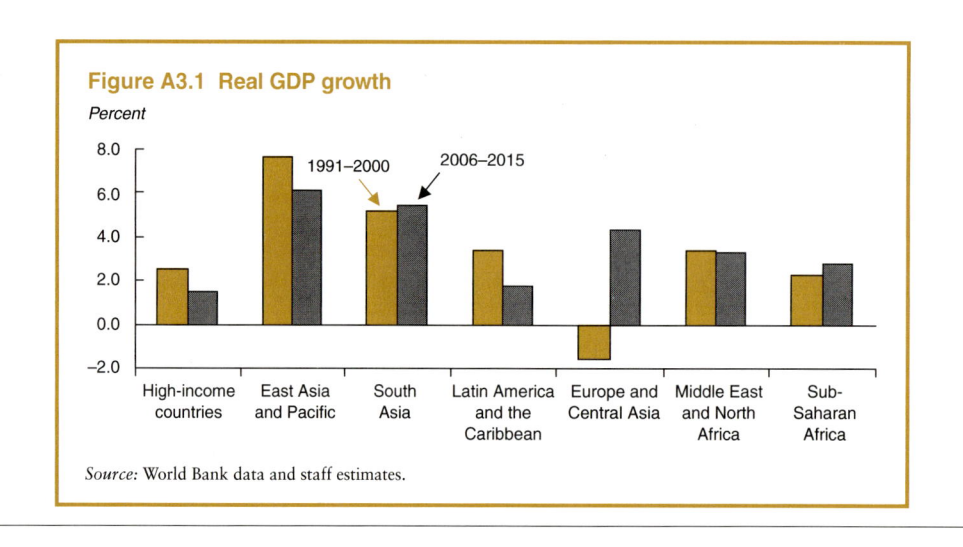

Table A3.1 Growth of Real GDP, 1971–2015
GDP in 1995 prices and exchange rates, average annual growth (percent)

	GDP in 2002 (current billions of dollars)	Growth percent 1971–80	1981–90	1991–00	Estimate 2002	2003	Forecast 2004–2005	2006–2015
World	32,016	3.7	3.0	2.6	1.9	2.0	2.9	3.2
High income economies	25,937	3.5	3.1	2.5	1.6	1.5	2.5	2.7
Industrial countries	25,190	3.4	3.1	2.4	1.6	1.5	2.4	2.6
G-7 countries	21,350	3.4	3.1	2.3	1.4	1.4	2.3	...
United States	10,446	3.3	3.2	3.2	2.4	...	...	...
Japan	3,997	4.5	4.1	1.4	0.2	...	...	...
G-4 Europe	6,172	2.9	2.4	1.9	0.8	0.7	1.9	...
Germany[a]	1,990	2.7	2.2	1.7	0.2	...	...	...
Euro Area	6,633	3.2	2.3	2.0	0.9	0.7	1.9	2.2
Non-G-7 industrial	3,840	3.2	2.9	3.0	2.4	1.8	3.0	...
Other high income	747	7.6	4.9	5.4	2.4	2.1	4.3	4.5
Asian NIEs	531	9.5	7.4	6.0	3.0	2.2	4.6	...
Low and middle income economies	6,079	5.0	2.6	3.3	3.3	4.0	4.9	4.6
excluding CE.Eur / CIS	5,147	5.6	3.1	4.7	3.0	4.0	5.0	...
Asia	2,403	5.3	6.9	7.0	6.1	5.9	6.3	...
East Asia and Pacific	1,757	6.7	7.3	7.7	6.7	6.1	6.6	6.2
China	1,237	6.2	9.3	10.1	8.0	...	...	...
Indonesia	173	7.9	6.4	4.2	3.8	...	...	...
South Asia	646	3.1	5.9	5.2	4.2	5.4	5.4	5.4
India	515	3.0	6.1	5.4	4.4	...	...	...
Latin America and Caribbean	1,658	5.9	1.1	3.4	−0.8	1.8	3.8	3.8
Brazil	452	8.5	1.5	2.7	1.5	...	...	...
Mexico	637	6.7	1.8	3.5	1.0	...	...	...
Argentina	102	3.0	−1.5	4.5	−10.9	...	...	...
Europe and Central Asia	1,114	3.9	1.5	−1.6	4.6	4.3	4.3	3.4
Russian Federation[b]	347	3.9	1.5	−4.0	4.3	...	...	...
Turkey	183	4.1	5.2	3.6	7.8	...	...	...
Poland	188	5.1	−1.7	3.7	1.3	...	...	...
Middle East and North Africa	587	7.0	2.5	3.4	3.1	3.3	3.7	4.3
Saudi Arabia	193	10.3	0.3	2.3	0.8	...	...	...
Iran	108	2.6	2.7	4.2	6.3	...	...	...
Egypt	90	6.6	5.5	4.3	3.0	...	...	...
Sub-Saharan Africa	316	3.5	1.7	2.3	2.8	2.8	3.7	3.5
Republic of South Africa	104	3.5	1.3	1.7	3.0	...	...	...
Nigeria	44	4.7	1.1	2.6	1.9	...	...	...

Notes: growth rates over intervals are computed using compound average methods;
a. data prior to 1991 covers West Germany
b. data prior to 1992 covers former Soviet Union

Figure A3.1 Real GDP growth

Percent — bar chart comparing 1991–2000 and 2006–2015 growth rates across: High-income countries, East Asia and Pacific, South Asia, Latin America and the Caribbean, Europe and Central Asia, Middle East and North Africa, Sub-Saharan Africa.

Source: World Bank data and staff estimates.

GLOBAL ECONOMIC INDICATORS

Table A3.2 Growth of real per-capita GDP, 1971–2015
GDP in 1995 prices and exchange rates, average annual growth (percent)

	GDP per capita 2002 (current dollars)	Growth percent 1971–80	Growth percent 1981–90	Growth percent 1991–00	Estimate 2002	2003	Forecast 2004–2005	2006–2015
World	5,297	1.8	1.3	1.2	0.7	0.8	1.8	2.2
High income economies[a]	27,185	2.6	2.5	1.8	1.2	1.1	2.1	2.5
Industrial countries	27,710	2.6	2.5	1.8	1.2	1.1	2.1	2.4
G-7 countries	30,256	2.7	2.5	1.7	1.0	1.1	2.0	...
United States	36,224	2.2	2.2	2.2	1.7	...	...	...
Japan	31,437	3.3	3.5	1.2	0.1	...	...	...
G-4 Europe	23,856	2.6	2.1	1.5	0.8	0.7	1.9	...
Germany[b]	24,123	2.6	2.0	1.4	0.3	...	...	...
Euro Area	21,721	2.7	2.1	1.7	0.8	0.7	1.9	2.3
Non-G-7 industrial	18,879	2.2	2.2	2.4	2.0	1.5	2.8	...
Other high income	16,577	5.0	3.1	3.8	1.1	0.9	3.1	4.2
Asian NIEs	15,891	7.2	5.9	4.7	2.0	1.3	3.7	...
Low & middle income economies	1,194	2.9	0.7	1.7	1.9	2.7	3.6	3.4
excluding CE.Eur / CIS	1,066	3.2	1.0	3.0	1.5	2.5	3.6	...
Asia	742	3.0	4.9	5.4	4.8	4.6	5.1	...
East Asia and Pacific	956	4.6	5.6	6.4	5.8	5.2	5.7	5.4
China	966	4.3	7.7	9.0	7.2	...	...	...
Indonesia	817	5.4	4.4	2.5	2.4	...	...	...
South Asia	461	0.7	3.6	3.3	2.5	3.7	3.8	4.1
India	491	0.7	3.9	3.6	2.8	...	...	...
Latin America and Caribbean	3,149	3.3	–0.9	1.7	–2.3	0.4	2.4	2.5
Brazil	2,593	5.9	–0.4	1.2	0.3	...	...	...
Mexico	6,314	3.6	–0.3	1.7	–0.8	...	...	...
Argentina	2,694	1.3	–2.9	3.2	–12.0	...	...	...
Europe and Central Asia	3,374	2.9	0.6	–1.8	4.5	4.3	4.2	3.3
Russian Federation[c]	2,405	3.2	0.9	–3.9	4.6	...	...	...
Turkey	2,626	1.7	2.8	2.0	6.3	...	...	...
Poland	4,859	4.2	–2.4	3.5	1.2	...	...	...
Middle East and North Africa	1,917	4.0	–0.6	1.2	1.1	1.3	1.7	2.5
Saudi Arabia	8,727	5.1	–4.8	–1.1	–2.2	...	...	...
Iran	1,641	–0.6	–0.7	2.5	4.6	...	...	...
Egypt	1,354	4.4	2.9	2.4	1.4	...	...	...
Sub-Saharan Africa	460	0.7	–1.1	–0.2	0.5	0.6	1.5	1.6
Republic of South Africa	2,392	1.2	–1.2	–0.2	1.7	...	...	...
Nigeria	328	1.7	–1.9	–0.2	–0.8	...	...	...

Notes: growth rates over intervals are computed using compound annual methods;
a. regional aggregates computed as sum(GDP$_i$)/sum(POP$_i$), where "i" indicates country in the region, and are unweighted by population or other measures;
b. data prior to 1991 covers West Germany;
c. data prior to 1992 covers former Soviet Union

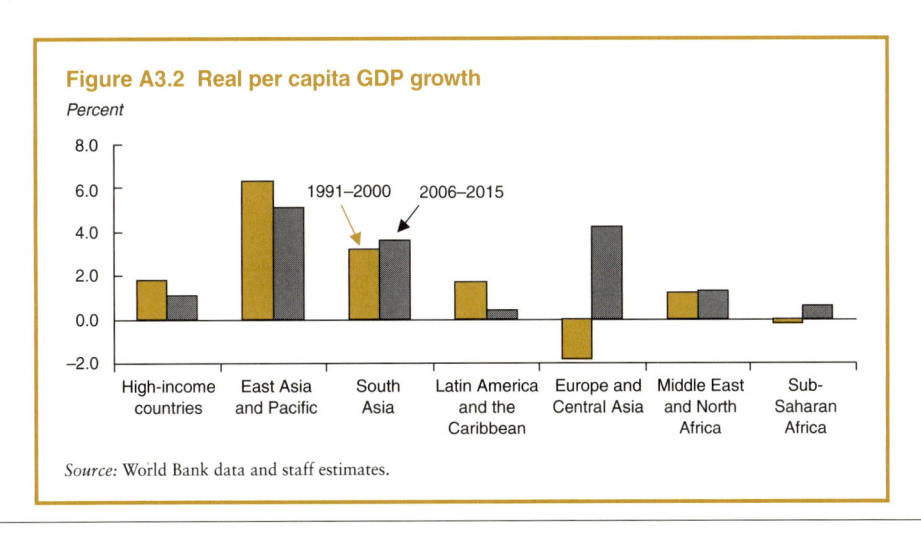

Figure A3.2 Real per capita GDP growth

Percent

[Bar chart comparing 1991–2000 and 2006–2015 real per capita GDP growth across: High-income countries, East Asia and Pacific, South Asia, Latin America and the Caribbean, Europe and Central Asia, Middle East and North Africa, Sub-Saharan Africa]

Source: World Bank data and staff estimates.

GLOBAL ECONOMIC PROSPECTS

Table A3.3 Inflation: GDP Deflators, 1971–2005
Deflators in local currency units; 1995=100; percentage change[a]

	Growth percent			2001	Estimate 2002	Forecast 2003	2004–2005
	1971–80	1981–90	1991–00				
World	9.1	5.9	3.7	2.2	1.5	1.6	1.8
High income economies	8.9	5.3	2.0	1.5	1.0	1.0	1.2
Industrial countries	8.7	4.6	2.0	1.5	1.0	1.0	1.2
G-7 countries	8.3	4.2	1.7	1.2	0.8	0.8	1.0
United States	7.0	4.3	2.1	2.4	1.1	1.5	1.5
Japan	7.8	2.0	0.1	−1.6	−1.6	−2.1	−0.5
G-4 Europe	9.9	5.7	2.6	1.9	2.2	1.8	1.5
Germany[b]	5.3	2.6	2.6	1.4	1.6	1.2	0.9
Euro Area	9.6	6.1	2.8	2.4	2.3	1.9	1.5
Non-G-7 industrial	11.1	7.1	3.3	3.1	2.3	2.4	2.1
Other high income	19.6	33.7	3.7	0.1	−0.6	0.5	1.8
Asian NIEs	9.5	4.7	2.4	−0.4	−1.4	−0.7	1.3
Low and middle income economies	9.8	8.8	11.8	5.2	4.0	4.0	4.1
excluding CE.Eur / CIS	11.6	10.7	9.4	4.8	4.1	4.0	4.2
Asia	10.2	7.7	7.6	2.9	2.6	4.4	4.9
East Asia and Pacific	9.8	6.6	6.8	2.6	3.3	3.7	3.7
China	0.9	5.4	6.3	0.0	0.4	...	...
Indonesia	20.6	8.8	14.9	12.6	7.2	...	...
South Asia	11.9	9.0	7.8	3.0	1.8	5.1	5.2
India	8.9	8.5	8.0	3.0	2.6	...	...
Latin America and Caribbean	15.6	20.4	12.0	5.5	4.7	4.1	4.0
Brazil	39.7	330.8	206.1	8.8	8.5	...	...
Mexico	18.1	63.7	18.1	5.4	4.9	...	...
Argentina	117.7	439.5	10.2	−1.1	30.8	...	...
Europe and Central Asia	0.2	1.0	76.0	6.1	4.0	5.8	4.6
Russian Federation[c]	0.0	31.6	104.5	18.0	10.7	...	...
Turkey	32.8	46.4	71.7	57.1	48.2	...	...
Poland	4.4	72.1	24.6	3.9	−3.5	...	...
Middle East and North Africa	11.7	8.4	7.5	2.6	3.8	4.0	4.0
Saudi Arabia	23.8	−3.1	3.8	−2.4	2.4	...	...
Iran	19.3	15.6	26.6	8.8	5.2	...	...
Egypt	11.0	13.1	8.7	3.8	4.0	...	...
Sub-Saharan Africa	10.7	10.0	10.5	5.8	4.2	3.7	4.5
Republic of South Africa	13.3	15.1	9.9	7.6	8.5	...	...
Nigeria	13.4	16.6	28.6	6.0	15.0	...	...

Notes: growth rates over intervals are computed using compound annual squares method;
a. High-income group inflation rates are GDP-weighted averages of local currency inflation; LMIC groups are medians; world is GDP-weighted average of the two groups.
b. data prior to 1991 covers West Germany
c. data prior to 1992 covers former Soviet Union.

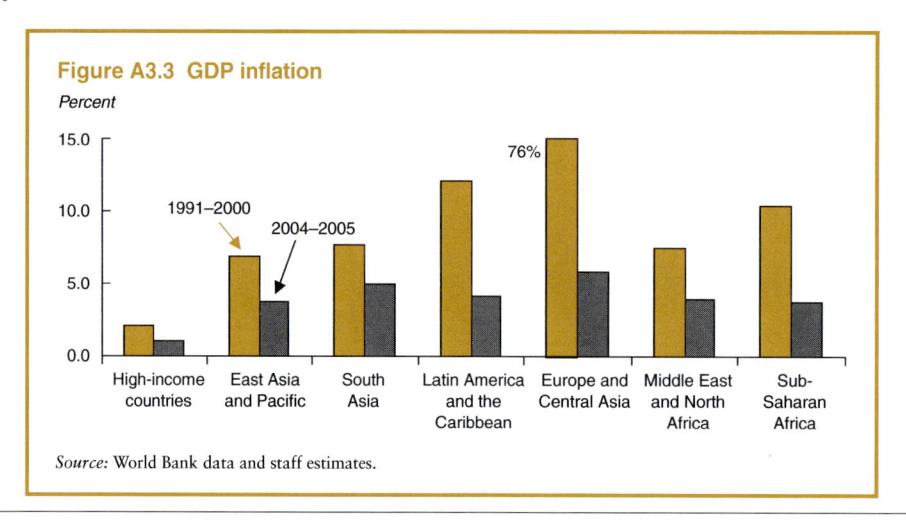

Figure A3.3 GDP inflation

Source: World Bank data and staff estimates.

GLOBAL ECONOMIC INDICATORS

Table A3.4 Current Account Balances, 1971–2005
Expressed as shares of GDP (percent)

	2002 Current Account (billions of U.S. dollars)	Shares percent 1971–80	1981–90	1991–00	2001	Estimate 2002	Forecast 2003	2004–2005
World[a]	–106	–0.1	–0.6	–0.2	–0.5	–0.3	–0.5	–0.6
High income economies	–177	–0.1	–0.3	0.0	–0.6	–0.7	–0.7	–0.7
Industrial countries	–238	–0.2	–0.5	–0.1	–0.9	–0.9	–0.9	–0.9
G-7 countries	–304	–0.1	–0.4	–0.3	–1.4	–1.4	–1.4	–1.4
United States	–481	0.0	–1.9	–1.8	–3.9	–4.6	...	...
Japan	112	0.3	2.3	2.4	2.1	2.8	...	...
G-4 Europe	54	0.1	0.3	–0.2	0.1	0.9	1.0	1.1
Germany[b]	46	0.5	2.4	–0.9	0.0	2.3	...	...
Euro Area	54	0.0	0.3	0.5	0.5	0.8	1.1	1.3
Non-G-7 industrial	65	–1.1	–0.8	1.2	1.9	1.7	1.8	2.0
Other high income	62	7.6	6.9	3.2	7.2	8.3	6.8	6.4
Asian NIEs	62	1.8	1.2	4.1	9.0	11.6	10.6	10.5
Low & middle income economies	70	0.2	–1.7	–1.6	0.1	1.2	0.5	–0.1
excluding CE.Eur / FSU	58	0.6	–1.8	–1.6	0.2	1.1	0.3	–0.2
Asia	59	–0.3	–1.7	–0.2	1.8	2.5	1.5	1.2
East Asia and Pacific	56	–0.1	–1.5	0.4	2.7	3.2	1.9	1.6
China	29	0.1	0.2	1.6	1.5	2.4	...	...
Indonesia	7	–2.3	–3.3	–0.4	4.7	4.2	...	...
South Asia	3	–0.4	–2.0	–1.5	–0.5	0.5	0.4	0.0
India	3	0.2	–1.7	–1.1	–0.7	0.7	...	...
Latin America and Caribbean	–14	–1.4	–1.7	–2.7	–2.7	–0.8	–0.5	–0.9
Brazil	–8	–4.4	–1.6	–2.2	–4.6	–1.7	...	...
Mexico	–14	–3.9	–0.8	–3.7	–2.9	–2.2	...	...
Argentina	9	–0.4	–2.2	–3.1	–1.7	8.8	...	...
Europe and Central Asia	13	–0.8	–0.5	–2.5	–1.4	1.1	0.6	–0.2
Russian Federation[c]	33	2.1	3.5	4.7	11.3	9.5	...	...
Turkey	0	–2.1	–1.3	–1.1	2.3	0.0	...	...
Poland	–7	–0.9	–1.4	–3.7	–3.0	–3.5	...	...
Middle East and North Africa	20	6.8	–1.5	–1.9	4.2	3.5	0.3	–2.0
Saudi Arabia	12	21.1	–7.3	–6.5	7.6	6.2	...	...
Iran	4	11.8	–0.4	1.9	3.5	3.1	...	...
Egypt	–1	–0.6	–2.6	1.5	–0.4	–1.3	...	...
Sub-Saharan Africa	–8	–2.1	–2.7	–2.0	–2.2	–2.2	–2.7	–2.6
Republic of South Africa	0	–1.3	0.4	–0.2	–0.3	0.3	...	...
Nigeria	0	1.5	–0.6	–0.2	–0.7	0.0	...	...

a. Current account as defined in BOP version 5.0, world represents statistical discrepancy; shares over intervals are period averages;
b. data prior to 1991 covers West Germany;
c. data prior to 1992 covers former Soviet Union.

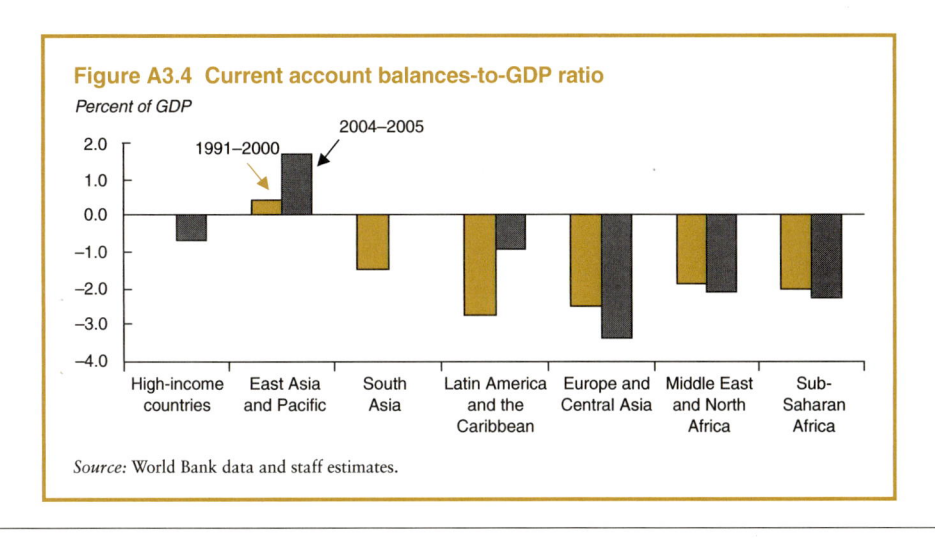

Figure A3.4 Current account balances-to-GDP ratio

Percent of GDP

Bars shown for 1991–2000 and 2004–2005 across: High-income countries, East Asia and Pacific, South Asia, Latin America and the Caribbean, Europe and Central Asia, Middle East and North Africa, Sub-Saharan Africa.

Source: World Bank data and staff estimates.

Table A3.5 Exports of goods, 2002

Merchandise exports (FOB), millions of dollars; average annual volume growth 1993–2002 (percent); effective market growth (EMG) 1993–2002 (percent)

	Exports	Growth	EMG[2]		Exports	Growth	EMG[2]		Exports	Growth	EMG[2]
World	6,285,029	6.3	6.6	Europe and Central Asia (continued)				High income countries	4,666,260	6.1	6.9
All developing countries	1,618,770	7.1	7.2	Belarus	8,035	−2.9	7.8				
				Bulgaria	3,512	5.1	6.3	Industrial countries	4,431,191	6.2	6.8
Asia	663,348	11.4	7.0	Czech Republic	26,977	4.5	6.3				
				Estonia	5,992	11.0	7.6	G-7 countries	2,857,740	5.4	7.0
East Asia	595,377	12.0	7.0	Georgia	748	24.5	6.5	Canada	263,777	7.3	8.9
China	325,574	17.3	6.8	Hungary	27,305	3.9	6.1	France	339,050	6.1	5.9
Fiji	511	3.6	7.3	Kazakhstan	10,590	17.2	8.0	Germany	592,010	5.9	6.6
Indonesia	56,922	5.1	7.0	Latvia	2,718	7.4	8.5	Italy	284,552	5.5	6.2
Malaysia	93,364	8.2	7.1	Lithuania	4,365	2.4	7.9	Japan	395,662	3.6	7.8
Philippines	34,455	10.4	7.4	Poland	36,115	13.5	6.0	United Kingdom	279,140	5.4	6.4
Thailand	68,902	8.0	7.1	Romania	12,820	1.2	5.8	United States	703,549	5.3	7.0
Vietnam	16,159	18.4	6.9	Russian Federation	79,059	−0.4	7.9				
				Slovak Republic	18,023	7.1	8.7	Other industrial	1,253,846	7.4	6.2
South Asia	67,972	7.1	6.9	Turkey	35,904	8.4	6.0	Australia	64,988	6.2	6.5
Bangladesh	6,374	11.6	7.0	Ukraine	19,260	−0.3	7.5	Austria	69,422	7.9	5.9
India	46,129	7.6	6.8	Uzbekistan	7,005	4.3	7.2	Belgium[1]	200,696	6.7	5.9
Nepal	733	8.2	6.4					Denmark	53,531	2.1	5.8
Pakistan	9,699	3.0	6.8	Middle East and N. Africa	161,597	2.3	6.6	Finland	7,507	7.7	7.0
Sri Lanka	5,036	7.4	7.2	Algeria	17,648	2.7	6.4	Greece	3,158	10.8	5.8
				Egypt, Arab Rep.	7,323	6.1	6.3	Iceland	2,150	2.8	6.3
Latin America	351,966	5.6	7.7	Iran, Islamic Rep.	24,203	−0.3	6.4	Ireland	88,970	9.7	6.2
Argentina	25,348	2.8	6.7	Jordan	2,466	7.0	5.8	Korea, Rep.	162,412	14.4	7.5
Bolivia	1,241	7.1	5.9	Morocco	7,427	3.6	6.1	Netherlands	198,624	6.3	5.8
Brazil	60,362	−2.9	5.9	Oman	11,508	5.0	7.9	New Zealand	14,860	3.7	7.1
Chile	18,340	5.1	6.7	Saudi Arabia	73,691	1.3	6.8	Norway	61,761	2.8	6.3
Colombia	12,803	4.5	7.3	Syrian Arab Rep.	6,173	5.1	5.4	Portugal	26,731	9.2	5.6
Costa Rica	5,007	11.0	7.8	Tunisia	7,676	5.0	5.5	Spain	121,572	7.7	6.1
Dominican Republic	5,142	24.5	7.9	Yemen, Rep.	3,483	9.4	8.8	Sweden	85,304	3.7	6.1
Ecuador	5,279	3.9	7.7					Switzerland	92,161	3.7	6.1
El Salvador	2,526	17.2	7.8	Sub-Saharan Africa	91,060	3.1	6.8	Other high income	554,674	7.0	8.3
Guatemala	2,850	7.4	8.7					Bahrain	5,529	3.4	5.6
Jamaica	1,466	2.4	7.7	Angola	7,582	4.4	8.7	Hong Kong, China	200,285	6.3	10.2
Mexico	160,834	13.5	9.0	Cameroon	1,917	−1.2	6.2	Israel	29,435	7.6	7.3
Panama	5,778	1.2	7.3	Côte d'Ivoire	4,275	2.8	5.6	Kuwait	15,477	6.2	6.7
Paraguay	2,176	−0.4	6.3	Ethiopia	326	10.3	5.1	Singapore	125,172	8.8	7.5
Peru	7,551	−0.4	7.3	Gabon	2,403	−2.1	8.3	Taiwan, China	130,666	6.9	7.1
Trinidad and Tobago	4,214	7.1	8.2	Ghana	1,402	6.9	6.4	United Arab Emirates	38,386	3.1	5.6
Uruguay	1,850	8.4	6.7	Kenya	2,028	5.6	5.7				
Venezuela	26,735	−0.3	8.8	Madagascar	962	10.9	5.9				
				Nigeria	16,333	0.7	7.4				
				South Africa	31,085	2.4	6.2				
Europe and Central Asia	306,543	5.6	7.2	Sudan	1,332	22.1	6.3				
Armenia	435	2.8	5.2	Zambia	1,057	6.1	5.0				
Azerbaijan	2,333	7.1	4.3	Zimbabwe	1,519	−0.4	6.2				

1. Includes Luxembourg.
2. Effective market growth (EMG) is a weighted average of import volume growth in the country's export markets.
Source: see technical notes.

GLOBAL ECONOMIC INDICATORS

Figure A3.5a Merchandise exports as share of GDP, 2002

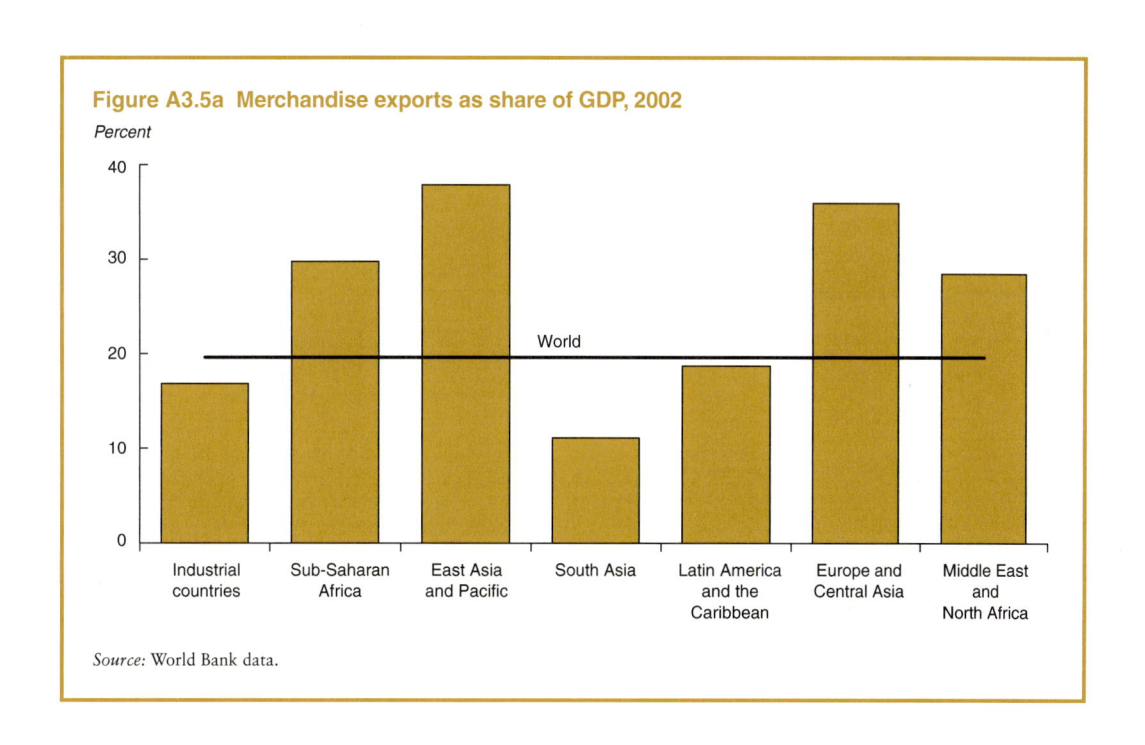

Source: World Bank data.

Figure A3.5b Annual growth rate of export volumes, 1993–2002

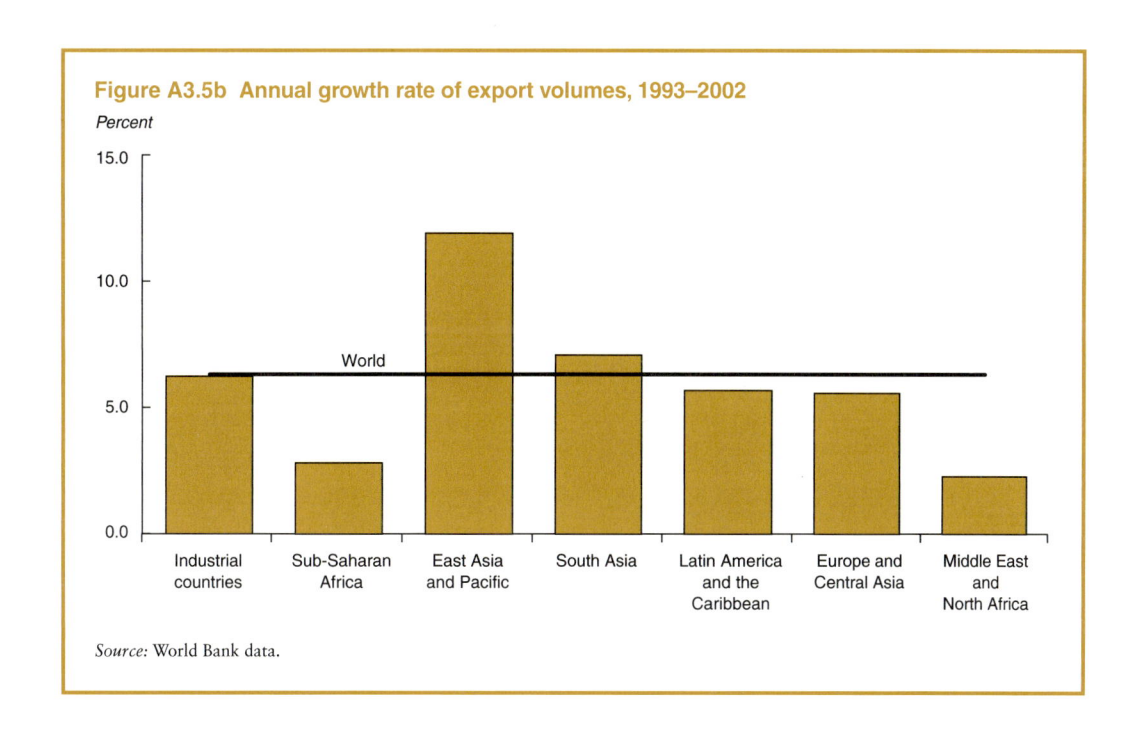

Source: World Bank data.

Table A3.6 Imports of goods, 2002
Merchandise imports (CIF), millions of dollars; average annual volume growth 1993–2002 (percent); merchandise imports share of GDP (percent)

	Imports	Growth	Share		Imports	Growth	Share		Imports	Growth	Shares
World	6,232,809	6.6	19.4	Europe and Central Asia (continued)				Sub-Saharan Africa (continued)			
All developing countries	1,441,537	7.5	23.5	Belarus	7,909	7.8	59.4	Zimbabwe	798	−7.7	6.4
				Bulgaria	6,106	6.3	43.6				
				Czech Republic	40,176	6.3	65.1	High income countries	4,791,272	6.4	18.5
Asia	579,564	9.6	23.7	Estonia	4,768	7.6	83.6				
East Asia				Georgia	885	6.5	27.9	Industrial countries	4,620,406	6.6	17.6
China	501,706	10.2	28.3	Hungary	34,619	6.1	62.5				
Fiji	613	−0.1	36.2	Kazakstan	7,106	8.0	27.8	G-7 countries	3,099,228	6.6	14.5
Indonesia	31,242	1.2	17.5	Latvia	3,623	8.5	45.3	Canada	226,994	6.7	30.9
Malaysia	75,043	7.2	78.9	Lithuania	6,188	7.9	47.1	France	316,953	5.8	22.1
Philippines	32,547	7.1	41.8	Poland	53,993	6.0	29.6	Germany	486,062	4.4	24.4
Thailand	64,317	4.8	50.8	Romania	15,527	5.8	35.1	Italy	244,491	4.6	20.7
Vietnam	16,599	19.5	44.8	Russian Federation	63,956	7.9	19.3	Japan	302,246	4.8	7.6
South Asia	77,858	5.6	11.5	Slovak Republic	11,980	8.7	49.6	United Kingdom	330,862	6.7	21.1
Bangladesh	8,514	9.1	17.0	Turkey	29,933	6.0	17.5	United States	1,191,620	9.4	11.4
India	52,114	7.0	9.6	Ukraine	14,079	7.5	32.1				
Nepal	1,521	5.4	27.9	Uzbekistan	3,523	7.2	32.5	Other industrial	1,166,814	5.9	30.4
Pakistan	9,937	−0.8	16.6					Australia	70,178	8.1	17.6
Sri Lanka	5,772	5.9	33.3	Middle East and N. Africa	114,003	1.4	17.2	Austria	67,958	5.3	33.2
Latin America	329,697	7.8	19.7	Algeria	11,378	4.2	19.8	Belgium[1]	184,178	5.6	74.8
Argentina	8,988	−4.7	8.8	Egypt, Arab Rep.	14,364	4.3	15.0	Denmark	46,896	2.9	27.2
Bolivia	1,492	2.2	17.8	Iran, Islamic Rep.	20,260	−2.1	16.3	Finland	5,277	3.8	4.0
Brazil	47,237	8.4	10.4	Jordan	4,349	3.5	46.2	Greece	10,207	4.8	7.8
Chile	15,827	4.9	23.8	Morocco	10,630	3.1	29.4	Iceland	2,206	3.0	25.9
Colombia	12,304	7.2	14.3	Oman	5,614	4.1	24.4	Ireland	52,381	8.7	42.8
Costa Rica	6,533	11.3	38.7	Saudi Arabia	30,418	0.0	15.8	Korea	151,768	9.2	33.8
Dominican Republic	8,428	14.6	37.4	Syrian Arab Rep.	4,576	4.0	5.0	Netherlands	177,228	6.0	42.4
				Tunisia	9,864	4.5	47.4	New Zealand	13,132	3.8	23.6
Ecuador	6,240	11.0	32.8	Yemen, Rep.	2,550	2.4	25.9	Norway	35,619	2.2	18.6
El Salvador	4,702	11.8	32.7					Portugal	39,530	3.3	32.8
Guatemala	4,895	7.7	24.4					Spain	155,190	7.9	23.7
Jamaica	3,063	7.2	38.1	Sub-Saharan				Sweden	65,809	5.7	27.5
Mexico	168,731	11.0	26.6	Africa	79,907	3.5	25.3	Switzerland	89,257	2.4	33.3
Panama	6,435	1.5	61.3	Angola	3,383	4.6	29.4				
Paraguay	2,460	0.6	34.1	Cameroon	1,866	5.7	20.8	Other high income	525,229	6.4	70.4
Peru	7,271	0.6	12.5	Côte d'Ivoire	2,339	1.1	22.5	Bahrain	3,972	−0.8	46.7
Trinidad and Tobago	3,541	5.5	38.1	Ethiopia	1,494	5.6	23.0	Hong Kong, China	205,337	6.9	127.1
				Gabon	1,113	2.5	25.3				
Uruguay	2,067	13.3	12.1	Ghana	2,513	6.1	45.1	Israel	33,317	5.8	29.6
Venezuela	15,204	−1.8	13.0	Kenya	3,202	6.8	27.4	Kuwait	7,341	0.0	21.6
				Madagascar	1,076	8.3	22.1	Singapore	110,256	6.4	126.8
Europe and Central Asia	318,748	7.2	30.5	Nigeria	11,570	4.7	24.7	Taiwan, China	112,957	5.9	40.0
Armenia	807	5.2	33.0	South Africa	26,712	3.5	24.8	United Arab Emirates	41,882	9.2	104.1
Azerbaijan	1,787	4.3	26.6	Sudan	1,306	6.5	9.9				
				Zambia	1,021	2.8	27.3				

1. Includes Luxembourg.
Source: see technical notes.

GLOBAL ECONOMIC INDICATORS

Figure A3.6a Merchandise imports as share of GDP, 2002

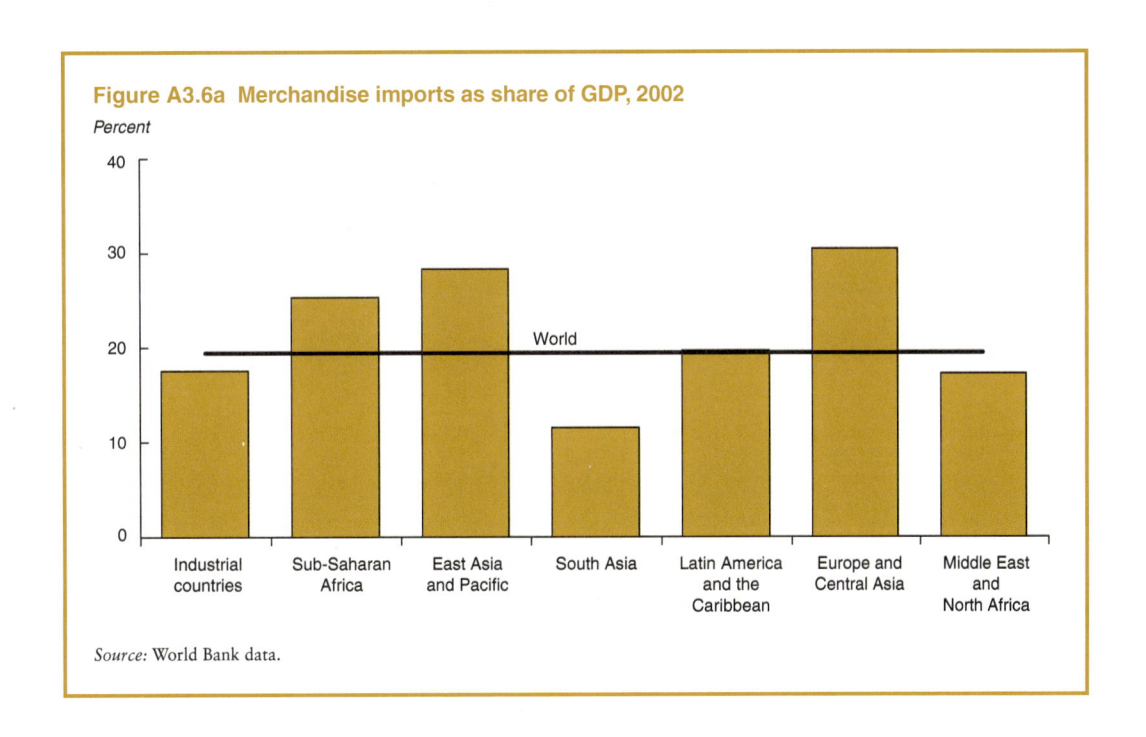

Percent

[Bar chart showing merchandise imports as share of GDP by region, with World reference line near 20%:
- Industrial countries: ~18
- Sub-Saharan Africa: ~25
- East Asia and Pacific: ~28
- South Asia: ~12
- Latin America and the Caribbean: ~20
- Europe and Central Asia: ~31
- Middle East and North Africa: ~18]

Source: World Bank data.

Figure A3.6b Annual growth rate of import volumes, 1993–2002

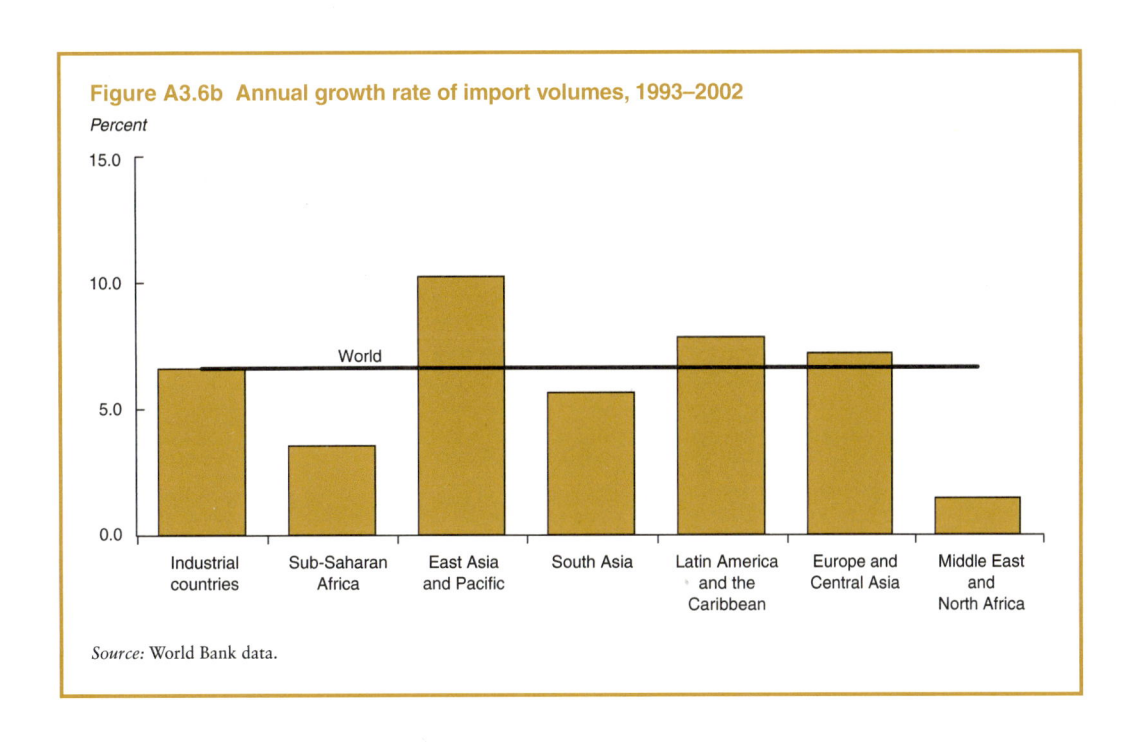

Percent

[Bar chart showing annual growth rate of import volumes by region, with World reference line near 6.5%:
- Industrial countries: ~6.5
- Sub-Saharan Africa: ~3.5
- East Asia and Pacific: ~10.3
- South Asia: ~5.7
- Latin America and the Caribbean: ~7.8
- Europe and Central Asia: ~7.3
- Middle East and North Africa: ~1.5]

Source: World Bank data.

287

Table A3.7 Direction of merchandise trade, 2002
(percentage of world trade)

Source of exports	High-income importers							Low- and middle-income importers							World
	United States	EU-15	Japan	Other industrial	All industrial	Other high-income	All high-income	Sub-Saharan Africa	East Asia and Pacific	South Asia	Europe and Central Asia	Middle East and North Africa	Latin America and the Caribbean	All low- and middle-income	
High-income econ.	12.3	27.4	3.0	6.5	50.7	5.5	56.2	0.8	6.5	0.7	3.7	1.5	4.0	17.1	73.4
Industrial	10.7	26.2	2.2	6.2	46.6	4.3	50.9	0.7	4.1	0.5	3.5	1.4	3.8	14.1	65.0
United States	0.0	2.3	0.9	3.3	6.9	1.0	7.9	0.1	0.8	0.1	0.2	0.2	2.5	3.9	11.8
EU-15	3.7	20.6	0.7	2.2	27.4	1.3	28.7	0.5	0.9	0.2	3.1	0.9	0.8	6.5	35.2
Japan	2.1	1.0	0.0	0.3	3.9	1.2	5.2	0.0	1.4	0.1	0.1	0.1	0.2	1.9	7.1
Other industrial	4.3	2.0	0.4	0.3	7.1	0.3	7.4	0.0	0.3	0.1	0.1	0.1	0.1	0.8	8.2
Other high-income	1.6	1.2	0.7	0.3	4.1	1.2	5.3	0.1	2.3	0.2	0.1	0.1	0.2	3.1	8.4
Low and middle-income economies	6.7	6.5	2.2	1.0	17.1	3.1	20.3	0.5	1.7	0.4	1.9	0.5	1.3	6.4	26.6
Sub-Saharan Africa	0.3	0.5	0.1	0.0	0.9	0.1	1.0	0.2	0.1	0.0	0.0	0.0	0.1	0.4	1.4
East Asia and Pacific	2.2	1.4	1.5	0.4	6.0	2.4	8.3	0.1	0.9	0.2	0.2	0.2	0.2	1.9	10.2
South Asia	0.3	0.3	0.0	0.0	0.7	0.2	0.8	0.0	0.1	0.0	0.0	0.0	0.0	0.3	1.1
Europe and Central Asia	0.3	2.8	0.1	0.2	3.4	0.2	3.6	0.0	0.2	0.0	1.5	0.1	0.0	1.9	5.5
Middle East and North Africa	0.3	0.8	0.3	0.1	1.7	0.3	2.0	0.1	0.3	0.1	0.1	0.1	0.0	0.6	2.6
Latin America and Caribbean	3.3	0.7	0.1	0.3	4.4	0.1	4.5	0.0	0.2	0.0	0.1	0.1	0.9	1.3	5.8
World	19.0	33.8	5.1	7.5	67.8	8.6	76.5	1.3	8.2	1.1	5.6	2.0	5.3	23.5	100.0

a. Expressed as a share (percent) of total world exports. World merchandise exports in 2002 amounted to some $6,300 billion.
b. Other high-income group includes the Asian newly industrializing economies, several oil exporters in the Gulf region, and Israel.
Source: IMF, *Direction of Trade Statistics.*

Table A3.8 Growth of current dollar merchandise trade, by direction 1993–2002
(average annual percentage growth)

Source of exports	United States	EU-15	Japan	Other industrial	All industrial	Other high-income	All high-income	Sub-Saharan Africa	East Asia and Pacific	South Asia	Europe and Central Asia	Middle East and North Africa	Latin America and the Caribbean	All low- and middle-income	World
				High-income importers						Low- and middle-income importers					
High-income econ.	5.6	1.2	1.8	4.0	2.7	3.9	2.8	1.5	8.3	3.7	11.1	0.1	5.7	6.5	3.5
Industrial	6.2	1.2	1.4	4.1	2.6	3.5	2.7	1.6	8.2	2.5	11.0	0.1	5.7	6.2	3.3
United States	0.0	1.9	0.7	5.7	3.5	3.7	3.5	0.8	8.2	5.2	2.9	−2.1	7.1	6.1	4.3
EU-15	7.4	1.1	2.8	2.6	1.9	4.7	2.0	1.5	6.6	1.3	12.1	0.6	4.7	6.4	2.7
Japan	2.2	−1.8	0.0	0.1	1.1	1.6	1.2	−2.9	7.2	−0.5	3.3	−3.9	−0.3	4.1	1.9
Other industrial	7.7	2.4	0.7	4.3	5.3	2.9	5.2	4.5	6.7	4.7	7.6	3.2	3.3	5.4	5.2
Other high-income	2.4	2.8	3.2	2.6	3.2	5.8	3.7	1.2	8.3	7.1	14.7	0.6	5.2	7.5	5.0
Low and middle-income economies	11.3	7.3	7.4	12.2	9.2	7.6	8.9	12.2	15.8	9.8	12.2	5.7	9.2	11.4	9.5
Sub-Saharan Africa	5.6	5.5	18.1	4.2	6.4	18.5	6.9	11.4	25.7	7.6	15.1	7.8	13.7	13.4	8.4
East Asia and Pacific	14.6	11.1	9.5	14.1	12.2	7.4	10.6	16.6	17.4	14.9	13.2	8.8	19.7	15.6	11.3
South Asia	10.8	4.8	0.0	7.5	7.0	10.1	7.5	11.1	13.9	8.1	5.9	3.2	20.1	9.1	7.9
Europe and Central Asia	17.8	9.7	2.8	12.7	10.2	15.9	10.4	10.0	9.9	8.6	13.4	4.6	9.8	11.8	0.0
Middle East and North Africa	1.8	2.5	2.9	2.1	3.0	5.3	3.3	15.3	16.3	4.8	0.0	3.9	−0.2	7.3	4.2
Latin America and Caribbean	11.3	2.5	2.1	16.7	9.2	3.5	9.0	4.6	13.9	11.2	12.8	5.4	8.1	8.6	8.9
World	7.3	2.1	3.8	4.8	3.9	5.1	4.1	4.3	9.4	5.7	11.5	1.2	6.4	7.6	4.8

Note: Growth rates are compound averages.
Source: IMF, *Direction of Trade Statistics.*

Table A3.9 Structure of long-term debt, 2001

Share of long-term debt (%): concessional debt; nonconcessional debt at variable interest rates; nonconcessional debt at fixed interest rates

	Concessional	Non-concessional Variable	Non-concessional Fixed		Concessional	Non-concessional Variable	Non-concessional Fixed
All developing countries	19.0	48.1	32.9	**Europe and Central Asia** (continued)			
				Czech Republic	2.0	72.8	25.2
Asia	32.0	44.5	23.5	Estonia	1.3	97.6	1.1
East Asia	24.2	52.0	23.8	Georgia	74.8	11.9	13.2
China	20.7	45.3	34.0	Hungary	0.5	63.6	35.9
Indonesia	27.4	63.8	8.8	Kazakhstan	2.9	86.1	11.0
Korea, Rep.	..	..	..	Kyrgyz Republic	65.2	27.7	7.1
Malaysia	8.3	56.9	34.8	Latvia	1.6	82.1	16.3
Myanmar	80.1	10.9	9.0	Lithuania	3.0	51.7	45.3
Papua New Guinea	34.1	55.9	9.9	Moldova	19.9	54.7	25.4
Philippines	25.1	42.5	32.4	Poland	11.2	76.7	12.2
Thailand	16.2	65.6	18.1	Romania	2.6	72.4	25.0
Vietnam	73.2	11.7	15.1	Russian Federation	0.4	34.7	64.9
				Slovak Republic	3.3	48.8	47.8
South Asia	52.0	24.9	23.0	Tajikistan	85.6	12.5	1.9
Bangladesh	96.4	0.0	3.6	Turkmenistan	19.4	67.4	13.3
India	38.9	29.4	31.7	Turkey	5.0	50.3	44.7
Nepal	99.8	0.0	0.2	Ukraine	24.4	50.8	24.8
Pakistan	68.8	24.8	6.3	Uzbekistan	23.5	68.1	8.4
Sri Lanka	81.7	10.2	8.1				
				Middle East and North Africa	36.1	32.8	31.1
Latin America and the Caribbean	4.6	59.1	36.3	Algeria	13.0	49.7	37.3
Argentina	1.3	38.5	60.2	Egypt, Arab Rep.	77.2	6.1	16.7
Bolivia	54.4	32.9	12.7	Jordan	48.4	34.1	17.5
Brazil	1.4	72.4	26.2	Morocco	31.6	44.7	23.7
Chile	0.9	94.1	5.0	Oman	18.5	64.7	16.8
Colombia	2.7	56.9	40.4	Syrian Arab Rep.	93.0	0.0	7.0
Costa Rica	15.1	23.1	61.8	Tunisia	25.4	31.6	43.0
Dominican Republic	35.2	33.0	31.9	Yemen, Rep.	94.1	2.0	4.0
Ecuador	15.8	32.5	51.7				
El Salvador	31.8	35.3	32.9	**Sub-Saharan Africa**	48.3	15.1	36.6
Guatemala	40.3	31.7	27.9	Angola	21.1	8.5	70.5
Jamaica	19.4	20.7	59.9	Botswana	69.0	7.1	23.9
Mexico	0.8	62.1	37.2	Côte d'Ivoire	38.9	46.8	14.3
Nicaragua	59.0	20.0	21.0	Cameroon	58.6	12.2	29.2
Panama	4.2	42.7	53.1	Ethiopia	91.4	0.1	8.5
Paraguay	32.7	47.4	19.8	Gabon	42.3	8.7	48.9
Peru	15.0	61.5	23.5	Ghana	78.6	5.4	16.0
Trinidad and Tobago	0.7	38.3	60.9	Kenya	78.4	5.1	16.6
Uruguay	3.0	47.0	50.0	Madagascar	72.8	5.0	22.2
Venezuela, RB	0.1	51.9	48.0	Nigeria	4.6	5.6	89.9
				Senegal	87.0	5.5	7.5
Europe and Central Asia	5.7	54.3	40.0	South Africa	0.0	55.5	44.5
Armenia	74.1	12.7	13.2	Sudan	50.1	17.9	32.0
Azerbaijan	55.4	41.0	3.6	Zambia	78.5	7.8	13.7
Belarus	12.6	59.7	27.7	Zimbabwe	45.7	20.3	34.0
Bulgaria	4.2	86.0	9.8				

Note: Nonconcessional debt data are available only for countries which report to the World Bank's Debtor Reporting System. For aggregate figures, missing values are assumed to have the same average value as the available data.
Republic of Korea is not included in the aggregate figures.

GLOBAL ECONOMIC INDICATORS

Figure A3.9a Structure of long-term debt, by group, 2001

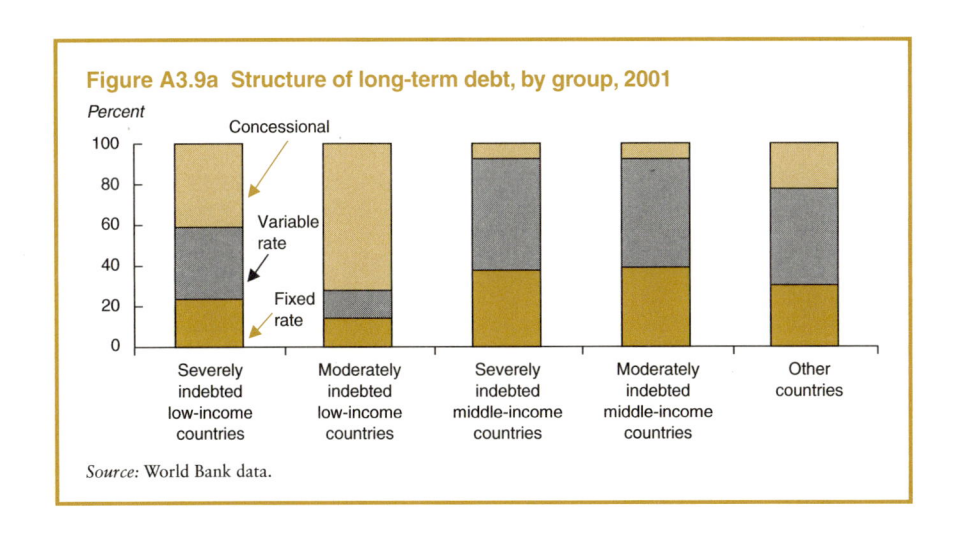

Source: World Bank data.

Figure A3.9b Structure of long-term debt, by region, 2001

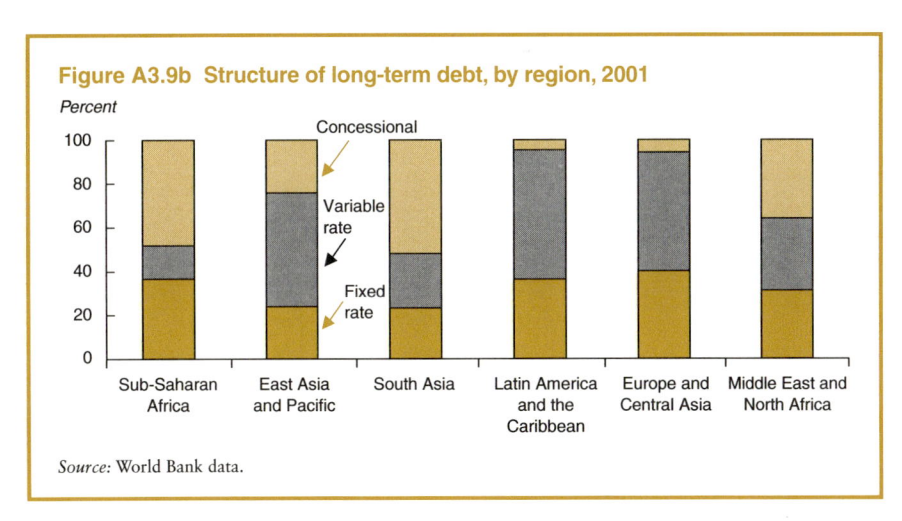

Source: World Bank data.

Figure A3.9c Top ten ratios of nonconcessional debt to GDP, 2001

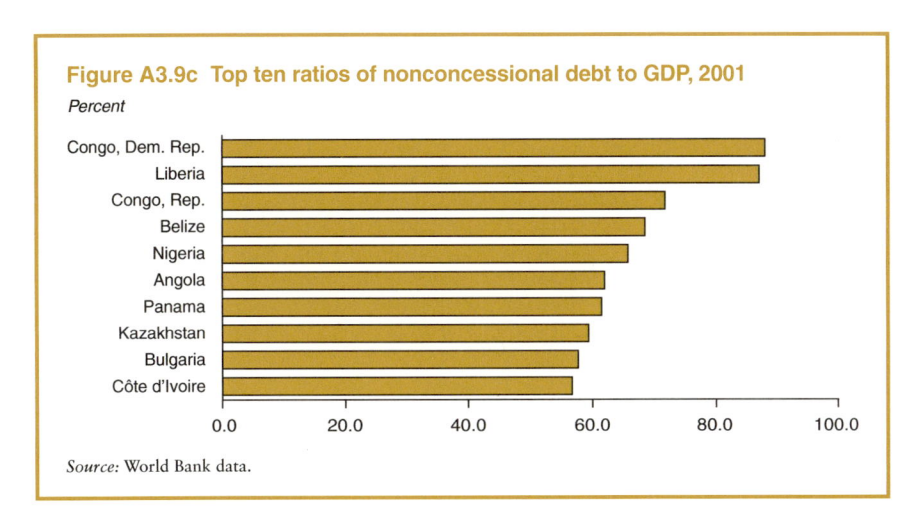

Source: World Bank data.

Table A3.10 Long-term net resource flows to developing countries, 2001
(millions of U.S. dollars)

	Total millions $	Percent GDP	Private Total	Debt flows (net)	FDI	Portfolio	Official Total	ODA	Other
All developing countries	207,063	3.3	169,003	−8,648	171,693	5,958	38,060	37,875	184
Asia	54,524	2.4	40,616	−16,898	52,979	4,535	13,909	12,359	1,550
East Asia	45,028	2.7	36,817	−15,025	48,913	2,930	8,211	6,649	1,561
China	45,635	3.9	43,238	−4,017	44,241	3,015	2,396	874	1,522
Indonesia	−6,446	−4.6	−7,312	−4,198	−3,278	164	866	955	−89
Korea, Rep.	9,046	2.1	9,279	−4,084	3,198	10,165	−233	−56	−177
Malaysia	3,004	3.4	855	951	554	−650	2,149	1,413	736
Myanmar	210	..	145	−63	208	0	65	65	0
Papua New Guinea	150	5.2	2	−61	63	0	148	78	70
Philippines	2,014	2.8	2,077	−98	1,792	383	−62	164	−226
Thailand	−2,977	−2.6	−3,052	−6,891	3,820	18	76	534	−458
Vietnam	1,946	5.9	710	−590	1,300	0	1,236	1,222	14
South Asia	9,496	1.5	3,798	−1,873	4,066	1,606	5,698	5,710	−12
Bangladesh	1,305	2.8	304	230	78	−4	1,002	1,007	−5
India	4,383	0.9	3,534	−1,608	3,403	1,739	849	813	36
Nepal	255	4.6	19	0	19	0	236	236	0
Pakistan	1,639	2.8	−308	−561	383	−130	1,947	2,066	−120
Sri Lanka	525	3.4	243	71	172	0	282	271	11
Latin America	79,898	4.2	72,067	500	69,309	2,258	7,831	3,495	4,336
Argentina	−2,770	−1.0	−3,897	−7,030	3,214	−81	1,127	−225	1,353
Bolivia	1,217	15.3	637	−26	662	0	580	549	32
Brazil	26,159	5.1	23,337	−1,781	22,636	2,482	2,823	398	2,424
Chile	5,634	8.5	5,727	1,470	4,476	−219	−93	8	−101
Colombia	4,768	5.8	3,597	1,312	2,328	−43	1,171	81	1,090
Costa Rica	451	2.8	630	176	454	0	−179	−31	−148
Dominican Republic	1,719	8.1	1,729	530	1,198	0	−10	−31	21
Ecuador	1,549	7.4	1,444	113	1,330	1	105	54	51
El Salvador	982	7.1	674	406	268	0	308	132	175
Guatemala	577	2.8	403	−52	456	0	174	102	71
Jamaica	1,344	17.3	1,385	771	614	0	−41	−4	−38
Mexico	27,429	4.4	28,079	3,198	24,731	150	−650	−64	−586
Nicaragua	820	..	13	−119	132	0	807	822	−15
Panama	1,806	15.0	1,799	1,287	513	0	7	−17	24
Paraguay	6	0.1	−14	−93	79	0	19	−13	33
Peru	2,317	4.3	1,400	294	1,064	42	917	184	733
Trinidad and Tobago	819	9.0	830	−5	835	0	−11	3	−14
Uruguay	880	4.7	796	478	318	0	84	−37	121
Venezuela	1,734	1.4	2,644	−730	3,448	−74	−910	0	−910
Europe and Central Asia	40,319	4.0	36,162	5,774	30,130	258	4,157	7,347	−3,191
Armenia	174	8.2	74	4	70	0	101	110	−9
Azerbaijan	348	6.1	216	−11	227	0	132	140	−7
Belarus	87	0.7	83	−13	96	0	5	20	−16
Bulgaria	1,028	7.6	1,043	360	692	−9	−15	170	−185
Czech Republic	5,481	9.6	5,194	−346	4,924	616	287	150	137
Estonia	658	11.9	625	54	539	32	34	43	−9
Georgia	307	9.6	173	13	160	0	134	147	−13
Hungary	3,935	7.6	3,952	1,378	2,440	134	−17	31	−48
Kazakhstan	5,009	22.6	4,947	2,128	2,763	55	62	57	6
Kyrgyz Republic	52	3.4	−73	−78	5	0	125	145	−19
Latvia	977	12.7	880	697	177	6	97	80	17
Lithuania	625	5.3	521	91	446	−16	104	91	14
Moldova	125	8.4	70	−27	94	4	55	64	−9
Poland	6,205	3.4	9,611	4,205	5,713	−307	−3,406	462	−3,868
Romania	3,002	7.6	2,633	1,468	1,157	8	369	236	133
Russian Federation	526	0.2	1,488	−1,524	2,469	543	−962	414	−1,376
Slovak Republic	447	2.2	303	−1,173	1,475	0	144	63	81
Tajikistan	179	17.0	39	17	22	0	141	134	6
Turkmenistan	..	..	..	..	..	..	..	..	..
Turkey	2,329	1.6	906	−2,281	3,266	−79	1,423	−302	1,725
Ukraine	815	2.1	426	368	792	−734	389	126	263
Uzbekistan	346	3.0	46	−25	71	0	300	217	83
Middle East & N. Africa	9,543	1.4	7,462	2,134	5,460	−132	2,082	2,553	−471
Algeria	−595	−1.1	243	−953	1,196	0	−838	−143	−695
Egypt, Arab Rep.	2,073	2.1	2,067	1,519	510	39	5	130	−125
Iran, Islamic Rep.	1,101	1.0	1,049	1,016	33	0	52	−28	80

Table A3.10 Long-term net resource flows to developing countries, 2001 (continued)
(millions of U.S. dollars)

	Total millions $	Percent GDP	Private Total	Debt flows (net)	FDI	Portfolio	Official Total	ODA	Other
Middle East & N. Africa (continued)									
Jordan	548	6.2	−114	−70	100	−145	662	472	190
Morocco	2,346	6.9	2,633	−17	2,658	−8	−286	46	−332
Oman	−557	−2.8	−867	−905	42	−3	309	9	301
Syrian Arab Rep.	167	2.1	204	−1	205	0	−37	−25	−12
Tunisia	1,568	7.8	1,108	666	457	−15	460	247	213
Yemen, Rep.	−118	−1.3	−210	−5	−205	0	92	113	−22
Sub-Saharan Africa	22,778	7.2	12,697	−157	13,815	−961	10,081	12,121	−2,040
Angola	1,793	18.9	1,924	−222	2,146	0	−131	−109	−23
Botswana	41	0.8	55	−2	57	0	−14	8	−22
Côte d'Ivoire	173	1.6	137	−110	246	1	36	155	−120
Cameroon	254	3.0	−16	−91	75	0	270	277	−7
Ethiopia	857	13.7	10	−10	20	0	847	860	−13
Gabon	−12	−0.3	170	−30	200	0	−182	−45	−138
Ghana	818	15.4	244	154	89	0	574	567	7
Kenya	188	1.6	−37	−43	5	0	225	371	−146
Madagascar	257	5.6	9	−2	11	0	248	247	1
Nigeria	−454	−1.1	920	−184	1,104	0	−1,374	92	−1,466
Senegal	439	9.5	167	41	126	0	273	294	−21
South Africa	6,842	6.0	6,627	427	7,162	−962	215	211	4
Sudan	716	5.7	574	0	574	0	142	143	−1
Zambia	518	14.2	126	54	72	0	392	401	−9
Zimbabwe	56	0.6	−28	−33	5	0	84	71	13

Note: Republic of Korea is not included in the aggregate figures.

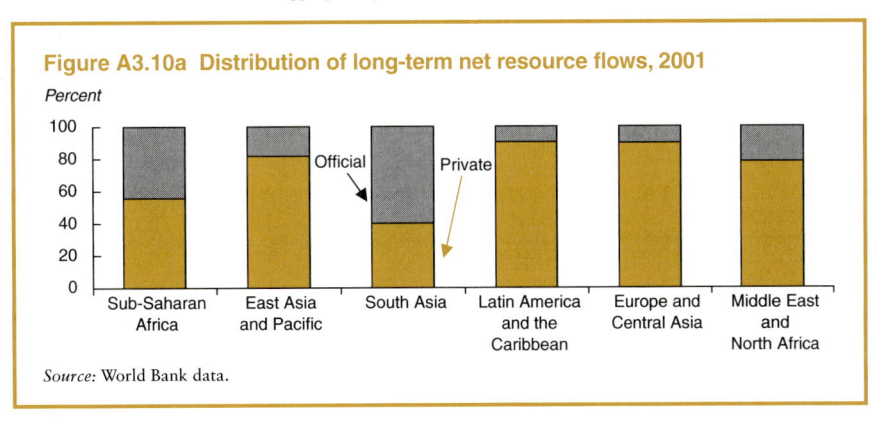

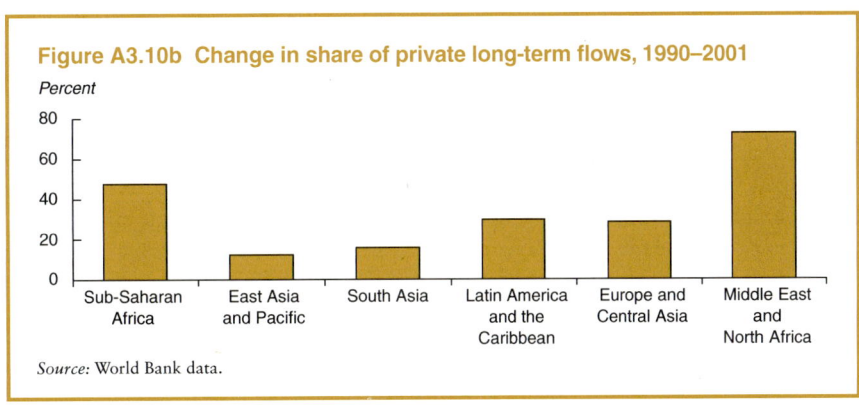

Figure A3.10a Distribution of long-term net resource flows, 2001

Source: World Bank data.

Figure A3.10b Change in share of private long-term flows, 1990–2001

Source: World Bank data.

Technical Notes

The principal sources for the data in this appendix are the World Bank's central databases and several International Monetary Fund databases, combined with data sourced from the OECD and from Oxford Economics Inc. (OEF), covering the industrial and other high-income economies. The cut-off date for data updates was July 16, 2003. Data revisions and new releases since that time have not been incorporated in the tables. Regional aggregates are based on the classification of economies by income group and by region, following the Bank's standard definitions (see country classification tables that follow).

Debt and finance data (tables A3.9 and A3.10) cover the 138 countries that report to the Bank's Debtor Reporting System (DRS), supplemented by data for non-DRS countries, for which commercial market information has been utilized. Small countries have generally been omitted from the tables, but are included in the regional totals. Current price data are reported in U.S. dollars.

Notes on tables

Tables A3.1 through A3.4. Historic data sourced from the databases noted above, while projections are consistent with those highlighted in chapter 1 and appendix 1.

Tables A3.5 and A3.6. Merchandise trade data is sourced from combined IMF, World Bank, OECD, and OEF sources. Merchandise exports and imports exclude trade in services. Imports are reported on a cost-insurance-and-freight basis. Trade values are expressed in millions of current U.S. dollars, while growth rates are based on constant price data, which are derived from current values deflated by relevant price indices or unit value measures. Effective market growth (EMG) in table A3.5 is the export-weighted growth of each country's trading partner imports.

Tables A3.7 and A3.8. The IMF's Direction of Trade database serves as the underlying source for the bilateral trade share and growth information highlighted in these tables. Growth rates are compound annual averages, and are computed from current U.S. dollar measures of trade.

Table A3.9. Long-term debt covers public and publicly guaranteed debt but excludes IMF credits. Concessional debt is debt with an original grant element of 25 percent or more. Nonconcessional variable interest-rate debt includes all public and publicly guaranteed long-term debt with an original grant element of less than 25 percent, whose terms depend on movements in a key market interest rate. This item conveys information about the borrower's exposure to changes in international interest rates.

Table A3.10. Long-term net resource flows are the sum of net resource flows on long-term debt (excluding IMF) plus non-debt-creating flows. Foreign direct investment refers to the net *inflows* of investment from abroad. Portfolio equity flows are the sum of country funds, depository receipts, and direct purchases of shares by foreign investors.

Classification of Economies

Table 1 Classification of economies by income and region, July 2003

Income group	Subgroup	Sub-Saharan Africa — East and Southern Africa	Sub-Saharan Africa — West Africa	Asia — East Asia and Pacific	Asia — South Asia	Europe and Central Asia — Eastern Europe and Central Asia	Europe and Central Asia — Rest of Europe	Middle East and North Africa — Middle East	Middle East and North Africa — North Africa	Americas
Low-income		Angola Burundi Comoros Congo, Dem. Rep. Eritrea Ethiopia Kenya Lesotho Madagascar Malawi Mozambique Rwanda Somalia Sudan Tanzania Uganda Zambia Zimbabwe	Benin Burkina Faso Cameroon Central African Republic Chad Congo, Rep. Côte d'Ivoire Equatorial Guinea Gambia, The Ghana Guinea Guinea-Bissau Liberia Mali Mauritania Niger Nigeria São Tomé and Principe Senegal Sierra Leone Togo	Cambodia Indonesia Korea, Dem. Rep. Lao PDR Mongolia Myanmar Papua New Guinea Solomon Islands Timor-Leste Vietnam	Afghanistan Bangladesh Bhutan India Nepal Pakistan	Azerbaijan Georgia Kyrgyz Republic Moldova Tajikistan Uzbekistan		Yemen, Rep. of		Haiti Nicaragua
Middle-income	Lower	Namibia South Africa Swaziland	Cape Verde	China Fiji Kiribati Marshall Islands Micronesia, Fed. Sts. Philippines Samoa Thailand Tonga Vanuatu	Maldives Sri Lanka	Albania Armenia Belarus Bosnia and Herzegovina Bulgaria Kazakhstan Macedonia, FYR[a] Romania Russian Federation Serbia and Montenegro Turkmenistan Ukraine	Turkey	Iran, Islamic Rep. Iraq Jordan Syrian Arab Republic West Bank and Gaza	Algeria Djibouti Egypt, Arab Rep. Morocco Tunisia	Bolivia Brazil Colombia Cuba Dominican Republic Ecuador El Salvador Guatemala Guyana Honduras Jamaica Paraguay Peru St. Vincent and the Grenadines Suriname
	Upper	Botswana Mauritius Mayotte Seychelles	Gabon	American Samoa Malaysia N. Mariana Islands Palau		Croatia Czech Republic Estonia Hungary Latvia Lithuania Poland Slovak Republic		Lebanon Oman Saudi Arabia	Libya	Argentina Belize Chile Costa Rica Dominica Grenada Mexico Panama St. Kitts and Nevis St. Lucia Trinidad and Tobago Uruguay Venezuela, RB
Subtotal	152	25	23	24	8	26	1	9	6	30

CLASSIFICATION OF ECONOMIES

Table 1 Classification of economies by income and region, July 2003 (continued)

Income group	Subgroup	Sub-Saharan Africa — East and Southern Africa	Sub-Saharan Africa — West Africa	Asia — East Asia and Pacific	Asia — South Asia	Europe and Central Asia — Eastern Europe and Central Asia	Europe and Central Asia — Rest of Europe	Middle East and North Africa — Middle East	Middle East and North Africa — North Africa	Americas
High-income	OECD			Australia Japan Korea, Rep. New Zealand			Austria Belgium Denmark Finland France[b] Germany Greece Iceland Ireland Italy Luxembourg Netherlands Norway Portugal Spain Sweden Switzerland United Kingdom			Canada United States
	Non-OECD			Brunei French Polynesia Guam Hong Kong, China[c] Macao, China[d] New Caledonia Singapore Taiwan, China		Slovenia	Andorra Channel Islands Cyprus Faeroe Islands Greenland Isle of Man Liechtenstein Monaco San Marino	Bahrain Israel Kuwait Qatar United Arab Emirates	Malta	Antigua and Barbuda Aruba Bahamas, The Barbados Bermuda Cayman Islands Netherlands Antilles Puerto Rico Virgin Islands (U.S.)
Total	209	25	23	36	8	27	28	14	7	41

a. Former Yugoslav Republic of Macedonia.
b. The French overseas departments French Guiana, Guadeloupe, Martinique, and Réunion are included in France.
c. On 1 July 1997 China resumed its exercise of sovereignty over Hong Kong.
d. On 20 December 1999 China resumed its exercise of sovereignty over Macao.
Source: World Bank data.

Definitions of groups

For operational and analytical purposes, the World Bank's main criterion for classifying economies is gross national income (GNI) per capita. Every economy is classified as low income, middle income (subdivided into lower middle and upper middle), or high income. Other analytical groups, based on geographic regions and levels of external debt, are also used.

Low-income and middle-income economies are sometimes referred to as developing economies. The use of the term is convenient; it is not intended to imply that all economies in the group are experiencing similar development or that other economies have reached a preferred or final stage of development. Classification by income does not necessarily reflect development status.

This table classifies all World Bank member economies, and all other economies with populations of more than 30,000. Economies are divided among income groups according to 2002 GNI per capita, calculated using the World Bank Atlas method. The groups are: low income, $735 or less; lower middle income, $736–2,935; upper middle income, $2,936–9,075; and high income, $9,076 or more.

Table 2 Classification of economies by income and indebtedness, July 2003

Income group	Sub-group	Severely indebted	Moderately indebted	Less indebted	Not classified by indebtedness
Low-income		Afghanistan, Angola, Benin, Burkina Faso, Burundi, Central African Republic, Chad, Comoros, Congo, Dem. Rep., Congo, Rep., Côte d'Ivoire, Ethiopia, Gambia, The, Guinea, Guinea-Bissau, Indonesia, Kyrgyz Republic, Lao PDR, Liberia, Madagascar, Malawi, Mauritania, Moldova, Myanmar, Nicaragua, Niger, Nigeria, Pakistan, Rwanda, São Tomé and Principe, Sierra Leone, Somalia, Sudan, Tajikistan, Zambia	Bhutan, Cambodia, Cameroon, Ghana, Haiti, Kenya, Mali, Mongolia, Papua New Guinea, Senegal, Tanzania, Togo, Uganda, Uzbekistan, Zimbabwe	Azerbaijan, Bangladesh, Equatorial Guinea, Eritrea, Georgia, India, Korea, Dem. Rep., Lesotho, Mozambique, Nepal, Solomon Islands, Vietnam, Yemen, Rep.	Timor-Leste
Middle-income	Lower	Brazil, Cuba, Ecuador, Guyana, Iraq, Jordan, Peru, Serbia and Montenegro, Syrian Arab Republic	Bolivia, Bulgaria, Colombia, Honduras, Jamaica, Kazakhstan, Philippines, Russian Federation, Samoa, St. Vincent and the Grenadines, Thailand, Tunisia, Turkey, Turkmenistan	Albania, Algeria, Armenia, Belarus, Bosnia and Herzegovina, Cape Verde, China, Djibouti, Dominican Republic, Egypt, Arab Rep., El Salvador, Fiji, Guatemala, Iran, Islamic Rep., Kiribati, Macedonia, FYR[a], Maldives, Morocco, Namibia, Paraguay, Romania, South Africa, Sri Lanka, Suriname, Swaziland, Tonga, Ukraine, Vanuatu	Marshall Islands, Micronesia, Fed. Sts., West Bank and Gaza
	Upper	Argentina, Belize, Gabon, Lebanon, Panama, Uruguay	Chile, Croatia, Dominica, Estonia, Grenada, Hungary, Latvia, Malaysia, Slovak Republic, St. Kitts and Nevis	Botswana, Costa Rica, Czech Republic, Libya, Lithuania, Mauritius, Mexico, Oman, Poland, Saudi Arabia, Seychelles, St. Lucia, Trinidad and Tobago, Venezuela, RB	American Samoa, Mayotte, N. Mariana Islands, Palau

CLASSIFICATION OF ECONOMIES

Table 2 Classification of economies by income and indebtedness, July 2003 (continued)

Income group	Sub-group	Severely indebted	Moderately indebted	Less indebted	Not classified by indebtedness	
High-income	OECD				Australia Austria Belgium Canada Denmark Finland France[b] Germany Greece Iceland Ireland Italy Japan	Korea, Rep. Luxembourg Netherlands New Zealand Norway Portugal Spain Sweden Switzerland United Kingdom United States
	Non-OECD				Andorra Antigua and Barbuda Aruba Bahamas, The Bahrain Barbados Bermuda Brunei Cayman Islands Channel Islands Cyprus Faeroe Islands French Polynesia Greenland Guam Hong Kong, China[d]	Isle of Man Israel Kuwait Liechtenstein Macao, China[c] Malta Monaco Netherlands Antilles New Caledonia Puerto Rico Qatar San Marino Singapore Slovenia Taiwan, China United Arab Emirates Virgin Islands (U.S.)
Total	209	50	39	55	65	

a. Former Yugoslav Republic of Macedonia.
b. The French overseas departments French Guiana, Guadeloupe, Martinique, and Réunion are included in France.
c. On 20 December 1999 China resumed its exercise of sovereignty over Macao.
d. On 1 July 1997 China resumed its exercise of sovereignty over Hong Kong.
Source: World Bank data.

Definitions of groups
This table classifies all World Bank member economies, and all other economies with populations of more than 30,000. Economies are divided among income groups according to 2002 GNI per capita, calculated using the World Bank Atlas method. The groups are: low income, $735 or less; lower middle income, $736–2,935; upper middle income, $2,936–9,075; and high income, $9,076 or more.

Standard World Bank definitions of severe and moderate indebtedness are used to classify economies in this table. *Severely indebted* means either: present value of debt service to GNI exceeds 80 percent or present value of debt service to exports exceeds 220 percent. *Moderately indebted* means either of the two key ratios exceeds 60 percent of, but does not reach, the critical levels. For economies that do not report detailed debt statistics to the World Bank Debtor Reporting System (DRS), present-value calculation is not possible. Instead, the following methodology is used to classify the non-DRS economies. *Severely indebted* means three of four key ratios (averaged over 1999–2001) are above critical levels: debt to GNI (50 percent); debt to exports (275 percent); debt service to exports (30 percent); and interest to exports (20 percent). *Moderately indebted* means three of the four key ratios exceed 60 percent of, but do not reach, the critical levels. All other classified low- and middle-income economies are listed as *less indebted*.